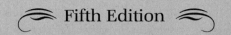

Fifth Edition

Total Learning

Developmental Curriculum for the Young Child

Joanne Hendrick
University of Oklahoma, Emerita

Merrill,
an imprint of Prentice Hall
Upper Saddle River, New Jersey • Columbus, Ohio

Library of Congress Cataloging-in-Publication Data

Hendrick, Joanne
    Total learning: developmental curriculum for the young child /
  Joanne Hendrick. — 5th ed.
     p. cm.
    Includes bibliographical references and index.
    ISBN 0-13-652009-X (case)
    1. Education, Preschool—Curricula. 2. Curriculum planning.
  3. Child development.   I. Title.
LB1140.4.H45 1998
372.19—dc21   97-12818
                         CIP

Cover photo: Joanne Hendrick
Editor: Ann Castel Davis
Developmental Editor: Carol S. Sykes
Production Editor: Sheryl Glicker Langner
Design Coordinator: Karrie M. Converse
Text Designer: Rebecca M. Bobb
Cover Designer: Brian Deep
Production Manager: Laura Messerly
Electronic Text Management: Karen L. Bretz
Director of Marketing: Kevin Flanagan
Marketing Manager: Suzanne Stanton
Advertising/Marketing Coordinator: Julie Shough

This book was set in Novarese by Carlisle Communications, Ltd. and was printed and bound by Quebecor Printing/Book Press. The cover was printed by Phoenix Color Corp.

 © 1998 by Prentice-Hall, Inc.
Simon & Schuster/A Viacom Company
Upper Saddle River, New Jersey 07458

Photo credits: Photos by the author from Institute of Child Development, University of Oklahoma; Children's Place of Baptist Medical Hospital, Oklahoma City, OK; Tinker Air Force Base Child Care Centers, Midwest City, OK; Starr King Parent Child Workshop, Santa Barbara, CA; San Marcos Parent Child Workshop, Santa Barbara, CA; The Oaks Parent Child Workshop, Santa Barbara, CA; Discoveries, Santa Barbara, CA; Metrotech Child Care Center, Oklahoma City, OK.

Printed in the United States of America

10 9 8 7 6 5 4 3 2

ISBN: 0-13-652009-X

Prentice-Hall International (UK) Limited, *London*
Prentice-Hall of Australia Pty. Limited, *Sydney*
Prentice-Hall of Canada, Inc., *Toronto*
Prentice-Hall Hispanoamericana, S. A., *Mexico*
Prentice-Hall of India Private Limited, *New Delhi*
Prentice-Hall of Japan, Inc., *Tokyo*
Simon & Schuster Asia Pte. Ltd., *Singapore*
Editora Prentice-Hall do Brasil, Ltda., *Rio de Janeiro*

⇒ Preface ⇒

Total Learning is a practical book that explains how to develop and present curriculum for young children that is comprehensive, developmentally appropriate, and culturally sensitive. Because it focuses on the developmental needs of the child rather than on specific subject areas, it is divided according to the emotional, social, creative, physical, and cognitive selves. To be sure, such topics as science, art, and emergent literacy are included, but they are incorporated into discussions about the self they predominantly benefit. The text advocates curriculum that is age-appropriate, nourished by play, and intended to encourage children to become independent, creative people.

Inviting Features of This Textbook

New to This Edition

- The author, who recently edited *First Steps Toward Teaching the Reggio Way*, includes explanations of the *Reggio Emilia Approach* and suggestions for integrating aspects of that philosophy into the text where appropriate.
- Vygotsky's educational theory is explained.
- Piaget's and Vygotsky's theories are compared.
- The material on teaching the cognitive self now emphasizes a comparison between using the *emergent approach* and the *conventional approach*, explaining why it is desirable to include both approaches when teaching young children.

- The popular annotated references feature includes hundreds of new references for further reading for both beginning and advanced students.
- An increased emphasis is placed on recognizing and honoring parental preferences.
- Suggestions for including children with exceptional needs into the life of the school are integrated throughout the text.
- Where desirable, important new research studies (such as Hart and Risley's) have replaced former, more familiar ones.

Continuing Features

- *Total Learning* includes a strong emphasis on multicultural, nonsexist education.
- It emphasizes teaching the *whole* child—not just the child from the neck up.
- It stresses the value of play as an avenue of learning.
- It provides developmental comparisons that show how curriculum differs for 2- to 3- and 4-year-old children.
- It is written from a practical, hands-on, how-to-do-it point of view.
- References for Further Reading are located at the end of every chapter.
- Content-Related and Integrative Questions are provided to help students review, as are discussion questions for use by the class as a whole.

Acknowledgments

Writing a book of this kind is a major undertaking that requires not only the work of the author but other people's support and contributions as well. In particular, I want to thank the staff of the Children's Center at Santa Barbara City College, Donna Coffman, Clevonease Johnson, Marilyn Statucki, and Zoe Iverson. Since my transfer to the University of Oklahoma, head teachers Cené Marquis, Jane Vaughn, Ruth Ann Ball, and Deb Parkinson have also contributed mightily to my enlightenment. Over the years these people have shared so many ideas and suggestions, and our philosophies are now so entwined, that it would be impossible to say any longer who was responsible for what. The same thing can be said of the students: if students like this book, it is because of what former students have taught me they needed and wanted—and many of their ideas and requests are incorporated here.

Several instructors reviewed the previous edition of *Total Learning* and offered valuable suggestions for improving it:

Nancy A. Benz, South Plains College; Janice K. Ewing, Colby Sawyer College; Karen L. Peterson, Washington State University-Vancouver; and Linda C. Sluder, Texas Woman's University.

The staff at Merrill/Prentice Hall have been of great assistance. I am especially grateful to Ann Davis, editor; Sheryl Langner, production editor; and Laura Larson, copy editor, for their understanding and encouragement as well as their professional expertise during the book's production.

I am most indebted as well as thankful for the forbearance of many staffs and children from a variety of children's centers and nursery schools who permitted me to invade their privacy by taking pictures for the book. These include the Institute of Child Development, University of Oklahoma; Children's Place of Baptist Medical Hospital, Oklahoma City; the East and West Tinker Air Force Base Child Development Centers, Midwest City; Metrotech Child Care Training Center, Oklahoma City; and the Starr King Parent Child Workshop, San Marcos Parent Child Workshop, Oaks Parent Child Workshop, and Discoveries, all located in Santa Barbara.

The quality of the photographs was much enhanced by my friends at Color Chrome Photographic Laboratories, who continue to make my work look much better that I have any right to expect. To them goes a special thank you!

Contents

4

Planning for Total Learning: Creating Supportive Curriculum Plans and Schedules   57

5

Designing the Supportive Environment   83

6

Planning with Individual Children in Mind: Using Educational Objectives in the Preschool   103

7

Practical Methods of Recording and Evaluating Behavior   113

8

Keeping Children Safe and Well Fed   133

9

Developing Physical Competence   157

10

Helping Children Understand and Value Life   185

11

Achieving Emotional Competence   201

12

Getting Along Together: Achieving Competence in Interpersonal Relations   **229**

15

Developing Verbal Competence 327

16

Putting It All Together for a Good Group Time   355

17

Helping Children Learn to Think for Themselves: Using the Emergent Approach   377

Appendixes

Have you ever

- Wondered what young children really should learn in preschool?
- Been questioned about your philosophy of teaching and felt unable to give a clear answer?
- Wanted to know how to plan curriculum more effectively?

If you have, the material in this chapter will help you.

When it comes to working well with children, respect must be informed by understanding—understanding of children's development, children's needs, the individuality of each child, the way the world looks to a child, what childhood is all about. The more understanding there is, the greater the pleasure, the greater the delightful mystery of children.

Respect informed by understanding allows no place for seeing children as objects for our amusement, as "cute," as less than human. Respect informed by understanding leads to empowerment of children, even babies and toddlers.

Ann Stonehouse (1995, p. 20)

This book concerns itself with answering the following questions: (a) What is the purpose of early education? and (b) What should curriculum for young children include?

What Is the Purpose of Early Education?

The answers to these questions can be deceptively simple. The purpose of early education is to foster competence in young children, though not only competence in intellectual areas. Competence should be thought of as relating to all aspects of self: learning to live comfortably with others, learning to master and safely express one's feelings, and learning to love life and welcome new experience. The purpose of education, then, is to foster competence in dealing with life.

What Should Curriculum for Young Children Include?

Curriculum, which is the design of experiences and activities developed by teachers to help children increase their competence, should be thought of as including everything that happens

to children during their time at the preschool, nursery school, day care home, or children's center. The teacher's task is to develop curriculum that enables such total learning to take place.

But how can teachers go about this? How is it possible to promote creativity, emotional health, physical prowess, social expertise, and cognitive skills in a few brief hours each day? Moreover, how is it possible to weave these into a consistent whole? At first glance it may appear an overwhelming task. However, if we break the task into smaller parts, we will see that it is possible to develop curriculum that does accomplish these goals and brings satisfaction and fulfillment to children and teachers.

The most common way of breaking curriculum into parts is according to subject matter (Bredekamp & Rosegrant, 1995; Day, 1994; Maxim, 1993; Seefeldt & Barbour, 1994). This approach may feel natural and sensible to us because we have been brought up in an educational tradition in which curriculum is divided according to that system. As children we moved from art class to science class to history class, seeing little relationship between subjects and often ignoring our feelings.

But life is not like that. In life many kinds of learnings happen together and affect each other. Feelings often strongly influence learning ability, and the need for social involvement takes priority over the acquisition of information. In real life all aspects of the person must be treated together and educated together. Only when this is recognized and provided for in the curriculum can true learning and competence develop. For this reason, I prefer to discuss curriculum in terms of these aspects, or *selves*, and to design curriculum that provides the various learning experiences that are most suitable for the development of competence for each of these selves. This life-oriented approach places the emphasis where it belongs—on the child, not on impersonal subject matter.

In this book, the selves are identified as the physical, emotional, social, creative, and cognitive selves. The physical self is discussed first because a healthy body provides the foundation that enables the other selves to develop and flourish. Curriculum for the physical self covers not only recommendations for the development of physical abilities but also discussions regarding nutrition, cooking, caring for the body, and understanding the cycle of life and death.

The emotional self is emphasized because emotional stability contributes so much to children's sense of well-being and self-confidence. Emotionally healthy children do not need to put their energies into defending themselves from worries and insecurities; instead, they are free to channel their energy into developing their total being, thereby enriching the growth of all five selves. Curriculum for the emotional self involves the planning of experiences that inspire trust, autonomy, and initiative and that teach children to remain in contact with their feelings. Such curriculum uses dramatic play to clarify these emotions and help children understand that other people have feelings, too.

The social self is vital to consider because children must live with other people all their lives. The earlier children can gain skills that help them get along easily and happily with others, the more likely they are to enjoy life and to feel successful. Learning for the social self usually depends on interpersonal encounters between the child and other people, both grown-ups and children. Curriculum to aid such learning promotes the ability to control antisocial impulses. It helps children get along in a group, enjoy playing with other youngsters, and learn to lend them a helping hand from time to time. If this curriculum is well presented, it encourages children to treasure their own ethnic and sexual identities and those of other people as well.

The creative self is another vital aspect because creativity greatly contributes to children's sense of self-worth and individuality and increases the probability of unique contributions that they may ultimately make to society. Curriculum for the creative self contains materials that encourage self-expression and pretend play and strategies that enhance the growth of original thought.

Finally, the curriculum for the cognitive self must be as carefully considered as the rest because the ability to reason and put the results of this reasoning into words enhances children's potential for later academic success. Therefore, the cognitive self, though discussed last here, has an important place in preschool curriculum.

Such curriculum includes experiences and activities that enhance verbal fluency and elicit the use of particular mental abilities. Ideally, it should also encourage children to generate their own ideas and solutions to problems for themselves. Fostering this independent habit of mind is an invaluable aspect of developing the cognitive self.

But while thinking of the individual selves, also remember that a sound curriculum not only provides opportunities to enhance the individual selves. In some ways, children are like bicycles: they are greater than the sum of their parts. It is the way the selves of the child operate together that produces the personality, just as gears and wheels operate together to become the bike. Therefore, well-designed curriculum should be planned to foster this kind of wholeness by providing opportunities for integrating learning.

Hard to believe that 4-year-old Anthony could be this competent, but he performed this feat a number of times. (He is also the son of a basketball coach!)

Teachers should intend that every subject they include, whether it be cooking, carpentry, or caring for an animal, educates all the selves, even though it may emphasize only one in particular.

What Is Competence?

This chapter began with the statement that the purpose of education is to foster competence in dealing with life. But what is competence, and why is it of such value? Competence can be defined as the wonderful feeling of assurance exemplified by the statements "I can do it," "I am able," "I know how," and "I am an effective person." These reveal a security and belief in oneself that are the fundamental cornerstones of self-esteem. The fortunate possessors of such confidence are willing to risk and explore for the sake of learning because they believe themselves to be worthwhile, competent people.

According to White (1968), the desire for competence is one of the basic motivators of human behavior. He postulates that in addition to needing to satisfy hunger, thirst, and other basic physiological needs, human beings have an inherent drive for mastery and competence. It is this drive, White maintains, that urges the infant on in the relentless practice of rolling over or sitting up, and it is the same drive that motivates many adults to pursue evening education classes after a long day's work.

Competence may also be considered in terms of its opposite: helplessness. Nelson (1987) reviewed a number of studies that demonstrate that feelings of helplessness result when children find that their personal efforts have little impact on how things turn out. In other words, when children experience consistent failure, some of them conclude that nothing they do makes any difference, and, as children grow older, they are more likely to draw the conclusion that they are ineffective in coping with circumstances. People often express this helplessness by acting anxious and depressed and becoming unable to take action (Peterson, Maier, & Seligman, 1993). They just stop trying.

On the other hand, when individuals feel competent, they see themselves, at least to some degree, as in control of their own destinies, and as a result, they feel good about themselves. Bronson (1974) claims that the person who sees himself as competent expects that "under most conditions he is likely to encounter, he will be able to cope with whatever demands he meets, and to derive joy from the encounter" (p. 243). What a marvelous educational goal this is for teachers—to help children attain competence so they may experience joy. And what a powerful antidote this could be for children of the poor, whose helplessness is often a hallmark of the family's attitude toward life.

How Is Competence Acquired?

Granted that competence is a fundamental goal desirable for education, the question remains, What do teachers need to know and do to foster competence in young children?

What Do Teachers Need to Know to Foster Competence?

First, *teachers need to understand the general capabilities and interests common to each age of childhood so that they can plan curriculum that is neither so difficult it is discouraging nor so easy it is uninteresting* (Bredekamp & Copple, 1997). They also require knowledge of each child, because every youngster, although like other children of the same age in some ways, is unique in others.

Studies and checklists are available that identify general developmental levels and characteristics for particular ages. One such list is included in Appendix A. To appreciate the uniqueness of individual children, however, teachers have to rely on themselves and their developing sensitivity and expertise, as much as on these more objective measures. For example: a teacher needs to know what cultural values the child's family holds dear. What do they anticipate or prefer that the school experience will be like? Are they undergoing hard times? Has there been a recent crisis of any kind? How does the child's family feel about her? What do they expect in the way of behavior?

And what is her neighborhood like? With whom does she play? How much television does she watch, and what kinds of programs does she see? All these bits and pieces garnered by the teacher contribute to understanding the child and her family and interpreting her behavior accurately. Actually, it is all these individual circumstances and variations that make teaching fascinating.

Teachers need to know how young children learn. The question of how to enable all children to learn as fully and completely as possible, without pushing them too hard or letting them drift into boredom, remains the continuing challenge of education. Because of a persistent pressure to push formal academic learning on young children before they are ready for it (Elkind, 1990a & 1990b; Greenberg, 1992; Rescorla, Hyson, & Hirsh-Pasek, 1991), teachers must be knowledgeable about what constitutes developmentally appropriate curriculum.

Fortunately, the National Association for the Education of Young Children has issued a publication entitled *Developmentally Appropriate Practice in Early Childhood Programs Serving Children from Birth through Age 8* that spells out in considerable detail what is and is not appropriate teaching practice for children of that age (Bredekamp & Copple, 1997; Bredekamp & Shepherd, 1990).

Unfortunately, a recent study has revealed that *only one in seven centers* (14%) included in the survey could be rated as being developmentally appropriate (Helburn, Howes, Bryant, & Kagan, 1995). The vast majority of the centers did not meet children's needs for health, safety, warm relationships, and learning. This shocking information makes plain just how important it is for teachers to study and learn as much as they can about providing education for young children that is humane, caring, and appropriate.

Once teachers have a reasonable knowledge of what young children are like, they need to understand how to teach them effectively, because the more easily children learn, the more competent they will feel. Although recent evidence indicates that this is a complex question and that the answer varies from child to child, some basic principles about how all young children learn are generally regarded as true.

One such principle is that children pass through a series of developmental sequences as they grow. Children learn to sit up before they learn to stand and to use their fingers before learning to hold a spoon. Such stage-related development has been substantiated by such

Challenges for children should be hard enough to be interesting but not so hard they teach defeat.

widely diverse researchers as Allen and Marotz (1990); Brittain (1979); Erikson (1963); Fox and Tipps (1995); Piaget (1983); and Thelen, Ulrich, and Jensen (1989).

Another related principle is that children learn things a step at a time. This step-by-step learning is often termed *hierarchical learning* because the child moves up a hierarchy rung by rung as skill is acquired. Teachers therefore should plan to teach skills gradually, first teaching simple skills and then more advanced ones as the children gain competence. An important implication of this principle for teaching is that the curriculum must offer a variety of levels of challenge concurrently, because different children in the same group are at different steps on the learning ladder during the same period.

Still another basic principle of learning is that children and adults learn best through actual experiences and participation. John Dewey's concept of learning by doing is as true today as it was 40 years ago (Cuffaro, 1995). The truth of this can be seen by reflecting on the process of learning to teach. One can read about teaching forever, but all the reading and discussion in the world cannot substitute for the learning that results from actually encountering the liveliness and variability of young children in the classroom. It is learning by doing, not learning by talking about it, that makes the difference.

For young children who cannot read and for whom language is still new and tenuously grasped, the value of experience-based learning is even more crucial (Fosnot, 1996; Piaget & Inhelder, 1969). Discussion and verbal learning that are isolated from actual experience have little educative power for such young learners. Instead, learning must be accomplished through all the sensory channels. Children must live through, explore, and try things out to attach meaning to them. As Bruner says, competence in the form of objective intelligence comes from knowing how, not knowing that (Connolly & Bruner, 1974).

The final principle to remember is that preschool children learn by using play to translate experience into understanding (Pellegrini & Boyd, 1993; Piaget, 1962). As Frank (1968) remarks, "Through play, children learn what no one can teach them" (p. 3). For young children, play *is* the lifeblood of learning, so it is vital that teachers provide extensive opportunities for children to learn through play every time they come to school.

Teachers must realize that parents are the most important influence in the child's development. Teachers sometimes fail to see that they have a limited role in the child's educational experience. The truth is that parents and the cultural/ethnic background of the home exert a much more profound influence than teachers do, particularly during the early stages of development (Hildebrand, Phenice, Gray, & Hines, 1996; Powell, 1989; Swick, 1991). This is true not only because of the greater amounts of time children and parents are likely to spend together but also because of the strong emotional bonds that exist between them. Teachers therefore need to keep their perspective about their relative importance and to realize the benefits of including parents in the life of the school. As an aid to teachers, suggestions concerning this home-school cooperation are made throughout this book, and chapter 2 is devoted entirely to this subject.

What Do Teachers Need to Do?

First, *teachers have to work hard.* Occasional newcomers to the field of early childhood education have the impression that young children are easier to teach or less challenging to control than older children are. Of course, this is not true. Teaching 2-, 3-, and 4-year-olds requires very special energies. As Farnham-Diggory (1992) says so aptly:

> The common denominator of our good teachers is available, well-directed energy. Energy to notice and attend promptly to the individual needs of children; energy to be pleasant and cooperative despite numerous demands from the children; energy to direct aides and volunteers cheerfully and sufficiently; energy to plan, plan, and replan ways of keeping the children busy and independent; energy to keep

> track of the effectiveness of lessons and other kinds of activities, to keep notes and written guides; energy to explain details of the program to parents and administrators; and, above all, energy to respond warmly and sensitively to children. (p. 54)

The hours are long, and the responsibilities are great because research indicates it is during these very early years that much of the child's basic intellectual ability is formed. Indeed, neurologists now confirm what we early childhood teachers have known on a practical level for a long time. It is that successful development of the brain depends not only on adequate nutrition and health but also, crucially, depends on the quality and repetition of experience provided to the child during the preschool years (Nash, 1997). We must never forget that the work of early childhood teachers and parents carries a very special responsibility with it—and the next day it is there to do all over again.

Teachers need to pay attention to research and apply the results of research findings when it is appropriate to do so. This book includes a summary of a research study in almost every chapter. Some of these studies were included because they are well known, while others were selected because they provide a variety of different and occasionally ingenious ways of finding out answers to questions about children. They were also selected to demonstrate the wide variety of forms research can take, ranging from recording observations of the way children behave to experimenting with changing their environments or carrying out long-term follow-up studies. Well known or not, all these studies contain valuable implications for teaching.

I hope that reading them will convince the student that research can be fascinating and that teachers need to pay attention to it because it can produce results that are directly relevant to what happens every day in early childhood classrooms. My frustration is that the studies could not be presented in their entirety. Perhaps these overviews will stimulate readers to pursue the original publication or, better yet, resolve to carry out research themselves in the future. The field of early childhood offers endless opportunities for such activity.

Teachers should take pride in knowing that preschool education can make a difference. In the past, the value of preschool education was often ignored or denigrated, and even today teachers must still fight the stereotype of being "just baby-sitters."

Unfortunately, many people are still unaware of the growing body of evidence that quality preschool child care programs can produce substantial, long-term benefits for children who participate in such environments. For this reason, it is important for all of us to know about the landmark study described in this chapter. We must be well informed so we can stand up for the value of what we do and be able to cite the research findings that prove its worth.

Teachers must present learning within a climate of caring. Although climate is composed of many elements, it is primarily a product of the teachers' attitudes toward the children and their work and the children's response to these feelings (Elicker & Fortner-Wood, 1995). We must ask ourselves, therefore, what kind of teacher attitude is most likely to promote learning in the classroom. Is it warmth or positive regard or even love? Surely all these qualities are of value in teaching. Who would not prefer a warm teacher to a cold one or an approving teacher to one who rejects children unless they conform to his or her demands?

The difficulty with advocating warmth and acceptance does not lie in whether they are desirable. The difficulty lies in asking teachers to feel this way at times when they cannot do it

Research Study

Early Education Can Make a Difference

Research Question   The Consortium for Longitudinal Studies asked the basic question, Can quality preschool education produce long-term, lasting benefits for children who attend such programs?

Research Method   This follow-up study gathered data about how young children turned out who had attended high-quality experimental preschool programs in the early 1960s. These 11 programs were distributed over the entire United States and included center-based, home-based, and combined center- and home-based programs. Most of the children came from low-income families. The total number of children included in the follow-up study was 2,008.

All the studies offered the advantage of experimental groups (children who had attended the programs) and reasonably similar control groups (children who had not attended the programs). This circumstance was crucial to the success of the follow-up study because researchers could compare what happened to the children who had attended preschool with what happened to the children who had not attended preschool.

The investigators checked school records, scores on intelligence tests, and interviewed the parents and young people who ranged from 9 to 19 years of age at the time of the follow-up study.

Results   The results of the follow-up study clearly indicated that the preschool programs *did* provide the following long-term benefits for the children who attended them:

1. The children were more competent in school. Although results varied from program to program, children in the preschool programs were only half as likely as children in the control groups to be assigned to special education classes, and fewer of them were required to repeat a grade in school. (Only 13.8% of the preschool children were assigned to special education classes as compared with 28.8% of the control children. Only 25% of the preschool children had to repeat a grade as compared with 36.6% of the control children.)

sincerely—times, for example, when a child has deliberately twisted the rat's paw to see it wince or bitten another child hard enough to draw blood. In such circumstances can one feel warm or accepting? And if not, what is left? Is it possible to advocate *any* attitude that is genuine and can be evoked in such highly charged situations that promotes positive growth for teacher and child?

It *is* possible, and that attitude is best described by the word *caring*. Perhaps it is really this quality that Harry Stack Sullivan (1940) has in mind when he comments, "Love exists when the satisfaction or security of another person becomes as significant to one as is one's own" (p. 20). I prefer to substitute the word *caring* for *love* because in our society the word *love* has so many different connotations (Stonehouse,

1995). Thus, we can say that caring exists when the satisfaction or security of another person becomes as significant as one's own. This attitude fits even difficult circumstances, because it is possible for the teacher to continue to care, and to care intensely, about a youngster even while being appalled at what he has done. In tense confrontations, it is deeply reassuring to children to sense this true concern. It assures them that no matter what they have done, they are important to the teacher and the teacher will not abandon them. Moreover, this reaction has the additional virtue of being absolutely genuine, which thereby makes unnecessary such false declarations of approval as "I like *you* but not what you do."

One final aspect of the Sullivan definition requires comment. The reader may recall the

2. Children who had attended preschool programs scored significantly better on intelligence tests during their early years in school; however, those differences disappeared after 3 to 4 years, so the final conclusion was that the effect of early education on intelligence test scores was not permanent.
3. Early education had an effect on the family—mothers of the preschool group were more satisfied with their children's performance in school and had higher occupational aspirations for their children than did mothers of children in the control groups.

Implications These findings are important because the effect on the children themselves is significant. How much better it is for children's self-esteem to remain in regular school classes than to be made to repeat a grade or suffer the potential humiliation of placement in a special education classroom.

The financial savings to society must also be taken into account. Providing special education and having students repeat grades costs a lot of money, and any time this can be avoided legislators and school administrators sit up and take notice. Therefore, educators can use these research results in their fight for additional quality preschool programs.

Finally, the Consortium study was the first longitudinal study to provide solid, well-researched evidence that early education actually does produce tangible, positive, long-term results. Thanks to it and to numerous additional studies since that time (Fuerst & Fuerst, 1993; Garber, 1989; Gotts, 1989; Schweinhart, Barnes, & Weikart, 1993), legislators and administrators now look more favorably toward providing preschool programs for young children because the research has made them aware that providing quality early education has lasting benefits for society.

Note. From "Lasting Effects of Early Education: A Report from the Consortium for Longitudinal Studies" by I. Lazar, R. Darlington, H. Murray, J. Royce, and A. Snipper, 1982, *Monographs of the Society for Research in Child Development*, 47(2–3, Serial No. 195).

Providing many opportunities for children to figure things out for themselves is a hallmark of the constructivist approach.

definition states that caring exists when the well-being of another becomes as important as one's own. Good teachers give much of themselves to the children and families whom they serve, but this should never be accomplished at the expense of caring for themselves. That is why it is so important to remember the second part of the definition, which makes it plain that it is necessary and acceptable to care for oneself as well as for other people. Caring should never be offered in a spirit of self-sacrifice, lest it become martyrdom.

Teachers need to develop a clear philosophy of teaching. This involves identifying those educational values they consider to be most worthwhile and determining the methods of instruction that will implement these values most effectively.

Educational Philosophies

Two points of view about how children learn are particularly valuable for early childhood teachers to understand. These are the *behaviorist* approach and the *constructivist* approach. In actuality, no preschool is likely to be purely behaviorist or purely constructivist; rather, individual schools tend to follow one approach more than the other while remaining somewhat eclectic.

The Behaviorist Approach

This approach maintains that the basic principles of learning operate according to the laws of classical, operant conditioning. Proponents of this approach advocate changing children's behavior by using behavior modification techniques based on those principles.

The teachers' role is to select out and reward behavior that they wish to continue and to ignore or negatively respond to behavior they wish to extinguish. Therefore, behaviorists recommend that teachers wishing to change a child's behavior should begin with a careful observation of the current behavior, determine which rewards are preferred by that child, develop a description of what behavior would be more desirable, and develop and implement a reinforcement plan or schedule that uses the preferred rewards to select and reinforce the more desirable behavior. Two examples of programs that have used this theory are the Bereiter Englemann program (Bereiter and Engelmann, 1966) and the Portage project (Shearer, 1993).

Nowadays it is particularly important to understand the value and uses of behavior modification as an educational approach because of the passage of the Americans with Disabilities Act (Child Care Law Center, 1994b). This legislation not only mandates that more children with disabilities be included in ordinary preschool classrooms; it also mandates that these children be provided with special support services. The vast majority of the specialists who constitute this support personnel use the behavior modification approach because they have found that it can have certain very positive results (Neisworth & Buggey, 1993). Therefore, it is important for preschool teachers to understand and accept the value of these strategies because they will be used increasingly as we welcome children with disabilities into our classrooms.

Although many early childhood teachers say they dislike this rather cut-and-dried, calculated approach to working with children, there is no denying that all teachers, either consciously or unconsciously, use the principles of positive reinforcement every time they smile in approval at what a child has done, just as they use negative reinforcement when they reprimand a child. One advantage of understanding behaviorist learning theory is that it may prevent naïve teachers from unwittingly causing unwanted behavior to continue because they fail to perceive and put a stop to the rewards a behavior holds for a child.

Another advantage of the behavior modification approach is that it encourages teachers to make careful observations of what the child is actually doing, develop clear-cut teaching goals, and formulate plans for how to reach those goals. The written Individual Educational Plans that regulations require be used when working with children who have disabilities are classic examples of this sort of behavior-based goal setting and planning that often embrace the tenets of behavior modification to carry out the plan.

Despite these strengths, there are certain *limitations* to this approach that must also be noted. According to Franklin and Biber (1977), these include (a) whether specifically trained behaviors generalize to other behaviors, (b) how long the reinforced behavior is likely to continue once the reward is removed, and (c) how tangible rewards (such as candy or gold stars) can be exchanged for more intangible ones later on.

In addition, I raise the problems of how such a reward system can be translated into internal rather than external gratifications, so that the child ultimately becomes inner rather than other

controlled. Nor does this learning theory satisfactorily explain how children generate novel sentences they have not heard before and, therefore, could not have acquired through imitation and reinforcement. Also, this kind of extensive advance planning tends to kill any spontaneity and spur-of-the-moment learning that might otherwise occur. Indeed, Franklin and Biber comment that programs presently based on behavior modification techniques seemingly value the more traditional, academic forms of education. These programs often emphasize the use of learning drills and rote memory as educational techniques: The Bereiter Englemann program (1966) was a particularly clear-cut example of this.

The Constructivist Approach

Because of such problems, many people feel that the strategies of behavior modification provide only partial explanations about how individuals learn, so they favor a perspective termed the *constructivist approach* that stems from the work of Piaget (1983) and Vygotsky (1978). Constructivists see the child as the source of action combined with interaction with the environment rather than being mainly manipulated from the outside as the behaviorists do. They maintain that as the child interacts with the environment, he gradually develops (constructs) inner cognitive structures that help him make sense of his world and that influence his response to the social and physical world in which he lives.

The earliest advocates of constructivism relied mainly on the philosophy of Piaget for support. Some examples of Piaget's contributions to constructivist theory include his emphasis on the value of direct exploration and handling of objects, his focus on the child's inner construction of what he knows, his identification of the various stages of cognitive and moral development, and his demonstrations that the thought processes of children and adults really *do* differ from each other. For these reasons his primary contributions to constructivism lie mainly in the cognitive realm.

Recently, as the work of Vygotsky has become more widely known, his theories have further enriched the constructivist base. While acknowledging the active role of the child in learning and developing meaning for himself, Vygotsky emphasized the social influences—the roles other people play—in what and how the child learns. He maintained that through discussion and experiences provided by other people—either children or adults—a child can be encouraged to reach beyond what he currently knows and move closer to the edge of what he "almost" knows, thereby adding to his store of knowledge. The art of teaching, then, is to perceive the child's current intellectual status and sensitively enable him to advance beyond that place through dialogue and questioning.

Although some debate continues on the relative contributions of these men, consensus appears to be building that incorporation of Vygotsky's theories has placed constructivist learning in a helpful, broader context of cognitive/social learning (Cobb, 1996). The schools of Reggio Emilia in northern Italy partially exemplify this point of view about learning and teaching.

Philosophy of this Book

Total Learning and its companion book, *The Whole Child* (Hendrick, 1996), are based primarily on the constructivist philosophy. They emphasize the value of children figuring things out for themselves as they interact with the environment and support the idea that children construct their own knowledge of the world from their interaction with it and the people it contains.

This interpretation of the constructivist approach views interaction as taking place not only between the child and the environment but also between the various aspects or internal selves within the child. The way the child sees and feels about herself influences her ability to learn, just as her potential sense of mastery over cognitive materials increases her positive sense of self-worth.

Children flourish when they know the teacher truly cares about them.

It also incorporates the concept that children pass through a number of predictable, orderly sequences in their growth. It uses Erikson as the model for emotional development, Piaget and Vygotsky in relation to cognitive growth, and Gesell and other more recent authors for sequences of physical development.

The constructivist philosophy emphasizes that it is important to enhance the child's sense that he is a competent, autonomous person in all aspects of his being. The child who sees himself as socially adept, emotionally self-possessed, physically skilled, and intellectually able feels secure and masterful—ready to cope with changes in his environment as they occur, ready to relish life and welcome new experiences.

Although it is necessary to discuss these different aspects of the child's self individually as this book progresses, the overall intention is to blend the needs and education of all of them together into an integrated, total curriculum and to deal with the child as a whole being. With such a philosophy, learning through play and actual experience is as essential to the curriculum as is the planning that provides for many choices within a carefully arranged yet flexible overall structure.

Throughout this book, emphasis is placed on *process learning*. This learning helps children acquire skills that enable them to cope with many situations rather than to merely learn facts or content (though the teaching of facts and content is included). Environments that favor such process learning are often spoken of as being "open," but this should not be interpreted as meaning haphazard. Indeed, the sensitivity needed for planning for self-selection and open choice that truly meets the needs of children requires more thought on the teacher's part than does the teacher-dominated approach in which children are conveniently marshalled from one activity to another according to the clock and the teacher's wish.

What *open* actually means according to the philosophy of this book is that a variety of carefully selected learning opportunities based on the children's needs and interests are offered. These are geared to the appropriate developmental level and are intended to develop all five selves. Some of these, particularly in the area of cognitive activities, may involve active participation by child and teacher; some are more child centered. The environment is open in the sense that children are encouraged to involve themselves in these experiences as their needs and desires dictate, provided that they do not injure themselves or others or damage property. But this is not just a case of child plus activity. The social milieu provided by other children and adults con-

tributes much to the richness and value of this learning experience. It is the people, both grown-ups and children, who provide the opportunities for the questions, interchanges, and compromises that are the essence of successful open education.

Summary

Because they are an essential part of that environment, parents exert a profound influence on the way children develop (Powell, 1989). Research shows that when preschool teachers provide high-quality education, they can also have an important effect on how children develop (Helburn et al., 1995; Schweinhart et al., 1993). The philosophy of *Total Learning* is an eclectic, constructivist one that acknowledges the contributions of the behaviorist approach but is primarily based on the philosophies of Piaget and Vygotsky.

The purpose of education is to foster competence in all aspects of life, so curriculum should provide opportunities for total learning. This is best accomplished by considering the five aspects of the child's personality (the physical, emotional, social, creative, and cognitive selves) when planning curriculum.

To make this a reality, teachers need to know what children are like. They must be knowledgeable about developmental sequences and individual differences to keep the curriculum both age- and child-appropriate. They need to remember that children learn things a step at a time, learn best through experience, and use play to interiorize knowledge. Teachers also need to value the family as the most important educational influence in the child's life.

Teachers need to work hard; they need to pay attention to research findings and their implications for the classroom; they need to know that what they do can make a positive, long-term difference in the lives of the children they teach; they need to develop a clear philosophy of teaching; and they need to present learning in a climate of caring, in which the well-being of the children is as important to them as is their own. This climate of caring is fundamental to the growth of competence.

Self-Check Questions for Review

Content-Related Questions

1. According to the author, what is the basic purpose of education?
2. Should curriculum focus mainly on cognitive, intellectual learning?
3. Name the five selves, and mention some areas of curriculum that belong to the separate selves.
4. Why is a feeling of competence so valuable?
5. Name three important principles about how all young children learn. Why do teachers need to know what these principles are and how to apply them?
6. Are teachers or parents more important influences in children's lives?
7. Name two important research findings produced by the Consortium for Longitudinal Studies. Why are these findings so important?
8. Give a brief description of the strengths and weaknesses of the behavioristic philosophy of education.
9. Describe some cornerstones of the constructivist approach that underlie teaching young children.
10. What is the second part of Sullivan's definition of love or caring, and why is it as important as the first part?

Integrative Questions

1. Select one activity, such as playing with blocks, and give examples of how creativity, emotional health, physical prowess, social expertise, and cognitive skills can be enhanced while the children are participating in that activity.
2. Give some real-life examples of teacher behaviors that might contribute to a child's feelings of helplessness, and compare these with some examples of behaviors that would increase a child's sense of competence.
3. Taking into account the factors discussed in chapter 1, discuss your own personal requirements that you feel a child-care situation should meet before you could accept a staff position.

Questions and Activities

1. Nobody is competent at everything. Think of an area in which you do not regard yourself as skilled, such as playing tennis, using a power tool, or giving a talk. How do you respond when asked to participate in such an activity? And how do you feel when forced to participate?
2. Watch closely the next time you teach. See if you can spot any circumstances in which a child feels incompetent. Was there some way you could have helped him or her cope more satisfactorily? What might be the best thing to say or do when a child says, "I can't"?
3. Considering the opposite of what should be done often stimulates thought. For this reason, suppose you wanted to make children feel as helpless as possible. What could you do to make them feel this way? Give several everyday examples.
4. What would you say the effect of helplessness is on self-esteem?
5. Put the difference between knowing *how* and knowing *that* into words. Use an example to illustrate what you mean.
6. A mother has just entered her child in your preschool. She asks whether he will be learning to write his name, the alphabet, and other skills that he needs to learn before entering elementary school. How would you explain the learning program at your school so that the mother understands what kinds of learning will take place?
7. Do you agree that caring is the most valuable attitude for a teacher to express? What other attitudes are important to project to children?
8. Is there any difference between the "openness" in a preschool setting as described in the text and allowing children to do anything they please when they please? Where should the teacher draw the line?

References for Further Reading

Overviews

Ayers, W. (1989). *The good preschool teacher: Six teachers reflect on their lives.* New York: Teachers College Press. This book is a collection of interviews given by six very different teachers of preschool children combined with descriptions of events in their child care situations. It provides insights into a variety of viewpoints about what good teachers of young children think about and how they put their philosophies into action.

Beardsley, L. (1990). *Good day, bad day: The child's experience of child care.* New York: Teachers College Press. This book contrasts fictitious good and mediocre schools by describing imaginary situations and how the schools handle them. These are followed by knowledge-based comments. *Highly recommended.*

Bredekamp, S., & Copple, C. (Eds.). (1997). *Developmentally appropriate practice in early childhood programs* (rev. ed.). Washington, DC: National Association for the Education of Young Children. This carefully done revision takes the necessity of adapting to a variety of ethnic and cultural expectations into account as well as defining generally agreed-on desirable early childhood education practices. It is also valuable because it includes helpful overviews of developmental characteristics of young children at various ages and for various selves. *Indispensable.*

Griffin, E. F. (1982). *Island of childhood: Education in the special world of nursery school.* New York: Teachers College Press. Griffin conveys a sense of the atmosphere that should surround children and teachers during these early years. *Highly recommended.*

Read, K., Gardner, P., & Mahler, B. C. (1987). *Early childhood programs: Human relationships and learning* (8th ed.). New York: Holt, Rinehart & Winston. This book remains the best description of the underlying attitude and approach I hope teachers can achieve when working with young children.

Competence

Fowler, W. (Ed.). (1986). Early experience and the development of competence. In W. Damon (Ed.), *New directions for child development.* San Francisco: Jossey-Bass. This paperback from the New Directions series considers competence from a variety of viewpoints. A useful place to begin.

Sternberg, R. J., & Kolligian, J. Jr. (Eds.). (1990). *Competence considered.* New Haven, CT: Yale University Press. A readable, comprehensive discussion of competence is offered here.

White, R. W. (1968). Motivation reconsidered: The concept of competence. In M. Almy (Ed.), *Early childhood play: Selected readings related to cognition and motivation.* New York: Simon & Schuster. In this classic discussion, the author reviews various theories about the nature of motivation and then proposes that certain behaviors are motivated by the need to achieve competence rather than by hunger or thirst.

Descriptions of Various Programs and Philosophies

Lay-Dopyera, M., & Dopyera, J. (1990). *Becoming a teacher of young children* (4th ed.). New York: McGraw-Hill. Chapter 9 provides an excellent overview of the behaviorist and constructivist approaches to early childhood education.

Morrison, G. (1988). *Early childhood education today* (4th ed.). New York: Merrill/Macmillan. Morrison offers a useful overview of the kinds of early childhood settings available in the United States.

Caring

Buscaglia, L. (1984). *Loving each other: The challenge of human relationships.* New York: Holt, Rinehart & Winston. Buscaglia offers some sensible advice about what loving really means.

Fosnot, C. T. (Ed.). (1996). *Constructivism: Theory, perspectives, and practice.* New York: Teachers College Press. This book provides an excellent introduction to constructivist philosophy. Of particular interest to early childhood teachers are the chapters on theory and the one on the project approach. *Highly recommended.*

Hendrick, J. (Ed.). (1997). *First steps toward teaching the Reggio Way.* Upper Saddle River, NJ: Merrill/Prentice Hall. *First Steps* includes clear descriptions of the Reggio Approach followed by many chapters depicting steps taken by American teachers to implement aspects of that philosophy in their classrooms.

Hohmann, M., & Weikart, D. (1995). *Educating young children: Active learning practices for preschool and child care programs.* Ypsilanti, MI: High/Scope Press. This updated version of an old favorite translates Piagetian philosophy into everyday practice.

Neisworth, J. T., & Buggey, T. J. (1993). Behavior analysis and principles in early childhood education. In J. L. Roopnarine & J. E. Johnson (Eds.), *Approaches to early childhood education* (2nd ed.). Upper Saddle River, NJ: Merrill/Prentice Hall. The authors clearly describe the basic principles of behaviorism and provide several helpful examples of how behavior modification techniques would be applied in specific situations with young children.

Warren, R. M. (1977). *Caring: Supporting children's growth.* Washington, DC: National Association for the Education of Young Children. This pamphlet, which is filled with wise observations on fostering the emotional health of children, illustrates many aspects of caring related to preschool education.

For the Advanced Student

Bellack, A. S., Hersen, M., & Kazdin, Q. E. (Eds.). (1982). *International handbook of behavior modification and therapy.* New York: Plenum. This is a very long book that offers a tremendous variety of articles related to the subject of behavior modification. For serious students of this approach, it is an outstanding reference.

Driscoll, A. (1995). *Cases in early childhood education: Stories of programs and practices.* Boston: Allyn & Bacon. Driscoll describes a wide variety of early childhood programs that, through various, have one thing in common—a quality experience, for children, teachers, and families. A not-to-be-missed description of what can and should be possible to offer young children.

Goffin, S. G. (1994). *Curriculum models and early childhood education: Appraising the relationship*. Upper Saddle River, NJ: Merrill/Prentice Hall. Goffin provides in-depth appraisals of several early childhood education models: Montessori, developmental-interaction, direct instruction, High/Scope and Kamii/DeVries constructivist. She includes excellent appraisals as well as a thoughtful discussion of implications for future investigations. *Highly recommended*.

Harter, S. (1985). Competence as a dimension of self-evaluation: Toward a comprehensive model of self-worth. In R. L. Leahy (Ed.), *The development of the self*. New York: Academic Press. Harter's chapter explores the relationship between competence and feelings of self-esteem.

Helburn, S., Howes, C., Bryant, D., & Kagan, S. L. (1995). *Cost, quality, and child outcomes in child care centers: Executive summary* (2nd ed.). Denver: Economics Department, University of Colorado. After defining quality care, this study reveals the distressing fact that only one in seven centers studied in this landmark research met developmentally appropriate standards. It closes with a list of suggested steps to remedy this serious situation.

Peterson, C., Maier, S. F., & Seligman, M. E. P. (1993). *Learned helplessness: A theory for the age of personal control*. New York: Oxford University Press. The authors offer a persuasive review of research documenting the results of succumbing to feelings of helplessness.

Roopnarine, J. L., & Johnson, J. E. (Eds.). (1993). *Approaches to early childhood education* (2nd ed.). Upper Saddle River, NJ: Merrill/Prentice Hall. This indispensable book presents discussions of theories/philosophies related to early education followed by descriptions of programs that exemplify the theories.

Schweinhart, L. J., Barnes, H. V., & Weikart, D. P., with Barnett, W. S., & Epstein, A. S. (1993). *Significant benefits: The High/Scope Perry Preschool Study through age 27*. (High/Scope Educational Research Foundation, Monograph No. 10). Ypsilanti, MI: High/Scope Press. For readers who desire more thorough information on the currently determined benefits of this particular intervention program, this is the best resource.

Slavin, R. E., Karweit, N. L., & Wasik, B. A. (Eds.). (1994). *Preventing early school failure: Research, policy, and practice*. Boston: Allyn & Bacon. For readers who are looking for a review of the lasting or ephemeral effects of various infant/preschool programs, this will be a helpful resource. *Highly recommended*.

Vygotsky, L. (1978). *Mind in society: The development of higher psychological processes*. Cambridge, MA: Harvard University Press. Vygotsky sets forth his basic theories in this very readable book.

2

Including Families in the Life of the School

Have you ever

- Wanted to get to know the parents in your center better but felt uncertain about how to achieve this?
- Fretted over how to produce an interesting parent meeting?
- Become angry when a parent asked you a critical question?

If you have, the material in this chapter will help you.

Glooskap and the Baby

Now it came to pass when Glooskap had conquered all his enemies, even the Kewahqu', who were giants and sorcerers, and the M'teoulin, who were magicians, and the Pamola, who is the evil spirit of the night air, and all manner of ghosts, witches, devils, cannibals, and goblins, that he thought upon what he had done, and wondered if his work was at an end.

And he said this to a certain woman. But she replied, "Not so fast, master, for there yet remains one whom no one has ever conquered or got the better of in any way, and who will remain unconquered to the end of time."

"And who is he?" inquired Glooskap.

"It is the mighty Wasis," she replied, "and there he sits; and I warn you that if you meddle with him you will be sorry."

Now Wasis was a baby. And he sat on the floor sucking a piece of maple sugar, greatly contented and troubling no one.

As Glooskap had never married or had a child, he knew little of the way of managing children. But he was quite certain, as such people are, that he knew all about it. So he turned to the baby with a bewitching smile and bade him come to him.

The baby smiled again, but did not budge. And the Master spoke sweetly and made his voice like that of the summer bird, but it was of no avail, for Wasis sat still and sucked his maple sugar.

Then the Master frowned and spoke terribly, and ordered Wasis to come crawling to him immediately. The baby burst out crying and yelling, but did not move for all that.

Then, since he could do but one thing more, the Master turned to magic. He used his most awful spells, and sang the songs which raise the dead and scare the devils. The Wasis sat and looked admiringly, and seemed to find it very interesting, but all the same he never moved an inch.

So Glooskap gave up in despair, and Wasis, sitting on the floor in the sunshine, went "Goo! Goo!" and crowed.

And to this day when you see a baby well contented, going "Goo! Goo!" and crowing, and no one can tell why, you will know it is because he remembers the time when he overcame the Master who had conquered all the world. For of all the beings that have ever been since the beginning, the baby is alone the only invincible one.[1]

Penobscott Indian Legend

Peter Anastas (1973)

There can be no doubt the family is the most important influence on the way children grow and develop (Dunst, Trivette, & Deal, 1994; Hart & Risley, 1995). This is true not only because parents provide the environment that surrounds the child most consistently but also because profound emotional ties exist between parents and children. When that potent influence is combined in a positive way with what goes on in the preschool, the outcome for the child is enhanced even further (Gonzalez-Mena, 1993). This is the reason *Total Learning* begins with a discussion of practical ways teachers can welcome families into the life of the school right from the first days of their teaching careers.

It is also true that beginning teachers do not always welcome the added complexity of relating to parents. Simply getting through group time, managing various behavior difficulties, and putting the children back on the Head Start bus seem like more than enough to cope with without thinking about parent conferencing and home visiting. Indeed, many teachers might prefer not to deal with parents at all.

But we must recognize that such a choice is not possible. Teachers need to acknowledge

there is an ever-increasing trend in the United States that advocates building a consistent closeness between families and those of us who care for their children outside the home (Berger, 1996; Slavin, Karweitz, & Wasik, 1994).

Building that closeness can take many forms, ranging from encouraging more volunteer participation by parents in the classroom to maintaining toy lending libraries. Some newer ways to build closeness are even resulting in new kinds of jobs for early childhood teachers. For instance, resource and referral agencies are increasing all over the United States. These agencies serve a variety of useful functions for parents and caregivers by providing information on child-care vacancies, training for providers, and other benefits. A number of states have also instituted programs of home visitors who regularly visit families in their homes to offer suggestions about how to help the children develop to their fullest potential.

Still another way of building closeness between families and preschools comes under the heading *family support systems*. This newer approach stresses the importance of coordinating services to families for the sake of not only convenience and better service but also greater economy (Kagan & Weissbourd, 1994).

Such programs make it very plain that parents can no longer be ignored or delegated to a minor role in education. That is why this chapter is

---

[1]From *Glooskap's Children* (pp. 14–15) by P. Anastas, 1973, Boston: Beacon Press, 1973. Copyright © 1973 by Peter Anastas. Reprinted by permission of Beacon Press.

*Time can stretch to an eternity when waiting for parents'
return.*

devoted to discussing ways of building bonds
between home and school so that children will
feel their world is a consistent whole rather than
split into the unrelated halves termed *home* and
school (Swick, 1991). It is best to include parents
"right from the start," as Boyer (1992) advocates.

There are many ways of enriching this parent-
school bond, and strategies must necessarily
vary to suit individual school situations. But all
schools, whether they are parent-child cooperatives or full-day centers, should strengthen three
basic home-school strands. These are weaving
strands of human relationships that let parents
know we care about them and their children,
strands that accept help from families so that
the lives of the children at the center are enriched, and strands that offer help to families to
strengthen family life.

Letting Parents Know We Care about Them and Their Children

Building a Climate of Trust

There is no substitute for the gradual establishment of trust that can be built between teacher
and parent when it is based on easygoing, consistent daily contact between them. It takes time
and personal contact to make friends. To accomplish this, the teacher should make deliberate
plans to be available while children are arriving,
to make each youngster personally welcome and
have a friendly word with the parent, too.

Strange as it may seem at first thought, the
very beginning of the day is *not* the time for the
teacher to be preoccupied with the children. If
parents are truly part of the life of the school,
this transition should be thought of as being the
part of the daily curriculum intentionally devoted to "family time." This is the part of the day
when the teacher takes a genuine interest in the
small details of each family's life. Needless to
say, it takes a good memory to remember to ask
about the anticipated kittens or how the grandparents' visit is coming along, but doing this
helps build the friendliness that fosters trust. It
also makes it more likely that the parent will
have opportunities to share helpful information
about the child. Maybe Jasmine has just gotten
a new pair of shoes, or Aaron has lost a tooth.
Perhaps the parent is worried because a youngster has been having nightmares, or the child is
very tired because he stayed up late to meet his
father's plane the night before. These tidbits can
contribute a lot to the teacher's understanding
of the child's behavior, as well as build bridges of
deepened understanding between the home
and center.

Building trust also means that the teacher re-
frains from talking about a family's affairs with
other people. This requires good judgment, since
sometimes families are in a position to help each
other if they know that such help is needed.

However, it is always wise to check with the family in difficulty before violating their privacy. Good judgment is particularly necessary when discussing "problem children." Certainly the parent who is concerned because her child has a big bite mark on his shoulder has a right to know the general steps the school is taking to prevent that from happening again, but if trust is to be maintained with everyone, privacy must be preserved at the same time. The teacher should particularly avoid "running down" the members of one family to members of another, because they are likely to assume that she will do the same thing about them behind their back. As one of my students put it, "Bad mouthin' makes bad feelin's."

First impressions can have a crucial effect on establishing a climate of trust and caring, also, and this is one of many reasons that the careful preparation for separating parent and child advocated in chapter 11 is so important. The teacher who takes time to explain the reasons for gradual rather than sudden separation and who helps the parent through this experience with a mixture of assured kindness and sympathetic concern demonstrates to the family right at the start of the relationship that she can be trusted because she has the child's best interests at heart.

Making Visits to the Children's Homes

The Missouri Parents as Teachers Project (Allen, Brown, & Finlay, n.d.), Iowa's Family Development and Self Sufficiency Project (Smith, Fairchild, & Groginsky, 1995), and the Infant Health and Development Program (Liaw, Meisels, & Brooks-Gunn, 1995) are current examples of successful home visiting programs that remind us, once again, of the effective results regular visits can produce. In the majority of preschool programs, visits happen less frequently partly because of the time involved and partly because of teachers' shyness and their other responsibilities. Even though such visits take time and extra effort, it is also true that making even occasional home vis-

its is one of the best ways to build trust and make friends with the families.

Although space does not permit a lengthy discussion of how to conduct successful visits, a few reminders can help get visitors off to a good start. For one thing, always let families know before stopping by—this can be done by telephone or even postcard if a phone is not available. Remember, it is the family's right to refuse, and occasionally people feel such visitors are intrusive spies, not friendly guests. During the visit anticipate the child will be thrilled and after some initial hesitancy will want to show you personal treasures. The child will enjoy receiving a name tag or some other little token from you to help bridge the gap between home and that unfamiliar place called school.

It is also helpful to have in mind a handful of nonthreatening, get-acquainted questions to ask family members about the youngster—perhaps what his favorite foods are, what he likes to do best, and how you can help him feel comfortable at school. This is also a fine time to explain that the family members are always welcome to come, too.

If refreshments are offered, be sure to accept them freely since it is likely the parent has gone to special trouble to provide these. (I once consumed three pieces of cake, a brownie, and a glass of wine all in one afternoon of such visits.)

Finally, for the sake of the teacher's time and also the family's, it is important to limit the length of each encounter. If the teacher politely mentions at the beginning of the visit she can stay only half an hour and has just stopped by to get acquainted, that will help the family know what to expect and not feel slighted when it is time to go.

Keeping Parents Informed

A somewhat more impersonal but still useful way of emphasizing that the school cares about families, as well as the children, is by providing information to parents about what the children are doing in school. Many schools use a bulletin board by the sign-in sheet for this purpose, but some parents never seem to read this—and they certainly will not continue to check it unless the material is eye-catching and frequently changed. When kept current and relevant, bulletin boards have real, practical value. For example, it is constantly necessary to make certain that parents understand that early childhood education is purposeful, and a weekly curriculum chart posted on the bulletin board will emphasize that teachers are not baby-sitters.

Many centers also make use of a monthly newsletter, and these are excellent public relations vehicles (Diffily & Morrison, 1996; Jones, 1996). One month a newsletter might concentrate on the cognitive skills the school is developing, and another could focus on ways the school fosters emotional health. In addition, it might include a calendar of events, recipes from the potluck dinner, general news about what the children will be doing during the coming month, or requests for "freebies" for the school. If bilingual families are part of the school, it is important to include material in both languages to make them feel welcome and let them know what is happening. Otherwise the language barrier may persist and perpetuate a feeling of being outside and apart from the school.

Accepting Help from Families That Will Enrich the Lives of the Children at the Center

Perhaps the words *accepting help* in this heading may seem peculiar at first glance, but they were chosen deliberately because sometimes teachers do not find it comfortable to accept such assistance.

Accepting and Using Criticism

Although it can be difficult to regard critical comments and questions as a form of help, it is important to pay attention to parents when they express such concerns and to benefit from what they have to say. Sometimes, if teachers listen instead of rushing in with a lot of defensive remarks, it can lead to changes in procedures or policies that are better for the children and more satisfactory for parents. Teachers should remember that if one parent complains, possibly others are also dissatisfied but are too intimidated to speak up. For example, we recently had a parent complain after her little boy arrived home for the third time in 2 weeks wearing someone else's sneakers. (At least one other family must have been unhappy.) She had a well-taken point, which we ultimately solved by color-coding 11 identical pairs of dark blue sneakers with dabs of tape so that children could match them up themselves.

Sometimes parents criticize policies because they do not understand what is going on. A father may be uneasy when he finds his little boy trucked out in a dainty petticoat. Another parent may wonder (as many do) when the children are "really going to learn something." It is best to view such critical-sounding queries as presenting opportunities for explaining the educational purposes behind what is going on at school. Parents are entitled to such information. *If, by chance, teachers find themselves unable to produce sound reasons for the inclusion of particular activities, it should indicate to them that they should think further about whether something else might be more profitably substituted for these activities in the future.*

Of course, it is not always possible for family and school values to coincide (Jacobs, 1992). The staff of our center believes that parents' wishes should be honored whenever possible, and so we are willing to cut naps short when a parent tells us her 4-year-old will not go to bed until 10 if we do not, or to help children follow religious dietary rules, or to change an occasional youngster into school clothes before letting him play in the mud.

On the other hand, we would not be willing to allow a child to roam around the room during

It is important to provide activities that parents are comfortable with when they participate in the classroom.

lunch, eating as he goes, nor would we ever spank a child who has messed her pants, no matter what the parent advised. When this kind of conflict occurs between home and school values and, for one reason or another, neither side feels it can compromise, we just say clearly to the child, "Well, there are home rules, and that's what you do at home, and there are school rules, and this is what the rules say you do here." In other words, when necessary, we are frank about the fact that different places have different rules; this is not too difficult for children to understand. We feel that teaching them this is better than undercutting parents by secretly defying their standards or implying to the children that the school is totally right and their homes are totally wrong.

It is interesting to note that some research in the area of teacher/parent values questions whether teacher disapproval of parenting skills affects the way the teachers act toward the children of those parents. The research study by Kontos and Wells (1986) that is included here provides reassuring evidence that teachers do not hold grudges against the children because of such differences.

Drawing on Parents as Resources

Examples are cited throughout this book of ways parents can serve as resources for enriching the children's lives, so I will only provide an overview of such possibilities here. It is remarkable the kinds of contacts parents have within the community and the amount of help they can offer once they are aware of what is needed. When asking about such resources, remember to be precise about what is needed and to furnish examples so that people really understand what you are looking for.

In addition to unearthing sources of free materials, parents often know of special animals, or they are acquainted with people who would be of interest to the children, or they may know of a fascinating place to visit, such as the back room of a bakery or a goat farm, and will help make the arrangements. Then, too, families themselves are so varied and have so many talents, it would be a pity to overlook them. Remember that family members include grandparents, aunts and uncles, and brothers and sisters, as well as parents, and these people often have special talents and free time they enjoy sharing with the children. In the past few weeks our center has had a flute player, the owner of a large, interesting snake, and members of a Boy Scout troop all spend time with the children, while their young relatives basked in the reflected glory.

Parents as Volunteers

Not all parents like working directly in the preschool (after all, a perfectly valid reason for sending children to school is so mothers can have time to themselves, and many other parents work all day), so it makes sense to emphasize to families that volunteering can take many different forms. Producing the resources we discussed earlier is such a variation. Serving on a parent advisory board, working on a potluck, or participating in a cleanup and painting day are other valuable contributions preferred by some parents.

Participating in the Classroom

When parents *do* want to participate directly with the children, several basic things can be done to make them feel truly accepted and welcome. Always bear in mind that the primary purpose of having the volunteer at school is to provide a situation that *both the volunteer and children will enjoy* and not just to comply with a mandated parent involvement component. This means that whatever activity is selected, it has to be something that does not entail a lot of potential discipline problems, it should not be demeaning (cleaning the animal cages, e.g.), and it should not be something that demands an expertise the visitor may not have (such as being in charge of an entire group time). It *should* capitalize on the interests and strengths of the volunteer, and if you have made a consistent point of becoming acquainted with the families, you can usually develop a pretty good idea of what these abilities are.

It works best to get volunteers together ahead of time to talk over basic school ground rules and ask them what they would like to do. A list of possibilities can help stimulate ideas. These might include reading to the children, cooking

something with them, bringing a baby to share, or coming along as the additional adult needed on a field trip. If the volunteers can choose what they prefer doing, they will be more at ease than if such activities are simply assigned to them.

When volunteers come to school, it is important to pay attention to them so they feel truly welcome. The book by Miller and Wilmshurst (1984), *Parents and Volunteers in the Classroom*, is packed with useful suggestions about how to do this even when the teachers are very busy.

Teachers sometimes fail to appreciate that being a volunteer is stressful. To feel competent, volunteers need specific instructions about what to do, and they also deserve to be thanked sincerely upon departure. Probably the best advice to give teachers working with volunteers is that they should ask themselves from time to time how *they* would feel if they were the volunteer and what they would say the staff could do that would make them want to return for another day. Then, of course, those teachers should accept their own advice and proceed accordingly.

Offering Help to Families to Strengthen Family Life

Suggestions for Conferences with Parents

Private conferences with families are one of the most satisfactory ways of providing help on a personal basis, but they do have the unfortunate tendency to make both teacher and parents nervous. Realizing that this nervousness is typical and acknowledging this to the parents can help overcome such feelings. The daily informal chats recommended earlier help, too, but it really takes more than one conference to get past this hurdle.

Conferences are primarily useful because they provide private, uninterrupted opportunities for conversation, and there is no chance that the child might overhear the discussion. They

**Research
Study**

Can Teachers Separate Their Attitudes toward Parents and Children?

Research Question   The investigators wanted to find out whether teachers act differently toward children according to whether they thought the children's parents had good or poor parenting abilities. Does a negative attitude toward parents carry over to the children?

Research Method   In an earlier, related study, Kontos and Wells asked directors of several centers to identify parents whose parenting skills they held in low or high esteem. Upon completion of the first investigation, the researchers turned next to observing the behavior of the teachers toward the children of those parents. The sample consisted of 17 children whose parents demonstrated high parenting skills and 10 children whose parents demonstrated low parenting skills. Their ages ranged from 20 to 73 months, and the average age of both groups of children was not significantly different.

   Each child's behavior was observed three times for 5 minutes each time. The observer did not know whether the child's family was included in the high- or low-skills group. The children were observed for task involvement, the way they used materials, cooperation, verbal behavior, and consideration of others.

   The teachers' behavior was also observed and recorded. They were checked for such behaviors as being absent or present with the child, participating with the child, and for the quality of their verbal responses to the youngster.

Results   When the observations of the children's behavior was analyzed statistically, the behavior of both groups of children was very similar—the children with parents in the low parenting skills group rated slightly more likely to be considerate in relation to using materials and taking turns, and they engaged in somewhat more recitation/task talk than did those children with parents who possessed high parenting skills.

   When the behavior of the teachers was analyzed, once again their behavior toward both groups of children was more similar than it was different. In almost all aspects, teachers did not favor one group of children more than they did the other. Where differences *did* show up, they were ones that favored the children who belonged to the low parenting skills group. Teachers were present more of the time where low-group children were and also engaged in more social talk with them.

Implications for Teaching   It is good to know that at least the teachers in question did not carry over their disapproval of parental child-rearing skills into dislike or avoidance of the children. If anything, they may have compensated for that dislike by paying extra attention to them. Or perhaps the child rearing judged less appropriate by professional teachers produced behavior in children that required more teacher attention to correct! Whatever the reason for the added attention, it is reassuring to learn that teachers, at least in this study, are able to separate their feelings about children from their feelings for the parents and are able to behave in generous and unbiased ways toward the children in their care.

Note. From "Attitudes of Caregivers and the Day Care Experiences of Families" by S. Kontos and W. Wells, 1986, *Early Childhood Research Quarterly, 1*, pp. 47–67.

are appropriate places to review the youngster's progress and to produce the checklists, observations, or portfolios that document that development (Bundy, 1991). If begun early in the year

when the teacher is just becoming acquainted with the child, conferences can help establish mutual respect between teacher and family. This is because the parents can be cast in the role of

Conferences should present an opportunity for sharing information and discussing alternative solutions.

knowing more about the child than the teacher can possibly know at this point.

Inevitably, conferences are also used to discuss problems, and if that is the case, it is sensible for the teacher to avoid giving the impression of taking the parents to task for their child's foibles. Each child has a unique temperament from the time of birth, and it is not always within the parents' ability to change some of these characteristics. The child is a powerful agent in creating his or her own behavior (Maccoby & Martin, 1983). That is why this chapter opens with the Glooskap legend; it is intended to remind adults to retain their sense of proportion and remain aware of that personal, individual power that comes from within each person.

More productive than indulging in the shaming-blaming syndrome (which is likely to elicit a similar retaliatory attack on the teacher by the parent) is using conference time for the mutual purpose of sharing information and discussing alternative solutions.

In general, the teacher who has a listening ear and a quiet tongue will find the most positive

changes taking place for the children and the families, should these be needed. Parents often know deep inside what would be a good solution; the well-done conference can provide parents with the chance to talk the situation through, weigh alternatives, and decide for themselves what action to take. Only in this way are changes really brought about. Listening more than talking does not mean that teachers should not contribute suggestions and ideas drawn from professional experience and training—they should. It does mean that the right to make the decisions rests with the parents.

Meetings about Parenting

Many parents also benefit from opportunities to learn more about children in a general way, and, for this reason, parenting meetings are an additional helpful service offered by many preschools. A few cooperative schools meet every week for discussion, which provides splendid opportunities to develop an informed population of parents who form close bonds with the other families, as well as with the school. Parents in most schools do not meet that frequently, so special attention must be paid to keeping a thread of relationships and continuity stretching from one meeting to the next (Foster, 1994).

Finding Appropriate Topics

A good opening topic for the year might be a discussion of the curriculum and philosophy of the school, replete with visual aids. It often works well to ask parents at that meeting what they would like to discuss at the next one and to build continuing meetings from their input. Some additional topics that are usually of interest to parents include building inner controls in children, understanding the father's influence in children's development, coping with jealousy in youngsters, defining nonsexist education, learning how to teach sharing, helping children through crisis situations, being a single parent, recognizing the characteristics of good toys, and fostering mental ability in young children.

We have found that using an informative videotape as a basis for discussion is particularly helpful early in the year, because it gives a group who may not be acquainted with each other something in common to talk about. Such media can be rented or purchased from various university media centers or other sources and are well worth the fees. Write to the ones at the universities nearest to your school and request a media catalog.

Another effective way to entice parents to attend a program is to use slides of their children participating at school. This is an especially effective approach when discussing why various activities are included during the school day— just remember that parents will be looking for pictures of their particular child, so it is a wise teacher who makes certain that every youngster is included.

Presenting the Topic

Many teachers feel very anxious about leading such meetings and so, time after time, fall back on guest speakers. Although such visitors can bring special expertise and information with them, they have no way of knowing the people in the group and the particular significance of questions they may ask. The presence of visitors also reduces the chance for parents and teachers to talk together about a topic of general, mutual interest.

For these reasons, it is more desirable for teachers to pluck up their courage and lead the meetings themselves. They must remember that these do not have to be, and really *should not* be, presented as lectures anyway. People learn much more from a combination of discussing and sharing information than they do from just sitting and listening.

The secret of leading successful discussions is identifying the important points for people to learn before beginning, making certain that these points are covered during the discussions, developing a good selection of thinking questions in advance to pose to the group, and having the patience and courage to wait for the replies, particularly at the beginning of the discussion when people are feeling shy. It is really the same strategy recommended in chapter 17 in which the generation of creative thinking skills is discussed in relation to young children and to emergent curriculum.

Role playing, breaking into small groups to discuss special points, and participating in panel discussions are additional, effective ways to produce interesting parent nights.

Including Time for Socializing to Take Place

Although education is often the ostensible reason for holding parent meetings, another important value should not be overlooked. Meetings can also provide valuable social opportunities for parents. These are especially nice for young homemakers, who may not get out much and are feeling isolated and lonely. The chance to be with other people who have similar problems and concerns can furnish real emotional support for such people, as well as simply providing fun. Therefore, part of every meeting should allow time for human friendliness. Refreshments offered beforehand or at a break give people something to do with their hands so they feel less self-conscious and furnish chances for them to become acquainted, too.

Sometimes it can be worthwhile to dispense with the program altogether and have a potluck dinner instead. There is no better way to build a comfortable, relaxed bond between home and school than by eating together. It is easy to run a successful potluck if attention is paid to the kinds of details discussed in chapter 19.

Helping Families in Nontraditional Settings

Nowadays families come in a fascinating array of configurations, and it is absolutely vital for the teachers of their young children to take these variations into account as they welcome them into the life of the school. The old stereotyped picture of Father going off to work while Mother stays home and bakes cookies lies far from present-day reality for many people. (Please refer to chapter 11 for a discussion of handling crises and to chapter 13 for information on families from various cultural and ethnic backgrounds.)

Some information to bear in mind about the real circumstances of families in the United States at this time includes the following points:

- One in every four children lives below the poverty level (Children's Defense Fund, 1995).
- Although the rate of divorce has stabilized during the past few years, the rising rate of unmarried motherhood has continued to cause the ranks of single-parent families to increase (Kagan & Weissbourd, 1994).
- In 1994, the Census Bureau reported that the number of single-parent families amounted to 30% of all families surveyed. Twenty-six percent of these were headed by mothers and 4% by fathers (*Education Week*, 1995).
- Nearly one in four children now lives with one parent (Kagan & Weissbourd, 1994).
- In 1994, 60% of married women with children younger than 6 worked outside the home (Children's Defense Fund, 1996b). Seventy

percent of employed mothers with children younger than 6 and 69% of those with children younger than 3 worked full-time (Children's Defense Fund, 1994).
- In 1991, 32.3% of young children with employed mothers were cared for in child-care centers, 25.1% in family child-care homes. The remainder were cared for by nonparental relatives or an unrelated caregiver at home (Children's Defense Fund, 1996b).

If we really pay attention to these facts, it means we must also rethink the kinds of services we offer to parents, because their needs are changing and will continue to change in the coming decade. For this reason, some specific suggestions are offered next about ways to assist these families while their children are at the center or preschool. (Chapter 13 provides suggestions for relating to families from differing cultures.)

Some Suggestions for Helping Families in Which Both Parents Work Outside the Home

- Adapt center hours as much as possible to meet parents' needs in a realistic way.
- Plan events so that working parents can attend. Perhaps a Saturday visiting day could be included; night meetings are also helpful.
- Set aside an evening or early morning for parent conferences. If conference times are planned for late afternoon, be sure to provide a bite to eat during the conference also to reduce fatigue.
- Develop a list of people who are willing to care for children who are ill, and make this available to parents. (A handful of schools make provision for sick child care on their own premises. Some hospitals also provide daily care for sick children at reasonable cost.)
- Be careful to keep the emergency call list for each child up-to-date so that permission is on file when parents have someone else pick up the child from school.
- Reassure parents that good parenting is a matter of spending "quality time" with their children and does not depend on the total

amount of time—and help them define what "quality time" means.

- Keep informed on tax information so that you can furnish correct information about the Earned Income Credit and the Child and Dependent Care Credit tax deduction for parents who ask about them.[2]
- Make it clear that you respect whatever kind of work the parents do. If possible, arrange for a group of children to visit the workplaces. Encourage parents to come and explain their jobs to children at the school.

Evening programs of special interest might include these:

- Spending quality time with my child: what does this mean?
- Balancing work and family life
- Finding time for myself
- Where can I turn when I must work and my child is ill?

Some Suggestions for Helping Families Headed by a Single Parent

Speaking as a single parent myself, I want to point out that a stigma is still attached to being divorced. Therefore, try to overcome whatever critical feelings you may have about the pros and cons of divorce. Problems related to that situation are complex enough for the parents without having to deal with your prejudice, too. The following are some suggestions:

- Avoid using such terms as *broken home* and *fatherless children*. A more acceptable term could be *single-parent family*, because being a family does not necessarily depend on having a mother and father present in the home.
- Avoid taking sides with one parent or the other; it is likely that neither is all right or all wrong.

---

[2]Contact the Internal Revenue Service or the National Women's Law Center, 11 Dupont Circle, Suite 800, Washington, D.C. 20036.

- Remember that single-parent families are very likely to have low incomes. Newly divorced families may experience special problems in this regard and will benefit from referral to appropriate social agencies.
- Many single parents are lonely; they find themselves gradually excluded from contact with couples and at a loss to know how to handle holidays without a former spouse. Suggestions and information can be very welcome if tactfully presented.
- Notices about community activities such as meetings of Parents without Partners or We Care (for those whose spouse has died) should be routinely posted.
- Make it a point to introduce single parents to each other. They could be encouraged to develop a support group of their own within the school.
- Avoid deploring the fact the parents are divorced. Instead, be on the lookout for the strengths demonstrated by the single parents and comment on these in an encouraging way.
- Be sure to send notices offering parent conferences to *both* parents. Occasionally both will attend the same meeting, but frequently the parents prefer to come separately, and so conferences will require more of your time.
- *Be sure you are aware of the custody provisions for the child.* Know who is permitted to take the child from the school. Although this is often a friendly arrangement between divorced parents, sometimes it is not, and the school is legally responsible for the child's safety while on those premises.

Programs of interest to single parents might include these:

- Opportunities for meeting single parents of the opposite sex
- What should we tell the children?
- The strengths of single parents
- Legal rights of women
- When fathers have custody: how to make a go of it

- Dealing with children who are feeling emotional pain: how can parents help?

Some Suggestions for Helping Blended Families

Often considerable stress arises when parents remarry and blend families together. Centers can at least avoid contributing to such stress by doing some of the following:

- Understand that children going through the blending process may be confused or upset. They have to deal with feelings related to loyalty, jealousy, anger about possible rejection, confusion over authority, and so forth (and so do all the parents).
- Joining a blended family often means a child's birth order shifts dramatically. For example, a former "only" child might become a middle child with both older and younger siblings.
- Be aware that stepparents often are not legally entitled to grant permission for medical treatment. Clarify this with the families *before* an emergency happens.
- Offer the children the opportunity to make something for both stepparents and natural parents at holiday times.
- Remember to include the stepparents in school functions. They are often ignored, and it should be their and the child's choice whether they will actually attend.
- Avoid the temptation to pass judgment on which reconstituted side of the family is doing the better job with the child in your care.

Programs of special interest to blended families might include these:

- Living with other people's children
- Sharing children between two families
- Joint custody: how can we make it work?
- When the chips are down: who disciplines whom?
- Dealing with stepparent stereotypes
- Coping with jealousy

Some Suggestions for Helping Families Who Have Very Low Incomes

- Be matter-of-fact, not condescending or pitying.
- Be especially careful not to offend parents. Families on food stamps may not appreciate artwork made from macaroni or chocolate pudding finger painting. Nor do they feel comfortable with pictures of children who have heaps of presents around them during the holidays.
- Process agency papers, such as applications for child-care vouchers, as quickly as you can. Families' reimbursement or income may depend on your efficient paperwork.
- Be particularly aware of community resources—when and where food stamps are available and what the hours are for the county health clinic, for example.
- Deliberately build acquaintance with various social agencies yourself. A friendly call from you will often help a parent use the system more effectively.
- Provide a clothing exchange for outgrown but not worn-out children's clothing.
- Offer a food coupon exchange in which people can leave or take whatever coupons they wish.
- Acquaint yourself with the state welfare aid regulations. There may be portions of those regulations that parents do not know about that could benefit their children if used.

Programs of interest to families who are poor might include these:

- A speaker from the social welfare office, explaining rights and obligations
- Speakers from unfamiliar agencies, such as those that sponsor special Christmas stores for low-income families
- Very practical discussions on child rearing (Although it is always important to be practical, these families are particularly likely to dislike theoretical, head-in-the-clouds, professorial-type meetings.)
- What to do about specific community problems, such as how to get vicious dogs off the street

Visiting grandparents add special delight to the day.

Some Suggestions for Helping Families Who Have a Child with a Disability

The enactment of the Individuals with Disabilities Education Act (IDEA) combined with the Americans with Disabilities Act (ADA) means that more and more preschools will be gathering children with disabilities and their families into their schools, so some suggestions for helping those families fit comfortably into the group are worthwhile to include here. (Please note that many additional recommendations are incorporated throughout the text to help these youngsters participate successfully as part of the group.)

- Always remember that children with disabilities are more like other children than they are different. It is important to see past the atypical qualities of the child to the typical qualities as well.
- Remember that participation in your preschool may be the first major encounter the family has

with an organized group of so-called "normal" children. These first encounters are often particularly stressful for the families because of possible contrasts in behaviors or abilities that may be apparent between their youngsters and others in the group.

- Brief, matter-of-fact explanations of the child's disability may be needed by the other children and/or their parents to satisfy their concerns and curiosity about the child's brace, inability to hear, or unusual behavior, for example.
- It is vital to be truthful as well as kind and gentle when discussing the child's accomplishments with the parents. Although it is delightful to rejoice in what the child has learned, it is also important to acknowledge limitations to keep reality in focus.
- Be aware that the child's siblings, who may also be attending your school, may be suffering from an intense and painful mixture of feelings about the special-needs child. These emotions

can include protectiveness, jealousy, feeling left out, plus a multitude of other ambivalent feelings. Such conflicting emotions, often expressed as anger or a high level of frustration, may require special patience and attention from the teacher.

Programs of interest to parents who have a child with a disability might include these:

- Helping all children deal with a child who is different from themselves
- How can I help my child cope with teasing or comments about the disability?
- Facing facts: what is fair to expect my child to accomplish?
- Speaking up in my child's behalf: what are my rights? To whom may I turn for help?
- Letting go: ways to help children become independent

Summary

Review of the Knowledge Base
Gonzalez-Mena (1993) and Powell (1989) provide excellent rationales for including families in the life of the school. Berger (1995) also offers a strong base of information on such matters as conferencing, home visits, and the value of parent education. Probably the most accessible and therefore most useful source of statistical data about the status of young children and their families can be obtained from the Children's Defense Fund (see Appendix G).

Parents are a tremendously significant part of the child's life, and children's centers should make every effort to weave bonds between home and school that make the fabric of that life complete and whole. A basic strand in this process is letting parents know that teachers care about them and their children. This can be accomplished by establishing a condition of trust between home and school through consistent, daily contact, handling separations with caring concern, and keeping parents posted on school

activities by means of bulletin boards and newsletters.

Accepting help from families is not always easy, particularly when the help comes in the form of critical comments and questions, but even these can benefit the school and the parent-teacher relationship if handled maturely. Two other less threatening ways parents can offer the school help are by providing resources of various kinds and by participating directly in the school with staff and children. Such participation requires special preparation and planning by staff so that the volunteers and children gain feelings of competence and happiness as a result of that experience.

The third way of drawing families and teachers together is by offering help to families to strengthen family life. This should include adjusting the center's services for families who do not fit the traditional middle-class stereotypes of family life. Conducting individual conferences is one way of providing such help; making friendly visits to the home and sponsoring meetings on parenting concerns can also be effective. Potluck suppers and visiting days at school offer additional excellent opportunities for staff and families to become better acquainted so that more interchange can take place.

Self-Check Questions for Review

Content-Related Questions
1. Why should teachers not be preoccupied with children at the beginning of the center day?
2. List some practical things teachers can do to help establish a feeling of trust between themselves and parents.
3. Do you agree with the statement that children's misbehavior is usually the result of the way the child is handled at home? Be sure you can give reasons for your position.
4. Describe some important points to remember when planning a parent education meeting.
5. What does the author suggest teachers should do when home and school policies cannot agree?

6. Select an example of a nontraditional family, and provide some suggestions about how the school could help the family function effectively.
7. Regulations require that 40% of the parents in your center participate in the center in some fashion. Create a checklist of various ways parents might participate. Be sure to include such items as sharing resources from home and serving on the parent board.
8. List three things teachers should remember when making an initial visit to a child's home.

Integrative Questions

1. Just suppose that a teacher did not want to have much contact with parents. Suggest some ways she could arrange her program so that it would be difficult for parents to have informal chats with her. How do your suggestions compare with the behavior of some teachers you recall from your days in elementary school?
2. You are now the teacher in a Head Start center, and you want to keep the parents informed about what is happening in your classroom. If you could *not* use a newsletter to do this, what other practical means of communication could you use to relay news to the families?
3. If the Kontos and Wells (1986) study had revealed that teachers were less helpful and friendly to children when they disapproved of their families' parenting skills, what would you suggest as a remedy? Would simply telling teachers they should "behave better" be enough?

Questions and Activities

1. Do you think all teachers should be required to have parents participate in their rooms? What might be some of the drawbacks to such a requirement?
2. One of your friends, who is in her first year of teaching, and feeling very depressed, calls you. She went to some lengths to plan a special parenting meeting, and only half the parents actually showed up that night. What would be your response to her depression?
3. The next time your college class is shown a video, take a few minutes and develop questions based on it that would encourage good discussion in a parenting group.

4. You are now a teacher in a full-day center, and a parent who lives near another one of the center's families takes you aside and tells you a lengthy story about the mischief the other child leads her son into at home. (They are no angels at school either!) She asks you not to allow the boys to play together at school anymore and threatens to withdraw her child if this is not enforced. As a teacher, how do you think you should handle this kind of request? What if her son, in your opinion, is actually the ringleader?
5. Think of a policy parents might legitimately complain about at a children's center or at the school where you are teaching. Now try role-playing various responses to such complaints. These responses could include attacking back, refusing to listen, reflecting parent feelings, and explaining the reasons for the school policy.

References for Further Reading

Overviews

Berger, E. H. (1995). *Parents as partners in education: Families and schools working together* (4th ed.). Upper Saddle River, NJ: Merrill/Prentice Hall. This comprehensive textbook provides in-depth discussions of ways to generate the teacher-parent partnership. *Highly recommended.*

Swick, K. J. (1991). *Teacher-parent partnerships to enhance school success in early childhood education.* Washington, DC: National Education Association and the Southern Association for Children under Six. This book focuses on a down-to-earth discussion of ways to enhance these relationships coupled with substantiating research evidence.

Parent Involvement

Boutte, G. S., Keepler, D. L., Tyler, V. S., & Terry, B. Z. (1992). Effective techniques for involving "difficult" parents. *Young Children, 47*(3), 19–27. The authors include capsule descriptions of various kinds of difficult parents along with specific recommendations on ways of encouraging them to participate at school.

Brand, S. (1996). Making parent involvement a reality: Helping teachers develop partnerships with parents. *Young Children, 51*(2), 76–83. The author includes several useful ideas as she describes how a special project increased teacher's skills in relating to parents.

Hendrick, J. (1996). *The whole child: Developmental education for the early years* (6th ed.). Upper Saddle River, NJ: Merrill/Prentice Hall. The chapters "What Parents Need" and "Tender Topics: Helping Children Master Emotional

Crises" contain considerable information and recommendations about effective counseling with parents.

Making Friends with Parents from Other Cultures

Although the "Who Am I?" chapter covers cross-cultural education in detail, I cannot resist including a handful of helpful references specifically focusing on families here.

Lee, F. Y. (1995). Asian parents as partners. *Young Children*, 50(3), 4–9. Lee suggests many practical ways to reach out effectively to parents who may otherwise feel reticent about approaching their children's teachers. *Highly recommended.*

Lopez, A. (1996). Creation is ongoing: Developing a relationship with non-English speaking parents. *Child Care Information Exchange*, 107, 56–62. This sensitive article focuses on the Latino point of view. Very helpful.

Wilson, M. N. (Ed.). (1995). African American family life: Its structural and ecological aspects. *New Directions for Child Development*, 68 (entire issue). A good range of information on African American family life from a variety of perspectives is included here—useful reading.

Working with Parents in Special Circumstances

Crosbie-Burnett, M. (1994). The interface between stepparent families and schools: Research, theory, policy, and practice. In R. K. Pasley & M. Iniger-Tallman (Eds.), *Stepparenting: Issues in theory, research, and practice* (pp. 199–216). Westport, CT: Greenwood. Despite the somewhat daunting title, this rare chapter offers a number of practical suggestions that all teachers should put into practice because of the blended families in their classrooms.

Hildebrand, V., Phenice, L. A., Gray, M. M., & Hines, R. P. (1996). *Knowing and serving diverse families*. Upper Saddle River, NJ: Merrill/Prentice Hall. *Knowing and Serving Diverse Families* should be in every teacher's library because it offers hard-to-find information on a wide range of family backgrounds from various ethnic groups to single parents and gay and lesbian families. *Highly recommended.*

Kennedy, M., & Ing, J. S. (1994). *The single-parent family: Living happily in a changing world*. New York: Crown Trade. This short book is filled with sensible advice and would be a useful reference for the parent information shelf.

Lawler, S. B. (1991). *Teacher-parent conferencing in early childhood education*. Washington, DC: National Education Association. Down-to-earth, humane approaches to conferencing with parents are suggested. The list of do's and don'ts about conflict resolution is particularly helpful. *Highly recommended.*

Swadener, B. B., & Lubeck, S. (Eds.). (1995). *Children and families "at promise": Deconstructing the discourse of risk*. Albany: State University of New York Press. Various authors analyze and attack the concept of "risk" and argue the value of emphasizing the construction of success instead. This is important reading for everyone.

Reaching Out to Parents

Berger, E. H. (1995). *Parents as partners in education: Families and schools working together* (4th ed.). Upper Saddle River, NJ: Merrill/Prentice Hall. Already cited under "Overviews," this book offers a particularly good chapter on parent education.

Diffily, D., & Morrison, K. (Eds.). (1996). *Family-friendly communication for early childhood programs*. Washington, DC: National Association for the Education of Young Children. Ever wish you had a quick way to explain some aspect of early childhood philosophy or practice to parents? If so, this book is the answer to your problem. It includes more than 90 brief "articles" that may be reprinted without permission to be used with families.

Fenwick, K. (1993). Diffusing conflict with parents: A model for communication. *Child Care Information Exchange*, 93, 59–60. Fenwick provides a clear, brief discussion of how to respond to an angry parent by reflecting, reframing, and reviewing what the parent has said.

Fox-Barnett, M., & Meyer, T. (1992). The teacher's playing at my house this week. *Young Children*, 47(5), 45–50. Although focusing on child-centered home visits, this article also offers practical suggestions about home visiting in general.

Wasik, B. H., Bryant, D. M., & Lyons, C. M. (1990). *Home visiting: Procedures for helping families*. Newbury Park, CA: Sage. A rare book on this subject, *Home Visiting* reviews a variety of programs and includes practical chapters on managing visits and visiting in stressful situations.

Wellhousen, K. (1993). Children from nontraditional families: A lesson in acceptance. *Childhood Education*, 69(5), 281–288. Wellhousen reminds us to be sensitive regarding potential family structure when talking with children.

For the Advanced Student

Behrman, R. E. (Ed.). (1994). Children and divorce. *The Future of Children*, 4(1), 4–254. This material from the Packard Foundation provides comprehensive, up-to-the-minute information on the subject. *Highly recommended* for the serious student.

Dunst, C. J., Trivette, C. M., & Deal, A. G. (Eds.). (1994). *Supporting & strengthening families. Vol. 1. Methods, strategies and practices*. Cambridge, MA.: Brookline. The emphasis on recognition of inherent family strengths and on the practical assessment of ways to help makes this a valuable resource.

Kagan, S. L., & Weissbourd, B. (Eds.). (1994). *Putting families first: America's family support movement and the challenge of change*. San Francisco: Jossey-Bass. The broad scope of this subject is exemplified in this helpful review—readable yet comprehensive.

Mallory, B. L., & New, R. S. (Eds.). (1993). *Diversity and developmentally appropriate practices: Challenges for early childhood education*. New York: Teachers College Press. The authors point out the truth that parents who come from a variety of cultures may hold very different points of view about education from that of the teacher. Thought-provoking reading.

Powell, D. R. (1989). *Families and early childhood programs*. Washington, DC: National Association for the Education of Young Children. Powell presents a research-based discussion of these relationships from children's, parents', and teachers' points of view.

Weissbourd, R. (1996). *The vulnerable child: What really hurts America's children and what we can do about it*. Reading, MA.: Addison-Wesley. This book should be read by everyone who hopes to work effectively with children and their families. It is filled with readable matter-of-fact analyses and recommendations. *Highly recommended*.

Other Resources of Special Interest

Child Care Information Exchange, PO Box 2890, Redmond, WA 98073-9977. CCIE invariably contains a wealth of useful information on child-care practices and management. It is listed here because it often includes practical information about working with parents.

Play

The Integrative Force in Learning

Have you ever

- Fumbled for words when a parent says, "Well, I'm glad they're having fun, but when do you really teach them something?"
- Known that play was an important mode of learning but doubted whether it contributed much to mental development?
- Wondered what you could do to encourage the children to get more out of their play experiences?

If you have, the material in this chapter will help you.

In play a child is always above his average age, above his daily behavior: in play, it is as though he were a head taller than himself. As in the focus of a magnifying glass, play contains all developmental tendencies in a condensed form: In play, it is as though the child were trying to jump above the level of his normal behavior.

Lev Vygotsky (1966, p. 16)

Protecting the child's right to play is no easy job. It goes far beyond setting up an environment where play can occur. It includes knowing a great deal. It means knowing what goes on when children play, so that the environment can, in a sense, grow with the children, both as a group and as individuals. It means knowing when and how to intervene in the play and when to stay on the sidelines. It means comprehending the limits of play, knowing when play is not enough, knowing when children need the satisfaction of accomplishment in the real world and when soaring on the imaginations of others is more appropriate.

Patricia Monighan-Nourot, Barbara Scales,
Judith Van Hoorn with Millie Almy (1987, p. 9)

Chapter 1 advocates not only planning curriculum for each of the child's selves but also considering the child as a whole, because the whole is more than the sum of the individual parts. We never want to lose sight of the child as being this complete human being. So, as we plan our teaching, we must ask ourselves, What method do we use to bring about this sense of wholeness for children? What glue can we supply that will stick the parts of that small person together to form a complete, fully functioning person?

To answer this perplexing question, we have only to go to the children and observe what they use to accomplish this integration. The answer is that children use play to achieve this goal. Play provides children with unparalleled opportunities for integrating their personalities, because when children play, all the selves are used simultaneously. Thus, a child taking the father's role in house play may be developing the physical self by practicing eye-hand coordination as she pours pretend juice, practicing social skills as she ingratiates herself with the group, developing emotional insight when the recalcitrant baby protests, "No! No! Baby not go to bed," and using her cognitive creative abilities as she substitutes a necktie for a leash while walking the family dog. I can think of no other experience in the child's life that provides the same opportunity for all the selves to interact and grow simultaneously as does the opportunity for play.

Trying out adult roles is one of the benefits of pretend play.

Play further acts as an integrative force by providing opportunities for children to clarify who they are and who they are not. Playing the role of a police officer, mother, baby, or bus driver is one way of doing this, of course, but the ordinary social interactions that occur during play also help children form concepts of their total self. During play they may define themselves, or may be defined by others, as someone who is liked, or disliked, or good at climbing, or a crybaby, or a myriad other things. Such labels tend to push a child into a particular mold or framework that can be desirable or undesirable.

Play also acts as an integrative force by helping children discriminate not only between who they are and who they are not but also between what is real and what is not. Two- and 3-year-olds, in particular, may require the teacher's help in remembering that dramatic play is "just pretend" and that they are acting "as if" something were true. For example, I recently helped a child work out some of his fear of dogs by allowing him to hit a stuffed dog at nursery school while stuttering out all the terrible things he would like to do to it because it had bitten him. Suddenly he stopped and said uncertainly, "But if I bite him, he won't bite back, will he?" He needed me to ask him, "Is the puppy real?" before he could continue with his play. That moment of uncertainty demonstrated how thin the line can be between reality and fantasy in young children's play and how important the teacher is in providing reassurance when it is necessary.

As children mature, they learn to handle the real/not real continuum themselves and need less frequent direction from the teacher. Garvey (1983) explains that they do this by developing ways of signaling between themselves when they begin to play and make the transition from reality to pretend. For example, they may begin an interchange with "Pretend that . . ." or "I'll be the mommy and you be the daddy, OK?" This kind of gambit is an accepted social signal among preschoolers that they are entering a period where literalness is suspended and imaginative play substituted in its place.

But What Is Play?

There are as many differing theories and definitions of play as there are people who write about it, and the arguments continue (Frost, 1992a; Pellegrini, 1995). Schwartzman (1978) is still accurate when she said, "Today we are still flying theoretical 'kites' in the study of play—only now there are more of them. This is as it should be because play requires a multiperspective approach . . . and resists any attempts to define it rigidly" (p. 325).

Definitions of Play

Definitions range from Montessori's "Play is a child's work" to Dewey's "Play is what we enjoy while we are doing it. Work is what we enjoy when we have accomplished it." Views on the purpose of play also vary, ranging from Freud's contention that play provides opportunities to clarify and master emotions, to Piaget's proposal that play enables children to substitute symbols in place of reality (Nourot & Van Hoorn, 1991). Vygotsky contends that play is valuable because it enables the child to approach the growing edge of the zone of proximal development and because it provides opportunities for learning to control impulsive behavior since play requires the child to conform to the rules and roles assumed while playing. He maintains such advancement is most likely to occur when the play is guided by an adult (Bodrova & Leong, 1996). Like Piaget, Vygotsky values play because it encourages children to substitute pretend objects for real ones, thereby helping them separate thought from concrete objects.

Johnson and Ershler (1982) offer a definition with particular merit for preschool teachers: "Play may be defined as behavior that is intrinsically motivated, freely chosen, process-oriented, and pleasurable" (p. 137). This definition is useful because it provides us with a set of standards against which we can measure the play activity in our classrooms. It is only necessary for us to translate these standards into a series of questions to use them in this way. For example:

- *Play is intrinsically motivated* (interpretation)—Will children choose to become involved in the curriculum I have planned because the activities are inherently satisfying or because they will be rewarded by the teacher?
- *Play is freely chosen* (interpretation)—Does this play allow children to choose freely what they wish to do for at least a portion of the time they are at school? Does it encourage them to use their own ideas?

- *Play is process oriented* (interpretation)—Will children find satisfaction while doing the activity and not just in the end result?
- *Play is pleasurable* (interpretation)—Will the children have fun while they are participating in the activity?

We need to ask ourselves these questions continually because all too often teachers lose sight of them when planning to include play in the curriculum. For example, teachers may set up a block corner to carry out a particular theme such as farm animals or transportation, which thereby stifles the children's opportunities for freely choosing how they wish to play with blocks that day.

Sutton-Smith (1987) speaks of such guided play as the "domestication of early childhood play." He suggests that some teachers tend to see "educational play" as being the only really good, worthwhile kind and the more spontaneous, vigorous, child-instigated play as less desirable and hence not worthy of encouragement.

Although there can be a place for controlled play experiences in the curriculum, we must always remember that guided play does *not meet the criteria of being child generated or freely chosen* because teachers tend to push children into following the theme and the teacher's idea.

Children are no fools about this—in fact, the most salient way they define the difference between work and play is that work is something you *have* to do whereas play is something freely chosen you *want* to do (Wing, 1995). So, if we wish children to feel they are genuinely playing, we must provide many opportunities for them to play freely and spontaneously as their own ideas and internal states dictate. It is only when such open opportunities abound that children can fully develop their ideas and passions. It is this kind of open play that provides the best opportunities for integration of all the selves.

Stages of Play

Researchers do agree that play passes through a series of developmental stages, although once again they differ in their categorization of these.

One tried-and-true categorization still in use today, which investigates the social aspects of play, was developed by Parten (1932, 1996). She viewed play as advancing from *solitary play* (playing alone, with little reference to what other children nearby are doing—characteristic of very young children), to *parallel play* (playing beside but not with a companion child with toys that are similar—often seen in the play of 2- and 3-year-olds), to *associative play* (playing together but not subordinating their individual interests to a common goal—often witnessed in the play of 3½- to 4½-year-old children), and finally to *cooperative play* (playing together for a common purpose—often apparent in the play of 4- and 5-year-olds who organize themselves into a group). These stages are not mutually exclusive, however. Rubin (1977) demonstrated that solitary play can be quite sophisticated and that the same child may use various forms and combinations of these stages at different times of the day and in various circumstances throughout early childhood. Therefore, teachers should not view solitary and parallel play as necessarily being evidence of immaturity.

Another well-known way of categorizing stages of development in play was developed by Smilansky (1968) following Piagetian theory. This categorization has also been widely used by researchers (Henniger, 1985; Howe, Moller, & Chambers, 1994; Roopnarine, Bright, & Riegraf, 1994). Smilansky divides play according to *functional play* (the child makes simple use of movements to provide exercise—characteristic of infants and young toddlers), *constructive play* (the child works toward a goal of some sort, such as completing a puzzle or picture—characteristic of children up to about 3½ years), and *sociodramatic play* (the child assumes roles and uses language for pretending). By age 7 the child reaches the stage of *games with rules*, which is described as the highest form of cognitive play.

Smilansky used one of the Piagetian stages, *sociodramatic play*, in the research study described in this chapter. It is included here not only because the results are valuable but also because her work pioneered an entire new generation of research studies on play and is still widely cited today.

The value of understanding and identifying these stages is that it allows teachers to plan play activities that are appropriate for the ages of the children they are teaching. It is as inappropriate to expect a 2-year-old to understand how to play duck-duck-goose as it is to expect a 4-year-old to be satisfied with a rattle and set of nesting blocks. Knowledge of developmental levels prevents boredom or frustration in young children because it enables teachers to suit experiences to the child's developmental capabilities.

Principles for Encouraging Play

Play flourishes best in an atmosphere of acceptance and approval. Children sense when teachers are not fully convinced of the worth of play and just tolerate rather than accept it in a wholehearted way. On the other hand, teachers who fully understand that play is a productive avenue for learning and thus make a commitment to it subtly convey this message to children. In this climate, play and all its attendant benefits thrive and children lead rich, engrossed, and happy lives at school.

In addition to commitment, some more obvious and generally applicable principles can be incorporated into the teaching repertoire by teachers who wish to encourage play. One such principle is that *planning enough time for play to be generated is essential* (Ward, 1996). It takes time for children to develop their play ideas fully—to move all the way in their play from packing their suitcases to trundling them through the school, visiting their friends, pretending to have a snack, and finally returning.

Equipment must be stored in readily accessible areas. Teachers should feel free to move with the children's play and produce materials on request rather than say, "It's in the shed—we'll get it tomorrow."

Plentiful materials also encourage children to play freely because having enough equipment to go around promotes comfortable, harmonious play. This does not mean it is necessary to have 20 little red cars so that everyone can have one, but it does mean it is wise to try to have at least two of whatever items are very popular.

Equipment should also be age appropriate. Appendix F offers many suggestions for the kinds of age-appropriate materials and equipment children love to use in their play.

Wherever play takes place, teachers should be aware of it and seek to continue and extend it. We sometimes think of pretend play as occurring only in the housekeeping area or in the block corner, and it is true that these are highly popular places for such activity to take place. However, play can occur anywhere: in the sandbox as children imagine they are digging to the bottom of the earth, on the climbing gym as it becomes an eagle's nest, or at the manipulative table as they play zoo with small models and cubical counting blocks. Play can also be a wagon transformed into an ambulance, a young parent nursing a doll, or two children laughing together as they do stunts on the crawl-through blocks.

Nourishing such play requires a delicate balance between knowing when to intervene and when not to. Too intrusive, insensitive interventions by adults can actually spoil it, as the research by Fiese (1990) reveals. She found that when mothers did too much questioning and were too intrusive with their suggestions, their children retreated to less mature, simple play. In their zeal to use play to advance learning, it seems to me that proponents of Vygotskian theory need to be particularly sensitive to this kind of excessive intrusion.

On the other hand, research by Howes and Clements (1994) reports that most teachers do not intervene enough. "Teachers used free play and outdoor times in the child care center to step back and visit with their own peers. They tended to monitor peer play *only for safety believing that children learn best when they solve their own peer problems*" [italics added] (p. 33). Clearly, if the children are to obtain maximum benefit from playing together, either extreme of over- or underinvolvement should be avoided.

Encouraging play is like pulling taffy. Just as the accomplished taffy puller can stretch and bend the candy as far apart as his arms will reach, so the accomplished teacher can do the same thing with play—drawing it forth, stretching it out, extending it, so that children can obtain the maximum benefit from the experience.

To do this successfully, the teacher should anticipate what the children might go on to next in their play. Offering a mild suggestion as the play begins to wane or falter can save and continue it by adding an additional episode. ("Well, here you are, sitting at the cash register! Has anyone phoned in an order? Oh, here comes Ryan. Are you the man picking up the hamburgers?") Teachers can find inspiration for this by assuming the children's perspective and asking themselves what they would enjoy doing next if they were that age.

A note of caution: be prepared to accept rejection of your idea by the children without feeling offended. Remember, it is *their* play and you are the supporter, not the creator, of it.

Remember it is important for teachers to allow some space between themselves and the children so that the youngsters do not feel suffocated by too much close attention. Yet, at the same time, it is necessary to *remain alert and willing to set limits* when these are needed. Two- and 3-year-olds may require intervention for the sake of their own safety. Four-year-olds are more likely to benefit from restraints for the sake of others' safety, as when they are involved in such activities as monster play.

In summary, when children are involved in play, the ideal attitude for teachers to assume is that of attentive approval. Teachers with this attitude remain aware of what is happening, are willing to contribute ideas and materials when this seems desirable, can clarify and interpret

**Research
Study**

Teachers Can Help Children Learn to Play More Effectively

Research Question   In a previous study, Smilansky observed significant differences in the play activity of middle-class European Jewish children and lower-class Jewish children who came from Middle Eastern countries. She became interested in what could be done to improve the quality of play for the less developed second group.

Therefore, she formulated the question, What methods of adult intervention are most effective in developing the ability for sociodramatic play in children from culturally deprived backgrounds? (The term *culturally deprived* is no longer used because everyone comes from a culture. The children Smilansky designates by this term were Jewish children from low-income families who emigrated to Israel from various Middle Eastern countries.)

Research Method   Three groups of "disadvantaged orientals" (Groups A, B, and C), totaling 420 children of kindergarten and preschool age, and two control groups were included. Control Group D was composed of children matched to the experimental group ($n = 362$) and Control Group E was composed of European children ($n = 427$). Teachers in Group A were trained to enrich the children's informational background by taking them on field trips, talking over experiences, and so forth. Teachers in Group B concentrated on teaching the children how to play by using active intervention and suggestions, and teachers in Group C combined enriching experiences with techniques for improving the quality of the children's play. In the control groups the children played as they usually did. All the teachers used the same themes: visiting the health clinic, going to the grocery store, and a theme based on a storybook.

Each child in the experimental and control groups was classified at the beginning of the experiment according to the level of his or her sociodramatic play skills based on a series of observations. Following 9 weeks of the experiment, the level of the children's play was observed for a second time.

Results   The sociodramatic play of Group A, who had only experiences and discussions, did not improve significantly. Nor did the play of Control Groups D or E change significantly.

On the other hand, the level of sociodramatic play of Group B (who were exposed to direct instruction in developing play skills) and Group C (who were exposed to direct instruction combined with experiences) improved to a significant extent. Group C improved the most.

Implications   This study is important for two reasons. First, it demonstrates that children from so-called "deprived backgrounds" can learn to enrich their styles of play. It also supports the idea that play combined with experience and teacher interaction is an effective way of changing children's play behavior.

A second, even more important result came from Smilansky's work, however, and it is the reason why a study done in 1968 is included in this book. It is important because it marks one of the first times a fairly rigorous research study focused on play! Until then, many investigators assumed that the activity of play was too difficult to evaluate, so almost no research was conducted on that subject. Inspired by Smilansky's work, however, studies have proliferated, and we now possess a respectable, though sometimes tantalizing, body of research on this vital topic.

Note. From *The Effects of Sociodramatic Play on Disadvantaged Preschool Children* by S. Smilansky, 1968, New York: Wiley.

Asking just the right question at just the right time is part of the art of teaching.

the children's actions to each other should this be necessary, and appreciate the value of this activity as the play unfolds.

Additional Benefits of Play

If the integrative function of play were its only value to children, this would be reason enough to include it as a basic element in planning curriculum. But, when analyzed, play provides many additional benefits (see Table 3–1). When children play, they are more completely themselves than at any other time. Play leaves chil-

dren free to express ideas and to play things out safely with no penalties attached. While playing, they make choices and decisions for themselves, they assume command, they are masterful and in control of what is happening, and they are able to seize endless opportunities to try out, experiment, and explore. Moreover, they can subtly regulate their play, so that it offers challenges that are neither too difficult nor too easy. Knowledge of these benefits is important to teachers, because they need to be able to explain to parents and administrators why play is a vital ingredient when planning learning situations for young children.

TABLE 3–1
Potential Learning Benefits from Pretend (Dramatic) Free Play*

Creative	Emotional	Social	Physical	Cognitive
Encourages:	**Encourages:**	**Encourages:**	**Encourages:**	**Encourages:**
Enjoyment of process, not product	Clarification and better understanding of own personal feelings	Ability to get what child wants by peaceful means: negotiating, bargaining, trading, waiting, using a substitute	Practice of newly emerging physical skills	Ability to extend and expand on ideas and to solve problems
Generation of new possibilities and ideas	Ability to express and control own feelings		Use of small-muscle skills such as buttoning doll's dress or water pouring	Use of symbols in place of real objects (emergent cognitive and literacy skill)
Use of the mental process of imagination	Expression of feelings in "safe" nonretaliatory environment	Generation of skills related to entering an ongoing group	Use of large-muscle skills particularly on climbing or balancing apparatus	Ability to tell real from pretend
Flexibility of thought	Feelings of delight and satisfaction	Development of cooperative skills: taking other people's desires and needs into account, sharing	Coordination of subskills	Ability to use imagination
Problem-solving skills: "How can we?" "What could we use for . . . ?"	Feelings of relief when anxieties are played through		Attempts at more challenging new skills while pretending (e.g., sliding down pole while playing firefighter)	Development of advance plans and scenarios (e.g., "You be the cat doctor, and my cat just throwed up!")
Expression of personal uniqueness— self-expression	Feelings of freedom from adult standards and expectations	leadership role with others, sharing equipment		Clarification of information about world beyond the home
Use of pretend and "as if" situations	Sense of mastery and control over what's happening	Grasp of social roles such as doctor, teacher, mother and rules that govern that role	Acquisition of new motor skills	Experimentation and drawing conclusions from trying things out
Increase breadth of repertoire of possible responses to situations	Development of empathy, insight into how other people feel	Differentiation between self and others: who child really is or is not	Experimentation with taking risks while in a safe environment	Use of language to express ideas to others during play
Unfamiliar uses of familiar equipment		Insights about others' cultures if teacher encourages this (see chapter 13)	Integration of language with physical action (directions, finger plays, etc.)	Use of signs and labels (emergent literacy skill)
Creation of new roles				

*For analyses of potential learning benefits from specific activities (such as blocks or self-expressive materials), please refer to the appropriate chapter.

Encourage the Development of the Physical Self through Play

The joy, freedom, and vigor that are so characteristic of children as they use their bodies in physical play is certain evidence of how deeply satisfying this is to them. Knowing what one's body can do and feeling physically confident enhances the basic feelings of security and self-esteem in a special way.

How Can Teachers Help?

It is important to maintain a reasonable balance between allowing children to experiment with tak-

---

 Surefire Pretend Play Activities

Here are a few suggestions for settings that will spark dramatic play among the children.

- *Playing house*—A trusty standby that holds endless appeal for children. Try an apartment set up with two houses side by side made from hollow blocks; this often facilitates social interaction between groups of children and quells arguments as well. A nice variation on this play can be moving to a new house or apartment. Children decide where they would rather have the house be, use wagons to transport furniture, and so forth.
- *Marketing*—Offer paper bags, empty cans and boxes, imitation fruits and vegetables, play money, and something to use as shopping carts (e.g., doll buggies and wagons). Children enjoy both the buyer and seller roles. Marketing works well as an enrichment to house play.
- *Running a fast-food restaurant*—Although some of us may deplore certain aspects of this industry, there is no denying that children are very familiar with placing orders, take-out features, and the virtues of "with pickles or without." Ride 'em trucks or possibly trikes, as well as cash registers, trays, sacks, containers, order blanks, and hats, add joy to the play.
- *Camping*—Bedspread tents hung on A-frames and whatever camping equipment is available such as canteens, firewood, or sleeping bags make this play lots of fun. Flashlights also add delight.
- *Hospital play*—Children are deeply interested in participating in this activity. Inclusion of a stethoscope, some kind of shot needle (turkey basters or large eyedroppers can be used to represent these), and masking tape and gauze for bandages add interest. When one of our students as-

sembled a transfusion unit from a plastic bottle and tubing, the children played with it repeatedly.
- *Business office play*—Old typewriters past the possibility of repair, calculators, stamps with stamp pads, used envelopes, paper clips, and surplus paper bring appeal and realism to this play.
- *Baby washing*—Baby play combines the delights of water play with family life. Because boys often can be enticed into this activity, it is particularly valuable as a way of providing experience in a nurturing role. Towels, bar soap, cornstarch powder, and diaper wipes add reality.
- *Birthday party play*—Boxes (either with or without something inside) and recycled party wrappings, cards, pretend birthday cakes (styrofoam bases with candles stuck in them), paper plates and cups, and possibly hats provide a surprising amount of rather ritualized, yet satisfying, play on this theme. Children enjoy wrapping up the "presents" as much as unwrapping them—perhaps because adults often restrict such activity so that gifts will "look nice."
- *Taking a trip play*—Children find great pleasure in packing suitcases and lugging them around. Play may include plane tickets, maps, magazines, peanuts for snack, and special hats for the pilots and flight attendants to wear. Discussions about destinations, possible weather anticipated there, and so forth, can encourage children to do a little thinking and planning ahead.
- *Baptisms*—A student suggested we name and baptize our newest doll. To my surprise our children were both knowledgeable and enthusiastic about the process and played it repeatedly. The combination of dressing up plus copious amounts of water and snack served as a "party" was irresistible.

ing risks and practicing common sense control. A sound rule to follow is to intervene in any play that is genuinely dangerous to the child or to others nearby while encouraging as much movement and freedom as possible. More protection is necessary for 2-year-olds than for 4-year-olds because the former are less experienced and consequently have poorer judgment. Although 4-year-olds are thirsty for risks and infatuated with challenges, they can be asked to evaluate dangers for themselves rather than being constantly controlled by the teacher.

Adding variety to the possibilities for outdoor play will also support it in a positive way. When the same trikes, swings, and climbers are present day after day, no wonder children succumb to boredom and wild behavior. However, a bedspread tent over the climber or lengths of hose and a ladder combined with the tricycles can suggest new play potential that will sustain their interest and cultivate new ideas, as well as encourage continued physical effort.

Finally, play emphasizing physical activity between children can be influenced by the choice of equipment available. Large, portable items they can haul together, such as boards and hollow blocks, encourage cooperative, physical play. These "open-ended" materials (sometimes called "loose parts") allow children to work together to construct all kinds of play situations, which constitutes an added bonus for the creative self. (For further discussion of curriculum for the physical self, please refer to chapters 8, 9, and 10.)

Enhance the Emotional Self through Play

We hear repeatedly that play can be the great reliever of feelings, and there is no denying the truth of that statement. Play does permit unacceptable impulses to be expressed in acceptable ways. Its value for the emotional self goes far beyond that, however. Playing out difficult situations provides prime opportunities for reducing stress and feelings of anxiety (Curry & Arnaud, 1995). For example, when opportunities for play

are provided to children who are hospitalized, Kampe (1990) points out that

> play provides a context for understanding and creating meaning, for regaining a sense of self-control in a strange environment, for building relationships, for learning new information, and for making pain and discomfort more bearable or waiting more tolerable. (p. 168)

On a more positive note, play promotes feelings of healthy delight. What fun it is to become absorbed in building an oven in which to bake the sandbox cookies or to feel satisfied when at last the blocks balance or the car runs through the tunnel all the way. What joy it is to play with another child and feel she has become your friend.

Of course, other feelings also arise in play: anger, when someone else becomes dominant; pain, when one is left out; fear, when an activity becomes too scary. The virtue is that play allows children to experience this wide range of emotion under relatively safe circumstances and to learn to deal with these feelings bit by bit. How valuable it is to learn that sadness and anger can be coped with and that they do not last forever.

How Can Teachers Help?

First, teachers can allow the expression of feelings while drawing the line when necessary between feeling like doing something and actually doing it (see chapter 11). It is just as acceptable to feel angry while playing as it is to feel silly or happy or excited. As a matter of fact, a child most probably will experience all these emotions when playing with other children. It is far better to realize this and to encourage children to express these safely through words than to insist they conceal or suppress such feelings, thus causing children to act them out by hurting someone else.

Second, teachers can help the child's emotional self grow during play by providing play experiences that draw out a problem when a child seems blocked from dealing with it independently.

During social play, children learn about getting along together; sharing power, space, and ideas with other people; and cooperating to gain satisfaction.

Perhaps, for unknown reasons, a child has become afraid of the dark. The teacher might provide some large boxes and flashlights in a darkened corner of the playroom so that the youngster can control the situation and play through her fear. Of course, if the fear appears to be increasing or extreme, the teacher would take some additional steps besides providing opportunities for such play. Depending on the severity of the behavior, these steps might include talking with the child, reading some stories during group time about how other children coped with similar concerns, or having a parent conference.

Usually, however, providing appropriate play opportunities will clarify feelings and provide relief, particularly when teachers realize how helpful such experiences can be. Teachers should also remain aware of their limitations in such circumstances. They are not professional psychologists. When a child's play appears to be

anxiety ridden or highly ritualized and repetitious, they should recognize these signals as calls for help that go beyond their training. At this point, referring the family for psychological consultation is usually the wisest step.

Help the Social Self Develop through Play

Although children gain many benefits from playing by themselves (solitary play) or side by side (parallel play), it is when they play together in associative or cooperative play that the social self benefits most because these kinds of play provide the richest opportunities for social learning. Preschool teachers typically spend a large part of each day helping children develop this aspect of themselves. During such play, children learn about getting along together, entering a group, handling exclusion and dominance, sharing power, space, and ideas with other people, making compromises, driving bargains, and cooperating to gain satisfaction.

Children also learn about the social world that lies beyond childhood as they assume the role of a mother or a teacher or Godzilla during play. Moreover, some researchers (Rubin & Howe, 1986) maintain that such role taking has the additional benefit of allowing children to put themselves in another's place, which probably encourages children to understand other people's feelings and to develop their ability to feel empathy for them. Social play therefore presents an unsurpassable means by which the social self can develop.

How Can Teachers Help?

The most important contribution teachers can make to social play is to pay attention to what is happening so they can facilitate this in a beneficial way. Perhaps one child is hovering on the edge of the play and needs a suggestion on how to enter the group; perhaps an argument is brewing over who will drive the truck and who will ride; perhaps someone is crying angrily because she thinks her friend tripped her on purpose. To deal with these situations, teachers must act as arbitrator, negotiator, and clarifier. At the same time, they model strategies that the children will eventually learn to use for themselves as teachers gradually encourage them to take over the demonstrated roles.

When seeking to facilitate social play, teachers have to walk a fine line between being at the center of attention and withdrawing too far from what is going on. The teachers' behavior must vary with the needs of the group. Some children, as Smilansky (1968) and Shefatya (1990) point out, are so inexperienced that they need help even to begin play. For such youngsters it may be necessary for the teacher to participate very directly by suggesting possibilities for play ("My goodness! It looks like there are some babies here that need to be fed. What shall we make them for dinner? Shredded Wheat? Oh, that would be delicious. What can you use for bowls?") For other inexperienced children, supplying equipment as the need arises is the answer. For older 4-year-olds it may be sufficient to extend their play by asking questions, such as "Now you've got the carriages loaded up—are you fellows going on a trip, or what?" Through it all, teachers should remember the goal of promoting play *among* the children rather than between the children and themselves. They should be ready to intervene quickly when it is necessary but remain attentive observers when it is not.

Some kinds of activities and equipment appear to promote social interaction among children, whereas others do not. For example, Rubin (1977) reports that children usually engage in solitary or parallel play while using play dough, clay, and sand and water. On the other hand, some equipment invites or even requires participation by more than one child to be maximally satisfying. Parachutes, rocking boats, balls, long jump ropes (for slightly older children), wagon and trike combinations, and horizontally hung tire swings are all examples of equipment that encourage play by more than one child at a time. Teachers who wish to foster cooperative social

interaction among children and help them develop their social selves as fully as possible should search for and acquire such equipment.

Foster the Creative and Cognitive Selves through Play

Reviews of research concerned with finding a possible link between divergent thinking (the ability to produce more than one answer to a problem) and play report that children who have been involved in free play before being asked to participate in situations requiring divergent thinking produce more various and creative answers to those problems than do children who were exposed to structured experiences before the problem was posed to them (Görlitz & Wohlwill, 1988; Johnson, 1990; Russ, 1996). For example, Pepler (1982) set up an experiment using 3- and 4-year-olds in which the children either played with pieces that could fit into formboards (a convergent, only-one-correct-way activity) or played with these pieces without the board (a more-than-one-correct-way activity). The control groups just watched the experimenter engage in convergent or divergent activities. The results indicated that the children who had played freely with the block pieces gave more unique responses when presented afterward with a divergent thinking task than did the children in the other three groups who had not been involved in free play.

How Can Teachers Help?

The most important thing to do is to remain open-minded about possibilities and recognize the value of creative ideas as they appear in such free play. Such positive support by teachers reinforces and encourages this kind of behavior in children.

Welcome the unconventional use of equipment whenever possible. Just the other day, as I waited in line at the bank, I watched a number of youngsters playing with one of those velvet-covered ropes that banks use to designate where people

Encourage the use of equipment in unconventional ways whenever possible.

should stand. Although adults saw only this function for the rope, the children saw a number of other possibilities. These included brushing their hands back and forth along it (a blissful sensory experience judging from one little girl's face), playing follow-the-leader and winding back and forth between its poles, hitting it with a little stick and making it swing, and running under it in a game of tag. The children's behavior clearly illustrated the playful, creative powers children bring to almost any situation.

Teachers should generally accept unconventional uses of equipment by young children, because these are of great value to the children's

creative selves. Thus, children should be permitted to ride tricycles backward, balance along the handle of a broom left on the sidewalk, or go down the slide toboggan-style on a bit of carpet.

Unfortunately, the same inexperience that enables children to perceive unusual possibilities in the equipment may also make it difficult for them to assess potential dangers, so teachers must remain alert to such potentially dangerous situations if they arise. The child who attempts to convert a tier of dresser drawers into a set of stairs may be in for a painful surprise.

Encourage imaginative substitutions. Although children's activity can at times genuinely cause harm or destroy property and teachers must intervene, far more often the unconventional, original use of equipment would not be damaging or dangerous, and teachers need not discourage the children's idea. For example, there is really no reason that unit blocks cannot be used on a table instead of the floor or a hat cannot double as a shopping bag.

Sometimes this original, unconventional approach is expressed by the imaginative substitution of something for something else. Piaget (1983) terms this activity *symbolic play* and maintains that this representation of reality on a symbolic level is an important step in mental development. Pretend play almost always makes use of this kind of creative imagination at some point. For instance, the guinea pig may represent a lion, the doll carriage may become a hospital cart, or an oatmeal carton can become a drum. By age 4, children often do not need the object at all, and we see pretend coffee being poured into a nonexistent cup or an imaginary rocket taking off with all the appropriate sound effects (Nourot & Van Hoorn, 1991).

Such creative, symbolic play can be particularly encouraged if the children's center makes a point of offering unstructured equipment, because the less structured (less reality bound) the equipment is, the more imagination the children are free to put into it. This is because whenever something looks like something in particular, it generally will be used as the thing it resembles, which thus restricts the children's imaginations. If a series of boxes in the play yard is painted to look like a series of quaint houses, the children are likely to play house in them, but not as likely to think of turning them over and converting them into a boat or train, as they would if the boxes were plain and accompanied by some boards, blocks, and old tires.

One February, for example, our staff decided that the housekeeping corner was not really attracting children anymore despite its enchanting array of beds, artificial fruit, lifelike replicas of stoves and iceboxes, and charming little dishes. So we took it all away. In its place we set out boards and large, hollow blocks and sawhorses and then neatly laid out a few dolls, blankets, and dishes on one of the boards. We said nothing and just waited. It was really interesting to see the children expand on the possibilities. The creative play began at a very primitive level, with the "furniture" consisting of a bed of blankets arranged on a couple of blocks and a kind of picnic set up on the floor. Over the weeks the children played more and more intensely and for longer periods of time as they developed and extended their ideas and perceived additional possibilities. Their play varied on different days and included the construction of an elaborate, two-room house, a two-deck camper, and an operating room. As their enthusiasm mounted, they added unit blocks, cubical counting blocks, pictures from our file, and rug scraps. This became one of the most satisfying experiences for the children at our school.

Rasmussen (1979) sums it up well:

> Perhaps the most incalculable error that adults make in respect to children's play is assuming that expensive, fixed structures are somehow better than inexpensive or discarded raw materials. Such notions could be dispelled if adults would open their eyes to children at play and see for themselves the genius of imaginative creative minds at work, transforming the simplest material into the stuff of excitement and joy. (p. 39)

Ask questions that encourage children to think for themselves. Free play time is the time par excellence to foster the development of thinking by asking children questions. The right question at the right time can stimulate creative solutions by children and also allows them to realize that the teacher values their ideas. Some examples of questions that can encourage young children to think creatively include "We don't have a truck. What could you use instead?" or "Is there some way I could help you? Something I could get for you?" and "I've been wondering, how will you figure that out?"

Helping Children with Disabilities Join in the Play

Although space does not permit extensive discussion of ways to facilitate the play of children who have specific disabilities, some general principles are worthwhile to bear in mind.

The most basic of these is the fact that fostering play for children with disabilities is of *great value* (Frost, 1992a). This is because a common educational pattern for these youngsters is divided schooling, in which the children spend part of their time in classes where they receive special instruction adapted to their unique needs and the remainder of their time mainstreamed with groups of more "typical" children. Observation has taught me that in the special instruction classes children can be expected to work particularly hard at tasks that may be quite difficult for them. That is why the relief provided by the free-play situations offered in the second school is especially precious for them. Free, pretend play provides the indispensable balance to other pressures to learn and achieve.

Welcoming children with special needs into their play also benefits more typical children. As recent legislation concerning fair treatment of people with disabilities reminds us, the time is past when people who differ from the usual are

Welcoming children with special needs into an activity benefits all the children.

hidden away or regarded as helpless. In the United States everyone is to be welcomed and employed according to their abilities, and there is no better time to instill that truth than in the early childhood years.

However, it is not enough to simply place a child with a disability in the company of more typical children and expect play to automatically occur, and yet Tobias (1994) found this to be the typical expectation of adults she observed during free play. She found that, without adult assistance, the children did not mix much less play together. Tobias concluded that teachers have to provide opportunities that are deliberately planned and structured to include *all* the children if such play is actually to take place. Otherwise, little benefit accrues from the experience for anyone.

Adapting Play to Fit the Capabilities of Children with Special Needs

The most obvious way to adapt play situations is to change the physical environment. For example, adding a nonslip surface to a ramp plus a

lower railing makes it possible for a child with braces to walk down unassisted, or reducing the noise level of the room can keep a blind child from becoming overly distracted. The references at the end of the chapter list several books that provide more information on this subject.

Even more important than such physical adjustments, however, is adapting teacher expectations to the level of the child's particular abilities. *The teacher must think of the child in terms of mental or physical developmental level, not in terms of actual chronological age.* Unfortunately this is harder to do than to talk about. Who, for instance, has not fallen into the trap of expecting more mature social behavior from a child just because she was taller than the other children?

It can be even more difficult to remember this when children have disabilities because some of their needs may not be immediately apparent to the naked eye, either. For example, a 4-year-old who cannot hear well or who is developmentally delayed may appear "perfectly normal" and yet may need special help working his way into the group playing dragons. Fortunately, many play activities such as water play, housekeeping, and blocks adapt well to the differing levels of ability of all kinds of children as long as the teacher remembers to suit expectations to what the particular child is ready to learn next. Perhaps a child is just learning to trade something rather than grab it or to wait a little while for a turn. These newly acquired skills should be commended instead of expecting the youngster to propose a more complicated bargain.

At the same time, do not make too many allowances for the child. It is as easy to underestimate abilities as it is to overestimate them. Either extreme breeds unfortunate results. It is as true for children with special needs as for more typical children that part of the teacher's responsibility is providing opportunities for consistent but not impossible growth.

Facilitating Play with Other Children

Of course, children are wary of individuals who look or act unusual, but a matter-of-fact explanation that Jamie's eyes look funny because he needs very thick glasses so he can see to string the beads will help reduce the uneasiness. Reducing feelings of apprehension goes a long way toward increasing the acceptability of the child who seems different.

Children do tend to be frank about their feelings, but they can also be taught that such frankness may hurt other people's feelings. A 4-year-old should no more be permitted to tell another youngster, "You're too dumb to do that" than he would be permitted to call someone a "dirty nigger." It is best to take the speaker aside and explain the child's difficulty while pointing out it makes her feel bad to be called dumb and it is unkind to hurt someone's feelings.

Fortunately, even young children can be genuinely kind and sympathetic to those who need their help if the teacher models that behavior and also offers suggestions about ways to be thoughtful. Perhaps she can point out how important it is to face the hard-of-hearing child when telling him something or thank the youngster who agrees to let a developmentally delayed child hold the hoop while the others roll the ball through it.

Summary

As Frank (1968) remarks, "Play is how children learn what no one can teach them." To this I would add that the activity of play is what children use to integrate their experiences and themselves into a meaningful whole.

Many definitions and purposes are ascribed to play, and all reflect some degree of truth. One definition is especially useful for preschool teachers to use: "Play may be defined as behavior that is intrinsically motivated, freely chosen, process-oriented, and pleasurable" (Johnson & Ershler, 1982, p. 137). Teachers can profit by using the elements of this definition as standards against which to measure the freedom and richness of play in their schools.

Investigators agree that play develops through a series of stages as children mature. Two examples of these stage theories are presented in the text because an understanding of them helps teachers plan age-appropriate play experiences for the children.

Some general ways teachers can encourage rich, full play include creating an atmosphere of acceptance and approval, providing enough time for play to develop fully, storing equipment in accessible places, providing enough of it, and extending and prolonging play.

Teachers can foster the development of the physical self through play by helping children keep a reasonable balance between taking risks and being safe, adding variety to outdoor activities, and providing equipment that encourages them to use their bodies in different ways. Play that promotes the development of the emotional self can be encouraged by providing ample opportunities for play and permitting the expression and ownership of the full range of feelings by children. Teachers can enhance the social self by paying close attention to play and teaching social skills to children as the need arises. While doing this, teachers must avoid becoming the center of attention, yet they must be ready to stimulate and extend play if it begins to falter.

Play offers excellent opportunities for children to develop their creative and intellectual faculties. This is particularly true when teachers remain open-minded about unusual but harmless uses of equipment, establish a climate of acceptance and admiration for the children's ideas, provide plenty of unstructured equipment, ask helpful questions, and avoid distracting the children by interrupting too often.

When drawing a child with disabilities into play activities, the teacher should try to adapt the play situation to make it as usable by the child as possible. This should include keeping activities physically accessible and developmentally appropriate to enhance their attractiveness. It is also important to encourage the other children to welcome the child with a disability into their play. This is best accomplished by matter-of-fact acceptance and explanation of the child's disabilities and by stressing the role of kindness and helpfulness by the other children.

Self-Check Questions for Review

Content-Related Questions

1. Name three ways play acts as an integrative force for children's personalities.
2. List the four standards recommended by the author that should be applied when evaluating whether a teacher's idea about a play activity is truly play from a child's point of view.
3. One of the principles for encouraging play is that the teacher needs to accept its value in a wholehearted way. Name four or five additional principles listed in the text.
4. Pretend you are giving a talk to a group of parents and that you wish to explain to them why play is important in the lives of young children. (You will probably give this particular talk many times during your teaching career!) Give some reasons why play benefits the physical, emotional, social, creative, and cognitive selves of the child.

5. What are some practical things teachers can do to foster play for each of the child's five selves? (These are the physical, social, emotional, creative, and cognitive selves.)
6. Why is it specially valuable to offer play opportunities to children with disabilities?

Integrative Questions

1. It is Easter time and the children have been to visit a family that raises rabbits. Upon return, the teacher passes out rabbit-ear hats and encourages the children to hop around like rabbits. What do you think Sutton-Smith would say about that activity?
2. If you agree with the definition of play provided in this book, then how would you define work?
3. Compare the suggestions about what teachers can do to help foster emotional growth in play with suggestions for fostering physical growth through play. How do the suggestions differ?
4. Propose two ways you might adjust an ordinary 4-year-old classroom to accommodate the needs of a child in a wheelchair. Now propose two ways you might modify the same room to accommodate a child who requires crutches to get around. Would the same adjustments facilitate the play of both children? If not, how might they differ?

Questions and Activities

1. You are planning your first parent meeting of the year, and you want to base it on play and its value as a mode of learning. Think of two or three different ways you might present this topic so that it would be genuinely interesting to the parents.
2. You have a group of young Mexican American boys in your room who spend most of their time playing "Bullee, Bullee" (a game where one boy acts the part of the bull by holding finger horns at the side of his head, and the other boys play matador). What would you do about this kind of play? Does it encourage cruelty to animals? Is it too aggressive? What about the other children who do not join in?
3. Some pieces of play equipment always seem to be rarely used by the children because they are stored in inaccessible places. Think about the storage where you are teaching. How could some of the less used but potentially play-full materials be stored so that they would be more readily available to teachers and children?

4. Take time to observe some children playing at the water table. Record what they do, and then identify what they are learning from the activity while enjoying themselves. Compare your notes with others who have also observed the activity.

5. A new 3-year-old who has cerebral palsy will be joining the children in your group two mornings a week. You have met her and think she will fit in all right except you are worried that her unusual way of moving—her movements are somewhat uncoordinated, and sometimes she drools a little—will attract the other children's curiosity. Do you think you should discuss this child with the children before her arrival? What should you say? Do the parents need preparation? What if someone makes an unkind remark?

References for Further Reading

Overviews

Isenberg, J. P., & Jalongo, M. R. (1996). *Creative expression and play in the early childhood curriculum* (2nd ed.). Upper Saddle River, NJ: Merrill/Prentice Hall. This book is filled with practical suggestions about incorporating play and self-expressive materials into the classroom. *Highly recommended.*

Stone, S. J. (1995). Wanted: Advocates for play in the primary grades. *Young Children, 50*(6), 45–54. For readers who require additional explanations of the benefits of play for all children, this article is an excellent resource. *Highly recommended.*

The Teacher's Role

Jones, E., & Reynolds, G. (1992). *The play's the thing: Teachers' roles in children's play.* New York: Teachers College Press. This excellent book provides thoughtful discussions of various ways teachers can inhibit or support the play of young children—filled with examples. *Highly recommended.*

Ward, C. D. (1996). Adult intervention: Appropriate strategies for enriching the quality of children's play. *Young Children, 51*(3), 20–25. Useful tips on when and when not to intervene are provided here.

Encouraging Play for
Children with Disabilities

Linder, T. W. (1993). *Transdisciplinary play-based intervention: Guidelines for developing a meaningful curriculum for young children.* Baltimore: Brookes. If the reader can have only one book dealing with children who have special educational requirements, this is the one to get! In addition to many other subjects, Linder provides detailed information on play and play materials discussed in relation to developmental levels categorized according to cognitive, social-emotional, communication, and sensory-motor disabilities. *Highly recommended.*

Sheridan, M. K., Foley, G. M., & Radlinski, S. H. (1995). *Using the Supportive Play Model: Individualized intervention in early childhood practice.* New York: Teachers College Press. Another very *practical* book filled with specific suggestions about how to integrate children with disabilities into the life of the school through play. *Highly recommended.*

Spodek, B., & Saracho, O. N. (1994). *Dealing with individual differences in the early childhood classroom.* New York: Longman. In a generally excellent book, the authors' chapter on "Using Educational Play" is outstanding because it provides concrete examples of ways to stimulate play for children with many differing disabilities.

Practical Advice about Facilitating Play

Brokering, L. (1989). *Resources for dramatic play.* Belmont, CA: Fearon. *Resources for Dramatic Play* has an outstanding opening chapter detailing the value of such play followed by a wealth of ideas about how to embellish it.

Cherry, C. (1976). *Creative play for the developing child: Early lifehood education through play.* Belmont, CA: Fearon. This book deals with play in the broadest sense of the word and includes discussions of such topics as gross- and fine-motor activities, science experiences, and dramatic play. *Highly recommended.*

For the Advanced Student

Berk, L. (1994). Vygotsky's theory: The importance of make-believe play. *Young Children, 50*(1), 30–39. This article not only provides a clear description of Vygotsky's reasons for valuing play but also describes recent research findings about play and its influence on development. *Highly recommended.*

Curry, N. E., & Arnaud, S. H. (1995). Personality difficulties in preschool children as revealed through play themes and styles. *Young Children, 50*(4), 4–9. The authors identify children's behaviors during play that may signal they need special help and understanding.

Gowen, J. W. (1995). The early development of symbolic play. *Young Children, 50*(3), 75–84. Gowen provides a detailed yet readable account of how children develop their ability to use symbols in place of concrete objects as they mature.

Klugman, E., & Smilansky, S. (1990). *Children's play and learning: Perspectives and policy implications.* New York: Teachers College Press. Excellent summaries of the relationship of play to social and cognitive development are included as well as broader views concerning the status of play. *Highly recommended.*

Pellegrini, A. D. (Ed.). (1995). *The future of play theory: A multidisciplinary inquiry into the contributions of Brian Sutton-Smith.*

Albany: State University of New York Press. This fascinating array of articles discusses everything from the benefits of rough-and-tumble play to the marketing of toys. *Highly recommended.*

Piaget, J. (1962). *Play, dreams and imitation in childhood.* New York: Norton. In his classic description, Piaget discusses how children assimilate knowledge of the world around them by means of imitation and the use of symbolic play. Rather difficult but interesting reading.

Roopnarine, J. L., Johnson, J. E., & Hooper, F. H. (Eds.). (1994). *Children's play in diverse cultures.* Albany: State University of New York Press. The first in a series on play in society, this book covers eight cultures ranging from Japanese to African. Generally based on research studies, the chapters often include the school's attitude toward play as well as that of the larger society. Very interesting reading.

Other Resources of Related Interest

Play, Policy and Practice Connections, c/o Tri-C-AEYC, PO Box 104, Meadville, PA 16335. The newsletter, sponsored by the Play, Policy, and Practice Caucus of the National Association for the Education of Young Children, offers articles of current interest.

United States Affiliate of the International Association for the Child's Right to Play (Nancy Eletto, 616 Kimbark St., Longmont, CO 80501). This interdisciplinary, internationally linked group holds conferences, conducts study tours, and sponsors special projects related to play. Publications are available.

4

Planning for Total Learning

Creating Supportive Curriculum Plans and Schedules

Have you ever

- Had exciting ideas of what to offer the children but been puzzled about how to begin making a curriculum plan?
- Needed an example of a basic schedule for a full- or half-day program?
- Wondered how to manage a rainy day successfully?

If you have, the material in this chapter will help you.

At no other level of education does a teacher have so much freedom and so few constraints concerning content, method and expected outcomes. Inherent in this freedom is both challenge and responsibility for careful, imaginative, resourceful planning for the education of young children.

Oralie McAfee (1981)

Traditionally, I had made monthly plans, consistently fine-tuning procedures to make them more developmentally appropriate and process oriented. Materials were usually brought out for only one day, with new activities being introduced daily with hopes of keeping the children's interest stimulated. The ideas were teacher generated and carefully planned to avoid problems and keep conflict among the children to a minimum.

Inspired by Reggio, I totally abandoned this carefully worked out curriculum. One of the most important things that we did when making this change was *slow down* and tackle fewer activities on which we could emphasize more in-depth research.

Cheryl Breig-Allen (1997, p. 128)

You got to be very careful if you don't know where you are going because you might not get there.

Yogi Berra, as quoted in M. P. Zuckerman (1992, p. 88)

Discussing how to plan a curriculum for total learning before discussing the basic elements that compose it is somewhat like explaining how to plan a nourishing meal before teaching anything about good nutrition, cooking, or even shopping for food. I believe, though, that it is helpful to see the intended whole before going on to discuss the individual elements. For this reason, this chapter concentrates on planning curriculum (*what* will happen) and developing schedules (*when* it will happen). Chapter 5 discusses constructing environments for children (*where* it will happen).

The Basic Ingredients of Planning: What Should Be Included in the Curriculum

Know What You Want the Children to Learn

Chapter 1 states that the basic purpose of education is to enhance children's feelings of being competent and cared for. Because later chapters describe in detail how to achieve such feelings of security and self-worth for each of the five selves, we will content ourselves here with

Good planning includes planning for opportunities for children to identify and stay in touch with all their feelings.

reviewing a basic list that is intended only as a summary of the most valuable skills children should begin to acquire as they move through a well-planned day at preschool. Teachers need to be aware of these skills to include them consistently when planning curriculum.

In addition to those activities that provide for the health and safety of the children and help them understand and value life, there are those activities specifically for the *physical self* that should be included in the preschool curriculum. These include activities that provide practice in the following:

- Participating in movement and locomotion activities
- Practicing static and dynamic balance
- Developing body and space awareness
- Practicing rebound and airborne activities
- Fostering rhythm and temporal awareness
- Engaging in throwing and catching activities
- Using daily motor skills

- Participating in relaxation and tension-releasing activities

A curriculum that favors the development of *emotional health* in children should include opportunities for learning to do the following:

- Separating comfortably from their families
- Achieving the basic attitudes of trust, autonomy, and initiative
- Remaining in contact with their feelings while maintaining emotional control
- Using dramatic play and other self-expressive materials to come to terms with emotional problems
- Facing reality
- Beginning to understand how other people feel and feel empathy for them

Learnings for children's *social selves* should encompass the following:

- Learning to feel what they want but control what they do

- Acquiring socially acceptable strategies for getting what they want
- Learning to function successfully as a member of a group
- Finding satisfaction in helping each other
- Finding pleasure in accomplishing meaningful work
- Understanding their place in the world, and feeling good about their gender roles and ethnic heritages

Opportunities for children to develop their *creative selves* should include the following:

- Using a wide range of self-expressive activities
- Participating in imaginative dramatic play
- Engaging in creative thinking and problem solving

Finally, the children's *cognitive selves* should be enhanced by the following:

- Fostering *verbal ability* by (a) putting their ideas into words throughout the day and enjoying communicating with other people and (b) participating in carefully planned group times
- Developing *cognitive skills* by (a) analyzing choices and making decisions, (b) figuring out answers for themselves, and (c) pursuing interesting subjects (pathways) in depth
- Using the midlevel mental abilities of matching, perceiving common relations, grouping, temporal ordering, graduated ordering (seriation), and determining simple cause-and-effect relationships

Know How to Teach These Skills

Teachers should ask themselves two questions when thinking about how to teach any particular skill to a young child: (1) What activity can I include that provides the best opportunities for learning this skill? and (2) How can I help the child experience success in that activity?

I recall a teacher who had a 4-year-old in his group named Angie who went out of her way to tease Jeanne, a Down syndrome child. So he asked himself, "How can I stop the teasing and turn Angie's attitude into a more positive one?" and, even more important, "How can I help her understand a little about Jeanne's difficulties?" Although he was puzzled at first about how to accomplish these goals, he finally decided to encourage Angie to hold Jeanne's coat every day. He explained to Angie privately that although Jeanne looked as big as the other children, she was actually younger *inside* and so needed help just as Angie's little sister did. She did learn to help Jeanne with some quiet coaching from him (and some louder coaching back to him from Angie). "Not that way, dummy," she once said to him in exasperation. "It works best if you hold it this way for her. Here, you'd better let me do it." Eventually this led to Jeanne putting her coat on by herself, much to Angie's satisfaction. Thus, the activity resulted in a growth in competence for both children. Although these were different kinds of competence, each was well suited to the different ages and abilities of the children.

Design the Plan: Decide How to Incorporate the *What* and *How* into an Overall Plan*

It is vital to realize right from the start of this discussion of curriculum planning that developing a curriculum plan requires a combination of structure and flexibility.

Careful structuring is the more usual, conventional aspect of planning curriculum content. This structure is essential to include because it ensures that all aspects of learning are covered. Table 4–1 provides an example of how a structured, comprehensive weekly plan could be developed, and we will talk more about how to do this later on in the chapter.

But there is another side to good content planning in addition to this sort of structured curriculum chart. *Really good planning* also allows for the curriculum to develop and change in a

TABLE 4–1
Weekly Curriculum Analysis Chart*

Focus of Interest: Bodies & Hospitals†

Part of Self Being Developed		Monday	Tuesday	Wednesday	Thursday	Friday
Physical self	Activity	Creative dance	Obstacle course	Beanbag game: throw in tires / Practice La Raspa	Health examinations; carpentry	Health examinations
	Educational Intention	Emphasize rhythm, tension release, creative self-expression	Emphasize balancing, bouncing (airborne), and body-perception skills	Projectile management; coordinate movement with music	Health screening / Carpentry: small-muscle skills	Health screening
Emotional self—mental health	Activity	Read *Curious George Goes to the Hospital* / Talk about Kevin's fracture	Hospital play	Group time: pass around a stethoscope and tongue depressor; discuss their use	Water play in bathroom	Block play with rubber people as accessories
	Educational Intention	Use discussion to broaden understanding and overcome fear	Play out concerns and fears about hospital	Prepare children for brief health examinations on Thursday and Friday	Tension relief: important because of doctor's visit	Perhaps play family or hospital with them
Social self	Activity	Make dough	Visiting mother shares twins' baby book	Group makes card for child in hospital	Doctor's visit: help doctor set out instruments	Doctor's visit: help set out instruments
	Educational Intention	Older children "read" the illustrated recipe to younger ones, thereby helping them	Enhance twin's self-esteem; strengthen home bonds with school	Pleasure in doing something for someone else; maintain social bonds with absent child	Opportunity for meaningful work / Career education	Opportunity for meaningful work / Career education

*Note. This chart includes only special activities. Standard activities such as sand, tricycles, books, and so forth, are assumed to be present.
†Focus of interest for mixed group of 3- and 4-year-olds, including four Mexican American children. This topic was selected because Kevin was hospitalized with a fractured pelvis.

61

TABLE 4-1
continued

Focus of Interest: Bodies & Hospitals†

Part of Self Being Developed		Monday	Tuesday	Wednesday	Thursday	Friday
Multicultural and nonsexist emphasis	Activity	Field trip: Cinco de Mayo celebration; see dance group dance La Raspa, return to center and dance	African American mother brings twins' book to share with group	Dance: Practice La Raspa	Female doctor conducts examination	Male doctor conducts examination
	Educational Intention	Generate positive feelings toward Mexican American culture	Emphasize that babies from various cultures have a lot in common	Pleasure in another culture—Mexican American	Teach principle that both men and women can be doctors	Teach principle that both men and women can be doctors
Creative self	Activity	Using dough; dancing	Hospital pretend play; easel painting	Large collaged get-well card; dough	Repeat hospital play; carpentry	Finger painting
	Educational Intention	Using dough is creative; making it is not	Foster creative, dramatic play, and self-expression	Collage: design and arrangement; dough: free, self-expression	Opportunities for self-expression	Relaxation, tension release; free, non-demanding experience
Language development (Also see "Think About" questions)	Activity	Group time: read and discuss *Curious George Goes to the Hospital* "Read" dough recipe—measure ingredients	Use book about babies at group time	Emphasize "Think About" questions	Teacher turns page of *Curious George Goes to the Hospital* Have children retell the story.	Have children dictate stories about seeing doctor Subject: "What happened when the doctor examined me."
	Educational Intention	Provide information on what a hospital is like and facts for later, realistic play Add vocabulary Develop emergent literacy & math skills	Encourage children to discuss "When they were little. . ."	Foster development of alternative answers; identify emerging curriculum possibilities	Practice recall and temporal ordering	Use language to describe experience to express feeling; emergent literacy skill

Cognitive self	Activity	Follow dough recipe: illustrated for children to "read" by themselves	Compare pictures of twins	Discussion in large group: "What helps us keep well?"	Lotto game: occupations—what equipment goes with what occupation? [include doctor equipment]	Compare baby pictures with current children
Midlevel abilities	Educational Intention	Practice temporal ordering, use of symbols, common relations (tools with materials)	Practice matching: discuss whether twins are identical	Practice cause and effect	Practice common relations	Practice temporal ordering
Possible emergent pathways—"Think About" questions	Activity	Provide outline drawings of body shapes; ask children to draw what they think is inside	Introduce X-rays of human & animal bones, some broken	How can we let Kevin (in hospital) know we miss him? Then, make get-well card or present	Help arrange room for doctor visit	Offer raw chicken foot with tendons exposed to pull
	Questions	In your opinion, do we really need a head and stomach? What if we did not have any bones—what then?	How could you grow bones back together? Are bones blood? What's the difference? Do only small animals have small bones?	What's a practical present for someone in traction?	What will help the doctor feel comfortable and able to work well?	What makes the claw contract or expand? Do hands work the same way?
	Educational Intention	Find out what children know &/or are wondering about	Foster problem-solving skills	Foster social concern for another person; empathy; problem-solving skills	Meaningful work & concern for someone else's comfort	Foster problem-solving skills—insight
Special activities for children with special needs	Activity	Try new support table with Evan so he can stand while making play dough	Share twins' baby book	Special notice of child in hospital	Work on Ellen's self-control during carpentry	Encourage Timothy to play with others in block corner
	Educational Intention	Increase Evan's sense of mastery	Build twins' self-esteem	Help Kevin feel he still belongs to the group	Increase ability to exercise a little patience—not "explode"	Overcome shyness; learn strategies for entering group

flexible way as the children's interests in a subject develop and take direction. This is often spoken of as being *emergent curriculum* because it arises or emerges as the topic develops (Jones & Nimmo, 1994) and is negotiated between teacher and children. It is this willingness to move with the children's interests while, at the same time, analyzing those interests and singling some of them out to focus on that provides the best cognitive learning opportunities.

But doing this is not easy. Gould (1996) sums the challenge up well when she says:

> Collaborating with pupils and negotiating the curriculum with them is not easy. It requires a considerable degree of flexibility and an ability and readiness to meet the needs of children by providing information and materials that children will be interested in and wish to pursue. It also demands a constant creative stance with children—receptivity to children's ideas and a willingness to take them seriously, even when, from an adult point of view, they seem naïve or immature. At the same time, creating an authentic learning environment requires clear thinking and planning in relation to broad, long-term goals and imagination in finding specific themes, activities, and materials that will spark fresh interests and make connections between those that have already been developed. (p. 93)

The problem confronting the novice teacher is how to maintain structure in the overall curriculum while remaining open to changing some aspects of it as the children's interests develop. The easiest way to do this is to think of a portion of the curriculum as being a pathway down which you and the children walk together. Some teachers speak of this as doing *projects*. For myself, I prefer the term *pathway* because to many people, *projects* implies a concrete preordained unit the children are expected to complete, whereas *pathway* implies an adventurous journey. As the path rounds a bend, sometimes new visions of learning possibilities are revealed to both teacher and children.

Although it is extremely worthwhile to follow these burgeoning interests, this does not mean that overall curriculum plans should be abandoned. In the words of Carlina Rinaldi (1994), it is best to regard premade plans as being a compass, not a train schedule. Table 4–1 includes "Think About" questions that might lead to the development of investigatory pathways depending on whether the children become interested in following up on them. Chapter 17, "Helping Children Learn to Think for Themselves," discusses how to generate such emergent cognitive curriculum in more detail.

Planning *What* Will Happen[1]

The same steps should be followed when thinking about the curriculum plan whether planning the advance portion or the more emerging aspects of it. Developing a curriculum plan is accomplished most easily by dividing the process into a series of steps.

Step 1: Begin with an Aspect of the World That Has Caught the Children's Interests

The initial, spontaneous interest that comes from the children should be the magnet that draws teacher and children together when settling on a subject to pursue. It might be what becomes of rain when it vanishes down the sewer or what makes shadows change their shapes or what are babies really like.

Although most of us would agree that basing curriculum on the children's concerns and interests is the best way to motivate learning, the truth is that most curriculum ideas are chosen by teachers because they already have a box of learning materials available or because they have an activity book that offers lots of ideas on that subject. The reality of the daily teaching grind forces me to admit it may be necessary to rely on such embalmed resources from time to

---

[1]The material in the following pages draws on many of the ideas from the municipal schools of Reggio Emilia, Italy.

time, but every teacher should also cultivate opportunities that arise from the spontaneous interests of his or her current group. Doing this assures the topic is relevant and will sustain the children's interests. It is also much more stimulating and creative for the teacher.

Step 2: Brainstorm Ideas About Ways and Things to Teach the Children That Are Related to the Topic

This is the point in curriculum development where the fancy should be allowed to wander and entertain all sorts of possibilities. The resulting list usually turns out to be a mixture of figuring-out questions and activities.

For example, many children in Oklahoma are very interested in and afraid of tornadoes because they occur so frequently there. A teacher of 4-year-olds might list some of these possible pathways to investigate:

- What can tornadoes do?
- Practice safe tornado drills.
- Compare fire drills and tornado drills.
- How can we tell how hard the wind is blowing?
- Talk about places to go to be safe from tornadoes.
- Can you draw a tornado sound?
- Visit a TV station and see weather-reporting equipment.
- Experiment with different kinds of fans—hand-held, electric, and so forth.
- Make a rain gauge to measure the amount of rain in a storm.
- Buy an anemometer to measure wind speed and have the children help hook it up.
- Where does wind come from? What makes wind?
- Can we make wind ourselves?
- How can we make wind blow harder or more gently?
- Fly kites with no wind and with some wind.
- Investigate bubbles—through straws in water, soap bubbles, balloons.

- How do you know whether a tornado is coming?
- Can we see wind?

Other children might be equally interested in (though not as afraid of) rain. Potential pathways might be these:

- What would rain-type music sound like? Could you write it down some way?
- Where does the rain go that falls on the streets?
- What if it never rained—what could we do to get water?
- If we did not have boots and slickers, what could we use to stay dry?
- Are hail and snow really rain?
- How can we tell how much it has rained?
- What makes puddles dry up? Do they dry up faster in the sunshine or under a tree?
- Why does it only rain when there are clouds in the sky?
- Experiment with different size holes in cans to make softer or harder rain.
- Use squirt bottles to discover how to make water pressure.
- See if we can make water fall up instead of down.
- Change water into its different forms—ice, steam.
- Can we make a rainbow?
- What could we use to make a rainy picture?

Or the children in the 3-year-old room might be particularly interested in babies because of several new little brothers and sisters. Possible pathways for them might include the following:

- How do mothers take care of babies? (You might want to consider various animal mothers as well as humans.)
- Do rat mothers and bird mothers care for their babies the same way?
- Read books about babies.
- Talk about how it feels to be a baby.
- How can we take good care of baby animals?

- Bathing babies: Have Father visit and do this.
- How could we tell whether a baby is growing?
- How are babies different from children?
- Get out baby equipment and play house.
- Try on baby clothes—see how children have grown.
- Keep track of new skills as baby acquires them.
- Use picture puzzles of baby animals and their mothers.
- Invite Mom to school to feed baby with bottle and by nursing.
- Serve baby food at snack.
- Do all babies eat the same thing—animals and humans? How are the foods alike and different?
- Explore feelings that siblings may have about baby brothers or sisters.

Step 3: Narrow Down the Possibilities by Facing the Reality of What Is Possible and What Is Not

It is clear from scanning these lists there are many possible pathways to investigate. Indeed, the problem may lie in choosing which of a number of attractive possibilities to select to develop in depth. Asking the following reality-based questions will make those choices easier.

Reality 1: Which Ideas Are Most Developmentally Appropriate for the Children in the Group?
Older fours might feel reassured by talking to the meteorologist and finding out how he or she keeps everyone safe during a storm, whereas young threes would rather know a safe place to go is available that will protect them. Two-year-olds are more likely than 4-year-olds to be intrigued with actually trying on baby clothes and seeing how much they have grown, whereas 4-year-olds may think the answer so obvious the idea is silly. On the other hand, the fours might enjoy thinking of additional ways to measure and keep track of the baby's growth, whereas this might be too difficult a concept for young threes to explore.

Reality 2: How Feasible Is the Idea?
How far away is the TV station? Does the teacher know where to locate fertile eggs to hatch? What if there are no mothers available who are willing to nurse a baby in front of an audience?

Reality 3: Are the Activities Reasonably Connected to Each Other?
The teacher should be aware that sometimes pathways become so diffuse there is no focus or common avenue or theme that ties the information together. This is the problem that sometimes arises with *webbing* (Workman & Anziamo, 1996). When ideas are too loosely "webbed" or linked together, the pathway is lost sight of and teacher and children just wander around in ever-widening circles. For example, the children might be interested in how to find out what their guinea pig prefers to eat; this widens to how to grow plants for them, which then spreads to ideas about celebrating the harvest, which branches out to a discussion about Pilgrims.

The teacher's responsibility is to keep things on track while at the same time remaining sensitive to developing the areas that catch fire from the children's enthusiasm. Therefore, he or she must consider whether some wonderful but extraneous ideas could best be used at another time. Perhaps the ideas about harvest and Pilgrims would fit in someplace else, for example.

Reality 4: Are There Enough Possibilities Related to the Topic to Provide for Continued Interest by the Children?
Sometimes a pathway peters out because of lack of ideas or interest from either the teacher or children. These should be allowed to die a natural death.

On the other hand, many pathways turn out to be richly productive, and it is worthwhile to take as much time as necessary to explore those in depth. In the Reggio schools such interests may extend over weeks or even months. Allowing for such in-depth investigation, as Katz and Chard (1991) emphasize, permits children to experi-

Flexibility in presenting activities is as important as flexibility in adapting plans to the needs of the moment.

ence the satisfaction of knowing about one subject in depth rather than flitting from subject to subject in more superficial, less satisfying ways.

Reality 5: Can This Topic Be Used to Provide Curriculum That Develops All Five of the Children's Selves?

The answer to this question is probably not. It is usually necessary to plan some additional activities to make certain the curriculum is sufficiently comprehensive.

For example, the topic of rain offers many opportunities to develop the cognitive self, such as finding out whether hail and snow are really rain, or experimenting with changing water into its various states, or figuring out how to represent rain by using drums or tambourines to imitate its sound. It is more difficult to think of ways the physical self might be developed when rain is used as the investigative pathway.

Reality 6: Can the Topic Be Presented so That It Is Not Too Stimulating or Overwhelming for the Children?

Student teachers in particular are sometimes so excited (and worried) about their curriculum that they plan too much in one day or even in one week. The result of too much variety can be

distracted, fatigued, confused children who have had no time to savor each of the experiences to their fullest extent or have time and opportunity to go forward with their own ideas. Therefore, it is necessary to caution beginning teachers to practice moderation in their planning, while at the same time hoping that, as they become more experienced, they will retain their sense of enthusiasm every time they plan learning experiences for the children.

Reality 7: Does the Curriculum Take the Needs of Individual Children into Consideration?

For example, the teacher could ask the shy child to bring his baby sister to school. Or the unpopular youngster who tends to bully the weaker children could be asked to help those youngsters punch holes in the cans when doing the water investigation. Is there some way a particularly intelligent little girl can pursue an interest related to the topic in more depth? Perhaps she would enjoy measuring the amount of rainfall over a month's time and making a flannel-board graph that shows the results. Or perhaps she might like to videotape different kinds of clouds and learn to identify each type by its special name.

*Reality 8: Does the List Include Anything
That Can Be Used to Promote a Multiethnic
or Nonsexist Approach?*

If the subject is babies, discussing pictures during group time of how Hopi mothers carry their babies on cradle boards, for instance, would satisfy the multiethnic requirement, or teaching about the role of both parents in conception would satisfy the nonsexist aspect (see chapter 10 for more details).

*Reality 9: Does the Plan Allow for Opportunities
for Change to Follow the Children's
Interests as These Develop?*

Plans are absolutely essential when developing curriculum, but their great weakness is that, once made, they may seem cast in concrete. If a basic purpose of curriculum is fostering the enthusiasm to find things out, then the teacher must remain open and flexible to the children's questions and interests as they bubble up. This means he or she must be willing to adjust or even scrap carefully thought-out plans as the curriculum develops. Collaborating with the children in their quest for knowledge is the surest way to whet their appetite for further learning.

After Analysis, Relist the Remaining Topics.

As the realities of planning are considered, some ideas are removed from the list, some are simply deferred, and some are added as inspirations strike the teacher. At this point the process moves to Step 4.

Step 4: Block in Activities Throughout the Week

In this step of curriculum design, teachers must block in the potential activities over a week's time. The simplest way to do this is to prepare a chart, such as the one shown in Table 4–1.

Although experienced teachers may clearly see the purposes for each activity they plan, beginning teachers often do not have this clear perception, so it is essential that they identify the educational purpose for the activity. This pinpoints the reason by providing an explanation for its inclusion in the curriculum. For example, the activity of cooking banana bread might fulfill the cognitive purpose by providing experience in temporal ordering as the children follow the order of the recipe and in understanding cause and effect by putting some batter in the oven and comparing what happens to it with the way the raw batter looks. Making the bread could also satisfy the need to provide for the social self because the children are doing something that benefits the entire group and also enjoying the experience of doing meaningful work.

I strongly recommend that *beginning teachers write out the purpose for each activity as is done in this chart for at least several weeks.* This is valuable to do for two reasons. First, pinpointing the major reason for including the activity clarifies the teacher's purpose and helps emphasize that aspect when presenting it. Second, providing examples of the educational reasons for including activities makes it easier for parents to understand why activities that look like "just being fun" are actually worthwhile learning opportunities.

Step 5: Fit Activities into the Daily Schedule

In the fifth step of curriculum design, teachers must fit the content-curriculum plan into the schedule. Remember, a schedule is *not* a curriculum plan. It just provides the framework of time in which the activity will take place during the day. Such schedules can be a blessing if they are used to help teachers and children know what comes next and to contribute to the feeling of security such knowledge produces. Or they can be a burden if they are allowed to dominate the day in a rigid, minute-by-minute fashion that ignores children's needs and prevents teachers from exercising good judgment. A well-designed schedule not only provides for orderly planning but also allows for flexibility so that time periods can be extended or contracted depending on whether the children are deeply occupied or particularly restless.

Step 6: Evaluate What Happened and Decide How to Improve the Activity Next Time

Nothing is more satisfying than finishing a day with children and knowing that it was a good one—that the children learned something worthwhile and that everyone has grown a little toward decency and happiness. When that happens, it can be a temptation to leave well enough alone and simply bask in the pleasure of work well done.

On the other hand, everyone has days when just the opposite occurs and nothing seems to have gone right. The temptation then is to wallow in misery and see everything in shades of gloom.

Actually, neither of these responses is desirable. What is preferable to either of them is taking a more clear-sighted view of how the children responded to each activity and then asking oneself what can be done next time to make the activity more effective.

Table 4–2 provides an example of how one student teacher evaluated some of the activities she included on a particular day she taught.

Devise the Daily Schedule: Planning *When* It Will Happen

Meeting the Needs of the Children

The schedule should provide for alternating periods of quieter and more active experiences. A sound schedule provides a daily pattern of activities that reduces the possibility of excitement escalating to the point of wild exhaustion. This is accomplished by interspersing quieter times, such as group or snack, with more vigorous experiences, such as outdoor play or dance.

In addition to this overall alternation, it is also important to plan for a variety of quieter and more vigorous activities within the larger time block, because individual children have different activity level requirements. Sometimes, for example, a child needs to be allowed to leave the group early, just as another youngster may relish the chance to withdraw to a shelter of blocks when the rest are rolling giddily down the hill outside. All schools should provide cozy book corners and rocking chairs to which children can retire when they wish to find peace and quiet.

The schedule should provide for indoor and outdoor play. While thinking about the value of alternative quiet and active learning situations, it also makes sense to consider whether the schedule will require all the children to be inside or outdoors at once or whether they will be free to move in and out as they desire.

If the staff is large enough and weather permits, allowing children to go in and out at will provides the best mix of large- and small-muscle activities. Schools in warm climates often operate on this kind of plan year-round, but schools situated in more wintry areas usually prefer to go through the routine of snowsuits, boots, and mittens only once a morning and afternoon. What these colder climate schools sometimes forget, however, is that it might be possible to operate on a more open plan during early fall and late spring. If the staff is limited in number, part of the indoor and outdoor areas can be blocked off so that supervision remains adequate. The increased freedom and reduction of tension that results can make the effort of modifying the schedule well worth the trouble.

Sometimes, however, all-indoor or all-outdoor scheduling is necessary. Staff who must operate according to this plan should take special pains in planning the schedule to see to it that large-muscle activities are planned for inside and small-muscle activities are included outside to maintain a satisfactory balance in the curriculum.

70

TABLE 4–2
Activity Analysis Sheet: A Morning with 2-Year-Olds*

	Theme: The five senses	Age: 2-year-olds	Time: Tuesday morning
Name of Self	**Activity**	**Purpose**	**Evaluation**
Physical: small-muscle	Making orange juice	Develop eye-hand coordination: squeezing and pressing; tasting sweet and sour.	Children were extremely interested in this activity. They loved squeezing the oranges and tasting them. *Next time* I will offer this activity at beginning of self-select (individual choosing) time, instead of in the middle (we had to wait for the cook to be free to help). That way, more of the children could have participated.
Physical: large-muscle	Obstacle course	Foster coordination of bodies in crawling, balancing, climbing, and spatial awareness. Talk about feeling body as it moves.	Children really enjoyed crawling through the tunnel and climbing up the stairs. I emphasized feeling how hands hold on, feet sting after jumping down. They modified the activity to satisfy their love of throwing beanbags into the tires. They rearranged the large hollow blocks and balance beam in a row and threw the beanbags into the tires. *Next time* I will have the beanbag throwing separate from the obstacle course so the activities won't interfere with each other. If both require close supervision, I'll move one outside for later play.
Social	Washing dishes in the water table	Encourage children to play side by side; encourage conversation and meaningful work. Have warm soapy water and cold rinse water; ask children to sense the difference.	The children enjoyed washing dishes (including the orange juice ones) and playing with the bubbles. Some brought more dishes from the dramatic play area. Children tried to feel the bubbles. *Next time* I would offer this activity right next to dramatic play to facilitate play in both places. Use only warm water — children disliked the contrast, even though it did fit the theme.

Nonsexist	Wood train and blocks	Encourage both girls and boys to use blocks and train.	Children were engrossed with the trains — both boys and girls enjoyed building the track and using the little people and animals I added. *Next time* I might have more blocks out and try harder to interest girls. It helps immensely to have a teacher in that area.
Emotional	Hiding in large box included in obstacle course	Work on fear of dark; controlling strength of experience by self-regulation. Talk about seeing better in light than in dark.	Children played cooperatively, shutting each other inside the box. It was too scary and/or stimulating for several of them. There was considerable screaming and excitement. *Next time* I'd do this as a separate activity; perhaps with flashlights. It was too much to supervise, so I finally pushed the box over to the wall and closed the flaps so the children couldn't get in. We talked about feeling scared in large group afterward. Tried shutting our eyes to make it dark.
Creative	"Finger painting" with feet	Provide semicreative experience. Concentrate on sensation via feet as compared to sensation via hands.	Painting was very slippery. Children had to sit on chairs, not walk on paper. Required lots of supervision because of safety and cleanup and putting on shoes and socks. *Next time* I would talk about it first — prepare children for "sitting" rule. Offer only if plenty of help is available.
Cognitive	"Smell" cannisters used in Let's Find Out. Asked children to match identical smells and to label smells they knew.	Practice concept of matching using a different sensory mode. Attach names to smells.	Most children were cautiously interested. *Next time* it's important to keep correct lids on cannisters so smells don't get mixed up. Color-coding tops and bottoms would make this easier to do.

*Based on work by Jill Staab, student teacher, University of Oklahoma. Reprinted by permission

Research

Study

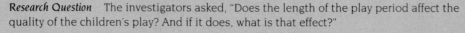

Which Is Better: More *Play* Times or More *Time* to Play?

Research Question   The investigators asked, "Does the length of the play period affect the quality of the children's play? And if it does, what is that effect?"

Research Method   Christie, Johnsen, and Peckman conducted an observational study in which they observed thirty-four 4- and 5-year-old children during times when the indoor play period was 15 minutes long. They also observed the same children during times when the indoor play period was 30 minutes long. The same care givers and play equipment were present during short and long episodes. Using the Parten/Piaget play categories, they took time samples of the play behavior until they accumulated 15 minutes worth of observations for each child during both short and long play times and compared the results.

Research Results   The results indicated that the length of play time definitely did affect the quality of the children's play. During the shorter periods, there was more standing around and watching and more functional and parallel-dramatic play. When the play period was longer, the children became engaged in more mature forms of play. They were more involved, played more together, and utilized more constructive and group dramatic play. Moreover, most of the more mature play occurred during the second 15 minutes of the play periods.

Implications for Teaching   Teachers who value play must realize it takes quite a while for children to warm up and experience maximum richness from play. Little dabs of play experience during the day are *not* enough. As Christie and Wardle (1992) point out, it is much more valuable to schedule at least one longer play period every day than several briefer ones. Otherwise the children will not be able to derive the full benefit from that play opportunity.

Note. From "The Effects of Play Period Duration on Children's Play Patterns" by J. F. Christie, E. P. Johnsen, & R. B. Peckover, 1988, *Journal of Research in Childhood Education*, 3(2), 123–131.

The schedule should provide for a reasonable pace throughout the day. I began this section by mentioning the beneficial effects of adjusting the tempo of particular days to the needs of the children as these become apparent, but it is necessary also to allow enough time overall, every day, in the schedule to permit children to become truly engrossed in what they are doing. That is why the research study by Christie, Johnsen, and Peckover (1988) is included here. It is so important to provide enough time for children to become engrossed in what they are doing. Plans that cause children to be constantly shifted back and forth from one thing to another reduce their chances for concentration and deep involve-

ment, to say nothing of the general feeling of harassment they promote throughout the school.

Besides planning long enough play periods, think about planning transitions from one activity to another. Too many of these during the day can be exhausting for children and staff. As Neugebauer (1988) points out:

Each day we must make many transitions from one space or activity or interaction to another—reorganizing our thoughts and emotions to deal with each situation. How much does each of these transitions cost us, in terms of psychological and emotional energy? How many transitions can we withstand in one day? If we agree that they're hard on us, how many should we expect children to make?

Maria has a daily schedule for her class posted on the bulletin board—it looks interesting, filled with activity and movement. If we count the transitions, there are over 18 that children in her class must deal with every day—from one classroom to another, from inside to outside, from circle to free play, from bathroom to snack time, from home to center and back. Many of these transitions are compounded by staffing rotations.

How much energy does each transition cost a child? How many of these transitions are really necessary? How can we make each transition less taxing? (p. 31)

Transitions also require time. Little children do not "hurry" well. It takes time for them to shift gears from one activity to the next, and the wise teacher allows for this when making out the schedule. Particularly at the beginning of the year or in complicated change situations, a transition may require as long as 15 minutes.

A reasonable pace for transitions also means that staff has time to create those intimate moments of relationship with each youngster that lie at the heart of the preschool learning experience—a truly vital ingredient in early education.

Finally, the schedule should provide for a balance between individual self-selected learning experiences and participation in more regulated group experiences. Another way of saying this is that the day should provide a combination of self-selected, open-choice activities combined with more whole-group participation ones. Whole-group activities include such experiences as eating together and circle time. The open-choice times are desirable so that children learn to make responsible choices, develop their autonomy, and have many opportunities to pursue their long-term interests in particular areas. The more structured group experiences are needed to help them learn to function as members of a group and to ensure comprehensive coverage of some areas of curriculum that might otherwise be shortchanged.

Meeting the Needs of the Adults

Adults, as well as children, have needs, and it is important that the schedule take these into con-

sideration as well. For example, beware of the schedule that assumes that the same staff member will be at the same place at the same time each day. Adults need variety just as children do. Changing areas frequently and encouraging staff to decide among themselves in which area they will be teaching during the coming week help ensure cooperation and enthusiastic participation.

Particularly in full-day centers, teachers also need respite from being constantly with the children. They need this not only to go to the restroom, take a coffee break, or talk to a colleague; they also need time to prepare materials and hold staff meetings. Unless such opportunities are deliberately included in the schedule, such times are often nibbled away, morale and energy decline, and both teachers and children suffer from the results.

Finally, as noted in chapter 2, the schedule must provide time for teachers to greet and chat with parents at the beginning and end of the day. These friendly, comfortable contacts are indispensable in creating the bonds between home and school.

Reviewing the Schedule from Time to Time

Children change during the year, and a schedule that suits them in the fall more than likely requires modification in the spring. For example, the time allocated to large group probably should be lengthened as the children's abilities to concentrate and get along together increase, and transition times can be shortened because the children have learned to move easily through such routines.

It is also useful to examine the schedule from time to time for trouble spots where things are not going smoothly and consider whether an adjustment might alleviate the difficulty. Perhaps congestion and scuffling in the toilet room might be reduced by sending the 3-year-olds through first and feeding them a little sooner than the 4-year-olds are fed, or restlessness at group time might be alleviated by offering it earlier in the morning when the children are less tired. Remember, it is always possible to experiment with a variation for a week or two and then go back to the previous pattern if the change fails to solve the difficulty.

Some Comments on Half- and Full-Day Schedules

Half-day schedules, in particular, require attention to the comments about pacing the day well. If long enough blocks of time are to be included, the pattern that usually works best is two large time periods divided in the middle by snack and group time.

Short days also mean that most of the preparation must be done before the children arrive or after they go home, and, to be realistic, staff time for this purpose should be scheduled and paid for.

A *Schedule for a Half-Day Center for 2-Year-Olds*

Here is an example of a schedule for 2-year-olds. The teacher who shared this with me stressed that it is just the latest in a continuing revision based on the children's changing needs and the dictates of the classroom environment. For example, she commented that she changed group time from starting in the morning until later on because, to reach the group time area, the twos had to walk across the activity areas and were beguiled by those attractions, thereby finding it difficult to come to group. Later on, she is thinking about rearranging the room, and the schedule may change in accordance with that rearrangement. Her goal is to have as few transitions as possible during the morning.

9:00–9:15 or later

   Arrival

9:00–10:15

   Self-select activities: art, gross-motor, blocks, cooking, dramatic play, book and writing cor-

ner, woodworking, and so forth

10:15–10:25

   Clean-up and transition to group

10:25–10:35

   Group (may last longer)

10:35–10:50

   Snack (includes washing hands)

10:50–11:00

   Transition to outdoors (allows time for outdoor dressing)

11:00–11:30

   Outside activities and go home

A *Schedule for a Full-Day Center*

Full-day centers are blessed with many scheduling advantages: among these are the leisurely pace the longer day affords combined with plenty of time for involving children in activities and for forming close relationships with them.

7:30–9:00

   Children arrive, play indoors until it warms up; time of going outside varies, also, in accordance with children's energy needs.

9:00–9:15

   Transition: wash hands, toileting, move to snack tables

9:15–9:45

   Breakfast or substantial snack—everyone sits down together; transition, including brief large-muscle activity

9:45–10:15

   Planned experience group time (most intellectually challenging group time of day presented at this point)

10:15–11:45

   Activity time, indoors and out; pursue special pathways, field trips, and so on

11:45–12:00

A Special Problem in Scheduling: What To Do When the Weather is Terrible

It is one of those difficult days that happen in every child-care facility. The weather has not been good all week, but until now the children have been able to go outside at least for a little while. Not today—it is only Thursday, with the weather forecaster predicting more of the same on Friday. (One thing teachers cannot count on is having fewer children in school on a day with bad weather. Under such circumstances parents are more faithful than mail carriers, and neither rain nor sleet nor snow seems to stay them from their appointed rounds of car pools.)

Long-Term Remedies
Make out an emergency daily schedule well in advance so that you are not caught in a frenzy of last-minute planning.

Develop a list of volunteers and substitutes who have said they would be willing to rise to the occasion and help out on days that are especially taxing. When these people arrive, be certain you have simple but worthwhile activities for them to do with the children, such as reading to them or cooking with them. It is important for these people to feel successful enough so that they want to return. Try to give them advance warning, if possible, and be prepared for some excuses and refusals.

Consider having some kind of shelter constructed in the play yard: an outdoor covered area is both a summer and winter blessing, as is a wall that blocks out prevailing winds.

Short-Term Remedies
Stay as positive as possible. Help the children savor the day—after all, it *is* special. Get out special weather poems, stories, and pictures. Encourage

them to watch the thermometer or rain gauge. Serve hot soup for snack (keep some dehydrated packets on hand for this purpose). Put a pan of ice outside and see how many days it takes to melt.

Find some extra space and use it for "spill-over" activities, such as water play in a large bathroom, tricycles in the hall, carpentry on a covered porch, or block off part of an indoor room for trikes. Be willing to make some exceptions for rambunctious behavior. Look around—sometimes available space will surprise you.

Large-muscle activities are essential. Dancing and marching offer controlled opportunities for active, large-muscle play. Remember to combine it with relaxation experiences.

Offer absorbing favorites. Water play, cornmeal in tubs, or wheat kernels to pour will occupy children for hours, and the cornmeal and wheat activities require little supervision. Cover some tables or A-frames with old bedspreads or sheets and ask the children to furnish these houses with what they need.

Divide and conquer. If you teach in a self-contained classroom, suggest trading some children for part of the day with another teacher; the change can provide relief for both groups. Or if the weather permits travel but not outdoor play, send part of the group on an excursion to the library or market.

Control the noise level. Noise tends to escalate particularly on such days. Be sensitive to this. Lower your own voice, turn the phonograph off, and insist that everyone use indoor voices.

Finally, treat yourself to something special when you go home. Congratulate yourself for a job well done and reward yourself with a luxurious bath, a good book, or a favorite TV program. After all, you deserve it.

Transition: cleanup, toileting, wash hands, gather for lunch

12:00–12:30

Lunch

12:30–12:45 or 1:00

Toileting, wash hands, brush teeth, gradually settle down for nap

1:00–2:30

Nap: children are expected to at least rest quietly for 30 to 45 minutes. Most will sleep

A well-planned schedule allows time for children to experience quietness—a real chance to be themselves.

a bit longer than that; children get up gradually as they waken.

3:00

Last child up by this time

2:30–3:15

Snack set out: children may come to table and eat as they are ready.

2:30–4:30

Activity time, indoors and out; includes opportunities for field trips, purposeful play, and so forth

4:30–5:15

Story time for those who desire it, quiet play, get cleaned up with hands washed, hair smoothed, ready to go home with families

The major problem in scheduling that full-day centers must take into account is the problem of monotony and lack of variety in curriculum that results from teacher fatigue and burnout. This is likely to be particularly true in the afternoon portion of such programs when all too often children are simply turned loose on the playground for hours at a time.

Rather than allowing this to happen, the staff should face the problem of teacher burnout squarely and attempt to solve it in two ways. First, make certain that the schedule provides respite for teachers from continual contact with children. The second effective scheduling strategy is to combine full-time and half-time staff so that some half-time people arrive in the afternoon armed with new ideas and equipped with the energy to see these through. (Young teachers in training and volunteers are both good sources for such afternoon help, but if these resources are drawn on, supervising teachers must play fair and make certain they provide them with sufficient guidance and support.)

TABLE 4–3
Activity Schedule for Fifteen 4-Year-Olds* in a Full-Day Center

Date: Tuesday, November 12, 1993
Topic or theme for week: Babies and hospitals (chosen because of new baby in one family and because another child is due for a hernia repair the next week)

Time	Staff[†]	Activity	Purpose and Notes
7:30–9:00	Two staff	*Welcome children*	Ease transition to school; conduct health check.
		Collecting baby pictures	Use pictures for bulletin board and group discussion—continues interest from yesterday.
		Tabletop activities, including books about babies	
		Outdoor play for a while if warm enough	Weather is nice, better take advantage of it.
9:00–9:15	Two staff	*Transition*	Everyone to toilet if necessary and wash hands; get one adult seated with children as quickly as possible; make sure cook has breakfast ready as children sit down.
9:15–9:45	Two staff	*Breakfast* (or snack) Fruit, cereal, and milk with buttered toast.	Special event: serve fruit in baby food jars, baby cereal, and milk to fit baby theme.
9:45–10:15	Two staff with divided group, or one adult sets up while other conducts group	*Planned experience time* Book: *Curious George Goes to the Hospital*	Generate questions about hospital; may read half of book, rest later if too long; during hospital discussion point out that doctors and nurses can be of either sex.
		Song: "Rock A Bye Baby"	Use *B* sound at beginning of each word for fun and for auditory training.
		Discussion: What was it like when you were a baby?	Use baby pictures to discuss "now and then" (temporal ordering).
		Poem: "Five Little Monkeys"	Use flannel board—may lead to doctor discussion; also talk about bouncing on mattress, which the children will do later outside.
		Transition—dismissal	Dismiss according to who is wearing sneakers, jeans, and so forth; provides practice in mental abilities of grouping or matching.

*Group is composed of seven Anglos, four Mexican Americans (all English speaking), and four African American children (including a pair of twins).
[†]The identity of staff changes as their shifts are completed.

TABLE 4–3

continued

Date: Tuesday, November 12, 1993
Topic or theme for week: Babies and hospitals (chosen because of new baby in one family and because another child is due for a hernia repair the next week)

Time	Staff[†]	Activity	Purpose and Notes
10:15–11:45	Two staff	*Highlights of self-select activity time*	
		Hospital and baby play	Set up outside if weather permits.
		Blocks	Accessories: ambulance and biracial wooden medical figures.
		Make salad	Salad made with childrens' help if cook has time.
		Dough	Made by children with a little teacher help; illustrated recipe encourages left-to-right "reading" and provides practice in temporal ordering.
		Outside: swings, trikes, dampened sand, and obstacle course	Balance on low wall, jump off onto mattress, bounce, throw ball into tire, run up ramp, repeat (while they are jumping, remind children of "Five Little Monkeys"); practice in dynamic balance, locomotion, rhythm, rebound, throwing and catching activities.
11:45–12:00	Two staff	*Transition*	Toilet, wash hands (teachers, too), calm down, move transition along by singing and discussing what is for lunch.
12:00–12:30	Two staff	*Lunch* Tortillas with beans, green salad, yogurt with fresh fruits for dessert, milk	See if cook has time for children to help make salad during self-select; meal is multicultural emphasis for day—use one of the Mexican American family's recipes for beans.
12:30–12:45 or 1:00	Two staff	*Transition to nap*	Toilet, wash hands, brush teeth; emphasize quiet.
1:00–2:30	One staff during nap. Two staff as children wake up (in nap room)	*Nap*	Children get up gradually as they wake up. Second staff preparation time.
2:30–3:00	One staff	*Transition*	Last child up by this time; toilet, wash hands.

Date: Tuesday, November 12, 1993
Topic or theme for week: Babies and hospitals (chosen because of new baby in one family and because another child is due for a hernia repair the next week)

Time	Staff[†]	Activity	Purpose and Notes
		Snack	
2:30–3:15	Two staff	Orange quarters and raisins; water if desired.	Children come to eat as they get up and move on to play; second staff member sets up afternoon.
		Self-select activity time	
2:30–4:30	Two staff (after supervising nap and snack)	Water play outdoors; then get out baby buggies, plus usual outdoor activities.	Wading pool with hoses (requires supervision with both staff); fun, coolness, social play, and facts about volume and what the power of water can do.
		Indoor activity time	
4:30–5:15	Two staff and visitor	Story time, quiet play; children cleaned up to go home	Offer drinks of water to thirsty children. As crowd diminishes, one staff sets up for morning activities.
		Special visit from mother of African American twins who brings their baby book to share with the group	Builds self-esteem of twins who are shy and tend just to play together; provides practice in concept of matching (do the twins look the same as babies and now?) and cross-cultural learning.

Translated into an actual schedule, the plan might appear as shown in Table 4–3. Note that this plan uses the material included for Tuesday in Table 4–1.

Summary

Careful planning lies at the heart of all well-run early childhood programs. To accomplish this task successfully, teachers need to do two things. They must preplan curriculum so that it includes activities that foster the development of all five selves of the child. While honoring that plan, they must also remain open to moving with the children's interests and questions as they venture down a variety of investigatory pathways together.

Drawing up an effective curriculum involves going through a series of steps. These include selecting a topic related to the children's interests and brainstorming a large number of possible activities related to that topic, analyzing these possibilities according to a number of realities that must be considered when planning, blocking out the activities over a week's time, making certain there is a worthwhile purpose or reason for including each one, fitting the activities into the daily schedule, and evaluating the day when it is over.

Once the *what* of the curriculum has been identified, then the *when* must be considered. A sound daily schedule provides for alternating periods of quiet and active experience, proceeds at a reasonable pace throughout the day, and includes a balance between self-selected and group times. Examples of schedules and plans complete the chapter.

Self-Check Questions for Review

Content-Related Questions

1. Think of the five selves and list some skills for each of them that should be included in a curriculum plan.
2. Why is it most satisfactory to select a topic for a curriculum theme drawn from the children's interests?
3. Describe the five steps to follow when developing a curriculum plan. Why is each one important?
4. A number of reality tests proposed in the chapter should be applied to curriculum ideas to make certain the activities are practical and appropriate. List and discuss as many of these as you can.
5. Why is it valuable for teachers to pinpoint the purpose or reason why they are offering a particular activity for the children to do?
6. When planning the schedule, what are some of the children's needs the teacher should take into account? And what are some of the adult's needs that must also be considered?
7. Discuss some practical ideas teachers can use to make a spell of bad weather more tolerable in their classrooms.
8. Finish the following sentence: "The research study by Christie, Johnsen, and Peckover found it was important to schedule longer play periods because during the longer periods the children. . . ."

Integrative Questions

1. Assume that you are teaching a group of 2-*year-olds* and that you intend to use birds as a theme because one of the children wants to bring her pet canary to school. Read through the following list of activities and evaluate them in terms of the nine realities discussed in the text. Which ideas would you select? Which ones would you discard? Explain your reasons for each decision.[2]

   - Use a stuffed or dead bird for close observation.
   - Ask children to discuss the differences between robins and eagles.

   - Put a bird feeder outside the window for the children to check on every few days.
   - Raise a baby wild bird who has fallen from its nest.
   - Provide tubs of feathers and other objects to contrast how they feel on the children's feet or hands.
   - Offer a snack (popcorn and water in flat bowls) so that children can eat and drink as birds without using their hands.
   - Visit the bird room in the museum.
   - Have children make a birdhouse.
   - Emphasize the Native American culture since birds have always held a place of importance in that culture.

2. Think of a topic and pathway down which you and the children in your group might journey together and propose several possibilities that could be investigated.
3. You are making a decision about which of two jobs to accept. One is in a full-day center, and the other is in a half-day center. Based on the discussion of scheduling in this chapter, assess the advantages and disadvantages of each kind of schedule, explain which one you would choose for employment, and why you personally prefer it.
4. Compare the behavior and kinds of play identified by Christie, Johnsen, and Peckover during the 15- and 30-minute play periods and explain why they concluded that the activities during the 30-minute periods were superior to those taking place during the 15-minute periods.

Questions and Activities

1. Is there anything wrong with turning children loose on the playground in the afternoon? After all, don't they need this free time to generate creative play ideas?
2. This book has talked a good deal about the benefits of using a focus of interest as a center for developing curriculum, but is there another side to it? What might be the disadvantages of centering on a particular topic?
3. Are there some consistent trouble spots (times of day when teachers seem consistently to discipline or control the children) in teaching situations you have observed or in which you have worked? Share some of these with the class and consider possible

---

[2]Bird ideas kindness of Cené Marquis, Head Teacher, Institute of Child Development, University of Oklahoma.

rearrangements of the schedule that might alleviate these situations.

4. Assume that the Quick Check Curriculum Chart (Table 4–1) is a useful planning tool for you to employ. If you wanted to use it for planning a group time or for just one morning, explain how the headings might be modified to make this possible.

5. It is 4:30 in the afternoon at your day-care center. The children have been through snack time, they have done the special activity for the afternoon, and they have played outside until they are exhausted. Now they are fighting and bickering among themselves, and there is still an hour to go. What activity would you recommend scheduling that would enable the children to remain in at least partial control of themselves during this time rather than spending it in a state of tantrums, attacks, and just galloping around?

References for Further Reading

Overviews

Bredekamp, S., & Rosegrant, T. (1992). *Reaching potentials: Appropriate curriculum and assessment for young children* (Vol. 1). Washington, DC: National Association for the Education of Young Children. Volume I interprets the guidelines cited below. It includes discussions of helping children, including those with disabilities, as well as helping staffs reach their full potential.

National Association for the Education of Young Children and the National Association of Early Childhood Specialists in State Departments of Education. (1991). Guidelines for appropriate curriculum content and assessment in programs serving children ages 3 through 8. *Young Children, 46*(3), 21–37. Basing their conclusions of a review of how young children learn, this position paper provides an authoritative overview of what curriculum should contain for this age group. It includes recommendations on what constitutes appropriate assessment techniques. *Highly recommended.*

Developmentally Appropriate Planning

Bredekamp, S., & Copple, C. (Eds.). (1997). *Developmentally appropriate practice in early childhood programs serving children from birth through age 8* (rev. ed.). Washington, DC: National Association for the Education of Young Children. Although this has been cited previously, it is such a valuable reference it merits noting again because of its emphasis on planning curriculum that is developmentally appropriate for children.

Gestwicki, C. (1995). *Developmentally appropriate practice: Curriculum and development in early education.* Albany, NY: Delmar. This book includes a useful discussion of what *is* and what is *not* developmentally appropriate practice followed by clear descriptions of what constitutes nurturing physical, social/emotional, and cognitive environments for various ages. *Highly recommended.*

Developing Overall Plans and Schedules

Larson, N., Henthorne, M., & Plum, B. (1994). *Transition magician: Strategies for guiding young children in early childhood programs.* St. Paul, MN.: Redleaf. This book is filled with delightful, practical ideas about ways to smooth children's and teacher's transitions from one activity to the next. *Highly recommended.*

Taylor, B. J. (1995). A *child goes forth:* A *curriculum guide for preschool children* (8th ed.). Columbus, OH: Merrill/Prentice Hall. Taylor discusses planning curriculum and fitting that content into the time frame schedule.

Developing Curriculum Based on a Topic or Theme

Dolinar, K. J., Boser, C., & Holm, E. (1994). *Learning through play: Curriculum and activities for the inclusive classroom.* Albany, NY: Delmar. The authors provide 27 examples of theme-based curriculum that are exceptional because each one includes specific suggestions for ways to include children who have various disabilities.

Isbell, R. (1995). *The complete learning center book.* Beltsville, MD: Gryphon House. A wealth of possibilities for every learning center is included here. Of special note is inclusion of relevant children's books, endless suggestions for enriching the children's activities, and ways to add spark when play interest wanes. *Highly recommended.*

Developing Emergent Curriculum

Jones, E., & Nimmo, J. (1994). *Emergent curriculum.* Washington, DC: National Association for the Education of Young Children. An open, enthusiastic example of how to make emergent curriculum work is provided here.

For the Advanced Student

Bredekamp, S., & Rosegrant, T. (Eds.). (1995). *Reaching potentials: Transforming early childhood curriculum and assessment* (Vol. 2). Citing national curriculum standards developed by a variety of professional disciplines, this book provides discussions and examples illustrating how those standards can be appropriately implemented when teaching children aged 3 to 8 years.

Hendrick, J. (Ed.). (1997). *First steps toward teaching the Reggio way.* Upper Saddle River, NJ: Merrill/Prentice Hall. Various authors explain how and where they are beginning their attempts to integrate some of the emergent Reggio approach into their own philosophy and practice. Exciting reading.

Wien, C. A. (1995). *Developmentally appropriate practice in stories of teacher practical knowledge*. New York: Teachers College Press. This qualitative research study describes the conflicts experienced by teachers who wish to use developmentally appropriate practices in their teaching yet also feel pulled toward a more teacher-centered classroom..

Relevant Journals

Child Care Information Exchange. P.O. Box 2890, Redmond, WA 98073-9977. The timely, practical articles in CCIE fill a gap in the literature on how to work in and operate child-care centers. Topics range from dealing with staff burnout to informing parents about tax exemptions. A valuable publication.

5

Designing the Supportive Environment

Have you ever

- Hated the room in which you teach?
- Needed to save money when buying equipment?
- Wished there were more interesting things for the children to do when they played outside?

If you have, the material in this chapter will help you.

Children took weeks to think about, plan, purchase, bring from home, or make items to put in their cubbies. This was an excellent example of looking at the image of the child. Most often the teachers decide what will be in the child's cubbies: usually some type of sign for a name or some kind of symbol, but when thinking about children's capabilities, if children are supported and their ideas are respected, they are more than capable of planning and decorating their own cubbies. This is a small example of allowing the children to do for themselves what they are capable of doing and not robbing them of an opportunity. The children had many ideas for their cubbies as evidenced by photos of families, drawn pictures, cut-out pictures from magazines, miniature mobiles, miniature painted wood cut-outs, stuffed animals, and mirrors. Everyone wanted a mirror installed in their cubby.

Karen Haigh (1997, p. 161)

Now that we have the elements of a good curriculum in mind and understand how to plan and schedule it, there is one more thing to consider: what to do about arranging the physical setting and materials so they facilitate and support the curriculum. This means that as teachers plan this physical environment, they must review once again the basic educational purposes that they consider important to make certain that this plan embodies their philosophy.

Some Yardstick Questions to Apply

For example, if teachers believe that the purpose of education is to increase competence for each of the child's selves, they might apply the following yardstick question to evaluate the environment: *Will this arrangement help children be competent and successful?* Accomplishing the goal implied by this question might involve something as simple as placing a row of tires as a barrier between the tricycle activity and the sandbox area so that riders need not be contin-

ually reprimanded for intruding on the diggers' space, thereby preserving their self-esteem by avoiding criticism of their behavior. It also might involve using small, transparent pitchers at snack time to make it easier for children to pour skillfully without spilling. Or it might involve enlarging the block corner so that children are less likely to antagonize each other by stumbling over each other's constructions.

If teachers believe that children learn best when all their senses are involved, they will continually incorporate these kinds of opportunities into the physical environment. They will tie visual experiences to concrete ones whenever possible. Perhaps they will start by opening a book to an exquisite drawing of a growing plant and placing it beside plants that the children have started for themselves or ones that they can touch and handle. Perhaps they also will encourage the children to listen to the silkworms chewing on their leaves and to feel their soft, dry bodies as well as to look at them. A good yardstick question to ask here might be, *What will the children be able to do with what is set out here?* When the answer is "Just look," this is a clue that something should be modified.

If teachers believe that curriculum topics should stem from the children's interests, they will listen to these concerns carefully and create not only a curriculum that is based on these interests but also a physical environment that reflects them. An example of a good question to ask here is, *Where did this idea come from?* Did it come from the children, or is it simply a piece of "embalmed" curriculum I find convenient to get out once again? Although physical settings often benefit from the use of resources accumulated from past years, they also derive great benefits from the addition of new resources. Adding these fresh items sustains both the teachers' and children's interest in the subject and helps ensure that teaching materials will be relevant to the interests of the current group of youngsters.

Finally, if teachers are convinced that children learn to appreciate beauty by experiencing it, they will ask themselves these questions regarding the entire environment:

- What does the room look like today? Is it colorful but not garish?
- Is it orderly and clean but not bare or stark?
- Is it interesting without being overwhelming?
- Is it beautiful?

Does Room Arrangement Really Matter?

In addition to considering the empowering and aesthetic values related to arranging indoor and outdoor environments, teachers should consider this subject with care for another practical reason. The way the environment is arranged definitely affects children's and adult's behavior. A number of studies (Babcock, Hartle, & Lamme, 1995; Petrakos & Howe, 1996; Trawick-Smith, 1992) confirm that this is true.

For example, in a recent study researchers found that the size of an activity area made a substantial difference in the length of time children played in an activity and how quickly they became involved in complex play. Small and sheltered was definitely better (Tegano, Moran, DeLong, Brickley, & Ramassini, 1996). The authors make a good case for including nooks and crannies, a loft, screening, or even a closet with the door removed as potential sheltered spaces. At the Institute, we used an old fireplace filled with pillows to partially satisfy this need. The children loved it.

This area of study is often spoken of as the *ecology* of child-care centers because ecology has to do with the relationship between living things and their environments. The research study by

Here are the cubbies designed by the children that Karen Haigh describes in the opening quotation.

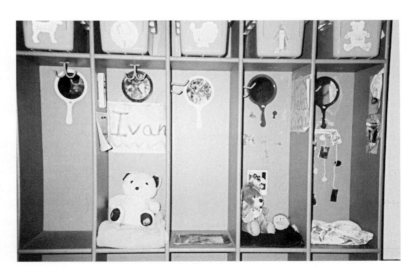

Teets that is included here provides an example of how these studies are carried out.

Suggestions for Arranging the Environment

Starting from Scratch

Occasionally teachers have an opportunity to design a children's center right from the start. Even though such opportunities are relatively rare, such a design is included here (Figure 5–1) because so much interest has been displayed in this particular center by visitors.

This center is a good example of a building planned to meet many needs during the day. Each of the indoor play areas can be, and frequently is, divided into smaller spaces by flexible dividers, and a third "special activities" room is used for children's large-muscle activities as well as college classes and parent meetings. The large storage units placed in the center of the indoor play rooms make fre-

quently used equipment readily accessible. Note also the numerous storage closets. Outdoors the fixed play apparatuses, such as swings and climbing complexes, have been deliberately situated in the far corners of the yard to encourage the children to make use of the entire space. The building accommodates 55 children as well as numerous student teachers and staff members.

Planning the Indoor Environment

Suppose that the building is already there and that you, the teacher, are stepping into the room for the first time, and it is completely empty. (Sometimes when teachers have been teaching in the same room for a while, they find it worthwhile to put everything out in the hall and simply experience the empty space while thinking about it and the children who will occupy it.) Now take note of such unchangeable items as the location of doors, windows, built-in cabinets, water facilities, and light plugs, and examine how these

Special safety glass provides toddlers with a wider view of their world.

FIGURE 5–1
Sample Design for a Children's Center

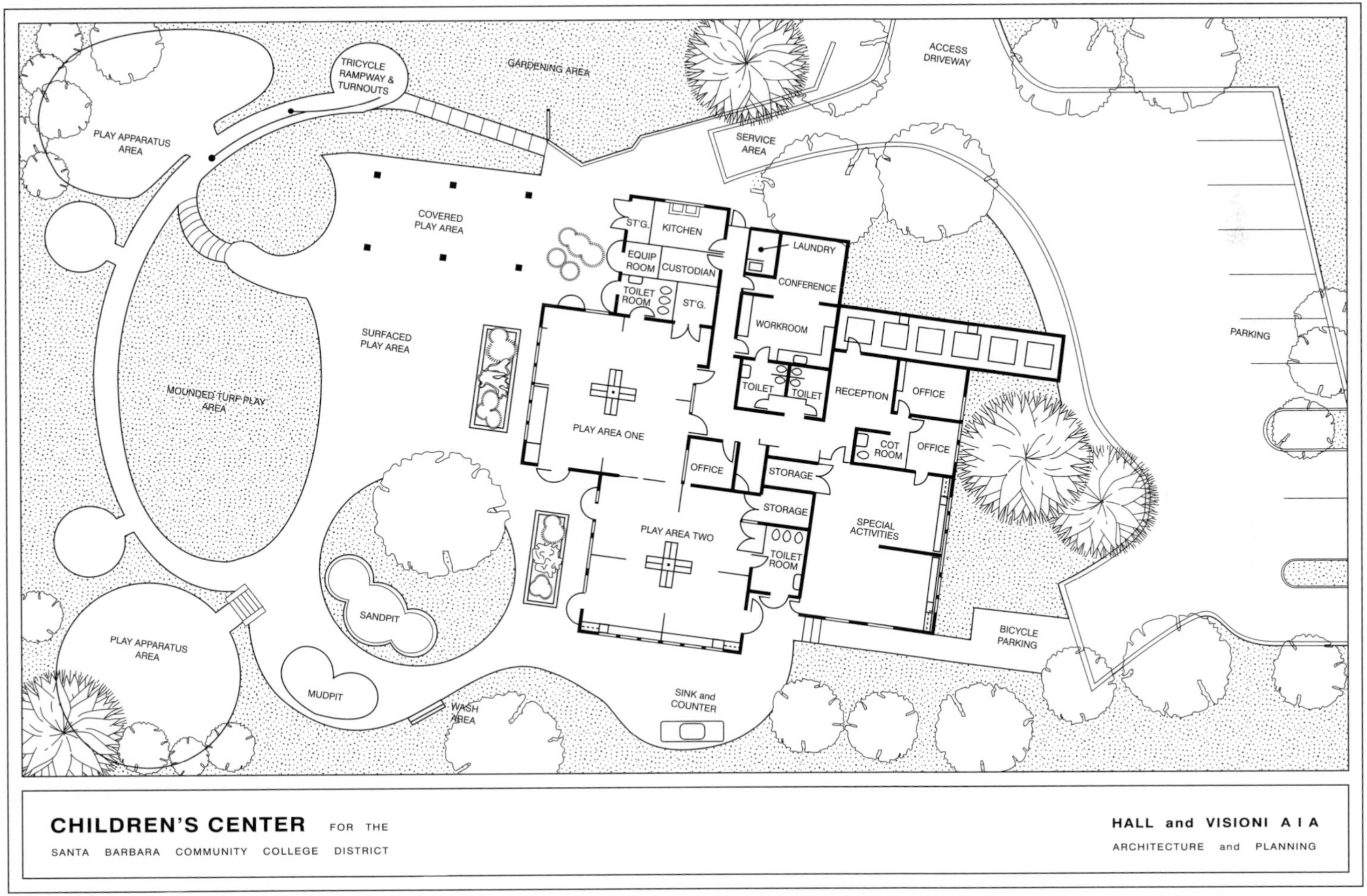

HALL and VISION! A I A
ARCHITECTURE and PLANNING

PARKING

ACCESS
DRIVEWAY

SERVICE
AREA

GARDENING AREA

BICYCLE
PARKING

LAUNDRY

CONFERENCE

WORKROOM

TOILET

TOILET

RECEPTION

OFFICE

OFFICE

COT
ROOM

SPECIAL
ACTIVITIES

STORAGE

STORAGE

TOILET
ROOM

OFFICE

STG.

KITCHEN

CUSTODIAN

STG.

EQUIP
ROOM

TOILET
ROOM

PLAY AREA ONE

PLAY AREA TWO

SINK and
COUNTER

TRICYCLE
RAMPWAY &
TURNOUTS

COVERED
PLAY AREA

SURFACED
PLAY AREA

MOUNDED TURF-PLAY
AREA

PLAY APPARATUS
AREA

PLAY APPARATUS
AREA

SANDPIT

MUDPIT

WASH
AREA

CHILDREN'S CENTER FOR THE
SANTA BARBARA COMMUNITY COLLEGE DISTRICT

87

"givens" affect the way things must ultimately be arranged in the room. (For example, the most convenient place for the cooking table is near both the sink and a power supply.)

Next, think about the traffic patterns. Can furniture be arranged to provide unimpeded pathways to the "go-home" door, bathrooms, and outdoor play areas? Can it be used as buffers and dividers to prevent undesirable patterns from developing so that block and book corners and the dramatic play area are protected from unnecessary intrusions?

Then go out in the hall and look at the available furniture with a fresh perspective. Try to see the playhouse stove or the book cabinet in terms of its potential as an area demarcator or as an empty space on which a child's picture could be displayed or as a countertop for holding an interesting exhibit. Sometimes it is helpful to play the game, "If I couldn't . . . ": "If I couldn't use this cabinet as a bookcase, what else could I use it for?" Doing this can allow you to discover new possibilities in even the most mundane furnishings.

Noise levels must be considered, too. It is wisest to separate noisy areas as far from each other as possible. For example, if carpentry cannot be done outside, consider placing it at one end of the room, which will keep it out of the traffic pattern and will prevent (at least partially) the sound of hammering from rocketing through the school. Consider also whether it might be possible to use part of the hall for this purpose, since a teacher must devote undivided attention to it anyway.

Quiet areas must be created to balance the more noisy, high-activity ones. Consider how tiring it is even for an adult to be in the constant company of other people. Although we think of children as generally seeking the company of other children, they find it equally exhausting to endure the continual stimulation and adjustments from constant contact with other people. Children need quieter, somewhat secluded places to which they can withdraw when they have had enough contact. Such arrangements may vary from a comfortable sofa with books nearby to an unused fireplace where children snuggle down into a mass of pillows.

Finally, think about the various activities you want to include and where these would be most sensibly placed, taking into consideration the unchangeable givens, the desirable and undesirable traffic patterns, the need for noise and stimulation control, and the available equipment. Remember also to place activity areas with an eye to the accessibility of storage, the level of illumination needed, and the desirability of distributing activities throughout the room. Plan also for open spaces into which activities and children can spread as needed.

Typical Indoor Activities

Particular activity areas commonly included indoors are the unit block area, a reading and story corner, one or more places for dramatic play (this usually includes a housekeeping area but should be able to accommodate many other pretend play situations from time to time), space for creative self-expressive activities and tabletop activities, and a let's-find-out exploration area that varies with the current focus of interest. Less frequently provided for, but of great importance, is an area for parents that includes a comfortable place to sit and useful reading materials.

Many areas in the children's center serve more than one purpose during the day. The carpeted block area, for instance, readily converts to a comfortable group time spot, and most full-day centers must use all available floor space for cots and mats at nap time.

Planning Environments for Aesthetic Appeal

Now that the functional aspects of the arrangement have been considered, it is time to consider the aesthetic aspects of the environment. A room should be beautiful and appealing as well as practical.

Some examples of ideal preschool environments are found in the Italian city of Reggio Emilia where outstanding preschool education has been developing since the end of World War II (Katz & Cesarone, 1994; Hendrick, 1997). Briefly stated, the child-centered philosophy of these schools is based on respect for the child that emphasizes collaborative learning among child, teacher, and family.[1] The physical environment of the school is seen as a vital element in facilitating the relationship of children to the world around them, and teachers often comment that "the environment is the third teacher."

For this reason, the schools are designed with much emphasis on reducing the sense of barrier between outdoors and indoors through the use of large windows, airy ceilings, white walls, and pale woodwork. There are often windows between interior spaces as well, and even talking tubes are included between rooms to facilitate communication. The rooms themselves are colorful and filled with light while not seeming gaudy. Examples of the children's work are displayed throughout the buildings. Mirrors abound and are set at many unusual (to us) angles to encourage children to familiarize themselves with more than simple frontal views of their bodies. Everywhere there is a sense of space, color, light, joy, and growing things. What inspiration these rooms can provide if we, too, give thought to the important role beauty plays as we create room environments for our children.

Of course, careful attention to design and texture when purchasing basic equipment is important.[2] But it is not necessary to put off improving the environment until a good fairy produces a flush budget for us. A bright pillow, a lovely painting, or a blooming plant can enliven a room

Take another look at your environment—sometimes something as unpromising as a blank wall can be used with relish by the children.

with fresh color that delights both heart and eye during the day. We must never forget the next generation's taste is being formed by the environment with which we surround them.

Wall coverings such as bulletin boards deserve special mention here when discussing environments because some teachers put so much emphasis on their design. If well done, these boards can tell children something valuable about how the school views their abilities. When their work is attractively presented and changed frequently, they can see that their work is valued and respected. In the Reggio schools, for example, the teachers take many photographs of the

---

[1]Please refer to chapter 14, "Freeing Children to be Creative," and chapter 17, "Helping Children Learn to Think for Themselves," for further discussion of the Reggio approach to learning.

[2]Bronson (1995) and Moyer (1995) are good resources to use when selecting such equipment.

Sometimes children create their own quiet places!

children's work to document its progress and mount these on boards so everyone can remember and appreciate what is happening.

The material on bulletin boards should be placed low enough that short people (i.e., children) can see it easily. Often adults unthinkingly place items of interest at their own height, and the children do not benefit from such displays if they must crane their necks to see them. It is a sound principle to get right down to the children's height when planning wall arrangements and take a look at them from the children's position—the results can sometimes be surprising.

In their delightful books on teaching-learning environments, Jones (1977) and Jones and Prescott (1978) speak of the hardness-softness dimensions in the school environment. Softness should surely be a part of the aesthetics of the center. Cozy furniture, carpeting, sand, rocking chairs, and laps all fall into this category, as do play dough, animals, and strap swings. These might all be thought of as simply "soft to touch," but the authors define their common quality in a different way. They describe a "soft" environment as one that is sensorily responsive. For example, a playground with grass, sand, and tires to bounce on is more sensorily responsive than is an asphalt one with metal play equipment. If we wish to make this sensorial responsiveness part of the room itself as well as part of the curriculum, we must strive for an overall effect that is homey and comfortable—"soft" in every sense of the word.

Including Multicultural Elements in the Design

It also contributes to the feeling of homeyness and comfort when the ethnic and cultural backgrounds of children are matter-of-factly represented in the physical environment of the school. The inclusion of multiethnic pictures, books, and artifacts will contribute to the children's overall feelings of being valued for their own cultural richness, but the inclusion of such things should constitute just the bare beginnings of multicultural experiences. Opportunities for learning about other cultures, as discussed further in

In the Reggio Emilia schools mirrors abound. Note how the small cutouts enable children to see just a little bit of themselves and how the mirrors that intersect at the corner encourage children to view more than one aspect of themselves at the same time.

chapter 13, should be provided on a continuing basis throughout the year and should stress two things: first, that all people have many things in common—they get sleepy, feel hungry, and sometimes are sad or happy; second, that everyone has different, unique, and valuable contributions to make to the life of the group.

Even though teachers should be casual and matter-of-fact about teaching these values, they also should be persistent in planning for their inclusion as part of the environment. For example, the fact that all kinds of people have some needs in common could be taught by borrowing a tatami mat and quilts from a Japanese friend and encouraging the children to play "going to bed" using the Japanese bed and also using a Western-style sleeping bag. Meanwhile, the teacher could point out that everyone gets tired and sleepy and that they satisfy this need in different but equally practical and comfortable ways.

Adapting the Environment to Include Children with Disabilities

Total Learning begins with the statement that the purpose of education is to increase competence, and that statement is as true for children with disabilities as for more typical youngsters. When such children are mainstreamed into the ordinary preschool, one of the easiest ways to increase their competence is to take a good look at the physical environment and do what is possible to maximize the mainstreamed child's independence and ability to be self-sufficient.

It is good to realize that making such adjustments is no longer a matter of choice now that the Americans with Disabilities Act has become law. This act requires all public agencies, including children's centers, to make their services accessible to all people with disabilities (Rab & Wood, 1995). Part of being accessible has to do with removing physical barriers to access. For example, an obvious barrier might be a flight of steps up to the school, so it might be necessary to build a ramp to replace it. Or it might be necessary to rearrange the room to make it easier to maneuver a wheelchair around the other furniture.

Although space does not permit extensive recommendations on adapting environments for specific disabilities, there are some useful general principles to remember. More specific recommendations may be found in the References for Further Reading.

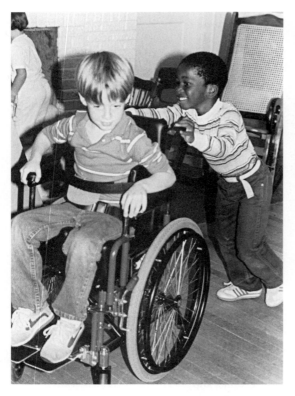

Including children in wheelchairs makes construction of a ramp essential.

Common sense coupled with keen observation by the teacher are indispensable when seeking solutions for special problems. We had a partially sighted 4-year-old at the Institute who always sat on the stairs and inched her way down them on her bottom despite the fact there was a rail nearby. Once we took a closer look at the stairs we realized they were painted gray and all blended together. Adding a black strip at the edge of each step made them much more visible (and safer for everyone!) and also enabled her to walk down them with confidence because she could see where the edge was.

Another helpful thing to do is to ask the family and the child development team for suggestions. These people are usually gold mines of ideas. Or they may have access to references that would be helpful.

It is also valuable to make a special effort to reduce confusion and clutter wherever possible. Occasional teachers, for example, keep music playing all day long or are insensitive to an escalating volume of noise. Such environments are particularly difficult for children who do not hear well or are exceptionally distractible. Other teachers unthinkingly allow a clutter of abandoned dress-up clothes or blocks to accumulate that will surely trip up a child who cannot see.

Sometimes a special piece of equipment, such as a U-shaped table to accommodate a wheelchair, will enable a child to participate more readily. On the other hand, some youngsters who are developing more slowly than most do not require special equipment but just need materials that are appropriate for their developmental level (e.g., puzzles with fewer, larger pieces or climbing equipment that does not require careful judgment about potential risks).

Whatever physical changes are contemplated, there is one most important thing to remember to do when thinking about modifying the environment: ask yourself the right question. That question is not, How can I keep this child protected and safe?—although safety for all children is important. The *most* important question to ask is, How can I help this child be successful today? Effective modification of the physical environment offers great potential for accomplishing that goal.

Evaluate and Reevaluate the Results

Once you have decided where everything should go and which aesthetic components should be included, then it is time to move it all into place and observe how the staff and children live within this environment together. Ask yourself if the plan is achieving the desired purposes. If not, why not? Never hesitate to rearrange things once again to achieve the educational goals you deem most desirable.

Both the *Early Childhood Environment Rating Scale* (Harms & Clifford, 1996) and the *Accreditation Criteria and Procedures of the National Academy of Early Childhood Programs* (National Association for the Education of Young Children, 1991) provide useful ways to assess the quality of a preschool's physical environment.

It is refreshing to rearrange rooms from time to time for the sake of variety, in addition to more functional reasons, by changing materials from one place to another or moving indoor equipment outside or vice versa. It also can be exhilarating to empty the room and encourage the children to do the arranging for a change. One school that experimented with this reported that the children scarcely used the tables at all in their own arrangements, and yet some preschools are positively littered with tables. A side benefit reported by this staff was that, as they paid particularly close attention to what the children were telling them and as they encouraged the children to carry out their own ideas, the amount of conflict between children was reduced and they began to solve more of their social difficulties for themselves (Pfluger & Zola, 1972).

Planning the Outdoor Environment

The outdoor play area is just as valuable and important to plan and arrange wisely as is the indoor area. Too often teachers who take pains over their interior rooms think of outdoor play as primarily having large-muscle values, but a well-arranged play yard includes opportunities for the development of all the child's selves (Frost, 1992a, 1992b). Therefore, in addition to swings, sandboxes, slides, and wheeled toys, outdoor areas should contain gardens, animals, and places for water and mud play. Opportunities for pretend play can be especially rich outdoors if a plentiful supply of sturdy boxes, boards, ladders, and perhaps a parachute is available. Science activities, particularly those in natural science and physics, fit in well outside if equipment such as water, pul-

leys, ropes, and living materials is included in the environment. Many art activities such as finger painting are also better suited to the more easily cleaned and less restrictive outdoor area.

Schools in colder climates lack the freedom of having some of these activities take place outside in winter months, but they do possess the advantage of vastly changing weather conditions, which can provide an appetizing variety of activities—if teacher and children dress warmly enough! A well-planned environment contains dry outdoor playing areas that are larger than usual and surfaced with asphalt, cement, or shredded bark so that the children do not become wet and chilled. Particular attention should be given to wind protection so that the children can spend considerable time outdoors almost every day.

Many of the principles mentioned in regard to indoor planning apply equally to outdoor planning. It is important to provide clear pathways that invite children to move to different areas. Planning to prevent congestion by dispersing interesting areas throughout the yard is also valuable, and placing activities near their storage units makes effective use of equipment more probable. Shaded areas and a diversity of surfacing materials where possible are important to consider, too.

In addition, the analysis of kinds of outdoor equipment done by Kritchevsky, Prescott, and Walling (1996) has particular merit, because there tend to be many more "simple" units used there than inside. According to these researchers, a *simple unit* has "one obvious use and does not have sub-parts or a juxtaposition of materials which enable a child to manipulate or improvise. (Examples: swings, jungle gym, rocking horse, tricycle.)" (Kritchevsky et al., 1996, p. 146). This kind of equipment is limited in play value because of the number of children it can interest at one time and the length of time it is likely to keep even one child occupied. A *complex unit* is defined as one "with sub-parts or juxtaposition of two essentially different play materials which enable the child to manipulate or improvise. (Examples: sand table with digging equipment; play house with supplies.) Also included in this category are single play ma-

Research Study

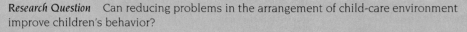

Changing the Environment Can Change Behavior

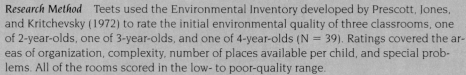

Research Question   Can reducing problems in the arrangement of child-care environment improve children's behavior?

Research Method   Teets used the Environmental Inventory developed by Prescott, Jones, and Kritchevsky (1972) to rate the initial environmental quality of three classrooms, one of 2-year-olds, one of 3-year-olds, and one of 4-year-olds (N = 39). Ratings covered the areas of organization, complexity, number of places available per child, and special problems. All of the rooms scored in the low- to poor-quality range.

Then the children's behavior was observed and scored for 2 weeks according to the amount of child-child interactions, teacher-child interactions, use of materials in appropriate areas, and level of involvement with material. Twenty behavior samples were gathered for each child.

Next, the rooms were arranged so they qualified for high scores on the Environmental Inventory, and the children's behavior was observed and scored under those conditions for another 2 weeks.

Finally, the rooms were returned to their original condition, and the children's behavior once again recorded.

Examples of the changes made during the second, high-quality phase included moving tricycles outside that had been stored near the door where children were tempted to ride them in the room, and separating interest areas so that, for example, music and science activities were not located in the same place. Rugs and soft cushions were added to a library area to increase its usage.

Results   The investigators reported that during the time the rooms were arranged to meet high-quality standards, the children talked more together and did less standing around than during the times when the rooms were poorly arranged. The children used materials in ap-

terials and objects which encourage substantial improvisation and/or have a considerable element of unpredictability. (Examples: all art activities such as dough or paints; a table with books to look at; an area with animals such as a dog, guinea pigs, or ducks.)" (p. 146). A *super unit* is a complex unit that has "one or more additional play materials, i.e., three or more play materials, juxtaposed. (Examples: sand box with play materials and water; dough table with tools; tunnel, movable climbing boards and box, and large crates)" (p. 146). These units can involve more children at the same time and sustain each child's interest longer. Jones (1977) reported in another publication that "a super unit is about eight times as effective in holding a child's attention as a simple unit; a complex

unit about four times as effective" (p. 12).

Certainly teachers who wish to promote positive social action, creative problem solving, and richer play as part of their outdoor curriculum will do well to assess the outdoor play equipment and convert it to complex and super units where possible. One of the easiest and most productive ways of doing this is to acquire the supply of boards, sawhorses, crawl-through blocks, mattresses, and large hollow blocks recommended in chapter 9. If these are moved to various areas at different times and are used in conjunction with other, less movable equipment, they add instant complexity and play possibilities to areas as diverse as the sandbox and jungle gym. Adding dramatic play props, such as

propriate areas more of the time, the amount of constructive play increased, and random and deviant conduct decreased. All of these results met a satisfactory level of statistical significance. When the rooms were restored to their original condition, the children returned to their earlier, less desirable behaviors.

Therefore, Teets concluded that the study demonstrates that good-quality environments *can* produce positive changes in children's behavior.

Implications   Previous studies of child-care environments, such as that by Smith and Connolly (1980), had centered on the effects of overcrowding but had not demonstrated that such effects can be corrected by changing the environment. Teets's study goes beyond that work and offers evidence (and hope!) to teachers that they can change what is happening in their classrooms by paying careful attention to the effect room arrangement has on children's behavior.

When children seem rowdy or at loose ends or consistently get in trouble, the wise teacher should stand off and review the way the room is arranged. Are the children running back and forth because they're "naughty," or are they running because the room is arranged like a long, narrow tunnel? Are they stomping on each other's blocks because they're destructive or because there's insufficient space for them all to build as they wish? Are they standing around doing nothing because they're withdrawn or because there isn't enough for them to do?

Although not all undesirable behavior can be attributed to poor design of the environment, some of it certainly can be. Teachers can make their own lives and the lives of the children they teach so much easier if they will take care when planning how to arrange their rooms.

Note. From "Modification of Play Behaviors of Preschool Children through Manipulation of Environmental Variables" by S. T. Teets, 1985, in J. L. Frost and S. Sunderlin (Eds.), *When children play: Proceedings of the International Conference on Play and Play Environments*, Wheaton, MD: Association for Childhood Education International.

---

dolls, housekeeping paraphernalia, or fire hats and hoses is another easy way to change a simple unit to a complex or super one.

When arranging and developing the outdoor activity areas to increase their potential for richer play, teachers should ask themselves these questions:

- What direction is the play taking? What is there in reserve that might be added to deepen and extend it as it progresses?
- How can I involve the children in concocting solutions to items needed in their play?
- What is there on the playground that could be combined to produce a *complex* or *super unit* instead of several *simple* ones?

- How can I arrange this area so the children will be encouraged to play together?
- Is there a way to modify the setting to make it more accessible for our children with disabilities?

Maintaining the Total Environment in Good Order

Another aspect of the development of the physical environment is worth considering: the overall impression that the physical environment conveys is of great significance. Mundane as it may seem, orderliness and cleanliness play vital roles in that impression.

Here are helpful ideas for solving some common problems.

96

Of course, some items, such as the plastic cover used at the clay table, are better left uncleaned. Maintaining good order should not become a fetish in a children's center, but cleanliness is appreciated by experienced visitors who have all too often come across schools with sticky chairs, smudged blocks, and grubby puzzles. Days at a center move at a quick and ever-changing pace, which makes it difficult, though not impossible, to keep things looking

TABLE 5–1
Money-Saving Tips on Maintaining and Preserving Equipment

Preservation and Maintenance	Additional Comments
Furniture	
Buy varnished or lacquered shelves, cabinets, and so on, rather than painted ones. They require less frequent refurbishing.	Buy furniture with casters whenever possible to aid movement. Avoid "built-ins" when you can; they reduce flexibility.
Look for easily cleaned plastic surfaces on tabletops and chairs. Chairs, in particular, soil easily, so purchase ones that will hold up under frequent washing and do not require repainting; ones with plastic backs and seats are good choices.	Scratched and marred surfaces can be recovered with plastic similar to Formica, but which can be cut with scissors and glued with a special adhesive.
Check all furniture regularly to make certain that nuts and bolts are tight.	Buy good-quality, substantial items or have them made; it saves money in the long run.
Wax all wood and plastic furniture with paste wax before using initially and after washing. This cuts work and saves surfaces. (Children like to help polish the result.)	Haunt thrift shops and rummage sales for low dressers, shelves, old tables, and so forth. Tables are easy to shorten—all it takes is a saw, muscles, and careful measurement. It makes money go further.
Floors	
Use linoleum as the basic surface (carpeting is impossible to keep clean in eating or art areas), but provide carpeted spaces where possible. (Keep carpets away from outdoor entries.)	Carpeting adds warmth, comfort, noise control, and "softness" to the room; tightly woven ones are best for easy vacuuming. Small area rugs that can be shaken out and moved easily are nice if they do not wrinkle too much; use nonskid mats underneath.
An old-fashioned carpet sweeper is very handy for quick rug cleanup by children or teachers.	
String mops are more effective than sponge mops to use after water play.	
A drain in the bathroom floor facilitates frequent cleaning and disinfecting; it makes indoor water play more welcome.	
Files (Picture, Poetry, Flannel Boards, Songs)	
Mount them on stiff cardboard or mat board. (Rubber cement is most satisfactory adhesive.)	These files are invaluable educational resources, cost relatively little, and provide instant access to curriculum when a sudden interest arises from the children.
Spray with clear, flat, acrylic spray.	
File under topic headings for easy identification.	

TABLE 5–1
continued

Preservation and Maintenance	Additional Comments
Books	
Purchase durable, library-grade bindings to start with or cover with clear contact paper.	It adds variety to put some books away for use another day.
Repair books promptly with mending tape.	Keeping books sorted according to some simple classification system makes finding that "special" book easier.
Teach children to handle books with loving care.	
Unit blocks	
Wax with paste wax before use.	Stack on shelves according to kind; never dump in bins.
It is occasionally necessary to wash really dirty blocks. Do *not* soak. Dry immediately to avoid roughening and raising grain.	Use on flat, "tight" carpeting: it deadens noise, is warmer for children to sit on, and protects corners of the blocks.
	Use homemade soft wood blocks as money stretchers. They do not wear well but will do in a pinch—so will sealed and stapled milk cartons if money is really tight. Be sure you provide a lot of them.
Tabletop Activity Materials	
Mend broken corners of storage boxes immediately. Children can help.	Storage in see-through plastic boxes is ideal.
Have a special, centrally located little pot or box, and drop stray bits and pieces into it for weekly sorting; include nuts and bolts, Tinker toys, puzzle knobs, and so forth.	Presenting some items, such as colored bears, pegs, and cubical counting blocks, in a shallow basket makes them readily visible and appealing.
Label puzzle pieces with individual symbols on back for rapid sorting and reassembly.	When cardboard boxes are used for storage, draw a picture on the side or top so children can "read" what is inside.
Teach children to keep small, many-pieced items on the table; do not permit these to scatter. Using carpet squares, one per child, helps keep an activity focused in one place.	
Count pieces of some items before setting out, mark quantities on box, and recount before putting away (e.g., doctor's kit and simple games).	
Protect teacher-made activities with acrylic spray or clear contact paper.	
Inspect all items regularly for cleanliness, and wash when necessary.	
Tools (Cooking, Woodworking, Gardening)	
Keep tools out of the weather, and keep them oiled and painted when necessary.	Purchase sturdy equipment that really works. Store tools of all kinds with care; do not just dump in a box.
Teach children to use them for their intended purpose; do not discourage experimentation, but do not permit destructive abuse.	

Preservation and Maintenance	Additional Comments

Self-Expressive Materials

Present messy activities away from carpeted areas.

Store cleanup materials used together in the same place; for example, keep sponges, detergent, and scrub brushes assembled in the fingerpainting bucket.

Wash glue and paintbrushes thoroughly, every time; store on end, wood tips down.

Stack large sheets of paper on a series of narrow shelves rather than on one deep one for easy access; paper is heavy to lift.

Store construction paper in closed cabinets to reduce fading.

Sort donated materials as they arrive.

Buy art materials in quantity whenever possible (test quality first; tempera paint varies a good deal, as does paper).

Consider forming a purchasing co-op with other schools; bargain for discounts.

Wheel Toys

Always store under cover.

When possible, buy toys that do not require painting.

Check nuts and bolts frequently; oil occasionally.

In the long run it pays to buy the expensive preschool-grade quality of this equipment; check warranties.

Outdoor Equipment (swings and slides)

Avoid buying painted equipment; if you have it, sand, prime, and paint it regularly.

Repair instantly, for safety's sake and to discourage further abuse.

Wooden jungle gyms placed on grass or dirt rot quickly.

Inspect rigorously for safety.

Purchase removable, fiber swing seats with extra hooks.

If affordable, rubber matting under such equipment is wonderful.

Hollow Blocks, Boards, Sawhorses, Boxes, and So On

These should be lacquered with a product such as Deft every year.

Use only on grass or carpet to prevent splintering (indoor-outdoor carpeting or artificial turf can be used for this purpose when the entire play area is paved).

Some brands of large plastic blocks are reported to bow in or out or to be too slippery to be satisfactory for climbing on and for stacking.

Store molded plastic items in a warm place and wooden equipment in a dry place.

Animal Cages

Bottoms should be made of mesh to be self-cleaning. No animal should have to live in squalor.

Outdoor cages require shade, wind protection, and ventilation.

Protect from vandals by keeping cages carefully mended and using quality padlocks.

fresh and well maintained. Table 5–1 contains many suggestions for keeping maintenance simple and for saving money, too.

Materials

Recommendations for the actual presentation of various materials to children are included throughout this book, so here in closing we will content ourselves with the remarks by Harms (1972) on the importance of how materials are maintained and displayed:

> Everything present in the environment, even the spatial arrangement, communicates to the child how to live in that setting. Materials that are in good condition and placed on open shelves tell a child that the materials are valued, that they are meant to be considered, and that a child may take them off the shelf by himself. When they are taken off the shelf, they leave a big empty space so it is easy to put them back where they belong. What kind of message does a child get from open shelves crowded with an odd assortment of materials, few with all the pieces put together? What kind of message does he get from a closed cupboard? (p. 59)

When materials are plentiful, whether they be collage supplies or blocks, this tells children they need not pinch and scramble for their share, which thus allows them to be more generous. When materials are changed regularly, this tells them that school is a varied and challenging place. When they are complete and well cared for, this teaches them to take care also. When they are in good taste or, better yet, beautiful, this helps form children's taste for things of beauty and quality. When materials are multiethnic and nonsexist, this reminds them repeatedly of the fundamental equality and worth of every human being.

Summary

When planning the arrangement of indoor and outdoor space in the preschool, it is important to consider immovable "givens," traffic patterns, noise levels, and ways to control the level of stimulation. Beauty should also be an important component of the environment. Special thought should be devoted to including multiethnic and nonsexist areas, and the needs of children with disabilities must also be taken into consideration.

All of these factors are involved in the careful arrangement of the physical setting and contribute in substantial ways to the overall effect, the *ambience*, of the school. But, like the children themselves, ambience is more than the sum of its parts. Ambience is composed of many things: it includes the intangible glow the staff radiates in the morning, the feeling there is time for everyone, the splash of color on the walls, the rocking chair in the corner, and the blooming plant on the windowsill. These all contribute to the sense of caring, personal concern, and beauty that careful planning and sound room arrangement convey to the children.

Self-Check Questions for Review

Content-Related Questions

1. Two "yardstick questions" are recommended to use when evaluating the environment. What are those questions? Why are they worthwhile ones to ask?
2. List some points that should be considered when arranging equipment in a classroom, and give practical examples of how equipment could be arranged to take these factors into consideration. For example, suggest a variety of purposes a bookcase might fulfill in addition to holding books.
3. What are some ways a teacher could add touches of beauty to her room?
4. Suppose you have a child from Nicaragua in your room. Suggest some items you might include that would help him feel culturally at home.
5. Think of the room where you are teaching and of the equipment included there. Using the suggestions in Table 5–1, suggest some practical ways to preserve and maintain that equipment.
6. Give some practical examples drawn from the research study that illustrate how rearranging a room can affect the children's behavior.

Integrative Questions

1. Select a piece of outdoor play equipment and explain how it could be used as a simple, complex, or super play unit.
2. The text emphasizes that the environment should reflect the teacher's underlying philosophy. Give four examples of the way *you* would set up an early childhood room so that it would reflect *your* philosophy.
3. If using the bulletin board areas as spaces for sharing what the children have made conveys the message their work is valued, what might the use of the cardboard, cartoonlike characters such as Power Rangers or Disney-type animals convey as messages?
4. You have agreed to welcome a 4-year-old boy who has only partial vision into your group. He can tell dark from light and is aware of large objects when these are in his path. Using your common sense, suggest several ways you could adapt your room environment to make it possible for him to function as independently as possible.

Questions and Activities

1. You are now the teacher and you have six Vietnamese children as part of your preschool group. In terms of creating the physical environment, what multiethnic touches would you add from their culture to help them feel at home?
2. Halloween is coming soon, and you want to give your room a festive air in honor of that season. What would you do to make this a truly *participatory* environment for the children?
3. Draw a floor plan of your ideal preschool room, suitable for 15 children. Show how you would arrange the major elements to foster positive social interaction between the children.
4. What is the best storage idea you have observed in a child-care center? Share it with the class.
5. Estimate what you think the costs of the following items of equipment are likely to be and then look up the actual costs in an equipment catalog: (a) a large set of hollow blocks, (b) an aluminum tricycle, (c) a set of rubber wild animals for the block corner, (d) a dozen building boards approximately 10 inches × 60 inches each, and (e) a starter set of hardwood blocks.

References for Further Reading

Overview

Caples, S. E. (1996). Some guidelines for preschool design. *Young Children, 51*(4), 15–21. This article by a practicing architect provides sensible, general advice about constructing interior and outdoor child-friendly spaces.

Greenman, J. (1988). *Caring spaces, learning places: Children's environments that work.* Redmond, WA: The Exchange Press. Greenman offers an original and refreshing book that should not be missed by anyone interested in the care of young children. *Highly recommended.*

Weinstein, C., & David, T. (1987). *Space for children: The built environment and children's development.* New York: Plenum. This is an extraordinarily useful book that covers topics ranging from the physical environment in child-care centers to playgrounds for able and disabled children. Children's participation in planning is also discussed. *Highly recommended.*

Designing Indoor Spaces

Church, E. B. (1996). Your learning environment: A look back at your year. *Scholastic Early Childhood Today, 10*(8), 28–35. Church combines assessment questions with helpful tips about improving several aspects of the environment.

Houle, G. B. (1987). *Learning centers for young children* (3rd ed.). West Greenwich, RI: Consortium. Houle provides thorough discussions of 18 potential learning centers, all illustrated. *Highly recommended.*

Readdick, C. A., & Bartlett, P. M. (1995). Vertical learning environments. *Childhood Education, 71*(2), 86–90. Interactive suggestions for using vertical space are advocated in place of old-fashioned bulletin boards.

Designing Outdoor Spaces

Frost, J. L. (1992). *Play and playscapes.* Albany, NY: Delmar. *Play and Playscapes* is *the* authoritative work in the field of playground design. Beginning with theoretical discussions of play, Frost devotes intensive discussion to the all-important areas of safety before discussing design, per se. *An indispensable reference.*

Moore, R. C., Goltsman, S. M., & Iacofano, D. S. (1992). *Play for all guidelines: Planning, design and management of outdoor play settings for all children* (2nd ed.). Berkeley, CA: Communications. A basic reference in the field, this revised edition remains a treasure trove of playground design while adding valuable information on how to comply with the Americans with Disabilities Act, thereby welcoming all children to the delights of playing outdoors. *Highly recommended.*

Wilson, R. A., Kilmer, S. J., & Knauerhase, V. (1996). Developing an environmental outdoor play space. *Young Children, 51*(6), 56–61. Practical ways to emphasize nature in outdoor play spaces and extend children's appreciation of it are included here.

Adapting Environments for Children with Disabilities

Note the book by Moore et al. (1992) recommended earlier.

Bailey, D. B., & Wolery, M. (1992). *Teaching infants and preschoolers with disabilities* (2nd ed.). Upper Saddle River, NJ: Merrill/Prentice Hall. Chapter 7 provides a rare in-depth discussion of adapting preschool environments for children with special needs.

Miller, R. (1996). *The developmentally appropriate inclusive classroom in early education.* Albany, NY: Delmar. In this first-rate book, Miller provides a wealth of suggestions of ways to use/or adapt typical preschool equipment to suit special requirements of children with disabilities. *Highly recommended.*

Information about Equipment

Bronson, M. B. (1995). *The right stuff for children birth to 8: Selecting play materials to support development.* Washington, DC: National Association for the Education of Young Children. Bronson opens each chapter with a list of developmental characteristics and then recommends equipment for six ages, categorizing materials as fostering social/fantasy, exploration/mastery, music/art/movement, and gross-motor materials. *Highly recommended.*

Moyer, J. (Ed.). (1995). *Selecting educational equipment and materials for school and home.* Wheaton, MD: Association for Childhood Education International. This updated version of a dependable old favorite provides lots of sensible advice about choosing equipment, including a chapter on selecting microcomputers and software. It features explicit lists of equipment for various-aged children, separating items into "essential" and "extensions." *Highly recommended.*

Evaluation of Preschool Settings

Harms, T., & Clifford, R. M. (1996). *Early childhood environment rating scale.* New York: Teachers College Press. Ever wonder how the environment you teach in might measure up in terms of how effectively it is meeting the needs of children and adults? The Harms/Clifford Scales are simple to use and cover seven areas, ranging from personal care routines of children and creative activities to how well the needs of the adults are met.

National Association for the Education of Young Children. (1991). *Accreditation criteria and procedures of the National Academy of Early Childhood Programs* (rev. ed.). Washington, DC: Author. This is another very useful set of criteria for measuring many aspects of quality programs, including the physical environment.

For the Advanced Student

Brett, A., Moore, R. C., & Provenzo, E. B. (1993). *The complete playground book.* Syracuse, NY: Syracuse University. For a useful overview of playgrounds past and present, this is an excellent resource. Particular attention is paid to European playgrounds, and plentiful illustrations enrich the text.

National Association for the Education of Young Children Information Service. (1991). *Facility design for early childhood programs: An NAEYC resource guide.* Washington, DC: Author. The guide includes an annotated bibliography, organization list, and NAEYC accreditation standards. Deals with both indoor and outdoor physical facilities.

6

Planning with Individual Children in Mind

Using Educational Objectives in the Preschool

Have you ever

- Heard someone mention behavioral objectives and wondered what they were?

- Felt like you knew in a general way what was important for little children to learn but had trouble translating general goals into specific curriculum?

- Wanted to make a plan to help a particular child behave better?

If you have, the material in this chapter will help you.

Once upon a time the animals had a school. The curriculum consisted of running, climbing, flying, and swimming, and all the animals took part in all the subjects.

The Duck was good in swimming, better, in fact, than his instructor, and he made passing grades in flying, but he was practically hopeless in running. Because he was low in this subject, he was made to stay after school and drop his swimming class in order to practice running. He kept this up until he was only average in swimming. But average is acceptable, so nobody worried about that except the Duck.

The Eagle was considered a problem pupil and was disciplined severely. He beat all the others to the top of the tree in climbing class, but he used his own way of getting there.

The Rabbit started out at the top of the class in running, but he had a nervous breakdown and had to drop out of school on account of so much makeup work in swimming.

The Squirrel led the climbing class, but his flying teacher made him start his flying lessons from the ground instead of the top of the tree down, and he developed charley horses from overexertion at the takeoff and began getting C's in climbing and D's in running.

The practical Prairie Dogs apprenticed their offspring to a Badger when the school authorities refused to add digging to the curriculum.

At the end of the year, the abnormal Eel that could swim well, run, climb, and fly a little was made valedictorian.

Anonymous

Now that we have looked at the overall schedule and environment in terms of the entire group of children, it is time to think about individual children and their needs. Many preschool teachers store an informal list of such needs and the ways they intend to meet these in their heads. Some examples might include these:

- Next time I'll turn over the rocking boat, creating an arch of stairs, to give Cecile (who is 2 years old) practice in alternating her feet as she climbs up them.
- I think I'll serve soba (Japanese noodles) for snack to help Fumie feel more at home with us.

These teachers believe that such mental notes are sufficient and that they allow them to be flexible and adjust quickly to children's needs as they change from week to week.

For some teachers, however, such casual lists of what they intend to do about a problem do not suffice. They make a good case for the value of pinpointing what individual children need to learn. They maintain that, once these needs are clearly stated, it is much easier to make individualized curriculum plans that will help particular children acquire specific skills and become more competent. For example, a teacher who prefers this more definite approach might add the following objective to a little boy's record: "When Miles builds in the block area, he will do it with another child twice a week." Then she might include a few notes or a plan for helping Miles play with others in this area:

1. Suggest that another child carry some blocks over to help him build.
2. Get out the large boards that require two children to lift them together.
3. Add the small cars to block play—these seem to encourage interaction between the children.

When children's learning needs are stated in this specific way, they are called *educational* or *behavioral objectives*.

After a decline in the 1980s, the ability to understand and compose these more specific objectives has once again increased in importance. This is because of recent legislation that mandates inclusion of youngsters with disabilities into typical school settings, including preschool settings. Additional legislation also requires these youngsters be equipped with individualized educational programs (IEPs) that specify what each youngster is supposed to learn next. These expectations are typically written in the form of educational objectives. Preschool teachers who welcome such youngsters into their classrooms will find they are often expected to help formulate such objectives for the children in their care or, at the very least, understand what they are and be able to translate the stipulated behaviors into reality. It is for this

reason that the classic, "purist" approach to writing objectives is included at the beginning of this chapter.

Pros and Cons of Using Behavioral Objectives

Objections to the Use of Behavioral Objectives

Ever since the 1970s, the pros and cons of using such objectives has been hotly debated (Ebel, 1970; Eisner, 1969), and the argument continues today (Howe, 1995; McCollum, 1995). Some believe that using them stifles and narrows educational programs. They disapprove of objectives because they believe that they encourage a cut-and-dried approach to teaching based mainly on the principles of behavior modification and that such intensive preplanning deadens spontaneity. Others argue that some of the more valuable kinds of social and emotional learning cannot be made specific in behavioral terms.

Responses to These Arguments

There is no denying that objectives can be miswritten or misused. However, when objectives are correctly employed, they can also help teachers think seriously about which of them have the greatest value and how to tell when the objective has been accomplished. The clear-sightedness that results is a welcome antidote to the high-minded pronouncements that abound in education and that give the reader a pleasant glow but do not actually mean much when given careful attention.

Consider the following excerpt from a center brochure: "Our little school, nestled amid the rustic pines and hills of _____ , has as its goal the development of the whole child———we want him to be mentally healthy, physically able, authentically creative, and socially sensitive." There is nothing wrong with this statement as a long-range, general foundation for an educational program. But many teachers never bother to ask themselves seriously what practical steps they will take to translate such lofty goals into the daily reality of the children's lives. Behavioral objectives can help teachers bridge this gap between broadly stated, general goals and actuality.

Another difficulty teachers cite is that objectives deaden spontaneity and make responding to the children's developing ideas impossible. But this is not necessarily true. Another, softer word for *objectives* is *intentions*. If we think about objectives as crystallizing our intentions, as is described later in the discussion of constructing informal objectives, then it is easy to see how the teacher's desire to remain responsive to shifting interests need not interfere with her educational intentions and hopes regarding the development of individual children. The fact that the children's interests have changed from hatching ducklings to solving the problem of how to provide a pool for them does not change the teacher's intention, for example, that Brad needs to learn to ask another child for a toy (or duckling!) instead of just grabbing it.

Definition of Behavioral Objectives

Behavioral objectives are not as appalling as they may sound. An *objective* is simply a clear statement that identifies a behavior the teacher deems important. It usually consists of one or two sentences describing how the child will behave or perform when he has reached the desired behavior. The outstanding characteristic of behavioral objectives is that *they must be based on behavior that the teacher can actually see.*

Objectives can and should cover many areas of learning rather than just the cognitive domain (Gronlund, 1995). Thus, a teacher who believes that originality of ideas is important might write this objective: "When presented with a problem that requires a solution, Claire will think of and

try out a variety of ways to solve it until she has found an effective solution. For example, when unable to get into a swing that is too high, she will think of and try out several ways to reach the seat until she achieves success." Another teacher who believes that physical development is valuable might compose this objective: "Given one or two trials, Jackie will be able to catch a large ball thrown to him from a distance of 5 feet."

The worst pitfall for beginning teachers is a tendency to select insignificant behaviors to document. This is probably because certain behaviors, such as finger snapping or color naming, are easy to observe and count. Fortunately, it is equally possible to write behavioral objectives for the affective or cognitive domain that identify richer, more significant behaviors, as illustrated by the examples used throughout this chapter.

Moreover, it is not necessary to write objectives in a stiffly classical form for them to be explicit and useful. Although that approach is included in this book because it is still required by many school systems as being the standard form for writing IEPs, this chapter also illustrates how to write objectives that say the same thing in a less stilted manner more palatable to teachers.

Steps in Writing Behavioral Objectives

There are four steps to writing an objective. The first step is to identify the desired, broad goal. The next step is to translate this goal into several behaviors that reflect the accomplishment of the goal and to write specific objectives for the most significant of these behaviors. The third step is to add the conditions and performance levels of the objectives, that is, where, when, and how often the child must exhibit the behavior for the teacher to decide he or she has attained the objective. The final step, which may or may not be included because it is not really a part of the objective, is a list of possible activities the teacher could use to help the youngster reach the objective.

Step 1: Select the Broad, General Goal

Selecting a broad goal is the most logical starting point because this requires teachers to think carefully about what they really want children to learn. If they consider the area of mental health important, then they must identify a series of broad goals that contribute to mental health. Identifying these long-term goals also helps ensure that they cover every area of curriculum it is valuable to include.

One approach that helps ensure thorough coverage is to use outlines of educational goals. These outlines are often called *taxonomies* (several are listed in the references at the end of this chapter). It is not necessary to use taxonomies devised by other people, however; the staffs of many centers feel they are quite capable of developing their own outlines of goals. Working together to write such outlines has the advantage of tailoring the goals to the specific philosophy of the school and to the particular needs of the children's families as well.

Some examples of broad goals that might be selected by full- or half-day children's centers include the following:

Physical Development

1. The child will be able to demonstrate or acquire physical skills appropriate to his age.
2. He will develop a sense of himself as being physically competent both in relation to his personal aspirations and in comparison with his peers.

Emotional Stability and Mental Health

1. The child will remain in touch with the full range of feelings, including positive and negative ones, within herself and will be encouraged to recognize and acknowledge their presence and express them in appropriate ways.
2. The child will develop a sense of identity by learning who she is in relation to other members of her family and their cultural background, and in relation to the children and staff in the school.

Creative Self-Expression

1. The child will express her own ideas and feelings through the use of self-expressive materials and play.
2. She will use a variety of different mediums (such as paint, play, dance, and collage) to express herself.

Social Competence

1. The child will gain the ability to care about the rights and needs of other people.
2. She will develop the ability to play with other children by accepting leadership from others on occasion and also by contributing her own ideas when desirable.

Language and Cognitive Development

1. The child will be able to express herself verbally by increasing her vocabulary and by gradually extending the length and complexity of her syntax.
2. She will increase her communication skills by learning to listen to other people and grasp what they mean.
3. She will learn to produce alternative solutions to problems when this is necessary.

Step 2: Compose an Objective That Describes the Desired Behavior

After identifying the broad goals, the next step is formulating the objectives. This involves deciding what behaviors can be used to indicate that the child has reached the goal. For example, in the first goal from the area of social competence ("The child will gain the ability to care about the rights and needs of other people"), it is necessary to think of several more specific situations that would require the child to consider the rights and needs of other people. One such occasion might be lunchtime when everyone is entitled to a fair share of food. Other possibilities include respecting the privacy of other children's cubbies, being quiet at nap time so that all may sleep, not breaking other children's toys, or refraining from constantly demanding to be the center of attention. Let us suppose that sharing food at lunchtime has been picked as one of the situations to use when assessing whether the goal of caring about the rights of others is being attained.

Write the Objective

After considerable trial and error, an objective to fit lunchtime is developed: "When given a bowl of a favorite food, Terry will show he cares about the rights of others by serving himself a portion and leaving enough for the other children, too." There are two special points to note about this objective. The first is that the teacher used *action* verbs to describe the way Terry will behave when he has accomplished the goal; that is, instead of the objective being written as, "Terry will *think* of others and *be aware* that everyone is hungry at lunchtime," it is written as, "Terry will *show* he cares . . . by serving himself . . . and leaving enough food. . . ." Good verbs to use when writing objectives include *identify, name, describe, show, tell about, construct, arrange in order, show what comes next,* and *demonstrate.* These are far superior to verbs like *think, be aware, understand,* or *appreciate* because such action verbs describe behavior that can actually be seen; they make it unnecessary to guess at what is happening.

The second point to note about this objective is that it does not explain how the child will learn to take some and leave some. Because teachers are likely to be teachers before they become objective writers, they often fall into the trap of trying to explain how the goal will be reached. Such teachers might formulate the following objective: "The child will learn to share food at lunchtime by having to wait until last when he grabs out of turn." Aside from whether this describes a sound teaching technique, it explains how the teacher intends to reach the goal of teaching social concern. This is incorrect. *An objective should state only the desired outcome, not the means by which it is to be attained.* It specifies only how the child will behave once he or she has reached the objective.

Here is an objective written by a hard-pressed preschool aide with a particular little boy in mind: "At snack time Henry will wait until the basket of fruit is passed to him. He is not to grab or yell, 'Give me!' If he can usually wait until the basket has been passed to two other children before him, the goal is accomplished." Note how specific her goal is. Note also that the objective does not describe how to teach him "not to grab or yell, 'Give me!' " Note particularly the last sentence of this objective because it is an example of the final items that must be included to make an objective complete.

Step 3: State the Conditions and Performance Level of the Objective

Once the desired behavior is identified, two more items must be added to make the objective complete: the conditions and levels of performance the child is expected to reach to accomplish the objective. In Henry's case the condition is that he can "wait until the basket has been passed to two other children before him," and the level, or frequency, of performance is "usually."

This portion of the objective, which stipulates when and how frequently a child must display the behavior, can be one of the most significant parts of writing objectives, because such statements of expectations force teachers to examine underlying values, as well as standards of performance. Consider an objective that states, "The child will provide evidence that she likes to eat by eating everything on her plate at each meal." Another example, written for a group of 3-year-olds, might be, "The children will sit quietly during story time. They will never interrupt the reader or talk to their neighbor while the story is being read." But are "eating everything on her plate" and "sitting quietly during story time" truly desirable educational goals? Are there more desirable ones that could be selected in place of these? What are the most fundamental values that should be stressed and turned into goals?

Sometimes it takes direct intervention by the teacher to help children learn to "take some and leave some."

Consider the level of expectation in these examples. No one can be expected to be perfect. It is unreasonable to demand that a youngster *always* clear her plate or that a group of 3-year-olds *always* sit quietly during story hour. Unless these objectives are modified, they imply an expectation of perfection. For the behavioral objective to be successful (and to enhance the self-esteem of the children), it is necessary to take the children's developmental level into account and to set a reasonable standard of performance for them to attain.

Step 4: Create a List of Activities to Help the Child Reach the Objective

After teachers have formulated an objective for a youngster, they often go on to develop a plan for reaching it. When such a plan of action is desired, it should be included as a separate fourth step. Remember, it is not technically a part of the objective per se.

For the objective we have been discussing ("When given a bowl of a favorite food, Terry will show he cares about the rights of others by serving himself a portion and leaving enough for the other children"), a plan might include the following:

1. I will check the kitchen and make sure the amount of food supplied will be plentiful.
2. I will delegate Terry as the one person to return to the kitchen for seconds to show him there is plenty.
3. When the food is passed, I will remind him to take some and leave some, showing him what I mean if this is necessary.
4. I will make sure he has a second helping when he wants one.
5. I will praise Terry when he does help himself and remembers to leave enough for the other children.

Creating Informal Objectives

Writing objectives in the manner described here often seems so cold and unnatural to teachers that they become hostile to the whole idea of using or writing them. As mentioned previously, this view is particularly unfortunate because it may color their attitudes when working with children for whom such objectives are required. That hostility may also blind teachers to the genuine virtue of objectives, which is that they *do* pin down what the child needs to learn.

As proposed earlier, one solution to this problem is to retain the fundamental concept of using objectives while thinking of them as representing your hopes and intentions and then write them in a more informal way to express that intention. When doing this, it often works well to begin with the words I *want* followed by what you want the child to learn.

For example, a formal objective might be phrased, "While playing in the sandbox, Lotus will add her own ideas to our play activities two times each day." When this same objective is translated into an informal objective, it might be phrased, "I want Lotus to be more confident and tell us her ideas a couple of times a day when the children play together in the sandbox."

The joy of this more informal approach is that it lends itself to a final step that feels natural, too. It is the addition of an objective for the teacher that clarifies her plan (objective) for her own behavior, that is, what she intends to do to turn the plan into reality. In this case it could be, "I'll watch for a problem-solving situation—Lotus is so smart—and ask her what she'd do about it. Maybe the children will need to carry water, or something like that, and they'll need a way to transport it. I think if I asked her directly, she wouldn't be too shy to tell or show me what she thinks."

Note that the less formal way of writing the objective still focuses on what the child will actually be doing when she has reached the objective, it says how frequently the behavior is expected to take place, and it tells the circumstances in which the behavior will occur. The informal objectives also keep the plan of action separated from the child objective by including it in the teacher objective instead.

Following are a few more examples illustrating the two forms of objective writing.

Formal objective for child: Maggie will participate in an interpersonal activity with at least two other people this week.

Informal objective or intention for child: I want Maggie to play with a couple of other children sometime during the week.

Teacher objective or intention: I'll invite Maggie, Mike, and Lisa to tell me what we need to play "going camping." I'll see if I can generate some togetherness that way.

Jeff has recently reached an objective identified by his teacher. Can you guess what it is? And can you formulate an informal objective that would define what she wanted him to learn to do?

Formal objective for child: Jonelle will try out the medium slide this month.

Informal objective or intention for child: I want Jonelle to overcome her fear of the medium slide and be willing to use it when we go outdoors, hopefully by the end of this month.

Teacher objective or intention: I must think of some way to help Jonelle understand that going down slides is fun and that she doesn't need to be scared. I guess I'll start with sliding the dolls down the little slide. I'll also offer to slide down with Jonelle on my lap. I have to remember to take it easy and not push her too hard.

Formal objective for child: Brad will ask for a toy when he wants it at least once today.

Informal objective or intention for child: I want Brad to learn to ask instead of grabbing everything he wants at least once a day.

Teacher objective or intention: I will stay with Brad when he plays in the block area. When the chance comes up and I can see that he wants a block another child has, I'll coach him how to get it instead of just grabbing it and point out how much more friendly the other child acts when he behaves that way.

Carrying the Objectives Through: Final Comments

Remember that objectives, whether formally or informally stated, must be viewed as being continually "in process." As the children's abilities increase and their interests and needs change, objectives must change, too. The clarity that the use of objectives can provide, coupled with flexibility and the willingness to change them as the children change, is a hallmark of effective teaching.

Also remember that in addition to keeping pace with the children's development, goals and objectives will have little effect on the actual program unless they are reviewed from time to time to make certain the curriculum is focusing on them. If the review indicates that they do not match what is actually being taught in the school, then they should be rewritten in terms of the actual program or the program should be modified to reflect the desired goals.

Summary

The use of behavioral goals and objectives in curriculum planning can be a helpful strategy. If properly developed, they can help teachers examine their value systems, select goals they feel are significant, and translate lofty ideas into practical behavioral expectations for the children in their groups.

A well-written objective confines itself to specifying behavior that can be readily observed and to stating the frequency and conditions under which the behavior is expected to take place. Although many school districts prefer teachers to use more formal objectives, they may also be written according to a less formal style and phrased in terms of what the teacher wants the child to accomplish. When these are accompanied by objectives for the teacher, the resulting changes in behavior can be very rewarding.

However, it is not sufficient only to write objectives. Checks must be made during the year to find out whether the objectives are being implemented in the actual curriculum, and evaluations of children's behavior should be carried out to determine whether the teaching has been effective.

Self-Check Questions for Review

Content-Related Questions

1. List some pros and cons about using behavioral objectives.
2. Explain the difference between a goal and an objective, and give an example of a goal. Then show how you might change that goal into several objectives.
3. There are two special points to remember when writing an objective. One is that it is important to use action verbs. List some action verbs. Also list some that should be avoided because they are not verbs that describe behavior that can be seen.

4. What is the second important point to remember when writing an objective?
5. In this text, what do the terms *conditions* and *performance level* mean?
6. Write a formal objective. Then demonstrate how it could be turned into an informal objective. Next, write an objective for the teacher to accompany the informal objective.

Integrative Questions

1. Read over the parable at the beginning of the chapter. What is the meaning or moral of this tale?
2. Write a goal and an objective for some aspect of social behavior. Compare them and explain what they have in common. Also explain how they differ from each other.

Questions and Activities

1. What educational values do you think would be most likely to be overlooked when writing a set of behavioral objectives for a young child?
2. What might be some important educational values that are so intangible that you feel it might not be feasible to write objectives that could cover them?
3. Identify and explain the differences between the broad goals listed in the first part of the chapter and the behavioral objectives discussed later.
4. Select one of the broad goals and practice identifying specific activities that would represent the goal in action, then write objectives based on the satisfactory performance of these activities.
5. One of the most effective ways to learn to write good objectives is to use negative practice; therefore, write the very worst objective you can think of. Be sure to make it an objective that is difficult to observe and that represents a value you feel would be inconsequential. Share these morsels with the class.
6. Which of the two forms of writing objectives do you prefer? Explain why this is the case. What might be the advantage of using the unpreferred form?

References for Further Reading

Writing Effective Objectives

Gronlund, N. E. (1995). *How to write and use instructional objectives* (5th ed.). Upper Saddle River, NJ: Merrill/Prentice Hall.

This sensible book describes in plain language how to write objectives for a variety of the selves.

Mager, R. F. (1984). *Preparing instructional objectives* (2nd ed.). Belmont, CA: Pitman Learning. Mager's short book explains in a clear and amusing way how to write instructional objectives.

Notari-Syverson, A. R., & Shuster, S. L. (1995). Putting real-life skills into IEP/IFSPs for infants and young children. *Teaching Exceptional Children,* 27(2), 29–32. A series of standards and recommendations for writing IEPs are presented in a useful way. *Highly recommended.*

Seefeldt, C., & Barbour, N. (1994). *Early childhood education: An introduction* (3rd ed.). Upper Saddle River, NJ: Merrill/Prentice Hall. In their chapter on planning, Seefeldt and Barbour include numerous examples.

Taxonomies

Beaty, J. J. (1994). *Observing development of the young child* (3rd ed.). Upper Saddle River, NJ: Merrill/Prentice Hall. Beaty begins each chapter with a list of skills children should acquire. These skills could be readily translated into objectives. She then suggests many activities that might be provided for practice in skill acquisition.

Beaty, J. J. (1996). *Skills for preschool teachers* (5th ed.). Upper Saddle River, NJ: Merrill/Prentice Hall. This text lists specific objectives for teachers for many areas of curriculum.

Gronlund, N. E. (1995). *How to write and use instructional objectives* (5th ed.). Upper Saddle River, NJ: Merrill/Prentice Hall. Gronlund includes a readable adaptation of the taxonomies listed for advanced students.

For the Advanced Student

Bloom, B. S., Engelhart, M. D., Furst, E. J., Hill, W. H., & Krathwohl, D. R. (1956). *Taxonomy of educational objectives. Handbook I. The cognitive domain.* New York: McKay.

Krathwohl, D. R., Bloom, B. S., & Masia, B. B. (1964). *Taxonomy of educational objectives: Handbook II. The affective domain.* New York: McKay. The Bloom and Krathwohl taxonomies are listed here because they are frequently referred to in the literature on behavioral objectives. However, these particular taxonomies do not specify overt behavior outcomes, and it may be difficult to translate the sophisticated skills listed in them into behavior that is characteristic of preschool children.

Tyler, R. W. (1950). *Basic principles of curriculum and instruction.* Chicago: University of Chicago Press. Tyler's work is a famous example of the behavioral objectives movement.

Practical Methods of Recording and Evaluating Behavior

Have you ever

- Had a parent ask you how her child was getting along and been unable to say anything concrete or specific in reply?
- Read an advertisement for a new preschool test and wondered how to tell whether it was any good or not?
- Been asked to prove that the children in your group were really learning?

If you have, the material in this chapter will help you.

During the past year as we have studied the Reggio Approach, the staff and I have been looking at our image of children with the intention of seeing their capabilities, not their deficiencies; seeing their interests, not the adults' interests; and seeing their potential for learning, not their potential for making mistakes. It is difficult for teachers to become listeners and observers who notice children's capabilities and interests and then plan or wait for opportunities to support their learning. It is difficult for teachers to know when to step in and offer a challenging question, when to offer advice, when to stand back and watch and let the child discover, when to set limits, and when to support opportunities for children to advance on their own. These are some of the most challenging aspects of teaching.

Karen Haigh (1997, p. 164)

The subject of evaluation—how to find out what young children know and what they are able to do—has become a matter of such intense concern that three major early childhood organizations have published position papers on this subject in the past few years. These include the Association for Childhood Education International (Perrone, 1991), the National Association for the Education of Young Children (1988), and the Southern Association for Children under Six (1990, now, the Southern Early Childhood Association).

All three organizations agree it is very important to know as much as possible about the abilities of every child in the group. What they object to so vehemently is depending on a standardized test to reveal that information. They maintain there are many other more appropriate ways to find out what young children know and what they can do. Many of these ways will be discussed later in this chapter. First, however, it is important to understand why children need to be evaluated at all.

Purposes and Advantages of Using Evaluation Procedures

Evaluation as a Way to Know the Children Better

Evaluation serves two basic purposes. First, it can describe the child's current abilities, and, second, if repeated, it can show ways she or he has changed over a period of time. When data on a number of children are combined, the results can also provide a picture of the current status of the group, as well as identify changes that have occurred since the previous evaluation. This is essential information to have when planning what should happen next in the curriculum.

Do not picture this process as requiring the services of a psychologist who comes in and administers a series of commercially developed tests. Although such formal measures have a definite place in sophisticated research programs or when working with children who appear to have special problems, useful information can also be obtained by means of simpler, less costly procedures that teachers can employ themselves as part of their ordinary routine. The drawback to developing such procedures is that it takes time and effort, but if the advantages of assessing children are fully understood, teachers may be better motivated to include this process in their busy schedules.

Purposes of Evaluation

Evaluation can increase the quality and specificity of the curriculum by targeting it. Once the degree of the children's skills is known and their strengths and weaknesses are identified, the planning of a curriculum becomes easier and more focused. For example, the majority of the children in a Head Start group might be evaluated in September as "usually showing interest in field trips." However, the majority also might be placed in the "hardly ever" category on "able to tell a connected story." A curriculum that uses the group's strength (shows interest in field trips) to help remedy the weakness (inability to tell a connected story) could then be planned. Perhaps one such activity would be a field trip in which the teacher takes the children to visit a car wash and afterward asks them to tell what happened when the car went through the wash and she forgot to roll up the windows.

Moreover, *evaluation permits specific abilities and inabilities of particular children to be noted,* and plans can then be developed to work on these difficulties or use particular strengths. For instance, a staff member at our center noted in her running observation record that one of her lively little boys had a difficult time sitting through lunch. Rather than criticizing and constantly restraining him, she resolved to ask him to be the kitchen messenger. This individualized, prescriptive activity helped him contribute to the well-being of the group, made him feel genuinely important, and gave him an opportunity

to move around. This approach did help him eventually to become less restless and better able to settle down to his meals.

Evaluation can improve teacher morale. It is surprising how easy it is to forget in May what a child was like in September. Many center teachers have been left at the end of the year with only the hazy impression that the children have learned a good deal and a few more specific memories, such as Leroy no longer bites or Elizabeth no longer screams when her mother leaves. It was not until I participated in a research project that measured certain abilities in the fall and again in the spring that I realized how much tangible records of progress can raise teacher morale by substituting concrete evidence of progress for a handful of memories.

Evaluation aids the compilation of reports to parents. Parents are always concerned about the welfare of their young children at school and like to know how they are getting along. In addition to the daily chats that are such a valuable part of binding home and school together, occasional conferences are also helpful. There is an obvious advantage to being able to produce carefully kept records at such times. Parents really appreciate having the information, and they are also reassured when shown evidence that the teacher has cared enough to make this special effort to know about their child.

Evaluation is an invaluable resource to draw on when compiling reports to boards and funding agencies. The trend that requires preschools and children's centers to be accountable to qualify for continued public support means it is important that teachers in such schools use sound, relevant evaluation procedures to measure change and growth. The following methods may not only serve the attractive purpose of directly benefiting children in the group but also may be used to furnish evidence that progress has taken place and that further financial support of the facility is justified.

Basic Principles of Evaluation

Before reviewing the actual methods of evaluation, the teacher needs to understand some general principles that apply to all forms of evaluation.

Observe confidentiality and professional discretion at all times. All records concerned with children and their families must be regarded as confidential. This means that they must never be left lying around for someone to pick up and read even while the teacher is working on them. The competence of individual children should never be discussed with people outside the school or with other parents who do not have a right to know about it. Above all, results of evaluations should be interpreted with caution and mercy, because it is very possible the teacher may have reached an incorrect conclusion about the child's abilities.

Select evaluation measures that match the educational goals and objectives of the school. The dangerous results from the early days of Head Start when tests that were *not related to the curriculum* were used to measure the program's effectiveness remind us just how vital it is to select measures that are closely related to what the teachers are teaching. Head Start was almost scuttled as a result of those early, incorrectly selected tests (Cicerelli, Evans, & Schiller, 1969; Smith & Bissell, 1970).

Perhaps the staff has selected the development of self-esteem as one of the most important educational goals. To find out whether the children are developing good self-esteem, it is vital that the teacher use either a school-developed measure of objectives or a commercial test that evaluates this specific trait. General measures of socialization, personality, or intelligence should be avoided, because they are unlikely to reveal progress in specific areas. However, if a list of formal or informal behavioral objectives has already been developed to define more clearly what is meant by self-esteem, that list would be a fruitful source for developing adequate evaluation measures.

Be sure to carry out more than one evaluation. Sometimes teachers employ measures of evaluation only at the end of the year. This provides a summing up for the family and for the next teacher (who may or may not read it) but is of little value to the teacher who has done the work. It is more useful to employ evaluative measures shortly after the youngster enters the program and again later on. Early assessment helps the teacher quickly become acquainted with the child and begin to plan around the youngster's needs and interests. It also provides a pretest to be used as a comparison at the middle and end of the year. Without this measurement at the beginning, there is no way to show how much the child has learned during her time at school.

Select evaluation measures that take varying ethnic/cultural backgrounds into account. Unfortunately, taking differing cultural characteristics into account is easier said than done by most middle-class, white teachers or anyone else who is expected to assess people who come from backgrounds different from their own. A beginning has been made in the realm of some commercial tests that are now normed on populations that represent a bigger assortment of children than former ones did. *Much remains to be done in this area, however.*

A special advantage preschool teachers have is that we are likely to become well acquainted with families as well as their children, and, if we are at all open-minded, over time we have the opportunity to become comfortable with and knowledgeable about differing cultural values that influence the children's behavior. For example, white, middle-class teachers often value children's ability to sit quietly and raise their hands when they have something to say, whereas the children in Reggio Emilia are encouraged to benefit from sharing their ideas via lively discussions. Young Japanese children are socialized into the importance of blending in and not "having their heads stick out above their friends" to a degree that would be unheard of in most "American" homes. Many Russians view the American habit of easy smiling as being close to dim-wittedness. It is easy to see how these behaviors could be regarded as positive or negative aspects of behavior when viewed by a teacher who lacks cultural awareness.

Our other advantage is our openness to using alternative methods of assessment when assessments are necessary. Using a variety of measures provides a better picture of the child, revealing who he is and what he can do more fully than "single-shot" assessments can.

Include a variety of measures that gives a picture of all the child's selves. If the intention of the assessment is to provide a fair and reasonably complete picture of the youngster's abilities, then it is vital to think carefully about what measures can be used to provide information about the child's physical, emotional, social, and creative selves as well as her cognitive/language self. All too often the use of commercial tests concentrates the focus on just the cognitive area. Because young children are busy developing and learning in so many areas, narrowing the evaluation to that one area is nothing short of tragic.

In recent years an encouraging trend has developed, exemplified by the work of Howard Gardner and Samuel Meisels. These theorists have stressed the value of looking at children's abilities from a number of perspectives. For example, Project Zero, which is based on Howard Gardner's (1993) work, identifies seven intelligences or ways of knowing (linguistic, logical/mathematical, kinesthetic, visual/spatial, musical, interpersonal, and intrapersonal). Meisels's Work Sampling System (Meisels, Liaw, Dorfman, & Nelson, 1995) covers seven domains (personal and social development, language and literacy, mathematical thinking, scientific thinking, social studies, the arts and physical development).

Appropriate Evaluation Measures to Use in the Preschool

In keeping with this broadening of significant domains, an accompanying trend advocates what is termed *authentic assessment.* When this approach is used, the emphasis is on keeping track of what children are able to do in real-life classroom situations rather than on how they perform on standardized tests.

Using "Documentation" to Mark What the Children Are Doing and Learning

The term *documentation* has come to have a particular meaning in recent years as a descriptor for a method of assessment used in the schools of Reggio Emilia (Gandini, 1997; Tarini, 1997). The teachers there keep running track of what the children are doing by consistently recording dialogues and comments made by children and adults, taking frequent photographs of what the children are doing as well as saving

Documentation boards help children recall how their ideas developed and keep parents and other visitors informed, too.

actual, concrete examples of their work. This material is then compiled on "documentation boards" that are hung throughout the school. The result is a beautiful, colorful, respectful record of how the curriculum is developing and what the children are learning about together.

Keeping track of children's development and learning in this fashion offers many advantages. The boards stimulate the children to further effort by recognizing what they have already achieved, they help the children recall how their ideas developed, they inform parents and other visitors about what the children and teachers are accomplishing together, and they contribute a great deal to the general impression of beauty and excitement that pervades these Italian schools.

However, some disadvantages to using these boards must also be admitted. Chief among these for American teachers (Goldhaber, Smith, & Sortino, 1997; Williams & Kantor, 1997) appear to be finding enough time to construct them on a consistent basis, finding the money for ongoing photographic documentation, and producing boards that are as aesthetically pleasing as the Reggio ones are. However, even though they may be dissatisfied with their results when comparing them with the Italian boards, many Reggio-inspired teachers in the United States are persevering in their use of this approach to documentation because it is an extremely valuable way of assessing and demonstrating what their children are learning (Hendrick, 1997; Saltz, 1997).

Using the Portfolio as a Method of Authentic Assessment

One of the easiest authentic ways to keep track of how all five selves are developing is to assemble a portfolio for each youngster. The word *portfolio* may sound fancy, but actually it just means the collection of information about the child gathered during the year from all available sources (Gullo, 1994; Southern Association for Children under Six, 1991). Note that the list given here of possible items to include contains a wide array of materials and that teacher-made and commercial tests represent only two of a great many possibilities for assessing the child's development.

This collection should be started promptly in the fall so that the child's beginning level of accomplishments can be used as a point for comparisons as skills are developed during the year.

Suggestions of what to include are as rich and various as the imagination and energy the teacher can devise. For example, the following items might be included:

Child-Produced Material

Photographs of block structures

Self-expressive efforts such as paintings, drawings, collages, and so forth

Dictated stories

Interviews with the child—favorite books, pets, things to do

Videotapes or audiotapes

Parent-Produced Material

Questionnaires about child's development, preferences, and health

Summaries of conferences

Noteworthy family events

List of family members who are emotionally significant to the child

Emergency contact list

Anecdotes and other information the parent wants to include

Records from Community Resources

Physician reports: immunizations, allergies, other relevant information

Information from the Child Development Team and IEPs if the child uses these services

Teacher-Produced Records

List of formal or informal individualized objectives for the child, perhaps in the form of checklists

Evaluation of achievement of the objectives and/or the IEPs

Height, weight, vaccination, and possibly attendance records

Summaries of parent interviews

Observations and anecdotal records

General checklists of achievements that apply to the entire class

Standardized commercial tests

Composing Teacher-Produced Records

The advantage of many of the suggested items in the folio list is that quite a few of them, such as health records, summaries of parent-teacher interviews, and results of the child's self-expressive activities, require no more extra work than simply putting them in the portfolio.

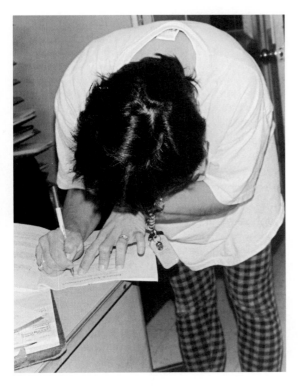

Careful record keeping is an unavoidable part of being a professional early childhood teacher.

Many schools suggest to parents that they add comments and records of their own in addition to the material contributed by the school. For example, it is both fun and enlightening to send a return-mail postcard home once a month asking parents to note some way their child has developed during the month and something he has particularly enjoyed doing.

When objectives have been previously agreed on by parents and teachers together, it is also helpful to have the degree of achievement of that objective evaluated at home as well as at school for inclusion in the portfolio. Meisels et al. (1995) use the terms *not yet accomplished, accomplished*, or *highly accomplished* in the Work Sampling System, and these are such friendly, unnegative terms they would be good ones to use in other evaluations, too.

It is all too easy when discussing the teacher-contributed records to advocate methods that, though excellent in many respects, are simply not practical for daily use by most teachers. If the method of record keeping requires too much time and effort, it is almost certain to be dropped by the wayside as the year progresses and the teacher puts it off in favor of preparing for the parent potluck or Valentine's Day. Occasionally schools have access to extra help (parent cooperatives and laboratory schools are particularly fortunate in this regard) and are able to employ a more elaborate system of recording behavior, but this is not the case in most working situations. For this reason, elaborate case studies, long written observations, and even the suggestion that the teacher carry a little notebook in which to jot down bright sayings and astonishing incidents are not advocated here as practical methods of evaluating children at the center. There is a valuable place for such activities in teacher training and for occasional studies of children who have special needs, but I do not believe it is realistic to suggest that such lengthy methods be used as primary ways of gathering information on the majority of the children.

Fortunately there are four briefer kinds of evaluation that have proven useful and feasible:

the parent interview, maintenance of brief anecdotal records, the inclusion of checklists related to the educational objectives of the school, and the use of an occasional commercial test.

Use of Parent Interviews as a Source of Information

The parent interview remains one of the outstanding means of collecting information about the child. Some information may be obtained in written form, but some is best gathered by means of personal interviews. Effective methods of talking with parents are discussed in chapter 2, but the interview deserves special mention here because it is such a good way to find out about a child's skills. Children's behavior is sometimes quite different at school and at home. For instance, a child who is silent as a sphinx at school may be quite talkative at home. This is important for the teacher to know when evaluating language development, as well as when deciding what to work on next.

Maintaining Anecdotal Records

Basically, anecdotal records are the notes made by teachers about individual children recording behaviors that they think are particularly important to remember. Probably the simplest method of maintaining these records is to use large index cards, one for each child. These should have the child's name, birth date, and date of entering school at the top. The observer's name or initials should be included also.

Notes about what the child does or says that is important or revealing are added on these cards as often as possible. Some teachers like to add to each of these cards once a week so that they can be aware of every child and of any progress being made. Others prefer to do half the children one week and the other half the next.

In addition to noting behavior that seems particularly significant, it is also useful to draw some conclusions about what the behavior probably means. Such conclusions need to be somewhat tentative, because it is always possible for observers to draw incorrect conclusions about the

If you were observing the child in the striped dress, what is her behavior telling you?

reasons for behavior. Nevertheless, drawing conclusions may help teachers see what the child is ready to learn next so that they can develop appropriate, timely objectives for the youngster. These objectives, which may change from week to week as the child gains skills, make the formulation of simple, practical plans much easier.

In the example that follows (names have been changed to protect the children's privacy), note how the teacher describes the behavior in one section and then enters his interpretation (conclusions) separately in the summary. This is done to keep the behavioral record as factual and unbiased as possible. The learning objective for the next week is written very simply in the informal "I want" form discussed in chapter 6. Many teachers find this kind of phrasing easier to use than the more formal objective, "Dean will play with Charlie at least two times in the block corner during the coming week," which was described in the previous chapter.

> Dean W.; birth date: August 2, 1993; entry to school: September 1997; observer: H.B.J.

Week 1: September 5

Dean is new to Center. Tall for age, slender, a little pale. First day stayed by door with mother, looked uncertain—stoic. Mother took off work to spend morning with D. She took him home after lunch, which he was unable to eat. Hid head when urged to say good-bye. During week, hardly knew he was there. Quiet, watchful, and attracted to book corner. Liked *Billy Goats Gruff* story a lot.

Summary: D. seems anxious, not sure he likes Center. Has made little contact with other children.

Objective: I want him to feel more at home and join in some of the activities this coming week.

Plan: Build bond with him myself. Talk with him about books he likes; suggest he bring one of his favorites to school for me to read to children. Don't push him too hard to join in.

Week 2: September 11

D. refused to bring book. However, at group time he brought me *Billy Goats Gruff* from our shelf and was delighted when I read it and told the children he had chosen it for the group. Spends most of time alone; used easel as vantage point for watching other activities. Able to eat more at lunch, especially bread and milk. Played a long time in blocks at end of day when Charlie (a vigorous block builder) had gone home.

Summary: D. is still a loner but is becoming interested in what is going on. Eating better so he's probably less anxious. Likes blocks.

Objective: I hope he will move into activities more and relax.

Plan: Make sure there's as much bread and milk as he wants until he's comfortable enough to eat the rest of the meal. Work on security bond. Read him special story. He likes trucks; add them to block corner. Invite him to go with small group to story hour at library.

Week 3: September 18

Turned down library—not surprising. Blocks are D.'s passion. Used trucks and blocks, built bridge. Said trucks were billy goats and they would fool the ogre. Later in week built elaborate structure; it was near 5:00 and he couldn't finish so left it for the next day. He arrived *smiling* and set to work; Charlie joined him. Boys worked together until every block in school was used. Dean was even noisy as they knocked it down afterward.

Summary: Seems D. is mastering anxiety by playing out the Billy Goat's Gruff theme. Wonderful he's making friends with Charlie; relationship would be a good balance for each.

Objective: I hope D. will play with Charlie at least some of the time next week.

Plan: Suggest boys feel free to use cardboard blocks and boards with unit blocks if they need more scope. Show them pictures of other children building with all sorts of blocks in *The Complete Block Book* (Provenso & Brett, 1983) to encourage them. Seat them together at lunch table.

Week 4: September 25

Had a setback with Dean. At mention of the practice fire drill he began to look anxious. Since everyone else wanted to hear the alarm, I turned it on. D. covered ears, scrunched down to bury head in carpet. I told him it was only practice, but he still looked worried. Retreated to book corner. Next morning cried as he came in door. I tried to reassure him. When drill came, I took his hand and he huddled against me. That afternoon he told his mother he didn't want to come anymore. I explained what had happened. She said she would explain at home, too.

Summary: The noise and fire talk frightened him—reawakened his anxiety. I think maybe I would have been smarter to have had fire drill right after hearing the alarm so that he wouldn't worry about it over the night.

Objective: I want D. to play through his fears about fire so he wants to come to the Center again.

Plan: Not sure, but must be careful not to make things worse. Start gently with fireman book. Be steady and not act overly concerned. Stress we can keep ourselves safe by knowing what to do when we hear the alarm.

Week 5: October 2

D. wouldn't let me read the fire book to him, but *did* look at it behind the bookcase by himself. What really worked was Charlie, Heaven bless him! He asked for the fire trucks to use in the block area. Dean hovered on the sidelines. Charlie said, "Hey, Deano—I'm squirtin' you with the hose," and he made fire siren sounds. Instead of retreating, D. said, "No you ain't—I'm squirtin' *you*," and he grabbed up another truck and shoved it at Charlie. They laughed hysterically at this, rolling on the floor (I could see Dean's relief on his face). Played in blocks with fire trucks, staked out fire area. Wouldn't let anyone else come in to get burned up. Play lasted intermittently rest of the week.

Summary: Never underestimate the power of play. I'm relieved for him. He is mastering his anxiety once again and building a friendship, too.

Objective: I want Dean to continue to play through his fear of fire and his anxiety during the coming week—and to play with Charlie.

Plan: Get out fire hats and some hoses. See if children will use them with the trikes when they go outside to play.

Construction and Use of Checklists and Rating Scales

For potential comprehensiveness of coverage in the preschool, nothing beats the checklist rating scale. Checklists may be developed on almost any conceivable aspect of child development of behavior. Because they are criterion referenced, which means that they are designed to match specific objectives, checklists are congruent with what is going on in the teacher's own classroom. They offer an excellent means of assessing whether educational objectives have been accomplished, and they can be filled out at the teacher's leisure and need not be completed in one sitting.

For example, one of the objectives for D. during week 2 is "I want him to move into activities more and relax." This makes an excellent checklist item, not only for D. but for many children. It is readily observable, it has worthwhile social value, and it is developmentally appropriate.

Possible Ways to Use and Develop a Checklist. A checklist should be thought of as being just that! It is *not* a test—it *is* a way to keep track of how the child is progressing and to remind the teacher of the important purposes and intentions of the curriculum envisioned for the year. When developing this kind of checklist, the teacher should list the educational goal first and then include several kinds of behaviors, preferably defined in behavioral objective terms, that are likely to be present when the goal is accomplished, as discussed in chapter 6.

Thus, when the staff of our children's center chose the general goal of fostering emotional health in the children, the following behaviors were selected as representing several coping behaviors related to emotional health: able to express liking for other children and adults, able to express anger in a way that does not damage people or equipment, able to confront an adult directly when the adult has caused the child to feel angry, able to maintain sustained friendships with other children.

Next, the process of making the checklist was refined by including measures of how often the behavior occurred. For our purposes we selected the following categories of frequency as quantitative measures we could all understand: *no opportunity to observe, not yet accomplished, accomplished,* and *highly accomplished.* The addition of these measures of frequency changed our modest checklist into a more useful measure—a checklist rating scale.

Because we knew how desirable it is to assess the child's abilities shortly after school begins, as well as at midyear and year's end, we found it helpful to allow space for the three evaluation periods on one sheet of paper. This made comparison simpler and also reduced the bulkiness of the file for each youngster.

Finally, additional items were added to cover other aspects of emotional and social behavior that the staff felt were important. Bear in mind that there is nothing holy about this particular list; other staffs would select other items suited to their own goals and children.

A sample of the final form of our chart looked like the one shown in Figure 7–1 (p. 124), "Suggestions about Compiling Checklists." Although going through the checklists of other schools to garner ideas is often helpful, each school should really develop its own set, because each school has its own philosophies about what they think is most important. The checklists should be designed to fit these objectives. It is astonishingly easy to become trapped into evaluating children on skills that have not been emphasized in the curriculum. Results of such mismatched evaluations can only be disappointing.

The teacher should be as explicit and clear as possible when describing the behaviors that will be evaluated. For example, suppose that the following formal educational objective has been selected by the school: "Following an initial period of adjustment, the child will demonstrate emotional independence by tolerating separation from meaningful family members during her day at the center." Which of the following checklist items should be selected as the most explicit one to use as a measure that the child is achieving independence?

1. The child rarely demonstrates her anxiety.
2. The child can wave good-bye to her mother without undue stress.
3. The child enters into a nursery school activity within 10 minutes after her mother's departure.
4. The child exhibits a favorable attitude toward her teachers.

Numbers 1 and 4 are not clearly related to the stated goal. Number 2 is probably a good item to use, although the phrase "without undue stress" may vary in interpretation from teacher

to teacher. Number 3 is the clearest statement of the four and should be included on the list.

When composing such lists, the teacher also must keep them within reason in terms of developmental levels. It can be frustrating and discouraging to both a child and teacher if the teacher expects behavior that lies beyond the child's developmental ability to achieve. For this reason, it cannot be recommended too strongly that developmental charts, such as the one included in Appendix A, be consulted when checklists are being constructed. Several resources are listed at the end of this chapter. Where such material is not available, the lists should be based on recommendations of experienced early childhood teachers.

One final admonition about the construction of checklists must be added. If the list is to be used in the manner suggested at the end of this chapter to summarize data for fiscal reports, it is necessary to phrase the behavior items so they are all positive behaviors that the teacher desires to have increase during the school year. An item should be phrased "able to share teacher with others" rather than "clings to teacher, fights other children off from her." If a positive form is not followed and a mixture of positive and negative descriptions is used, some of the behaviors will be marked as increasing and others as decreasing during the year. The result should be that the losses and gains cancel each other out, and no improvement could be revealed by the final scores.

Be careful to present checklist material to each child in the same way. Sometimes it can be a temptation to change the way a checklist item is presented in accord with the personality or skills of a particular child. For instance, a teacher might unconsciously take a few steps forward to shorten the distance when throwing a ball to a younger child, or in recording balance beam walking she might allow more accomplished children to walk on the narrow beam but use the wider side for a less able child, yet she will mark all the children as successful on the checklist. Such inconsistencies

FIGURE 7–1

A Sampling of Some Social-Emotional Competences for 4-Year-Olds

	Not able to observe	Not yet accomplished	Accomplished	Highly accomplished	Not able to observe	Not yet accomplished	Accomplished	Highly accomplished	Not able to observe	Not yet accomplished	Accomplished	Highly accomplished
Name _____												
Date of Birth _____												
Social Competence												
Able to share teacher with others												
Willing to bargain to attain goals												
Able to share when he or she has enough for him- or herself												
Able to show or express concern for other people												
TOTAL												
Coping Techniques												
Able to express liking for other children and adults												
Able to express anger in a way that does not damage people or equipment												
Able to confront adult directly when adult has caused child to feel angry												
Able to maintain sustained friendships with other children												
TOTAL												
Self-Confidence												
Able to hold his or her own when challenged (confident, not unduly intimidated)												
Likes to try new things												
Takes criticism and reprimands in stride												
Able to adjust to change in routines or people in the center												
TOTAL												
Autonomy and Independence												
Enters into center activity within 10 minutes after mother's departure												
Spends more time with own age group than with adults												
Relates to more than one adult at school												
Appears independent—when given the opportunity, able to make decisions for him- or herself												
TOTAL												
GRAND TOTAL												

Date: _____ Date: _____ Date: _____
Recorder: _____ Recorder: _____ Recorder: _____

Note. From Santa Barbara City College Children's Center, 1975.

make comparison between children impossible and spoil the accuracy of the group report. Hardhearted as it may seem at first, if a specific measure of accomplishment is included, it is essential to measure all the children against the same standard. The way to adjust a checklist to include less skilled children is to provide several different task levels, ranging from easier to more difficult, for the children to attempt. In the case of the balance beam, this might mean that all children are asked to try both the broad and narrow beams.

Sometimes also the teacher gradually changes the method of presenting a checklist item as she becomes more experienced using it and figures out a "better" way to do it. Doing this must also be avoided. Every item must be presented in the same manner from the first test to the last if comparisons are to be drawn between subjects or even if comparisons are to be made between early and later performances of the same child. To draw valid conclusions, the teacher must compare the same behaviors, not different ones.

Beware of the getting-better-and-better syndrome. Although it is a happy fact that many children will make progress, it is also true that some children will not, at least not in all areas. To avoid tester bias, which may view every child as getting better and better all the time, the teacher must discipline herself to observe behavior objectively so that she sees it as it is rather than as she wishes it to be. The development of explicit descriptions of behavior as checklist items will help the teacher be objective in her judgment. It is also helpful to have another teacher participate in the evaluation when possible.

A different kind of tester bias that must also be guarded against is the tendency of some teachers to check the same level of accomplishment for most items on a child's checklist. This is sometimes termed the *halo effect*. Again, the teacher must discipline herself to consider each item on the list on its own merits to resist the influence of the halo effect as much as possible.

Using Commercial Tests

Before deciding to use commercial standardized tests, consider the drawbacks carefully because they raise many objections.

We have only to ask ourselves, as adults, why we dislike taking tests to gain insight into some of the reasons we should avoid using them with little children. Test situations create tension and anxiety; tests often do not find out what the person knows but what they do *not* know; the result is that tests often make us feel inadequate.

Some of the reasons for restricting their use cited by the National Association for the Education of Young Children (1988) and the Southern Association for Children under Six (1990) are that such tests provide extremely narrow assessments of skills, the form of the tests and the methods of administration are often developmentally inappropriate, people put too much trust in the results, tests tend to label children unfairly or prematurely, and the testing situations are unrealistic.

An inspection of test information compiled by Johnson (1979), Bracken (1987), and Meisels and Atkins-Burnett (1994) reveals additional weaknesses. The majority of commercial preschool tests are of poor quality and do not meet adequate standards of reliability and/or validity; they require one-to-one administration, which can be time-consuming and inconvenient to arrange, even for a class of 15 children; many tests have professional restrictions requiring that they be administered by a psychologist, a service rarely available to centers or preschools; the tests are expensive to purchase; and tests that measure exactly what the early childhood teacher wishes to measure can be difficult or impossible to find.

Finally, there is the disadvantage that many commercial tests appear to favor the white, middle-class child and are inappropriate to use with children who come from poor families, who are bilingual, or who come from backgrounds that differ from that of middle-class, white society (Bernal, 1993; de Barona Santos & Barona, 1991).

Since there are so many disadvantages, does this mean teachers should never use a commercially developed test?

Despite all the drawbacks it is also true that it is sometimes useful to include a good-quality standardized test as *part* of the information included in the child's portfolio (Mindes, Ireton, & Mardell-Czudnowski, 1996). If the teacher selects a test that has been normed on many other children of varying ethnic groups and cultural backgrounds, a well-designed test enables the teacher to compare that child's performance with what other children of the same age are able to do. This can help determine who may be either lagging behind or so far ahead they would benefit from special assistance.

Using a standardized measure also enables the teacher (and other people such as administrators) to compare the performance of the group with a larger, national sample. Although this practice is often criticized because it may encourage teachers to teach to the test instead of to the needs of the children, the truth is that many school systems still require this kind of numerical data as part (or all) of their accountability procedures. This makes it even more crucial that the tests selected be as good quality as possible.

Criteria for Selection of Commercial Tests

It is never safe to assume that just because a test has been published somewhere or is offered in a glossy brochure it is good quality. One has only to look at the ratings of 40 currently available screening tests listed by Grace and Shores (1991) to be reminded of the extreme variability of quality.

Well-developed tests will always include information on what kinds of children and how many of them were included in the original standardization of the test. For the test to be fair, it is of great importance that this original sample include an adequate mix of youngsters from various economic levels and ethnic groups in our society.

High-quality tests also make a point of reporting *validity* and *reliability*. The *content validity* of a test has to do with whether the test measures what it says it does. For example, if the test claims that it measures self-esteem, is that what it really measures? Another kind of validity, known as *predictive validity*, has to do with how well the test predicts future outcomes (e.g., how well the test might predict future performance of the child in school).

Reliability is the degree to which test scores can be counted on to be consistent when the test is repeated. For example, if the same child took the test again within a few days, would the score be about the same?

Occasionally tests publish this information in their brochures, but usually it is necessary to write to the publisher and request data on the test's population sample, reliability, and validity. These reports should be shown to someone who is knowledgeable about test construction and administration. School psychologists, for instance, are usually glad to help with this kind of evaluation and can determine whether the standards are high enough to make the test of real value.

Several Different Kinds of Commercial Tests

Generally speaking, there are four kinds of commercial tests used to assess young children; the first two are of special concern to preschool teachers (adapted from National Association for the Education of Young Children, 1988, p. 45):

- *Screening tests* (also called *developmental screening tests*)—tests used to identify children who *may* be in need of special services, as a first step in identifying children in need of further diagnosis; focuses on the child's ability to acquire skills. It is very desirable to include hearing and vision assessments as part of the screening procedures.
- *Readiness tests*—assessments of child's level of preparedness for a specific academic or preacademic program. Screening tests and readiness tests typically measure skills and

behaviors previously found to be typical of a large group of children of the same chronological age.

- *Achievement tests*—tests that measure the extent to which a person has mastery over a certain body of information or possesses a certain skill after instruction has taken place
- *Intelligence and other diagnostic tests*—a series of tasks yielding a score indicative of cognitive or other types of functioning

The Pros and Cons of Using Screening and Readiness Tests

The purpose of screening tests is to assist administrators in finding children with disabilities who need special services and in identifying those children who are "developmentally immature" and not ready for kindergarten. Once children who appear to be lagging behind their peers are identified, they can be provided with whatever special services they require. That function is particularly useful when conducting "Child Find" searches intended to locate youngsters who would benefit from special services because they are disabled in some way.

As the research report on page 128 reveals, it is always necessary to regard these preliminary screening results with caution. If circumstances warrant, screening tests should always be followed by more intensive examinations and whatever special help is found to be necessary. The sooner such help is available, the more effective it is likely to be.

However, the other purpose—determining maturity and readiness for kindergarten entry—is currently the subject of considerable controversy (Graue, 1993; Hewit & Baker, 1995). For example, the position paper on school readiness of the National Association for the Education of Young Children (1990) states:

> It is often assumed that tests exist to reliably determine which children are "ready" to enter school. Because of the nature of child development and how children learn, it is extremely difficult to develop reliable and valid measures of young children's abilities. When tests are used to make decisions which have such considerable impact on children's lives as denial of entry or assignment to a special class, they must offer the highest assurance of reliability and validity. No existing readiness measure meets these criteria. *Therefore, the only legally and ethically defensible criterion for determining school entry is whether the child has reached the legal chronological age of school entry.* (p. 22)

Despite such strong statements, some people continue to argue in favor of providing extra time for a child to mature (Gesell Institute, 1987). This is thought to be particularly true for boys born during the second half of the year before kindergarten entry. Just about every teacher can cite examples of children who made satisfying growth during that extra year—growth that enabled them to function more effectively when they entered more formal schooling a year later.

Another side to the issue, however, also has merit. This is the argument that simply allowing extra time for a child to mature is not enough (Meisels, 1996). Healthy development entails more than maturation. Children, particularly those who are immature, require stimulation and the opportunity to learn. When children are "held out" or "kept out," there is no accurate way to tell whether they might have caught up and benefited from their year in kindergarten because they have not had the opportunity of attending. Proponents of this side of the argument maintain that it is the *school* that should change, not the child (Southern Regional Education Board, 1994). At the very least, it seems sensible that children with delayed admission have the opportunity for appropriate preschool experience during the year of deferral.

This argument over the value of delayed admission is not completely settled yet, and because both sides have merit, it remains up to the reader to decide with which faction to agree. But whichever side is selected, it is important to remember that when a screening test singles out a particular child as needing help, the screening test must be regarded as just the first step in the

Research Study

How Much Should We Really Rely on the Results of Screening Tests?

Research Questions Glascoe and Byrne wanted to find out how accurately three commonly used screening tests identified children with developmental problems. They wanted to see whether the three tests underselected (i.e., missed children who had problems and needed extra help) or *overselected* children (i.e., singled children out as needing help who actually were developing adequately). In other words, the investigators wanted to find out how *sensitive* the tests were to identifying youngsters with special developmental problems.

Research Method The investigators selected three widely used screening tests: the Developmental Profile—II (Alpern, Boll, & Shearer, 1986), the Denver—II (Frankenburg et al., 1990), and the Battelle Developmental Inventory Screening Test (Newborg, Stock, Wnek, Guidubaldi, & Svinicki, 1984). The sample was composed of 89 children and their parents. Forty-three girls and 46 boys participated, ranging from 7 to 70 months of age. The majority of the children were black and came from low-income families.

One investigator administered the three screening tests to each youngster, and a different investigator administered a group of highly researched diagnostic tests to the same children. The diagnostic tests were used as comparison measures for the screening tests.

Results Of the 89 children, 18 were identified by the more thorough and reliable *diagnostic* tests as being disabled. Seventy-one youngsters were identified as nondisabled. Then these results were compared to the results from the three screening tests.*

The investigators found that "the Academic Scale of the Developmental Profile—II failed to identify the majority of children with developmental difficulties " (p. 375). "The Denver—II produced more incorrect than correct identifications" (p. 376). The Battelle Developmental Inventory Screening Test "appeared to out perform the other two measures although it, too, is not immune from inaccuracies . . . |since| over-referrals were somewhat higher than is desirable" (p. 376).

Implications Few would disagree with the premise that it is worthwhile to identify children who have special developmental difficulties and arrange to provide them with the help they need as early in their lives as possible.

However, we must always remember that important decisions about children's lives are often based on the results of tests, so it is extremely important to understand the limitations and problems inherent in their use. *This is particularly true of brief, poorly researched screening instruments.* At best, such testing should be regarded as the first, very tentative step toward identifying children who need or do not need special help. This is because, as Glascoe and Byrne point out, "All screening tests contain error. Minimizing this error is essential due to the high costs involved: children may be under-detected and miss crucial opportunities for early intervention, or they may be over-referred, which is expensive, anxiety provoking for parents, and a waste of limited diagnostic resources" (p. 377).

The moral for teachers is plain—even when reputable, standardized screening tests are used, great care must be taken in their selection and interpretation because, as this study reveals, their quality is often inadequate.

*Space does not permit a more detailed report of the investigators' findings. Readers who require that information are referred to the original article: "The Accuracy of Three Developmental Screening Tests" by F. P. Glascoe and K. E. Byrne, *Journal of Early Intervention,* 17 (4), pp. 368–379.

diagnostic process. As the research by Glascoe and Byrne (1993; see p. 128) reminds us, screening tests are notoriously brief and inaccurate (Meisels & Atkins-Burnett, 1994). Therefore, follow-up, in-depth testing is essential before any final decisions are made.

Using the Information That Has Been Collected

Developing an Individualized Curriculum

For the individual child's well-being, the most important use of checklists, observations, and interviews is the use of the portfolio to identify strengths and difficulties so that learning activities may be provided that will help the youngster develop as well as possible.

For example, when the teacher looked over one such checklist, she was alerted to the fact that Jeannie had several "hardly ever" ratings on a portion of her Social-Emotional Competence Scale. A further perusal of the anecdotal records contributed to the picture of a 4-year-old girl who was new to school and who, though appearing to like the other children, stuck close to the teacher and was unable to share whatever she played with. The parent interview added the information that Jeannie was an only child who lived in a neighborhood where there were no other children. When these pieces of information were put together, Jeannie emerged as being a socially inexperienced 4-year-old rather than the "spoiled little girl" she might have seemed at face value. The information not only increased the teacher's understanding but also her liking for the child. It also helped her plan a curriculum that was built on Jeannie's liking of other people and that sought to develop her confidence and trust. This enabled Jeannie to gradually let go of teachers and equipment more easily and make friends with the other youngsters.

Making Reports to the Family

Preparation for a parent conference is much easier when records have been kept in a systematic manner. The material is already at the teacher's fingertips and needs only to be reviewed before the family's arrival. Such records may be referred to in a general, summarizing way or in terms of more specific behaviors as the occasion warrants. When these materials are shared with the parents and, hopefully, the parents have also contributed to the array, the resulting discussion can be much more revealing and satisfactory than presenting the family with a report card.

Indeed, I never think of "report" cards without recalling a quotation from John Gatto (1992) in *Dumbing Us Down*:

> A monthly report, impressive in its provision, is sent into a student's home to elicit approval or mark exactly, down to a single percentage point, how dissatisfied with the child a parent should be. The ecology of "good" schooling depends on perpetuating dissatisfaction. . . . Although some people might be surprised how little time or reflection goes into making up these mathematical records, the cumulative weight of these objective-seeming documents establishes a profile that compels children to arrive at certain decisions about themselves and their futures based on the casual judgment of strangers. (p. 10)

It would do no harm if every teacher would read this quote over before every parent-teacher conference.

Preparing Reports for Official Boards and Funding Agencies

With increasing frequency, teachers and directors of day-care centers are being required to present annual summaries of the children's progress to justify continuation of funding. Many staff members are uncertain about how to present such information effectively, even though they have faithfully kept track of the children's growth during the year. A useful method of summarizing data when such reports are required is found in Appendix B. It shows how checklist information can be converted to numerical data to provide evidence for those reports.

Summary

Evaluation is a valuable process that early childhood teachers can use for describing children and measuring changes in their behavior. However, great care must be taken when selecting such measures. Teachers must be careful not to place too much confidence in the results of preliminary screening devices. They should also restrict conclusions based on their own teacher-made tests.

Practical methods of recording and evaluating behavior include the use of parent interviews, anecdotal records, checklists, and occasional commercially developed tests.

Evaluation that is systematically carried out increases knowledge of the individual child, facilitates the planning of an individualized curriculum, and makes reporting to parents a simple matter. It also provides useful data on which to base reports to advisory boards and funding agencies.

Self-Check Questions for Review

Content-Related Questions

1. What are the advantages of including evaluation procedures in an early childhood program?
2. The text lists some basic principles of evaluation. Tell what these are and explain why each is important.
3. Parent interviews are one useful source of information about children. Name three additional sources teachers can use to obtain useful information about children.
4. Commercial tests can be helpful to use, but they also have potential drawbacks. Discuss the pros and cons of using such tests.
5. What are the desirable and undesirable aspects of using screening tests with young children?

6. What are the reasons the National Association for the Education of Young Children gives for objecting to the use of readiness tests to determine when children should be admitted to kindergarten?

Integrative Questions

1. You are a kindergarten teacher in a school district that requires you to use the Batelle Developmental Inventory as a screening test. According to Glascoe and Byrne's (1993) research, what kinds of scores should you be particularly wary of believing when looking at the results of that screening test?
2. Compare checklists and rating scales. How are they alike and how do they differ?
3. The people who argue against the value of holding "developmentally immature" children out of school for a year maintain that it is the school that should change rather than the child who should wait. Which solution do you think is the more practical way to deal with the maturity variability of young children? Should they be held out of school for a year? Or should the expectations of the school be changed?

Questions and Activities

1. Testing and keeping checklists are a lot of work and also time-consuming. Are these activities really worth the time and trouble? What other equally satisfactory methods of identifying skills or lags in development might be employed in place of these?
2. Your school is funded by a state that requires you to administer a variety of pretests and posttests to the children to determine the effectiveness of the program. This year you are horrified to discover that the posttest results indicate that the children have made little improvement in language development when compared with the national norm included with the test information. You are in charge of the program. What would you do about this result?
3. In your opinion, what should become of evaluative records once the child has left the preschool? Should they be forwarded to the next school, for example? Should they be destroyed? Should they be saved for a number of years? Think carefully about the pros and cons of taking any of these actions.
4. Assess the needs of some youngsters in your school as they have been revealed by your evaluation

materials. On the basis of these findings, suggest activities that you feel could be used to develop the youngsters' weaker areas by drawing on their strengths as identified by the evaluation procedures.

5. If you were the teacher and had written the following notes in Patty's anecdotal record, how would you summarize her behavior? Then what objective might you pick for the following week, and what plans would you suggest to implement that objective?

When our new child, Willie, hit Patty and grabbed the book she was holding, she said,"You stupid! You spastic!—give it back!" Later on I heard her call someone else a "dummy" because they wouldn't play with her. Last week she called a teacher a "nerd" because he wouldn't let her go outside.

6. You have been appointed to work with another staff member to develop a checklist to evaluate what the children have learned in the Let's Find Out corner. She has a friend who works in another school that also offers a discovery area, so she suggests that you just use their checklist for the evaluation because it would save so much work. Would you agree to do this? Explain why or why not.

7. You are now a parent and you have a child getting ready to enter kindergarten. You have heard that the district is considering using a prekindergarten screening test for the first time. Would you encourage or discourage the adoption of this policy? Explain the basis for your preference.

References for Further Reading

Overviews

Gullo, D. F. (1994). *Understanding assessment and evaluation in early childhood education.* New York: Teachers College Press. This brief book provides a simple overview of the subject. A good place to begin.

McAfee, O. I., & Leong, D. (1994). *Assessing and guiding young children's development and learning.* Boston: Allyn & Bacon. This book covers just about everything you might ever want to know about this subject, including an appendix that lists examples of behaviors to look for, four of the five selves, plus developmental chronologies. *Highly recommended.*

Wortham, S. (1995). *Tests and measurement in early childhood education.* (2nd ed.). Upper Saddle River, NJ: Merrill/Prentice Hall. Wortham provides helpful discussions of standard-

ized testing and how to develop checklists and conduct observations.

Position Papers from Various Organizations

National Association for the Education of Young Children. (1988). NAEYC position statement on standardized testing of young children 3 through 8 years of age. *Young Children, 43*(3), 42–47.

National Association for the Education of Young Children. (1990). NAEYC position statement on school readiness. *Young Children, 46*(1), 21–23.

National Association for the Education of Young Children and the National Association of Early Childhood Specialists in State Departments of Education. (1991). Guidelines for appropriate curriculum content and assessment in programs serving children ages 3 through 8. *Young Children, 46*(3), 21–37.

Peronne, V. (1991). On standardized testing. *Childhood Education, 67*(3), 132–142.

Screening Tests

Meisels, S. J., & Atkins-Burnett, S. (1994). *Developmental screening in early childhood: A guide.* Washington, DC: National Association for the Education of Young Children. This invaluable guide explains clearly what standards must be applied when selecting a screening test, limitations to their use, and how to use follow-up procedures. It includes a copy of NAEYC's position statement on standardized testing.

Developmental Checklists

Beaty, J. J. (1994). *Observing development of the young child* (3rd ed.). Upper Saddle River, NJ: Merrill/Prentice Hall. Beaty offers many examples of appropriate checklist items.

Bentzen, W. R. (1991). *Seeing young children: A guide to observing and recording behavior* (2nd ed.). Albany, NY: Delmar. This is a how-to book distinguished by the inclusion of lists of developmental characteristics.

Portfolios

Grace, K., & Shores, E. F. (1991). *The portfolio and its use: Developmentally appropriate assessment of young children.* Little Rock, AR: Southern Association for Children under Six. *The Portfolio and Its Use* includes assessment of many commonly used assessment measures together with a clear description of how to assemble a portfolio of children's work. *Highly recommended.*

Meisels, S. J. (1992). *The work sampling system: An overview.* Ann Arbor: Center for Human Growth and Development, University of Michigan. The overview describes how to compile a work sample or portfolio for a child. The checklists range from preschool through grade three and cover seven areas of development.

Wesson, C. L., & King, R. P. (1996). Portfolio assessment and special education students. *Teaching Exceptional Children*, 28(2), 44–48. This is a very practical article that focuses on elementary-age children but offers many points that can be adapted to preschool youngsters.

Taking Diversity into Account

Bergen, D., & Moseley-Howard, S. (1994). Assessment perspectives for culturally diverse young children. In D. Bergen (Ed.), *Assessment methods for infants and toddlers: Transdisciplinary team approaches*. New York: Teachers College Press. The authors point out various ways differing cultural backgrounds can affect assessment results—a valuable resource.

For the Advanced Student

Bondurant-Utz, J. A., & Luciano, L. B. (1994). *A practical guide to infant and preschool assessment in special education*. Boston: Allyn & Bacon. Although targeted to readers concerned with children who have possible disabilities, this book offers a wealth of information about cultural diversity, working with families, and so forth, valuable for everyone. An appendix lists a selection of preschool tests together with brief descriptions and information about reliability and validity.

Goodman, J. F. (1992). *When slow is fast enough: Educating the delayed preschool child*. New York: Guilford. Goodman relates the results of a 3-year ethnographic study and presents potent evidence that children with developmental delays are often taught inappropriately. This is a thoughtful book that early childhood educators will appreciate and that will antagonize some special education teachers for the same reasons.

Jervis, K. (1996). *Eyes on the child: Three portfolio stories*. New York: Teachers College Press. Jervis traces the way teachers in three very different settings went about defining and using portfolios as a means of assessing what their children were learning.

Mallory, B. L., & New, R. S. (1994). *Diversity and developmentally appropriate practices: Challenges for early childhood education*. New York: Teachers College Press. This seminal book produces more questions than answers about the effects of culture on development and teachers' sensitivity and consequent undervaluing of those effects on the children in their care. Several chapters are particularly relevant to the problem of fair assessment.

Neill, M., Bursh, P., Schaeffer, B., Thall, C., Yohe, M., & Zappardino, P. (n.d.). *Implementing performance assessments: A guide to classroom, school and system reform*. Cambridge, MA: FairTest: National Center for Fair & Open Testing. This is a good, concise guide to performance assessments. Like most publications in this field, it focuses on older children, but the basic approach and suggestions are useful.

Resources of Further Interest

FairTest: The National Center for Fair & Open Testing. 342 Broadway, Cambridge, MA 02139. This organization offers a number of stimulating books and booklets and publishes a quarterly newsletter, *FairTest Examiner* ($20 a year).

8

Keeping Children Safe and Well Fed

Have you ever

- Worried how to tell whether something was safe for the children to do?
- Wondered whether there was any way to stem the tide of colds sweeping over your center?
- Wanted to include cooking for the twos but thought they were too young to do it?

If you have, the material in this chapter will help you.

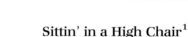

Sittin' in a High Chair[1]

Sittin' in a high chair, big chair, my chair,

Sittin' in a high chair, bang my spoon!

Sittin' in a high chair, big chair, my chair,

Sittin' in a high chair, feed me soon!!

Bring on the plate, bring on the cup,

Never going to fill this baby up!

Bring on bananas, bring on the bread,

Mama's gotta get this baby fed!

Sittin' in a high chair, big chair, my chair,

Sittin' in a high chair, bang my spoon!

Sittin' in a high chair, big chair, my chair,

Sittin' in a high chair, feed me soon!

Bring on the carrots, bring on the peas,

Mama come serve this baby please!

Bring on the pancakes stacked in a pile,

Papa's going to make this baby smile!

Sittin' in a high chair, big chair, my chair,

Sittin' in a high chair, bang my spoon!

Sittin' in a high chair, big chair, my chair,

Sittin' in a high chair, feed me soon!

Bring on the napkins, bring on the sponge,

Clean me up cuz I'm all done!

Hap Palmer and Martha Cheney (1984)

I love this song because of its lustiness. If only we can convey this same sense of gusto and delight to children, we will transmit a worthwhile value about the pleasures their bodies can provide.

There are really two ways of helping children feel good about their bodies. The first consists of all the things we do to foster good health, safety, and sound physical development while we care for children during the day. The second comprises the curriculum we plan that encourages children to understand, cherish, and care for their bodies. Both approaches, however, should have the same basic goals: keeping children safe and healthy, feeding them well, teaching them to understand and value life, and providing plenty of pleasurable opportunities for the growth of physical expertise.

---

[1]To be sung to the tune "Shortnin' Bread."

Keeping Children Safe

Good teachers must be unceasingly aware of what children are doing and occasionally move quickly to forestall an accident because unfortunately every year in the United States one child in three is injured severely enough to require medical attention (Children's Safety Network, 1996). The problem for beginning teachers is to know when to intervene and when not to. It is very easy for them to be so overprotective that the children absorb their apprehension and, interpreting this as a vote of no confidence, lose confidence in themselves. This is surely undesirable. On the other hand, there is no doubt that children must be stopped quickly from running in front of a moving swing or stepping backward off the playhouse roof. The question is, How can you as a teacher tell when an activity should be stopped and when it should be allowed to continue?

Use common sense and learn to worry about the right things. If whatever the child is doing is likely to seriously hurt himself or someone else, then it is time to stop him; but if the danger is relatively slight and he is likely to learn something valuable from the experience (such as it is a good idea to keep your fingers out of the way when using a hammer), then let him continue. Anytime you are truly dubious about the safety of a particular activity, it is wiser to stop it temporarily and ask the master teacher to help you and the child evaluate the situation. Certainly it is better to be safe than sorry.

Look over the play yard with a critical eye for safety before the children arrive. Tricycle handle bars unprotected by rubber end guards can deliver nasty cuts to the forehead of a child who tips over on them, wooden swing seats can loosen teeth, and rickety climbing equipment can come to pieces and really harm youngsters. Glass bottles (no matter how small and sturdy) at the water table may cut, as may rusty cans and metal toys in the sandbox. Splintery boards literally leave painful reminders behind. Constant vigi-

Buying equipment that has safety features "built in" allows children to make the most of their opportunities to be independent.

lance is needed to make certain that all decaying equipment is either removed or repaired immediately (Aronson, 1992; Frost, 1992a).

It is particularly important to make certain all swing seats are made of canvas or rubber because 25% of all playground injuries result from children being struck by or falling from this piece of equipment. In addition, it is vitally important to maintain a resilient surface under swings and climbing equipment. Most of us do not realize that "when a 4 foot tall child falls from a height of 5 feet, he may hit the ground at 16 miles per hour" (Frost, 1992a, p. 239). This fact explains why falls often produce serious head injuries. A number of commercially developed products on the market are developed to cushion falls safely, or many utility companies will provide large quantities of shredded plant materials free of charge. The amount of

If the danger is relatively slight, let him continue.

On the other hand, sometimes the teacher must move quickly!

shredded bark needed to prevent injuries varies from 6 to 12 inches depending on the height of equipment, but it is always better to have too much rather than too little (Kendrick, Kaufmann, & Messenger, 1995). Sand can also be used but tends to create problems because children like to play in it and may put themselves in dangerous proximity to equipment as they play.

Enlist parents in the campaign to keep children safe. Two examples of possible safety programs that parents should attend include fire safety in the home and the use of safety car seats for young children.

Fire departments are usually delighted to send speakers and pamphlets on fire safety. All families should discuss and practice ways of leaving their homes in emergencies, and all children should be taught to "stop, drop, and roll" rather than run should their clothing catch fire.

If a parent program presents this material in a calm, matter-of-fact way, it can be done without arousing too much anxiety, and, more important, it may save lives or the terrible pain and disfigurement resulting from burns.

Fortunately, in the past few years many states have passed legislation encouraging the use of safety car seats. As an early childhood teacher who sees families deliver children by car every day, you are in an excellent position to remind and encourage parents to obey this law. The teacher should become acquainted with the resources in the community that make these seats available free to families who could not otherwise afford them. An evening program could emphasize this information and make it available to all (Child Health Alert, 1996).

Teach children to think about safety for themselves; this is probably the best way to keep them safe. Help

Gates must be closely supervised at all times.

them anticipate consequences and evaluate *beforehand* what the result will be of what they want to do. This is hard to accomplish without moralizing. A frightened teacher finds it easy to blame a child for an accident by saying something like, "See, I told you not to run with your socks on. I told you the floor is slippery—I was right, wasn't I? See, you hurt yourself, didn't you?" How much better it would have been if the teacher had said before the accident, "Our rule is, 'We only dance in bare feet.' Now why do we have that rule?" The teacher also should demonstrate how slippery the floor is when wearing socks. Or, when out of doors, she might say, "That looks pretty high to me. Try jumping from lower down first and see what that feels like, then we'll decide together whether it's safe to jump from higher up in the tree."

Prepare an emergency plan in advance. These plans need to cover a variety of possibilities, such as what to do when a child is seriously hurt, how to leave the building safely and where to go should a fire break out, and how to deal with other unanticipated emergencies such as earthquakes or tornadoes.

Emergency instructions should be posted in several places throughout the school together with emergency phone numbers by the telephone, and these must be periodically reviewed during staff meetings. Parents, in particular, need to be reassured about how their children will be kept safe and where the children will be taken for safety should a crisis occur.

Both staff and children must have regular opportunities to practice how to behave in a potential disaster. This crisis proofing, if carried out in a matter-of-fact manner, does a lot to prevent panic. For example, if the children have heard the fire alarm before and know they should drop everything and go immediately to the door where the teacher is standing, they are not as likely to be paralyzed into inaction, and if the teacher practices in advance taking the attendance sheet and family reference file with her, she is more likely to remember them when they are sorely needed.

Of course, as our local disaster in Oklahoma City reminds me, it is impossible to anticipate all catastrophes in advance, and there are additional, long-term aspects of coping with them that space does not permit discussing here (Copeland, 1996). The most important thing to remember is that having an emergency plan and practicing it are essential parts of keeping children safe that must not be put off or ignored.

Keeping Children Healthy

Teaching Children to Follow Simple Rules of Hygiene

Perhaps because health and cleanliness do go together and "cleanliness is next to godliness," teachers tend to get preachy when they talk about health. At least at the preschool level, good health practices are generally better taught by example than taught in such units as "Our Friends, the Teeth" or "Milk Makes Strong Bones."

Very young children are largely unaware of their bodies as such and completely ignorant of how to care for them, so teachers can help them learn about good health care by setting a good example and by making sure the children follow certain basic rules of hygiene.

One of the most important of these is washing hands after toileting and before handling food. The importance of washing hands and learning to keep them away from eyes, noses, and mouths cannot be emphasized strongly enough for both children and adults. Doing this not only sharply reduces the number of colds in children's centers but also has been shown to lower the number of hepatitis A infections (Kendrick et al., 1995). Yet teachers frequently supervise hand washing by the children and fail to take advantage of this opportunity to wash their own, or they allow children to cook food without scrubbing up first.

Adjusting the amount of clothing to changes in temperature is another health rule well worth observing. Although doctors swear that becoming chilled is not related to catching a cold, experience has taught me that it is tempting fate to allow hot, sweaty children to get up from a nap and run outside into a cold wind. Unless temperature changes are called to the children's attention, it is unlikely that they will notice them and take

their sweaters off or put them on as needed. Teachers must remind them to do this.

Conducting a health check as children arrive is a mandatory part of the regulations of many states and should be carried out whether mandated or not. Parents are often hurried in the morning and fail to take a close look at their youngsters in the rush of getting off to the center. Moreover, a sick child presents a terrible dilemma for parents who may be torn between needing to go to work and needing to stay home to care for an ailing child. This is a dilemma for teachers, too. However, we must remember that the welfare of the group must be taken into account, as well as the needs of a particular family. Children who are contagious cannot be allowed to stay in the group even if they seem to feel up to doing so. (Refer to Appendix C for a chart of communicable diseases and methods of control.)

Some schools attempt to resolve this problem by maintaining lists of people who will care for children in such emergencies, but most schools just encourage parents to make plans in advance to handle such emergencies. Another solution for sick child care is the development of daily outpatient hospital care for children who are too sick to come to school and whose parents must go to work. Many families feel that the charges for this service, which are generally a few dollars more an hour than the usual provider care, are well worth the cost. When these resources fail or when the child becomes ill during the day, he should be isolated from the other children and kept comfortable and quiet until he can be taken home.

Keeping immunization records up-to-date also prevents the spread of various contagious diseases in the center and protects the community at large. Children's centers and nursery schools are typically the first institutions entered by young children; therefore, they can act as the first line of health checks for immunizations provided that they enforce their licensing requirements for admission.

Teachers often take immunizations for granted and do not realize that it is still necessary to be

It is important to take special care of children who have been sick.

very careful to make sure every child entering the program is fully immunized. At latest count, only three of four children in the United States had been immunized against the commonest infections. Although this is a desirable increase from the slightly more than half of them immunized in 1991, it still means that one in four 19- to 34-month-old youngsters were not protected from such scourges as diphtheria/tetanus/whooping cough, measles/mumps, and rubella (Children's Defense Fund, 1996a).

In recent years another disease nicknamed HIB (*Haemophilus influenzae*, type B) has come to the attention of pediatricians because of its potential seriousness for children of preschool age. HIB attacks 1 of every 200 children in the United States before age 5 and is responsible for over half of all cases of meningitis in children. It also produces joint infections that result in arthritis-like conditions and is thought to be responsible for the majority of ear infections as well. Fortunately, a new, safe vaccine is available for this disease, and although most states do not presently require it, the American Academy of Pediatrics and the United States Public Health Service recommend its administration. This protection is particularly desirable for chil-

dren in day care and kindergarten because they come into close contact with so many other children every day (Aronson, 1991). Teachers should be aware of this potentially serious disease and encourage parents to discuss the possibility of having their children vaccinated against it.

The fifth important health rule to follow is to take special care of children who have been sick. When a child returns to school following a bout of flu or an earache or something as serious as chicken pox or measles, he must be watched carefully for signs of complications, be kept warm, and not be allowed to become overtired. Even though his doctor has said that he can come back, this does not mean that he is in tip-top shape.

Feeding Children Well

Children, like the army, march on their stomachs. Yet all too many schools still rely on the old juice-and-cracker routine to see youngsters through the morning. Often today this is not even real fruit juice but some dye-laden, sugar-saturated synthetic. The only advantages of this policy are that it is quick and cheap, neither of which is in the best interests of children. Instead of settling for such trash, think of food as being one of the most important parts of the curriculum and plan for it accordingly.

Problems of Malnutrition

Perhaps the reader feels that the significance of good food is being emphasized unnecessarily because in many parts of the world children suffer from malnutrition to a much greater extent than they do in the United States. However, it is also true that hunger is far from unknown in our own land (Food, Research and Action Council, 1995). This is the case particularly among families of the poor (Cheung, 1995), but malnutrition also exists in special forms among more well-to-do families who allow their children to feast on the junk foods so persistently touted on television. Such inadequate diets result in decaying teeth, lowered resistance to infection, a reduced ability to pay attention, and (in more severe cases) general lethargy and slower-than-normal physical development.

Two Specific Health Problems

In the United States, two aspects of malnutrition among children of all economic levels deserve special discussion: dental decay and iron deficiency.

It has been estimated that 99% of all American children are affected by dental decay at one time or another (Williams, 1990). Although decay is related to a number of factors, including a child's inherent ability to resist infection, it is well substantiated that a diet high in refined sugar is *directly associated* with increased tooth decay. The most destructive sweetener is sucrose (common table sugar), the same sugar that occurs in brown sugar and molasses (Pipes, 1985). Sweet food that is sticky, such as candy, should be particularly avoided, because it stays on the teeth for a long time.

It is also important to realize that it is the *frequency* of eating sugar, rather than the total

Ninety-nine percent of American children are affected by dental decay at one time or another.

amount consumed, that makes the difference. Indeed, I have heard a children's dentist say desperately that he did not care how much sugar children ate if only they would eat it just once a day. But if a child eats jam or sweetened cereal for breakfast, then is fed a snack of graham crackers (think of how sticky they are), and then has pudding for lunch, sugar has been added at convenient 2-hour intervals to nourish the bacteria that secrete the acids and enzymes that make teeth vulnerable to decay. This is the reason it is worthwhile to plan snacks of popcorn, homemade peanut butter (most commercial peanut butter contains sugar), or carrot sticks with cottage cheese dip. Desserts of fresh fruit should also be featured. Reducing the sugar intake by these means controls bacteria by starving them. Day-care centers also should require tooth-brushing after lunch so that teeth are cleaned at least once a day. The brushes should be stored out of reach and exposed to light and air so that they dry as quickly as possible.

Iron deficiency anemia, according to Woteki and Filer (1995), is the most prevalent nutritional deficiency in the United States today, especially among children under 3, adolescent girls, and women during the childbearing years. It is also common among preschool children, particularly African American youngsters in whom 1 in 10 is likely to be anemic.

Insufficient iron produces pale, apathetic children who tire quickly and who catch cold easily. Teachers should watch for children who match this description, because such young-sters are probably in their rooms. When this condition is suspected, it should be drawn to the parents' attention so that they can discuss it with their physician. Meanwhile, the school can do its part in preventing anemia by planning meals that include organ meats (especially liver), meats, egg yolks, whole wheat, seafood, green leafy vegetables, nuts, dried fruit, and legumes.

We all can remember situations like this when the last thing in the world we wanted to do was "clear the plate"!

Planning Nutritious Food

One of the best things about children's centers is that most of them still retain the privilege of planning their own meals and snacks. This is ideal because it allows the director and staff to combine what they know about the food preferences of young children (plain familiar food, small portions, and finger foods are preferred) with knowledge of good nutrition. Appendix D provides examples of a set of menus that appeal to young children and satisfy nutritional requirements as well.

The Food Pyramid Guide (Figure 8–1) reminds us that well-balanced meals for children and adults should rest on a strong foundation of bread, cereal, and pasta and that the inclusion of fruits and vegetables is very important, too. These foods are generally low in fat and high in vitamins, minerals, and fiber and are important sources of sustained energy. Note that fats, oils, and sweets should be kept at a minimum. Although this balanced approach remains important throughout our lives, it is particularly important to honor when feeding young children. This is true not only because they are growing so fast but also because food preference habits formed in childhood persist into adulthood.

For meals to have maximum appeal, they should reflect the children's cultural backgrounds as well as be nutritious. Nothing fills a newcomer's heart with such despair as the sight of bowls and bowls of food he does not recognize and fears to eat. With a little imagination

FIGURE 8–1
Food Guide Pyramid

A Guide to Daily Food Choices

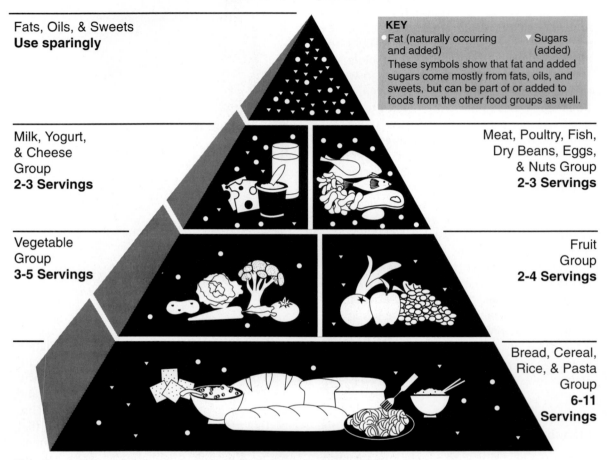

Fats, Oils, & Sweets
Use sparingly

KEY
○ Fat (naturally occurring   ▼ Sugars
   and added)   (added)
These symbols show that fat and added
sugars come mostly from fats, oils, and
sweets, but can be part of or added to
foods from the other food groups as well.

Milk, Yogurt,
& Cheese
Group
2-3 Servings

Meat, Poultry, Fish,
Dry Beans, Eggs,
& Nuts Group
2-3 Servings

Vegetable
Group
3-5 Servings

Fruit
Group
2-4 Servings

Bread, Cereal,
Rice, & Pasta
Group
**6-11
Servings**

Note. From U.S. Department of Agriculture/U.S. Department of Health and Human Services.

and sensitivity on the teacher's part, the misery of this experience can be avoided.

Young African American children, for example, may find mustard, turnip, and collard greens especially appealing and may like black-eyed peas and hominy grits. Mexicans, on the other hand, may find tortillas, *pan dulce*, salsa, and chili more to their taste. Japanese youngsters may prefer food flavored with soy sauce and may particularly enjoy fish, rice crackers, and soba (whole-wheat noodles). Although

these dishes are likely to be special favorites of children from these backgrounds, it is probable that *all* the children will come to enjoy them if they are gradually included in the menus. Because the majority of the group may be unfamiliar with these foods, the best approach may be to serve only one unfamiliar item at a time. Remember that to some of the children who come from differing backgrounds, most of the food at the center may be unfamiliar at least at first.

Can Children's Food Preferences Be Changed?

Research Study

Research Question   Birch asked the following questions: Can the attitude of peers change a child's attitude toward a particular food? If it can, is this a temporary change, or does the change in attitude persist?

Research Method   The sample consisted of 39 middle-class 3- and 4-year-olds. Each child was asked to rank nine vegetables from most to least preferred. (Vegetables such as corn, peas, raw mushrooms, and carrots were included.) Then a child who ranked corn, for example, as least liked and peas as most liked was seated for 4 days at lunchtime with three or four children who ranked corn as most liked. Each day the teacher offered a choice of corn or peas to the children. The first day the corn hater chose first. The next three days the corn lovers chose first, and the child who disliked corn chose his vegetables after seeing the other children's selection.

Results   Twelve of the 17 children who had originally disliked a particular vegetable showed an increased preference for it following exposure to children who preferred it. This result was statistically significant at .05.

More of the younger children changed their food preferences than older children did. There was no difference in behavior between boys and girls. Later on, when children were again asked to rank the same nine foods, the change in preference rankings continued for at least several weeks.

Therefore, it is reasonable to conclude that the attitude of peers *can* affect a child's attitude toward certain foods and that these changes in attitudes are not short-lived but have at least some lasting effect on a child's food preferences.

Implications   Birch says it well when she concludes, "If children were routinely exposed to children with differing food preferences, the set of foods they prefer could be enlarged" (p. 495).

I would add that if this positive result is true, a negative one may also be true. If a child hears a number of his peers being consistently negative about a particular food, he might also shift his opinion to an unfavorable one. For this reason, it is wise to encourage positive comments at snack and lunchtime and to discourage negative comments about food such as "This looks like dog poo-poo" while casually but quietly permitting children to refuse foods they dislike.

Note: From "Effect of Peer Models' Food Choices and Eating Behavior on Preschooler's Food Preferences" by L. L. Birch, 1980, *Child Development*, 51, pp. 489–496.

An example of one approach to dealing with children's unfamiliarity and/or having to confront foods they might dislike is detailed in the research study included in this chapter. Note in the report that there was no pressure on the teacher's part to encourage the children to enjoy or even taste the unpreferred food. Instead, the children were merely exposed to the example set by the other children.

One final word on nutrition. Children and adults need to drink plenty of fluids. Little children do not always realize they are thirsty, and so they often translate their discomfort into crabbiness. Although teachers may have to discourage children from filling up on milk and skipping the rest of their lunch, they should make certain that plenty of liquids are offered during the day. It is especially wise to be aware of this on hot afternoons and to offer every child a *cup* of water—a few swallows from a drinking fountain are insufficient.

Keeping Costs Down

As in all aspects of preschool management, costs must be taken into consideration with preparing menus. Table 8–1 presents a thoughtful plan that can keep down costs and still provide solid nutrition. Many schools, either privately or publicly supported, can also obtain additional funds for feeding children if they serve low-income families. More information on this subject may be obtained from the U.S. Department of Agriculture. School systems can usually supply the nearest address of this government agency.

Including Cooking in the Curriculum

Feeding children well in terms of snacks and lunches is important, but this is only half the nutrition story. The other half relates more directly to the children, because it centers on involving them in understanding about good food through cooking activities.

The value of providing such experiences frequently in the preschool is extraordinary because cooking offers so many different kinds of learning for all the child's selves, as Table 8–2 reveals. For the cognitive self there is learning how to measure and weigh, learning temporal sequence (first break the egg, then beat it, then mix it with the margarine), and learning the different flavors, tex-

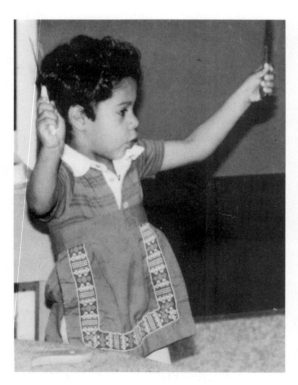 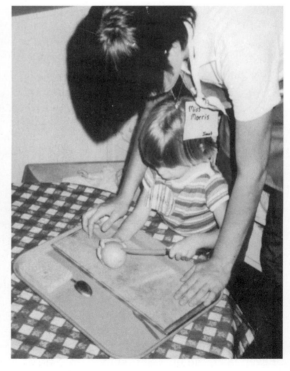

Children need careful, continuous supervision when using knives. Standing directly behind them provides good protection and control for everyone.

TABLE 8–1
Money Stretchers to Make Food Dollars Go Further

Food Groups	Usually Less Expensive, More Food Value for the Money	Usually More Expensive, Less Food Value for the Money
Milk products	Concentrated, fluid, and dry nonfat milk, evaporated, buttermilk	Fluid whole milk, chocolate drink, condensed milk, sweet or sour cream
	Mild cheddar, Swiss, cottage cheese	Sharp cheddar, Roquefort or blue, grated or sliced cheese, cream cheese, yogurt
	Ice milk, imitation ice milk, imitation ice cream	Ice cream, sherbet
Meats and meat substitutes		
Meat	Good and standard grades	Prime and choice grades
	Less tender cuts	Tender cuts
	Home-cooked meats	Canned meats, sliced luncheon meats
	Pork or beef liver, heart, kidney, tongue	Calf liver
Poultry	Stewing chickens, whole broiler-fryers, large turkeys	Poultry parts, specialty products, canned poultry, small turkeys
Fish	Rock cod, butterfish, and fresh fish in season, frozen fillets, steaks, sticks	Salmon, crab, lobster, prawns, shrimp, oysters
Eggs	Grade A	Grade AA
Beans, peas, and lentils	Dried beans, peas, lentils	Canned baked beans, soups
Nuts	Peanut butter, walnuts, other nuts in shell	Pecans, cashews, shelled nuts, prepared nuts
Vegetables, fruits	Local vegetables and fruits in season	Out-of-season vegetables and fruits, unusual vegetables and fruits, those in short supply

tures, and consistencies that teachers love to bring to the attention of children. Much cause-and-effect learning also is related to cooking, such as "Is it the water or the heat that made the egg hard?" Many plain facts are presented, too, such as the fact that eggs come from chickens.

Information about health and nutrition can be incorporated casually, but persistently, into cooking activities. This helps children understand the value good food has for keeping their bodies in good condition and helps them learn to take care of their physical selves.

Other, even more basic values than those listed here are inherent in the preparation of food, and these are closely bound up with the psychological value of nourishment. Young children equate food with love. This arises from their early feeding experiences in which love was embodied by the mother relieving the child's hunger with milk. What better ways, then, to continue to express caring and love to children than by feeding them well and allowing them to cook for themselves and other people? Cooking permits children not only to satisfy

TABLE 8–1
continued

Food Groups	Usually Less Expensive, More Food Value for the Money	Usually More Expensive, Less Food Value for the Money
Vegetables, fruits, *cont'd.*		
Vitamin A–rich	Carrots, collards, sweet potatoes, green leafy vegetables, spinach, pumpkin, winter squash, broccoli, and in-season cantaloupe, apricots, persimmons	Tomatoes, brussels sprouts, asparagus, peaches, watermelon, papaya, bananas, tangerines
Vitamin C–rich	Oranges, grapefruit, and their juice, cabbage, greens, green pepper, cantaloupe, strawberries, tomatoes, broccoli in season	Tangerines, apples, bananas, peaches, pears
Other	Medium-sized potatoes, nonbaking types	Baking potatoes, new potatoes, canned or frozen potatoes, potato chips
	Romaine, leaf lettuce	Iceberg lettuce, frozen specialty packs of vegetables
Breads, cereals	Whole-wheat and enriched four	Stone-ground, unenriched, cake flour
	Whole-grain and enriched breads	French, Vienna, other specialty breads, hard rolls
	Homemade rolls and coffee cake	Ready-made rolls and coffee cakes, frozen or partially baked products
	Whole-grain or restored uncooked cereals	Ready-to-eat cereals, puffed, sugar-coated
	Graham crackers, whole-grain wafers	Zwieback, specialty crackers, wafers
	Enriched uncooked macaroni, spaghetti, noodles	Unenriched, canned, or frozen macaroni, spaghetti, noodles
	Brown rice, converted rice	Quick-cooking, seasoned, or canned rice

Note: Revised by M. J. Ferree and C. C. Groppe. From *Balanced Food Values and Sense* (pp. 6–7) by F. Cook, C. Groppe, and M. Ferree, 1975, Berkeley: University of California, Division of Agricultural Sciences, Leaflet 2220. Used by permission.

their own needs but also to experience the satisfaction of nourishing others—an excellent opportunity for encouraging the development of the social self.

Moreover, because of the intense gratifications involved, cooking is one of the most ideal ways to incorporate multicultural values into the lives of young children. How better to learn that Jewish or African American or Italian or Mexican people are attractive than by preparing and eating something delicious that is typical of their culture? For example, our children have not only enjoyed the process of grinding, stirring, and baking that the following recipe requires but have also relished eating the result with a glass of orange juice for snack.

TABLE 8–2
What Can Children Learn from Experiences with Cooking?

Physical	Emotional	Social	Creative	Cognitive/Language
Encourages:	Encourages:	Encourages:	Encourages:	Encourages:
Good physical health produced by sound nutrition	Sense of satisfaction with life because of eating well	Working together to produce a result	Experimentation with changing flavors	Understanding of cause-effect relationships (application of heat, cold, additional liquid; effect of different cooking methods on same food — whipping or boiling eggs)
Learning through many sensory channels (tastes, smells, textures, temperatures; can you hear it? How does it sound when you chew it?)	Taking pleasure in activity — cooking is fun	Satisfaction of doing something to benefit the group	Use of own ideas with some foods: pizzas, tacos, fruit salad	
	Development of self-control while using kitchen tools, working with hot pans, etc.	Satisfaction in doing real, meaningful work (both cooking and cleaning up)	Arranging prepared food attractively	Understanding of measurement by various methods: temperature, liquid and dry measures (cups, spoonfuls), length of time, weight, development of increased vocabulary
Development of fine-muscle skills (chopping, mashing, peeling, stirring, kneading)	Ability to take (well-supervised) risks while handling tools such as knives, hot plates, etc.	Widening positive acquaintance with other cultures by experiencing their good-tasting foods	Note: Many people think of cooking as a creative experience; however, to purists there is a difference between "making" something and "creating" something. "Creativity" implies more self-expression than is intended by many recipes.	Practice in temporal ordering (sequence)
Understanding that good food helps you grow well and strong	Willingness to risk trying new flavors and unfamiliar foods	Learning that people meet the same need in different ways (e.g., make bread and compare with other kinds of breads)		Practice in classification skills
		Trying out adult role of parent in kitchen		Development of emergent literacy skills: "reading" picture recipe left to right; understanding value of number: how much, and how many?
		Idea that food is important to everyone in the world. We must share and not waste it.		Acquisition of facts about various foods (milk comes from cows; it provides butter, cheese, yogurt, ice cream, etc.)
				Acquisition of facts about nutrition
				Extended experiences: gardening, toothbrushing; going to the market; visiting ethnically oriented delicatessens; visiting a farm; seeing a cow milked at county fair

147

Zuni Bread

1½ c whole-wheat flour
1 c shelled, ground sunflower seeds (a food grinder will do)
1 T baking powder
1 t salt
2 eggs
4 T shortening
4 T honey
1 c milk
½ c whole unsalted sunflower seeds

Mix together dry ingredients. Beat eggs, shortening, and honey thoroughly and add to flour mixture with milk. Stir until smooth. Fold in whole seeds. Grease bread pan and flour bottom, and spoon in batter. Bake at 350° for 1 hour. Cool on rack for 10 minutes in pan. Remove, but do not slice until cold.

Basics for Choosing a Recipe

Pick a recipe that is not too delicate. Part of the cooking experience for children inevitably includes tasting everything, and this does take its toll in proportions. For this reason, it is often best to begin the cooking year with some items whose proportions do not matter much. For example, scrambled eggs with cheese, fruit salad, green salad, spaghetti, and vegetable soup all turn out well no matter what gets sampled along the way. (Incidentally, a good base for vegetable soup is tomato juice; this provides body, color, and flavor, without requiring that meat be added.)

Pick a recipe that has a lot of things for the children to do. Many recipes for little children seem to concentrate only on stirring, which usually means that everyone waits impatiently while each child takes two whacks with the spoon. To counteract this, look the recipe over and note whether there is enough variety to it. For example, compare the following two recipes and ask yourself these questions: How many different things will the children be able to do in each? What is the learning potential of each recipe? What is my opinion of the nutritional benefits to be obtained from each? Which would I choose as providing the most desirable curriculum opportunities for the children?

Nutritious-Delicious Cookies[1]

Measure and stir together the dry ingredients:

1⅓ c flour (unbleached)
1 t baking soda
½ t salt
½ t cinnamon
½ t (or less) nutmeg
¼ t (or less) cloves

Put the following in bowl and beat, combining first margarine and honey, then adding egg, and last the zucchini:

½ c margarine, softened
⅔ c honey
1 c grated zucchini
1 egg, beaten

Combine blended ingredients with dry ingredients. Then add the following:

½ c rolled oats
1 c dates, finely chopped
1 c walnuts, chopped
½ c coconut (optional)

Drop by heaping spoonfuls onto an oiled cookie sheet. Bake at 325° for 15 minutes until cookies are golden brown. Makes 36 cookies.

Instant Pudding[2]

Pour 2 cups cold milk into leakproof 1-quart container. Add one package (four-serving size) Jell-O Instant Chocolate Pudding; cover tightly. Shake vigorously at least 45 seconds. Pour at once into dishes. Pudding will thicken quickly. Ready to eat in 5 minutes. Ingredients: sugar, cornstarch modified, cocoa processed with alkali, sodium phosphates (for thickening), artificial flavor, hydrogenated soybean oil, titanium dioxide (for color), mono- and diglycerides (prevent foaming), red 40, yellow 5, natural flavor, blue 1, BHA, and citric acid (preservatives).

[1]From *Zucchini Cookbook* by V. Lemley and J. Lemley, 1976, Cave Junction, OR: Wilderness House. Copyright © 1976. Used by permission.
[2]From *Instant Jell-O Pudding & Pie Filling* (1996). Kraft General Foods, Inc., White Plains, NY.

Whenever possible, choose recipes that avoid refined flour and sugars because these have a deleterious effect on teeth. The use of whole grains, fresh fruits, and vegetables provides good sources of fiber while also providing wonderful opportunities to talk with children about eating those foods that both taste good and are good for them. Two examples of good cookbooks that stress nutrition are Jacobson and Hill's (1991) *Kitchen Fun for Kids* and Wilson's (1989) *The Good-for-Your-Health All-Asian Cookbook*. But nourishing recipes can be found anywhere. One of my student teachers modified a standard recipe and came up with the following:

Basic Muffins[3]

Measure and combine the dry ingredients:

2 c whole-wheat flour
3 t baking powder
½ t salt

Mash four ripe bananas—several children can do this in several small bowls. Put the following together in a bowl, combining first margarine and honey, then adding milk and beaten eggs:

½ c margarine (soft and warm)
¾ c milk
½ c honey
2 eggs, beaten

Stir in mashed banana. Combine wet and dry ingredients and pour into oiled muffin tins. Bake at 400° for 20 to 30 minutes. Yield: 18 large muffins.

Age-Appropriate Cooking Activities

Recipes must also be appropriate for the developmental levels of the child, and even children as young as 2½ enjoy cooking. Table 8–3 offers some examples of activities that are appropriate for children of various ages.

In addition to being durable, nutritious, and age appropriate and providing opportunities for participation, the recipe should be multiethnic if possible. Here is an example from *Kitchen Fun for Kids* (Jacobson & Hill, 1991) that offers a Mexican recipe that combines sound nutrition with regional background.

Soft Bean and Cheese Tacos[4]

6 soft corn tortillas
A chunk of Monterey Jack cheese
1 c home-cooked or canned pinto or kidney beans
3 medium-sized tomatoes
1 medium-sized onion
1 c chopped lettuce
½ c bottled salsa

Wrap tortillas in aluminum foil and place in middle of center rack in 275° oven. This will make the tortillas soft and warm.

Grate cheese to fill about ⅓ cup, using large-holes side of grater. Drain and rinse beans and place in bowl. Mash beans with potato masher or fork until slightly lumpy.

Wash tomatoes and remove stems; cut into bite size pieces. [For younger children, the teacher can remove skin first to make chopping easier. Plunge tomatoes into boiling water and then ice water to facilitate skin removal—children can help peel off the skin.] Peel away outer skin of onion and chop into very small pieces. [Cutting onions in half first makes peeling *much* easier.] Mix with the tomato or leave separated.

Shred lettuce and put salsa into low bowl.

Take warmed tortillas from oven; spread each with 1 heaping tablespoon of beans, then top with cheese, tomato, onion, lettuce, and salsa. Serves 3.

Per serving: calories, 313; protein, 15 g; carbohydrates, 4 g; sodium, 168 mg; fat, 7 g (21% calories).

Recipes that come from teachers' families are always cherished by the children. At Thanksgiving our head teacher shares a recipe and tradition from her Louisiana family.

---

[3]From Andrea Davis, class of 1978, Santa Barbara City College.

[4]From *Kitchen Fun for Kids* (pp. 42–43) by M. Jacobson and L. Hill, 1991, Washington, DC: Center for Science in the Public Interest. Copyright © 1991 Center for the Public Interest.

TABLE 8–3
Cooking Activities for Young Children of Differing Ages

Ages of Children	Suggested Cooking Activities	Comments
2- to 3-year-olds	Washing and scrubbing vegetables Peeling hard-boiled eggs Tearing lettuce for salad Fruit milkshakes (mash fruit, shake in plastic bottle) Mixing cottage cheese dips Fondue (grating cheese, etc.) Squeezing orange juice (press-down-type electric juicer) Potato salad (begin with boiled potatoes) Bananas rolled in honey and wheat germ Arranging pizza ingredients Deviled eggs Kneading bread Nachos	Utensils that work well with twos include wooden spoons, dull knives (for spreading things and for cutting soft substances, such as bananas), vegetable brushes, graters (particularly four-sided plastic ones), and sieves. Twos are interested in contrasting substances, such as cornmeal compared with unbleached flour and molasses with milk. Be prepared for a great deal of tasting and touching. Although fairly conservative about trying new foods at the table, they are often willing to taste bits of less familiar items while cooking them. Although these rules are important for all ages to remember, twos must be taught the simple rules of hygiene — you must wash your hands before cooking, and you must not touch your nose and then touch food the group is going to eat.
3- to 4-year-olds	Vegetable soup Scrambled eggs French toast (with whole-wheat bread) Fruit salad	Threes are able to use utensils, such as measuring cups and spoons, sharper knives, graters, peelers, juice squeezers, manually operated rotary egg beaters, and rolling pins. They like to

I want to thank Donna Coffman, former Director of the Santa Barbara City College Children's Center, for some of the suggestions included in this table.

Teachers who are uneasy about using heat while cooking with young children may want to refer to *Cool Cooking for Kids: Recipes and Nutrition for Preschoolers* by P. McClenahan and I. Jaqua (Belmont, CA: Fearon Pittman, 1976).

Sweet Potato Pie[5]

2 c cooked sweet potatoes
1 t cinnamon
¼ c sugar
2 T butter
3 eggs
¼ c evaporated milk

[5]From Clevonease Johnson, head teacher, Santa Barbara City College Children's Center. (We make special exceptions to the ban on sugar when other positive values make this necessary.)

Mix all ingredients together and pour into an 8-inch uncooked pie shell. Bake 30 minutes or until done in a 375° oven.

Sometimes a member of a child's family will join the class and reminisce about how they cooked when she was little, and this intensifies the children's interest when they make the same recipe.

Children also enjoy bringing some special foods from home to share with the group. At

Ages of Children	Suggested Cooking Activities	Comments
3- to 4-year-olds, *cont'd.*	Frozen juice bars (allow them to squeeze oranges first) Applesauce Filled celery stalks Meatballs Tacos Tabouli Asian dishes that require chopping and cutting Hamburgers Greens with bacon	mash, mix, measure, and talk about the order in which things go together. They can use recipes that require more heat, although they will need close watching. They are able to wait a bit longer for results. They enjoy doing things that help the entire group, such as making part of the snack for everyone to enjoy later.
4- to 5-year-olds	Bread Quiche Ice cream Anything grown in their garden Butter Beef jerky Fruit leather Read-for-yourself recipes Recipes from other cultures *	Fours, particularly if this is their second year in school, are accomplished cooks and can do just about everything except deep fat frying. They are able to use tongs and pancake turners, assemble equipment, such as ice cream freezers and food grinders, use a barbecue grill, and even separate eggs. If recipes are illustrated with cups, spoonfuls, and labels, they will enjoy following these with only minimal help from the teacher.

*Recipes from the UNICEF book *Many Friends Cooking* by T. T. Cooper and M. Ratner (New York: Philomel Books, 1983) are particularly appropriate to use with the fours because it contains information on the eating customs of the countries from which the recipes come.

Thanksgiving they find it fun for each to bring a piece of fruit for a gigantic fruit platter. This helps them appreciate the bounty and plenitude of the earth and also encourages the idea, once fundamental to the holiday, of sharing with others. Because we like the idea of the school also sharing with families, our center prepares quantities of cranberry-orange relish and sends a cup home with each youngster to share at Thanksgiving dinner.

Suggestions for Making Life Easier

When cooking, overcrowding should be avoided because this means that each child gets to take only one stir. It may even be dangerous if the children start shoving for the knife or arguing over a hot pan. Overcrowding can be prevented if at least one other, very attractive activity is deliberately offered at the same time—preferably as far away from the cooking area as possible. Crowding can be reduced also if two adults make

Things sure taste better when you've made them yourself.

the same recipe at separate tables or if one adult repeats the recipe twice so that additional children can participate the second time. Choosing a recipe that offers many things to do that do not require close supervision or that an additional staff member can supervise also alleviates crowding. Finally, the best way to reduce overcrowding is to offer cooking frequently enough that the novelty wears off, while the satisfaction remains. When children know there are plentiful opportunities to take part in an experience, they lose that desperate "I gotta do it now" feeling.

Avoid recipes that are too difficult, and allow plenty of time for the children to participate fully. The test of whether a recipe is too difficult is how much of the work the teacher ends up doing and whether most of the children remain interested throughout the process. Roll-and-cut cookies seem to me to be a prime example of an activity that requires too much teacher assistance and supervision, although some teachers seem to thrive on making these.

It is always wise to try out a recipe at home before using it with the children. This enables the teacher to anticipate problems and also provides a time line. It is a pity to hurry children through a cooking experience that has such rich learning possibilities, so it is wise to plan plenty of time on cooking days.

Remember that clean-up is half the fun, and plan enough time for children to participate in this process. Children love to do dishes and mess about with soapy sponges, and cooking gives them a fine opportunity to do this while experiencing the satisfaction of meaningful work as well. Think of clean-up as being an integral part of the cooking experience and plan so that children can usually participate in this satisfying aspect of the activity.

Integrate Information About Food into the Curriculum

Besides actually cooking, it is desirable to include talking about food and good nutrition during the day. So many delightful books about food are available that it is impossible to mention them all, but such treasures as *Blueberries for Sal* (McClosky, 1948), *The Enormous Turnip* (Parkinson, 1986), *Gregory the Terrible Eater* (Sharmat, 1980), *Tops and Bottoms* (Stevens, 1995), *If You Give a Mouse a Cookie* (Numeroff, 1985), and *Bread and Jam for Frances* (Hoban, 1964) tie in well with cooking and eating and are great fun besides.

Parents appreciate knowing what their children are eating during the day, so posting menus in a prominent place helps assure them that the children are being well fed. At the institute, where we have a general policy of serving no-dye, sugar-free, low-fat, and low-salt foods, we have made a point of telling parents about the policy and why we follow it. We couple this with suggestions of nourishing treats they can supply in place of the sticky birthday fare so often provided. Most parents are pleased to comply with our requests for these wholesome substitutes that can include popcorn, trail mix, fresh and dried fruits, and nuts.

Summary

There are many ways of developing the physical well-being and competence of young children. This chapter stresses two of them—keeping children safe and healthy and feeding them well.

When considering physical safety, teachers must use their common sense to decide when to intervene and when not to intervene. They must also continually assess the condition of school equipment to make certain that it has not deteriorated, and they should teach children gradually to think about safety for themselves.

Basic rules of health include consistent hand washing by children and adults, conducting daily health checks, excluding children from school when they are contagious, maintaining up-to-date immunizations, and taking special care of children who have been ill.

Feeding children well is best approached from two points of view—planning meals and snacks that are nutritionally sound and offering cooking as a continuing part of the curriculum. Eating well deserves a good deal of attention in children's centers because problems of malnutrition, particularly dental decay and iron deficiency anemia, are widespread among children in the United States.

When choosing recipes to cook with the children, the teacher should select ones that are not too delicate, that offer many things for children to do, that are nourishing and age appropriate, and that come from a variety of cultures.

Recipe for a Happy Day[6]

1 cup friendly words
2 heaping cups of understanding
4 heaping teaspoons time and patience
A pinch of warm personality
Dash of humor

Mixing:

Measure words carefully. Add heaping cups of understanding. Use generous amounts of time and patience.

Cook on front burner, but keep temperature low; do not boil.

Add generous dash of humor and personality. Season to taste with the spice of life.

Serve in individual molds.

Self-Check Questions for Review

Content-Related Questions

1. What is a good rule of thumb to follow when deciding whether an activity is safe for a child to continue?
2. Name some items that would be dangerous to allow in a play yard.
3. Explain why it is becoming even more important than it used to be to insist that children have their immunizations up-to-date before admission to school.
4. What is HIB? And how is it best controlled?
5. List some valuable ways of keeping children healthy.
6. What are the two most important health problems related to malnutrition among children of all economic levels in the United States?
7. What are the changes recommended for food selection and preparation that could lead to better health for everyone?
8. List some expensive and less expensive kinds of food that offer adequate nutrition.
9. Explain some helpful points to consider when choosing a recipe to cook with young children.

---

[6]From *Recipes for Busy Little Hands* by D. J. Croft, 1967, Palo Alto, CA: Author. Copyright © 1967. Used by permission.

10. Imagine you are teaching a group of 2-year-olds. Suggest some cooking activities that are appropriate for them. Now do the same thing for 3- and 4-year-olds.
11. Suggest some policies you would follow when planning a cooking experience with children that would make the experience fun and enjoyable for everyone.
12. List some wholesome substitutions for birthday cake that you could suggest parents bring to the center to celebrate their child's special day.

Integrative Questions

1. A mother is enrolling her child in your school and explains that although the youngster's immunizations are not up-to-date, she will take care of them as soon as she can get around to it. Would you or would you not allow that child to enter school? Explain the reasons for your decision.
2. The research study in this chapter on the influence of peers presents interesting possibilities. Could there be other situations where peer example might influence a child's preferences? Propose a possible situation where this might be the case.
3. Give an example of something you might say to a child after an accident that would be moralizing. Then rephrase it in a more appropriate form.
4. Refer to the recipes for instant pudding and soft tacos and compare the opportunities for children to participate in making those recipes. Compare the recipes, also, in terms of their nutritional values.

Questions and Activities

1. Do you think women teachers are more likely to be overprotective than men teachers are? Be ready to explain why or why not you think this is true.
2. Elizabeth's mother arrives with her child in tow and says, "Oh, by the way, Elizabeth threw up in the middle of the night, but she seems to be all right now— I'd appreciate it if you'd keep an eye on her today." How would you handle this situation? Should Elizabeth be allowed to stay at school? Should she be sent home? What would you say to the mother?
3. Suppose you are in charge of planning snacks for the coming week. As a consciousness-raising activity, develop five different snacks that have minimal food value but that the children would like a lot. Now develop five with sound nutritional values that children would also relish.

4. What was the most serious accident that has occurred at your center or at one where you were observing in the past month or so? Benefit from this experience by analyzing what could be done to prevent its happening again.
5. You are now teacher in a day-care center, and there is a youngster in your group whose family are strict vegetarians—they eat no animal protein at all, including milk. You serve not only a snack and lunch, but also breakfast. Do you think that you should provide this youngster with a special diet? Should he merely make do with the fruits and vegetables the other children eat, ignoring the animal proteins they also have as part of the planned nutrition program? How do you think you should handle this situation?
6. *White Elephant Corner*: What was the most awful cooking experience you ever had with children? Give the class the fun of hearing all the reasons why it was so awful.
7. Share a recipe with the class that represents your own cultural background.
8. Maintaining adequate immunity against infectious diseases is important for everyone. This is particularly true for young women who may be contemplating pregnancy because rubella (3-day measles) can have such a disastrous effect on the fetus. How up-to-date are your own immunizations? Investigate the services of your county health clinic and report to the class. Which immunizations are available there at nominal cost?

References for Further Reading

Health and Safety

Copeland, M. L. (1996). Code blue! Establishing a child care emergency plan. *Child Care Information Exchange*, 107, 17–22. This is such an excellent article I think it should be read by every child care person. It covers what to do before, during, and *after* a disaster occurs.

Frost, J. (1992). *Play and playscapes*. Albany, NY: Delmar. The chapter on playground safety is "must" reading for early childhood teachers.

Kendrick, A. S., Kaufmann, R., & Messenger, K. P. (Eds.). (1995). *Healthy young children: A manual for programs* (3rd ed.). Washington, DC: National Association for the Education of Young Children. If you can have only one reference on health in your library, this is the one to have. It offers a comprehensive, practical mix of information ranging from safety and preventive health to nutrition and caring for children with special needs. *Highly recommended*.

Nutrition—General Information

Berman, C., & Fromer, J. (1991). *Meals without squeals*. Palo Alto, CA: Bull. A user-friendly book that should not be missed, it includes recipes, information on nutrition, cleanliness, recycling, feeding practices, and more! *Highly recommended*.

Endres, J. B., & Rockwell, R. E. (1993). *Food, nutrition and the young child* (4th ed.). Upper Saddle River, NJ: Merrill/Prentice Hall. This book is full of practical, extensive information covering everything from menu planning, to nutrition education, to preparing baby formula.

Garland, A. W., with Mothers & Others for a Livable Planet. (1993). *The way we grow: Good-sense solutions for protecting our families from pesticides in food*. New York: Berkley Books. These people outline the potential dangers resulting from the overuse of pesticides and also present effective ways of advocating for pesticide-free food.

Advice on Menu Planning

Aronowitz, V., & Turner, S. (1989). *Health wise quantity cookbook*. Washington, DC: Center for Science in the Public Interest. Contained here are 200 particularly healthy recipes, each serving 50 people.

Dunkle, J. L., & Edwards, M. S. (1992). *The no leftovers child care cookbook*. St. Paul, MN: Redleaf. This book explains the Child and Adult Care Food Program and offers quantity recipes for 6, 20, 25 or 100 children.

Hodges, S. (1994). *Healthy snacks: Low fat, low sugar, low sodium*. Everett, WA: Warren. In addition to describing the snacks, this book has an appendix that tells necessary quantities and which food component of the Child and Adult Care Food Program component it fills.

Edelstein, S. (1992). *Nutrition and meal planning in child-care programs: A practical guide*. Chicago: American Dietetic Association (available from the Association, 216 W. Jackson Boulevard, Suite 800, Chicago, IL 60606-6995). Edelstein bases her recommendations on Department of Agriculture guidelines, which makes this book particularly helpful for centers receiving federal nutrition grants. It highlights important basic nutrition information and endears itself to me because the menus take into account diverse cultural food preferences ranging from Hispanic, to lacto-ovo vegetarian, to Jewish. *Highly recommended*.

Teaching about Good Nutrition and Cooking with Young Children

Berman, C., & Fromer, J. (1991). *Teaching children about food: A teaching guide and activities guide*. Palo Alto, CA: Bull. This excellent book takes a multicultural world-view approach and offers many suggestions for teaching about food as well as how to cook it. It includes a first-rate list of references. *Highly recommended*.

Ferreira, N. (1982). *Learning through cooking: A cooking program for children two to ten*. Palo Alto, CA: R & E Associates. If you could afford just one such book for your school, I believe this would be the one to choose. All the recipes pay careful attention to nutrition and have been used with children of prekindergarten age.

Jacobson, M., & Hill, L. (1991). *Kitchen fun for kids*. Washington, DC: Center for Science in the Public Interest. Although theoretically for older children, there are many recipes included that are appropriate for younger children to make. Excellent nutritional values—low fat, low salt, low cholesterol, high fiber—are stressed. Child tested. *Highly recommended*.

Katzen, M., & Henderson, A. (1994). *Pretend soup and other real recipes: A cookbook for preschoolers and up*. Berkeley, CA: Tricycle. Mollie Katzen of *Moosewood Cookbook* fame has produced a delightful, well-illustrated, child-tested cookbook. Each recipe is pictured so that very young cooks can "read" what to do. Sensible advice is also included.

Lakeshore Learning Materials. (n.d.). *Multicultural cooking with kids*. Carson, CA: Lakeshore Equipment. This spiral-bound, plastic-coated book offers two to three recipes from each of several diverse cultures—Mexican, Japanese, and German, for instance—plus a cultural fact about each recipe.

Taking Cultural Food Preferences into Account

Copage, E. V. (1991). *Kwanzaa: An African-American celebration of culture and cooking*. New York: Morrow. Copage's book is rich with discussions of various aspects of celebrating Kwanzaa, as well as providing delicious recipes.

Cox, B., & Jacobs, M. (1991). *Spirit of the harvest: North American Indian cooking*. New York: Stewart, Tabori & Chang. This book features attractive American Indian recipes classified according to region. Overviews of Indian tribes and handsome photographs of some recipes are included. Every effort has been made to keep the material as authentic and respectful as possible.

Crocker, B. (1993). *Betty Crocker's Mexican made easy*. Upper Saddle River, NJ: Prentice Hall. Reasonably authentic Mexican recipes are featured that use readily obtainable ingredients.

Parham, V. R. (1993). *The African-American child's heritage cookbook*. South Pasadena, CA: Sandcastle. Parham provides a good array of recipes including ones specifically identified as African, Creole, Jamaican, soul food, and healthy ways to fix old favorites. A specific section is devoted to the legacy of George Washington Carver. *Highly recommended*.

Wilson, M. (1989). *The good-for-your-health all-Asian cookbook*. Washington, DC: Center for Science in the Public Interest. Two hundred and twenty recipes are drawn from Korea, Indonesia, Malaysia, Pakistan, India, the Philippines, Singapore, Thailand, Vietnam, Japan, and China. Emphasis is on good nutrition as well as ethnic background.

Dealing with Eating-Related Problems

Satter, E. (1987). *How to get your kid to eat . . . But not too much.* Palo Alto, CA: Bull. Satter provides sensible, expert advice on establishing normal feeding patterns for children and suggestions about what to do when the pattern is not normal. Helpful for teachers and indispensable for parents.

For the Advanced Student

Bearer, C. F. (1995). Environmental health hazards: How children are different from adults. *The Future of Children: Critical Issues for Children and Youths*, 5(2), 11–26. Bearer documents many ways children are particularly susceptible to insults from the environment. For example, did you realize "The average infant consumes 6 ounces of formula per kilogram of body weight—for the average male adult, this is equivalent to drinking 35 cans of soda pop a day" (p. 15). Information like this really makes one think about how important it is for young children to drink uncontaminated water.

Birch, L. L., Johnson, S. L., & Fisher, J. A. (1995). Children's eating: The development of food-acceptance patterns. *Young Children*, 50(2), 71–78. An interesting summary of research is presented here that documents the effects of social action on food preference and intake regulation. *Highly recommended.*

UNICEF. (1993). *Child malnutrition: Progress toward the world summit for children goal.* New York: UNICEF, Statistics and Monitoring Section. This report is included to remind us how fortunate most of us are in the United States in relation to the hunger that exists in so many other parts of the world.

Journals and Organizations of Particular Interest

Center for Science in the Public Interest, 1875 Connecticut Avenue, NW, Washington DC 20009-5728. CSPI publishes a first-rate bulletin entitled *Nutrition Action* plus various attractive charts and books about nutrition. The Jacobson and Hill book and the Wilson book previously listed are some of their publications.

Child Health Alert. Box 610228, Newton Highlands, MA 02161. This monthly publication covers subjects ranging from what to do about head lice to sports and their effect on the epileptic child. It provides a quick way to keep up-to-date on a wide variety of child health issues.

Child Health Talk. Published by the National Black Child Development Institute, 1023 15th St. N.W., Suite 600, Washington, DC 20005. The Institute newsletter features health and nutrition advice about young children.

Have you ever

- Thought that although preschool teachers paid a lot of attention to creative and social development, they did not do much to help children develop their perceptual-motor skills?

- Wondered what should be offered to enhance those skills?

- Wondered not only how to start a dance experience but also how to prevent it from turning into chaos?

If you have, the material in this chapter will help you.

What joy is in the body! The joy of work and of hard purposeful effort, the joy of singing, the joy of sport and activity, the joy of tenderness and physical touch, the joy of controlling physical things. Children have a tendency toward them all. Softly feel a baby's head, rough-house with a two-year-old, watch a three-year-old squeeze shapes from a square block of clay, and you'll see the opening melodies of the body's joy.

Inhibition and fear take away the body's joy. Children learn inhibitions and fear from us. How can we avoid it? First, we must help them to try physical things without intimidation, embarrassment, or fear. We must help them begin to sense the simple enjoyment of the functioning of their bodies. Then beyond that, we must help them find and concentrate on the particular physical things that they do especially well, the things in which they are gifted, be they sports, music, crafts, dance, or whatever their own particular gifts suggest.

Linda Eyre and Richard Eyre (1984, p. 26)

In addition to making sure that children's bodies are well nourished and that the children are learning to cherish and care for them, teachers also need to do all that they can to encourage sound physical development through exercise. This is because studies indicate that physical fitness is declining among young children in the United States. For example, 40% of 5- to 8-year-old children show at least one of the following risk factors for heart disease: elevated blood pressure, higher than desirable cholesterol ratings, or low levels of physical activity (Javernick, 1988). This situation is bound to become worse as children spend longer and longer hours squatting in front of television sets and playing with computers.

Nor is it correct to assume that just because children are playing outdoors every day that they are involved in enough vigorous exercise. A recent study that observed the activity level of 4- and 5-year-olds at free play outside revealed that the children spent more than 60% of their time in sedentary activities such as sitting, standing, and talking/socializing and only 11% of their time in truly vigorous activities (Sallis, Patterson, McKenzie, & Nader, 1988). Clearly, if we want to instill a taste for healthy, vigorous exercise in the children we care for, we must do more than turn them loose on the playground.

Physical Activity Benefits All the Selves

As Table 9–1 illustrates, no other kind of activity offers such rich opportunities for the development of all the selves. Obviously the body benefits—and so does the emotional self, as the child acquires feelings of competence through the acquisition of new skills, or uses physical activity as an acceptable channel for aggressive feelings, or becomes involved in creative dance and explores a wide range of emotions. The cooperative interplay between children and the satisfaction

TABLE 9–1
How Can Physical Activity Promote Development of the Whole Child?

Physical	Emotional	Social	Creative	Cognitive/Language
Encourages: Development of skills: Locomotion Dynamic and static balance Body and space perception Rhythm and temporal awareness Rebound and airborne activities Projectile management Fine-motor skills Physical fitness: Endurance Heart rate Muscular strength Flexibility Good health Development of coordination: Eye-hand Eye-foot Kinesthetic awareness (knowledge of what body is doing as it moves; body "cues") Sensory awareness Bilateral and cross-lateral physical activities Ability consciously to relax	Encourages: Positive attitude toward attempting challenges (trying new things) Being persistent Sense of physical competence Ability to channel aggression Relief of tension through acceptable physical activities Safe expression of wide range of feelings in dance Willingness to take moderate risks	Encourages: Cooperative play Cooperative use of equipment (trike and wagon; round tire swing; rocking boat) Social give-and-take (sharing trike track) Acknowledgment of other children's physical skills Development of competitive attitude toward other children under some circumstances Development of conflict resolution skills	Encourages: Vigorous pretend play Unusual ways to use familiar equipment Generation of tricks and stunts Expression of own ideas in dance Use of imagination Original solutions to "problems" in movement exploration activities Aesthetic appreciation of combined music and movement experiences	Encourages: Coordination of language with physical activity (Miss Mary Mack; finger plays; simple singing games) Knowledge of fundamental principles of good health; i.e., exercise makes bodies strong Knowledge of spatial relationships (in, under, etc.) Ability to estimate in advance: depth and distance; potential risks Ability to conform to simple rules for safety Ability to understand rules of simple group games, such as Farmer in the Dell Use of movement to communicate ideas

Vigorous outdoor play should be encouraged at every opportunity.

of doing things together develop the social self. The cognitive self is enhanced as children learn about body image and spatial relationships, and the creative self is provided with opportunities for original thinking that are encouraged by movement exploration activities and also nourished by the marvelous creative opportunities inherent in dance experiences and play.

Because of all these benefits, physical activity is of great value to the young child, and it behooves teachers to think carefully about its educational potential to help children make the most of its possibilities (Gallahue, 1995a, 1995b). What is needed is the development of a comprehensive physical development program that does not regiment the children but does provide opportunities to practice many different kinds of skills.

The best way to achieve this lies in acquiring general knowledge of the likely ages for acquisition of various skills and specific knowledge of the developmental needs of the individual children. This information should then be used to plan a comprehensive program using perceptual-motor activities, movement exploration, and creative dance. These experiences should be offered in attractive forms so that children will seek them out rather than having to be coerced into participation.

Identifying Levels of Development

It only makes sense to plan physical activities that fit the developmental abilities of the children. Threes, for instance, are a lot more likely to be interested in simple climbing skills and riding tricycles than they will be at catching balls or skipping rope.

For the approximate ages at which the average preschooler attains various skills, Table 9–2 provides a useful index.

Once the teacher has an idea of the general level of ability in the group and is also aware of children who have special talents or who lack motor skills that most children have acquired by their age, a solid foundation exists for knowing what level of activities should be included in the program. One word of caution is in order, however. Although the sequence in which children develop physical skills remains fairly constant, the time of acquisition varies considerably, and this must be taken into account when evaluating developmental status (Fox & Tipps, 1995; Gallahue 1995b). Just because a child is 6 months ahead or behind the time listed in Table 9–2, the teacher should not conclude that she is either an athletic genius or a potential klutz. Gross deviations, on the other hand, should be cause for further investigation by a pediatrician.

TABLE 9–2
Sequence of Emergence of Selected Stability Abilities

Movement Pattern	Selected Abilities	Approximate Age of Onset
Dynamic Balance Dynamic balance involves maintaining one's equilibrium as the center of gravity shifts	Walks 1-inch straight line	3 years
	Walks 1-inch circular line	4 years
	Stands on low balance beam	2 years
	Walks on 4-inch-wide beam for a short distance	3 years
	Walks on same beam, alternating feet	3–4 years
	Walks on 2- or 3-inch beam	4 years
	Performs basic forward roll	3–4 years
	Performs mature forward roll*	6–7 years
Static Balance Static balance involves maintaining one's equilibrium while the center of gravity remains stationary	Pulls to a standing position	10 months
	Stands without handholds	11 months
	Stands alone	12 months
	Balances on one foot 3–5 seconds	5 years
	Supports body in basic 3-point inverted positions	6 years
Axial Movements Axial movements are static postures that involve bending, stretching, twisting, turning, and the like	Axial movement abilities begin to develop early in infancy and are progressively refined to a point where they are included in the emerging manipulative patterns of throwing, catching, kicking, striking, trapping, and other activities	2 months–6 years
Walking Walking involves placing one foot in front of the other while maintaining contact with the supporting surface	Rudimentary upright unaided gait	13 months
	Walks sideways	16 months
	Walks backward	17 months
	Walks upstairs with help	20 months
	Walks upstairs alone—follow step	24 months
	Walks downstairs alone—follow step	25 months
Running Running involves a brief period of no contact with the supporting surface	Hurried walk (maintains contact)	18 months
	First true run (nonsupport phase)	2–3 years
	Efficient and refined run	4–5 years
	Speed of run increases, mature run*	5 years

*The child has the developmental "potential" to be at the mature stage. Actual attainment will depend on factors within the task, individual, and environment.

TABLE 9–2
continued

Movement Pattern	Selected Abilities	Approximate Age of Onset
Jumping Jumping takes three forms: (1) jumping for distance; (2) jumping for height; and (3) jumping from a height. It involves a one- to two-foot takeoff with a landing on both feet	Steps down from low objects	18 months
	Jumps down from object with one foot lead	2 years
	Jumps off floor with both feet	28 months
	Jumps for distance (about 3 feet)	5 years
	Jumps for height (about 1 foot)	5 years
	Mature jumping pattern*	6 years
Hopping Hopping involves a one-foot takeoff with a landing on the same foot	Hops up to 3 times on preferred foot	3 years
	Hops from 4 to 6 times on same foot	4 years
	Hops from 8 to 10 times on same foot	5 years
	Hops distance of 50 feet in about 11 seconds	5 years
	Hops skillfully with rhythmical alteration, mature pattern*	6 years
Galloping The gallop combines a walk and a leap with the same foot leading throughout	Basic but inefficient gallop	4 years
	Gallops skillfully, mature pattern*	6 years
Skipping Skipping combines a step and a hop in rhythmic alteration	One-footed skip	4 years
	Skillful skipping (about 20%)	5 years
	Skillful skipping for most*	6 years
Reach, Grasp, Release Reaching, grasping, and releasing involve making successful contact with an object, retaining it in one's grasp, and releasing it at will	Primitive reaching behaviors	2–4 months
	Corralling of objects	2–4 months
	Palmar grasp	3–5 months
	Pincer grasp	8–10 months
	Controlled grasp	12–14 months
	Controlled releasing	14–18 months
Throwing Throwing involves imparting force to an object in the general direction of intent	Body faces target, feet remain stationary, ball thrown with forearm extension only	2–3 years
	Same as above but with body rotation added	3.6–5 years
	Steps forward with leg on same side as the throwing arm	4–5 years
	Boys exhibit more mature pattern than girls	5 years and over
	Mature throwing pattern*	6 years

*The child has the developmental "potential" to be at the mature stage. Actual attainment will depend on factors within the task, individual, and environment.

Movement Pattern	Selected Abilities	Approximate Age of Onset
Catching		
Catching involves receiving force from an object with the hands, moving from large to progressively smaller balls	Chases ball; does not respond to aerial ball	2 years
	Responds to aerial ball with delayed arm movements	2–3 years
	Needs to be told how to position arms	2–3 years
	Fear reaction (turns head away)	3–4 years
	Basket catch using the body	3 years
	Catches using the hands only with a small ball	5 years
	Mature catching pattern*	6 years
Kicking		
Kicking involves imparting force to an object with the foot	Pushes against ball; does not actually kick it	18 months
	Kicks with leg straight and little body movement (kicks *at* the ball)	2–3 years
	Flexes lower leg on backward lift	3–4 years
	Greater backward and forward swing with definite arm opposition	4–5 years
	Mature pattern (kicks *through* the ball)*	5–6 years
Striking		
Striking involves sudden contact to objects in an overarm, sidearm, or under-hand pattern	Faces object and swings in a vertical plane	2–3 years
	Swings in a horizontal plane and stands to the side of the object	4–5 years
	Rotates the trunk and hips and shifts body weight forward	5 years
	Mature horizontal pattern with stationary ball	6–7 years

*The child has the developmental "potential" to be at the mature stage. Actual attainment will depend on factors within the task, individual, and environment.

Note. From *Understanding Motor Development: Infants, Children, Adolescents, Adults* (p. 229), by D. Gallahue, 1995, Dubuque, IA: Brown & Benchmark. Used by permission.

It is also of interest to refer to the box from Cratty and Martin on the following page to obtain a general feeling for the kinds of things children are able to do and not do by the time they enter kindergarten.

Equipment for Physical Development

It was stressed in previous chapters that equipment should be durable, safe, and well maintained (Taylor & Morris, 1996). (See also the discussion of outdoor equipment in chapter 5, and note particularly the discussion of simple, complex, and super play units there.) We often think of *equipment* as meaning large, permanent structures, and some sorts of vigorous activity do require this kind of installation. However, many activities suggested in Table 9–3 do not require large, elaborate equipment at all.

As the research study presented in this chapter substantiates, the best resource for physical play activity remains the child's ideas and body, combined with a variety of readily obtainable accessories, such as boards, ladders, tires, barrels,

Evaluation Criteria for a 5-Year-Old Child

A 5-Year-Old Child Should Be Able:

1. to balance on his preferred foot, with eyes open, with arms folded, for at least 4 seconds.
2. to catch a 16-inch rubber ball bounced chest high from distance of 15 feet, four out of five times.
3. to jump forward and to hop forward on one foot three consecutive times.
4. to identify body parts, limbs, front, back, and sides.
5. to run in a coordinated manner, with integration of arms and legs.
6. to jump over a 10-inch high barrier.

It Is Unlikely That a 5-Year-Old Will Be Able:

1. to identify his left and right body parts better than would be expected by chance (i.e., better than 50% correct responses).
2. to alternately hop from foot to foot, without undue hesitation or placing both feet on the ground simultaneously, in either a 1/2, 3/3, or 1/3 pattern.
3. to touch a ball swinging on a 15-inch string through a 180° arc, arm's distance away.
4. to jump or hop with accuracy into small squares.

Note. From *Perceptual-Motor Efficiency in Children: The Measurement and Improvement of Movement Attributes* (pp. 41, 85) by B. J. Cratty and M. M. Martin, 1969, Philadelphia: Lea & Febiger. Used by permission.

boxes, and blocks. These kinds of materials have the capacity for infinite rearrangement necessary for the generation of creative, large-muscle play (Rivkin, 1995).

Some of these items, such as hollow blocks, are best purchased, though I once saw a very substantial painted set that had been made from old whiskey boxes. However, much portable equipment can be built. Some can even be wheeled for free from businesses such as milk companies that donate old milk crates or tire companies that give away worn tires.

When large structures are needed, there is no other place in the preschool where one can spend so much money so quickly. There is no denying there are some beautiful, physically satisfying structures available for purchase, but fortunately there are also many ways of achieving equivalent play value without spending a fortune. Several good resource books on this subject that demonstrate how to apply ingenuity and free labor to the problem of building satisfying play equipment for children are listed at the end of this chapter.

Adding ropes to this low-cost piece of equipment brings variety and zest to outdoor play.

Each community offers its own potential for free materials for such construction. Among ones frequently available are railroad ties, logs sawn into various heights, boulders for climbing, chipped sewer pipes for tunnels, and strong dead trees.

People, too, are good resources. Park and street department people are often generous with advice and surplus materials if contacted by day-care centers. Park and recreation people, in particular, are deeply interested and knowledgeable about large-muscle play equipment. Ask them for suggestions about planning and for community sources of free materials—they are used to making dollars stretch.

It is of utmost importance to ensure that whatever is built is safe and that it is *twice* as strong as you think it should be. Never assume that just because the children are small, equipment need not be well braced and firmly built. In fact, young children are very hard on equipment. They use apparatus vigorously and constantly, and construction must take this into account if the equipment is to be safe and to last more than a few months.

Finally, every center has its own unique potential for physical experiences. It may be a large, blank wall to bounce balls against, or a gentle slope for children to roll down, or something as seemingly undesirable as a completely paved playground that also means a quickly drying surface in almost all weather. The point is that every situation has hidden assets if teachers will take a fresh look at their environment from time to time and then put these possibilities to work.

Making a Plan for Comprehensive Physical Development

Besides identifying the current level of the children's physical skills, the teachers also need some kind of comprehensive outline (taxonomy) to follow to make certain that they are not leaving out an important motor ability. I favor using the outline originally proposed by Arnheim and Sinclair (1979) and Arnheim and Pestolesi (1978) as a guide because it requires relatively few categories, is reasonably comprehensive, and is easy to understand.

These categories include *locomotion*, which encourages various ways of moving from one place to another, and *balance*, which pertains to balancing either while standing still or while moving. Awareness of one's body (where it is and what it can do) not only is important in such activities as gymnastics but also is significant to children's sense of identity and self-esteem; thus, *body and space perception* is a third category. *Rhythmic activities* help children integrate and pace their physical movements, as well as add pleasure to what they are doing. *Rebound and airborne activities* refer to the bouncing and jumping so dear to preschoolers, and also to the stretching and swinging movements entailed in the use of hand-over-hand exercise bars. *Projectile management* is a somewhat fancy term for throwing, catching, and otherwise moving an object through space by hitting it. Daily motor skills comprise what early childhood teachers speak of as fine-muscle skills.

It will be evident from examining Table 9–3 that some kinds of activities, such as climbing activities and swinging, are best included through informal, spontaneous play and are usually available in most children's centers. Others, such as relaxation strategies, balancing techniques, and beginning throwing and catching skills, may be less familiar and require planned inclusion.

Teachers should supply appropriate vocabulary along with each activity, since children are unlikely to possess such language without such assistance. This helps children identify what they are doing, extends their range of information, and may enhance, in some fashion that is not yet completely understood, their motor planning skills by tying the cognitive/verbal component to the action. This vocabulary may be as simple as this statement to a young two: "Jumpy, jump, jump!" or as elaborate as this

TABLE 9–3
Some Suggestions for Perceptual-Motor and Movement Education Activities

Physical Ability	Perceptual-Motor Activity		Movement Education Activity
	Easier	More Challenging	
Tension Releasers — Relaxation Strategies See discussion in text: Helping children learn to relax			
Locomotion			
Rolling (5 months) (mats are nice but not essential)	Roll over and over, sideways — both directions Roll downhill (and try rolling up!)	Roll with arms overhead or do forward roll somersault (age 5), arms around knees — roll "butterball" style. Roll about, balanced on top of very large ball. Be rolled by someone else while braced in large tire.	Roll to music "I roll myself over and over." Roll toward sound of drum with eyes closed — changing directions as drummer moves.
Creeping and crawling (10 months)	Can use legs straight or bent Crawl with arm and leg on same side of body parallel or in opposition (X) movement. Encourage crawling on textured surfaces for increased sensory input.	Crawl while pushing a ball with head or following a line. Wriggle across floor using only arms (GI crawl).	Play at being various crawly animals — snakes, lizards, turtles, bears, cats, etc. For control, creep slowly and then pounce — while singing "Old Grey Cat Goes Creeping" — or be spider singing "Eensy Weensy Spider." Ask children whether they can crawl under, over, through, and so forth. Try big cardboard boxes for this.
Climbing (as early as age 2; proficient at 4; ladder climbing mastered by age 6)	Slide ladder is often only fixed ladder on playground; can also use jungle gyms, arched climbers, cargo nets, or A-frames — good to encourage hand-over-hand, foot-over-foot activity.	Rope ladder or fireman's ladder Ladders with more distance between rungs are more difficult. Steeper is harder. Ramp to top of sewer pipe, jump off Attach rope to top of slide and climb up hand over hand.	For children who know the story, "Jack and the Bean Stalk" provides lots of pretend climbing.

Skill	Notes	Activities
Jumping (28 months)	Jumping is easier than hopping. Jump over lines or off low heights.	Jump over low objects. Jump off higher things onto mattress. Jump rope swung in half arc slowly, or whirled in circle on ground. Jump and land "on target" marked with tape or carpet square. Rabbits, grasshoppers, popcorn, and birds all jump. Can act out motions of animals, such as a scared rabbit. Position in space by jumping in and out of hoops; more advanced form, one child jumps in as another jumps out; be a frog jumping on a lily pad; jump in something sticky like molasses.
Hopping (age 3 — hop two or three times, same foot)	Hop one or two steps on one foot, over lines, etc.	Hop several times, same foot. For alternate hopping activity, Claire Cherry suggests Native American dancing. What can you do on one foot? On one arm?
Skipping		14% of fours and 22% of fives can skip; therefore, not appropriate to stress at nursery school level.
Running and leaping (children are accomplished runners by age 4)	Very desirable to have large open space for this — conveys marvelous feeling of pleasure and freedom	Can foster agility by encouraging figure-8 runs; this is quite difficult for fours. Crouch down and "explode" on signal by leaping up; run and stop in time to music or play "freeze"; leap over "puddles" on floor. Can you run like a mouse? Like an elephant? Run as if the wind is pushing you. Run as butterflies fly. Do shadow running and leaping, moving as partner does.
Balance		
Static (balance while still)	Stand on tiptoe; try balancing lying on side.	Balance on hollow block. Balance on one foot. Stand still with eyes closed. Hold still as long as drum doesn't beat. Can you balance on three parts of your body? Without touching the floor? Without using your feet? Play "statues."

TABLE 9–3
continued

| | Perceptual-Motor Activity | | |
Physical Ability	Easier	More Challenging	Movement Education Activity
Balance, *cont'd* Dynamic (balance while moving) (both feet on beam, walk partway, 38 months)	Use a balance board — wider is easier. Walk, with one foot on, one foot off beam; walk along log, curb, edge of wall, or thin chalk line.	Both feet on beam (4-inch beam or, if proficient, use narrow side of beam), or walk sideways, foot over foot on beam. Visit a "clatter" bridge (may overwhelm some children). Walk on well-anchored gangplank between A-frames. Skate on one roller skate. Use a scooter. Walk around an edge of tire or "toober" (big inner tube). Step over thin ropes laid across balance beam. Walk on edges of ladder. Roll a hoop.	How can you get to end of balance beam without walking on it? Imagine you're on a tightrope. Dance on tiptoe — slowly for greater challenge.
With object	Roll a tire. Crawl with beanbag on back. Walk with beanbags, arms extended from sides.	Balance beanbag on back of hand. Balance balloon or small ball on hand. Walk on wide plank — with one weighted pole on one side or carrying bottle of sand on one side. Walk carrying something spillable in bowl.	Dance with hoop or paper parasol or very large fans (can be obtained from stores specializing in oriental goods) and retain balance. What can you do with the fan? How far can you bend over with it?
Body and space perception	How many people can fit in the box? Guess, then try it.	Play "Simon Says." Use screen that just lets shoes show — guess who the shoes belong to.	Any activity requiring movement in space, varied in *tempo* (pace and rhythm); *force of motion*, particularly where awareness is stressed

How high can you reach? Any activity that fosters knowledge of body parts such as "Head, Shoulders, Knees, and Toes"

Shut eyes — guess who you are touching by touch alone.

Do something with body and tell what you did in words.

Work on identifying more difficult body parts — eyebrows, elbows, toenails, eyelids.

Traffic course on bikes requiring careful steering.

All body-object relationships — "on," "under," "behind," and so on, i.e., directionality

How slow can you creep? How fast can you run?

Practically any kind of finger play

Move in water if a pool is available.

All activities where expression of emotion or physical states is encouraged — a "tired" dance, e.g.

Have child move like an animal of his choosing — ask others to guess animal.

Use "mirror" or shadow dancing.

How close can you get to your partner and not touch him?

Ask "What can you do with your toes?" and "Anything else?"

Have children propose ways to use the parachute.

Rhythm and Temporal Awareness

(Even newborns are sensitive to different rhythms.)

For further discussion, see text: Movement education and Helping children enjoy creative dance

Any activity that has a regularly recurring rhythm to it — rocking boats, swings, even tricycles, rocking chairs

Any kind of bouncing equipment (see Rebound and airborne activities below)

Finger-paint to music.

Ride bouncy horses to music.

Jump over rope.

Jump rope swung in half arc.

Galloping has definite rhythm (rudiments acquired by age 4).

Can clap hands in pattern — knees, hands, head.

Rock with partner — singing "Row, Row, Row Your Boat."

March and do other moving to music activities that emphasize response to "beat."

Shaking activities — like wet dog, like salt shaker, "Looby Lou" (rhythm band is a conforming, not creative, rhythmic activity).

Dance to holiday music — contrasting rhythm of "Jingle Bells" to "White Christmas," e.g.

Move according to poetic chants — John Brown's Body" has a lot of appeal.

Marching and using instruments at same time is more difficult.

TABLE 9–3
continued

Physical Ability	Perceptual-Motor Activity		
	Easier	More Challenging	Movement Education Activity
Rebound and Airborne Activities			
Jumping activities	Involves jumping skills combined with timing	Jump on "toober."	Can you bounce another way? Sitting down? Squatting?
	Equipment such as mattress, box springs, bouncing boards are appropriate.	Try turning while jumping.	Bouncing activities are particularly satisfying when music is added.
	Do not use trampolines; they require too much supervision and training. (Many insurance companies now refuse insurance on this equipment.)	Jump on and off low mattress.	Vary tempo to encourage variety of kinds of bounces.
	Bouncing has added value as an aggression reliever.		
Hanging and stretching activities	Simply hang and stretch from exercise bar.	Use hand-over-hand exercise ladders.	
		Use trapeze for swinging and hanging.	
		Hang by knees from exercise bar.	
Projectile Management			
Throwing (easier than catching — children not really proficient until 5)	Roll large balls to partner.	Roll at target — large empty bleach bottles.	Pretend you are rolling something big and heavy — or as light as thistledown.
	Throw soft balls, such as Nerf balls.	Throw at target or through hoop.	Use scarves and streamers for waving in air.
		For advanced children, try combination of running and throwing.	
Catching (also not well developed at preschool level)	Begin with catching a rolled ball between legs; encourage child to keep eyes open.	Catch slightly smaller ball.	Catch soap bubbles (watch out for slippery floor).
	Requires adult to throw ball to child for proper chance of catching; best to use large ball.	Bounce and catch ball.	
		Try a pitchback net.	

170

Skill			
Kicking (requires ability to poise on one foot)	Bounce ball with two hands. Kick large, still ball.	Kick gently rolling ball. Roll faster to increase challenge.	
Striking (makes teachers nervous but children enjoy it even though it takes close supervision)	Keep balloons in air with hand. Hit punching bag mounted on spindle. Hit whiffle ball poised on traffic cone with plastic bat.	Hit balloon with paddle. Hit ball hung from string with paddle. Use large plastic bat and ball; adult pitches.	Dance with balloons.
Fine-Muscle Skills (essentially tool manipulation skills that require not just eye-hand or eye-foot coordination, but also eye-finger coordination)	Use of tools that do not require extremely fine control, including such cooking utensils as potato mashers and spoons; carpentry tools, such as hammers and saws; and self-expressive items, such as paintbrushes and gluing activities; also manipulative items, such as pegs, puzzles, blocks of various descriptions	Tools that require more control such as scissors, braces and bits, rotary egg beaters, tweezers, and large needles	
	Skills, such as simple buttoning	Self-care skills—fitting zipper parts together, buttoning small buttons, and occasionally, shoe tying	
	Bead stringing—large beads	Bead stringing—small beads	
	Puzzles—large pieces, few in number, within a frame	Puzzles—smaller pieces, more numerous ones, greater variety of types.	
	Simple manipulation of scissors	Use scissors to cut on lines or to cut fabric.	
	"Bristle" blocks, cubical counting blocks	Play with Lego blocks, Tinker Toys, Lincoln Logs	
	Pegs in peg hole boards		

These ladders are notched so they hook safely over other pieces of equipment and can be used in many different ways.

comment to a 4-year-old: "See how your toes are gripping the edge of the tire underneath—they're inside, and you're outside." Either statement identifies and enriches the child's experience at an appropriate level.

Note that Table 9–3 includes easier and more difficult items to demonstrate how curriculum can be developed to suit the developmental levels of younger and older children.

It is particularly important to be aware of fine-muscle skills. These skills are so inherent to and pervasive in activities of the early school years that teachers sometimes fail to think of them as psychomotor skills and take them more or less for granted. We must realize however that such fine-muscle skills are not equally easy for all youngsters to master and that *expecting young chil-*

dren to work at such skills for too long at a time without relief can be a real source of strain. Moreover, teachers should regularly take a careful look at all the children as they are handling small manipulative items, such as beads or puzzles, and be on the alert for undue clumsiness, excessive frustration, and for children who habitually hold such work too close to their eyes or who avoid such activities altogether. *All these behaviors are indications that children may be having special eye-hand coordination problems. Such youngsters should be referred promptly to their pediatricians, ophthalmologists, or optometrists for further identification of the difficulty.*

Presentation of Activities

In general, the more informal the presentation of such activities is, the more ideal, because an easy-going, casual approach is the antithesis of regimentation. However, the reader should not construe *informal* to mean *unplanned*. A good physical development program *does* require careful planning to make certain that opportunities for practice are provided for developing each of the listed skills at various levels of challenge.

Of course, planning should remain flexible and subject to change in accord with what the children spontaneously attempt. There is no better place in the curriculum to practice sensitivity to their ideas than in the realm of physical activity. Teachers who see their role as listening and responding to the children's ideas as well as taking responsibility for proposing possibilities themselves will find their physical activities program vastly enriched.

Basics to Remember

No matter which skill and level of skill the teacher has selected, there are some general principles to remember that apply to all of them.

1. Remember to welcome ideas and variations suggested by the children. In the final analysis

they know better than the teacher what they are ready to learn next.

2. It is necessary to offer *repeated* opportunities for practice when children are learning new skills—once is not enough.

3. Encourage movement backward and sideways, as well as forward. Keep possibilities open—do not settle for "visual, frontal, and flexed" activities.

4. Encourage children to try the same movement on each side of the body.

5. Plan activities that use more than one level in space (e.g., lying on floor, sitting, kneeling, standing).

6. Ask children to stop and change direction while moving.

7. Include movements, such as finger painting or playing elephant, that require swinging arms or legs across the midline of the body. It is thought that these movements enhance shifting control centers between the hemispheres of the brain.

8. Look for ways to increase tactile input (input from sense of touch), such as dancing barefoot on a variety of surfaces.

9. Keeping safety in mind, encourage children to try activities with their eyes closed to help them be more aware of their kinesthetic sense (sensory information coming from joints and muscles).

10. Include movements that sometimes require parallel and sometimes cross-action patterns of arm and leg movements.

11. Do not emphasize teaching the concept of left and right—preschool children are too young for this to have much meaning.

12. Remember to include a variety of activities that provide quietness and relaxation, as well as more energetic ones.

13. Keep movement sessions short enough to be fun. Do not push children to the edge of exhaustion.

14. Remember to keep safety in mind—and help children think about it, too.

Including Activities in the Daily Schedule

Plan Specific Activities

One way to include activities is to refer to Table 9–3 and make certain that one or two activities are offered each day that enhance the specific skills listed there. This not only helps ensure coverage but also breaks the sterile monotony of many outdoor play times in which the only variations may be the way hollow blocks are used or a few new toys in the sandbox. Children appreciate the changing opportunities and often work seriously and persistently until they have mastered the new skill—a sure indication that the activity has more to offer than mere novelty.

Develop Obstacle Courses

Another way to present perceptual-motor activities is to offer obstacle and action courses once or twice a week. This can put both the teacher's and children's ingenuity to work if the teacher asks, "Let's see, what could we use to jump into today?" or "What would be fun to balance on?" It is interesting to note that the children often concoct things to do that are a lot harder than what the grown-up considers reasonable.

Some general things to remember about obstacle courses are that they require a large, maneuverable area, that they should be supervised carefully (particularly if the teacher has some specific skills in mind for the children to practice), and finally that it is fun to change them while they are being used.

Honoring Developmental Tastes and Preferences

Two-year-olds love to crawl (through tires, plastic snap-together blocks, and large, open pipes), climb (sets of stairs and A-frames), and jump from low heights onto mattresses or other spongy materials. They love balancing tasks on low, wide boards but are easily frightened of being too high up or of being shut in tunnels or

Research Study

What Kinds of Play Equipment Do Children Prefer?

Research Question   Which kind of outdoor play environment is most attractive to young children during free play?

Research Method   The subjects consisted of 138 middle-class Anglo children enrolled in kindergarten, first, or second grade in a private school.

The children had the choice of using three differing outdoor play environments. Environment A was a wood structure containing interior and exterior space for climbing and dramatic play, including tire swings, a slide, and a fireman's pole and ladder. It was basically a single structure with several activities included. Cost was about $5,000.

Environment B offered an array of 16 wood structures including balance beams, chinning bars, obstacle climbers, a suspension bridge, slide, jungle gym, and so forth. Equipment was linked together, and the primary intention was to promote gross-motor activity. Cost was about $5,000.

Environment C was made by parents and staff of the school according to a design furnished by the researchers. It consisted of a slide, fort, boat, car, storage, picnic table, three types of climbers, wheel vehicles, and used materials including tires, spools, barrels, railroad ties, and utility poles. It provided a wide range of experiences with opportunities for self-expression combined with action-oriented equipment (wheel vehicles and some movable items). Cost was $1,425, with some materials donated.

The children's choice and use of the three environments was recorded for one 30-minute free-play session a week for 6 weeks, and each child was recorded three times during that 30-minute period. Selection of play area was left entirely to the individual children.

Results   During these observations, Environment C (the most varied one) attracted the most children, comprising over 63% of choices. Environment A (the single structure) attracted the

boxes. Repetition of basic physical activities can be such a passion with twos that it may seem almost obsessive to the adults in charge.[1]

Three-year-olds enjoy activities similar to those enjoyed by twos, but they are much more competent, particularly in the domain of balance and coordination. They like to develop their own ideas of how to build tunnels and construct other exciting physical experiences.

Whereas 2-year-olds require careful supervision because they are inexperienced and cannot always anticipate results adequately, 4-year-olds require supervision because they enjoy taking risks and doing daring stunts. It is as though,

now that they have acquired basic physical competencies, they feel impelled to test these to the utmost. They enjoy tumbling activities, balancing on more difficult beams, hanging upside down by their knees, and jumping from considerable heights. Of all the ages of children, fours are the ones for whom teachers need to offer the most challenge and variety.

Table 9–4 (pp. 176–177) is an example of a student assignment illustrating how the full range of activities may be incorporated into the daily schedule.

Helping Children with Disabilities Participate

Teachers sometimes overlook the pressing need for physical activity felt by children who have

---

[1] I am indebted to Paula Machado, former specialist in 2-year-olds for the Santa Barbara City College Children's Center, for these comments.

next most, with over 23%, and Environment B (the "linked" gross-motor unit) the least, with just over 13%. In terms of total numbers of choices made by the children, Environment C attracted 1,641 children, A attracted 600 children, and B attracted 345 children during the time of the study.

The younger children chose C much more frequently than they chose A or B. As grade level increased, A and B became more popular as did play involving games with rules.

Implications for Teaching   The investigators concluded that, particularly for children of kindergarten age, providing a single-play structure (Environment A) or a combination that only elicits gross-motor play (Environment B) is not sufficient for meeting the free-play needs of young children.

Children prefer complex structures that offer several play options and equipment that is movable and does something. They also prefer play equipment that they can change to meet the requirements of their play, rather than having to adjust to an immovable arrangement where they must conform to the dictates of the structure. If teachers want to promote balanced outdoor play involving dramatic and imaginative play as well as simple gross-motor activity, they need to provide a variety of equipment to promote such play.

It is also worthwhile to consider the cost/use ratio apparent in the three environments. For teachers of young children seeking the most play value for their dollar, clearly the design of Environment C not only provides the greatest variety of play experiences for the children but is also the most economical one to construct.

Note. From "Equipment Choices of Young Children during Free Play" by J. L. Frost and E. Strickland. In *When Children Play: Proceedings of the International Conference on Play and Play Environments*, edited by J. L. Frost and S. Sunderland, 1985, Wheaton, MD: Association for Childhood Education International.

various kinds of physical disabilities and tend to assume the children do not mind being so immobilized. However, their limited opportunities for physical activity mean that, if anything, they need more, not fewer, chances to use their bodies in every way that can be made available to them.

For example, sand tables and water tables at waist height can be used by youngsters in wheelchairs if the chair is turned sideways to favor use of the child's dominant hand, or well-anchored trays can be fastened to the chair itself (although this is not as much fun as using the larger table is). Or handholds can be provided on the edge of tables to enable children to pull themselves to a standing position. Or a slide can be installed on the slope of a hill with an easy-to-climb-up ramp beside it lined with textured material for traction. Children who have diffi-

culty with small-muscle activities can be more successful if magnetic "sticky" blocks are provided. Youngsters with impaired vision can use a lot of outdoor equipment such as hanging bars, swings, and climbing equipment once they have had a quiet chance to investigate such equipment by feeling it and having it described to them. Remember, though, that it is *even more important than usual* to shield these activities so that partially sighted youngsters cannot possibly walk in front of them and be struck—this is *especially* important to remember to do with swings.

What it mainly takes to increase the participation of such youngsters is a teacher who is sensitive to their needs and willing to look for creative solutions and who remembers to ask the parents and the other specialists associated with the children's care to contribute their ideas also.

TABLE 9–4
One-Day Physical Development Curriculum Plan

Physical Ability	Perceptual-Motor or Movement Education Activity	Modifications Needed	Children's Response
Locomotion	Roll about balanced on top of large balls on grass outside.	Needed more *really* large balls. Balls kept blowing away so might be better inside.	D. and J. used the one very large ball and repeatedly enjoyed it. Children kicked smaller balls.
	On the way to play outside, go on walk from east door around south of building. Go up and down stairs, take long giant steps, short steps, walk fast then slow, tiptoe, stomp, and jump over the cracks on sidewalk.	First in line did well. Later ones needed to hold back for space between so children could have freedom to move.	H. and J. did everything on suggestion with enthusiasm. P. had difficulty, partly because he did not have one hand free for balance (arm was in splint).
Balance	Place rope on floor in block area for children to walk down.	Had to demonstrate rope repeatedly; children couldn't understand instructions alone. Finally removed it.	L., J., and E. had no trouble once it was demonstrated, but lost interest quickly.
	Make orange juice. Ask children to go to large container of water at another table and fill a cup and carry back to table.	Moved container so children wouldn't spill in main walkway.	E. asked if she could take two turns. Almost everyone helped. Very few spills.
Body and space perception	"Head, Shoulders, Knees, and Toes" during group.	It should have been repeated since it was new. Should be slowed down.	Quite a few children participated, which is good for first time.
	Beanbag toss with body target (conversation about body) at rug 1.	Teacher had to hold bags in her lap to keep everyone from throwing at once or just dropping them in. A taped line on floor might have helped.	J. stayed with it for a long time and also counted the bags. R.refused to stand back as did many others. They preferred to get close or to just drop them in.
Rhythm and temporal awareness	Finger-paint with shaving cream to music.	Teacher in charge forgot to bring music.	H. stayed with it almost the whole time. Children washed hands a lot.

Rebound and airborne activities	Jump on mattress in block area.	Teacher had to participate to get them started. Added steps made out of blocks at one end to jump from.	E. is a strong jumper. L. jumped repeatedly once I held her doll.
Projectile management	Beanbag toss at body target.	See Body and space perception.	
Management of daily motor skills	Finger-paint with shaving cream.	See Rhythm and temporal awareness.	
	Make orange juice. Use tools such as juicer, spoon to stir, knife to cut oranges, pour and measure orange juice.	Substituted an electric juicer because children couldn't press hard enough to use customary type.	Children needed help learning to start juicer by pressing down. Did fine with spooning.
	Manipulative materials such as puzzles, seriation cylinders, and Bristle Blocks included during rug time.		
Relaxation	Finger-paint with shaving cream to relaxing music.	Teacher in charge forgot music.	
	Jump on mattress; relax on mattress.	Teacher tried to structure activity so only two were on mattress at one time, but explaining and carrying this out resulted in the children losing interest and walking away. Alternative of allowing the children to pretty much control number using mattress only got out of hand once.	Seemed relaxing to children even without music to set the pace. L. and J. really did relax.
	Rolling on large ball would be relaxing for some children.		Rolling on the ball did seem relaxing for D. and J.

Note. Plan kindness of Cené Marquis, sudent teacher, the Institute of Child Development, University of Oklahoma, 1982.

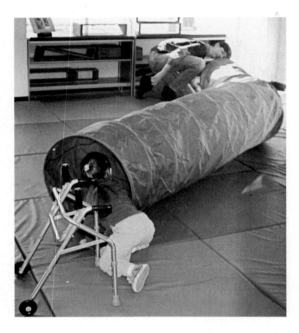

This equipment is well suited to various abilities and needs—and offers lots of playful fun.

Helping Children Learn to Relax

Early childhood teachers have long recognized the necessity of having quiet times during the day, such as nap or midmorning rests. The ability to make good use of these times by genuinely relaxing varies a good deal from child to child. The more tense the child, the more difficulty she will have letting go—and the more she needs to do so. We often think of tension as being revealed by restlessness or a strained facial expression, but there are many other signs to look for. These are seen in children who hold their bodies in tense positions (hunched shoulders or clenched jaws), who appear immobile, or who are awkward or inhibited in movement. Other indicators of tension that are familiar include the inability to eat or a compensatory need to eat more than necessary, breathing difficulties, blushing or turning pale, cold hands or feet, the need to urinate frequently, tension headaches, and insomnia. When one reviews this list, the value

of freeing a child from such burdens by teaching her to relax becomes apparent.

Teachers can help children learn to relax by using the simple method advocated by Jacobson (1976). Described in very general terms, this involves helping children learn to perceive how their bodies feel when they are tense and how they feel when they are relaxed and then helping them learn to relax at will. Young children can grasp this fairly readily if asked to make themselves as stiff and tight as possible or to walk like a robot, and then to make themselves as floppy as a soft rag doll or to melt like a Popsicle. Mirrors are helpful accessories because the children can observe their faces when they scrunch them up tight and then let them go soft. They can also be encouraged to look at other children and tell when they are tensing or relaxing. Emphasis should be placed on repeatedly contrasting tense and relaxed states until the children identify them easily and produce each state at will. Once they have mastered whole-body relaxation, they can work on isolated areas, such as legs or arms or hands.

Stretching and yawning are excellent relaxation inducers, as are simple yoga exercises for breathing that can be used with older fours and fives. Of course, using soothing music and reducing extraneous stimulation, such as that caused by children and staff going in and out of the room during rest period, are basic to achieving success when teaching relaxation.

Movement Education

In addition to the kinds of activities that have already been discussed, an additional activity teachers often use to foster the physical development of children is termed *movement education*. Table 9–3 offers many examples of how this approach can be used with children of preschool age.

Although not as free as creative dance, movement education does have creative aspects, because teachers using this approach stress creative thinking on the part of the children (Cleland, 1990). Movement education also helps children become more conscious of their bodies and what their bodies can do. Thus, the teacher might ask the children to demonstrate all the ways they can balance a beanbag or how they might get from one corner of the room to the other without using their feet. Because this approach often uses music, it is pleasurable to children and thus can make physical development seem less like exercise and more like fun. A combination of movement exploration activities and creative dance makes a good blend—movement education helps ensure that the range of perceptual-motor activities is complete and that concepts of body image are developed, and dance (discussed in a later section of this chapter) ensures opportunities for rhythmic improvisation and self-expression.

In my opinion, teachers must be careful that this kind of direction ("Can you put your body behind something or in front of something?") does not become overly academic and dull. Movement education can easily be corrupted and misinterpreted if the teacher is insensitive and allows the experience to degenerate into an instructional situation intended only to teach the meaning of adverbs.

Yoga exercises are an alternative approach to movement education that teachers might find interesting to use with young children if they have a good grasp of this philosophy. These exercises feel good and can be presented quite simply, as Rachel Carr's book (1980) demonstrates.

Helping Children Enjoy Creative Dance

By far the freest method of providing experiences that use some of these motor abilities is through creative dancing. This requires *combining some open-ended suggestions from the teacher with spontaneous activity generated by the children*. Beginning teachers (and more experienced ones, too) sometimes approach creative dance with apprehension. They usually fear two things—losing control of the group and not being able to get the children to participate. The problem may also be compounded by their feeling self-conscious about dancing themselves.

When the teacher played some lively waltzes outdoors, this dancing just "boiled up" spontaneously.

Maintaining Control of the Group

To keep control of the group, draw the line between active movement and wild running around. Fortunately, several things will help. Among them are keeping the group a reasonable size (for a beginning teacher this can mean as few as four or as many as eight children) and always having an idea about what you intend to do next. It is important to employ a variety of slower and quicker rhythms and to provide relaxation periods so that the session does not keep building and building to a disastrous climax. It will also help teachers retain control if they incorporate movements that involve sitting and lying down part of the time, as well as those that require standing and moving about. Life will generally be easier if an assistant is available to help with shoes, records, and so forth. (If dance activities are offered toward the end of the morning, often a parent can be prevailed on to return early and assist before picking up a car pool.)

How to Begin

Getting children to participate need not be difficult if the teacher does some planning ahead and also participates in the activities. Such enthusiasm is contagious. It often works out well to begin a dance session with some simple, sitting-on-the-floor activities, such as finger plays, dancing with the arms to music, and movement education activities. These "beginners" help overcome self-consciousness by not making everyone be up on their feet moving around right away. Sad to admit, even as early as preschool, some little boys have already decided that dancing is sissy. If this is the case, it is wiser to call it *movement time* or some other less prejudice-laden term than *dancing*.

Using simple props can help start the dance session also; scarves, balloons, tubes of stretchy jersey material, crepe paper streamers, tie-on skirts made of tulle sewn to ribbon waist bands, capes, and even piles of dry leaves may help distract the self-conscious child from thinking of him- or herself. It is better not to depend on props too much, though, because they can become distracting.

Thinking about the children instead of oneself is a good basic remedy for overcoming personal self-consciousness, but other activities will help, too. Taking a modern dance class where everyone is moving together is one way of working through this feeling. Another way to reduce the overall sense of anxiety is by planning everything well and having a reassuring reservoir of ideas on which to fall back. Some beginning teachers prefer to be left completely alone with the children and provided with the assurance that absolutely no one will interrupt them; others feel more comfortable if they pair with another person at the start.

Incidentally, dance experiences provide excellent opportunities for identifying children with possible hearing difficulties. Watch for children who do not respond at all to changes in rhythm, who lose interest as soon as softer music is played, or who seem to stay consistently close to the source of the sound. These behaviors may be indicators that the child is not hearing well and would benefit from a referral to a physician.

Using Music

Music contributes a great deal to the satisfaction of a dance experience. A piano and accompanist are ideal but not necessary. Probably the best solution to the problem of music is to make tapes of your own to fit various moods and rhythms. It is also possible to purchase records to fit these categories, but there always seem to be some selections on each record that you do not want to use, and it can be tedious to stop and hunt for particular items while the children stand, restlessly waiting.

Be wary also of a multitude of so-called children's records that feature vocals that are arch, condescending, and insincere. When listening to these recordings, it is obvious that the people who have produced them do not know much about little children, because so often the tempo is too fast, the pitch is too high, the lyrics inane, and the activities inappropriate. Remember that children's tastes are being formed by the music you use; do not settle for second-rate tripe when there are performers like Ella Jenkins, Marcia Berman, and Raffi available.

It is not necessary to use music the entire time. Percussion instruments, such as drums and tambourines, are very effective, and chants and songs are useful also.

Never forget that music offers fine opportunities for incorporating multiethnic materials into the center's day. Every culture has its own tradition of folk dances, drum patterns, and songs. Music can also bring the culture of the home to the school if children are invited to bring records or tapes of popular music from home to share. After all, most popular music is written to be danced to.

Folk dances have both strengths and weaknesses for the dance group at preschool. Because they follow prescribed patterns, we cannot deceive ourselves that they are creative, and they may also be too complicated or move too quickly if presented in their original form. It is important to remember that they can be simplified, that they do provide a way of honoring other people's culture, and that they offer opportunities for children to accomplish something together in a group. Therefore, they deserve their place in the dance experience as long as teachers realize their limitations as well as their virtues.

Expression of Ideas and Feelings

Once the children are moving freely, the time is ripe to draw suggestions from them about what the music is saying to their feet. From here it is but a short step to encouraging children to express their feelings and helping them make contact with those feelings, whose presence they may otherwise be denying to themselves. For example, the teacher might move from playing an action game based on the song "Here We Go 'Round the Mulberry Bush," featuring the things done at school (swinging, eating snack, hammering wood), to dancing the way they would dance if they felt sad when their mother left

To jump or not to jump—that is the question!

them at school, or if they felt a little angry about being left, or if they were happy to come. During the activity, the teacher also can comment casually that children often feel all these ways—a mixture of feelings. The same approach could be applied to going to the hospital, receiving a measles shot, or the new baby arriving.

Ingredients of a Good Creative Dance Experience

To sum up, then, a good plan for dancing includes some nonthreatening warm-up activities to begin with, some multiethnic music for cultural richness, at least one idea that encourages the expression of feelings related to the children's life experiences, and plenty of encouragement for the children to dance freely to a variety of tempos and rhythms (Stinson, 1988). A good plan also includes a reserve of ideas in the teacher's head in case something does not go as well as hoped and a good selection of records or tapes with which the teacher is so familiar that the needed music can be located quickly.

Summary

Activities that enhance their physical skills are very dear to young children, as well as vital to their growth and development. For this reason, it is well worth teachers' time and attention to plan a comprehensive program that develops each kind of basic perceptual-motor skill.

To do this successfully, teachers must know about general developmental levels and also know specific facts of physical development about each youngster. Once they have this information, they should refer to a thorough outline of perceptual-motor skills to make certain that their curriculum plans are truly comprehensive.

It is valuable to offer both portable and solidly fixed apparatus to encourage the growth of physical skills. Although all these items may be purchased, it is also possible to build many of them for reasonable sums of money.

The needed activities can be incorporated into the center's day in several ways: offering perceptual-motor activities per se, constructing changeable obstacle courses, and including movement education and creative dance activities on a regular basis. Learning how to relax should also be included as an important aspect of exercise.

Self-Check Questions for Review

Content-Related Questions

1. Give some examples of how physical activity benefits each of the five selves.
2. What are the approximate ages when children become proficient at letting go of something voluntarily (controlled releasing)? Catching a small ball using only their hands? Skipping skillfully?
3. Name some movable types of equipment that are inexpensive and useful to offer when developing a play space for children that stimulates large-muscle play.
4. What are some of the basics to remember that were cited in the discussion on presentation of activities?

5. Why is it important to teach children how to relax? Suggest some strategies for teaching relaxation that are helpful to use with young children.
6. List some helpful principles to remember when leading children in a creative dance experience.

Integrative Questions

1. Think of several outdoor play yards you have seen in children's centers. How does the equipment in those yards compare with that recommended by the research of Frost and Strickland?
2. Table 9–3 provides many examples of activities children can use to develop various physical abilities. Suggest an activity not included in the chart for each of the eight abilities. Explain how you could make the activity easier or more challenging, depending on the skill and age level of the children.
3. How do movement education and creative dance differ from each other? What are the benefits of each of these activities?

Questions and Activities

1. Suppose you wanted to make certain that all the children participated in every physical activity each day. Explain to the class what the value of doing this might be and what the drawbacks might be.
2. There is a little 3-year-old boy in your group who is terrified of going down your 7-foot slide. His father sees this as being "sissy" and urges his son to attempt the slide every time he brings him to school. If you were this youngster's teacher, what would you do about this situation?
3. If you could only add one piece of outdoor equipment to the preschool where you teach, what would it be? And why would you select it? How could you obtain it for the least cost?
4. Is there a piece of equipment where you observe or teach that the children rarely use or always use the same way? Suggest two things you might try with it to make it more attractive to them.
5. Play through your popular albums at home, and bring two contrasting ones to share with the class that you feel would be nice to use in a dance session with children.
6. The weather has been very bad for the past 4 days—so bad that no child or teacher has ventured outdoors. Can you suggest a number of

large-muscle activities that could be used indoors to provide relief? What if you put all the furniture out in the hall? Or could you use the hall?

7. You are just setting up a neighborhood day-care center that you expect about thirty 3- and 4-year-olds to attend. You have little money, but lots of strong friends who own some good power tools. List the most important pieces of equipment you think your play yard needs, and explain how you plan to obtain them.

8. If you could not use a newsletter or have a parents' night, how else might you keep the parents informed about the physical development program at your school?

9. You are the head teacher at last, and so you are in charge of scheduling. How would you design a simple, clear schedule for physical activities that would cover all the skills listed in Table 9–3?

10. Share with the class the most successful things you have done with the children so far to encourage creativity in dance.

References for Further Reading

Overviews

Frost, J. (1996). Joe Frost on playing outdoors. *Scholastic Early Childhood Today,* 10(7), 26–28. The leading authority in the field answers some relevant current questions about playgrounds and their purposes in early childhood.

Gallahue, D. L. (1995). Transforming physical education curriculum. In S. Bredekamp & T. Rosegrant (Eds.), *Reaching potentials: Transforming early childhood curriculum and assessment* (Vol. 2). Washington, DC: National Association for the Education of Young Children. This sensible chapter stresses suiting physical education instruction to the individual child while also recognizing that children progress through a series of phases and stages. Includes a list of national physical education standards and an example of a checklist that could be used for evaluating children's progress.

Rivkin, M. S. (1995). *The great outdoors: Restoring children's right to play outside.* Washington, DC: National Association for the Education of Young Children. Rivkin presents an overview of why outdoor play is so valuable and how to go about providing it for children in a satisfactory way.

Winter, S. M. (1995). *Outdoor play and learning for infants and toddlers.* Little Rock, AR: Southern Early Childhood Association. This pamphlet is filled with useful information and has a special emphasis on developing safe outdoor environments for very young children.

Information About Physical Development

Gallahue, D. L. (1995). *Understanding motor development: Infants, children, adolescents, adults.* Dubuque, IA: Brown & Benchmark. The best basic textbook in the field provides a comprehensive look at physical development. *Highly recommended.*

Activities

Benelli, C., & Yougue, B. (1995). Supporting young children's motor skill development. *Childhood Education,* 71(4), 217–220. These four pages are filled with so much practical advice about how to actually teach specific skills to preschool children that it is well worth seeking out.

Hammet, C. T. (1992). *Movement activities for early childhood.* Champaign, IL: Human Kinetics. Written by an obviously experienced teacher of preschool children, this book presents many activities for developing movement skills.

Kruger, H., & Kruger, J. (1989). *The preschool teacher's guide to movement education.* Baltimore, MD: Gerstung. Carefully divided according to developmental stages, this book is rich with ideas and practical suggestions for fostering movement exploration.

Miller, K. (1989). *The outside play and learning book: Activities for young children.* Mount Rainier, MD: Gryphon House. Many age-appropriate, attractive, fresh suggestions for outdoor activities are included here. Topics range from ideas for riding-toy play to snow and woodworking activities.

Werner, P., Timms, S., & Almond, L. (1996). Health stops: Practical ideas for health-related exercise in preschool and primary classrooms. *Young Children,* 51(6), 48–55. The authors provide practical advice about ways to increase the amount of vigorous exercise for young children. *Highly recommended.*

Movement Education

Benzwie, T. (1987). *A moving experience: Dance for lovers of children and the child within.* Tucson, AZ: Zephyr. The subtitle is somewhat misleading because this book deals more with what is often termed "movement education" than with creative dance. It offers many good ideas, including useful ones about how to move children gradually into the experience. It also includes a good list of appropriate records for various activities.

Sullivan, M. (1982). *Feeling strong, feeling free: Movement exploration for young children.* Washington, DC: National Association for the Education of Young Children. This book provides suggestions for children from ages 3 to 5 and 5 to 8. Sullivan does not hesitate to discuss how to obtain and retain control of the group. She also makes many suggestions for activities. *Highly recommended.*

Weikart, P. (1987). *Round the circle: Key experiences in movement for children ages 3 to 5.* Ypsilanti, MI: High/Scope. Weikart discusses eight aspects of helping children with movement experiences, ranging from using language to describe movement to moving with others to a common beat.

Weikart, P. (1988). *Movement plus rhymes, songs, and singing games: Activities for children ages 3 to 7.* Ypsilanti, MI: High/Scope. *Movement Plus* accompanies *Round the Circle* and offers many additional suggestions.

Dance

Overby, L. Y. (Ed.). (1991). *Early childhood creative arts: Proceedings of the International Early Childhood Creative Arts Conference.* Reston, VA: American Alliance for Health, Physical Education, Recreation and Dance. This publication includes several useful articles on using dance and movement experiences with young children.

Stinson, S. (1988). *Dance for young children: Finding the magic in movement.* Reston, VA: American Alliance for Health, Physical Education, Recreation and Dance. This book offers a helpful mixture of practical ideas, suggestions for themes, approaches with handicapped children, and sound dance theory.

Zukowski, G., & Dickson, A. (1990). *On the move: A handbook for exploring creative movement with young children.* Carbondale: Southern Illinois University Press. This helpful book is filled with simple, practical suggestions for generating dance activities. It includes a chapter on working with special needs children.

Teaching Children to Relax

Cherry, C. (1981). *Think of something quiet: A guide for achieving serenity in early childhood classrooms.* Belmont, CA: Pitman Learning. This is a truly rare book; it deals with various aspects of quietness, ranging from recommendations on presenting naps to suggestions for teaching relaxation.

Humphrey, J. H. (1988). *Teaching children to relax.* Springfield, IL: Thomas. After discussing the causes of tension, Humphrey provides instructions for progressive relaxation, meditation, and other techniques. Many of the suggestions could be used successfully with preschool children.

Including Children with Disabilities

Block, M. (1994). *A teacher's guide to including students with disabilities in regular physical education.* Baltimore, MD: Brookes. There are two chapters in this book that are particularly valuable for preschool teachers. One provides suggestions for adapting activities to specific disabilities. The other discusses how to draw preschool children who have disabilities into active physical participation—and shows how to translate an individual education program (IEP) into actual activities. *Very practical.*

Greenstein, D., Miner, N., Kudela, E., & Bloom, S. (1995). *Backyards and butterflies: Ways to include children with disabilities in outdoor activities.* Cambridge, MA: Brookline. This well-illustrated book describes numerous ways that equipment can be adapted to include everyone in the joys of outdoors. Appropriate for parents and teachers.

Moore, R. C., Goltsman, S. M., & Iacofano, D. S. (1992). *Play for all guidelines: Planning, design and management of outdoor play settings for all children.* (2nd ed.). Berkeley, CA: Communications. A basic reference in the field, this revised edition remains a treasure trove of playground design while *adding valuable information on how to comply with the Americans with Disabilities Act, thereby welcoming all children to the delights of playing outdoors. Highly recommended.*

Equipment Design—Money Savers

Werner, P. H., & Simmons, R. A. (1990). *Homemade play equipment for children.* Reston, VA: American Alliance for Health, Physical Education, Recreation, and Dance. There are many low- or no-cost ideas included here plus suggestions for original uses of materials that may inspire the teacher.

For the Advanced Student

Allen, Lady of Hurtwood. (1968). *Planning for play.* Cambridge, MA: MIT Press. Lady Allen, a progressive thinker, was among the first to advocate the development of adventure playgrounds. She describes the purpose of this book as being "to explore some of the ways of keeping alive and sustaining the innate curiosity and natural gaiety of children." It does that. A classic.

American Public Health Association/American Academy of Pediatrics. (1992). *Caring for our children: National health and safety guidelines for out-of-home child care.* Washington, DC/Elk Grove Village, IL: The Association and Academy. This publication lists hundreds of standards for out-of-home care together with the reason for advocating the standard. It is extremely thorough and includes a reprint of a Consumer Product Safety publication.

Brett, A., Moore, R. C., & Provenzo, E. B. (1993). *The complete playground book.* Syracuse, NY: Syracuse University. For a useful overview of playgrounds past and present, this is an excellent resource. Particular attention is paid to European playgrounds, and plentiful illustrations enrich the text.

Fox, J. E., & Tipps, R. S. (1995). Young children's development of swinging behaviors. *Early Childhood Research Quarterly,* 10(4), 491–504. For readers interested in how to research steps in development of a particular skill, this article provides an interesting example of an approach.

Associations with Related Interests

American Alliance for Health, Physical Education, Recreation and Dance. 1900 Association Dr., Reston, VA 22091. The Alliance offers many publications and media materials related to an astonishing range of physical activities.

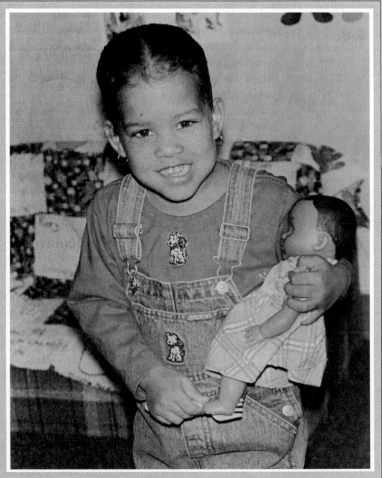

Helping Children Understand and Value Life

Have you ever

- Wondered whether little children understand anything about the cycle of life?
- Wished you knew how to avoid total chaos when an animal visits?
- Needed to know what to do when there has been death in a family and parents come to you for advice?
- Wanted to help young children avoid sexual abuse?

If you have, the material in this chapter will help you.

The nursery school is a place where the pulse of life is sensed and celebrated. Encountering the wonders of existence, the beauty and mystery of life and birth, the joy of music, and the fun of movement, pulses life-enabling energies. One of the goals of nursery school is to help a child feel life pulsing within, and animating his community and his world.

Martha Snyder, Ross Snyder, and
Ross Snyder, Jr. (1989, pp. 33–34)

Teaching children to understand and value life may seem too abstract or advanced a subject for such young children, but when it is broken down into specific topics, it becomes clear that we have many opportunities to establish basic attitudes toward life (and death) at this early age.

For example, even very young children are interested in their own bodies and what goes on inside of them. They often ask such questions as these: If we eat watermelon seeds, will they really grow out of our ears? When Sue broke her arm, did it really fall off? How did the doctor sew it on again? When I want a baby sister, why can't I buy one of those little jars at the market, take it home, and just water it real good? (The child who asked this was convinced that babies came from baby food jars.) Why doesn't the bird fly anymore? Why can't we wake him up? Why is our mouse so stiff, and why does he smell so funny?

These and innumerable questions like them provide evidence that questions about life and its cycle come up frequently and naturally in preschool classrooms. The difficulty with this subject matter is that some adults feel uncomfortable about dealing with it themselves, much less discussing it with young children. Then, too, despite recent polls showing that more than 90% of parents want schools to discuss sex education in particular (Flax, 1991), some families continue to feel strongly that such material should be handled only within the family, and not in the school.

For these reasons, individual teachers must decide what the appropriate approach is for their particular group of children and use the material in this chapter accordingly. It is to be hoped that most teachers will be able to include information about life and death in a matter-of-fact and wholesome way as the opportunity arises.

Teaching Reverence for Life

The most fundamental concept to bear in mind when teaching about the cycle of life is that the living things in the world around us should be valued and cherished for their beauty. The world is filled with exquisite life forms, and every time you teach children to step over a spider, or point out the fragile beauty of the rat's paw, or share the delicate wonder of a sprouting seed, you are helping them acquire this concept.

Our obligation to conserve and protect nature's wonders also should be a part of teaching reverence for life. Such mundane activities as building a compost heap, digging rabbit droppings into the garden, and returning a rotten pumpkin to the earth can all help children realize they can participate in a simple, practical effort to sustain natural life cycles (Wilson, 1995).

Best of all, teaching reverence for life can be woven beautifully into cross-cultural learnings from the Native Americans. These people have understood better than most how to live in harmony with nature, abusing neither animals nor earth.

In no other area of subject matter are so many books available that can be used to extend the child's feelings for the beauty of the world. Even when the text is too advanced, as is the case with the books by Holling Clancy Holling, the illustrations alone may be worth the price of the volume. There is even a magazine[1] published especially for prekindergarten children that stresses conservation and understanding nature. Teachers can make quite an occasion of its arrival each month.

Teaching about reverence for life also involves teaching about the entire life cycle of human beings. Children love the idea that they are growing bigger and stronger every day. They relish visits by babies, and they are quicker than people of many ages to appreciate the value of older adults, who can become treasured participants in the life of the school (Seefeldt & Warman, 1990). Not only do older people need children, but also children genuinely need them to enrich their understanding of the stages of human life. Most communities have organizations composed of older adults who can be approached in the search for congenial volunteers.

Helping Children Learn to Cherish Their Bodies

One of the most meaningful areas of life education for young children is learning about their own bodies and how to cherish them. Children like to know what is inside themselves. They are interested in seeing X-rays of arms and legs, listening to heartbeats, and comparing parts of their bodies that are soft such as ears and tongues with parts that are hard such as fingers

and heads. They love drinking a glass of water and then rocking in a chair to feel the splash inside, and they are fascinated with blood—what it is and what it does.

They are also interested in urination and bowel movements, because they went through toilet training not long before. Children often attach strong feelings to defecation, because toilet training remains a point of strain in some families. Indeed, some psychologists and teachers with Freudian backgrounds maintain that one of the most significant values of offering mud and play dough and finger painting is that these materials allow children opportunities to express some of their more hostile feelings about toileting in a socially acceptable (sublimated) way. For

Here Katie is performing major surgery on a model from the biology department.

---

[1]*Your Big Back Yard*, published by the National Wildlife Federation, 1400 16th St. N.W., Washington, DC 20036-2266.

this reason, they recommend that remarks likening these substances to bowel movements should be accepted casually rather than deplored, because such remarks are frequently a part of such play. On the other hand, a reasonable line must be drawn so that children do not spend their lunchtimes talking about how the gravy is made of poopoo lest it make the food seem unpalatable to the listeners.

Discussions about excretions should be frank, as should discussions about anatomical differences between boys and girls. The usual preschool practice of using the same bathroom for both sexes is a great aid in dispelling the mystery of sexual differences. Using correct vocabulary for various body parts and functions also is more desirable than using slang or street language, though teachers certainly need to understand what a child means when he urgently whispers "kaka" or "peepee."

The most wholesome attitude to encourage is that our bodies are sources of pleasureful feelings and that they deserve good care. It feels good to stretch and yawn, it feels good to eat and be satisfied, it feels good to wake refreshed from sleep, and it feels good to go to the toilet. Bodies are not parts of us to be punished by being ignored or mistreated; they should be carefully cared for and cherished. This includes allowing our bodies to rest when they feel tired, nourishing them well, and appreciating the joys of good health, pleasures that all too often are taken for granted. Teachers must help children learn to honor their bodies and treat them well so that they remain a source of delight to them all their lives.

What to Do When Children Masturbate

Sooner or later most children discover that one source of physical pleasure comes from masturbation. They may do this almost absentmindedly while watching television or listening to stories; they may masturbate as part of lulling themselves to sleep or as a means of passing time during a sleepless nap period; they may retreat to this activity when feeling anxious and insecure in new surroundings.

The difficulty is that this behavior, although natural, is not socially acceptable. Besides that, many of us adults feel very uncomfortable when we discover a masturbating child. On one level, we are acquainted with research about masturbation that reveals that the practice is commonplace among children and adults (both men and women) (Kinsey, Pomeroy, & Martin, 1948; Kinsey, Pomeroy, Martin, & Gebhard, 1953; Masters, Johnson, & Kolodny, 1994). We also know that masturbation is neither perverted nor self-destructive, that penises do not drop off as a result of it, that dark circles do not show under eyes because of it, and so forth. Therefore, at least intellectually, we would like to regard masturbation as being a simple, natural part of human sexuality. But, on an emotional level, our feeling selves may respond in quite a different way, and we may feel embarrassed, disapproving, flustered, and perhaps even angry when coming across a masturbating child (Lively & Lively, 1991).

The problem is how to handle these reactions in a way that does not mortify children or make them feel guilty and yet realistically takes into account society's expectations and our own feelings. At present, the best solution seems to be to teach children as calmly as possible that masturbation is something people do only in private, just like nose picking—neither activity is socially sanctioned behavior done in front of other people. Simply take the child aside and quietly explain this without making him or her feel like a criminal.

We must also be aware that many adults (both parents and teachers) would not agree with this point of view—they condemn masturbation entirely. But it is to be hoped that these people can at least learn to refrain from issuing those dire threats that some of us were subjected to in our own childhoods—threats about what happens to little boys and girls who "do that."

Teaching Children to Protect Themselves from Sexual Abuse

We cannot leave this discussion of caring for our bodies without including information on how to teach children to protect themselves from sexual advances. From evidence that has accumulated in the past decade about the sexual abuse of children, it becomes clear that such experiences happen far more frequently than we might expect.

Finkelhor (1994) reports that in 1993 approximately 150,000 *confirmed* cases of child sexual abuse were reported—this amounts to about 15% of the more than 1,000,000 confirmed cases of all child abuse and neglect for that year. Because many such cases go unreported, it is also helpful to consider data from retrospective studies of adults. Finkelhor's summary of 19 such studies reveals that one in five adult women in North America experienced sexual abuse during childhood and from one in 20 to one in 10 men reported such abuse.

Although the standard advice about never taking candy from strangers or getting into a car with someone you do not know remains sound, research reveals that in most cases of sexual abuse the perpetrator is well known to the child and is often a relative or family friend (Finkelhor, 1997).

In conducting education about sexual abuse, teachers must walk a delicate line between frightening children unduly and instructing them on what to do if they are approached. Children should be taught that their bodies belong to them alone and that their genitalia are private areas that no one has the right to invade in any way. If someone tries to do this and offers them presents or threatens them or their families, their best protection is to refuse and to tell their parents, teacher, or another adult immediately, regardless of how frightened they are.

Children need to understand there is a big difference between an abusive kind of touch and the physical affection of hugs and cuddling that both children and those who love them rightfully enjoy and require to feel emotionally fulfilled. Children need to be taught to discriminate between nurturant behaviors and those of a more frightening and unusual nature.

Teachers need to know that when they suspect abuse has taken place, whether it be due to sexual or other types of injury, law requires them to report it to the correct authority (Rothman, 1990). Working with such cases requires skill and delicacy and is best handled by people who have special training, so teachers should avoid confronting parents directly with their suspicions. Remember that abuse is highly likely to be repeated, so it must not be overlooked or ignored.

Because of recent publicity about sexual abuse taking place in day-care centers, some adult caretakers have become hesitant about showing physical affection to children. Fortunately, it appears that most trained early childhood educators understand that expressing affection *is* not only natural but also a necessary part of building sound relationships between adults and the children they care for. The research study included in this chapter makes these differing points of view plain. However, it is also necessary to understand how to protect both children and adults from experiencing or being accused of committing sexual abuse.

Protecting Teachers from Accusations of Sexual Abuse

The sensational publicity about incidents of sexual abuse in child-care centers has caused both parents and teachers to worry about this possibility (Mikkelsen, 1997). Although careful study of the prevalence of such incidents reveals that these episodes are rare, occurring at the rate of 5.5 children for every 10,000 children enrolled in such centers (Stephens, 1988), everyone agrees that even one such episode is one too many.

Besides that, there is the problem of false accusations. Experts tell us we should never ignore reports by children that they have been abused because it is unusual for children to make up such stories. However, such false allegations have been known to occur (Jones & McGraw, 1987). In my own relatively small community, two such episodes have happened in the past 3 years. Of course, such misunderstandings or false accusations can be disastrous for the accused staff member and the school, too, unless people are able to defend themselves by documenting the steps taken to protect both children and staff.

Basic precautions include making certain that parents know they are always welcome to visit at any time. They do not need to call ahead or alert the center in any way that they are coming. Parents should be educated about the difference between sexual abuse and the affectionate hugging and cuddling so necessary to children's well-being. They should be encouraged to become well acquainted with their children's teachers so that a bond of confidence can develop between them. They should be informed that staff always work in pairs, so there is always a "witness" to what is going on.

Arrange rooms and play yards so they are open to view, with no hidden corners or out-of-the-way unsupervisable spots. Stall doors in bathrooms (if they are used at all) should be either half-height or not go all the way to the floor. Finally, directors must be careful about whom they hire. They should follow up written references with telephone inquiries, and they should make background checks of criminal records in states where this is either required by regulation or at least permitted.

The suggestions given here concerning operation of the center should always be fol-

One winter day a well-informed child at the Institute decided her time had come, so she gave birth while our student teacher interpreted the event to an interested bystander.

**Research
Study**

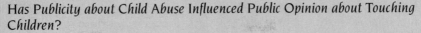

Has Publicity about Child Abuse Influenced Public Opinion about Touching Children?

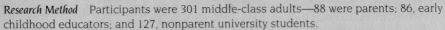

Research Question Does publicity about sexual abuse in day-care centers generate a negative attitude toward positive touching and physical affection in parents and teachers?

Research Method Participants were 301 middle-class adults—88 were parents; 86, early childhood educators; and 127, nonparent university students.

The investigators asked these groups to read material supporting the value of physical affection between adults and children *or* material that said "recent publicity about sexual abuse has made physical contacts between adults and children the focus of increased concern" (Hyson, Whitehead, & Prudhoe, 1988, p. 60). Next, half of the participants in each group were told they were to watch videotapes of day-care providers interacting with children, and the other half of each group were told they were to watch videotapes of parents and children interacting together. Actually, the same tape was used for both groups. The tapes presented a series of brief episodes showing adults being physically affectionate by touching children (e.g., hugging them) or being positive and friendly but not touching the children (e.g., watching a child on a climber). Viewers were asked to rate their degree of approval after viewing each episode.

Results Results indicated that publicity about child abuse can influence attitudes about the value of physical affection. The subjects who had read the comment about sexual abuse before viewing the tape disapproved more of affectionate touching and approved more of nontouching behavior. Viewers approved more of physical affection when it was done by a "parent" rather than by a "day-care provider." Men approved less of adult-child physical affection than women did, and early childhood teachers were more approving of physical affection than the other groups were.

Implications for Teaching People are rightfully concerned about the possibility of sexual abuse happening to young children wherever this might take place. In day-care centers, where parents may be uneasy or feel guilty about leaving their children anyway and are uncertain about what happens beyond the reach of their supervision, worry about this problem is particularly serious and has been exacerbated by recent reports that such abuse has taken place. The research points out how readily uninformed people are influenced by even the words *sexual abuse* and how quickly they tend to equate any form of physical affection with that concept.

This means that teachers must go out of their way to clarify the difference for parents between sexual abuse and physical affection. Teachers need to reiterate how important it is for young children to experience love and caring through touch as well as words, and they need to become well acquainted with every parent to establish bonds of trust between themselves and the families of the children they care for.

An encouraging fact is that the early childhood teachers who participated in this research remained convinced of the value of affectionate touching, despite the influence of negative publicity. Hopefully, such convictions will remain steady. Yet, if suspicions continue and incidents of abuse increase, teachers may eventually lose the confidence of their convictions and come to view the expression of physical affection with young children as something it is wiser to avoid. Hopefully, this outcome will never come to pass.

Note. From "Influences on Attitudes toward Physical Affection between Adults and Children" by M. C. Hyson, L. C. Whitehead, and C. M. Prudhoe, 1988, *Early Childhood Research Quarterly*, 3(1), pp. 55–75.

lowed as a matter of course. If all of these procedures are followed consistently, it is probable that both children and staff will be well protected and can go their happy, affectionate way without worrying that their behavior will be misconstrued (National Association for the Education of Young Children, 1997).

Answering Questions about Reproduction

Many adults feel uneasy about discussing sex and reproduction with children. (The development of sex roles and nonsexist curriculum is discussed in chapter 12.) Fortunately for those

---

 A Surefire Activity: Helping Children Understand and Appreciate the Wonder of Animals

Having animals at school can be a delight or a pain in the neck, depending on the manner of presentation. Most children love animals and are likely to be very excited when one comes to visit. The advantage of having the visitor stay a few days or at least several hours is that as some of the newness wears off, the children have time to become more familiar with the animal. This allows them to overcome either their intense excitement or possible apprehensions. Remember, never force an animal on a reluctant child or vice versa.

When presenting an animal, choose not only one that you enjoy yourself but also (if possible) one that is fairly slow moving and emotionally placid. Always consider safety first, and prepare for safety in advance. This is essential. Make certain that the animal can be adequately confined (we once had an octopus that escaped through an incredibly small hole in the mesh screen). A tippy, temporary cage increases the teacher's anxiety and the consequent number of warnings that she or he must naggingly give the children. Make certain that cages are secure and steady and that they require adult assistance to open. Because tired animals, like tired children, are more apt to lose control, make provisions so that the animal can be withdrawn from circulation and have a rest when it needs this.

When presenting the visitor, it is very important to have firm control over the situation. *Insist* that the children sit down and be as calm as possible. It can be helpful to have carpet squares arranged in a circle to mark where they should sit (chairs can also be used for this purpose). Remind the children of what gentleness means—sometimes telling them "Remember, use soft hands and quiet voices" helps

them understand this concept better than using the word *gentle* does. Remind them also to move slowly.

Crowd control will need to be considered as well. Older fours can manage suggestions and rules for themselves, but the younger children will need more direct teacher control. Offering something else of equal interest at the opposite end of the room, for example, will help. Perhaps water play with some new equipment can be offered, or having some children play outdoors while a few come in at a time may reduce pushing. Presenting the animal during large-group time is still another effective method of crowd control. When all else fails, the rule of "only three or four at a time—please come back later" can also be enforced.

Discussion before the animal arrives should include instructions about whether it can be held or should be watched, how to hold the visitor if this is possible, and how to refrain from frightening it. Animals that can be handled are the most desirable kind to have at school. Rabbits, guinea pigs, rats, land turtles, slow-moving snakes, puppies (who have had their shots), and even baby goats and lambs are all good candidates. If a young animal is to be studied, taking pictures as it grows or, better yet, measuring and weighing it every few days helps children relish and understand the growth process. (Ducks, rabbits, guinea pigs, and rats grow almost as swiftly as radishes.) In some instances, it works well to have the animals live at school during this time, but sometimes, particularly with puppies, it is best to have them visit periodically.

Give some thought to what you want the children to gain from the animal experience. The title of this

of us who feel awkward about this subject, the questions nursery school–age children ask are likely to be simple and not very distressing to answer. Young children often do not even realize that dogs always have puppies and cats, kittens.

They typically want to know where babies come from or why that lady is so fat. The answer to these queries is simple enough: a baby grows inside its mother in her uterus until old enough to be born and then comes out of a special place between her legs called the vagina.

What teachers usually fear is that youngsters will also want to know how the baby got in there in the first place. Actually this is a very uncommon

section intentionally contains the word *appreciate*. Think about how you can help children take time to really look at and appreciate the animal's wonderful qualities, to examine the delicacy of its paws, the beauty of its markings, the softness of its fur, and the whiteness of its teeth. (Children are extremely interested in teeth and whether the animal will bite.) Discuss how various features have helped it adapt to its particular environment: Why do rabbits need such large ears? Why do snails leave that trail of slime behind them? How can the snake move without any legs?

Books on natural history, such as the Golden Book series, are good sources of information on wilder forms of animal life, but often the adequate sources for more domesticated animals are the pamphlets found in pet stores or the local library. The 4-H Clubs sponsored by county extension programs also offer useful information on caring for various barnyard animals.

Whatever the source of information, you should be prepared to offer the children fascinating factual tidbits as they watch and hold the animal: Isn't it interesting that snails have 10,000 little, rough teeth on their tongues to rip up leaves? Imagine—that whole duck came out of a shell just this big! Do you know that some birds carry shells away in their beaks and drop them far from their nest to keep predators from finding their chicks?

Children love feeding animals, so it is wise to have an ample supply of food on hand. Guinea pigs and rats make very desirable pets, since their appetites are almost insatiable.

But with feeding inevitably comes the problem of keeping the animal clean. Nothing is sadder or smellier than a forgotten animal living in a cage badly in need of cleaning. Such a beast cannot help itself; it is up to us to care for it and keep it clean. If you wish to have animals as permanent tenants, you must be willing to work with the children in keeping the animals in immaculate condition.

Experiences with animals should be a pleasure for all the participants.

question for children under 5. In case it should come up, it is accurate to say that the father and mother start the baby growing in the mother by being very loving and close to each other. When they are feeling this way, the father fits his penis inside the mother's vagina and a fluid passes into her that helps start the baby growing. This kind of explanation is desirable because it incorporates both the importance of affection and biological facts.

It often confuses children to talk about planting seeds in relation to human babies. When teachers use this analogy, youngsters naturally think of gardening, which can lead to very odd misconceptions about conception.

In discussions about reproduction, teachers should find out what the children really want to know, make answers truthful and simple, encourage children to say what they think, and help them understand that warmth and caring should be important elements in the experience of intercourse.

Answering Questions About Death

No discussion of the life cycle would be complete without including information on the topic of death. Yet, for many people, this remains a subject even more taboo than sex and one that they prefer to avoid completely when teaching young children. They may believe that children should be shielded from experiencing sadness or that death is too difficult for children to understand. Perhaps the whole subject of death is so frightening and distasteful to them that the thought of mentioning it to children seems overwhelming.

If we face reality, however, we must admit that death is all around us, just as life is: animals die, insects die, flowers die, and people die—even people children know. If, as adults, we are able to acknowledge to ourselves that death is part of life, then we may be more willing to include the subject of death when talking about the cycle of life with children. This comes up very naturally when animals die, roses fade, or pumpkins rot.

Even young children can be allowed to investigate how a dead animal differs from a living one and to mourn its passing (Westmoreland, 1996). Moreover, this experience provides sound opportunities to learn that grief is more endurable when shared and that it does not last forever.

It is helpful to understand that preschool children view death as being a temporary condition from which people may return and continue living (Sprang & McNeill, 1995), a viewpoint unhappily encouraged by animated cartoons that feature exactly this happening. When discussing death with children, the early childhood teacher has to take this kind of magical thinking into account and realize that it is not necessarily an attempt to deny the reality of death but merely an indication that children do not grasp the irreversibility of the event. Because this idea of returning to life appears to be a developmental characteristic, about all the teacher can do is to reiterate patiently the fact that death is permanent.

Preschool children also tend to equate death with sleep—another concept unfortunately reinforced by some adults, which may induce a certain reluctance for bedtime among sensitive youngsters. For this reason, comparing death to sleep should be avoided.

Children are very interested in funerals and enjoy participating in burying pets and nursery school animals that have died. This behavior should be permitted because it contributes to understanding the life cycle and the process of mourning. Such interest should not be regarded as morbid or macabre—it is natural. It becomes morbid only when shocked adults force it to be clandestine.

These participatory understandings can be supplemented with books that touch on the subject of dying. Teachers can use such books to introduce matter-of-fact discussions that may dispel some of the more bizarre misconceptions children harbor about death, the worst one being that death is unmentionable. Several good books that serve this purpose, ranging from *Charlotte's Web* (White, 1952) for older children to

The Tenth Good Thing about Barney (Viorst, 1972) for some of the youngest ones.

Helping Families When Death Occurs

Inevitably there will be occasions during the year when a member of one of the children's family dies. Since families frequently turn to the teacher for advice about how to handle this situation with young children, it seems wise to include a few basic principles here. Some additional books on this subject are included in the references at the end of the chapter.

The most important thing for parents to realize is that the death should be neither restricted from conversations nor concealed from youngsters. Children always know when something is wrong (Furman, 1990; Schaefer, 1987, 1988), and their fantasies can be much more frightening to them than reality would ever be. Truthful statements are generally the best approach.

If possible, parents should prepare children in advance for the death of a loved one. This may be done by saying such things as "The doctors are doing everything they can to help your granny, but sometimes there's just nothing else to do, so she may die."

It is not necessary to try to conceal all grief from children—seeing others cry may help them be able to express their sadness and learn to cope with it (Westmoreland, 1996). As time passes, they also have the chance to realize that gradually the pain of losing someone lessens and life can continue.

Some Special Things to Caution Parents About

Parents should be informed that children (and adults) experience more than pain when someone dies. They are often angry at being abandoned. Sometimes this anger is mixed up with guilt. This may develop because children feel guilty about being angry—"I shouldn't feel mad"—or because they perceive themselves as having caused the death—"If only I hadn't stamped my foot . . ." or "If only I'd been quiet like Mommy said." When fam-

ilies and parents discuss these feelings with children, the youngsters are able to recognize that these are acceptable and natural and that they are in no way responsible for the person's demise.

It may take quite some time for children to grasp that the person is truly gone. For example, one of the youngsters at our center who seemed to have understood his aunt's death surprised us one day by telling us what he thought she would be sending him for his birthday.

Children also require honest reassurance about who will take care of them and how the family structure may change. They wonder, What will happen? What if the other parent dies? What about life will be the same? Occasionally, adults are shocked at what seems to them to be such a self-interested attitude. But young children *are* self-centered. Their experience is extremely limited, and the world as they know it does orbit around them. They also know very well how young and helpless they are. When life is disturbed in such a significant way, it is only natural that they require repeated reassurance and explanations that someone will continue to take care of them.

Finally, families should know that children benefit from recalling memories of the person who has died. Adults sometimes avoid doing this with children because it may also reawaken the pain of loss, but if the life cycle is to be understood and human relationships valued, recalling happy times with departed family members is most worthwhile. This also provides valuable opportunities to finish working through grief and clear up any misunderstandings or concerns the child may be harboring.

Coping with the Threat of AIDS

As discussions of AIDS (acquired immune deficiency syndrome) become prevalent on television and in other media, even children of preschool age are becoming aware of its existence and seriousness.

Although adults need to understand the basic ways that this condition is transmitted and the consequences of not taking precautions to avoid it, for young children it seems more important to concentrate on the aspects of AIDS most likely to concern or frighten them and their families.

One thing that will concern more and more centers as the AIDS epidemic increases is what to do about admitting children infected with the HIV virus (the virus that can lead to AIDS) to their centers. The plight of such youngsters cannot help but touch all our hearts. They are truly innocent victims of this plague, having acquired the condition before or during birth, while being breastfed, from transfusions, or from sexual abuse by an HIV-infected person (National Pediatric HIV Resource Center, 1992). It is also true that AIDS is difficult to transmit from person to person, and *not one case* of such transmission resulting from contact by child to child or contact at school, preschool, or child-care centers has been reported (Pressma & Emery, 1991). Nor have children in homes where an infected person is present, and who have been hugged and kissed by that person, become infected (Skeen & Hodson, 1987).

Despite fairly widespread acquaintance with these facts, one survey revealed that about a third of the parents and a fifth of the care providers questioned felt that children with the HIV virus should not be permitted to attend preschool (Morrow, Benton, Reves, & Pickering, 1991). If a real situation occurred, resistance would likely be even stronger. This resistant attitude to admitting these youngsters sooner or later is going to come into conflict with stipulations of the Americans with Disabilities Act, which states that no one may be excluded because of having AIDS (Child Care Law Center, 1994b).

It seems wisest to think procedures through in advance while heads are cool and emotions relatively in check. For this reason, knowledgeable people are suggesting that centers establish policies and procedures regarding employment, admission of children, and care of children who are so afflicted in advance (Pressma & Emery,

In times of family troubles, centers can be havens of stability for disturbed children.

1991). The policy should include "material on personnel; education and training; infection control; intake, assessment, and enrollment; testing for HIV infection; confidentiality vs. the need to know; record keeping; and an ongoing support continuum for caregivers, children and families" (Pressma & Emery, 1991, p. 12).

Once such a child is admitted, the importance of maintaining the privacy of the child and his or her family is stressed over and over, as is the necessity for following very conscientious policies related to hand washing, diaper changing, and wearing gloves when dealing with injuries involving bleeding (Aronson, 1987; Merahn, Shelov, & McCracken, 1988). It is also very important to protect HIV-positive children from exposure to such infectious diseases as chicken pox and measles because they have sharply reduced or no immune systems to combat these conditions. For this reason some authorities suggest that a small, more intimate child care arrangement may be the most desirable environment for them.

The second concern about AIDS that is directly related to the majority of young children in our care is what we should tell them about this terrible disease. It has been interesting to me, as I reviewed the literature on this subject, to note that although general information and reassurance abounds, most of the information about what to tell children about AIDS per se begins at kindergarten level (Moglia, Welbourne-Moglia, & Haffner, 1989; Quackenbush & Villarreal, 1988). Yet, even young children are bound to have questions about AIDS as we are flooded with information by the media, particularly television. They are also likely to pick up the tone of the messages and become frightened and/or confused by them.

The exception to this dearth of information remains an article by Skeen and Hodson in the May 1987 issue of *Young Children*. Following a lengthy discussion about what adults need to know about AIDS, they turn to the subject of young children and point out how important it is to be careful when we approach this topic with them. They remind the reader that young children know very little about sexuality, blood, or death and that we do not want to confuse or frighten them about these matters. At the same time, it will be necessary to deal with their worries about AIDS if these arise.

Skeen and Hodson (1987) suggest that "children [of preschool age] . . . need a little information and a lot of reassurance" (p. 69). Children should be told that the chances of their getting AIDS is very, very slight, that almost no children have it, and that they are safe. They recommend that if they want to know more, it is sufficient to say that AIDS " 'is caused by a virus, a tiny germ.' Issues of sexual transmission, the spread of the disease through the sharing of contaminated needles during drug use, and the transmission of AIDS through infected blood of mother to fetus, are issues that can be discussed when the child is older" (p. 70). I would suggest adding that "many grown-ups are working hard to learn how to take better care of these people and how to help them get well."

For most youngsters of preschool age, this will be enough. However, for the tragic few who must cope with a loved one's infection or death, much more extensive help will be needed than can be discussed in this chapter. Two resources for such help are listed in the footnote.[2]

Summary

Teaching children to understand and value life should be a basic element of curriculum intended to stress physical well-being. It includes often taboo subjects such as death, sex, sexual abuse, and AIDS and learning about other aspects of children's bodies—what is inside them, how they work, and how good they feel. In addition, even very young children can begin to develop a reverence for life; the chapter includes several suggestions of ways to teach this reverence.

Self-Check Questions for Review

Content-Related Questions

1. What is the wholesome attitude we want children to have toward their bodies?
2. Should masturbation be discouraged at all times? What is the recommended way to deal with a child who masturbates?
3. Why is it valuable to cuddle and hug little children? How have reports on sexual abuse in children's centers affected the behavior of some teachers in those centers?
4. Discuss some practical ways teachers can protect themselves from accusations of sexually abusing young children.
5. What are the results of the research conducted by Hyson, Whitehead, and Prudhoe on attitudes toward expressing physical affection? Discuss the implications for teachers that can be drawn from that research.
6. What is "reverence for life"? Give some examples of how this principle can be taught to young children.

---

[2]National Pediatric and Family HIV Resource Center. 15 S. Ninth St., Newark, NJ 07107. The Public Health Service also maintains a toll-free hotline: 1-800-342-AIDS. For Spanish access, call 1-800-342-7432.

7. What kinds of questions about reproduction are young children likely to ask? Name a couple and practice answering them.
8. How does the young child's concept of death differ from that of grown-ups? Why is it important not to conceal death from children?
9. Is AIDS a disease that is easily caught by young children?

Integrative Questions

1. Suppose you had a baby goat visit the children in your class. What plans and precautions would you take to make the visit most satisfactory to the children *and* the animal?
2. Parents are rightfully concerned about their children's safety while attending child-care centers. What will you do and say to reassure families that their children will be safe in your care?
3. Compare what young children need to know about AIDS with what adults need to know.

Questions and Activities

1. One of the 3-year-olds in your group comes to school in tears because a neighbor has run over her kitten with his car. How do you think this situation should be dealt with at school? The mother also wants to know whether they should stop at the pet store on the way home from school and get another kitten. What would you advise?
2. You suddenly realize that you are missing two or three of the 4-year-olds from your group. When you investigate, you find them hiding in the playhouse comparing differences in their sexual anatomies. How do you think this situation is best handled? What approaches do you feel should be avoided? Why?
3. You are devoted to cross-age grouping, and you have a grandma who volunteers regularly at the school where you teach. You also are devoted to the value of teaching reverence for life. One day you find the grandma outdoors leading the children in stamping all over a spider's nest. How are you going to cope with this situation so that (a) the volunteer is not humiliated and (b) the children do not kill any more spiders?

4. There is no denying that many teachers are still not at ease with such topics as life and death and sexuality. How would you advise them to go about becoming more comfortable with these subjects?
5. You are now teaching in a parent cooperative preschool, and the program committee has decided that the group would like a program on what all young children and their parents should know about sex. They want you to lead the group. Three families are very conservative and believe all sex education should take place in the home, and others believe the school should play a part in such education. What kind of program would you present? What do you believe yourself?
6. One of the children in your school is in an automobile accident. He is seriously hurt and after 4 days dies. How would you handle this situation with the children in your group? His twin sister is due to return to school in a few days.

References for Further Reading

Overviews

Carson, R. (1956). *The sense of wonder.* New York: Harper & Row. Rachel Carson was one of the first to awaken us to our responsibilities for maintaining the earth in a healthy state. In this classic, she is concerned with helping children learn to wonder about the world around them.

Eyre, L., & Eyre, R. (1980). *Teaching children joy.* New York: Ballantine Books. This book expresses a wonderfully positive point of view toward children and toward life. *Highly recommended.*

Wilson, R. A. (1995). Nature and young children: A natural connection. *Young Children,* 50(6), 4–11. Reading Wilson's article will inspire your efforts when helping children learn to enjoy and revere their natural world. *Highly recommended.*

Helping Children Appreciate Life

Kramer, D. C. (1989). *Animals in the classroom: Selection, care, and observation.* Menlo Park, CA: Addison-Wesley. This very good book includes interesting facts and excellent advice on the care of animals ranging from earthworms to rabbits. *Highly recommended.*

Rockwell, R. E., Williams, R. T., & Sherwood, E. A. (1992). *Everybody has a body: Science from head to toe: Activities book for teacher of children ages 3–6.* Mount Rainier, MD: Gryphon House. A wealth of appropriate activities based on experiences with the body are included here—for example, how long can you hold your breath, how big is your chest, and how far can you see? *Highly recommended.*

Seefeldt, C., & Warman, B. (1990). *Young and old together.* Washington, DC: National Association for the Education of Young Children. The authors include a convincing list of learning goals possible when older volunteers participate with young children and also offer excellent resource lists of related curriculum materials. *Highly recommended.*

Education About Sex

Leight, L. (1988). *Raising sexually healthy children: A loving guide for parents, teachers and care-givers.* New York: Avon Books. In this simply written book, Leight presents a sensible discussion of developmentally appropriate approaches to sex education.

Lively, V., & Lively, E. (1991). *Sexual development of young children.* Albany, NY: Delmar. As the title implies, this book focuses on children up to age 8. It uses vignettes to introduce discussion of a wide array of sexual topics ranging from normal development to abuse and the impact of AIDS.

Information on Sexual Abuse and Children's Centers

Koralek, D. (1992). *Caregivers of young children: Preventing and responding to child maltreatment.* Washington, DC: U.S. Department of Health and Human Services, Administration on Children, Youth and Families, National Center on Child Abuse and Neglect. For a brief yet comprehensive discussion of child abuse as it impacts abused children in children's centers, this publication is the most helpful I have found. It may be obtained by calling the Clearinghouse on Child Abuse and Neglect (800-FYI-3366) and should be in every center's library. It discusses recognizing and reporting child abuse, protecting the center from accusations of abuse, and working with abused children and their parents. *Highly recommended.*

Mikkelsen, E. J. (1997). Responding to allegations of sexual abuse in child care and early childhood education programs. *Young Children, 52*(3), 47–51. The author provides practical advice about dealing with false and genuine accusations of sexual abuse.

National Association for the Education of Young Children. (1997). NAEYC position statement on the prevention of child abuse in early childhood programs and the responsibilities of early childhood professionals to prevent child abuse. *Young Children, 52*(3), 42–46. The paper contains clear, practical advice on preventing all kinds of abuse from happening. *Highly recommended.*

Nelson, M., & Clark, K. (Eds.). (1986). *The educator's guide to preventing child sexual abuse.* Santa Cruz, CA: Network

Publications. This valuable book covers everything from issues to guidelines to bibliographies and programs. *Highly recommended.*

Young Children with AIDS

Child Care Law Center. (1994). *Caring for children with HIV or AIDS in child care.* San Francisco: The Center (22 Second St., 5th Floor, San Francisco, CA 94105). This organization, which specializes in counseling about legal problems for child care centers, here provides a guide about legal requirements for admission and accommodation of infected children, universal infection precautions, issues of confidentiality, and so forth.

Pozen, A. S. (1995). HIV/AIDS in the schools. In A. Boyd-Franklin, G. L. Steiner, & M. G. Boland (Eds.), *Children, families, and HIV/AIDS: Psychosocial and therapeutic issues.* New York: Guilford. Although focused on school settings of older children, the material on teacher attitudes applies to preschool teachers just as well.

Pressma, D., & Emery, L. J. (1991). *Serving children with HIV infection in child day care: A guide for center-based and family day care providers.* Washington, DC: Child Welfare League of America. If you require only one reference about children and AIDS in your library, this is the one to get. It covers inclusion of infected staff, precautions, and recommended care of afflicted children—outstanding.

Sprang, G., & McNeil, J. (1995). *The many faces of bereavement: The nature and treatment of natural, traumatic, and stigmatized grief.* New York: Brunner/Mazel. Because a growing number of us work in situations in which families are experiencing these deaths, readers may find the chapter on dealing with grief resulting from a death by AIDS particularly helpful.

Education About Death and Severe Illness

Fox, S. S. (1985). *Good grief: Helping groups of children when a friend dies.* Boston: New England Association for the Education of Young Children (35 Pilgrim Rd., Boston, MA 02215). In this sound, practical book, Fox covers just about every aspect of death and young children that the teacher needs to know. *Highly recommended.*

Greenberg, J. (1996). Seeing children through tragedy: My mother died today—when is she coming back? *Young Children, 51*(6), 76–77. Good advice is provided here about helping the individual child and the group through the experience of death.

Pristine, J. S. (1993). *Helping children cope with death: A practical resource guide for "Someone Special Died."* Carthage, IL: Fearon Teacher Aids. Written in simple terms, this book briefly discusses stages and behaviors related to children's experiencing death and, most valuably, suggests appropriate activities to offer them in various stages of grief.

Schaefer, D. J. (1987). The status of parent-child communication on death and early-stage grief and loss. In J. E. Schowalter, P. Buschman, P. R. Patterson, A. H. Kutscher, M. Tallmer, & R. G. Stevenson (Eds.), *Children and death: Perspectives from birth through adolescence*. New York: Praeger. This chapter provides excellent advice for parents from an experienced funeral director.

Wallinga, C., & Skeen, P. (1996). Siblings of hospitalized and ill children: The teacher's role in helping these forgotten family members. *Young Children*, 51(6), 78–83. A not-to-be-missed article helpful not only with children of hospitalized siblings but also with youngsters adjusting to a sibling with a more permanent disability.

Webb, N. B. (Ed.). (1993). *Helping bereaved children: A handbook for practitioners*. Following an overview, various chapters use case studies ranging from parental suicide to the death of a teacher or sibling to illustrate how to help. *Highly recommended*.

Westmoreland, P. (1996). Coping with death: Helping students grieve. *Childhood Education*, 72(3), 157–160. If you have time for only one resource, this is one of the best because it offers succinct information and practical suggestions.

For the Advanced Student

Essa, E. L., & Murray, C. I. (1994). Research in review: Young children's understanding and experience with death. *Young Children*, 49(4), 74–81. This article includes a summary of research as well as practical recommendations for helping children come to terms with death.

The Future of Children. (1994). Sexual abuse of children. Entire issue: 4(2). This issue provides in-depth, carefully researched information on this difficult subject. It is one of a continuing series of publications from the Packard Foundation concerned with children's well-being—all of which are *highly recommended* (The David and Lucile Packard Foundation, 300 Second St., Suite 102, Los Altos, CA 94022).

Kinnear, K. L. (1995). *Childhood sexual abuse: A reference handbook*. Santa Barbara, CA: ABC-CLIO. This one-of-a-kind book provides invaluable resources for readers seriously interested in this subject. Included are discussions of laws, court decisions, and an extensive annotated bibliography. *Highly recommended*.

Moller, D. W. (1996). *Confronting death: Values, institutions, and human morality*. Cambridge: Oxford University Press. This fascinating book considers death from a sociological point of view. An excellent chapter is included on children and death.

National Guidelines Task Force. (1992). *Guidelines for comprehensive sexuality education: Kindergarten–12th grade*. New York: Sex Information and Education Council of the United States. The guidelines are endorsed by the National Education Association, and they outline appropriate learning goals for four levels of development related to six aspects of sexuality education.

Papadatou, D., & Papadatos, C. (Eds.). (1991). *Children and death*. New York: Hemisphere. *Children and Death* includes material on children's understanding of death, the dying child, and effective ways of helping children, parents, and health professionals cope with death—a good but saddening book.

Resources of Special Interest

The Compassionate Friends. P.O. Box 3696, Oak Brook, IL 60522. An organization for parents whose child has died.

National Center for the Prevention and Treatment of Child Abuse and Neglect. 1205 Oneida St., Denver, CO 80220.

National Committee for Prevention of Child Abuse. 332 S. Michigan Ave., Suite 1250, Chicago, IL 60604-4357.

Siecus Report. Published by the Sex Information and Education Council of the United States, 130 W. 42nd St., Suite 2500, New York, NY 10036.

Have you ever

- Wondered how to help children express their feelings without hurting other children?
- Wanted to know some practical ways to reduce feelings of tensions and aggression in children?
- Worried over how to help a child through a family crisis?

If you have, the material in this chapter will help you.

A teacher with an open heart will be warm, alive, spontaneous, connected, compassionate—able to see the language of the body, hear the feelings between and beneath the words.

Shelly Kessler (1991, p. 6)

Sensitivity, responsive care, involvement, and emotional communication are important aspects of supportive relationships with infants and young children. . . . Teachers should find ways to spend special time with each child in their care, times when the focus is just on the child and the adult. Adults can share their feelings with children and encourage them to express their feelings, too. Caregivers can look for opportunities to make one-to-one moments with each child happen every day. Greeting children as they arrive in the morning, playing in the sandbox, pushing the swing, talking over juice, getting ready for naptime, taking time to share feelings when a child approaches to show that special creation—these are all opportunities to become more involved with a child, when relationship building is a priority.

James Elicker and Cheryl Fortner-Wood (1995, p. 76)

The difficulty with talking about curriculum for the emotional, or affective, self is that the very word *curriculum* has an academic ring that can lead us to overintellectualizing our teaching if we are not careful. We must guard vigilantly against this tendency by remembering that the most effective kind of learning and teaching about the emotional self is embedded in the everyday happenings of life rather than in self-conscious discussions of feelings in artificially contrived group times. To deal with feelings in the most effective way, we must seize teachable moments as they occur to help children perceive and cope with their feelings so they can lead comfortable, emotionally healthy lives.

Sometimes such learning is best accomplished at school by capitalizing on opportunities as they spontaneously arise between children and other children or between children and staff. Sometimes it is best accomplished by

working with parents to deepen their understanding of their children's emotional needs and how to meet them at home. But whichever approach is used, the competencies we wish children to attain are basically the same.

Help the Child Learn to Separate from the Family

The first competency the child has to acquire to survive away from home is the ability to separate from her parent with a reasonable degree of ease so she feels comfortable at school. Ideally, entrance to a children's center or nursery school will not be her first experience in separation, but even if it is not, the length of the absence combined with the unfamiliar environment makes some children uneasy and a few even frantic.

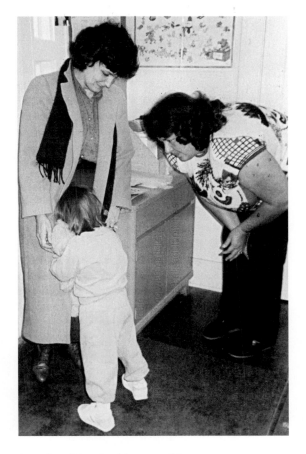

Sometimes it is so hard to say good-bye.

To make the transition as painless as possible, separation should be accomplished gradually. This allows the youngster to make friends with her teacher and possibly one or two of the children and be involved in activities before her parent "abandons" her. Some schools make friends by having staff visit the child at home, or they send each child a personal letter welcoming them to school (children get so little mail and enjoy it so much). Schools that begin anew each fall often invite small groups of children to attend at different times of the morning for the first day or two to provide personal attention for each youngster and prevent feelings of being overwhelmed.

A parent should be encouraged to stay for the first few times until the child has settled in, but he or she may also need to be instructed to be matter of fact and definite when ready to leave, since it increases separation difficulties considerably if the adult debates and vacillates between leaving and staying. However, no matter how well acquainted the child is and how well handled the departure, teacher and parent should realize that tears or a quivering lip are a possibility. Teachers who allow themselves to feel frightened and guilty when a child is upset surely add to the child's anxiety, whereas teachers who take these upsets in stride convey their own sense of security to the child and are thus reassuring (Godwin, Groves, & Horm-Wingerd, 1994).

Unfortunately, feeling secure in the midst of a disturbing scene is more easily recommended than attained by beginning teachers. This is particularly true because such upsets so often take place while other parents are coming and going. The way to become more at ease with these situations is to (a) resolve to see them through as calmly and confidently as you can, (b) comfort the child as well as you are able without pleading or acting apologetic, and (c) while acknowledging her grief, distract her as quickly as possible from her grief. Experience over a period of time helps most of all, for everyone, but the only way to obtain that experience is to work the separation situation through with the child and her family as it arises.

Families, as well as children, benefit from the teacher's assurance, and it can comfort worried parents if they are invited to telephone later to check on whether the child is still crying. Ironically, usually the parent who is the most prone to worry is also shyest of calling about the child unless specifically invited to do so. Fathers, in particular, may be wary of appearing too concerned.

Although it is vital to realize that little children can be desolated by a parent's departure, it may also help teachers feel better if they remember that there is sometimes a touch of drama in the experience. I well recall a young friend of mine, clinging pathetically to the door, while sobbing, "Goldilocks has lost her mama!" The moral of this tale is that it is important to discriminate between the child who is really distressed and the one who is less disturbed (even though making quite a fuss over the separation) and to respond accordingly.

For children who are deeply anxious, the basic task of teacher and parent is to establish a bond of trust between the three of them. Needless to say, the mother or father who sneaks away without letting the child know she or he is leaving is hardly establishing such a bond. *Teachers should be careful to see that this does not happen.*

For an anxious child, the separation should be kept short in the beginning. Sometimes it helps if the parents leave something tangible that belongs to them for the child to keep. (I know of one instance where the youngster wrapped himself in the mother's old sweater for several days.) Sometimes a surrogate comfort object, such as a favorite blanket or stuffed animal, helps bridge the gap. If the child is generally accustomed to toting such an item around, the first days of school are not the time to separate him from it.

Transition to school is also made easier if beginning days are kept simple and uncomplicated and if standards for behavior are not set too high. It can be difficult not to expect a new group of children to begin in the fall where the "sophisticated" former spring group left off. Teachers should bear in mind that the most vital learning tasks for the child's emotional self at the start of school are learning (a) that school is a comfortable place to be and (b) that the parent will return as promised.

Of course, even when children appear to have made the transition comfortably, they may be holding some feelings back. I am reminded of one of our Institute's children whose mother asked him how he had liked school that day. "Well," he replied, "you know, I've been playing a joke on the teachers." "You have?" she asked in

Caregivers should look for opportunities to create one-to-one moments with every child, every day.

surprise. "Yes," he said, "they think that I'm having a good time—but really I'm not!"

Foster Basic Attitudes of Trust, Autonomy, and Initiative in the Child

A second fundamental goal of curriculum for the emotional self is encouraging the child to be trustful, independent, and able to reach out and investigate the immediate world. Erik Erikson (1963, 1982, 1996) has made a valuable contribution to our understanding of the significance of these attitudes in the emotional life of the child and how to encourage their development.

Erikson hypothesizes that during their life span, individuals pass through a series of stages of emotional development in which basic attitudes are formed. Early childhood encompasses three of these stages: (a) trust versus mistrust, (b) autonomy versus shame and doubt, and (c) initiative versus guilt. Although children of preschool age are likely to be working on the second and third sets of attitudes, it is important to understand the implications of the first set, also. This is because Erikson theorizes that the resolution of each stage depends in part on the successful accomplishment of the previous one.

Trust versus Mistrust

In the stage of trust versus mistrust, the baby learns (or fails to learn) that other people can be depended on and also that she can depend on herself to elicit needed responses from them. This development of trust is deeply related to the quality of care that the parent provides and is often reflected in feeding practices, which, if handled in a manner that meets her needs, help assure the infant that she is valued and important. Although by the time she enters preschool, the balance between trust or mistrust will have been tipped in favor of one attitude or the other, the need to experience trust and to have it reaffirmed remains with people throughout their lives. This is also true for the other attitudes as they develop.

Therefore, it is vital that the basic climate of the center encourage the establishment of trust among everyone who is part of that community. If the teacher thinks of establishing trust in terms of letting the children know that they can depend on him, it will be fairly easy for him to implement this goal. For example, consistent policies and regularity of events in the program obviously contribute to establishing a trustful climate. Being reasonable also makes it clear to the child that she can depend on the teacher. In addition, if he is sensitive to the child's individual needs and meets them as they arise, the teacher can confirm the message of her infancy once again that she is worthy of love and thus further strengthen trust and self-esteem.

Autonomy versus Shame and Doubt

In our society the second stage, in which the attitudes of autonomy versus shame and doubt are formed, occurs during the same period in which toilet training takes place. During this time, the child is acquiring the skills of holding on and letting go. This fundamental exercise in self-assertion and control is associated with her drive to become independent and to express this independence by making choices and decisions so often couched in the classic imperatives of the 2-year-old: "No!" "Mine!" and "Me do it!" Erikson maintains that children who are overregulated and deprived of the opportunity to establish independence and autonomy may become oppressed with feelings of shame and self-doubt, which result in losing self-esteem, being defiant, trying to get away with things, and, in later life, developing various forms of compulsive behavior.

The desirable way to handle this strong need for choice and self-assertion is to provide an environment at home and at the center that makes many opportunities available for the child to do for herself and to make decisions. This is the fundamental reason that self-selection is an important principle in curriculum design. At the same time, the teacher must be able to establish decisive control when necessary, because young children often show poor judgment and can be tyrannized by their own willfulness unless the adult is willing to intervene.

Initiative versus Guilt

Gradually, as the child develops the ability to act independently, she embarks on building the next set of basic attitudes. Around the age of 4 or 5, she becomes more interested in reaching out to the world around her, in doing things, and in being part of the group. At this stage, she wants to think things up and try them out: she is interested in the effect her actions have on other people (witness her experimentation with pro-

Allowing children to do things for themselves helps foster their sense of identity.

fanity and "bad" language); she formulates concepts of what her family feels are appropriate sex roles; she enjoys imaginative play; and she becomes an avid seeker of information about the world around her. This is the stage Erikson has so aptly named initiative versus guilt.

To feel emotionally satisfied, a child of this age must be allowed to explore, to act, and to do. Children's centers are generally strong in meeting the children's need to explore and create, but they often underestimate the ability of

older 4- and 5-year-olds to participate in making plans and decisions for their group, or to attempt challenging projects. Of course, the teacher must make allowance for the fact that 4- and 5-year-olds are better planners and starters than they are finishers. Satisfaction in completing projects is more likely to be part of the developmental stage that follows this one: the stage of *industry versus inferiority*, which is characteristic of children during their early years in primary school. But encouraging the ability to initiate plans and take action will enhance children's feelings of self-worth and creativity, as well as their ability to be self-starters—all highly desirable outcomes necessary for future development and happiness.

Help Children Remain in Contact with Their Feelings While Learning to Control What They Do About Them

Unfortunately, much of our culture appears dedicated to teaching children to suppress and deny feelings. As early as age 2 or 3, some children have already learned that certain feelings are not acceptable for them to "own." These vary according to family standards and may include jealousy in one family, anger toward adults in another, or fearfulness expressed by crying in a third. Whatever they are, such denial, if imposed firmly enough, causes a child to disown part of herself and believe that some part of herself is not acceptable.

The reason for such denial and suppression seems to be that people assume that feeling inevitably leads to acting or that acknowledging a feeling will make it stronger. These assumptions are coupled with the conviction that if one pretends something does not exist, it will go away. But such assumptions are psychologically unsound. What *is* true is that repressing, denying, or ignoring feelings *increases* the probability that the child will act them out—either directly or indirectly. In other words, the child who is unable to *tell* someone how he feels is almost inevitably driven to *show* that person how he feels. Perhaps he hits someone; perhaps he messes his pants; perhaps he knocks over the block construction of an innocent bystander; perhaps he retreats to a quiet place and rocks there, endlessly, in a solitary way. None of these behaviors is an emotionally or socially productive solution, and many of them

could be avoided if parents and teachers would learn to take the risk of helping children recognize their feelings and express them safely. They should use simple terms that children can understand: "Feel what you wish, feel all your true feelings, but control what you *do*."

The problem is that, although the most effective way of dealing with feelings is by telling somebody about them, many adults do not welcome some disclosures. Monahon (1993) states this dilemma clearly when she says:

> If acknowledging a child's feelings were easy, I'm sure it would be done more frequently. It is, in fact, quite difficult to accept what children say about their feelings. There are so many feelings we wish children would not have. For instance, if little Marcie were to tell her mother that she hated that lady who squeezed her, would her mother feel she had said enough by simply replying. "I know, Marcie. You really hated her when she did that to you"? Most parents would want to add some instructive words about "hating." But sometimes when we add our own thoughts and reactions to what children tell us about their feelings, we unintentionally give them the message that we do not accept and respect those feelings. The ever-present temptation to lecture a child is one that we would all do well to resist. (p. 106)

Furthermore, little children are often unable to put feelings into words. Reality forces me to admit that some parents will always interpret this directness as insolence, but the success of such books as *How to Talk So Kids Will Listen, & Listen So Kids Will Talk* (Faber & Mazlish, 1980), *Unsmiling Faces: How Preschools Can Heal* (Koplow, 1996), and *Loving Your Child Is Not Enough* (Samalin & Jablow, 1987), as well as the Parent Effectiveness Training of Gordon (1976, 1989) provide encouraging evidence that it is also possible for many adults to learn to listen and respond to children's feelings without being unduly threatened by the experience. The research study presented here provides additional evidence of how valuable listening closely in order to reflect feelings can be.

Does Reflecting Children's Feelings Really Do Any Good?

Research Study

Research Question   Can using the techniques of recognizing and reflecting children's feelings affect children's ability to control themselves and help them engage in higher-level play behaviors?

Research Method   Forty-eight bilingual Puerto Rican children between the ages of 3 to 6 were randomly divided into groups of four each. Two boys and two girls were included in each group.

Before beginning the experiment, researchers ranked the children on a variety of measures, including one measuring intelligence, one measuring self-control, another evaluating the developmental level of the child's play, and a fourth that measured how well the child was liked by the other children. No significant differences were found between the control and the experimental groups before the experiment took place.

The children who served as the controls participated in unstructured free-play sessions supervised by their teacher for the same amount of time as the experimental children participated with the play therapist. Toys for the control groups were equivalent to those used by the experimental children.

The experimental groups participated once a week with a play therapist who used (a) recognition of the child's feelings and developmental stage, (b) structure of the play environment (by providing the same equipment and saying the same statements at the beginning and end of each session), (c) reflective responding, and (d) limits, when necessary, accompanied by appropriate consequences. She was careful not to use other teaching techniques such as asking questions or giving directions, advice, or praise.

Results   After 10 weekly sessions, the children were evaluated again using the same measures as before. Statistical analysis revealed that the behavior of the control groups did not change to a significant degree. On the other hand, the children who had experienced the recognition of feelings and reflective responding *did* show significant improvement in self-control and also exhibited higher developmental level play behaviors when compared to the control groups. In addition, the boys in the experimental groups became more accepting of other children than did the children in the control groups.

Implications for Teaching   It is important to bear in mind that these findings involved a specially trained person (a therapist) working with only four children at a time. However, it is also true this research provides evidence that taking time to describe and reflect children's feelings to them did have a beneficial effect on their behavior. The growth in the children's ability to control themselves is particularly noteworthy.

Although the more concentrated experience with a highly trained person may produce a stronger effect, there is no reason the use of these techniques should be limited to those situations. Any teacher who decides to use these methods of sensitively responding to the children by describing and reflecting their feelings to them is likely to experience beneficial results, also. For teachers who are willing to make this effort, the results will clearly be worthwhile.

Note. From "The Effects of Child-Centered Group Play Sessions on Social-Emotional Growth of Three- to Six-Year-Old Bilingual Puerto Rican Children" by S. L. Trostle, 1988, *Journal of Research in Early Childhood Education*, 3(2), pp. 93–106.

Hodges (1987) terms this process *active listening* and describes it beautifully:

> Active listening requires giving undivided attention to children and accepting what they say without blame, shock, or solving their problems for them. Giving undivided attention is signaled by positioning squarely in front of a child, getting close to the child's eye level, and leaning forward without crowding. Active listening enables us to reflect the feelings of the child, respond appropriately, and to check to see if we understand. Active listening communicates respect, warmth, and empathy. Children know that they are important and that they belong when they are heard. (p. 13)

Help Children Express Their Feelings

The clearest way to show the child that you have really listened is to take time to describe her feelings before saying anything else. This *paraphrasing* what you surmise she is feeling helps her substitute words for action, thereby fostering self-control. When attempting this, remember to keep sentences describing feelings *short, uncomplicated*, and *tentative*. It is particularly important to be tentative because identifying feelings involves sensitive guesswork. Because you have to surmise the child's probable emotion, there is always the painful possibility of injustice and inaccuracy. To avoid hurting the child through misunderstanding her, it is best to begin interpretations with such phrases as "You seem to me . . . ," "I wonder if you're feeling . . . ," or "Is your face telling me that . . . ?" In short, always remember that such interpretations should be offered as caring guesses rather than as dogmatic labels. Another advantage of concentrating on the child's feelings is that this also begins the lengthy task of teaching her the difference between self-report (telling another person how one feels inside oneself) and verbal attack (hurting the other person's feelings by name calling and so forth)—a valuable distinction, albeit difficult to learn.

Also, because young children's comprehension of language is so limited, it is better teach-

Children sometimes feel like they do not have a friend in the world.

ing to go beyond using an adjective such as *mad* or *happy* or *jealous* to describe the emotion. These words are only beginning to acquire meaning to children of such tender years. Expert teachers try to be more descriptive than that, so they may say, "You look to me like your stomach's all churned up inside" or "I think your eyes are telling me you wish you hadn't done that!" rather than telling a child she looks excited or remorseful.

Although teachers should make a point to recognize all kinds of feelings, not just unhappy ones, experience has taught me that it is the unhappy feelings that are most likely to be passed over—not so much unhappy, sad feelings as unhappy, angry ones. Yet taking time to identify the angry feelings of each child so that both youngsters hear them stated plainly should always be one of the first steps in settling a fight. Doing this takes some of the pressure to act out of an encounter. Once the teacher has stopped the actual battle, it only takes a minute extra to say something as simple and caring as, "Jon, you really want that rabbit badly, and, Jasmine, you aren't ready to give it up, and you don't want him to grab it—is that right?" Such teaching has to be done again and again, but if the teacher is persistent, this technique will gradually bear fruit. These brief descriptions of feelings let both children know the teacher or parent cares enough to understand and recognize their respective feelings without passing judgment on their worth—feelings are neither good nor bad, they simply are. But what we do about them is another matter, and so we are reminded once again of the importance of the second part of the basic mental health principle, "Feel what you wish, but *control what you do.*"

Young children frequently require clear reminding, sometimes coupled with physical restraint, that it is not all right to act out a feeling by socking somebody or biting them, no matter how angry they feel. To continue with the rabbit incident, the teacher might say, "Jon, I know you want that rabbit badly, and you, Jasmine, aren't ready to give it up, and you don't want Jon to grab it. I know it's hard to wait and hard to share, but I can't let you pull the rabbit's leg that way—it hurts him too much." In other words, *the pattern of intervention from the teacher should include a statement of the children's feelings, a statement of what they can or cannot do, and a simple, clear reason for the restraint.*

In addition to implementing sound mental health practices, this particular strategy has the added advantage of instilling the beginnings of internalized consciences in children. Research indicates that two of the most effective ways of building an internal conscience are combining warmth and control with simple reasons why a child must not act a particular way (Coopersmith, 1967; Hoffman, 1970). These occasions are not the time to moralize and talk about how good little girls would feel or what nice little boys would do. The teacher should state the reason firmly and briefly why the child cannot do as she wishes and move on with her to something else.

Avoid Long-Drawn-Out Discussions About Motives

One more thing about describing and discussing feelings must be emphasized: It just does not work to ask young children *why* they did a particular thing. I have occasionally heard well-intentioned students inquire, "Why did you hurt the puppy like that?" or "Why did you cry when your mother left?" It is a rare child who can deal with this question effectively and explain in any depth why she hurt the puppy or why he poured paint all over his neighbor's picture. An incident in my own family illustrates this point. My oldest child, then aged 4, pushed her brother down the cellar stairs one winter day. I still remember those terrible thumping sounds as he rolled down those stairs. After assuring myself that he was all right, I turned to her and roared that fatal question, "Why, Nancy, why on earth did you push him down the stairs? Don't you know that's dangerous? You could have killed him!" "Well," she said, looking at me sideways, "well . . . it's really just too complicated to explain." And that sums it up. The motivation for such acts *is* too complicated for most young children to explain.

Help Children Learn to Use Play and Creative Materials to Resolve Emotional Problems

Describing children's feelings to them is one valuable method of helping children remain in touch with their emotional selves, but its effectiveness depends on the sensitivity of the teacher, as well as on her being right on the spot. Fortunately, additional activities can be provided in the curriculum that also serve this purpose and do not require such close attention from the teacher. These are primarily pretend-play situations and self-expressive creative activities (Koplow, 1996). When such activities are provided, children make use of them in a very natural way to work through troubling situations, repeating them until they have diluted their impact to manageable proportions and have attained some mastery over them.

For example, children often play out hospital experiences, enact scenes from home in which they assume adult roles, or retreat to infantile behavior and roles as their feelings dictate. I even recall one youngster who consistently played at being the father: beginning with a dinner table scene, he would roughly shove his "wife" aside, tip over furniture, and dump the doll children from their beds before rushing out and slamming the door. Although no such violence had actually transpired in his own home, the mother and father had recently separated, and it seemed to the teachers that the child's own feelings and his perception of the father's feelings were mingled together in his angry play.[1]

Use Pretend Play to Strengthen the Emotional Self

Children can use almost anything that comes to hand for pretend play, and to help them exercise

their imaginations, it is best to choose equipment that lends itself to many possible uses. Blocks, for example, can be used to represent roads, cars, baby bottles, buildings, or fences. Scarves can be made into aprons, diapers, reins for horses, veils, or elegant sashes. Of course, it also facilitates certain kinds of play if some items of a more structured nature, such as dolls and dress-up clothes, are provided. These lend themselves beautifully to playing out episodes of domestic happiness as well as contention. Then, too, special circumstances can warrant inclusion of other structured items (we added leg braces and crutches shortly after a youngster with a disability joined our group), and equipment for general hospital play is always valuable to offer.

Use Specific Themes

It is also possible and occasionally desirable to stimulate play around a particular theme to meet a special problem. We once had a youngster at school who had been badly frightened at Halloween by some older boys who cornered her while wearing terrifying rubber masks. It is not exaggerating to say that this episode colored the child's life with terror, and she became apprehensive of many new experiences as a result. Gradually, we made simple masks available in the dramatic play area and then went on to make paper-bag ones and finally introduced the rubber, pullover kind. She learned to approach these with bravado and finally mastered her fear through the medium of play. I can still see her stalking up to another child, mask in hand, saying to him solicitously, "I'm going to frighten you, Frankie—are you ready?" and then slipping on the mask and growling at him fiercely while he coped in a very adequate fashion by growling back.

Encourage Storytelling by Children

Still another way of using imagination to help children understand how they feel is by encouraging them to dictate stories. Fours and

---

[1]It should be noted that the teachers did not simply let this child struggle through this alone in his play. Because they understood he felt abandoned and was living with both grief and anger, they offered some simple, understanding comments about how everyone feels like breaking things when families are separating and reassured him that he would often be able to see his father (something that was true in that particular case) and that both his mother and father still cared about him.

fives often relish dictating such accounts, and these are clearly influenced by their personal concerns.

This story was told by a 4-year-old in response to a picture of a little girl sitting alone on a beach playing:

> She's sad because she's out there by herself at the beach. And it's dark out there because she's been bad. She ran away and she got lost!

This one was in response to a picture drawn by another child, also aged 4:

> A kitten and a bluebird are talking about the sun. They think that the sun goes to a big barn at night. I think that's true! The bluebird gets the sun out in the morning. He punches the barn down. The end!

This story was accompanied by a kind of antiphonal chant from another youngster:

> **Joshua:** I've got a story—a scary one—about Godzilla. Oh, he's scary—in the dark, he glows! The shark makes him do it—and sharks are really scary, but Dracula was the scariest—and a fire hose is scary—he's really scary!
>
> **Angie** (who has been listening nervously): I'm not scared of dark or ghosts!
>
> **Joshua:** . . . and an alligator comes along—and King Kong. . . .

Even when it is too cold for water, playing with sand can relieve tension.

Angie: I dreamed about King Kong—and it was *dark*—but I wasn't scared—and I came out and I patted him and he was friendly!

Joshua: Let's see—hummmm! More scary—Aha! I got it! And the lizard came! Aha! And a crocodile!

Angie (firmly): But I'm not scared of anything!

Joshua (to me): Write this down! (looking disgustedly at Angie) And they all ate each other up—even the lizard! There, baby![2]

Finally, from a 3-year-old:

I saw a little snail and the snail got on him—on this little guy! And he went on him, and that guy ate the snail! That's all![3]

Sometimes the teacher can help focus the child's concern by starting the story in a particular vein. Perhaps she might begin, "Once upon a time there was a little girl who was supposed to stay at the baby-sitters, but she ran home instead. When she got there . . . ," or "Once upon a time there was a child named Henry who went to the doctor and he said, 'Henry, you're going to have to have your tonsils out.' Well, that was quite a surprise to Henry. . . ."

Or children may be drawn into playing out stories and experiences by using puppets or little rubber dolls. These items are often particularly successful with excessively "bland" children who permit themselves only sharply restricted ways of expressing strong feelings and who may find actual dramatic play in the housekeeping corner overwhelming. My guess is that using dolls and puppets has the advantage for such youngsters of allowing them to be bigger than the puppets and somewhat apart from them—conditions that are reassuring to children who are uneasy about getting too close to strong emotions.

In addition to meeting special needs, miniature dolls and puppets are also useful to employ with children in general, particularly those older than age 3. Besides fostering their imaginations, puppets give them the sense of being in obvious command of the play, and this contributes to their feelings of mastery and strengthens their ego controls. Note how evident the mastery theme is in some of the children's stories quoted previously.

Use Self-Expressive Materials to Express Feelings Safely

In addition to supplying materials for imaginative play and storytelling, teachers can provide for the socially acceptable expression of various emotions by offering expressive art materials such as paint and dough. These substances have additional cardinal virtues as outlets for creative ideas and aesthetic satisfactions, but they are without peer in the realm of expressing feelings. (Chapter 14 presents an extensive discussion of the creative possibilities offered by paint and dough.)

It is not realistic to expect most young children to use these materials to produce actual pictures of their problems. Nevertheless, the youngster who uses her fingernails to scratch tensely through the finger-painting paper or who limits herself to using only the center of the paper is expressing her feelings, just as the child swooping and squishing his way through a finger painting is expressing his happiness and lack of constriction. Some of these materials lend themselves particularly well to the sublimated expression of aggression, and some to the relief of more generalized tension.

Aggression-Relieving Activities

We may as well realize that the world is full of frustrating circumstances for young children (Murphy, 1987). Their wants are immediate, intense, and personal, and inevitably they are prevented numerous times every day from satisfying their desires. Such frustrations range

---

[2]These stories are from children in the California Preschool Program, Santa Barbara City Schools.

[3]From a child in the Santa Barbara City College Children's Center.

from seeing that another child already has the ball they want, to having a passerby stumble over their blocks, or to finding that lunchtime has cut short their play on the swings. The intensity of frustration and amount of ensuing anger and aggression vary from child to child, but all children need to learn to redirect their aggressive feelings into channels that harm neither themselves nor others.

Ways to Relieve Anger Harmlessly

One of the best ways of relieving such anger, as already discussed, is dealing with the feeling directly by letting the child know that you are aware of the anger and that you will help confront it squarely.

Other, less direct methods, such as vigorous physical activity, are also helpful. Jumping hard on a mattress or throwing beanbags can be useful. Vigorous crying is an outstanding way to achieve relief. Dancing—particularly if offered with therapeutic questions such as, "What's the strongest dance you do?" or "What's the angriest thing you can think of to be? Show us what that would look like"—provides a valuable avenue of expression. Hammering is still another excellent aggression-redirecting activity, particularly if large peg-and-hammer sets are used, because these can take brutal punishment while not requiring close supervision. Beating large drums also offers a safe aggression reliever, if the teacher can tolerate the noise (outdoors is infinitely preferable to indoors

Using Mud, Sand, and Water to Relieve Tension

Mud or sand, combined with water, provides an excellent example of a material that is both absorbing and relaxing for young children. Some psychologists and psychiatrists think that the smearing associated with messy materials such as mud has special emotional value to young children who have only recently passed through toilet training. They maintain that learning to conform to society's expectations by controlling their urine and bowel movement can be a difficult task for young children, and the opportunity to play with messy things seems to relieve some of the stress of this situation. Perhaps this is because the children can be allowed to do as they like (within reason) with the mud.

Whether one accepts this theory or not, there is no denying that these materials can settle down tense children to absorbed play for long periods of time. Water alone provides soothing pleasures to children, which, I believe, are unmatched by those of other materials. The opportunity to pour, swish, or generally delight in using water is one of the true joys of childhood. When combined with mud or sand, it is even more pleasurable (Betz, 1992).

Some schools are able to purchase special water tables for such play, but less expensive deep galvanized tubs work just as well. If the bathroom is large and has a drain in the floor, water play can

be set up there to make access to water and mopping up simpler. The addition of containers, shakers, sieves, funnels, spoons, and pans will furnish literally hours of deeply involved play, and they may be acquired very cheaply at rummage sales or thrift stores.

In addition to the tension-relieving aspects of mud and water, these materials have many other virtues, as Table 11–1 (p. 217) attests (Crosser, 1994; James & Granovetter, 1987). For example, children can learn such facts of physics as water always runs downhill and it can change from solid to liquid to solid again in wintery weather. Pouring, mixing, and experimenting with textures of sand and mud and with the properties of wetter versus drier mud offer additional learning experiences. The use of moist sand encourages construction of tunnels and towers, as well as all sorts of pretend bakery products, thereby fostering the imagination. Sand also provides excellent opportunities for cognitive learning.

In addition, opportunities for social cooperation abound in sand and mud play. Water play, in particular, is so absorbing and relaxing that it is often a time of pleasant harmonious interaction (I mention this because inexperienced teachers often dread water play, thinking it will make the children wild.

for this activity). Squirting water is still another satisfying, though milder, way of getting feelings of frustration and anger out of the system.

Regardless of what aggression reliever is provided, teachers should bear in mind that they need to be on hand to exert control if necessary. Children using these materials forcefully must still stay within the bounds of safety. It is important to be very clear with them about the rules, *before* they start. The hammer may be used only with the peg set, no matter how the child feels, and the water may be squirted on the fence or the tree, but not on another child or the teacher. (Note that direct methods of preventing and controlling aggression are discussed in the next chapter.)

Although such restraints are obviously necessary, it is important to remember also that the basic intention of such activity is to *reduce* frustration, not build it. For this reason, it is best to select materials that do not require much skill to use. This is why it is better to use a peg-and-hammer set rather than a hammer and nails for relieving aggression. Having to fiddle with a pesky nail in itself contributes to rage.

Tension-Relieving Activities

Some general tension-relieving activities are also of great value. Two of these are so practical that we often forget about them. They are (a) taking children who are acting restless to the toilet and (b) offering children something to eat or drink when they are out of sorts. I would not want these suggestions to be misconstrued so

---

However, if there is plenty of space and time and water to go around, this is not typically the case.)

Presenting These Materials Effectively
The most delightful kind of mud, sand, and water play involves warm days, trickling hoses, and barefoot, lightly dressed children. In these circumstances children can puddle and play to their heart's content. Cleanup is simple because it is easy to hose everything down at the end of playtime. The satisfaction evident on the children's faces as they muck and squish about makes it plain that this is an activity of great value to them.

Fortunately, such play need not be limited to warm weather. It is possible to teach children that they must keep their clothes and shoes dry when it is a chilly day. Board tables can be set up on sawhorses in the sandbox to keep pant knees from soaking through; or if the activity must be carried on inside, waist-high, indoor sand tables can be used and aprons provided. Cornmeal may be used as a variation for sand if the teacher does not want the sand inside; however, one must remember that cornmeal makes floors very slippery and so must be swept up continually while it is in use. Wheat is also delightful to pour and sift, though it cannot be molded.

Several points about sand require mentioning. First, because sand is so often offered to children in only its dry state, which is relatively uninteresting and useless for play, the sandbox or table should be checked every day to make certain that at least half of the sand is moist enough for molding and modeling. Second, although children love this material so much that they will uncomplainingly make do with the same old equipment day after day, the teacher should offer a variety of play equipment to stimulate imagination and attract more children to the sandbox. **Stout** shovels are important to provide, as are sturdy spoons. Big and small cars and trucks make wonderful additions, as do cooking utensils. Sifters and sieves with various-sized holes are also useful. The inclusion of sturdy, little plastic people or animals (or both) will stimulate the playing out of pretend adventures. We have also found that an old set of wooden blocks is interesting to add occasionally. Plumber's pipes and joints and sewer tile (particularly when combined with water) add a whole new dimension. Finally, a soft hand brush stored in the sand area makes it easy for children to brush off their clothes before leaving if their clothes are very sandy. Indoors, a brush and dustpan are essential for cleaning up both floors and children.

that every restless little boy is continually escorted to the bathroom or that food is used as a means of continually placating children, but sometimes these solutions are worth trying. Children are often unaware that physiological needs are making them cranky; they just know that nothing feels quite right, and sometimes this gets them into unnecessary trouble.

The value of crying as a tension reliever is often underestimated by adults, both for themselves and for children. But crying, as Solter (1992) points out, can "be a healing mechanism, a natural repair kit that every person has. It allows people to cope with stress" (p. 66).

Other tension-relieving activities include rhythmic ones such as swinging and rocking, which are very soothing to young children. The close physical contact while rocking in the teacher's lap, in particular, provides its own special relaxing comfort. Other, more specific relaxation techniques discussed in chapter 9 ("Developing Physical Competence") are also valuable. Finally, finger painting and dough, mud, and water play offer excellent opportunities for children to relax and mess about to their heart's content. (Finger painting and dough are discussed in chapter 14.)

Whatever is offered in the way of materials that relieve feelings, it must be remembered that such items are intended to help children over the inevitable humps and hollows of growth. As such, they are only temporary measures—first aid, not long-term cures. It is the overall environment of the school, where frustration is kept to a tolerable level by careful planning and by sound knowledge of children's needs and where overstimulation is avoided, that produces the basic facilitative climate that helps children gradually attain understanding and mastery of their feelings.

Help Children Learn to Face Reality

On first thought, it might seem to be ideal for children to experience childhood as a perfect, golden time devoid of frustration and anxiety, but many contemporary psychologists do not agree with this point of view. For example, in his classic work, *The Meaning of Anxiety* (1977), Rollo May maintains that properly harnessed anxiety can be a powerful incentive for creativity; and Lois Murphy (1976) cites children who cope well with anxiety as possessing the qualities of confidence, flexibility, resourcefulness, and definiteness in using the environment and managing their frustrations. It seems, then, that experiencing at least a certain amount of frustration and anxiety so often associated with facing reality can have beneficial results for young children, particularly if parents and teachers help them learn to cope with these situations in a productive way. Part of this learning to cope involves facing reality and accepting what cannot be changed.

Accepting What Cannot Be Changed

Everyone has to learn at one time or another that some things in life cannot be changed. No amount of tears can affect the fact that the cut must be stitched, any more than tears can bring about a reconciliation of parents determined to separate. This does not mean that the child should not protest or mourn. Such behavior is natural, but at the same time adults can provide reassurance and comfort by taking the position, "You may not like whatever is happening, and I can understand why you feel bad, but it is something that cannot be changed. It's going to be tough, but we'll see it through together. After a while, you'll feel better again."

Fortunately, most reality facing for young children is not so emotionally disturbing. Indeed, when speaking of facing reality, I am reminded of an old cartoon that pictures two men leaning up against a bar. One man says philosophically to the other, "Well, I've finally learned what 'facing reality' means—it means doing what my wife wants!" This kind of everyday situation is what facing reality means for most children, too. It means doing what grown-ups want.

TABLE 11–1
What Can Children Learn from Playing with Water, Sand, and Mud?

Physical	Emotional	Social	Creative	Cognitive/Language
Encourages:	Encourages:	Encourages:	Encourages:	Encourages:
Development of specific eye/hand coordination skills (pouring, squeezing, stirring, etc.)	Feelings of relief of tensions	Relaxed, harmonious playing together	Imaginative, pretend play (cooking, roads and tunnels, buried treasure, etc.)	Acquisition of concepts and vocabulary, such as wet/dry, sink/float, hot/cold, solid/liquid (emergent literacy skill)
Widening of sensory experiences: textures (gritty, pasty, etc.); temperature changes (hot/cold); contrasts of thick/thin; gradations of tones of scale (jars with differing amounts of water in them)	Sanctioned opportunities to be messy and/or wet	Cooperative play with water, sand or mud: negotiation; sharing equipment, space and materials; bargaining	Creating structures from sand and mud	Use of measurement and estimations: how much will it take? full/empty, heavy/light, more/less (emergent mathematical skill)
Relaxation	Concentration and absorption in an activity	Cooperative work with water: washing dishes, watering garden, bathing dog	Trying out ideas and solutions to problems	Practice that prepares child to move from preoperational to concrete operational stages of reasoning (Piaget): conservation of volume; reversibility (emergent mathematical skill)
	Working through potential emotional conflicts over toilet training	Opportunities to express and manage harmless aggression	Aesthetic appreciation of water's beauty	Understanding principles of physics: effects of force (increasing flow of hose increases force; use of water wheel); effects of gravity (water runs downhill); changes in state (solid, liquid, gas)
		Understanding that everyone from all cultures needs water (to drink, bathe in, grow food)		General information and vocabulary: What makes rain? Where does water come from and where does it go? sand used to be big rocks; adding water makes things runny
		Idea that conserving water and using it wisely is important for everyone		

Note. These suggestions are just a handful of examples; water, sand, and mud play offer many additional cognitive possibilities.

Sometimes withdrawal is quite literal.

Part of the art of teaching is keeping these adult demands within reasonable bounds so that children do not have to face the reality of conforming more than is truly necessary.

Learning to Accept Alternative Satisfactions

There can even be a silver lining to the dark cloud of learning to accept what cannot be changed. It is that children can learn to extend their coping abilities by creatively seeking alternative solutions (see also the section "Teach Children Socially Acceptable Ways of Getting What They Want" in the next chapter). For example, one alternative strategy they can acquire is the ability to accept compromises to get part of what they want. The child who wants to build a tower of blocks, for instance, may be willing to substitute the oblongs in place of the cylinders for this purpose if the cylinders are all in use. Or she can be encouraged to strike bargains with another youngster: she will let him use her truck if he will share some of the blocks with her.

(Four-year-olds are particularly adept at using this kind of solution.)

One additional comment about providing alternative satisfactions is in order here. Sometimes when a serious crisis strikes a family, the teacher is tempted to "make it up" to the youngster by becoming a surrogate parent. The teacher should realize, however, that it is neither possible nor desirable to fill this void by behaving this way. For one thing, the relationship between teacher and child is only temporary; it draws to a close at the end of the year, and so its value is necessarily limited. Besides that, the teacher has the obligation to be involved with all the children, not with one in particular. Finally, allowing such a relationship to become established is unfair to the family, no matter how kindly the teacher's intention, because doing this robs parents of their right of parenthood.

Using Mechanisms for Protecting the Emotional Self from Too Much Reality

Neither children nor adults learn to face reality in one fell swoop or with unwavering consistency.

All people develop ways of protecting themselves from time to time, and these methods of protection (or coping) serve the useful purpose of reducing stress to tolerable limits. In their book *Vulnerability, Coping and Growth* (1976), Murphy and Moriarity summarize a long-term study that presents a particularly interesting analysis of the coping strategies developed by young children. It is worthwhile to pay attention to this list because teachers do not always recognize that these particular behaviors serve the useful function of helping young children deal with stresses that might otherwise overwhelm them.

Some examples of coping strategies listed by Murphy and Moriarity (1976) include asking for help, conforming to routines, shifting to easier tasks, drawing on previous experience to help deal with a new one, avoiding situations, using humor, and protesting actively by crying or by using other emotional means of expression. They also discuss how preschoolers use what they term *self-protective devices*. Among such devices are the ability to fend off excessive stimulation by controlling the impact of the environment, timing rest periods, using strategic withdrawal, us-

ing delay to appraise a new situation, and forestalling danger by knowing when to stop.

All youngsters develop their own personal repertoire of coping skills for everyday life situations. It can be fascinating, as well as enlightening, to pick a particular event (such as arriving in the morning or settling down for sleep) and then note how individual children manage this event each day. A sensitive observer will find that there are likely to be as many different ways of making these transitions as there are children attending school. Part of the purpose of teaching is to help children extend their repertoires of adaptive coping responses, which thereby will increase their ability to adjust more easily to changing life circumstances.

Using Withdrawal and Regression as Ways of Coping with Reality

Two self-protective devices warrant special comment here because they appear so commonly in early childhood and are often regarded with undue alarm by teachers. These are withdrawal and regression (Barton & Zeanah, 1990). Both of these behaviors are indicators that the child

All too many children have run in terror from a masked firefighter trying to save their lives. Crisis proofing can forestall that panic reaction.

feels overwhelmed and needs to retreat for a bit. The goal of the teacher should not be to deprive the child of these strategies but to recognize them when they occur, appreciate their value, and also perceive them as signals by the child that all may not be well in his or her world.

Sometimes withdrawal is quite literal: the youngster hovers behind an easel, dabbling idly with a brush, or builds herself a corral of blocks and sits inside, or even hides under a table. Such children should not be forced into participation before they are comfortable, no matter how unsocial the behavior may appear to the teacher. Indeed, the more the teacher pushes, the more resistance may be incited. On the other hand, patience combined with enticing materials and a low-key approach that does not reward non-participation with attention will almost always draw such youngsters into activities.

Regression, the second of these two defense mechanisms, occurs when the child retreats to behavior appropriate for a younger child. Thus, we see examples of bed wetting when the new baby arrives, or wanting to be pushed on the swing, or insisting on being helped with boots and coat when only a week before putting these on herself was a jealously guarded prerogative.

Teachers are so growth oriented that they seem especially threatened by this kind of emotional backsliding. However, if they relax and meet this dependency in an understanding way by satisfying the child's emotional hunger rather than trying to starve it to death, the child will almost always return to a more independent status as soon as she is emotionally able to do so. Children have a compelling desire to grow, and wise teachers count on this fact as their most useful ally.

Help Children Cope with Crisis Situations

Give Children Credit for Being Resilient

Crises of one sort or another happen to all children from time to time. They can be as serious as

the death of a parent or as relatively mild as moving to a new neighborhood or starting nursery school. Sometimes crises are of long duration; sometimes they are as brief as having stitches in the emergency room. What is interesting about this subject is the fact that some children crumble under such experiences whereas others cope more effectively and recover quickly. What is it about these survivors that causes them to come through such difficulties sunny-side up?

Not too much is known about the factors that lie behind these effective copers. For all too long, the emphasis has been on the other kinds of children—the crumblers—and what to do to rescue them. It is the old medical model of dealing with illness rather than fostering wellness. Certainly, the crumblers need help, but it is also true that if we knew more about why some children do *not* crumble—why they remain stable despite adversity—we could use that information to help all children as they grow and develop.

Besides having confidence that many children possess some inner strengths that will help them cope with crises, teachers should also know how to help children make the most of these strengths when special problems arise. Although space does not permit an extensive discussion of specific crises, some basic principles that apply to most of them are detailed here. For further information, the reader is referred to materials listed in the references at the end of this chapter.

Prepare Children in Advance for Crises Whenever Possible

Some crises, such as accidents, occur so suddenly that advance preparation is not possible, and child and parent must simply see them through with whatever fortitude they can muster. Other potential emergencies can be prepared for, at least to a degree, by using a technique called *crisis proofing* (Furman, 1995b).

Crisis proofing seeks to arm the child against crises by providing the child with a mild, diluted form of the experience before a more serious crisis occurs. One example of such advance crisis proofing is the use of pet funerals, discussed in chapter 10. The opportunity to experience death in moderately saddening but not devastating circumstances can help prepare a youngster for a more serious experience later such as the death of a family member or friend.

Other crisis-proofing activities might involve having an ambulance visit the school so that the children can see what is inside, visiting a kindergarten before actually attending, or touring the children's ward before having surgery. Such experiences are included in the curriculum to provide opportunities for the children to gain advance understanding and knowledge, which thereby reduces their fear of the unknown and partially prepares them for similar but more powerful situations.

Reading topical books to children is an additional way to provide advance preparation for a crisis. (These can also be read after one has occurred.) This technique is called *bibliotherapy*, and it can be an excellent way to free children to ask questions and become involved in discussion. Some good reference resources for these books are included at the end of the chapter.

Before presenting such a book, it is important to read it through carefully. Make certain that it is appropriate for the particular group and situation. Anticipate questions that may arise from the children and consider how you might best handle these. Prepare some discussion questions of your own that would encourage the children to talk about the material. Perhaps you might want to supplement the book with some pictures from the picture file or with poetry. Plan to repeat the story or theme on additional days, just as you would any other theme. Children need time to understand new information; they need time to consider what was said and to ask questions that may occur to them later.

The purpose of crisis proofing and bibliotherapy is to help children gain strength and understanding without causing them to be excessively anxious. For this reason, it is important to point out the positive as well as the negative aspects of a situation. For example, when discussing hospitalization, although you should not gloss over the possibility of pain with false reassurances, you should explain that hospitals help children feel better and get well.

Encourage Parents to Explain the Crisis to Children

As mentioned in the discussion about death, it is important to include children as part of the family when crises arise. Children will sense tension and problems in the family anyway, and the uncertainty they experience of not knowing the reason for the strain is likely to be worse than the certainty of knowing what the trouble is (May, 1977). However, young children should not be expected to bear the burden of feeling responsible for either causing or helping cure the problem. We do not want them to blame themselves for the situation or feel that they must do something to correct it. Still, they do benefit from simple explanations about what the emergency is and what is being done to relieve it. If there is some not-too-burdensome way that they can be helpful, this will also provide comfort to children by enabling them to feel somewhat in control.

Children Also Benefit from Sharing Feelings

Parents should be informed that it is not necessary or desirable to shield children from all expressions of dismay, grief, or feeling upset *as long as reassurance is provided along with the expression of feeling*. Children learn about handling strong emotions partly by seeing how others cope with them. For example, a mother might say to her son, "I do feel bad about Aunt Mary. I love her, and when she's hurt it makes me cry . . . and then I feel a little better. We'll have to think of some way to help her." Sharing concerns, revealing a moderate amount of feeling, and showing children how to cope with that feeling is recommended. Exposing children to floods of adult emotion is not.

Provide Children with
Chances to Ask Questions

Sometimes questions about crises arise at home, sometimes at school. Whenever they come up, the adults in charge should make every attempt to answer them simply and truthfully: "Yes, when they take the stitches out, it will hurt a little—it will feel like a sharp little twitch or pinch, but then it will be over and your cut will have grown together again."

Rather than plunging into a lengthy explanation, it often works best to ask questions in reply to a question to find out what the child really wants to know. Does Jeremy really want to know all the details of the divorce, or is he actually most worried about whether he will see his father again?

Play Is the Great Healer

Earlier in this chapter, and in chapter 3 as well, considerable time was devoted to discussing how to use play to promote emotional health. When children are undergoing a crisis, provision for working through their feelings via play can bring them great relief (Monahon, 1993).

Curriculum that is particularly worthwhile to use with children in times of emotional stress includes tension-relieving activities and sublimated ways of expressing aggression. Pretend play involving relevant themes can often be sparked by the inclusion of items suggesting that theme in play. The inclusion of a grandmother doll, for instance, led one of our children to contrive a wheelchair from a market basket and to spend considerable time pushing the grandma up and down the halls of the pretend rest home.

Sometimes when families are troubled, play can also alert the teacher to the fact that the youngster needs special help. Curry and Arnaud (1982) list a number of signals to watch for, including (a) the use of themes that are not appropriate for the child's age, (b) single-minded repetition of one theme or role, (c) very unusual play themes, and (d) excessive preoccupation with one object.

The manner in which children play may also reveal to the teacher that they are having particular difficulties. Perhaps they seem particularly flushed or intense about the play, or perhaps they seem actually to become what they are playing and are unable to divest themselves of an assumed role. For instance, at one school in which I taught, there was a little girl who almost literally became a rabbit. Unless she had on her ears and tail and had her stuffed rabbit with her, she seemed frozen and unable to participate in the life of the school. What had begun as an amusing quirk ultimately became an obsession that required the help of a psychologist to correct.

Keep the Environment as Stable
and Reasonable as Possible

Children's centers can make a wonderful contribution to the child's well-being in the area of stability. The steadiness of routine and calm affection of the teacher can provide a haven for children who are living in stressful situations at home. Simply knowing what is going to happen next and what is expected in the way of behavior at school is comforting. When this is combined with the use of play to clarify feelings, children can return home strengthened and reassured.

While keeping the environment as stable as possible, it also may be necessary to reduce expectations of good behavior for children experiencing crises who may be feeling miserable. They may cry more easily or fly off the handle more readily; they are more likely to tire sooner; they may be unable to settle down at nap; and anxiety may reduce their appetites, making them feel even more fatigued.

When children display these behaviors, they require extra comforting combined with toleration. Yet, at the same time they cannot be allowed to become tyrants—a difficult balance to maintain. The best approach to balancing routines and expectations with children's special needs is to use common sense, mercy, and patience. As their lives return to normal, expectations can be readjusted accordingly.

Other Children May Be Aware of the Crisis

In numerous situations, families confide in teachers about intimate problems, and *teachers need to keep such information completely confidential.* However, a crisis often becomes known to other children in the group, as when someone's house has burned down, a car pool mother has fallen ill, or a child has had an accident. The children may feel quite distressed or anxious at the news, and they often wonder if such a thing could happen to them or their families.

Be aware that these youngsters need much of the same kind of help as that recommended for the individual children to enable them to come to terms with their anxieties. This includes crisis proofing, chances to discuss their concerns, and opportunities to deepen their understanding through play.

In addition, remember that such crises can provide very desirable opportunities to help children do something thoughtful for the child with the trouble. If the teacher asks children how they could help, they often have quite delightful ideas: "We could draw him a get-well picture," "We could give her hugs," "We could be nice and let her choose first at snack time," "We could let him feed the fish this week." These are suggestions I have heard from 3-year-olds. They are nice, practical ideas for expressing concern and offering comfort. Moreover, they benefit the children in the group by allowing them to do something kind for someone else.

Help Children Begin to Build Empathy for Other People

Throughout this chapter we have been concentrating almost exclusively on how children feel and how to help them gain understanding of their feelings, as well as competence in dealing with them. The chapter would not be complete, however, without discussing a different kind of goal, even though it is one that can be only partially achieved by such young children. This is the goal of instilling empathy in children—the ability to put oneself in another's place and feel as that person is feeling. This ability is related partly to the emotional self and partly to the social self.

As Piaget (Piaget & Inhelder, 1969) has indicated, this is a difficult task because young children are essentially centered on themselves and have great difficulty grasping how others feel. Instead, they imagine that everyone feels as they themselves do. Therefore, teachers must be patient and approach this learning step by step, keeping it on a simple level and allowing time for both learning and maturation to take place.

Bearing these limitations in mind, there are three fairly practical ways of beginning to foster empathy in young children: (a) self-report, (b) role playing in pretend situations, and (c) "remember when" experiences. (These strategies can also be used to deepen insight and empathy in adults. Self-report is an extremely valuable skill to use with other adults, as well as with children, and role playing and gaining insight by referring to one's own experience are excellent ways of increasing understanding of other's feelings.)

Using Self-Report

Self-report, which in this case really should be called "other" report, can be used in two ways to foster empathy when teaching young children. The first way of using it is to encourage other children to tell the child how they feel. Thus, you can ask a child being pushed off the bench by another youngster, "Do you like what he's doing? Well, tell him how you feel about it," or "Do you want him to do that? Well then, tell him you don't."

The second way to use self-report is to make a point of honestly reporting your own feelings to the children. This is valuable as long as you are not too forceful or use the report of a "bad" feeling as a threat to induce better behavior. An example of an undesirable threat is, "Boys and girls, you'd better watch out—I'm getting angry!" On the other hand, an appropriate self-report statement might be, "I'm worried you children won't remember to wait with me when we get to the curb," or "I feel irritated today because we have so much to do to get the presents ready to go home." It is even all right, when stopping a fight, to say, "Just a minute—I haven't decided what to do about this yet; I need some time to make up my mind." This is more satisfactory than making an impulsive decision that you regret later but cannot change without losing face. Honest self-reporting not only helps the children understand the teacher better but also sets a model for them to copy.

There are some reasonable limits to the use of self-reports by adults. One is that care must be taken so that they are not used as a means of justifying the expression of rage or abandonment to grief, since such flood tides of feeling from grown-ups frighten children too much. When properly used, self-reports allow grown-ups to present themselves as human beings who experience a range of feelings, just as children do. The books of Axline (1964, 1969), Koplow (1996), Faber and Mazlish (1980), and Samalin (1991) contain many wonderful examples of sincere communication between children and adults and can be read with benefit by every parent and teacher.

Using Role Playing

The cultivation of insight through imaginative role playing, which happens so often in dramatic play, is a second valuable way to begin building empathy for other people within the child. Although it is true that the child who is feeling brave while being the firefighter or petulant while being the baby is playing out his own feelings and ideas of that role, it is also true that he is obtaining a little insight into how other people act and respond in particular instances. This

helps lay a framework on which to build later understanding (Selman, 1971).

Using "Remember When"

Finally, it is possible to build understanding of how another child feels by using the "remember when" approach. For instance, the teacher might ask, "Remember when your mother left you here for the first time? Remember how you cried? Well, that's how Janie feels right now. [Wait a bit for this to sink in.] What do you think we could do to help her?" Or "Remember how mad you got when Scotty took that red car from you? Well, that's how Jim is feeling." Note that no moralizing is attached to these questions; they are asked to remind the children of how they felt and to help them understand that someone else feels that way, too.

This remembering approach is a much stronger teaching method to use with young children than is the following approach: "What if you were him—how would you like it if he took your truck?" Phrasing the question in this way (which we call "pulling a switch" at our center) is too difficult for a little child to grasp because it requires him to (a) imagine himself as Jim and (b) imagine Jim as being him—a difficult task indeed for a child who, as Piaget informs us, has not yet decentered. No wonder that the usual response to such a query is one of baffled indecision.

Summary

The emphasis of curriculum for the emotional self should be on helping children become as resilient as possible by using everyday life situations as the medium for teaching. Such situations should be used to build the following competencies in young children:

- Learning to separate from their families with a reasonable degree of ease
- Attaining basic attitudes of trust, autonomy, and initiative

- Remaining in contact with all their feelings while learning to control what they do about them
- Using play and self-expressive materials to clarify feelings and resolve emotional problems
- Facing reality
- Learning to cope with crises
- Beginning to build empathy and understand that other people have feelings, too

Self-Check Questions for Review

Content-Related Questions

1. It is August, and you are getting ready to welcome a new group of children on their very first day of school. List some procedures you would follow to help them adjust as easily as possible to their new surroundings.
2. Which stage of emotional development comes first—the stage of initiative versus guilt, or autonomy versus shame and doubt? What is the name of the first stage babies go through? Describe some characteristics of each stage.
3. How can play and other creative materials be used to help children resolve emotional problems?
4. Why is it helpful to offer mud, sand, and water to children who are emotionally upset?
5. Give some alternatives you could suggest to a child who wants something another child won't let her have.
6. Name some ways children protect themselves from having to cope with too much reality.
7. Trostle's research study described in this chapter reported that children with whom reflected feeling techniques were used showed increased gains in self-control. Explain the link between these two events; that is, why did recognizing the children's feelings increase their ability to control themselves?
8. What is self-report, and why is it a useful strategy to use with young children?
9. Why is it more effective to use "remember when" instead of saying to a child, "What if you were him? How would you like it if he took your truck?"

Integrative Questions

1. This chapter includes discussions about presenting mud, sand, and water play to children. Why are these activities included in the chapter on building emotional health? How would you explain the emotional value of such material to parents?
2. Why should teachers be optimistic about the inner strengths many children possess? Should teachers assume that all children will be able to cope with their problems successfully and, therefore, will not need help from time to time?
3. Describe a situation where someone you know was upset or lost her temper. Then put that person's feelings into words by describing what she felt or would like to do.
4. There are some general principles that are helpful to follow when dealing with almost any crisis. Think of a particular crisis situation you have come across, and explain how you would apply the principles in that situation.

Questions and Activities

1. Can you remember being allowed (or forbidden) to play with mud, sand, and water when you were a young child? How did you feel about this experience then? How do you feel about it now?
2. Does it seem to you that nowadays children are more restricted or less restricted in the amount of free playtime they have at their disposal?
3. Do you think that parents are sometimes right in setting limits on what they allow their children to say to them to express their feelings? If limits should be set, at what point should they occur?
4. You have had a 3-year-old girl in your school every weekday for 5 weeks, and every time she comes she cries bitterly for at least half an hour after her mother departs. Both you and the mother are quite concerned. Do you think this child should stay in school? If not, what other solution would you propose? Explain the reason for your particular position.
5. With a tape recorder, record yourself talking with various children. Listen to the results carefully, and identify some of your replies that were insensitive to what the children were feeling. Explain what you

plan to say next time to respond more effectively to their real feelings.

6. Set up some role-playing situations in class in which students play children who are acting out their feelings. These might include a coming-to-school situation, a sandbox situation, and a snack time interlude. Observe the "children's" feelings closely and then suggest various things you might say to the children that would describe what they are feeling. Try to go beyond just labeling the feelings as glad, mad, and so forth.

7. Take an hour or so and do nothing but sit near the block or housekeeping corner and keep track of all the different strategies children employ when needing to enter a new group of children. Note also how the other children cope with the newcomers.

8. Is there a child in your preschool class who has recently come through some kind of crisis? Suggest some activities that you could plan in the curriculum to help the youngster work through and understand his or her feelings about this crisis.

References for Further Reading

Overviews

Hyson, M. C. (1994). *The emotional development of young children: Building an emotion-centered curriculum.* New York: Teachers College Press. Hyson presents a good review of recent research on emotional development. The second half of the book provides sound advice on ways to honor and support the role of emotions in the classroom.

Keubli, J. (1994). Young children's understanding of everyday emotions. *Young Children,* 49(3), 36–47. This first-rate article summarizes recent research concerning what young children understand about emotions. It includes practical applications and a list of children's books about feelings.

Developmental Stages and Emotional Needs of Children

Erikson, E. H. (1963). *Childhood and society* (2nd ed.). New York: Norton.

Erikson, E. H. (1996). A healthy personality for every child. In K. M. Paciorek & J. H. Munro (Eds.), *Sources: Notable selections in early childhood education.* Guilford, CT: Dushkin. These two publications contain Erikson's original source material explaining his concepts of the eight stages of human development and the emotional attitudes of paramount importance at various stages.

Greenspan, S. I., & Greenspan, N. T. (1985). *First feelings: Milestones in the emotional development of your baby and child.* New York: Viking. The Greenspans propose six steps in emotional development occurring in the very early years. Interesting reading that also provides practical recommendations.

Riley, S. S. (1984). *How to generate values in young children.* Washington, DC: National Association for the Education of Young Children. Here is a sound book that is simply and clearly written. It contains many thoughtful suggestions on helping children stay emotionally healthy.

Communicating with Children (and Other People)

Faber, A., & Mazlish, E. (1980). *How to talk so kids will listen, & listen so kids will talk.* New York: Avon Books. Numerous examples of describing and sharing feelings make this book a treasure trove of helpfulness.

Koplow, L. (1996). *Unsmiling faces: How preschools can heal.* New York: Teachers College Press. This wonderful book is filled with examples of teachers working and talking with children in emotionally enhancing ways. I cannot recommend this book highly enough!

Samalin, N., & Jablow, M. M. (1987). *Loving your child is not enough.* New York: Viking. The chapter on acknowledging feelings provides many examples of how to reflect and paraphrase feelings to children. Helpful reading.

Advice About Helping Children with Common Emotional Difficulties

Balaban, N. (1985). *Starting school: From separation to independence.* New York: Teachers College Press. Every teacher of young children should read this practical, insightful book.

Godwin, L. J., Groves, M. M., & Horm-Wingerd, D. M. (1994). Separation distress in infants, toddlers, and parents. In K. M. Paciorek & K. G. Munro (Eds.), *Early childhood education 94/95.* Guilford, CT: Dushkin. Many practical recommendations for easing the transition from home to school are presented here.

Schaefer, C. E., & Millman, H. L. (1981). *How to help children with common problems.* New York: Van Nostrand Reinhold. This book focuses mainly on older children and covers everything from tantrums to nightmares to running away.

Resources for Bibliotherapy

Bernstein, J. E., & Rudman, R. R. (1989). *Books to help children cope with separation and loss* (Vol. 3). New York: Bowker. This useful reference includes annotated bibliographies of books for children aged 3 to 16 years covering every kind of separation—the first days at school, divorce, death, AIDS, suicide, homelessness, and so forth.

Hut, V., Dennis, B. Koplow, L., & Ferger, J. (1996). Lesson plans for emotional life. In L. Koplow (Ed.), *Unsmiling faces: How preschools can heal.* New York: Teachers College Press. In addition to guidelines and examples of overall daily activity plans, this chapter includes a lengthy list of books dealing with varying emotional states.

Use of Specific Materials to Foster Emotional Competence

Betz, C. (1992). The happy medium. *Young Children, 43*(3), 34–35.

Crosser, S. (1994). Making the most of water play. *Young Children, 49*(5), 28–32. Hopefully these articles will infect readers with the authors' enthusiasm for such play—delightful reading.

Hendrick, J. (1996). *The whole child: Developmental education for the early years* (6th ed.). Upper Saddle River, NJ: Merrill/Prentice Hall. The chapter entitled "Tender Topics: Helping Children Master Emotional Crises" deals with general and specific recommendations related to various kinds of crises.

Hill, D. M. (1977). *Mud, sand, and water.* Washington, DC: National Association for the Education of Young Children. Hill's booklet emphasizes the virtues of using these materials for play and learning.

James, J. C., & Granovetter, R. F. (1987). *Waterworks: A new book of water play activities for children age 1 to 6.* Lewisville, NC: Kaplan. Title is self-explanatory.

Dealing with Crises in Children's Lives

Farish, J. M. (1995). *When disaster strikes: Helping young children cope.* Washington, DC: National Association for the Education of Young Children. This pamphlet provides a concise, sound summary of what to do before, during, and following a disaster. A *must* for every children center's library.

Furman, R. (1995). Helping children cope with stress. In E. Furman (Ed.), *Preschoolers: Questions and answers: Psychoanalytic consultations with parents, teachers, and caregivers.* Madison, CT: International Universities Press. One of the best parts of this chapter is where Furman discusses helping parents learn to accept children's expressions of how they feel in an understanding way.

Monahon, C. (1993). *Children and trauma: A parent's guide to helping children heal.* New York: Free Press. Readers will find chapter 6, "The Healing Process," particularly helpful.

For the Advanced Student

Gratz, R. R., & Boulton, P. J. (1996). Erikson and early childhood educators: Looking at ourselves and our profession developmentally. *Young Children, 51*(5), 74–78. Reading this article should deepen one's understanding not only of Erikson's theory but also of one's own developmental stages.

Mash, E. J., & Barkley, R. Q. (Eds.). (1989). *Treatment of childhood disorders.* New York: Guilford. Another first-rate book, this one provides a thorough discussion of history, causes, and recommended treatments of children with a wide variety of serious emotional disorders such as extreme fears, obesity, encopresis, autism, and so forth.

Wassom, J. (1995). Turning bad press into prestige. *Child Care Information Exchange, 101,* 69–72. Wassom provides excellent advice for administrators about how to cope with crises in a children's center before, during, and after they occur.

Wenar, C. (1990). *Developmental psychopathology: From infancy to adolescence* (2nd ed.). New York: McGraw-Hill. The author offers a detailed overview of developmentally related emotionally based problems. The book includes a chapter on working with children from minority groups.

Zeanah, C. (Ed.). (1993). *Handbook of infant mental health.* New York: Guilford. Foundations for sound emotional health are established well before teachers meet these children in preschool. For this reason it behooves interested adults to acquaint themselves with the rapid growth of information about practices that foster or hinder the growth of emotional health in infancy. *Highly recommended.*

Journals and Resources of Continuing Interest

American Journal of Orthopsychiatry. American Orthopsychiatric Association, 49 Sheridan Ave., Albany, NY 12210. The journal describes itself as being dedicated to providing information "relating to mental health and human development from a multidisciplinary and interprofessional perspective."

Journal of Children in Contemporary Society. Haworth Press, 28 E. 22 St., New York, NY 10010. This journal concentrates on a specific topic for each quarterly issue.

Mental Health Law Project. 1101 15th St., N.W., #1212, Washington, DC 20005. MHLP is a national nonprofit advocacy organization that presses to end discrimination against people with mental disabilities. They provide many valuable position papers, guides, and a newsletter that include information on children's and adult's rights.

Pediatric Mental Health. P.O. Box 1880, Santa Monica, CA 90406. A bimonthly newsletter, this publication covers research and practice on such topics as supporting parenting, play, and preparation for hospitalization.

Getting Along Together

Achieving Competence in Interpersonal Relations

Have you ever

- Worried about what to do next when children continue to disobey?
- Wished that you knew how to teach children to get what they want without just grabbing it?
- Wanted to know how to help children get along well together in a group?
- Tried to think of ways children could be genuinely helpful at the center?

If you have, the material in this chapter will help you.

The important point to emphasize is that punishment does not teach a child self-discipline. Second, while fear of punishment may restrain the child from doing wrong, it does not make children wish to do right.

K. Owens (1995, p. 194)

[Teachers of young children should strive for] children who learn to reach out and empathize with others, to accept and celebrate differences between themselves, to communicate their feelings and resolve conflicts in constructive ways, and to love become contributing members of the community. We must set standards and expectations for our children that help them develop their intrinsic capacities to be honest, courageous, wise, and compassionate. If we return to teaching these basic values, both at home and in school, our society will be renewed and eventually childhood will become the great adventure that it used to be.

Judith Anne Rice (1995, p. 1)

One of the most frequent reasons families give for sending their youngsters to a children's center is that they want the children to learn to get along with other children and generally be "fit to live with." But social competence goes far beyond those general abilities and embraces many subskills. For example, one recent research study listed some 32 different ones, ranging from wanting to be with other children, to showing someone else how to do something, to waiting for a turn and making suggestions that facilitate group play (Babcok, Hartle, & Lamme, 1995). Another study that identified prosocial qualities valued by teachers and parents included cheerfulness, sensitivity, friendliness, and expressing affection (Bergin, Bergin, & French, 1995).

Such lists are valuable because they extend our views of what constitutes friendly, prosocial actions, thereby helping us be more aware of the many positive behaviors young children exhibit. At the same time, it is necessary to single out a few of the more basic skills to work on with the children that provide the underlying foundation for social competency. These include knowing they are able to control their aggressive impulses much of the time. Socially competent children also know and employ a number of methods of obtaining what they want from other children. They are able to form friendships, and they understand what constitutes acceptable behavior at the lunch table or during large group. They find satisfaction in helping other people from time to time, and they relish the ego-enhancing experience of occasionally performing what they think of as being grown-up work.

Of course, most youngsters do not arrive at school possessing all these skills. It is up to us, the teachers, to help them acquire these. How to do this is the subject of this chapter. (For a developmental chart that traces the growth of social and self-help skills from birth to age 6, please refer to Appendix A.)

230

When a child wants something, he wants it right now, he wants it a lot, and he wants it because he wants it!

Help Children Learn to Restrain Unsocial Impulses

The ability to control unsocial or asocial impulses is absolutely basic to getting along with others. When the recommendation is phrased in this way, however, it may sound simpler than it really is. In actuality, we must never forget or underestimate the fact that children's wants are *immediate*, *intense*, and *personal*. This means that when a young child wants something, he wants it right now, he wants it very much, and he wants it because *he* wants it. Yet, we continually expect him to wait, to defer gratification, and even to be pleasant while doing this. When comparing what children prefer to what adults prefer, I am always surprised at just how often youngsters are agreeable about going along with our expectations.

The most effective way to keep our demands and expectations within reason so that the child is not driven to desperation over the conflict between his wants and our expectations is to be quite clear in our own minds about what behav-

ior must be stopped and what can be overlooked. The rule of thumb to apply here is that we must not allow the child to seriously hurt himself or someone else or damage anyone else's property. The word *seriously* is used to make it clear that we should not err on the side of being overly protective. Children learn best through experiences—unpleasant as well as pleasant ones—and if the consequences are not too dangerous, it may be desirable to let children simply experience the consequences of their actions. For example, a child who shoves another youngster down in the play yard may learn more from getting shoved back than from our preventing this relatively harmless encounter. On the other hand, if it looks as though he is going to push someone off the top of the slide or poke another child in the face with a stick, immediate action must be taken to forestall this.

Besides the general rule-of-thumb standard, it is also necessary to have a set of well-defined rules that are agreed on and enforced by all the staff. All teachers new to the center should become acquainted with these rules and enforce them, also. Unfortunately, beginning teachers do not always realize the importance of consistency, and because they dread having to confront children, they promote inconsistency by allowing them to get away with behavior that the rest of the staff does not permit. The reason consistency matters so much has been explained by behavior modification research and borne out by practical experience with children. One of the principles of learning theory (behavior modification) is that reinforcing behavior intermittently is a very powerful way of causing it to continue. When children are sometimes stopped from doing something they want to do but sometimes allowed to do it (a positive reward), this intermittent gratification greatly increases the probability that the children will repeat that behavior at every opportunity—the very thing teachers hope to avoid.

Short-Term Methods of Controlling Behavior

Because beginning teachers are often most concerned about handling situations that require immediate control, it seems best to outline six steps for controlling impulsive behavior first and then discuss ways of working toward the longer-term goal of building inner controls. These steps are as follows:

1. Redirecting the child to more positive behavior and reminding her of the right thing to do (i.e., the rule—and the consequence for violating it)
2. Removing the child
3. Discussing feelings and rules
4. Waiting for the child to decide when she is ready to return
5. Helping her return and be more successful in an acceptable way

Boys do not have a monopoly on angry feelings!

6. When all else fails, taking firmer action

Usually it is not necessary to go through all six steps. Most children most of the time only need step 1 combined with step 3. That is, most children just need to be redirected and reminded of the right thing to do accompanied by recognition and acknowledgment of their feelings.

When it *is* necessary to actually remove the youngster from the situation (step 2), it is very important to pay special attention to following through correctly with the third and fourth steps because these steps are the ones that foster the development of inner- rather than other-controlled behavior. Step 3, taking time to describe the child's feelings to her, is vital because this says to the child, "I understand what you're feeling, even though I have to stop what you're doing. I care enough about you to take time to show you I understand by putting your feelings into words." This also means, as explained in the previous chapter, that the child does not need to continue *showing* you how she feels by acting out the angry feeling, which helps her control her behavior. In addition, telling her a simple rule helps the child see the sense and reason for the restriction.

Step 4, having the child decide when to return, is equally important because this puts the responsibility for her behavior on *her* shoulders, not on yours. If you want children to become *self-controlled*, allowing them to make these decisions for themselves has great significance.

Table 12–1 offers a sampling of possible things teachers might say to carry out this short-term method of controlling behavior. Bear in mind that steps 2 through 6 should be used only when other methods, such as distraction and redirection, have failed. (Note that, for practice, two examples of distraction and redirection have been included; can you identify them?)

Using Prevention Rather Than Cure: Longer-Term Methods of Building Inner Controls

As the sandbox example in Table 12–1 demonstrates, it is not always easy for little children to control their immediate, intense, and personal impulses, and adults must be ready to take swift, effective action. Helping children establish inner controls goes far beyond this immediate action, however. Teachers and parents can do several additional things to make life easier and more pleasant for everyone and, at the same time, build self-control within the children.

Sometimes physical control is necessary.

Emphasize Activity Centers That Foster Prosocial Interchanges

When planning activity centers, it makes sense to bear in mind that different centers elicit different kinds of positive social behaviors and some produce more prosocial action than others do. Although we are likely to assume that pretend-play situations would produce the most opportunities and, hence, the largest number of positive interactions, it may be surprising to find out that, at least in one study, that was not the case. When Babcock et al. (1995) kept track of such behaviors, they found that the creative activity centers (art, woodworking, and writing) produced 42% of the positive social interchanges they observed. This was followed by 19% at group activity centers (discovery, water play, and blocks). Eight percent of such activity occurred in the pretend-play centers (mainly housekeeping), with 7% taking place in the process centers (primarily reading). The individual activity centers that featured listening and computers had the lowest rates of interchange at 3%. They also reported that different kinds of positive social behaviors were common to different activities. For example, blocks elicit more proximity seeking and leadership behaviors, whereas the creative centers facilitated a lot of sharing and helping each other. Teachers who wish to foster positive social activities would, apparently, do well to make sure they are including plenty of art, woodworking, and writing activities to generate the greatest amount of social interchange.

Analyze the Reasons for Repeated Misbehavior, and Correct or Prevent Such Conditions When You Can

Some "discipline" situations have a way of recurring. For example, teachers may find themselves constantly telling two or three of the children not to run into the wall with their trikes or to stop tapping the table with their cups or not to poke their neighbor at group time.

When such situations happen again and again, change the situation rather than nag the child. A board on sawhorses in front of the wall or passing the cups just before milk is poured, for instance, will eliminate some of the difficulties. Rescheduling group time for when children are less tired or shortening it makes it easier for the children to be in better control of themselves. Why make it harder than necessary for children to obey?

Take Individual Needs into Account

Children misbehave for a variety of reasons: fatigue, illness, social inexperience, and immaturity are among them. Some of these causes can be mitigated with the teacher's help. For example, careful scheduling of activities can reduce the effects of fatigue, and inexperience can be modified by seizing on social learning experiences as they arise and by gradually teaching

children how to handle these without resorting to fighting. Other causes of misbehavior must be remedied by the processes of time, growth, instruction, and patience.

Realize That Children Misbehave Sometimes Because of Problems or Crises at Home

I have already spoken of the effect family crises may have on behavior in chapter 11, but even when not dealing with crises, puzzled parents may resort to using ineffective child management techniques. Sometimes, too, they feel at their wit's end and simply do not know what to do. Teachers can offer real help in these situations, particularly if they are sympathetic rather than seeming antagonistic or condescending by implying that the parents are to blame for all the child's problems. Chapter 2 provides many suggestions for offering such guidance to parents when this is needed.

Warn Ahead

Many noncompliance situations (and much misbehavior can simply be thought of as noncompliance with teacher expectations) can be avoided by giving children advance notice of what will be happening next. Doing this gives children time to adjust to the new idea. Perhaps the teacher might say, "Pretty soon it's going to be time for snack. I wonder what it will be today?" or "In a few minutes I'll be back to help you finish the puzzle because it's going to be group time," or "It's almost time to go in. Would you like to leave the snowman up and work on it some more after nap?"

Tell Children What They *Should* Do: Provide Positive Instructions Instead of Negative or Neutral Ones

This is another tactful way of encouraging desirable behavior. The teacher who says, "Put the sand in the truck" or "Keep the sand down"

TABLE 12–1

Six Steps toward Acquiring Self-Control: Dealing with Behavior Problems on an Emergency Basis

General Principles	Examples of What to Say
Step 1	
Remind the child, and redirect him if he will accept such redirection. For example, you might warn a youngster that if he continues to throw sand, he will lose the privilege of staying in the sandbox; then suggest a couple of interesting things he could do with the sand instead of throwing it. It is important to make the child understand that his behavior is up to him. It is *his* choice, but if he chooses to continue, see to it that you carry out your warning.	What could we get out that would be fun? How about some water? Or could you put the sand in the dump truck?
	Remember, Zac, keep the sand down — when you throw it behind you that way, it hits the other children. Why not turn around and dig the other way?
	Make sure you put the sand beside you here — if you throw it, it might get in someone's eyes.
	Do you need something to put the sand in? Let's look around and find something so you don't have to throw it.
	Our rule is "You have to keep the sand down so it's safe." If you throw it, you might get some in Beth's eyes. Then she'll feel bad and you'll lose the privilege of playing here for a while.
	Mae, I'm going to warn you once about keeping the sand down so it's safe — if you do that again, you'll have to come sit with me for a while until you decide you can control yourself.
Step 2	
Warn only once. If he persists in doing what he has been told not to do, act calmly and promptly. Remove him and insist that he stay with you, telling him he has lost the privilege of playing in the sand. This is much more valuable than just letting him run off. Having him stay beside you interrupts what he wants to do — a mildly unpleasant consequence of his act, which also prevents his substituting another, more pleasant activity.	Well, you decided you would throw it again, so you've lost the privilege of using the sand. Come and sit with me and we'll talk about it.
	That's really against our safety rules — up you come! [Pick up the child.] Sit over here with me until you can control yourself.
At the Institute, we prefer this method to putting the youngster off by himself because it allows the teacher to stay bonded to the child. This feeling of closeness seems to lend the child additional ego strength. He is also less likely to feel punished by being ostracized and feeling abandoned.	Jennifer, you've been warned about that, but you chose to keep right on doing it. You've lost the privilege of staying here for now — come sit with me awhile.
	I told you boys, we just can't have that kind of behavior with sand. It hurts too much when it gets in people's eyes. You'll have to come over here with me until you calm down.
Step 3	
Take time to describe his feelings in an understanding way, but state the rule and the reason for it clearly and firmly. Do not moralize or rub it in too much. Do not talk too much.	I guess you wanted to see whether I really meant what I said when I warned you. I can see you were very mad at Janie and you wanted to get even, but I can't let you hurt her. You must keep the sand down.

TABLE 12–1
continued

General Principles	Examples of What to Say
Step 3, *cont'd.*	It looks to me like you were so busy with that hole you just couldn't remember to think about where you were tossing the sand.
	I can understand why you feel that way — it's OK to be mad at Janie or me, but it isn't OK to hurt somebody. Throwing sand can hurt if it gets in people's eyes. We have to keep the sand down in the sandbox.
Step 4	
Allow the child to decide when he is ready to return to the activity. Many teachers say something like, "Now you sit here until lunch is ready," thus shifting the responsibility for the child's behavior to their own shoulders instead of putting the child in command of himself. It is better to say, "Now, tell me when you can control yourself, and I will let you go back." Some children can actually say they are ready, but others need help from the teacher, who can ask them when they look ready if they are ready to go back.	When you can remember to keep the sand down, tell me and then you may go back and play. It's up to you.
	[To a child who is too shy or young to put the intention into words] Are you ready to go back now? [Perhaps he just nods or looks ready.] Good, your eyes tell me you are. What would you like to do for fun there?
	When you decide you can use sand the safe way, nod your head and we'll think of something that it's all right to do with it.
Step 5*	
Return with the child and help him be successful so that he has the experience of substituting acceptable for unacceptable behavior. It will probably be necessary to take a few minutes to get him interested. Be sure to congratulate him when he has settled down.	Well, let's see what you've decided to do that's fun and safe.
	I'll help you get another bucket so that you don't need to take Lashonda's.

*I cannot help but think that if the teacher had done and said some of these things earlier, she might have avoided steps 2 through 4.

rather than "Don't throw the sand" helps children behave well because she has provided positive guidance before they get in trouble.

Be Alert to Potential Difficulties, and Step in Before Disaster Strikes

This advice to intervene promptly must be balanced against the value of letting children learn from direct experience. However, when teachers know that they ultimately will have to intervene, it is far better to do it when everyone is still relatively calm and no one has experienced gratification from aggressive action. Children learn much better under such circumstances than after everything has blown sky high (Greenberg, 1991a, 1992b).

General Principles	Examples of What to Say
	Would you like to use these little red cars? Maybe they need a tunnel to run through.
	That's the way to do it — now everyone's safe.
	Show me what's the safe way. That's right. Good for you!
	Now you're doing the right thing. I'm proud of you!
Step 6 Occasionally, the teacher will come across a more glib customer who says hastily when removed from the sandbox, "I'll be good, I'll be good!" but then goes right back to throwing sand when he returns. At this point, it is necessary to take firmer action. Have him sit beside you until he can think of something acceptable to do, but do not permit him to go back to the sandbox. After he has calmed down, have him select a different place to play. Go with him or alert another teacher to be sure that he becomes involved in an acceptable activity. The same may be done if two or more children are involved. However, it may be wiser to separate them. In this case, take them to different activities and provide an explanation to the attending teacher. Comment favorably on his regained self-control as soon as you possibly can.	What you did [be explicit] shows me that you haven't decided to do the right thing, so you'll have to come back and sit with me until you can think of somewhere else to play. You've lost the privilege of playing in the sandbox. [To the other teacher] Jane and Maggie have lost the privilege of playing in the sandbox. They have decided they'd like to push each other on the swing awhile. Could you get them started on that?

This advice also means that teachers must pay consistent attention to what is going on around them. Particularly for beginners it can be a real temptation to focus on only one amiable child and avoid watching a wider area, but good teachers learn to do both things at once. They retain a kind of peripheral awareness of the entire yard or room, no matter what other adult is present, and also pay attention to individual children at the same time. It is an art—but a very necessary one to learn.

Make a Point of Recognizing Good Behavior

This does not have to be fulsome praise. Such simple statements as "Thank you" or "That's ex-

actly the right thing to do!" or "I appreciate your help" are satisfying without being gushy or overdone.

Convey a Feeling of Warmth Along with a Sense of Firmness

Admittedly, this can be tricky advice to give novice teachers, because some misinterpret it and attempt to buy good behavior from the children by being too friendly or "chummy" with them. The role of teachers is different from this: they must set a tone of warmth and caring concern while also maintaining a posture of firm reasonableness that is quite different from being the children's buddy.

Children (and adults) flourish in this climate of sincere approval and warmth. When they sense the teacher likes them, they try harder to retain this approval by behaving in accordance with her wishes. On the other hand, if they feel continually criticized and attacked, they gradually abandon hope and give up the effort of behaving well (Gartrell, 1995).

They will also feel more secure and trustful if they know that the teacher cares enough about them to prevent them from doing anything seriously out of line. This is why there is often a feeling of comfort between child and teacher after they have worked through a "scene." Although an inexperienced teacher often fears that the child will avoid or hate her following an encounter, usually an increased sense of closeness and confidence between teacher and child is the result—but it certainly takes courage on the teacher's part to see the first two or three such storms all the way through. Perhaps it is not only

the child who feels more secure following such an encounter.

Be Reasonable

By this I do not mean reasonable in the sense of not expecting too much, although that is certainly important, too. *Reasonable* here means that a simple reason for conforming to the rules should always be included along with the prohibition. Supplying a simple, clear-cut reason not only makes it plain that the rule is not just a whim of the teacher but also puts into practice some well-supported research finding that firm control combined with warmth and *accompanied by a reason* are the most effective agents in building inner controls and establishing the beginnings of conscience in young children (Hoffman, 1970).

Remember, children learn by example. Modeling good behavior helps them do the right thing.

Be a Good Example Yourself

It is true that children learn from models and that they may express more direct aggression when they have witnessed a model behaving aggressively (Bandura, 1986; Molitor & Hirsch, 1994) or have been exposed to actual aggressive behavior (Knutson & Bower, 1994). Therefore, to reduce aggressive behavior, it is important to remain in control of yourself so that you do not model such behavior for the children to copy. Unfortunately, it is all too easy to pull two struggling children apart and angrily dole out instant punishment to both of the culprits as a way of relieving your own aggressive feelings—and then regret the severity of that punishment a few moments later. How much more desirable it is to stop what the children are doing immediately and say, before doing anything more, "Wait just a minute. I need to calm down myself and think this over—then we'll talk about it." Doing this stops the action, gives everyone a minute to draw breath, and allows you to proceed in a less aggressive, better-considered way while presenting an example of how to control oneself.

Profit by Your Experience

Of course, not all discipline situations work out perfectly, and adults often feel badly about this. Although mishandling a situation cannot be condoned, it is also valuable to realize that one poorly handled encounter will not result in permanent damage to child or teacher.

The important thing to do when this has happened is not to sink into the depths of self-abasing despair but to think the situation over carefully, learn from it, and *decide what you will do differently next time*. Doing this helps prevent the useless repetition of ineffective responses to misbehavior, and planning ahead confers an invaluable sense of assurance on the teacher. In an interesting way, children are similar to animals—both sense immediately who is afraid of them and who is not, and they respond accordingly. Confident teachers who know what their next step will be if matters go awry often find that such steps become unnecessary.

Teach Children Socially Acceptable Ways of Getting What They Want

Of course, we need to go far beyond simply stopping children from doing harm if we want them to learn to get along well in groups. Although it may sound as if we are teaching selfishness, one of the most valuable things to do is to teach them alternative ways of getting what they want, bearing in mind that children also have to learn to balance what they want with what reality makes it likely they can get.

When children resort to force, it is often because they know of no other way to get what they want. This is why it is so worthwhile to teach children the alternative strategies that are discussed in the following sections. Children who possess a number of these advanced social ploys are less likely to resort to physical attack. Moreover, having these skills increases their feelings of being competent and masterful.

Teach Alternatives

If teachers keep on the outlook for potential snatch-and-grab situations, they can use them as a basis for practical social teaching provided they are aware of the range of alternative solutions that can be proposed to children. These include teaching children to (a) ask to use something when the other child is done ("Ask him, 'Can I have that when you're through?' "), (b) trade one thing for another ("Maybe if you gave him your hat, he'd let you use the cane"), or (c) work out some kind of compromise in which each child obtains some satisfaction ("I know

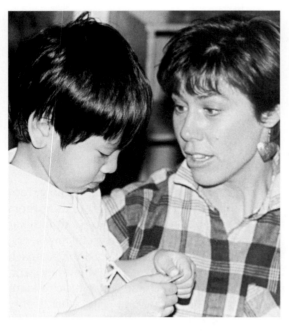

When the teacher puts a child's feelings into words for him, it helps him bring himself under control.

she's holding both crayons. Perhaps she'd let you use the orange while she's using red, and then you could swap"). Other alternatives include suggesting that the child use something else as a substitute or encouraging him to do something else while waiting ("The elephant puzzle's in use right now. How about doing the giraffe while you're waiting?"). Sometimes a genuinely cooperative arrangement can be worked out in which the play is enriched by the newcomer's contribution ("Janice, if they let you play, would you help them carry the blocks? Well, why don't you tell them that?").

When children are old enough (around age 3 ½ to 4), it is even possible to ask them to tell you what they could do instead. This helps them think up their own alternatives. For example, the teacher might ask, "It sure didn't work to tip over her trike, did it? Now she's mad and won't let you play. The next time you

want Tricia to let you ride, what could you do instead?"

At the preschool level, any of these alternatives generally work better than insisting that the children take turns regulated by the teacher or expecting that a youngster will gladly surrender something he is using just because someone else has asked for it. After all, why should he? Moreover, these alternatives are more desirable because they do not depend so much on adult enforcement, nor do they place an unreasonable expectation of generosity on either of the children involved.

Of course, these approaches do not always work—and when a youngster just begins trying them out, teachers need to remain with the child and lend their support to make them as effective as possible. It is also helpful to preface the suggestions with such phrases as "*Maybe it would work* if you tried trading him this truck for that little car," or "*Perhaps* he'd let you play if you'd sit on that side of the swing to balance it." This leaves the way open, if the other child simply refuses, to say, "Well, I guess she needs that herself right now. We'll just have to find something else for you to do instead. Maybe she'll come and tell you when she's through—would you do that, Susan?" (Incidentally, one thing that is almost certain *not* to work as a social approach for 4-year-olds is to coach them to ask, "Can I play?" There is such strong in-group feelings among fours coupled with the need for self-assertion that the answer to this plaintive inquiry will more than likely be a resounding "No!")

Finally, it is important to show approval when you see children accepting and using these alternatives: "I'm sure glad to see you ask Jim for that instead of biting him the way you used to—and he likes you better, too!" or "Well, that trade worked out pretty well, didn't it? Both you children got something you wanted." This makes the children more aware of what they are doing, and the positive reinforcement makes repetition of that behavior more probable.

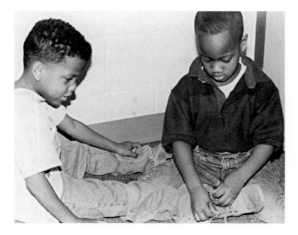

Children who are willing to help other youngsters are usually well liked.

Help Children Respond Generously

Children are more likely to feel generous about welcoming newcomers into their play or sharing equipment with them if they know that their own rights are protected. This is the reason many children's centers observe the rule "You can keep something until you're done with it, but if you've stopped using it, then someone else can have a turn." This policy helps reduce the need to cling jealously and vigilantly to things lest they be arbitrarily taken away by the teacher. It also means that when children are finished and have had enough, they give the item up willingly instead of grudgingly. In other words, they are sharing because they *want* to, not because they *have* to. There is a world of difference in what children learn in those two circumstances.

Children should also be taught how to stand up for their own rights because this, too, is an aspect of being socially competent, and, paradoxically, children who know they can protect themselves are likely to be less defensive and protective of their possessions. For example, the teacher might encourage a child to defend himself by asking an indecisively whimpering 3-year-old, "Do you want her to take your buggy? Well,

then, tell her you don't," or say to another child, "Hang on! You don't have to let him have that, you know. Tell him the rule!"

Generous behavior will be encouraged if the teacher occasionally points out to a youngster who has shared something that the other child is now feeling gratified and friendly: "Gee, you really made her feel good" or "Look how he's smiling at you. I think he's feeling friendly because you let him use that box." Perhaps a quick hug can be used to show pleasure in the child's altruistic behavior.

Finally, simply having enough equipment and materials to go around makes a difference that cannot be overlooked. As frustration increases, constructiveness in play decreases and nothing is more frustrating or breeds more closehandedness than having only enough blocks to build one tower or enough dough for tantalizing little fistfuls. It is not always necessary to have a large budget to provide plentiful amounts of materials and equipment. Many can be made or scrounged at reasonable cost if teachers and parents are willing to make the effort.

Increase the Child's Ability to Make Friends

What Makes a Good Friend?

One of the reasons it is valuable to teach children to get along easily with other children is that they are more likely to have friends when they are able to do this, and even for children of preschool age, having friends contributes to happiness (Ramsey, 1991).

Although some may have the impression that friendships between preschool children are largely temporary and haphazard, preschool teachers know this to be untrue, and studies of actual behavior bear this out as well (Axtmann & Bluhm, 1986; Howes, Unger, & Matheson, 1992). It is obvious that in most preschool groups there are children who prefer each other's company, as well as those who are more likely to be shunned or shut out of play.

When asked why someone is a good friend, preschoolers usually give quite simple answers that boil down to "Because I like him!" (Rubin, 1982). Hayes (1978) pursued this question in more depth and found that children gave additional reasons for friendship, including liking to play with the child, nearness (propinquity), and possession of interesting toys to play with. Some additional qualities that make a young child more likely to be selected as a friend include being physically attractive and acting friendly and outgoing (Hartup, 1983).

On the other hand, Hayes (1978) reported that youngsters disliked children who were aggressive, behaved in unusual ways, or broke the rules.

Sometimes reasons can be quite specific, as when one of our Institute children explained, "Well, you know—P.J., Grady, and I were born in the same hospital, we're the same tall [height] and the same age, so of course we must play together!"

Increase the Child's Likability

To help children make friends, teachers must realize that they can help with some factors but that other ones are part of the child's temperament. Some children, by temperament, are quiet and less outgoing than others are and so appear to be less friendly. Some children seem to feel most comfortable with one or two good friends, whereas others manage well with a number of different playmates.

While taking temperament into account, teachers can do some things that may increase a child's likability. One of the most important of these is helping children learn to control the way they express anger because research confirmed by common sense and experience shows that

other children dislike the perpetrators of hostile aggression. It is because learning to control the expression of hostile aggression is such a fundamental social skill that the steps toward acquiring self-control discussed earlier in the chapter are so important. The emphasis on fostering self-decision and self-regulation emphasized in those steps is intended to increase the child's ability to regulate his own behavior rather than relying entirely on the teacher to do that for him (Eisenberg, Fabes, Carlo, & Karbon, 1992).

Children who have developed a repertoire of alternative ways to get what they want are also less likely to resort to socially unpopular methods of snatch and grab and so are more likable. Generally speaking, increasing children's feeling of competence in any area helps them feel more confident, and this confidence helps them be more open, less defensive, and more friendly to others.

Sometimes even physical attractiveness can be increased if the teacher is very tactful about this. Some years ago, we had a 4-year-old youngster in the group who was very pretty and intelligent. Unfortunately, she smelled of urine. It got to the point where the children were telling her at snack time, "Sit somewhere else—you smell like peepee!" This was a delicate matter to bring to the mother's attention, to say the least. Yet, we could not go on allowing the child's feelings to be hurt. The teacher approached the problem by asking the mother if the little girl had ever had any previous urinary problems because we noticed that her panties were often just a little wet when she went to the bathroom. The mother agreed and said she had been concerned and had been meaning to take her daughter to the doctor. This conversation motivated her to take action, and it turned out that the child did have a physical problem, which they were able to correct.

Fortunately, not all friendship problems are this ticklish to handle. Teachers can do additional, simple things to help children form friendships. One is pairing children for special experiences. Asking a pair to help set up a cook-

About the worst thing a child can do under these circumstances is ask, "Can I play?"

ing experience may lead to their cooking together afterward, for instance. Others include restructuring a car pool or suggesting that a mother invite a child regularly to play after school. Sometimes finding a common interest helps generate a bond.

Occasionally, providing a clear explanation of how the child is offending other children becomes necessary: "You know, when you walk into the block corner and kick over their things, they feel really mad at you. That's why they won't let you play. Maybe if you got that truck, you could deliver some blocks when they need them. When you help people, they like you better."

Help Children Cope with Rejection

Although all children experience occasional rejection and exclusion by others, sometimes more extreme cases occur. This seems to happen more frequently with fours than with threes. The child continually hangs around a particular child, and the harder he presses the issue, the more vehement the rejection becomes. After trying some of the alternatives listed previously,

the teacher may just have to help the child accept the fact that a particular child does not want to be friends with him. There is no way to force such relationships. If he chooses to continue his wistful pursuit, that is his own decision, but the teacher can point out that other children are available to play with if he chooses to do that instead.

Increase the Child's Ability to Function Successfully as Part of a Group

Use Play Situations to Help Children Develop Group Social Skills

Children learn a lot about getting along with people by playing with them. They learn what others will tolerate and what they will not, how to maintain a balance of satisfaction so that everyone has enough fun that they want to stay and play, when to give in, and when to assert themselves. Maintaining this delicate balance between compromise and getting one's own

She did it!

way is an essential social skill that seems to come more easily to some children than it does to others as the research study by Trawick-Smith reveals.

Playing with other children varies in accordance with children's age, temperament, and amount of social experience. Two- and 3-year-olds play more frequently by themselves or alongside each other, whereas older threes and fours play more frequently together, often instructing each other quite specifically in the roles they should assume ("You be the mommy, and I'll be your little girl"), stipulating conditions ("I'll play, but you don't give me no shots!"), and using their imagination to set the stage ("This stuff over here is the tree, and we're the lions who live there"). Twos and threes tend to focus more on playing with objects and play materials, investigating their properties, sometimes investing them with imaginary play themes and sometimes not, whereas older threes and fours participate in more interactive dramatic play.

Research Study

The Social Value of Compromise

Research Question   Trawick-Smith asked, Why are some children more successful in leading play activities than other children are? What is it about the way they behave that causes other children to accept their ideas so readily?

Research Method   He studied the behavior of 32 preschool children while they engaged in natural free play at nursery school. While the children were playing together, he counted the number of episodes of leading and following behavior he observed.

Leadership behavior was defined as how frequently a child's directives, suggestions, or contributions to the play theme were actually accepted by the other children. Following behavior was defined as being the opposite of leadership behavior (i.e., how often a child accepted directives, suggestions, or contributions to the play proposed by the other child).

Research Results   Analysis of the results revealed something surprising. It was not the strongly outspoken, somewhat aggressive children who were the most effective leaders. Rather, the children who had the greatest number of their suggestions accepted by others turned out to be the ones who also accepted the most suggestions *from* other children. The high leadership children had many novel ideas to contribute, but they were also willing to concede some control of the play to the other youngsters.

On the other hand, unskilled leaders whose suggestions were not as frequently accepted fell into three categories. One group included the children who attempted to force their ideas on other children, whom the investigator classified as "bullies." The second

Once play has begun, teachers should bear in mind the value of prolonging and extending the interaction so children benefit from maximum social experience. It does take a delicate hand to know when to intervene and when not to. My impression is that some inexperienced teachers tend to participate too fully by acting childlike or make themselves the center of attention or become the source of too many of the ideas, all of which rob the children of the initiative.

On the other hand, some teachers lean too far in the other direction and do not encourage the children enough, with the result that the play falls apart too quickly or lacks richness. These people should acquaint themselves with the research by Smilansky and Shefatya (1990), which reports that intervention is particularly necessary with children from families of the poor who may lag behind in the development of their sociodramatic play skills and who need special modeling and encouragement in how to play to develop these skills more fully. Of course, limited richness of play may not be restricted to those children who are living in poverty. As more and more youngsters of all economic classes spend longer hours in front of television sets, their play may also require added support from teachers.

Such intervention may take the form of suggestions ("Perhaps you boys need a bag if you're going to go to the market. Let's see, I wonder what you could use?"), supportive comments ("You children are really busy in there" or "My goodness, little kitten, you *do* look snuggly—your mother is sure taking good care of you!"), or even direct participation and modeling ("Yum, yum, yum! Thanks for that delicious mashed potato cake! Should I feed some to the baby until you're not so busy?").

In general, if teachers remember that the purpose of intervening is not to dominate but to sustain and continue the play, as well as to foster positive social interaction among the children, they will not go far wrong.

group, which he named "boot lickers," were so eager to be included in the play they were overly compliant and did as they were told, while the third group, termed "isolates," usually played alone.

Implications for Teaching   This research highlights a particular social skill that is worthwhile for children to learn during their early years. This is the willingness to listen to suggestions from other children and incorporate them along with their own ideas as they play together—in short, to practice the art of compromise. In this sort of amiable situation, the value of everyone's ideas is recognized, and everyone gets at least a little bit of what he or she wants.

Additional conclusions drawn by the investigator include recommendations that bullies be taught to adopt more following behaviors, to ask for things rather than just demand them, to bargain, to accept compromises, and to understand the "futility of using force."

He suggests that boot lickers be encouraged to speak up for their own ideas and learn to exercise their right of choice and that isolated children be encouraged to play, at least occasionally, with other children.

In essence, a major goal to keep in mind when teaching children social skills is teaching them to maintain a balance between insisting on their own ideas and using the ideas put forth by others, a balance between compliance and self-assertion, and a balance between solitary and social play. It is the ability to maintain that balance that provides the key to playing successfully with other children.

Note: From "Let's Say You're the Baby, OK? Play Leadership and Following Behavior of Young Children" by J. Trawick-Smith, 1988 *Young Children*, 43(5), pp. 51–59.

TABLE 12–2

Ways to Increase Positive Social Interaction among Children

Approaches Likely to Induce *Positive* Social Action	Approaches Likely to Induce *Negative* Social Action

Dramatic Play Centering on the Home

Be prepared to suggest ongoing ideas from time to time when play appears likely to lag or fall apart. ("Hmmm, do I smell vegetable soup?")

Provide both male and female items in order to welcome both sexes and provide opportunities to try out other-sex roles. These might include shaving equipment, tools, wedding dresses, or boots.

Stimulate variety in the play by varying the equipment. Offer market supplies, hospital things, or the large blocks and boards.

Vary the location. Move equipment to a new area—perhaps outside or into a large bathroom for water play.

Include items that attract children particularly, such as water, several large empty boxes, or guinea pigs.

Foster cultural respect by offering multiethnic equipment, such as wooden bowls from Africa, a bedspread made of Guatemalan material, or dolls of various ethnic backgrounds, and speak casually, but respectfully, of such things as our "Mexican chair," our "Zambian bowl," and so forth.

Offer more than one piece of the same large equipment, such as two baby buggies or two suitcases.

Split the housekeeping equipment into two households, and encourage the children to improvise additional needed items.

Set up an office or a market in conjunction with the housekeeping area.

To encourage role playing, offer items large enough for the children to get into themselves, such as a regular high chair and a child-sized bed.

Increase the reality-information base of the play by having a baby visit, going to a real market, or actually visiting places where parents work to see what their mothers and fathers do there.

Offer a simple cooking experience, such as making peanut butter sandwiches in the housekeeping corner.

Encourage more than one age to play together. This is fairly easy to do in housekeeping because of the variety of family roles that are available.

Encourage the children to solve problems together. How could they turn the house into a camper? What could they use for bananas?

Pay attention to the children's requests and ideas. This helps them feel valued and important and encourages children to listen to each other, also.

Make the play area too small and congested so that the children get in each other's way much of the time.

Allow clothing or other equipment to accumulate on the floor so that the children stumble over it, mistreat it, or cannot find what they need.

Offer only female-type items, with the result that the boys feel subtly excluded. This makes attacks by the boys more likely.

Do not set up the homemaking area before the children arrive. Leave it as it was the day before.

Provide no physical barriers, so that children who are passing through intrude either intentionally or unintentionally.

Keep equipment skimpy so that children have to wait too long for a chance to use it.

Allow equipment to become broken or dirty. This tells the children that this play area and what happens there are not really important and that you do not care about them.

Approaches Likely to Induce *Positive* Social Action	Approaches Likely to Induce *Negative* Social Action

When necessary, help new arrivals enter the group successfully by suggesting how they could help, what they could be, or what they might say to the children who are already playing there.

Put all the regular equipment away and encourage the children to develop their own house, using blocks, boards, and accessories.

Outdoor Large-Muscle Play

Whenever possible, select equipment that invites or requires more than one child's cooperative use for best success, such as double rocking boats, a hammock, large parachute activities, jump ropes, wagons, and horizontally hung tire swings.

Offer several of one kind of thing, not only to reduce bickering but also to induce social play. Several bouncy horses together facilitate social congeniality, for example.

Provide plentiful equipment for dramatic play. In particular, a good assortment of blocks, ladders, sawhorses, and boards encourages the children to build things together. Smaller equipment, such as ropes, hats, and horses, also encourage this kind of social play.

Think of the sandbox as providing an interesting social play center (particularly for younger children), and provide things to do together, such as a fleet of little cars or a good supply of pans and sturdy spoons and shovels.

Stay alert and aware of what is going on to provide input and control in time when it is needed.

Occasionally encourage more physically proficient children to teach less skilled children how to do something.

Encourage children to help each other—push each other on the swing, for example.

Read and apply what Kritchevsky, Prescott, and Walling (1996) have to say about developing play spaces so that complex and super play units are offered rather than simple ones.

Offer outdoor sand, mud, and water play whenever possible. This encourages peaceful social interaction for lengthy periods of time.

Offer large-group projects that involve doing something together, such as painting a large refrigerator box to make something to play in, or gardening. This is not exactly play, but it is so much fun it feels like play to the children.

Provide no focus for the play—let the children mostly just run around.

Keep the children indoors so long that they are pent up and desperate for physical activity when they do get out.

Sit idly by.

Offer the same kind of large-muscle activities every day. This lack of variety breeds boredom and fighting.

Store equipment in inaccessible places so that it is difficult to get out and hence will not be frequently used.

Suggest competitive activities—who can run fastest, get there first, and so forth. This breeds ill feeling and hurt feelings.

Encourage games with many rules. This baffles the younger children, increases frustration and reduces spontaneity and creativity.

Permit the older, more powerful children to monopolize the equipment.

Table 12–2 (pp. 246–247) provides many suggestions for ways teachers can foster positive social interaction among children. Two areas of curriculum have been singled out to illustrate their potential for doing this. Actually, all areas of curriculum have equivalent potentials for positive and negative social learning. Consider what these might be when setting up each area—whether it be the block corner, the water play table, or the sandbox. Good planning facilitates desirable social learning.

Use Mealtimes to Foster Social Competencies

Sometimes we lose sight of the fact that eating together is one of the most profoundly social activities available to human beings. In many cultures around the world, the act of breaking bread together is a sign of peace and also lies at the heart of many celebrations. These lofty practices may seem far removed from a group of 3-year-olds spooning up fruit and yogurt. Yet, it is valuable for people working with children to keep the more profound social value in mind even while mopping up milk and showing children how to scrape their plates because it will help the adults remember that the fundamental goal of eating together is to have a congenial experience in which everyone is both physically satisfied and socially replenished.

Moreover, if well presented, mealtimes offer the best opportunity of the day to foster the feeling of home and family so important to young children and all too often missing from large day care situations. This feeling of "familiness" can be generated not only by the overall climate of warmth and human interchange but also by attention to such details as serving food that is culturally familiar (note that *familiar* comes from the same root as *family*) and by encouraging families to participate in meals at the center by occasionally having lunch with their youngsters or sending birthday goodies or sharing their surplus garden produce with the school (though there is a limit to the

amount of zucchini even a center can willingly consume).

Create a Climate of Intimacy and Calm
In addition to linking home and school, three other practices will help achieve a climate of easy comfort right from the start of the meal. First, *the group at the table needs to be kept as small as possible*: five children and an adult is ideal, though not always possible. Younger children require an even higher adult/child ratio because they need so much more help. What should be avoided at all costs is putting all 15 or 16 children around one table with no adult present, because pandemonium results. The children have to wait too long for food to be passed to them, and there is almost no way to generate conversation in such bedlam.

Second, *the food should be right there*, ready to be passed as soon as all the children are seated. The only drawback to this is that it may cool a little more than desired, but having a meal ready is infinitely preferable to nagging at children to sit still and stop tapping their cups or poking their neighbor.

Finally, *it is very desirable for adults to be present and sitting down* as the children come to the table. It is not the function of these adults to get up and run after sponges, go to the kitchen for refills, and so forth. The sponges should already be available on the service trays, and children should be allowed the social opportunity of going for refills. The adults are present to help generate a peaceful, welcoming, happy atmosphere in which each child has the chance to talk with the teachers and friends and also the opportunity to help others by passing food, mopping up, and so forth.

Keep Mealtime Policies Consistent with the Basic Educational Philosophy of the School
Nowhere in curriculum is the fundamental educational philosophy of the teacher revealed more plainly than in the way the food situation is handled.

Who makes the final decision on what to eat? Does the teacher decide by arbitrarily doling the food out on each plate and making the child eat everything? Or do the children decide by serving themselves and being allowed to go easy on food they do not like or are suspicious of?

Who passes the food around the table? Does the teacher move from child to child, or are individual children allowed to serve themselves and pass it on to their neighbors, learning social consideration by taking some and leaving some?

Who generates conversation? Is it always teacher centered, or does it become talk *between* children as a result of the adult encouraging that focus? Remember that conversation is thought to be one of the earliest (if not the earliest) forms of turn taking that children learn. Learning to allow space and time for others to reply is an intensely valuable social skill.

Use Group Time to Foster Social Competencies

Too often teachers think of group time as being primarily a time to read a book or two to the children, and books do have a valuable place in that activity, as discussed in chapter 16. But, in addition to the opportunities for language and cognitive growth inherent in group time, teachers should also use it to foster positive social interaction and learning.

This time of day offers excellent opportunities for children to become interested in other youngsters and what they have been doing. Perhaps someone has brought his pet mouse from home, or perhaps three or four of the children have just returned from seeing a poodle get its hair clipped at the groomer's. Such experiences are of genuine interest to children and delightful to share in the group. However, teachers get in trouble with having children share their experiences when they assume it is necessary to go entirely around the circle and have each child tell something each day. This takes too long, and instead of generating interest, this practice generates seething boredom because the children are pushed beyond their limits of self-control for holding still. Yet, if groups are kept small and ex-

periences are shared naturally by different children on different days, group time can be interesting and can also provide another opportunity to value things from home at school.

Occasionally discussing social problems also fosters social learning at group time, particularly with 4-year-olds (Beaty, 1995; Mize, 1995; Shure, 1994). For example, on the day before a new tricycle will be made available, the group might discuss how to work things out so that everyone will have a chance to use it, or they might discuss how to keep children from picking the tomatoes in the garden before they are ripe enough to eat. It is important that this kind of discussion not center on the past misdeeds of some small sinner in particular but focus instead on making a group decision that will bring about socially positive behavior.

The teacher who leads such a discussion should know that, as in many other aspects of child development, children's ideas of right and wrong (and hence their ideas of what constitutes justice) change as the child develops (Buzzelli, 1992). She should not be surprised if the rules they suggest are quite severe, definite ones, because children of this age believe what is right is right and what is wrong is wrong. Their idea of justice is one of reciprocity, the eye-for-an-eye and tooth-for-a-tooth variety, so the teacher may need to help the children temper their suggestions with mercy. However, if such group discussions are not overdone, they can help children think about the effect individual actions have on the group as a whole and what should be done about it.

Encourage Children to Find Satisfaction in Being Kind to Each Other, Helping Each Other, and Helping the Group

Encourage Kindly Actions

Encouraging children to be kind to each other is an important yet sometimes overlooked way

*A simple act of unexpected kindness
helps welcome a child to group time.*

to encourage positive social behavior and learning. Even though young children are largely self-centered in the sense that they see the world in terms of their own needs and point of view, they are also capable of offering comfort and help to other people if properly encouraged and if the example has been set for them in the past (Eisenberg, 1992; Katz & McClellan, 1991). This was brought vividly to my attention one day when I shut my hand in the door of the car. It hurt so much that I just collapsed on the seat of the car, tears oozing down my cheeks. At that point my 3-year-old climbed over, snuggled up close, and began to pat my back sympathetically, murmuring something over and over in my ear as I had done for her so many times before. When my senses cleared, I realized to my amusement that what she was crooning as she patted me was, "Pretty soon, pretty soon, you'll be all right—you're just tired and hungry! Tired and hungry!"

Help Children Begin to Gain Insight into How Other People Feel

Many opportunities arise every day at the center for children to experience the satisfying rewards of taking kindly, prosocial action in someone else's behalf—action that usually involves being considerate of other people's feelings and making efforts to help them feel comfortable and/or happy.

To do that, children have to realize that other people feel differently from the way *they* feel, and they also must be able to think up kindly ways to respond to those different feelings. One way to help children develop these skills is to follow Beaty's (1995) advice. She advocates asking a child directly, "How do you think *he* is feeling?" and then "How could you help him feel better?" Note that, as we descussed in chapter 11, this is very different from using the more confusing question, "What if you were him? How do you think *you* would feel?"

Another approach, as exemplified in Smith's (1993) book, is to incorporate various activities into self-select or small-group time that sensitize children to being more compassionate and loving toward other children in the group.

Encourage Children to Help and Comfort Each Other

If not overdone, older children can benefit by helping younger ones at school. This should not be construed as meaning that a four should surrender his doll to a three just because he is older, but it does mean that the four might hold the bunny's feet so it will not kick while the three is petting it, or that he might show the younger child where the napkins are kept or pull a towel out of the holder for him when it is too high to reach. This willingness to help others need not be limited to assisting younger children. The child who volunteers to open a door for a teacher whose hands are full or who helps his friend push a wagon up the hill is also demonstrating his ability to care for and help other people.

Children also feel very positively about caring for animals, and it is nice to give them this opportunity. Baby animals, in particular, elicit a kindly feeling in younger children, who are also likely to be concerned and critical about the quality of care the mother animal is providing.

Then, too, as early as 18 months of age children are quick to worry and feel concern when they see another child crying or when someone is hurt (Buzzelli, 1992). If the teacher welcomes this concern and involves the child in providing comfort and fixing the small injury, this not only helps reassure him but also lets him experience the benefit of helping another child feel better.

Meaningful Work Offers Opportunities for Helping

There are numerous places around a day care center where children can find real pleasure in working, as long as the teacher avoids turning the work into an onerous chore. Some examples include almost any kind of cleaning up that involves water, such as scrubbing easels, doing dishes, hosing off sidewalks or sandy toys, scrubbing chairs, or washing doll clothes. Working by fixing things, such as repairing pages from torn books, breaking up dried potter's clay with a hammer so it can be moistened and reconstituted, sawing off the handles of paintbrushes that are too long, tightening tricycle seats, decorating the picture file box with collage, and putting up the swing seats in the morning are other possibilities. Still another kind of work that contributes to the well-being of the group might be fetching second helpings from the kitchen, taking old material down from bulletin boards, spreading out the plastic door mats on snowy days, helping set up cots, feeding the fish, or reassembling a puzzle that the teacher finds too difficult. When more than one child has to cooperate to accomplish a task, the value is even greater. Perhaps two are needed to fold the larger blankets, or several children can work together to wash the teacher's car or carry the housekeeping equipment outside.

These kinds of opportunities should be available every day and will be most enjoyed by the children if the teacher allows them to choose how they want to help, keeps the jobs short, is not too critical of the results, and remembers to say "Thank you" afterward. It is particularly valuable to help them enjoy their feeling of accomplishing something genuinely worthwhile, which means that the job cannot be "make-work." Children love the sense of competence that comes from hard work well completed. It is one of the finest avenues for building self-esteem. As one youngster put it the other day, "I did it because I was so *big*! One of these days, Teacher, I'll be *so* big you won't even *know* me!"

Summary

If we want children to learn to balance their own needs and desires with concern for those of other people, we must have a clear grasp of the most basic social skills that are worthwhile to teach them so they will become happy, social people.

Among the most important of these competencies is the ability to control unsocial impulses and to use alternative ways of obtaining what they want rather than just snatching and grabbing. Learning to accept other children's ideas and incorporate them in the play is a particularly valuable social skill for children to acquire. Three group situations that occur during the center day offer fruitful possibilities for developing these social skills. These are sociodramatic play situations, eating together at mealtimes, and small-group sharing and learning times.

As the children gain experience and become more mature, they should also be encouraged to find satisfaction in helping each other and in doing things to help the group as a whole. Meaningful work can be used to provide this kind of satisfaction.

Self-Check Questions for Review

Content-Related Questions

1. What is the rule of thumb to apply about when to stop behavior?
2. Why is it important to be consistent in enforcing center rules?
3. List and discuss the six recommended steps when dealing with behavior problems. Illustrate each step with an example.
4. There are also many longer-term methods of building inner controls. What are some of those practical methods? Again, illustrate each with an example.
5. What are some alternative methods children can learn to use to get what they want?
6. What are some things teachers can do that may help a child be better liked by the other children?
7. According to the research study discussed in this chapter, what social skill separates the effective leaders from the other children?
8. Discuss some ways teachers can foster social competencies in the children during play, group times, or at meals.

9. Suppose you wished to *discourage* positive social interactions during dramatic play or outdoor time. Suggest some ways you could make this happen.
10. What are some ways children can be encouraged to help other people while they are at the center?

Integrative Questions

1. Sarah has just snatched some train track from Jan and is holding onto it fiercely while Jan is trying to tug it back. Both girls are crying loudly as they struggle. Describe how you would go through the six learning steps about discipline with Sarah, giving actual examples of what you would do or say. Then describe how you would use the situation to teach Jan what she needs to do next time.
2. Using the form on positive and negative social actions (Table 12–2), choose an indoor activity and show how you could arrange and manage it to foster either positive or negative behavior by the children.
3. Does the research carried out by Trawick-Smith have implications for adult as well as for child leaders? If so, what are those implications? Can you provide examples from your own experience of adults who fit the various categories of ineffective leaders that he describes in the study?

Questions and Activities

1. It is springtime, and you and the children have planted a vegetable garden. The children are really interested in this, and someone has been unable to resist pulling up the radishes to see if they are ready to eat. Because they are no more than little, pale pink roots and far from ready, you find them shriveled on the sidewalk where they have been tossed aside. Although you hope to have only a general discussion about this at group time, when the matter is brought up, one of the children says immediately, "Teacher, Teacher, I know who did it— Richard did it!" Thinking back over this particular situation, how would you handle it next time? And what do you plan to do about it right now?
2. Picking up the small blocks is often regarded as a real chore by both teachers and children. Suggest some things to do that would make this task more palatable.

3. What do you think of the idea of making a chart, listing on it all the jobs that must be done in school, and posting children's names before they arrive beside the items each day so they will know who is supposed to do what?

4. Describe some situations you have recently seen at your center in which it was *not* necessary to intervene in an argument between two children.

5. This book talks quite a lot about fostering alternatives to physically aggressive action. Pick out some of the more aggressive situations you have witnessed, and propose two or three alternative solutions that the children might have been encouraged to use.

6. Choose an area or activity in your own teaching situation, and list various ways positive social action could be increased.

7. Are there times when you now realize that you helped a child do something when another youngster might have helped instead?

References for Further Reading

Overviews

Bos, B. (1990). *Together we're better: Establishing a coactive learning environment.* Roseville, CA: Turn the Page Press. This book burgeons with fresh ideas about things children can do that encourage being together. *Highly recommended.*

DeVries, R., & Zan, B. (1995). Creating a constructivist classroom atmosphere. *Young Children, 51*(1), 4–14. Methods of fostering wholesome social relationships based on a Piagetian point of view are set forth here.

Gartrell, D. (1995). Misbehavior or mistaken behavior? *Young Children, 50*(5), 27–34. The author encourages us to view undesirable behavior as being "mistaken" and also analyzes similar behaviors, showing how they may stem from differing motivations. *Highly recommended.*

Read, K. H. (1996). Initial support through guides to speech and action. In K. M. Paciorek & J. H. Munro (Eds.), *Sources: Notable selections in early childhood education.* Guilford, CT: Dushkin. I believe this was the first material I ever read about working with young children, and this reprint is as sound today as it was 40 years ago! (It don't get no better than this!)

Wittmer, D. S., & Honig, A. S. (1996). Encouraging positive social development in young children. In K. M. Paciorek & J. H. Munro (Eds.), *Early childhood education 96/97.* Guilford, CT: Dushkin. A compendium of practical advice fostering positive social development is provided here. *Highly recommended.*

Helping Children Build *Self*-Control

Hewitt, D. (1995). *So this is normal too?* St. Paul, MN: Redleaf. This is a really useful book that singles out 16 common behavior problems and suggests effective (and different) things providers and parents can do to alleviate them. *Highly recommended.*

Marion, M. (1995). *Guidance of young children* (4th ed.). Upper Saddle River, NJ: Merrill/Prentice Hall. Marion's book is filled with a sound combination of research, theory, and practical advice on this subject.

Mitchell, G. (1982). *A very practical guide to discipline with young children.* Marshfield, MA: Telshare. Mitchell brings a world of experience to this useful book that discusses a general approach to discipline combined with discussions of typical problems.

Saifer, S. (1990). *Practical solutions to practically every problem: The early childhood teacher's manual.* St. Paul, MN: Toys 'n Things Press. My only problem with this book is where to place it in the references because it covers a wide range of problems such as gifted children, death, and biting, to name just a few. This is a good, useful book.

Aggression

Berkowitz, L. (1993). *Aggression: Its causes, consequences and control.* Philadelphia: Temple University Press. This is a very readable—almost chatty—yet very sound and comprehensive discussion of aggression. *Highly recommended.*

Integrating Children with Disabilities into the Social Life of the Center

Conroy, M. A., Langenbrunner, M. R., & Burleson, R. B. (1996). Suggestions for enhancing the social behaviors of preschoolers with disabilities using developmentally appropriate practices. *Dimensions of Early Childhood, 24*(1), 9–15. The authors show how following developmentally appropriate guidelines can help children with disabilities fit into ordinary early childhood settings. Noteworthy also because of good resource lists for further reading.

Direct Instruction about Social Skills

Beaty, J. J. (1995). *Converting conflicts in preschool.* New York: Harcourt Brace. Eight kinds of potential conflict situations are identified together with practical suggestions for their alleviation. Beaty advocates asking each child how the other one feels and what would make the other child feel happy as being a helpful way to settle these situations.

Mize, J., & Abell, E. (1996). Encouraging social skills in young children: Tips teachers can share with parents. *Dimensions of Early Childhood, 24*(3), 15–23. The authors suggest six practical ways parents and teachers can influence the development of sound social relationships with other children.

Shure, M. B. (1994). *Raising a thinking child: Help your young child to resolve everyday conflicts and get along with others.* New York: Holt. Shure explains in practical terms how to teach children as young as age 4 the "I can problem-solve" strategies of coming up with alternative solutions to social difficulties.

Helping Children Form Friendships

Lamme, L. L., & McKinley, L. (1992). Creating a caring classroom with children's literature. *Young Children, 48*(1), 65–71. This article offers a particularly rich resource of children's books demonstrating various facets of caring, ranging from caring for the sick, to caring for special friends, to caring for the environment. Some of the books may be too advanced for preschool children to grasp, but many are excellent.

Wolf, D. P. (Ed.) (1986). *Connecting: Friendship in the lives of young children and their teachers.* Redmond, WA: Exchange. In a series of easy-to-read articles, this book offers an overview of the value of friendship to young children along with comments on ways to enhance its flowering.

For the Advanced Student

Charles, C. M. (1992). *Building classroom discipline* (4th ed.). White Plains, NY: Longman. The most useful part of Charles's book as far as early childhood readers are concerned is the thorough descriptions of eight approaches to discipline that he presents.

Eisenberg, N. (1992). *The caring child.* Cambridge, MA: Harvard University Press. The many factors that affect the development of altruism (caring for and helping others) are discussed in this research based book.

Mize, J. (1995). Coaching preschool children in social skills: A cognitive-social learning curriculum. In G. Cartledge & J. F. Milburn (Eds.), *Teaching social skills to children and youth* (3rd ed.). Boston: Allyn & Bacon. Mize provides a practical, clear description of a research study in which she deliberately taught prosocially inept preschoolers how to be more socially effective. *Highly recommended.*

Rubin, K. H., & Asendorph, J. B. (1993). *Social withdrawal, inhibition and shyness in childhood.* Hillsdale, NJ: Erlbaum. Because evidence is mounting that "children who are extremely withdrawn relative to their age-mates tend to remain withdrawn and increasingly tend to manifest socioemotional difficulties as they grow older" (p. 117), it behooves serious students to learn more about this more negative side of the socialization coin. *Highly recommended.*

Schickedanz, J. A. (1994). Helping children develop self-control. *Childhood Education, 70*(5), 274–275. Schickedanz discusses recent findings concerning the development of moral understanding in young children and concludes with some practical recommendations on using discipline techniques that encourage development of that understanding in young children. *Highly recommended.*

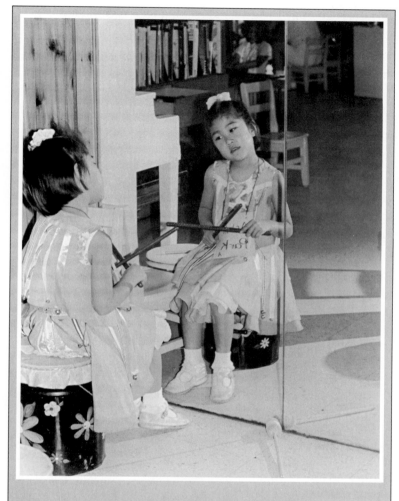

Who Am I?
Who Are You?

Developing Social Competence and the Sense of Self

Have you ever

- Wished that you knew how to help a child feel better about herself?

- Wanted to know what to say when a 4-year-old says to a Mexican youngster, "You can't play—you're dirty!"

- Racked your brain for what you could do besides offering cross-gender activities to reduce sex stereotyping in children?

If you have, the material in this chapter will help you.

In order to give other people the right or privilege of maintaining their own values, you have to confront what you do when those values conflict with yours. It's a two-layered process. One is to recognize what your own biases and belief systems are, and the other is to accept the possibility that they may not be right for everyone else. That's the hard one.

It seems to me that the only thing that teachers in classrooms realistically can do is gather parents and other community members around them and try to open the dialogue: "What do you want for your kids? What do you think is the best way to get there?"

Barbara Bowman (1995, p. 40)

Everything we do gives children messages about what it means to live with others. How we interact with other staff, how we communicate with parents, how we feel about ourselves, how we respond to exchanges between children—all give strong messages in verbal and nonverbal cues about what we believe. We cannot fool children and we dare no longer fool ourselves.

Bonnie Neugebauer (1992, p. 50)

So far we have been talking about social competence in terms of the interpersonal social skills that parents and preschool teachers can help little children develop. This chapter considers some additional aspects of social development that, though more subtle, are equally important. These have to do with how children develop a sense of who they are and of their place in the world.

How Do Children Develop a Sense of Self?

Theories about how a sense of self—of who am I?—develops remains a matter of debate (Cicchetti & Beeghly, 1990; Owens, 1995). In the beginning, it is thought that infants experience a sort of global oneness with their mothers and that an early task of infancy is to achieve a sense of separateness and a realization that the mother, as she comes and goes, continues to exist even when she is not within the baby's sight. As the infant gradually achieves this concept of mother separateness and continuing permanence, she also begins to sense herself as a separate, individual being. Piaget (1954) has called this sense of the separate other the concept of *object permanence*, and he regards it as being a fundamental prerequisite in the formation of later intellectual processes.

After infancy, children add to the sense of who they are by gaining identity from the people around them and becoming like them. This is the way children learn what constitutes basically acceptable ways for them to be and behave in their society (Cicchetti & Beeghly, 1990).

Freud (1962) postulated that this process of identification initially resulted from children being dependent on their mother and wanting to incorporate their strength into themselves. He maintained that the child gains security by acting as the mother acts, switching, if a boy, at about age 4 to identify with his father instead. Identification, then, as Freud sees it, is a complicated kind of substitution whereby a child comes to think, feel, and behave as though the characteristics of another person were her own. In a sense, she becomes as the other person is.

Proponents of behaviorism, on the other hand, subscribe to a different explanation of how children achieve a sense of identity and become like the people around them. Their approach, as exemplified in the work of B. F. Skinner (1954, 1974), favors the idea that, once the genetic endowment has been set, the individual's behavior is determined by external events. Put very simply, pure behaviorists maintain that behavior is repeated only if it has been rewarded in some manner. Parents and other members of the larger society reward behavior they approve of, causing children to repeat it and gain a sense of how they should behave.

Albert Bandura (1977; 1986) makes use of this theory of behaviorism but also notes that some behavior is internalized by children even when external reinforcement for repeating it is not evident. He theorizes that children learn to be like other adults in their society by observing them and imitating what they do, as well as by having their behavior reinforced. Apparently this kind of imitative learning takes place simply because children want to be like their parents, and this is a gratification itself.

Whether one subscribes to the Freudian, Skinnerian, or Banduran point of view, it is worth noting that all of them emphasize that adults are powerful influences in establishing the child's identity. Both Freud and Bandura stress that nurturing, attractive adults are the ones most likely to be imitated, and considerable additional research supports this con-

tention (Baumrind, 1989; Coopersmith, 1967; Harter, 1983). The implications of these findings for us as parents and teachers, who are all strong power figures in children's lives, is that if we want children to identify with us so that they want to "do as we do," we should be as warm and nurturing as possible, as well as being good examples.

One more factor worth mentioning is not directly discussed in these theories but also helps children develop a sense of self and of how to behave in their society. It is worth pointing out to teachers because adults frequently use it; that factor is direct instruction. Teachers and parents often tell children directly what are the acceptable and unacceptable ways to behave. How often adults say in essence, "We just don't do that. We never hurt animals," "It isn't right to bite people!" "Our family always . . . ," or "Our family never. . . ." (Although I do recall a neighbor remonstrating with his 4-year-old, saying, "Clark! We never spit on sidewalks!" to which his swaggering 4-year-old replied, "Well, Dad, boys do!" We must admit such admonishments do not always work!)

To sum up socialization theory, after infancy children appear to gain their basic sense of who they are and what their place is in the world partly through the process of identifying with admired others and behaving as much like them as possible, and partly through conforming to the expectations of others to obtain their support and approval. Both these factors contribute to children's ideas of what it means to be a boy or a girl, what it means to be a member of a particular ethnic group, and even as early as 3 or 4 years of age, what they can look forward to becoming when they grow up. (Witness this chilling statement from a 4-year-old who was asked what he would be if he were a girl: "A girl?" he asked. "A girl? Oh, if I were a girl I'd have to grow up to be nothing!" [Leifer & Lesser, 1976, p. 18]).

And these attitudes do not necessarily change over time. In 1994, the Sadkers reported that although 42% of the girls could see there would be some advantages to being a boy, 95% of the boys could see *no* advantage to being a girl. When they asked children how they would feel if they woke up and found they were members of the other gender, some of the boys replied, "If I were a girl my friends would treat me like dirt," and "I would *kill* myself *right away* by set-

ting myself on fire so no one knew" (pp. 83–84).

But teachers and parents must realize that, in addition to these basic processes of socialization, many other factors contribute to children's developing sense of self as they become aware of the world outside their homes. These include many elements over which teachers and parents may

---

  Is One Point of View Always Right?

Research

Study

Research Question   Lubeck asked the questions, How is culture transmitted in the classroom? Do the teaching styles of black and white preschool teachers differ from each other, and if they do, what are those differences and why do they exist?

Research Method   Over the period of 1 year, Lubeck studied two half-day preschool classrooms. One was a middle-class group of 24 white children, ages 2 to 4 ½ years, taught by white middle-class teachers presenting a traditional preschool program. The other was a working class group of 21 African American children, aged 4 years, taught by black working-class teachers at a Head Start center. The rooms were similar in the amounts of equipment and space provided for the children.

Lubeck gathered her information by observing the white preschool and by observing and ultimately participating as a volunteer teacher for the entire school year at the Head Start center. This participation gradually earned her the trust and acceptance of the Head Start staff. In both situations she took extensive, daily field notes. (This is termed the *ethnographic approach* to doing research.) Teachers at the Head Start center were given the notes to read and agreed that her observations were correct.

Results   Lubeck's study covered the teachers' use of time, space, activities, and teacher-child relations, but because of space limitations, only her conclusions about teacher-child relations will be included here.

She found that the black and white teachers did indeed teach differently and did teach different values to the children. This happened despite the overall Head Start policies of encouraging free play and individualized attention—basic educational values similar to the values of the white preschool.

The middle-class white teachers, who came from nuclear families themselves, concentrated on children during the day and did not have very much contact with the other teachers, whereas the black Head Start teachers, who came from extended families, were often involved in activities that were separate from what the children were doing. There was a sense of kinship among the black teachers that was not as apparent among the white teachers.

The white teachers stressed freedom of choice, permitted divergent answers, and encouraged children to be independent; whereas the black teachers emphasized the value of group solidarity and conformity rather than individual choice. Granting choices was feared as presenting opportunities for the children to get out of control. At the Head Start center, the importance of giving convergent, right answers was stressed, and the children were taught to obey authority unquestioningly.

In keeping with this sense of collective values, the language taught by the black teachers was generalized, also. For example, toys would be referred to as "toys" rather than

have little control. Current usage speaks of such influences as being part of the *ecology of childhood* (Brim, Boocock, Hoffman, Bronfenbrenner, & Edelman, 1975; Villarruel, Imig, & Kostelnick, 1995). Bansavage (1978) quotes Brim as defining this ecology as "the natural setting of developing children—the types of families, the types of com- munities, the friendship groups, the characteris- tics of their schools, contact with the adult world and similar environmental factors" (p. 119). This focus is useful, not only because it helps pinpoint influences but also because it reminds us that we must not underestimate the significance of slums, television, the neighborhood children, family size

> speaking of the little red truck or the puzzle with the two roosters on it as was done in the middle-class school.
>
> The white teachers typically influenced behavior by reasoning, suggesting, using indirect instruction and, when needed, firm, direct instruction. Lubeck comments that they appeared to believe that given time, reason would prevail. The black teachers typically told the chil- dren exactly what to do and had a strong air of authority as they issued such directives.
>
> *Implications*   When reading research, it is always important to remember its limitations. This study, intensive though it was, deals with only two classrooms of children. Therefore, it is inappropriate to conclude that every group of children in every other setting is taught using the same styles. On the other hand, it could also be the case that such differences may exist in many classrooms. If so, all teachers, whether they be African American or white, can benefit from thinking about the insights the study provides.
>
> One thing Lubeck documents is that it is not easy to change cultural values. Teachers are likely to reflect their own cultural values and styles as they teach children despite what the philosophical system encourages. Witness the split between Head Start philosophy and what actually took place in the African American classroom.
>
> It is easy for teachers who subscribe to the philosophy of the middle-class preschool to deplore the values taught by the black teachers, *but the truth is that these values have obvious worth as survival skills for black children.* The strong kinship patterns and the importance of conforming, following orders, and relying on the group for support have genuine short- term adaptive value for people growing up in a world where the most dominant group continues to be prejudiced against them. (Of course, there is also the possibility that teaching children to conform and take orders may not turn out to be to their ultimate benefit over the longer course of their lives.)
>
> Rather than merely deploring these findings or planning how things should change, perhaps, after careful consideration, readers of this research will be willing to move be- yond that point of view. Perhaps they may even begin to grasp what Lubeck said was her most profound learning from her study:
>
>> I have had to reconstruct the history of the people with whom I worked, people who shared my community but not my ways, people who reared children in ways different from my own. My reac- tions to our differences have changed over time: early horror that I could see only stereotypes in what was being done "wrong," later conviction that, if they could only be shown a (my) "better" way, they would change, *and later still appreciation for a way of life that had possibilities different from my own—and dawning realization of my own—and my own culture's—limitations.*
>
> Note. From *Sandbox Society: Early Education in Black and White America* by S. Lubeck, 1985, Philadelphia: Falmer.

and income, an urban or rural setting, persistent high levels of noise, overcrowding, climate, population density, and so forth, on the development of the children and their sense of who they are.

We must also not underestimate the positive effect home and school can have on the way young children see themselves (Wang & Gordon, 1994). As you read the description of Lubeck's research on the differing teaching styles of one group of African American and white preschool teachers (pp. 258–259), consider the effects the differing styles might have on the children in those classrooms. Reread Barbara Bowman's quote that opens the chapter and then ask yourself how it might be applied to the Lubeck findings

Enhance Children's Feelings of Self-Esteem

Beware of Overusing or Misusing Praise

If we define the sense of self as being the child's gradually developing idea of who she is, we can say that self-esteem is present when she feels this self to be valuable and worthwhile.

Many teachers think of self-esteem as being something they bestow on children by praising them or making them feel important, and it is true that merited praise and recognition are valuable ways of building self-esteem, because in the beginning these positive feelings come from outside the child. However, we certainly do not want children to remain eternally dependent on a constant barrage of "You're wonderfuls" and gold stars to feel good about themselves (Kohn, 1993; Wilt, 1996). Over a period of time, children need to develop feelings of self-worth and motivation that come from within rather than from without themselves.

The question is, What can teachers do to help children depend less on external, extrinsic rewards such as praise and depend more on internal, *intrinsic* rewards for satisfaction?

For one thing, avoid praising a child by comparing him with someone else—either by saying, "I sure wish Mariko behaved as well as *you* do," or using him as an example to the other children: "Look how well Cedric is putting the blocks away!" At best, this kind of praisee generates a priggish satisfaction in the praise and dislike from his peers. At worst, it violates some cultural attitudes of children from Native American and Asian backgrounds who have been taught never to stand above or surpass the accomplishments of their companions.

Another kind of praise to avoid is the gushing, insincere type. All this "blanket-type" praise does is smother children who soon learn that it really does not count for much.

When you *do* use praise, make it as specific as possible. For example, instead of telling a restless child, "You were a good kid at group time today," it is better to say, "You sat by Jose a whole 5 minutes without poking him at group time—that's terrific." This kind of praise has two virtues rolled into one: it singles out specific behavior, and, because it is specific, the child knows you *really* cared about him enough to see what he was actually doing. It also provides encouragement as well as recognition of accomplishments.

Build Self-Esteem by Showing Children That You Respect Them as People

Showing a child respect may seem like a difficult or intangible thing to do, but, actually, teachers translate that attitude into real behavior in many ways every day of their lives. For example, witness the contrasting behaviors a group of teachers identified in Goffin's (1987) article (see Table 13–1).

Build Self-Esteem by Discouraging the Use of Insults to Express Anger

In the chapter on emotional health, a big point was made about the importance of knowing what you are feeling and being able to say it out loud without hurting anyone else.

TABLE 13–1

Early Educator Responses to the Question "How Well Do We Respect the Children in Our Care?"

I show respect when:	I am somewhat disrespectful when:
• I listen to what a child has to say.	• I do not take a child's opinion seriously.
• I take time for a child when I'm very busy.	• I avoid an issue a child felt needed immediate attention.
• I play with children.	• I use time out.
• I color a picture with children.	• I leave the children alone.
• I recognize accomplishments.	• I walk away from a child while he/she is crying.
• I allow children to settle disputes between themselves.	• I don't stop to listen.
• I listen to a special song.	• I respond with "uh-huh."
• I show interest in a child's project.	• I use a "baby-talk" tone of voice with younger children.
• I make eye contact.	• I use angry words under stress.
• I encourage their viewpoints.	• I cut their conversations close.
• I allow them to make choices.	• I finish a task for them to hasten time.
• I try to arrange a schedule to be accommodating to a parent.	• I forget to follow through on something I promised.
• I allow for privacy.	• I answer for them when an unfamiliar adult asks them a question so they appear more articulate or seemingly more socially acceptable.
• I try to respond with words and actions to a child's uniqueness.	• I spend physical time with a child but am emotionally distant from the situation.
• I call children by their names.	• I behave impatiently.
• I know how to say "no."	• I use sarcasm.
• I encourage independence.	• I shout.
• I respond to their questions.	• I physically force a child into a situation in which he's uncomfortable.
• I allow a child to talk uninterrupted.	• My expectations are too high.
• I respect a child's choice of friend and play equipment.	• I rush children.
• I allow children to make mistakes.	• I don't take care of myself physically or emotionally.
• I realize their individuality.	• I call them names; e.g., dumbbell.
• I am flexible.	• I show frustration because their needs interfere with my schedule.
• I allow them to disagree.	• I focus on children's bad behaviors.
• I care for their property.	• I belittle their feelings.

TABLE 13–1
continued

I show respect when:	I am somewhat disrespectful when:
• I allow transition time.	• I sneak up on a child doing wrong.
• I listen to a child's problem and realize how upsetting the situation can be to a child.	• I ignore them.
• I talk to children as people.	• I stop a child who is really interested in a project.
• I give each child a chance to communicate.	• I don't allow a child to explain why or how a friend got hurt, or how an accident occurred.
• I ask a child for his/her solution to a problem.	
• I value their opinions.	
• I remember that play is of great importance in each child's life.	
• I prepare myself well for class so I don't have to "waste" children's time.	

Note. From "How Well Do We Respect the Children in Our Care?" by S. Goffin, 1987, *Childhood Education, 66*(2), p. 21. Used by permission.

Now, it is time to consider a special aspect of talking about feelings—not hurting anyone else—because there is a vast difference between saying how you feel ("I'm really mad at you—you took my car") and verbally attacking someone else by calling them a "dirty coon."[1]

There are three reasons why insults like this must be stopped. The first, most obvious one is that it is an example of hateful prejudice that wounds the other person's feelings—just as it is intended to do. The second is that it lowers the self-esteem of the child who is insulted (Kendall, 1996).

The third reason for preventing such remarks is more subtle but is, *in the long run, even more important*. It is vital for children to know and admit to themselves why they are *really* angry. This is because we do not want them to displace their anger on a false reason. Arvin is not mad at Jeff because he is black but because he took his red car. If the teacher allows Arvin to substitute a false reason why he is angry, *she is responsible for helping lay the foundation for further prejudice* by not getting to the heart of the matter. After all, Arvin has every right to be angry—Jeff *did* take his car.

For example, the teacher needs to say to Arvin, "I know you're mad at him, but we don't say things like 'dirty coon' at school. We tell kids *why* we're mad instead [pause]. What did Jeff do you don't like? Well, *tell* him that—tell him you don't like it and want the car back."

Next she turns to Jeff, reminding him, "Remember, Jeff, *just because somebody says you're something doesn't make it true!* You and I know you're really a good kid [pause]. Did you like what he called you? Well, tell him, 'Don't you call me that! I'm a good kid!' [pause]. Why do you think he's really mad at you?"

---

[1] In the following example, simply substitute the words *cootie, spaas, cripple,* or *bitch* when thinking about handling insults toward groups in our society.

Then, to both boys, the teacher says, "Now, how are we going to settle this fight?"

Build Self-Esteem by Providing Children with Skills so They Feel Competent

The child who is well coordinated and able to balance her way along a narrow wall or hang by her knees has a pleasant feeling of competence that "I'm good—I can do it," as does the youngster who can pull up his pants himself or carry the pitcher without spilling it. Acquisition of these skills requires that the teacher provide sufficient time and plentiful opportunities for practice and that he keep the level of challenge difficult enough to make things interesting, but not so hard that it scares children off from trying. If he also provides chances to carry out meaningful work and to help other people, as discussed in chapter 12, the teacher will enhance the children's feelings of mastery and satisfaction even further. *The goal in all these areas is to provide opportunities for children to feel successful so that they know deep inside that they are capable, adequate people.*

Encourage Self-Esteem by Helping Children Do Things for Themselves so They Feel Powerful

To paraphrase a better-known statement, children should be encouraged to do things "of themselves, by themselves, and for themselves" to increase their autonomy and gain a positive sense of self. This is really another facet of competence. Allowing this independence to develop can be especially difficult for teachers of such young children, because they must balance the children's needs for dependence and independence with their own need to keep the daily routines operating at a reasonable pace. It is not easy to tread the narrow path between lending a loving hand when it is needed so that children know we care and waiting quietly by when it is

The children loved using this hammock from Guatemala. "If I rolled up in this," said Veronica, "I'd feel just like a big banana!"

better for them to help themselves. Actually, waiting can be one of the hardest parts and most important skills in teaching. Even though teachers theoretically agree that the ultimate gains make waiting worthwhile, it may still be necessary for them to firmly remember this as they stand poised by the door while a group of threes fumble endlessly with their sweater buttons.

Encourage Self-Esteem by Providing Opportunities for Meaningful Work

Another way of enhancing children's sense of self-worth is to encourage them to be helpful by doing small jobs around the center. Young children love to participate in clean-up when it entails using water, just as they enjoy doing other "grown-up" jobs as long as these are reasonably within their abilities and are not too boring or long-drawn-out.

Unfortunately, adults often either underestimate children's abilities or pawn off the jobs that nobody really likes to do, such as putting all the blocks away. The kinds of jobs I have in mind are often one-time, short ones where the results are readily apparent. These might include washing the dishes after a cooking activity, sawing through a branch the wind has torn from the play yard tree and discarding it, or loading the wagon with hollow blocks to take outside. Or perhaps the birdhouse needs a spring cleaning, or leaves need raking in the fall, or the garden needs watering.

Many of these activities are so routine that adults do them just to get them over with, forgetting how much the children would love to participate. But such opportunities for participation should be seized on with joy by the teacher because they contribute to the welfare of the group and also because they can do so much to enhance children's sense of being competent, worthwhile people.

Being Creative Offers Satisfying Avenues for Building Self-Esteem

Early childhood teachers are generally quite strong in providing creative opportunities for children, although they do not always think of these as being esteem builders. Yet expressing ideas and feelings that come from within through the use of self-expressive materials can be a powerful source for enhancing self-esteem. Because creative activities are such esteem builders, it is particularly valuable to preserve the children's confidence that they are creative people so that this attitude and the resulting sense of personal worth can be retained in later life. What a pity it is that so many people, as they mature, come to feel apologetic and uncreative and close themselves off from one of the safest and potentially most rewarding avenues to self-satisfaction and self-esteem. Helping people retain the freedom to be creative probably is best accomplished by teaching children that the most important aspect of creating something is to be satisfied with pleasing themselves rather than other people. We will learn more about how to do this in chapter 14.

Strengthen Children's Positive Body Image

The whole subject of body image as it relates to people's sense of self is a fascinating one, and, even as adults, some of us are still plagued with body images that adversely affect our behavior. For example, some of us still secretly picture ourselves as being the skinny or fat or poor-complexioned adolescent we were several years ago rather than the more attractive person we are now, and we continue to feel insecure because of this negative image.

Developing Body Awareness

The degree of awareness of the body and what it can do varies a good deal with different children. It is necessary with some Head Start youngsters, for instance, to begin by teaching them to point to their eyes and ears and hair before going on to the fun of identifying eyebrows, cheeks, and ankles. Children also enjoy naming things inside their bodies, such as bones and blood. (We even had one youngster who wanted to know where his gallbladder was.)

In addition to developing body awareness by learning the names of various parts, we also want children to appreciate what the body can do and to gain skill in its control. Movement education is probably the best way of accomplishing this. It makes children aware of their bodies' position in space and relation to other people and objects, as well as encouraging them to devise creative ways of moving around in that space. Moreover, physical prowess is much admired by other children and becomes even more important in elementary school, where proficiency in games is a basic key to popularity. Chapter 9, which deals with the development of physical competence, provides many suggestions for helping children gain confidence and competence in controlling physical movement.

Developing a Positive Body Image

Finally, the whole delicate matter of what children think of their bodies is an interesting one to consider. At such an early age, this is not often a conscious matter, although there is evidence that preschool children are already aware of the color of their and other people's skins. Nevertheless, even young children are affected by how attractive they feel they are and by the influence their physical appearance has on the way people respond to them.

I recall a little 3-year-old in one of my own groups—a sturdy, red-headed, freckle-faced boy with the build of a wrestler but the personality of a retiring rabbit. I often saw fathers give him a playful poke as they passed by or jab his stomach or make playful sparring motions in his direction. Although initially dismayed, over a period of 2 years this youngster became increasingly aggressive—at least partially because of all these cues and expectations from men. His physique just seemed to elicit such responses.

Or how about the exquisite little girl with naturally curly hair, or the child whose nose is always runny, or the frail little boy with dark circles under his eyes? Nobody would dare poke him in the stomach, even though he might be yearning for this kind of masculine attention. I am not certain what teachers can actually do about these effects except try to see through the physical appearance of the youngster to the personality inside and encourage other people to do that, too.

It is not only physical characteristics that influence people's responses to children. Body postures influence responses and tell teachers a lot about how the child feels about herself. The child who shrinks behind her mother's skirts on the first day reveals more of her feelings than she possibly could with words. Often increased emotional and physical well-being is reflected in the easier, more open stance of chil-

dren as the year progresses. Teachers respond continually to these physical signals, sometimes termed *body language*, just as children respond to theirs. Since these postures reveal so much about children (and adults), it would be wise for teachers to make a deliberate effort to take time to look closely at what the children's body language is telling them. They could learn much about how the children feel about their world and about themselves if only they took time to notice.

Cultivate Positive Feelings in Children about Sexual Identities, Ethnic and Racial Heritages, and Children with Disabilities

Many principles of presenting curriculum intended to widen horizons and reduce negative attitudes apply equally well to nonsexist and multicultural education and to incorporating children with disabilities into the classroom. That is the reason a great deal of information is condensed into Table 13–2. It is so much quicker and easier for the reader to see such material concisely summarized than to wade through paragraph after paragraph of semirepetitive information.

Be on the Lookout for Opportunities to Confront Bias of All Sorts

Although this chapter confines itself to discussing nonsexist, multicultural, and antidisability education, we must remember that many other kinds of prejudice also exist. Some people are prejudiced against old people (witness the dearth of elderly characters on television), while others assume that poor people are always dirty or that early childhood teachers are "just babysitters."

Pacific Oaks, a college in Pasadena, California, has been a leader in advocating that even

TABLE 13–2

Creating Equal Learning Oportunities

Nonsexist Possibilities	Multicultural Possibilities	Special Needs Possibilities
Human Relations		
Employ teachers of both sexes who participate equally in the majority of activities; that is, the male teachers do not always supervise carpentry and female teachers do not always present cooking. Everyone pitches in to teach everything, clean up, take children to the toilet, and so forth.	Employ *teachers* from a variety of ethnic backgrounds. Make certain minority people are not relegated only to aide positions but are placed in positions of authority also. Children are shrewd assessors of such power rankings.	Make every effort to see past the exceptional to what is typical in the child, and treat her accordingly.
Know the preschool families well, and be on the lookout for members who have transcended the gender barrier in various occupations (female police officers, male nurses) and ask them to visit and acquaint children with what they do.	Know the preschool families well. Encourage them to share interesting customs and traditions with the children at school as they do with their children at home. This might have to do with favorite ethnic foods, holidays, trips, and so on.	If the child is accompanied by an aide or parent, integrate that person into the staff as much as possible. Encourage them to relate to all the children.
Be sensitive to men who have custody of their children. Offer assistance when they want it, but do not treat them as curiosities or objects of pity or condescension.	Make certain that all families are genuinely welcome. Help people meet each other, pick up each other for potlucks, and plan together for workshops.	Be sensitive to parental fears that their child is being rejected or that they feel blamed for the child's condition. Realize they are comparing their youngster to other more typical children in the group and are perhaps feeling pain as a result.
Arrange realistic visiting times at school when parents who work outside the home and siblings are free to attend — a Saturday morning play session, for example.	Remember that older family members are viewed somewhat as a culture apart in our society by some people. Make a point of including them and valuing their ideas and services.	Foster understanding and empathy in the children. Be truthful and matter of fact with other children about the child's disabilities.
Encourage children of both sexes to have access to the full range of their feelings (see chapter 11).	Visitors and field trips: Be on the lookout for people from many ethnic groups in a variety of occupations — particularly occupations thought of as professional or skilled ones. Be casual about this, but make sure children have a chance to become acquainted with such people.	Facilitate child-child relationships by encouraging communication and inclusion (e.g., provide techniques for talking with a child who is hard of hearing or explain to a partially sighted child what the children around her are doing so she can join in).
Visitors and field trips: It is worth mentioning once again that a point should be made of providing contacts with members of both sexes participating in a variety of occupations.	Take a small group and visit the homes of different families from time to time. This can emphasize both the things families have in common and special attributes, too.	
Many children have no idea what their parents do when they go to the office. Take a few youngsters to visit so they can find out what both mothers and fathers do who work outside the home.	Take the children to interesting places with a special ethnic flavor — the Greek delicatessen, the Chinese market, the Japanese kite shop.	

Room Climate and Environment

Use pictures that show both boys and girls doing active things — beware of sweet little toilet paper-type ads showing girls with kittens. Include pictures of boys in caring roles and pictures showing boys expressing feelings. Include pictures of fathers with children, mothers working outside the home, and so forth.

Follow a policy of "open toileting" (boys and girls using same bathroom together) to reduce clandestine sexual interests.

Manipulative materials, such as lotto games, puzzles, and block accessories, should be scrutinized to make certain they include men and women in a wide range of occupations. Make certain an equal number of boys and girls are pictured.

Offer boy and girl dolls and boy and girl dress-up clothes, and encourage both sexes to use all the equipment.

Use pictures that include children of all ethnic groups doing things the children in your school also do. (Incidentally, NAEYC offers a nice selection of multiethnic posters for sale using illustrations from *Young Children* covers.) Collect and use pictures of children in integrated groups doing things together.

Accumulate series of pictures showing how people of various cultures meet a universal need in a variety of ways — children taking baths in different ways, for example, or families eating together.

Make certain multicultural activities are consistently present throughout the curriculum and not confined to a week's unit on Indians or the Cinco de Mayo celebration.

Make certain pictures of older people in active roles are included. Beware of using only the grandparent stereotype.

Whenever possible, use furnishings and equipment at the school that come from a variety of countries — perhaps a Mexican child's chair in housekeeping or a bedspread from India with deer and elephants on it. Speak of these appreciatively to the children.

Manipulative materials, such as puzzles and block accessories, should include people from differing ethnic groups.

Dolls of various ethnic groups should be consistently available. Take a good look at these — are they true to ethnic type or just white dolls with different-colored paint on their faces? Many manufacturers are guilty of this sort of racial insult.

Include clothing typical of various cultures. Point out which culture they represent. Children's clothes are particularly appropriate.

Use pictures of children and adults who have various disabilities — show them participating in familiar activities.

Make necessary physical adjustments in the room — ramps, pathways for wheelchairs, equipment on low shelves.

Adapt equipment to increase usability: puzzles with knobs on nonskid mats or carpet squares, brushes with handles enlarged with wrapped masking tape.

It may be necessary to keep arrangement of furniture more static than usual, and make certain the floor is kept clear of clutter.

Avoid offering equipment that stimulates unusual behavior (such as things that spin readily if a child with autistic behaviors is attending).

Include dolls with disabilities in the housekeeping corner.

Include books about children with disabilities.

Post important sign language words at strategic places in the room to facilitate their use by everyone.

TABLE 13–2
continued

Nonsexist Possibilities	Multicultural Possibilities	Special Needs Possibilities
Activities		
In general, encourage children of both sexes to try everything — involve girls in science and boys in washing up, for example. Encourage both sexes to engage in vigorous outdoor play, self-expressive activities, and blocks.	If the school operates on a bilingual base, consider alternating days of each language rather than only translating back and forth.	Think of the child's abilities and be sure to include activities he *can* do easily and with satisfaction, as well as more challenging ones.
Occasionally keep a checklist to see if one area of the school is used more consistently by one sex than the other. Analyze why this is true, and attempt to correct it.	Foster children doing things together. When opportunities present themselves, pair ethnically different children together. Encourage intergroup mixing — sometimes, particularly when two languages are in use, children speaking the same language group together. Although this tendency is understandable, it is desirable to encourage children of all backgrounds to communicate as best they can while playing together. They manage surprisingly well.	Encourage children to include the child with the disability by finding him a role, helping him enter the group, etc. Story time: Encourage children who have vision or hearing problems or who need special control to sit close to you.
Story time: Examine books with care. Train yourself to spot books that present boys as heroes and girls as passive admirers. Check bibliographies listed in References for suggestions of non-sexist books available for purchase. Check Appendix E for guidelines on assessing books for sexist content.	Story time: Examine books carefully for racial stereotypes and overly quaint presentation of unfamiliar cultures, and also make certain that a balanced collection of books is purchased representing as many different kinds of children and adults as possible. Include ethnic folk tales. Check bibliographies in References for suggestions of resources, and also check Appendix E for assessment guidelines.	Be particularly aware of including opportunities for intensified practice of skills — for example, many children with differing disabilities benefit from extensive language stimulation; blind children need plentiful opportunities for vigorous physical activity. Take special scheduling needs into account. This might involve extra toileting, keeping routines very predictable, or providing for rest periods for children who become exhausted more quickly than is typical.
Music and dance: It may be necessary to call *dance* something else if boys have already learned to be wary of that "girl stuff." Widen the kind of material presented in dance so that it appeals to both sexes (see chapter 9).	Offer an occasional folk dance, keeping it simple and bearing in mind it takes considerable repetition for the children to learn it. Beware of perpetuating such stereotypes of ethnic dancing as putting feathers in the children's hair and dancing around doing war whoops.	Invite adults with disabilities to visit and demonstrate their prosthesis if they are comfortable doing this. Ask them to visit several times and involve them in attractive activities with the children.
Make certain to use male and female singers, ranging from Pete Seeger to Marlo Thomas. Also listen to what the lyrics are saying. Some of them are surprisingly sexist.		

Cooking: Although books on nonsexist education keep stressing that boys should participate in cooking, I have never seen a school in which this kind of participation was a problem. If it *is* a problem, boys should be deliberately drawn in to participate.

Blocks and other three-dimensional construction activities: For reasons described later in the section entitled "Foster Positive Attitudes toward Gender Roles," it is particularly valuable to encourage girls to use blocks more frequently than they may have done in the past.

Do not shun the music used in the children's homes. Popular music is very much a part of many families' culture.

There are many excellent folk music records available from all sorts of cultures and suitable to use with young children. Ella Jenkins, for instance, has made a rich contribution to this area. Some resources for these are included in the References.

Cooking: This is a wonderful way to learn to value other cultures as we discussed in chapter 8. Make certain ethnic food is not presented as peculiar or unappetizing. Remember, cooking can include going to specialty markets, cooking with culturally correct utensils, and eating in culturally appropriate style, such as using china spoons to eat egg noodle soup.

Provide experiences using assistance equipment, such as crutches, wheelchairs, and hearing aids for all the children to use.

Including all the children in play is one of the most desirable ways to express kindness towards them.

children as young as 2 and 3 years old should be presented with an antibias curriculum that actively takes a stand against all these forms of prejudice (Derman-Sparks, 1987, 1992; Derman-Sparks & the ABC Task Force, 1989).[2]

To make this both real and relevant, the antibias curriculum links such teaching to the children's lives and approaches the subject three different ways. To begin with, children are encouraged to explore physical differences and similarities. For example, Derman-Sparks (1987; 1995) suggests that 3-year-olds might be encouraged to note the differences in skin colors among children in their group, matching those colors with paint or crayons; hear and talk over a related story; take color photos of children and staff; and make a poster of the differing colors of their skins.

As opportunities arise, other situations that have a potential for confronting bias can be included. Children can try out a child's crutches, for example, and then list all the things they do that do not depend on running around.

The second approach advocated in the antibias curriculum is to explore cultural variations and integrate material into the curriculum based on the cultural backgrounds of the children in the group. This might include cooking favorite family foods, sharing accounts of trips back to Mexico to visit relatives, or comparing hair styles. Books that reflect stereotyped ethnic or sex roles can be read and then discussed—the teacher may ask children whether it is true that only men can be police officers or only women can take care of children.

Finally, the antibias curriculum of Pacific Oaks suggests that children learn to take direct action that challenges stereotypes and discriminatory behavior. For example, one group wrote a

---

[2]Please note that this description barely scratches the surface of the antibias curriculum. For further information refer to Derman-Sparks (1992).

letter to a bandage manufacturer protesting the use of the term "flesh colored" to describe their product, and another group scrubbed offensive graffiti from a playground wall. Direct action of this kind, providing it is developmentally appropriate, empowers children and teaches them they can take an active role in protesting unfair or biased behavior.

Foster Positive Attitudes Toward Racial and Cultural Backgrounds

All too often it appears that teachers think of multicultural education only in terms of using integrated pictures in their rooms or making certain that the books they are reading to the children are not racially biased or that tortilla making is included as a multicultural experience. No one denies that this approach has value, and some suggestions for incorporating such ideas into the curriculum are included in Table 13–2.

What is disturbing is that some teachers fail to understand that the real purpose of offering multicultural materials should be *to foster positive attitudes in children about their own and others' racial and cultural backgrounds*. The purpose, then, of inviting a Mexican mother to help the children make tortillas is not just to teach them that tortillas are made of a special kind of cornmeal called *masa harina* or that Mexican people eat tortillas and that tortillas taste good. The purpose is to provide a real, involving experience that is so much fun for the children that they attach pleasant feelings to being Mexican and eating Mexican food. In other words, *making tortillas is merely the medium through which the message of positive respect for someone's culture is conveyed.*

Attitudes Are Caught, Not Taught

Because it is attitudes that matter most and children can sense teachers' feelings so keenly, teachers must search their own hearts and monitor their behavior to make certain that they are con-

trolling the expression of their prejudices as much as possible. Of course, everyone prefers to believe they do not possess any prejudices, but it is more probable than not that we all do possess feelings of prejudice in some area (Jones & Derman-Sparks, 1992). For example, studies reveal that some teachers do not believe that Latino children are capable of academically demanding work and that instructional programs for such children tend to be remedial (Ortiz, 1988). The effects of segregation and prejudice on the self-esteem of various groups including African Americans, Latinos, and Native Americans have also been well documented by Nieto (1992).

Although it may not be possible to overcome deep-seated feelings of prejudice entirely, it is still valuable to know they exist inside oneself because once bias is recognized and "owned," it can also be controlled. Every time a prejudiced remark is suppressed, a tiny blow for fairness has been struck.

For those who wish to go further and weed such uncomfortable feelings from their hearts, a fairly effective way of overcoming prejudice is to learn more about people of other groups by taking courses on their culture, but getting to know them personally is best of all. Attempting to learn their language reduces the feeling of distance. Some encounter groups also work toward the goal of increasing racial understanding.

Remember, Families May Not Always Cherish the Same Values You Hold Dear

There is increasing recognition in the past few years that teachers do not always know what is best for every youngster, and so we must understand and incorporate the cultural values of the home if we intend to provide a truly multicultural environment. As the research study in this chapter demonstrates, we must recognize that sometimes these values differ from our own and that we may need to reconsider our own convictions from time to time (Mallory & New, 1993; National Association for the Education of Young Children, 1995; Nucci, 1994).

The question is, once such differences are recognized, what can we do about them? First of all, there are some times when parenting styles are in direct conflict with what we know is best for children. For example, just because a family advises the teacher to "slam him one when he don't behave" does not mean that the teacher should do that at school.

On the other hand, many times the teacher may find that family expectations and her expectations are "out of tune" and a genuine difference in cultural values of what is important arises. An example from my own experience was a young Japanese child in my co-op whose mother highly valued cleanliness and maintaining family pride through good appearance. Although she was genuinely eager for her little girl to participate in everything at school, her dismay (unspoken but in her eyes) was plain whenever she picked her up and beheld a somewhat muddy and/or painty offspring. We tried everything we could short of forbidding Fumi to participate—aprons, bare feet, rolled-up pants, and so forth—but the difficulty persisted together with gracious protests "Not to think of it" from her mother (respect for the teacher and social harmony being additional cultural values treasured by that family). So, what to do? Fumi was unhappy because of our hovering and her mother's (private) displeasure, I was uncomfortable, and the mother was torn by conflict. What we did was talk it over and negotiate—very politely and somewhat indirectly. We ultimately agreed that she would bring a change of clothes and I would change Fumi into a clean dress each day before it was time to go home.

Help Children Understand That All People Are Similar in Some Ways and Different in Others

Help Children Learn That Everyone Has Some Things in Common

Young children need to learn that people of every ethnic background have some human needs and characteristics in common: everyone needs shelter, rest, and food; everyone's knees hurt when they get skinned; everyone bleeds when cut; and everyone's blood is the same color. Children can begin to gain an appreciation of these truths from such simple activities as leafing through a scrapbook of pictures showing children of various cultures all sleeping, but sleeping in all sorts of beds, ranging from hammocks to trundle beds.

Be aware that, although matters have improved somewhat in regard to multiethnic materials, many manufacturers still seem to interpret multiethnic to mean only African American. It is still very difficult to find educational materials that picture people with accurate Latino, Japanese, or Native American features. Even many of the "black" materials are just white faces painted a different color. Multiethnic books also require careful evaluation and selection.

Learning will be even more meaningful if the preschool group is a racially integrated one, because opportunities to teach about common needs and likenesses abound when children are together.

Teach That Different Cultures Are Unique

Sometimes teachers who feel quite comfortable when teaching about similarities are confused about whether to teach children that people are not completely alike. They seem to fear that mentioning cultural diversity, sometimes termed *teaching cultural pluralism*, encourages the formation of prejudice or that it somehow "isn't nice" to talk about such things. Perhaps these teachers hope that if they avoid mentioning differences, the children will not notice them—but this is not true.

Considerable research reports that children as young as age 3 are aware of the skin color of African and Mexican Americans (Edwards & Ramsey, 1986; Ramsey, 1995; Williams 1990; York, 1991). Beuf (1977) states that this is also true for preschool Native American youngsters of the Southwestern and Plains tribes. Moreover, as children become older, awareness of ethnic group differences increases (Ramsey, 1995).

Because children *do* become aware of racial differences between people during their preschool years, it is only reasonable to conclude that teachers should be prepared to deal with questions about such differences in a positive way so that children learn to view diversity as a valuable part of being human.

Here is an example of how one teacher helped a youngster appreciate this truth as it relates to ethnic diversity:[3]

You're Black All Over? My Lab Experiences with Isabella
Reba Gordon

My experience in the lab was an interesting and memorable one. I was brought very close to a 5-year-old girl named Isabella. From our relationship, the impression I received is that she had never been in any contact with Blacks at all in her life.

My first contact with her was in the locker room. Isabella and Lynn were fingerpainting, and they had put it all over their faces. Afterwards I helped them wash up. Isabella then said, "You're a Black, you have Black hands."

I replied, "Yes," and that was the end of it. She didn't make any further comments for a while.

One day I sat down at the puzzle table with her and watched her complete a puzzle. She asked, "Were you born Black?"

"Yes, and my mother and father are Black, too."

She seemed shocked that I had parents, "You have a mother and father?"

"Yes, I also have a son, too, Isabella."

"Is your baby Black, too?"

"Yes."

Another day I wore my wig, and she was the only child that really noticed my hair was different.

"Why is your hair curly?"

"I'm wearing a different hairstyle today."

A week later I wore a semi-Afro hairstyle, and she said, "Why did you wear your hair like that?"

"I like it this way."

"I don't like it."

Every week or so I would change my hairstyle, and every single time she always noticed the change. She might say, "Your hair looks different," or "How come you changed your hair?"

During all this time I had been telling Mrs. Warner about this situation, and she later had a conference with Isabella's parents on their daughter's new discovery. After the talk Mrs. Warner informed me that Isabella's mother had bought her a Black doll and said she was going to buy some books with Black people in them.

A few weeks later, Isabella and some other girls were in the locker room switching clothes, and I had come out of the bathroom buttoning up my pants. My blouse was up enough that she could see my stomach. Isabella went on to say,

"You have on nylons."

"No, I don't. See, I'm wearing knee socks," as I pulled up my pants leg so she could see. All the other girls just sat and listened.

"Oh, you're Black all over!"

"Yes, I am." I was totally shocked by her statement. I took it for granted that she knew I was Black all over. From here on in it was definite to me that she knew absolutely nothing about Blacks. She did not seem to correlate the Black doll to human Black people, which means children need concrete evidence at times.

When we left the locker room, she asked me to help her zip up the jump suit she was wearing. She watched me intensely as I zipped it up. Out of the blue she said, "Some are Black, huh?"

---

[3]The child's name has been changed to protect her privacy. My thanks to the author, Reba Gordon, and to Helen Ross and Mary Warner of San Diego State University for sharing this material from their classes with me.

I didn't want to put any ideas in her head so I asked, "Some of what are Black?"

"Some skins are Black."

"Yes, they are, and some are White."

This statement showed me that Isabella's parents had been talking to her about Black people at home.

Many times when the class was outside on the playground, she would run past me and hit me on the arm and say, "Hi, Black."

And I would reply, "Hi, White." This did not affect her one bit.

Toward the end of the semester the class was being split up into four reading groups, and the children were assigned to different teachers every day. While they were assigning them she yelled out, "I wanta go with the Black."

During this same week my neighbor had corn-rowed my son's and my hair. I came to school the next day and many of the children made many comments.

"Why did you wear your hair like that?"

"What happened to your hair?"

"I don't like it that way."

"How did it get like this?"

And Isabella, to my surprise, said in a cool and calm way, "That's how Blacks wear their hair, huh?"

"Sometimes," I answered.

The next day I brought my son to the lab, and again the children noticed his hair was just like mine. Mrs. Warner asked Isabella if she had seen my son.

She replied, "Oh, yeah, the Black down there." She didn't really come around him much, but came over to the block area and said, "Your baby is Black, too," and left.

One more thing she said that I almost forgot was on a day I was head teacher and I was pinning on children's name tags. She hung around the table for a long while talking to me, at the same time keeping her face real close to my face whenever she got the chance. With a puzzled look on her face, she stuck out her lips and without sticking them back in their normal position she asked me, "Why do your lips stick out like this?"

Not really knowing how to answer her question, I said, "That is the way some Black people's lips are made."

Thinking about what she had asked me, I asked her why did her lips stick in. She answered, she didn't know why. She hung around a little bit more, examining my face, and then left to get involved in an activity.

At a picnic I wore my wig again and she ran past me and said:

"You got curly hair," and kept on running past.

One thing that sticks in my mind about the whole thing is that there was not any trace of viciousness in any of Isabella's comments. She never felt I was inferior compared to herself, which I felt was excellent, because many times I have come in contact with many White children, outside the lab, that are either frightened to death of Blacks or have some negative comments to make, which they probably picked up from their family or the street. I honestly believe she was very fond of me, and I too was very fond of her.

Isabella's mother talked to me one day and expressed she was embarrassed about the whole situation. I told her not to be, for Isabella had never tried to hurt my feelings. She went on to tell me that she had never been in contact with Blacks until she was in college, at the age of 20. She later went to teach at an all Black elementary school.

"I was so amazed by these Black children that I went around patting all their heads. And they are so rhythmic. But all in all I feel that you have been a great help to our daughter."

When she said that the children were "so rhythmic," I thought I would die. She sounded so typical of this day and age.

Since this situation has happened here and I know it has happened elsewhere, I hope it will help the present educator and future educators to see the importance of having multiethnic teachers and multiethnic education, for these types of children need to be exposed to people and cultures outside their own, along with this preschool experience. It is sad to see these same children go into adulthood and get jobs where they have to deal with society on the whole and not have any insight into any other race of people than themselves. I cannot see how they can represent all the people when they know nothing of all the people.

In conclusion, it was a good experience for me and I hope it was for Isabella also. I wish her all the luck in her future experiences and hope she keeps her beautiful curiosity and accepts all the new information as openly as she received my differences.

As this example demonstrates so clearly, the closer to home we can bring cultural diversity and richness to the actual lives of the children in our schools, the better will be our chances of substituting understanding and appreciation in place of prejudice. We do this in part by teaching each child that her own family and culture are worthwhile and in part by helping her enjoy the contributions of other families and cultures.

For instance, it can be interesting during holidays such as Thanksgiving to talk about the different ways families celebrate them. Do they have friends in or go to their grandparents'? Do they have mince or pumpkin pie? Is there a special way their family celebrates birthdays? How do some Native American families feel about celebrating this day? Are there religious occasions, such as Hanukkah or Ramadan, that the family observes and would be willing to tell the other children about? Might some of the children be invited to a home for a Japanese bath, or might a Hopi youngster be encouraged to bring some of his or her kachina dolls and tell the children about the characters they represent? Perhaps grandparents would come and tell stories to the children about what it was like when they were little ("You mean you didn't never even have television?"). All these kinds of opportunities have the potential for convincing a child

Although pictures, books, and equipment reflecting the ethnic heritage of the children are desirable to include, the most important ingredient in any cross-cultural curriculum is fundamental respect for every individual.

that his own cultural background is interesting and admirable, and they also help the other children see him as being special and having special things to share with the group.

Use Comparison to Demonstrate the Positive Aspects of Cultural Pluralism

At the Institute we have added comparison activities to such cultural sharings. These activities are intended to show the children that there is more than one way of reaching a common goal and that both ways are equally satisfactory. They always provide opportunities for real involvement and for positive comparisons to be made, too.

Some of the comparisons concocted by our student teachers have been quite simple; others have been elaborate, but all have been designed to encourage young children to compare their culture with another culture, see the advantages of each, and enjoy them both. These activities have included making the following comparisons:

1. African hair care with Anglo hair care
2. Cooking methods and eating styles of the West with those of Japan
3. Children's undergarments from the West with those from China
4. The open market of Jamaica with the supermarket of the United States
5. White bread (made into "French" toast) with Indian fry bread

The children loved participating in these experiences, and the adults have benefited, too. This is because our own horizons have widened as we have learned about the customs of other groups so that we could present them in an authentic way to the children.

Support Multicultural Learning Through Play

Of course, play presents delightful possibilities for including multicultural materials and instilling positive attitudes about ethnic and cultural differences into the lives of children. For instance, the multicultural addition one week might be Hawaiian clothes in the dress-up area. These should be introduced casually to the children: "Aren't these pretty? You're welcome to put them on. Leilani's family is sharing these for the fun of it this week. Did you know that she was born in Hawaii?" Or a hammock from Guatemala could be hung outside, and as the children enjoy swinging in it, the teacher could explain that it comes from another country, Guatemala, where it is so hot that people sleep this way to stay cool. He might say, "See, the air comes right through when you swing. Isn't that a practical idea? And it's fun, too."

Another aspect of multicultural play is the occasional problem encountered by teachers who have groups of children from different cultures in the same room. Of course, it is understandable that children who speak the same language find it convenient to play together. (I am thinking here of some Head Start situations in which I have worked, where the Spanish-speaking boys played together, apart from their English-speaking companions.) Sometimes teachers appear to make no effort to encourage the children to intermingle as they play. In fact, they sometimes seem completely unaware of the split in the group. However, children can and *should* be encouraged to overcome language barriers while playing, as well as while participating in more structured situations. A child does not have to speak fluent English or Spanish to enjoy building a block tower with another youngster, and the noises little boys make while pushing toy cars around the sandbox appear to stem from some universal reservoir of language.

Teachers should search for multicultural learning possibilities and encourage play among all the children whenever possible. Children are basically friendly, and teachers who provide tactful encouragement add one more building block to the bridge of interracial friendliness among people.

Foster Positive Attitudes Toward Gender Roles

We all know there are physiological differences between the sexes that make each sex unique, and it is necessary to help children understand genital characteristics and cherish their inherent sexuality, as discussed in chapter 10. The ability to feel good about his or her sexual role as it relates to procreation and childbearing should be a fundamental element in every child's sense of self.

Nonsexist Education

In addition to valuing the sexual aspects of the self, teachers should attempt to widen the horizon of both boys and girls so that they are no longer constrained and limited in their ideas about what activities are appropriate for children of either sex. This is what nonsexist education is all about. It teaches that people have many abilities, as well as needs, in common, no matter what their sex. Girls and women are encouraged to do things formerly the sole prerogative of boys and men, and vice versa.

At its best, nonsexist education opens new avenues for both boys and girls and helps them be complete, whole people. For example, girls are encouraged to see themselves as possessing a variety of potentials in addition to being wives and mothers, and boys are urged to remain sensitive to their caring and emotionally expressive side, a side that, in the past, our culture has frequently taught them to repress. As Honig (1983) says, "Caregivers need to celebrate competence in both males and females in *whatever* form competence appears" (p. 68).

What Can the Children's Center Do to Foster the Full Potential of Girls and Boys?

Many sexist attitudes are conveyed to children by their environments, as well as by other people's attitudes and behavior, and children's centers can make a positive contribution by being aware of this (Beal, 1994; Fagot, 1994). Although our schools are generally quite open to both sexes in offering such activities as outdoor play or cooking, there is still a long way to go in building sensitivity to the content of books, which continue to show a preponderance of boys as heroes taking an active role in stories and girls taking more passive ones (Wellhousen, 1996).

Inspection of many equipment catalogs also supports the claim that the majority of toys and teaching materials related to occupations continue to be sexist (Raines, 1991). For example, those stand-up cut-out models of people frequently used in the block corner teach all too well the lesson that girls are nurses, teachers, and mothers and that boys are doctors, police officers, and motorcycle riders.

Boys rarely object to participating in the cross-gender activity of cooking!

Moreover, teachers (often unintentionally) foster such attitudes, too. For many years I have observed the apprehension with which some of my young women students approach the carpentry table. Although it is true that such an activity requires careful supervision, there is little reason for it to arouse the degree of concern and even distaste I have seen reflected on their faces. They often protest that the children will hurt themselves with the saws or hammers, but I believe the real reason for their concern is that they know very little about the use of woodworking tools. In short, they are the victims of their previous sexist education. Instruction about the use of tools combined with a firm model of positive attitudes by the head teachers has helped overcome this concern, but it has also been necessary time and again to entice the adult students, as well as the girls and boys, to use carpentry materials. Otherwise, they may help perpetuate this particular kind of instrumental incompetence in the next generation. (Chapter 14 provides information on effective ways to present carpentry to all the children in the group.)

To encourage a variety of role models, do your best to encourage men to participate at the center. Sometimes this is as brief as asking fathers to schedule an hour in the morning once a month when delivering their child and stay to share a book or an interest with whomever is interested. Sometimes older male volunteers can be included on a weekly basis. Of course, when it is possible to employ male staff members, this is even more satisfactory because of the regularity and consistency of their contact with the children.

Suggestions from Research That May Enhance Nonsexist Teaching

Research also provides suggestions for ways teachers can reduce sexist practices in addition to simply encouraging cross-gender activities. A study by Honig and Wittmer (1982) documents that toddler boys more frequently used negative ways to elicit responses from teachers than the girls did. The caregivers, in turn, responded to this behavior from boys proportionately more often. Thus, the boys' less desirable behavior was reinforced by the caregivers' attention in such circumstances—and so perpetuated itself. There is much value in recommending that caregivers make more of a point of responding to the positive behavior of little boys if they wish to increase this instead.

Another study reveals that parents of both sexes interrupt little girls when they are speaking more frequently than they interrupt little boys (Grief, 1980). In a more recent study the author found the same behavior to be true of women teachers when they were observed talking with 4-

year-old boys and girls during snack (Hendrick & Stange, 1991). Not only did the boys interrupt the teachers more frequently than the girls did and were not corrected for doing this, the *teachers interrupted the girls much more often than they did the boys*. One may well ask what boys and girls learn from such subtle but consistent responses? Quite possibly, the boys are learning it is their role to be heard without interruption and also that it is acceptable for them to be assertive and interrupt adults, or at least female adults, when they wish to do so. And what of the girls? What might *they* be learning? As modeled by a wide variety of teachers, that role was to accept being interrupted more and also to interrupt less themselves when talking with males. Because what they had to say was treated with less respect, they may also have been learning they are less important than their male counterparts.

Still another study (Serbin, O'Leary, Kent, & Tonick, 1973) reveals that preschool teachers tend to provide boys with more help when they ask for it and also to give them more information than they do the little girls in the group. Again, this tendency requires monitoring of behavior to make certain that teachers are explaining things as carefully to girls as boys and offering them just as much encouragement in solving problems when they request it.

Finally, a series of studies by Serbin (1980) indicates that there are some three-dimensional materials, such as blocks, that are generally preferred by boys. It is believed that using these materials contributes to the ability to solve the kinds of cognitive problems that require spatial visualization. (Visual-spatial ability is the ability to picture in the mind's eye how to rotate an object or mentally transform its shape. Remember those items on intelligence tests that ask you to predict how many blocks there are in an irregular stack or whether a hand seen from an unusual angle is the right or left one?) As Serbin points out, these visual-spatial skills are the ones most needed by people who become pilots, engineers,

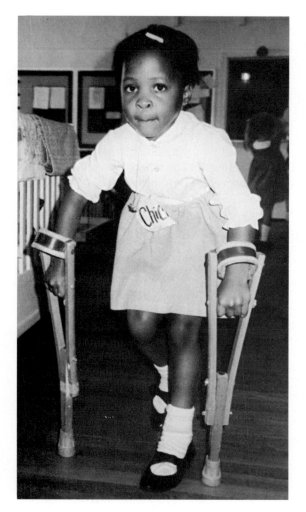

Providing opportunities to try out equipment helps generate understanding and reduces curiosity as well.

physicists, and architects—all fields in which few women currently excel. The question yet to be answered is, If girls used these materials more often, would their visual-spatial skills increase? And would new fields of endeavor be open to women as a result? Although we do not know the answers to these questions, we can reasonably assume that it would be worthwhile to encourage girls to play with blocks more often. Perhaps this

early experience would help equalize their chances; certainly it could do no harm.

Foster Acceptance and Understanding of Children Who Have Disabilities

Nowhere is the teacher's own attitude more important or infectious than when she is welcoming a child with a disability into her group. Frequently that attitude is an uncomfortable mix of apprehension and uncertainty combined with the good-hearted willingness to do one's best—if only one knew what "the best" was! (Heitz, 1989).

To complicate matters further, not only must the inexperienced teacher cope with her own feelings, she must also help the children in her group and the newcomer come to terms with theirs as well.

The Place to Start: Identify and Face Possible Feelings About Associating with a Person Who Has a Disability

Until quite recently, it has been true that children and adults who had disabilities spent their lives in relatively segregated circumstances (Chandler, 1994), but, as I have pointed out in previous chapters, this is no longer the case. We must realize that the previous segregation had a two-way effect—it not only isolated the disabled person from contact with many other people, but it also isolated we so-called normal or "differently abled" people from contact with our disabled peers. This means that most of us have known hardly anyone who has a disability, and, for that reason, we are uncomfortable and apprehensive when we meet them because we do not know how to behave. Indeed, we may even feel aversion or distaste when coming in contact with them. Or, possibly, we feel pity mingled with a certain relief we are not so afflicted ourselves. Because feelings like these are not attractive ones, many of us prefer to deny their presence, but it is more emotionally healthy to get them out in the open and confront ourselves about them. Doing this allows us to cope rather than use up energy attempting to conceal them from ourselves and other people. Hopefully, gaining insight into ourselves will help us appreciate how the children in our group may feel, too.

Familiarity and Information Can Help Overcome Initial Feelings of Apprehension

This holds true for teachers, families, and children. Whether the group should be prepared in advance about the new child remains an open question. Does the teacher follow that practice for all newcomers? Is there something so unusual about the child's appearance that it will cause a lot of immediate curiosity? Or should explanations be provided gradually and more casually as the need arises? Specific circumstances will dictate different answers to these questions at different times.

When questions do come up, of course, it is important to be truthful—"Ben's ears don't work very well. He'll hear you better if you stand right in front of him and make sure he's looking at you before you say something to him." "I know you told Shelly before not to grab your brush and she keeps doing it—it takes Shelly longer to remember things like that. Hold on to the brush, and tell her 'I'm using this one.' Then hand her another one instead."

One question children are likely to wonder about, particularly in the case of highly visible disabilities, is how the child got that way. Sometimes they are fearful the same thing might happen to them. Once again, the truthful, simple answer is best. "He was born that way—some people are," or "She had an accident," or—and this is often the case—simply "I don't know!" Explanations, of course, need to be combined with reassurance that things like that don't hap-

pen very often and that there are always ways to help the person overcome the disability.

Encourage Sensitivity to Other People's Feelings

Even young children know how it feels to have someone hurt their feelings, and they can learn to be sensitive to the effect cruel remarks have on the feelings of other people, also. "When you tell Jim he walks funny so he can't play Ninja turtles, it makes him feel bad. Remember when Shawntel said your shoes were weird? You felt bad, and we asked Shawntel not to say that again. Well, that's how Jim feels now. His feelings are hurt. I agree he can't run fast with those braces on, but isn't there some way he can play? Maybe he could be a turtle on a motorcycle and ride a trike instead?"

Above all, remember to be on guard for signs of rejection by the other children. Do your best to counteract that behavior or prevent it before it occurs. The basic point to emphasize firmly is that a child who has a disability is a lot like the other children—more like them than different from them. *Everyone* is better at doing some things and not as good at doing other things— and accompany that statement with examples.

Do Everything Possible to Integrate Children with Disabilities into the Group

Positive attitudes are certainly an important aspect of welcoming youngsters with disabilities into the group, but we must realize that attitudes are not enough. Once the child is admitted, it is very important to make certain he is genuinely included in as many activities as possible—and this requires constant monitoring on the part of the teacher—otherwise, many of the children will either ignore him or, sometimes, regard him as an irritating intruder if he lacks the social skills they have come to expect. True inclusion must go way beyond just having the child present (Bricker, 1995).

Unfortunately, space does not permit the detailed attention to the wide variety of other concerns and strategies needed for successful integration of children with disabilities into the ordinary preschool classroom. Suffice it to say here that, in addition to positive attitudes and deliberate efforts to facilitate participation, successful inclusion requires adequate support staff, an informed teacher, cooperative parents, and appropriate, adaptable, developmental curriculum (Bailey & Wolery, 1992; Bricker, 1995; Hendrick, 1996). It is a wise teacher who has the best interests of the child at heart who makes certain these ingredients are available before gathering such a youngster into her group.

Helping Children Learn Their Place in the World by Meeting Other People

Besides learning about their place in the world in relation to developing self-esteem, in relation to their cultural and ethnic background, and in relation to their gender role and varying abilities, children also learn about the world around them and their potential place in it by meeting people and finding out what they do. In children's centers this can be accomplished by having visitors come in and by going on field trips. If these experiences are presented well, children can really benefit; if done poorly, both children and grown-ups can have a miserable time.

In both learning situations it is important to remember to plan events so the children are as involved as possible and so they are not overwhelmed by adults talking too long and telling them things that do not interest them. I will never forget the firefighter who insisted on telling us the gallons per minute his truck could pump, the diameter of the nozzles, and the length of the fire hoses, when we could have been trying on coats and helmets, sitting in the engine's seat, and watching the light go around.

For such visits to be meaningful for the children, teachers must remember that many adults do not have the slightest idea about how to teach little children and that *they need to be coached beforehand to make the experience interesting for everyone.*

Having Visitors at School

Parents are wonderful resources for helping children learn about the world, so be on the lookout for ones who have skills or jobs that would appeal to the children. Some schools even inquire about these on their enrollment forms. Skills do not have to be extraordinary. The parent who has a camper and will let the children go through it or have a snack there or who will take time to let the children inspect a motorcycle adds real interest for the children and confers a certain glory on his or her own child, too. Some parents can play guitars, others may be able to demonstrate a potter's wheel, or they know someone who plays the flute. One of the mothers at our center was majoring in cosmetology and offered free haircuts occasionally. The children were enchanted—they loved watching, as well as having their own turn. Brothers and sisters can sometimes make special contributions, too. We recently had a 12-year-old bring in a garter snake and demonstrate what it could do.

Visitors offer a splendid way of widening children's occupational horizons—particularly if the teacher searches out women engaged in traditionally male vocations, such as telephone line "man" or physician. Visitors also provide good opportunities for cross-age grouping experiences. Families are so mobile these days that children are often deprived of contact with more mature adults, and some older people enjoy coming and reading to the children or sharing themselves in other ways in accordance with their talents and interests. Babies are also welcomed by children, who find their visits fascinating.

Still another value to having certain kinds of visitors come is that the experience helps children deal with their fears and apprehensions.

Such people as police officers and ambulance attendants are often best seen at school rather than on a field trip, because the children are more secure on their home ground.

The teacher should go over a few things with the visitor in advance. Explain that the children are very young and cannot be expected to sit still for lengthy explanations, and suggest that the visitor give only a *short* talk or simply come in and sit down and let the children gather around in small groups as their interest moves them. Ask them to bring something interesting for the children to look at or try out. The doctor, for example, might bring her stethoscope and "ear light." The police officer might let the children look over his police car (children are half appreciative and half dismayed by the siren), and he should be prepared to answer questions about where he has left his gun and what he does with it. The ambulance attendants might give the children rides on their stretcher.

Taking Field Trips

Young children can go many places on field trips, but the best have some qualities in common that are worth mentioning. These desirable destinations for field trips provide children with the opportunities to (a) move around fairly freely, (b) make some noise, and (c) participate in an activity rather than just look at something. Most excursions cannot meet all three of these criteria, but a few that do include wading in a brook, going to the park, beach, or lake, visiting a farm to help milk a cow or goat, and walking to the market to buy ingredients for a recipe.

Although children in all schools benefit from going on such trips, it is particularly important that full-day centers provide such excursions regularly. It is not natural or good for children to stay cooped up in one building and yard 5 days a week, 10 hours a day. They must be taken places and have contact with many experiences and people. If staffing is short, every effort should be made to find volunteers who can come along and assist the

teachers. Weekends at home with parents often cannot provide enough richness and variety for day care youngsters, unless the school helps, too.

Some examples of trips our center children have enjoyed include these:

- Walking to the library for a story hour
- Going to the Greek delicatessen to buy pickles
- Going to the pumpkin patch to get pumpkins before Halloween
- Taking a school pet to the veterinarian
- Collecting wood (with permission) at a nearby construction site
- Going to the nursery to buy little plants for Mother's Day
- Riding all the trikes around the block
- Attending a Cinco de Mayo celebration
- Visiting the cobbler's shop to see how shoes get fixed and buying polish to use on their own shoes back at school
- Visiting the teacher's house and having a snack there
- Visiting the college biology lab to see the skeleton
- Going to the post office to mail their valentines and visiting one of the parents who works there
- Walking to the office to pick up the mail
- Visiting the kindergarten they will attend in the fall
- Going to the wading pool in a nearby park
- Visiting a father at his pizza restaurant and making pizzas

Conducting a successful field trip requires careful planning. There are many matter-of-fact things to remember about this:

1. Keep excursion groups small but go frequently. Children have a better time in a small group, participate more, and are easier to control.
2. Notify parents in advance and obtain permission slips if necessary.
3. Leave a list at school of everyone who has gone on the trip. Put name tags on everyone.

4. *Visit first yourself* and, if necessary, obtain permission, check on appropriate times for the visit (find out, for example, when the park is sprinkled), and coach the adults about what will be expected of them.
5. Take two adults along if possible.
6. If going by car:
    a. Make certain the driver has adequate insurance.
    b. Talk rules over first. *Insist* that children remain seated in the back seat, and use seat belts at all times.
    c. If any misbehavior occurs, pull over to the side and wait. If it continues, do not hesitate to return to school. This ensures better cooperation next time.
7. Whether you are going by car or not, it is only fair to tell the children how they will be expected to behave before starting out. Perhaps they will have to sit in the waiting room at the vet's for a little while or say "thank you" to the butcher who takes them through his icebox. Telling them in advance helps avoid embarrassment by having to correct or prompt them in public.
8. Encourage children to use the toilet before departure.
9. Keep a record to make sure that certain tractable children are not going on many trips while other less cooperative ones are always staying at school.
10. Stick carefully to your promised time of return. Tired parents hate standing around waiting for children at the end of the day.
11. Be prepared to take advantage of unanticipated, fortuitous happenings as they turn up. Seeing a fire fighter test a hydrant may be of much more interest to the children than what you originally had in mind to do.
12. Remember that field trips need not be elaborate—repeated trips to the house that is being built next door and taking a look under the street when the manhole cover is removed are both fascinating experiences for preschoolers.

13. *Always remember to send a thank-you note afterward.* This is excellent public relations, and the recipients enjoy them so much, especially if they include a few choice comments made by the children. It helps the children learn good social manners, too, if they dictate what the teacher should say.

When the trip is over, use it as a base for continued learning. It is good practice for children to recall what they did, and talking it over will provide them with new vocabulary to describe the experience and exercise their memory, too. They will do some evaluating if asked what they liked best, what they disliked, or if anything scared them. Some trips lend themselves well to dramatic play afterward, also, and this can be encouraged if the teacher has a few props available and encourages the children to develop others on a spontaneous basis as they are needed.

If possible, it is a fine idea to take pictures during the trip. These can be used in many ways to remind the children of what happened. For example, some teachers bind these into storytelling books or use them as flannel-board stories. They can also be turned into a temporal ordering game that encourages users to arrange events in the order in which they occurred.

The following account written by a Head Start staff member is a good example of a successful trip that incorporates many of the recommendations listed earlier. As you read it, try to identify all the positive social things the children were learning.

A Day in the Carrot Fields

A lot of our kids' fathers work harvesting carrots up around here at this time of year, and we thought it would be good for them to see what their dads do. The kids don't always know this, because there is just one car in the family and he goes off to work in it lots of times before they get up. So we checked with the foreman, and he said we could come if we stayed away from the machine that does the digging.

We loaded the kids in the Head Start buses (borrowing one from the other school) and started out. The only trouble was we couldn't find the field right off and spent about half an hour driving around and looking, but we finally saw the harvester, and the kids all cheered.

Oh yes—I forgot to say we had talked about staying out of the way of the machine before we left—they were good about that—I think they were afraid of it. We walked down the rows and watched the men harvesting the carrots and the machine working, and two of the children saw their fathers. Along the way, Ramiro found a big caterpillar, which was nice after the way he's been so mean lately. We put it in the glove compartment so we could bring it back with us.

The soil was real rich and soft and sandy where the machine had dug, and it left a lot of carrots behind, just lying there—what a waste—so all the children could take as many as they liked. They filled their arms with as much as they wanted, and then we got back in the bus and so to school.

The carrots were real dirty, so we got out our laundry tubs and vegetable brushes and let the kids wash them off in there and ate carrots for a snack. Mrs. Sanchez (the cook) served them on orange paper plates we had left from Halloween with cheese slices and oranges. Maybe it tasted funny together, but it got the idea of orange across all right.

It worked out well at group time too because one group read *The Carrot Seed* (Krauss & Johnson, 1971) and the other group listened to the record about it. Next week we'll look at the snapshots we took and think about it again. I'm going to make them do like you said, and tell me which picture comes first.

When it was time to go, each kid had a big bag of carrots to take home. They were real fresh, and the children loved having so much of something. Their mothers were pleased, too. All in all, I'd say it was a good trip. The only thing I'd change is, next time we won't drive around so long looking for that field!

Summary

The children's sense of who they are and of their place in the world has important ramifications for building their sense of social competence. Children gain their basic sense of who they are by identifying with the people around them whom they admire and want to be like. As they enter child care outside the home, the models teachers provide may socialize children into additional ways of coping with their worlds. Teachers can influence children's feeling of self-esteem, their ideas of what constitutes appropriate sex roles for themselves, and what it means to belong to a particular ethnic and cultural group.

Teachers as well as families can help children build inner sources of self-esteem by (a) providing them with skills so that they feel competent, (b) including opportunities for them to do meaningful work, (c) helping them do things for themselves, and (d) encouraging them to be creative. A positive body image also contributes to children's sense of identity and can be developed in various ways.

Field trips widen children's horizons but also require careful advance arrangements to be successful.

In teaching about sexual and ethnic identity, the most important learning for children to internalize is a positive attitude toward members of the opposite sex and toward their own sex and toward their own and other's racial and cultural backgrounds. Children need to accept other youngsters with disabilities and see past those disabilities to the child within who is like themselves just as they learn that people of both sexes and various ethnic and cultural backgrounds are both alike and different from each other. There are many ways to make this teaching both positive and real for preschoolers, as the work done by Pacific Oaks College demonstrates.

Children also learn about their place in the world by coming in contact with interesting people, and these encounters should be a carefully planned part of the curriculum. When they are well done, visits and field trips become rich sources of pleasurable learning for the children and for the adults who participate with them.

Self-Check Questions for Review

Content-Related Questions

1. Briefly summarize three theories describing how identity is achieved.
2. Give an example of a way to increase self-esteem that comes from outside the child. Now list several other strategies teachers can use that will help generate self-esteem from within the child.
3. Cite an example illustrating how body image might affect an individual's sense of self.
4. What does the antibias curriculum developed by Pacific Oaks College advocate?
5. If the purpose of multicultural curriculum is not to teach facts about various cultures, what *is* the real purpose or intention?
6. In addition to teaching children that all people are similar in some ways, what is the second concept about people that should be taught?
7. What is the fundamental concept on which non-sexist education should be based?

8. Describe some of the research findings about ways teachers can reduce sexist practices in addition to encouraging cross-gender activities.
9. There is something important teachers should do before a visitor talks to the children to prepare that person for the encounter, whether this is at the center or on a field trip. What is it?
10. This chapter includes many suggestions of ways to help field trips be as successful as possible. Pretend you are helping an inexperienced teacher plan for his first trip. What suggestions would you give him to smooth the children's way?

Integrative Questions

1. Consult Table 13–1 where many parallels are drawn between nonsexist, multicultural, and antihandicapped education. Select a number of parallels and identify the common bond that links each pair together.
2. Review Lubeck's research in *Sandbox Society*. What strengths are present in the curriculum presented at the Head Start center that are lacking in the middle-class white school? How might these deficiencies be remedied in the white center? Then, switch centers and answer the questions again.
3. Explain why being able to wait patiently is one of the most important skills in teaching.
4. A Navaho child and a Hopi child are in your center, as well as a number of Anglos, and you have invited the Native American mothers to come and make Navaho fry bread and Hopi blue cornbread with the children. Explain what you want the children and their families to gain from this learning opportunity.
5. Compare the research study in this chapter entitled "Is One Point of View Always Right?" with the study in chapter 8 entitled "Can Children's Food Preferences Be Changed?" Both are research studies but the method of investigation differs. Explain what these differences are.
6. Table 13–2 lists many ways teachers do or do not show respect to children. If you could only select five items from that list, which ones would you choose as being the behaviors you would most like people to use to show that they respect *you*?

Questions and Activities

1. Every family has standards by which they expect their members to abide. Are you aware of some of

the ones in your own family? Think of some examples of things your family "never" does or "always" does and share them with the class. Some examples might be "Everyone in our family always goes to college," or "It just isn't a home to my mother without a cat in it," or "My dad makes the money, but my mother always pays the bills."

2. List several new skills you have seen children in your school learn this week that increased their feelings of competence.

3. Have your ideas changed in recent years about what constitutes appropriate ways for men and women to behave? Are there still some activities you think it is only all right for one sex to do, such as asking for a date?

4. You are now the director of a children's center, and a father comes to school somewhat concerned about your nonsexist approach to early childhood education. He is quite frankly worried, as are many people, that letting his son dress up in skirts may encourage him to become a homosexual. How would you reply to this concern? Might he be right?

5. Do you think it was all right for the little red-headed boy described in this chapter to be "roughed up" by the men? What might be the pros and cons of letting this kind of treatment continue?

6. Some students view themselves as having no cultural or ethnic heritage. They just say they are American. To demonstrate that you are more sophisticated than this, develop a project to do with the children that is based on some aspect of your own family's cultural or ethnic background.

7. As the children are assembling for group time, one of the little girls says distastefully, "I don't want to sit by Angelina—her skin's dirty!" (Angelina is brown because she is Puerto Rican, not because she is dirty.) How would you handle this incident? Be sure to think of practical, immediate and long-term approaches.

8. What was the best field trip you ever took children on? Share with the class what made it so successful and how you would ensure that it would be as worthwhile when you do it the next time.

9. What other age-appropriate activities besides those suggested in the material from Pacific Oaks can you think of that would enable children to take direct action against bias?

References for Further Reading

Overviews

Banks, J. A. (1994). *Multiethnic education: Theory and practice* (3rd ed.). Boston: Allyn & Bacon. Banks, a distinguished authority in this area, concludes this analysis of multicultural education by listing 23 guidelines curriculum should follow to be truly multiethnic.

Derman-Sparks, L. (1995). Children and diversity. *Scholastic Early Childhood Today*, 10(3), 42–45. Derman-Sparks reviews developmental stages of learning about racial identity and disabilities, providing some examples of antibias activities to clarify misunderstandings that accompany those ages.

Derman-Sparks, L., & the ABC Task Force. (1989). *Anti-bias curriculum: Tools for empowering young children.* Washington, DC: National Association for the Education of Young Children. *Anti-Bias Curriculum* explains in practical terms how that approach can be integrated into the early childhood curriculum. *Highly recommended.*

Edwards, C. P., & Ramsey, P. G. (1986). *Promoting social and moral development in young children: Creative approaches for the classroom.* New York: Teachers College Press. This readable book focuses on how children acquire social knowledge. It offers particularly useful chapters on understanding racial/cultural categories and gender and sex-role awareness. *Highly recommended.*

Kendall, F. E. (1996). *Diversity in the classroom: New approaches to the education of young children* (2nd ed.). New York: Teachers College Press. Chapter 3, "Taking the Emotional Risk," is particularly valuable because of its suggestions for identifying and confronting our own biases.

Ramsey, P. G. (1995). Research in review: Growing up with the contradictions of race and class. *Young Children*, 50(6), 18–22. Ramsey reviews what is known about young children's attitudes toward race and class and suggests some approaches teachers can use to foster positive attitudes.

Fostering Self-Esteem

Kohn, A. (1993). *Punished by rewards: The trouble with gold stars, incentive plans, A's, praise, and other bribes.* Boston: Houghton Mifflin. The author provides very persuasive arguments against depending on extrinsic rewards to obtain desired behavior and build self-esteem.

Owens, K. (1995). *Raising your child's inner self-esteem: The authoritative guide from infancy through the teen years.* New York: Plenum. This book provides a thorough discussion of the myriad ways our behavior with children can enhance or reduce their feelings of self-worth.

Honoring Cultural Differences

Hollins, E. R., King, J. E., & Hayman, E. C. (1994). *Teaching diverse populations: Formulating a knowledge base.* Albany: State University of New York Press. Chapters cover a variety of cultures, ranging from Appalachian to Puerto Rican to

American Indian. The majority of chapters have to do with teaching African American children, including an interesting one on characteristics of effective African American teachers. *Highly recommended.*

Sorti, C. (1989) *The art of crossing cultures.* Yarmouth, ME: Intercultural Press. Written by a former member of the Peace Corps, this book concentrates on adjusting to living abroad, but the lessons it teaches apply equally well to gaining understanding of people from other cultures in the United States. Delightful reading.

York, S. (1992) *Roots and wings: Affirming culture in early childhood programs.* St. Paul, MN: Redleaf. This truly useful book includes discussions of what might generate prejudice, age-appropriate activities, and an exceptional chapter illustrating how cultural standards are expressed in the child's experience coupled with suggestions of ways to increase the comfort level between school and home values. *Highly recommended.*

Sources of Information on Ethnic and Cultural Characteristics[4]

Brady, P. (1992). Columbus and the quincentennial myths: Another side of the story. *Young Children,* 47(6), 4–14. This article, combined with those in the same issue by P. Greenberg, "Teaching about Native Americans? Or Teaching about People, Including Native American?" and L. Soldier, "Working with Native American Children," provides a valuable overview of teaching Native American children.

Chisholm, J. S. (1996). Learning "Respect for Everything": Navajo images of development. In C. P. Hwang, M. E. Lamb, & I. E. Sigel (Eds.), *Images of childhood.* Mahwah, NJ: Erlbaum. Although written by an Australian, the author draws heavily on information from authentic Navajo sources. Noteworthy is a Navajo model of human development that is included.

Feng, J. (1994) *Asian-American children: What teachers should know.* Urbana, IL: ERIC Clearinghouse on Elementary and Early Childhood Education. Feng emphasizes the diversity of this group and suggests nine ways teachers can help them. A brief bibliography is included.

Hale, J. E. (1986). *Black children: Their roots, culture, and learning style* (2nd ed.). Baltimore, MD: Johns Hopkins University Press. A wealth of information about the similarities and differences that exist between middle-class White and Black cultures is included. *Highly recommended.*

Lee F. Y. (1995). Asian parents as partners. *Young Children,* 50(3), 4–9. Lee provides helpful information on communication and using interpreters with these parents.

Logan, S. L. (Ed.). (1996). *The black family: Strengths, self-help, and positive change.* Boulder, CO: Westview/HarperCollins.

This book singles out various strengths of Black families and provides recommendations on how to use them to foster better lives for all concerned.

Luangpraeseut, K. (1989). *Laos culturally speaking.* San Diego: Multifunctional Resource Center, San Diego State University. This rich resource covers everything from history to culture.

Ortiz, F. I. (1988). Hispanic-American children's experiences in classrooms: A comparison between Hispanic and non-Hispanic children. In L. Weis (Ed.), *Class, race and gender in American education.* Albany: State University of New York Press. The title is self-explanatory.

Promoting Gender Equity

Edwards, C. P., & Ramsey, P. G. (1986). *Promoting social and moral development in young children: Creative approaches for the classroom.* New York: Teachers College Press. In the chapter "Boys and Girls: Gender and Sex-Role Awareness," the authors define the difference between gender identity and sex-role identity. They include several activities that foster the development of both kinds of identity.

Levine, J. Q., Murphy, D. T., & Wilson, S. (1993). *Getting men involved: Strategies for early childhood programs.* New York: Scholastic. This rare book is filled with practical suggestions. *Highly recommended.*

Wellhousen, K. (1996). Do's and don'ts for eliminating hidden bias. *Childhood Education,* 73(1), 36–39. Although this article focuses on reducing gender bias, it applies equally well to eliminating other forms of prejudice. *Highly recommended.*

Information About Integrating Children with Disabilities

Bricker, D. (1995). The challenge of inclusion. *Journal of Early Intervention,* 19(1), 179–194. This longtime champion of integration of children with disabilities into preschool classrooms provides us with a thoughtful assessment of what is required for such integration to be truly successful. *Highly recommended.*

Chandler, P. S. (1994). *A place for me: Including children with special needs in early care and education settings.* Washington, DC: National Association for the Education of Young Children. Chandler provides a simple introduction suitable for early childhood teachers anticipating their first encounters with children who have disabilities. She provides an outstanding list of support organizations.

Activity/Idea Books

Please refer to chapter 8 for resources of multicultural recipes and to chapter 15 for lists of relevant children's books. Also, there is a real need and place for publications of the sort listed here, but I reiterate that *providing the kinds of environmental embellishments and activities suggested there should constitute only the beginning of true multicultural education.*

---

[4]For additional references, please refer to those in chapter 2, "Including Families in the Life of the School."

Crawford, S. H. (1996). *Beyond dolls & guns: 101 ways to help children avoid gender bias.* Portsmouth, NH: Heinemann. Crawford includes up-to-date information on gender stereotypes and behavior as well as suggesting many antibias, nonbias activities. Of particular note is a list of 15 ways to test for sexism. *Highly recommended.*

Hopkins, S., & Winerts, J. (1990). *Discover the world: Empowering children to value themselves, others and the earth.* Philadelphia: New Society. This unusual book offers numerous curriculum charts replete with ideas for integrating information about various cultures, friends, self-esteem, and so forth into the preschool day. Because it is published in cooperation with Concerned Educators Allied for A Safe Environment (CEASE), there is a refreshing emphasis on conflict management and peace-related concerns. *Highly recommended.*

Milord, S. (1992) *Hands around the world: 365 creative ways to build cultural awareness & global respect.* Charlotte, VT: Williamson. Every custom or activity described in this book is linked to something children can actually do themselves and to familiar behaviors where possible. A cheerful book that offers many opportunities for positive, respectful cross-cultural comparisons.

Raines, B. (1991). *Creating sex-fair family day care: A guide for trainers.* Philadelphia: CHOICE, Office of Research and Improvement, U.S. Department of Education; Newton, MA: WEEA Publishing Center (Distributor: 55 Chapel St., Newton, MA 02160). This curriculum guide was developed and field tested with family child care providers, *noteworthy in particular for its list of nonsexist children's books.*

Sprung, B. (1975). *Non-sexist education for young children: A practical guide.* New York: Citation. This paperback contains a wealth of practical ideas for conducting a nonsexist nursery school using five curriculum topics as examples. The best reference in the field.

York, S. (1991). *Roots and wings: Affirming culture in early childhood programs.* St. Paul, MN: Redleaf. Remember that York, described in the Overview, includes many excellent antibias activities also.

For the Advanced Student

Beal, C. R. (1994). *Boys and girls: The development of gender roles.* New York: McGraw-Hill. In this readable yet scholarly book, Beal provides balanced, comprehensive information about gender roles and what affects their development. *Highly recommended.*

Board on Children and Families. (1995). Immigrant children and their families: Issues for research and policy. *The Future of Children,* 5(2), 72–80. This invaluable publication provides a wealth of factual information concerning such youngsters.

Fagot, B. I. (1994). Peer relations and the development of competence in boys and girls. *New Directions for Child Development,*

65, 53–65. This article summarizes research on gender roles done by this distinguished investigator during the past 18 years. *Highly recommended.*

Greenfield, P. M., & Cocking, R. R. (Eds). (1994). *Cross-cultural roots of minority child development.* Hillsdale, NJ: Erlbaum. This book is filled with fascinating information about how differences in culture affect the way children develop. *Highly recommended.*

Hwang, C. P., Lamb, M. E., & Sigel, I. E. (Eds.). (1996). *Images of childhood.* Mahwah, NJ: Erlbaum. This book focuses on cross-cultural perspectives about raising children. (I particularly relished the chapter on proverbs, but everyone will develop their own favorite!) It discusses several cultures: Brazilian, Zambian, Japanese, Navajo, and Swedish.

Igoa, C. (1995). *The inner world of the immigrant child.* New York: St. Martin's. This book is well worth reading because of the insights it contributes about how to relate to children from other cultures. *Highly recommended.*

National Association for the Education of Young Children. (1995). *NAEYC position statement: Responding to linguistic and cultural diversity: Recommendations for effective early childhood education.* Washington, DC: Author. The title is self-explanatory.

Wellesly College Center for Research on Women. (1992) *How schools shortchange girls: The AAUW report: A study of major findings on girls and education.* New York: Marlowe. This landmark study on the "second place" girls and young women experience in education is followed by a series of recommendations for rectifying that condition.

Weber, S., & Mitchell, D. (1995). *That's funny, you don't look like a teacher: Interrogating images and identity in popular culture.* London: Falmer. Not only children are influenced by surrounding culture. This book documents the effects of culture on how we see the role of the teacher—amusing, informative reading.

Journals and Newsletters of Interest

The Black Child Advocate. 1023 Fifteenth St., N. W., Suite 602, Washington, DC 20005. This is the quarterly newsletter of the National Black Child Development Institute. It focuses primarily on current legislation that could affect the lives of all children and African American children in particular.

The MASC Spectrum. 12228 Venice Blvd., Suite 452, Los Angeles, CA 90066. With more than 1,000,000 multiracial families in the United States, the newsletter of the Multiracial Americans of Southern California is of increasing interest.

Native Peoples Magazine. Media Concepts Group, P.O. Box 36820, Phoenix, AZ 85067–6820. The magazine describes itself as "dedicated to the sensitive portrayal of the arts and lifeways of native peoples of the Americas." It is published in affiliation with many museums including the Smithsonian's National Museum of the American Indian. *Highly recommended.*

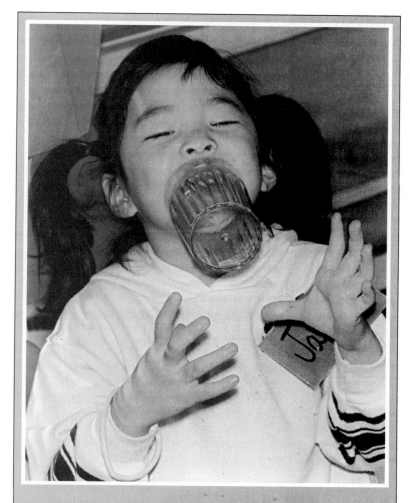

Freeing Children to Be Creative

Have you ever

- Dried up completely on ideas for creative activities?
- Needed to save money on art materials but did not know how?
- Wished you could explain more clearly why coloring books are not creative?

If you have, the material in this chapter will help you.

Of all the qualities we seek to nurture in children as they grow, use of the imagination must be one of the most important. Indeed, our imaginings grow more important with every passing year as our technology develops and becomes even more amazing. We must remember that every machine first has to be imagined by someone.

John Coe (1987, p. 75)

Creativity, as practiced by young children, is a dynamic, changing, fluid experience that derives its greatest satisfaction from the process, not the product. It is, in the best sense of the word, a state of "becoming." It is also an intensely personal process, since the wellspring of creativity lies within the child. For this reason, it contains the potential for both self-enhancement and self-despair. Because its manifestations are easily withered by disapproval, adults must be particularly careful to nourish rather than discourage creative self-expression in children, lest their criticism or domination blight its growth.

What Is Creativity?

Definitions of creativity vary widely according to the aspect being defined (Davis, 1983). For our purposes, the one proposed by Smith (1966) is most useful because it does not include the process of critical evaluation that is more appropriate to apply when working with older children and adults. He defines creativity as being the process of "sinking down taps into our past experiences and putting these selected experiences together into new patterns, new ideas or new products" (p. 43).

In preschool children, this putting together of new ideas and products based on past experience is expressed primarily through the use of self-expressive materials, through imaginative pretend play, and through creative thought. This chapter focuses on the first two of these approaches to creativity. Creativity in thought is discussed in detail in the section on the cognitive self.

Some New Ideas About Creativity from Reggio Emilia

In the past few years, interest in young children's artistic expressions has been stimulated by an exhibit touring the United States called "The 100 Languages of Children." This exhibit features the work of preschool-aged children from the municipal schools of Reggio Emilia, Italy, and has led many of us to be more aware of an additional benefit to using graphic materials besides the expression of feelings and aesthetic satisfactions. This additional value emphasizes the use of graphic materials to communicate to other people what the children are thinking about and what they know.

Indeed, the title "The 100 Languages" is intended to emphasize the multitude of possible materials children can use to communicate their knowledge. For example, if the children are interested in constructing a playground for birds, they might first draw their ideas of how to make a fountain for the birds to enjoy or construct a model of their ideas about that while using clay.

When American educators first beheld some of the Italian children's work, they greeted it with skepticism—it did not seem possible that such young children could produce such advanced and beautiful work. However, numerous visits to those schools have now convinced us that these products really are the result of the children's efforts and, therefore, have caused us to reexamine our ideas about what preschool children are able to do.

Some Contrasts Between the American and Reggian Points of View

Because various aspects of the Reggio Emilia philosophy have been discussed in previous chapters and will be touched on again in the cognitive sections, we will confine ourselves here to talking about some different emphases in the Italian approach to fostering creativity. The most obvious one is the result—the advanced quality of the children's work. This is due partly to plentiful opportunities for repeated practice with materials from a very early age and partly from teachers deliberately showing the children how to use materials successfully. But although these factors are important, there is a third one of even greater significance. Every lecture by Reggio staff begins with the statement that children are "rich, strong, and powerful" (Gandini, 1997; Rinaldi, 1994). They see children as possessing great potential—potential that is the privilege of the teacher to perceive and empower. They see children not as having needs but rather as having rights—as being entitled to good care and sound teaching because of who they are, not because of what they need.

How does this differ from the American point of view? On the surface, at least, we would certainly agree with it. But underneath, do we really see children as having such extraordinary ability at such an early age? It seems to me we view them from a much more protective and possibly restrictive vantage. For example, we often discuss "meeting children's needs" and "strengthening their weaknesses." Perhaps we have been so wrapped up in defending children's right to authentic childhoods that we may have unintentionally carried this defense too far, which has led us actually to underexpect what children can do. Certainly the accomplishments of the youngsters in Reggio Emilia offer many interesting examples of realizing creative potential we have not dreamed possible in the United States.

Attitudes About Creativity

Besides this most significant difference in attitude toward children, it is interesting to single out just a few of the many other differences between the Reggian and American approaches to creativity (Hendrick, 1996). One of the most obvious is the multitude and variety of materials the Italians make available for the children combined with the special work areas, typically separate rooms, they call *ateliers* where children come to construct their ideas. Moreover, a special staff person (an *atelierista*) is provided to facilitate that process. Although the majority of school staff in the United States would not find it difficult to extend the range of creative materials made available to children if they just thought about it, it is a rare school that could find the wherewithal to support the salary of an *atelierista* much less provide a permanent space for that person to hold forth. Nevertheless, as visitors behold the results made possible by this support, it leaves us hungering to provide similar opportunities for our children.

This admiration for the color, beauty, and quality of the Italian products often blinds the visitor to another real difference between American and Italian purposes in providing graphic materials. We value the creative process because it comes from within the child, is unique and original, and provides for the expression and possible relief of feelings.

The Italian setting appears to me to have a more cognitively oriented approach. The purpose of providing graphic materials leans more toward enabling children to express their ideas—to explain, for example, how the water actually gets to the fountain or what they think causes rain to fall.

We Americans hesitate to make suggestions to the children about what they are making, fearing we may stifle the children's spontaneity and creative original ideas if we intervene. We emphasize discovery and learning or figuring out how to use materials by trying them out. Therefore, we scrupulously leave children to discover on their own how to use materials effectively. The Italians, on the other hand, think nothing of showing a child how to wipe the brush on the edge of the cup to avoid dripping or how to wet the edges of clay so it will stick better.

For me, this was one of the most troubling aspects of watching that staff work until I understood their reasoning. They maintain that lending adult assistance when needed, whether it be bending a recalcitrant piece of wire or hammering in a nail, empowers youngsters to move ahead with their creations in a satisfying way. The way I have come to think about this is that there is a vast difference between showing a child how to use a brace and bit to make a hole and telling him where to put the hole or what to do with it once drilled. Although the Reggio teachers unhesitatingly teach skills and lend a helping hand when needed, they would never tell the child where to put the hole (though they well might ask her why she is putting it in a particular place).

Research Study

What Is the Relationship Between Choice and Creativity?

Research Question   Does providing choices of material motivate children to be more creative than giving them little or no choice does?

Research Method   Fourteen boys and 14 girls between the ages of 2 and 6 who were attending a day-care center participated in the study. The teachers ranked each child in relation to creativity, interest in art, and level of independence. Then the children were randomly assigned to the choice or no-choice groups. (The purpose of the ranking was to determine whether there was an initial difference in creative ability between the choice and no-choice groups. No significant difference in ability was found.)

During a collage experience, children in the choice group were allowed to select any materials they wished from 5 out of 10 boxes. They were then asked by the experimenter to make a design of their choosing. The experimenter selected materials for the children in the no-choice group. (Each no-choice child was provided with a group of five collage boxes previously selected by a child in the "choice" group. Thus, the pairs of choice/no-choice children were matched in terms of the materials used to make the collages.)

Then eight artists rated all the collages on a scale according to their being more or less creative.

Results   When the scores for the collages were analyzed statistically, the collages of the children who were encouraged to make their own choices were rated as significantly more creative than those of the children who had no opportunity for choosing their materials.

Implications for Teaching   This research supports the idea that allowing children to make choices from an array of creative materials rather than just telling them they must use particular materials can be an effective way of increasing the probability that they will express themselves more creatively.

Note. From "Children's Artistic Creativity: Effects of Choice in Task Materials" by T. M. Amabile and J. Gitomer, 1984, *Personality and Social Psychology Bulletin*, 10(2), pp. 209–215.

What Can We Learn from the Reggio Approach?

What does this exciting example of children's creative potential mean to us American preschool teachers? Does it mean that what we have been doing should be abandoned or regarded as undesirable practice?

Of course not—our essential treasuring of the creative process is quite correct, just as the value of fostering originality and the unique self-expression of feelings and ideas remains sound. Certainly we must retain these values.

At the same time, we can also welcome and include the more cognitive approach favored by the Reggians and encourage children to communicate their ideas through a variety of self-expressive materials. Even more significantly, we can strive to see children as they really are—not as unformed, weak, vulnerable people who require our protec-

tion but rather as strong, capable people. I believe it is this fundamental change in attitude toward children that will produce the greatest benefit for our children in the United States.

Some General Principles for Fostering Creativity

Later in this chapter we will discuss some quite specific approaches that apply to the presentation of particular kinds of self-expressive materials, but there are also some more general principles that apply to all of them. These will be covered first.

Create a Climate That Encourages Children to Feel Creative

A climate that encourages creativity is composed of a number of things; keeping anxiety low is cer-

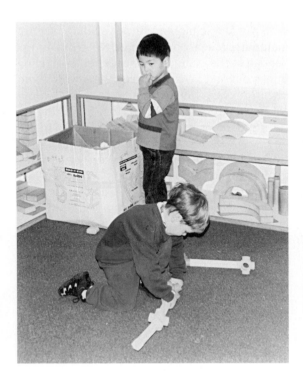 

Providing open, unstructured materials encourages children to express their own ideas. You can almost see the "Ah-ha" experience taking place as he thinks about how to make a hockey stick.

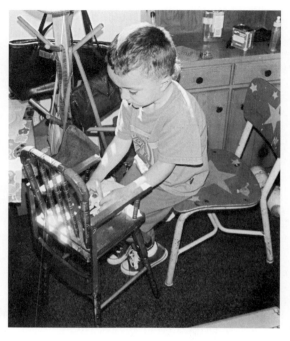

Allowing children to use familiar equipment in unconventional ways is an excellent way to foster creativity in thought.

tainly basic to it. When children feel they are living in a predictable environment where they know what is expected of them and the teacher is a reasonable person, they feel secure and so have more energy to devote to the pleasures of creativity.

Added to this is the general attitude of the teacher that could be summed up as "Let's try it!" or "Why not?" This attitude is expressed as an openness to suggestions from the children and a willingness to venture with them as they explore various creative mediums. It tells them that it is all right to try out something new and experiment with the possibilities of the materials being offered.

Teachers who wish to generate a creative climate must also be prepared to live with a certain amount of messiness. When children are caught up in the fever of creating things, their behavior is often somewhat helter-skelter, and it can really interfere with the creative process to insist that

self-expressive or play materials be maintained in nearly perfect order at all times. (Note also that comments on cleaning up are sprinkled liberally through this chapter to balance this behavior.)

Finally, a general air of approval and interested inquiry about what the children are doing does much to set the creative atmosphere for the group. This should be more a feeling of enjoying the experience *with* the children rather than singling out specific products for praise (Amabile, 1989). I still recall with pleasure a young three who turned to me after finger-painting, sighed blissfully, and confided, "You know, this experience was udderly dewightful!" Surely this is the climate we should aim for when building competence in the children's creative selves.

Remember That Process Is More Important Than Product

One reason it is better to emphasize the process is that young children are not skillful users of materials. Much of their creative effort is expended in the manipulative experience of trying things out and becoming acquainted with them (Schirrmacher, 1997). Moreover, little children are more interested in *doing* than producing results and rarely, if at all, betray a planned intention when they take up their paintbrushes or select collage materials. This sort of advance planning belongs to older children on the verge of kindergarten. The other very important reason it is sound to emphasize process is that this reduces the temptation to provide models for children to copy. Copies are not originals, and it is originality that is the hallmark of creativity.

Remember That Encouraging Choices Fosters Creativity in Children

For an experience to be creative for children, it must be generated from within them, not be an experience "laid on" from outside. Amabile and Gitomer's study (page 292) substantiates that it is important to encourage children to make

This creation done by children in the Reggio Emilia schools illustrates how permission to experiment combined with variety of materials can enrich creative play.

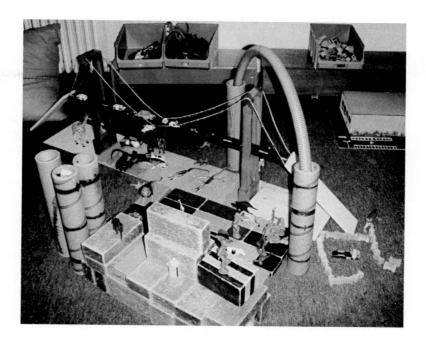

choices about the materials and activities for themselves. For example, rather than setting out three colors at the easel, why not suggest that each child choose which of four or five colors he wants to use, or select the nails she prefers, or pick accessories he requires in the block corner.

Encourage Children to Explain What They Mean by Illustrating Their Ideas Graphically

Of course, these depictions may not be on the advanced level we have witnessed at Reggio, but they are valuable, nonetheless. Donna Williams (1997) provides an encouraging example of what children can do in her description of a project she and the children carried out together after her return from Reggio. She was working with a group of 3- to 5-year-olds who were investigating various aspects of water. Part of the experiences involved evaporation.

> I brought in paper towels and water and asked the children to predict where water would go if we wet

the paper towels and left them out for a while. In spite of their previous "recitations," *not one child* predicted that water will evaporate. In fact, the group agreed that the paper towel would *never* dry, because "Paper towels are something that soaks up water." We wet the towels, children marked their own, and we recorded the day and time. The paper towels, of course, were dry when we returned the next day. The observations from the group were divided: four believed the air was causal in the drying, and four believed the "clothespins and air together did it." (Williams & Kanton, 1997, p. 118)

Offer Support When Needed, but Interfere as Little as Possible

Children are entitled to assistance with creative materials when they need it, just as they are entitled to help with their shoelaces or having their meat cut up. If materials are too difficult to manage, the end result is frustration, not creative satisfaction. Teachers should offer technical help when necessary but not usurp the children's right to make their own creative decisions.

Teachers can also offer support by providing enough time for children to have thoroughly satisfying experiences. It takes a while for them to become deeply involved in play or get deeply into finger painting, and if the scheduled time for such activities is too short, the children are deprived of the leisurely richness they require to lose themselves in it entirely.

Still another important kind of support to offer is the *provision of sufficient quantities of materials*, as well as plenty of opportunity to use them. Children should be allowed to paint as many pictures or make as many collages as their fancy dictates rather than "just making one so Mary can have a turn, too."

Fortunately, *many materials that are appropriate for self-expressive activities and for dramatic play are available free for the asking*, and their reuse has the added virtue of helping children appreciate the value of recycling (Drew, 1995). All it takes are an imaginative eye, the courage to ask for them, and the energy to collect them regularly.

Provide Enough Variety in Creative Activities

Providing variety is important because different activities appeal to different children. Variety can be obtained in many ways. Sometimes simply moving an activity from one place to another will attract different children. Little boys, for example, who may shun dramatic house play activities indoors often participate more readily if the equipment is moved outside, or young threes may use the large hollow blocks more freely if they are placed around a corner of the building where the older children are less likely to intrude on them.

It is also valuable to make a point of varying the activities themselves, not only by varying such basic materials as dough and paint recipes, but also by offering different levels of difficulty that suit different levels of maturation and skill. Table 14–1 lists activities suitable for various ages of preschool children.

One of the joys of offering creative, self-expressive materials to children with disabilities is that they offer such a variety of textures for the visually impaired youngster and can be used with delight whether or not a child hears well (Anderson, 1994). Adjustments can also readily be made for children with coordination problems. For example, adjustments might entail providing a table with a U-shaped cutout so a child in a wheelchair can reach the art materials without stretching or planning a particularly appealing collage experience for a youngster who needs lots of simple fine-muscle practice.

Make the Activity as Creative as Possible

Finally, when curriculum is developed that is intended to foster the creative aspect of the child's self, it is helpful for teachers to be quite clear in their own minds about just how creative the contemplated activity is likely to be. Table 14–2 provides some examples of materials that offer varying degrees of freedom of self-expression.

Those activities with the greatest potential for creative self-expression are characterized by requiring the least amount of control and instruction by the teacher. Examples of these are included in Column 1 in Table 14–2. They are most open to being used in a dynamic, fluid, "becoming" sort of way. Variations of these activities concentrate on varying the material rather than varying what is made from it. The materials might be thought of as being generally less refined or sophisticated than the ones in Column 2, because they do not require much skill for the children to have a satisfying experience using them. There is also more opportunity for direct involvement of the children with the materials, and there is more room left for them to express their intentions and feelings (their own, personal, creative selves), because they are not caught up in how to use the materials to such a marked degree. Because they are so satisfying, these materials can be offered over and

TABLE 14–1
Developmentally Appropriate Self-Expressive Activities

Two-Year-Olds	Three-Year-Olds	Four-Year-Olds
Easel Painting		
Twos like to experience using brushes, paint, and paper. First offer primary colors. Twos sometimes use only one color and often like to cover the entire sheet with a rich-looking mass of color. Experimentation with materials is an important facet.	Threes often experience some of the same things as twos, except that they may have an idea of what they intend to paint or may name it afterward when it looks like something. Threes appreciate some variation, such as different-sized brushes.	Older fours often have definite ideas of what to paint. They also like to use different types of brushes, textures of papers, shapes of paper, and a selection of many colors, and they enjoy mixing their own paints.
Finger Painting		
Twos work mostly with starch and paint on paper. They smear and spread paint, enjoying large-muscle movements. They sometimes watch a long time before beginning.	Threes can be encouraged to appreciate the possibility of making designs with their fingertips, palms, and so forth.	Fours enjoy variations in finger painting, as well as appreciating the possibility of making designs. Thick starch, negative prints from painting done on tables, or interesting scents such as vanilla or peppermint flavoring may be added to create variety.
Sponge Painting		
Twos tend to use sponge painting in the same way as finger painting. They squeeze paint out of the sponge and smear it on the paper — they do not grasp the concept of printing with a sponge.	Some threes will smear paint just as the twos do, but others will take time to make a sponge print.	Fours may take a conscious, active interest in the design they are creating. They deliberately experiment with using the sponge in different ways, such as dabbing lightly and pressing down hard.

My thanks to Cleavonease Johnson, head teacher, retired, Santa Barbara City College Children's Center.

over again, *and they should constitute the mainstays of the creative, self-expressive curriculum in the preschool.*

Column 2 also offers some valuable activities for preschoolers, typically the older ones in the school. However, these kinds of activities might be characterized as being more craftlike than creative. They generally require more skill on the part of the children and more instruction (at least initially) by the teacher. They tend to have more of a definite focus and direction, even though the teacher may meticulously avoid providing an actual model. Considerable latitude is allowed for individual ideas to be expressed (e.g., children might be left free to arrange their flowers in the May baskets any way they wish or to stamp the Christmas paper in any pattern that appeals to them), but they do restrict freedom of expression more than the Column 1 materials do. To be successful, these materials usually require repeated presentation so that the children can practice and gain skills in their manipulation,

TABLE 14–2
Creative Potential of Self-Expressive Activities

Column 1: Greatest Potential	Column 2: Medium Potential	Column 3: Very Limited Potential
Easel Painting (and its variations)		
Using materials as child wishes, provided she follows simple rules for positive social behavior, such as not painting her neighbor's picture or dripping paint on the floor. (Experience is varied by using several shades of same color, different-sized brushes, painting to music, and so on.*)	Painting in ways that allow less control by child, such as string painting, blowing paint around with straws, dropping food coloring on damp paper towels. Painting an object the child has made. Opportunities for genuine self-expression are sharply reduced because child cannot control the medium and express her own feelings and ideas.	Painting or coloring in coloring books or work sheets. Copying something the teacher has made, such as a sun, stick figure, or house.
Finger Painting (and its variations)		
Finger painting as it is usually presented. (Experience is varied by presenting different textures of paint, a variety of colors, and so on.)	Foot painting, because it requires sitting down and needs careful control to avoid slipping. Taking "negative" prints from tabletop finger paintings.	I cannot think of an example. One teacher commented that teachers are usually so busy helping the children "set up" that they do not have time to think up more managing strategies.
Drawing		
Drawing with simple materials such as chalk, crayons, soft pencils, crayon "relief," chalk with starch, or felt-tip pens.	Child encouraged to illustrate an experience, such as a previous field trip.	Drawing around stencils of animals, circles, triangles, and so forth. Using coloring books or duplicated worksheets, keeping carefully within the lines.
Dough Play		
Manipulating dough as child wishes and as an emotional release. (Variety is provided by many different kinds of doughs, colors, etc.)	Selecting whatever cookie cutters he wishes to make Christmas ornaments, decorating them as he desires with red and green felt-tip pens.	Making an ashtray according to a model provided by the teacher. Following a recipe for making biscuit dough.

*For more variations, refer to discussions of individual materials later in this chapter.

298

Column 1: Greatest Potential	Column 2: Medium Potential	Column 3: Very Limited Potential
Collage Making Child chooses from assortment of materials. (Teacher encourages child to consider qualities of design by asking what he thinks would look good together. Infinite variety is available in this medium through use of different materials and collage bases.)	Collage making centered on a theme — seaweed, shells, and sand after a visit to the beach; cotton balls, colored crushed egg shells, and Easter grass on lavender paper at Easter.	Cutting out pictures at the teacher's behest of all the chairs the child can find in a magazine and pasting them in a scrapbook. Gluing precut eyes, nose, and mouth on a precut pumpkin head.
Dancing Dancing freely as the music suggests or feelings dictate.	Participating in movement education activities — "How many ways you can you . . .?"	Folk dancing.
Puppet Play Using puppets just to "fool around with" and to express feelings.	Making up a story together and using puppets to present it after considerable practice.	Presenting a puppet play of a well-known story, such as "The Three Bears."
Woodworking Using different kinds of wood, nails, and so forth. (Technical advice is provided when necessary, but children are left free to use materials as they wish, provided that safety is observed.)	Making an airplane or boat at the teacher's suggestion with no model provided and materials chosen by child. (Advanced tools are provided that require considerable teacher instruction and supervision for successful use. As skill is gained, this activity probably moves over to Column 1.)	Nailing together a precut birdhouse or shoeshine kit.
Unit Block Play Playing with blocks that are available and well sorted and with accessories that are brought out at child's request or with several different kinds of accessories that are available on nearby shelves for selfselection.	Playing with rubber zoo animals that are deliberately set out after trip to children's zoo to provide focus for play.	Teacher setting up cages made of blocks with animals inside them after a trip to the zoo and encouraging children to do likewise.

yet they are frequently offered as only "one-shot" deals. They are valuable because they provide opportunities for purposefulness and challenges to skill that children appreciate. They also increase the variety of experience often needed desperately in full day centers.

Column 3 presents activities at the restricted end of the creative continuum. The advantages of offering these kinds of activities are that they teach children to follow directions, to conform, and to learn something the teacher has decided is valuable for them to learn (such as being able to discriminate between which furniture belongs in a living room and which belongs in a kitchen or how to coil clay to make a bowl like the teacher's).

I would be the first to agree it is necessary for children to learn how to follow directions. However, this kind of activity is all too often passed off as being creative by teachers who do not grasp the difference between *creating* something and *making* something. Such an activity may be creative for teachers who invent the instructional idea, but it offers children almost no latitude for expressing their own responses, ideas, and feelings and hence should not be thought of as providing opportunities to develop their creative selves.

Gaspar (1995) sums it up well when she says, "Many 'art projects' are really fabrication activities. Children enjoy copying and constructing, and there can be other developmental or educational value as well as their enjoyment. *However, it may be helpful for teachers to clarify which type of experiences they have designed for children in order to understand if their students are getting art experiences or copying and fabrication activities*" (p. 46, Gaspar's italics).

A Note About Expense

Throughout this book, suggestions are included about ways to save money while presenting a first-rate curriculum for the children. Nowhere is it more important to know how to stretch money than in the area of self-expressive activities, be-

Children benefit from many opportunities to try out techniques for themselves.

cause children can use up materials faster than the blink of an eye when they are involved in creative endeavors. For this reason, teachers need to develop their scrounging instincts.

The problem I have noticed is the way materials seem to pile up in an unsorted mess once they are collected. The most practical remedy (in addition to having adequate space for storage) is to take 5 minutes at the beginning of every staff meeting for everyone to sort out what has accumulated and toss it into the appropriate containers.

Table 14–3 lists a number of sources for free materials, and additional economy measures are also included with many of the discussions on materials in the rest of this chapter. Following these suggestions will help keep expenses down while providing the children with the plentiful amount of materials they require.

TABLE 14–3

Money Stretchers: Sources of Free or Almost Free Materials for Self-Expressive Activities

Materials	Sources
Empty ribbon rolls for wood gluing	Gift wrapping section of department stores
Wood shavings for collage	Scrap piles at building sites or cabinet shops
Scrap suede and leather pieces for collage	Leather stores
Boxes, large styrofoam pieces, and all sorts of things for construction	Trash bins of department and discount stores
Computer paper for coloring if the school uses crayons	Some computer places have reams of printouts used on one side — worthless paper (to them)
Empty fabric boards for large bases for group collages	Textile stores
Natural materials — bark, cones, seeds, leaves, dry flowers	Back yards (particularly in the fall) and hiking trails
Driftwood for collage	Beaches after a storm
Plastic and wood scraps for collage and woodworking	Plastic plants for trimmings, cuttings, and tubing; cabinetmakers
Five-gallon ice cream cartons for storage and for collaged wastebaskets as gifts	Ice cream stores
Rug scraps cut up to make wonderful textures for collage	Trash bins of carpet stores
Packing materials, including styrofoam, spongy materials, and excelsior for texture in collage and sheets of cardboard for collage bases	Electronic supply houses, china shops, and so on
Rolls from paper towels and toilet paper for glued constructions	Families' throwaways
Coated, colored bits of wire as accessories for wood construction and for collage	Telephone company (call public relations department)
Wood scraps for woodworking and gluing	Construction sites, cabinet shops, frame shops
Packing materials and large pieces of styrofoam for sawing	Hospitals, television stores, and electronic supply houses
Ends of newsprint rolls for easel paper and murals	Newspaper offices (may be a slight charge)
Wallpaper sample books for collage bases and as sources of interesting textures and colors for collages, stamping, and so on	Paint and wallpaper stores
Naugahyde and fabric samples; quite different textures from ordinary material	Upholsterers
Free "art" paper — usually small, various colors and textures	Print shops
Mat board for mounting poetry, or as collage bases; comes in lovely colors	Frame shops — cutouts from picture mats

TABLE 14–3
continued

Materials	Sources
Greeting cards and used gift wrapping for collage	Families' throwaways
Molded cardboard packing from apples, peaches, and pears, cut up to make interesting shapes for collage — smells heavenly	Markets on days fruit is unpacked
Styrofoam meat trays for sewing and for collage bases	Supermarkets and families' discards
Aluminum pie pans and TV dinner plates for glue	Families' throwaways
Plastic bottles for water play (wash thoroughly before using)	Beauty salons and homes
Egg shells, dried, crushed, and dyed, for collage, especially at Eastertime	Ask families to save.
Boxes, cotton, and packing materials for collage (do not use medicine bottles)	Pharmacies
Plastic tubing and containers for water play and boxes	Hospitals have portions of disposable, one-use items that were not used in patient care and would be discarded otherwise; nurses are wonderful sources.
Corks for collage and science experiments	Restaurants
Shingle scraps for collage bases	Houses under construction

Recommendations for Using Self-Expressive Materials to Foster Creativity

Easel Painting

One of the classic materials in almost all nursery schools and children's centers is the easel with its offering of tempera paint. Children of all ages enjoy this activity, and there are numerous ways to provide enough variety to sustain interest throughout the year.

Presentation of the Material
Needed equipment includes mixed paint, small containers for paint that fit the easel tray as nearly as possible, brushes, paper, a bucket, sponges and towels for washing hands, aprons, and a felt-tip pen for labeling the paintings.

Sometimes teachers like to start with only the three primary colors (red, blue, and yellow) in the fall and then add others in the second month or so. Large newsprint paper is best so that the children have plenty of scope to paint, and soft, floppy camel-hair brushes allow the children to swoop about the paper most freely. The stiff, flat kind of brush makes it harder to produce wavy lines. Although mixing paint in large quantities saves teachers time, the children enjoy making it so much, and this is so educational for them to do that mixing a fresh batch each day with one or two children helping stir is generally better. A surprisingly large amount of tempera is needed in relation to the quantity of water to make rich, bright, creamy paint; thus, it is best to dump the tempera into a pint container first and then add water bit by bit. Instead of water, some teachers prefer using liquid starch because it thickens the paint mixture. However, it does increase the expense. It is helpful to add a dash of liquid detergent, since this makes cleaning up easier.

A couple words of caution: Some blue paints smell like rotten eggs if mixed in advance, so it is best to mix blue fresh each day. Also, the use of a small electric hand mixer expedites paint mixing but is best used by the teacher before the children arrive.

Fruit juice cans make good paint containers, but only small amounts of paint should be poured in them at a time because many children put the same brush in different containers, which gradually turns all the colors dark gray. It is often necessary to cut off the wooden tips of the brushes because the tall handles get in the way of painting, they make it easier to tip the cans over, and they are hard for young children to handle. It is also helpful to stuff the empty end of the easel holder with newspaper to keep the cans from falling over. I do not favor the use of those lunch-size milk cartons for paint holders, unless the tops are cut off so that the children can see the color of the paint more easily. These containers also encourage some teachers to seal the spout and save the paint, which is generally of a questionable color, for the next day—a poor economy measure, in my opinion.

It will expedite matters if several pieces of paper are clipped to the easel at once. Many teachers prefer to write the child's name and date on the back of the paper to avoid the problem of having him paint over it. If a developmental portfolio is kept at school for each child, dating a few paintings and saving them delights parents at conference time because it enables them to see how the child's skills have developed during the year.

Cleanup

Children often enjoy helping clean up this activity. They can spend considerable time squeezing

*Hopefully this teacher is **not** asking, "What is it?"*

the colored, soapy water through sponges, wiping off easels and aprons, and so forth.

Economy Measures

Putting a small amount of paint in a can at a time is one way to avoid waste. Ordering paint in quantity once a year is another way to make money go as far as possible, and if schools combine their orders, sometimes an even lower cost per can is offered. Children should be taught some practical techniques for handling paint to avoid waste, such as wiping the brush on the edge of the can and returning paintbrushes to the same color paint each time. (There is a difference, however, between teaching children enabling techniques like these and limiting their ideas by suggesting what they should paint.)

Some Suggested Variations of Easel Painting

- Use a number of shades of one color.
- Use colored paper—colored newsprint comes in pastel shades, or the backs of faded construction paper can be used.
- Use the same color of paint with same color of paper.
- Use black and white paint (fun at Halloween).
- Use colors that are traditionally associated with the particular holiday season.
- Use various sizes of brushes, or both flat and floppy ones, with the same colors of paint.
- Paint objects the children have made in carpentry or paint dried clay objects.
- Paint large refrigerator-type boxes.
- Work on a long piece of paper together to produce murals.
- Paint the fence with water and large brushes.
- Draw firmly on paper with crayons and paint over it to produce "crayon resist" art.
- Paint with undiluted food coloring (this is expensive but lovely).
- Use all pastel colors (start with white and add color a bit at a time when mixing).
- Use cake watercolors (teach children to wash brush before changing colors).
- Cut paper into various shapes—leave a hole in the middle or cut it like a pumpkin, a heart, a Christmas tree, and so forth.
- Set up a table with many colors of paint and encourage the children to select the colors they prefer.
- Paint to music.

Finger Painting

Jean Stangl (1975) summarizes the value of finger painting very well:

> One cannot measure the satisfaction finger painting brings to the child who is tense, timid, autistic, shy, fearful, aggressive or hyperactive. It allows the child to get involved. It requires no help or skill, there is no fear of competition and the student is always successful. (How can the lesson fail?) Finger painting enables the individual to explore, to experiment, to be imaginative and creative, to be expressive and to get rid of many frustrations. It provides an opportunity for growth in self-confidence by allowing the student complete control over the paint. (pp. 4–5)

Finger painting seems to produce feelings of joy and peace more than any other activity. Thus, teachers should offer it frequently, even though cleanup is somewhat time-consuming.

Methods of Presentation

The quickest, simplest way to make finger paint is to combine liquid starch with dry tempera. This may be done by pouring a generous dollop of starch onto the paper and then sprinkling it with dry tempera. Alternatively, some teachers like to stir the dry pigment into an entire container of

Finger painting—a sensory delight!

starch base. However, I prefer to put spoonfuls of various plain bases onto the paper and then shake on whatever colors the children desire. No matter how the paint is originally prepared, teachers need to be ready to add more ingredients as the children work. The results to strive for are rich, brilliant color and sufficient paint to fill the paper completely if the child so wishes. Table 14–4 provides a number of pretested finger-paint recipes.

Needed materials include *waterproof* aprons (old shirts are not satisfactory because they al-

low paint to soak through onto the children's clothing), large sheets of glazed finger-paint paper, starch or some other medium to carry the color, pigment (either tempera or food color), and buckets of soapy water, sponges, and towels for cleanup.

Helping Children Who Feel Uncomfortable Enjoy the Experience

Although reluctant children should not be pressured unduly to participate in finger painting,

TABLE 14–4
Tested Finger-Paint Recipes

Method	Comments
Standard Finger Paint *	
Pour a puddle of liquid starch on glazed paper that is sufficient to cover it when spread, and shake on 1 to 2 tablespoons dry tempera to make a rich bright color. It may be necessary to add more starch or color as the children finger paint. Add more than one color in separate corners so children can enjoy blending them.	This is the quickest and easiest way to prepare finger paint. It dries dull and does not flake off. Liquid starch is somewhat costly. Try out the brand before buying a lot of it — a few off-brands curdle and are not satisfactory.
Cornstarch Finger Paint	
Dissolve ½ cup cornstarch in 1 cup cold water. Pour mixture into 3 cups boiling water (it thickens suddenly). Stir constantly until shiny and translucent. Allow to cool and use as finger-paint base, adding whatever color the children desire, or put in jars and stir in tempera or food coloring. This cornstarch recipe does not store particularly well. Recipes that *do* keep several days without caking are given below.	This is the least expensive form of finger-paint base to make and is very satisfactory. It feels slick, spreads well, and is not sticky. If it is colored with food coloring, it should be stored in the refrigerator. *It can only be kept 1 or 2 days* before caking occurs and is best used the day it is made. This paint has an attractive "clear" but not shiny look when dry provided it is used when fresh. It also works well when mixed with tempera.
Easy-to-Store Finger Paint 1	
Combine 2 cups water and ½ cup cornstarch, and boil until thick, stirring constantly. Add 1 cup Ivory Snow and coloring (if desired), cool, and use.	The addition of soap makes the base appear slightly curdled; material feels creamy when spread. Paintings, when dry, are dull and rich looking. Can be kept several weeks without refrigeration. Soap makes the cleanup easy.

Thanks to Cené Marquis, head teacher, Institute of Child Develpment, for retesting these recipes.

*Ready-made, premixed finger paint is also available for purchase but is generally too expensive to use as frequently as the children need it.

TABLE 14–4
continued

Method	Comments
Easy-to-Store Finger Paint 2	
Dissolve 1 cup cornstarch in 1½ cups cold water. Soak 2 envelopes plain unflavored gelatin in an additional ½ cup water. Add cornstarch mixture quickly to 4 cups hot water. Cook over medium heat, stirring constantly, until mixture is thick and glossy. Blend in gelatin and 1 cup powder detergent until dissolved. Store in refrigerator. This makes a whiter base than the other recipes do.	This recipe seems like a lot of trouble, but if you need one that keeps, this is it! It cleans up easily because of so much detergent in it.
Thicker Finger Paint (modified Rhoda Kellogg recipe)	
Combine 2 cups flour with 2 teaspoons salt; beat in 3 cups cold water with rotary egg beater. Add 2 cups hot water, and boil until mixture looks shiny. (Start it on low heat to prevent lumping.) Stir in 2 tablespoons glycerine. (The glycerine prevents this heavy mixture from being too sticky to spread and use easily.)	Use of dry laundry starch makes a thicker paint, but because it is often hard to find, try this recipe instead. If food coloring is used with this (and it takes a lot to make it bright), it eventually dries shiny. Tempera is also satisfactory. This paint is thick and takes a long time to dry, but it looks rich.
Soap Finger Painting	
Ivory Snow works well. Simply add water gradually while beating with a rotary egg beater until mixture is light and fluffy. Children enjoy making this as well as using it.	This mixture often appeals to children who resist getting their hands in "dirty" paint. It is best to use it directly on a plastic tabletop. Scrape it up and reuse it as different children want a turn. If it is used on paper, it flakes off as it dries and is very messy. It is lovely when tinted in pastel tones with food coloring. It cleans up more easily if vinegar is added to the cleanup water. Dispose of soap mixture by flushing it down the toilet or putting it in the garbage (it clogs sinks). Material turns slimy if kept.
Shaving Cream	
This can be used by several children if squirted on a plastic tray.	Shaving cream feels and smells nice, though it is expensive. When dry, it is dull and flakes off easily.

those who are uneasy about getting their hands "dirty" can often be induced to try soap painting. This is a variation of finger painting using Ivory Snow whipped with a rotary beater until light and fluffy. It is best presented as tabletop painting rather than paper painting because it cracks and flakes as it dries, and parents do not welcome getting this all over their cars on the way home from school.

Children who are wary of becoming involved in such a messy activity also need plenty of opportunity just to stand and look, plus the assurance that they can wash the paint right off whenever they want to. For these youngsters, teachers should avoid using permanent colors, such as purple or orange. Occasionally, a very shy child, who seems torn between wanting and not wanting to participate, is willing to begin by placing his hand on top of the teacher's as she paints. However, most children find this expressive medium irresistible—and teachers need only to make sure that the children are clad in waterproof aprons before they plunge in.

Economy Measures

There are a few noteworthy ways to save money on materials for finger painting. Because finger-painting paper is expensive, teachers may wish to substitute butcher paper, which also has a special finish (but does soak through faster than finger-painting paper does). Because it comes in rolls, butcher paper has the added advantage of being any size the teachers wish to cut. (It is also available in a number of beautiful, bright colors if the budget is liberal.) Painting directly on a plastic tabletop or large tray makes paint go further, requires less restriction of the children than painting on paper does, and can be very satisfying for children to clean up with lots of soapy sponges and warm water.

In addition, it is much less expensive for teachers to make their own paint than to buy it ready-made. To prevent waste, they should shake on the tempera themselves rather than allowing the children to do this, though the children should be allowed to select the colors that they prefer. On the other hand, teachers should *not* economize by using small sizes of paper and insufficient quantities of base and tempera. The purpose of finger painting is to encourage deep, sensual, expressive pleasure in rich, bright, large, free painting. *Skimpy, restricted dryness of the paint should be avoided at all costs.*

Additional Drawing Materials: Chalk, Crayons, Felt-Tip Pens, and Pencils

Teachers should not overlook the potential of chalk, crayons, pencils, and felt-tip pens, which are two-dimensional materials requiring fine-muscle activity, although these do require practice for successful use. All of them have the advantage of being easy to get out and clean up, and at the end of a long day this is important. Unfortunately, in a few schools they are the only expressive mediums readily available to the children, and this is certainly undesirable.

Sometimes teachers have unrealistic expectations about the drawing and writing abilities of young children. Table 14–5 provides a helpful list of what children at different ages can produce in the way of shapes and forms.

Are Ditto Sheets Creative?

Sometimes teachers succumb to the use of mimeographed materials, which one of my friends terms, quite aptly, "dictated art." Even though children are often permitted to use whatever colors they wish, such experiences are almost bound to stress staying within the lines, coloring in only one direction to "make it pretty," and using preselected subject matter. The result is a lesson in conformity, not in exploring one's own ideas and feelings and putting these down on paper.

I have heard beleaguered teachers say desperately that they hate using dittos but that the parents expect it. My guess is that parents expect dittoed work sheets because that is what they recall from their own early schooling experiences. I have found that once teachers explain the educational value of self-expression and originality and also what constitutes developmentally appropriate activities for preschool children, families no longer desire the mimeographed materials.

Chalk

Chalk is inexpensive and comes in pretty colors. Its most typical use is with blackboards, but little children do not seem to use it very effectively there. They do better if allowed to mark on the sidewalk with it—perhaps because the rougher texture of the cement more easily pulls the color off the stick, and the children seem more able to

TABLE 14–5
Developmental Continuum in Children's Drawings

Preschool (ages 2–5)

- Scribbles, loops, zigzags, wavy lines, jabs, arcs—often partially off the paper at first
- Chance forms or shapes
- Trying out different effects
- Meaning in the act itself, not in results or product
- Experimenting with leaving a mark, with colors and motions to leave a sign or have an effect
- Reflecting motion of hand/arm
- Separate lines, circlelike shapes, combined straight and curved lines
- Other basic forms, controlled marks, first schematic formulae, mandalalike shapes

Sources: Physical act of moving a hand and arm, basic concepts such as the circle, exploration of possibilities of line

Early Primary (ages 4–6)

- Shapes combined, becoming schemas; intentional image repetition of schemas; development of preferred schemas
- Beginnings of representation, often of people; letterlike forms; basic forms represented consistently—houses, flowers, boats, people; animals in profile
- Meaning (subject matter) increasingly readable
- Repertory or symbolic forms repeated, practiced, and new elements added
- Beginnings of individual style (e.g., typical way of drawing a house)

- Figures isolated, no context or baseline; each discrete (no overlapping of whole or of parts); size and details according to perceived importance or interest (e.g., long arms)
- Several figures on the page; beginning representing of events or narratives; schematic figures placed in a larger concept, for example, knowing an elephant is a four-legged animal with a trunk, the child uses a well-established routine, or schema, for drawing animals—cats, dogs, and so forth—and adds a trunk

Sources: Child's concepts and knowledge about the world, which take precedence over direct perception

Middle Primary (ages 5–8)

- Elaboration and variation of schematic figures and experimentation; repetition of imagery, practicing "set pictures" (always drawn the same way), such as racing cars
- Details often traditional or formulaic, such as windows with tie-back curtains, chimneys with smoke coming out at an angle, girls defined by skirts and long hair
- Narrative, illustrative, inventive; baselines often multiple; "see-through" houses; most figures in own space, without overlapping

Sources: Copying conventional renderings by other children, imagination, book illustrations, TV, cartoons, and so on

---

Note. From *Considering Children's Art: Why and How to Value Their Work* (p. 35) by B. S. Engel, 1995, Washington, DC: National Association for the Education of Young Children.

tell what they are doing as they squat down and draw. It is, of course, necessary to explain to them that they may "write" with chalk only on special places.

Chalk is also available in larger squares in a range of marvelous colors (be sure not to pur-

chase oil pastels, which are beautiful but will not wash away). These can be used with rough paper and a liquid starch base for an interesting variation halfway between finger painting and drawing. Buttermilk is also recommended by many teachers as being a good liquid base to use with this medium on rough paper. Liquid tends to seal the chalk, so teachers must rub it occasionally on a piece of old sandpaper to break this seal so the color will continue to come off readily.

Crayons and Nonpermanent, Nontoxic Felt-Tip Pens

Crayons are much more economical than pens (and who has not felt the thrill of pleasure over a new box of these), yet pens do come in beautiful clear colors. Compared with paint, they have the additional advantage of staying bright and unsullied until the children use them up.

Most schools set out crayons or pens jumbled together in a basket, but Harms (1972) recommends that they be kept assembled in separate boxes so that each user has an individual set. This cuts down on arguments and means that all the colors are available as the children require them. The use of thick crayons is general practice in preschools because they do not break as easily as thin ones do and, theoretically, because they are easier for children to hold. It is my opinion, however, that thinner crayons are probably easier to hold and manipulate. Perhaps preschool teachers should offer both varieties or try both out and decide for themselves.

Pencils

These require careful supervision. Children must not be allowed to run around with them, for they are somewhat dangerous. Previously our center did not offer them at all, until it became apparent that some of our children had almost no experience with them at home. Since they are widely used in kindergarten, it was evident that the children needed practice with them, so we have added them to the curriculum. For maximum success, teachers should purchase pencils with rich, soft lead cores and instruct children on the rules about where these can and cannot be used.

Printing and Stamping

Printing and stamping have some value in helping children develop a sense of design and understand cause-and-effect relationships, but the materials of these activities do not allow as much latitude for creative self-expression as other forms of self-expressive materials do. Nevertheless, information is presented here because so many questions are asked about how to use them effectively.

Several kinds of stamps are simple enough for little children to use, although any printing that involves paint is likely to change into finger painting as it smears—an indication of what the children would probably prefer to do. Commercially made rubber stamps work well with ink pads of various colors. Cookie cutters dipped in shallow paint trays print without distortion and can be used to stamp paper for various holiday events. Bits of sponges cut into different shapes can also be used effectively to create stamped designs. Clothespins make nice handles for these when clipped to one end of the sponge. Potato stamps can also be dipped in shallow paint and used for printing. These seem to work best if the design is incised very deeply rather than cut out. The best potato stamps I have seen were carved like pumpkins, with the features dug deeply into the round potato surface. It is a lot easier to use a pumpkin cookie cutter.

For those teachers who are feeling brave, here are some instructions for a more elaborate printing technique.[1]

Steps for Printing

Step 1: Squeeze some Speedball ink on the pane of glass (about as much as the amount of toothpaste you would use to brush your teeth, or an inch-long ribbon). Roll it with a brayer in several directions until it sounds sticky. This means the ink is thoroughly distributed and will print well.

---

[1] From *Foxtails, Ferns and Fish Scales* by Ada Graham, Four Winds Press. Copyright © 1976 by Ada Graham. Reprinted by permission of JCA Literary Agency, Inc.

Step 2: Take your leaf, flower, or grass and place it on the inked glass. Cover with a piece of scrap paper and press it into the ink.

Step 3: Lift the leaf and place it on the paper you wish to print. Cover the leaf with a sheet of clean paper. Follow the outline of the leaf through the paper with your fingers, pressing on the stem and veins and following them out to the edges. Lift the top paper and the leaf and examine print.

Aids: If your print is too dark and you cannot see the veins and outline, it means you had too much ink on the glass. Try printing it again. If the print is too faint and the veins and outlines do not show up, the leaf was not inked thoroughly.

If this technique is too advanced, Speedball ink can also be rolled out on the glass and children can place their hands on the inked surface and then make handprints on scraps of mat board acquired from frame shops. These make striking, personalized gifts on holidays. The ink can be wiped off their hands with vegetable oil.

Dough and Clay

As is true with finger painting, play with dough or clay offers direct contact with the material and provides particularly rich opportunities for the expression and relief of feelings as children push, squeeze, and pound. These materials are three-dimensional in effect, and clay, in particular, provides opportunities for "clean" smearing, which many children enjoy.

Suggestions for Making Dough

Children should participate in making dough whenever possible (the only exception being cooking the cornstarch mixtures, which become stiff so suddenly that they really require the teacher's strong arm and careful use of very hot materials). If allowed to help make the dough, children learn about measuring, blending, and cause and effect and also have the opportunity

to work together to help the school.

The doughs that require no cooking are best mixed two batches at a time in separate deep dishpans. Using deep ones keeps the flour within bounds, and making two batches at a time relieves congestion and provides better participatory opportunities. Tempera powder is the most effective coloring agent to add because it makes such intense shades of dough; adding it to the flour *before* pouring in the liquid works best. Dough can be kept in the refrigerator and reused several times. Removing it at the beginning of the day allows it to come to room temperature before being offered to the children; otherwise it can be dishearteningly stiff and unappealing. The addition of flour or cornstarch on the second day is usually necessary to reduce stickiness.

Variations

All the dough recipes in Table 14–6 have been carefully tested and are suitable for various purposes, as the comments explain. In preschool centers where process, not product, is emphasized, the dough and clay are generally used again and again rather than the objects made by the children being allowed to dry and sent home. For special occasions, however, it is nice to allow the pieces to harden and then to paint or color them. Two recipes are included in Table 14–6 that serve this purpose particularly well (Ornamental Clay and Baker's Dough).

Presenting Dough

Once made, dough is easy to get out and simple to supervise. Usually all the children have to remember is to keep it on the table and out of their mouths. It is a pleasant material to bring out toward the end of the morning or in late afternoon when children and teachers are tired and cleanup needs to be quick and easy.

For dough to be truly satisfying, children need an abundance of it rather than meager little handfuls, and they should be encouraged to use it in a manipulative, expressive way rather

TABLE 14–6
Tested Play Dough Recipes

Ingredients and Method	Comments
Basic Play Dough I [*]	
3 cups flour, ¼ cup salt, 6 tablespoons oil, enough dry tempera to color it, and about ¾ to 1 cup water. Encourage children to measure amounts of salt and flour and mix them together with the dry tempera. Add tempera *before* adding water. If using food coloring, mix a 3-ounce bottle with water before combining with salt and flour. Combine oil with ¾ cup water and add to dry ingredients. Mix with fingers, adding as much water as necessary to make a workable but not sticky dough.	Many basic recipes do not include oil, but using it makes dough softer and more pliable. It also makes it slightly greasy, and this helps protect skin from the effects of the salt. Dry tempera gives the brightest colors, but food coloring may be used instead if desired. Advantages of this recipe are that it can be totally made by the children, since it requires no cooking and it is made from ingredients usually on hand that are inexpensive. This dough stores in the refrigerator fairly well. It gets sticky, but this can be corrected by adding more flour. This is a good, standard, all-purpose, reusable dough. Others, listed below, are for special purposes and are nice to use for variety.
Basic Play Dough II [†]	
Combine 3 cups *self-rising* flour, 1 cup salt, 5 tablespoons alum (purchase at drug store), and 1 tablespoon dry tempera. Boil 1¾ cups water, add ⅓ cup oil to it, and pour over flour mixture, stirring rapidly. Use.	This dough is lighter and more plastic than the first one — feels lovely. It thickens as boiling water is poured in and cools rapidly so that children can finish mixing. It keeps exceptionally well in the refrigerator, oil does not settle out, and it does not become sticky — a paragon among doughs! Beautiful to use at Christmas, if colored with white tempera.
Basic Play Dough III [‡]	
Stir together 2 cups flour, 2 tablespoons cream of tartar, and ½ cup salt. Combine 2 cups water with 2 tablespoons oil, food coloring, and oil of cloves (if desired for scent). Combine wet and dry ingredients, stir, and cook over medium heat until it forms a ball.	This dough has an excellent texture and keeps well in the refrigerator.
Cooked Play Dough [§]	
Blend 1 cup flour, ½ cup cornstarch, and 1 cup water together to make a batter in top of double boiler. Boil 3 cups of water and 1 cup of salt together and pour it into cornstarch-flour mixture. Cook in double boiler until dough looks shiny and translucent, stirring firmly and constantly. Allow to cool enough so children can handle mixture, then stir in coloring. Gradually work in 3 to 4 more pounds (12 to 16 cups) of flour until of good handling consistency.	This is a resilient, springy dough, somewhat firm but not stiff, similar to commercial play dough in texture. Quantity is liberal for three or four children. Cooking must be done by adult because it gets very stiff quite suddenly and requires firm control of hot, slippery double boiler. This is a nice recipe because children can see and make the batter first and witness the dramatic change. It keeps well in refrigerator but does become firmer when chilled.

[*] From Santa Barbara City College Children's Center.
[†] Kindness of Sharon Brownette, California Preschool Program, Santa Barbara, California.
[‡] Kindness of Angie Dixon, parent of Dru Dixon, Institute of Child Development, 1984.
[§] Kindness of Barbara Berton, Happyland Preschool, Costa Mesa, California.

TABLE 14–6
continued

Ingredients and Method	Comments

Cornstarch Dough [II]

Mix thoroughly 1 cup salt, ½ cup cornstarch, and ¾ cup water to which food coloring has been added, and cook in a double boiler until thick and translucent. This happens suddenly, and it is very difficult to stir but worth it. Allow to cool to luke-warm on an aluminum pie plate.

This is one of the prettiest doughs I know. It sparkles while moist and resembles gumdrops! It has little grains of salt throughout so it feels mildly grainy but not unpleasant. For "gumdrop" effect, food coloring, *not* tempera, must be used. Quantity is sufficient for one child. It dries to a dull finish and does not break easily. Stirring *must* be done by an adult. It will keep overnight.

Ornamental Clay [¶]

Mix 1 cup cornstarch, 2 cups baking soda, and 1¼ cups water. Cook together until thickened, ei-ther in double boiler or over direct heat—*stir constantly.* When it is cool enough, turn it out and let children knead dough and make it into whatever they wish. If used for ornaments, make hole for hanging ornament while it is still moist.

This is a brilliant white dough that does well if dried overnight in an oven with pilot light on. It is quite strong when dry. If dried in air, it does not seem to be quite as strong. It has a kind of crisp though malleable texture when handled. Ideally it should be used same day it is made, preferably while still warm. If it is saved for next day, it can still be used, does not get sticky, but does become somewhat drier, crumbly, and a little stiff. It can be rolled very thin and cut with cookie cutters. Makes enough for one child or perhaps two, depending on what they do with it. When dry, it has a slight sparkle and is snowy white. It can be drawn on easily with felt-tip pens and is very lightweight if used for tree ornaments.

Baker's Dough [#]

Mix 4 cups flour, 1 cup salt, and 1 to 1½ cups water as needed to make dough nice to handle. Knead and handle as desired. Bake at 350°F for 50 to 60 minutes. Material will brown slightly, but baking at lower temperatures is not as successful.

This recipe makes enough for two or three children and keeps well in refrigerator. When baked, it becomes very light and very strong. It can be painted or drawn on with felt-tip pens to add color and requires no cooking, except for final baking if preservation is desired.

Thanks to Cené Marquis, head teacher, Institute of Child Development, for retesting these recipes (1984). Remember, flours vary. Adjustments, therefore, are sometimes necessary as dough is made. If too sticky, add more dry ingredients. If too dry, add more liquid.

[II] Modified from *A Curriculum for Child Care Centers* by C. Seefeldt, 1973, New York: Merrill/Prentice Hall.

[¶] Reprinted by permission of Doreen J. Croft (1967). *Recipes for Busy Little Hands*. Palo Alto, CA: Author.

[#] From *A Curriculum for Child Care Centers* by C. Seefeldt, 1973, New York: Merrill/Prentice Hall.

than in a product-oriented manner. For this reason, the usual practice of offering it with cookie cutters should be varied by offering it alone or only with rolling pins.

Cleanup

The cooked cornstarch recipes are the only ones that are particularly difficult to clean up because they leave a hard, dry film on the pan during cooking. However, an hour or two of soaking in cold water converts this to a jellylike material that is easily scrubbed off with a plastic pot scrubbing pad. If pans are soaked during nap time, the children will be quite interested in the qualities of this gelatinous material when they get up.

Other Molding and Modeling Materials

Potter's Clay

Potter's clay may be purchased at any art supply store in moist form. This is much easier to deal with than starting with dry powder. It is typically available in two colors, gray and terra cotta (terra cotta looks pretty but seems harder to clean up). Clay requires careful storage in a watertight, airtight container to retain its malleable qualities. When children are through with it, form it into large balls, press a thumb into it, and then fill that hole with water and replace in container.

Clay that is too soft for easy handling can be kneaded on a plaster "bat" board to remove excess moisture.

If oilcloth table covers are used, they can simply be hung up to dry, shaken well, and put away until next time. Formica-covered boards (sink cutouts left over from new counter tops) also make nice large surfaces to use with dough or clay.

Snow, Sand, and Mud

Remember that snow, sand, and mud also have modeling properties and that children enjoy forming shapes from these materials. In particular, do not overlook the real pleasure little chil-

dren take in making large snowmen, shoveling and hauling snow, and so forth. (See also the section "Using Mud, Sand, and Water to Relieve Tension" in chapter 11.)

Self-Expressive Materials Requiring Glue: Collage, Assemblage, and Wood and Box Gluing

Collage and assemblage (three-dimensional collage) offer the best available media in the center for helping children think about such qualities of design as the way colors, textures, and forms look when arranged together. For this reason, *collage should not be considered primarily a paper-on-paper experience*. Instead, it is best thought of as being a three-dimensional expressive experience that provides opportunities for children to become acquainted with innumerable materials and build their appreciation of and sensitivity to color, substance, and design.

Presentation

Collages and assemblages require a firm base of some sort for their construction. This can be anything from construction paper to large pieces of tree bark, scraps of wood shingles, meat trays, discarded mat board from frame shops, or bolt boards from fabric stores. The base should be large enough to allow plenty of space for the arrangement of materials; therefore, such picayune things as cottage cheese lids are unsuitable.

The only substance that really sticks well enough that it can be used to glue all kinds of collage is white glue. Though not cheap in any size, it is least expensive when bought in gallon jugs. It cleans up readily with hot water until it dries. After that, it is very difficult to remove, so be sure to clean up carefully when the collage experience is finished—and this includes wiping the neck of the glue bottle.

Children should be taught that glue is not paint (the use of brushes and its thick appearance encourage this notion) and that it should be used with care. It can be set out in flat, untippable TV dinner trays or in little, flat pans. Some schools use squeeze bottles, but these have to be watched closely and cleaned very carefully so they do not clog. Children should brush the glue onto the place where they want something to stick, but not all over the paper. An alternative to brushing is dipping the object to be glued lightly into a shallow pan of glue and placing it on the paper, but this tends to get fingers stickier and stickier!

Collage materials should be placed on a separate choosing table and sorted into shallow containers, such as baskets, so that the children can readily appraise the kinds of things that are available and consider how they will look when arranged together. Teachers can foster this awareness, particularly with older threes and fours, by asking them what they think would make an interesting contrast, what colors would be attractive together, and so forth. Children also should be encouraged to modify the materials to suit their needs. Perhaps they want to cut off just a snippet of styrofoam to use, or scrunch up a twist of tissue paper rather than leaving it flat, or bend a piece of wire to just the right shape.

Some Suggested Variations for Collage

The range of materials for collage is almost endless, and teachers should devote careful thought to selection of the materials presented together so that variety, contrast, and harmony are all present. The following are some possibilities for materials:

- All shades and colors of yarn, strings, ribbons, pipe cleaners, and colored wire
- All varieties of paper—corrugated, tissue, dull rough cardboard, old blotters, gilt papers from greeting cards, print shop papers, can labels, used gift wrapping papers, and so on
- Buttons of all sizes and colors
- Bottle caps and corks
- All forms of styrofoam packing (the white makes a nice contrast to other materials), including foam egg cartons

- Rock salt sprinkled on as the collage is completed for a snowy effect (can be colored by shaking it in a bottle with a little food color)
- All kinds of natural materials are exquisite— small pine cones, seeds, berries, leaves, twigs, bits of bone, bits of bark, small lustrous pebbles, feathers (though these can be difficult for small, gluey fingers), shells, pods, starfish, and so on
- Small tiles (require a strong collage base)
- Leather scraps and trimmings
- Spongy materials
- Wood chips and interesting wood shavings
- Netting and other see-through materials, such as cellophane, and old theatrical gelatins
- Beads from broken strings (colored beads make handsome accents)
- Cloth and wallpaper for adding patterns and textures—particularly fleeces, burlaps, velvets, and cloth and paper with interesting patterns
- Scraps and trimmings (such as rickrack), lace, and embroidery ends
- Colored glue with tempera for an interesting accent

The following are additional variations closely related to collage:

- Offer wood gluing, using styrofoam meat trays or roofing shingles to provide firm support. Painting or shellacking these later is a real pleasure and extends the experience for fours who can endure waiting for their constructions to dry before going on to the next step.
- Small boxes (hearing aid boxes and film boxes, for example), combined with other bits and pieces of things, provide satisfying, quick methods of "assemblage."
- Arrange flat materials such as bits of tissue paper between layers of waxed paper and iron. The melted wax intensifies the colors. The result can be taped to a window and can be quite beautiful.
- Use felt pieces of a flannel board for a more temporary kind of collage. Many children like to do this, and it fosters an interest in design.

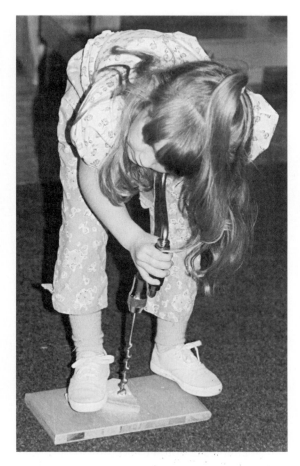

Encouraging girls to enjoy working with wood is particularly important because so many women are apprehensive about using such tools.

Woodworking

Some schools shun presenting carpentry, perhaps because some teachers have had little experience with woodworking tools and therefore think they are dangerous, but the activity is so satisfying for children that teachers should learn to use tools with care and competence so they can help children be successful, too. Women teachers who use tools in a confident, competent way provide good behavioral models for the children to emulate—models that may be par-

ticularly important for little girls who, in the past, have all too frequently been instrumentally incompetent in the area of woodworking.

Tools can be frustrating and tempers can mount as a result, so it is important to provide continual, attentive supervision for safety's sake. Teachers should be aware of children who are finding the activity too frustrating and offer help and encouragement in time to prevent explosions. As with the other self-expressive activities, it is possible to help children learn techniques in working with wood without restricting what they are creating with it.

Basic Tools

The most basic woodworking tools are hammers and saws. The hammers should be good, solid ones—*not* tack hammers. The saws should be crosscut ones so that they can cut with or across the grain of the wood, and they should be as short as possible. A well-made vise in which to place wood securely while sawing is invaluable. Preferably, there should be two of these, one at each end of the table. (C-clamps can be also used for this purpose and are less expensive, or a board can be nailed to the table while the child saws it, but this leaves the troublesome chore of removing the nails afterward.)

As the year progresses, additional tools should be added from time to time. A brace and bit are desirable (much better than "egg beater" drills, which are almost hopeless for little children to use); the brace and bit can be taken apart by the children, and different-sized bits can be inserted for variety. Rough and fine rasps and a light plane are also worthwhile. (Stanley Surform rasps are particularly good because they can be held with two hands and are very safe.) At our center, we have never had much luck using screws or screwdrivers. A general and important principle to remember is that, whatever tools are selected, they must be of good quality and really work. *Never* give children miserable little toy replicas; they are too unsatisfying to use.

Very young children enjoy sawing up the large pieces of styrofoam that come as packing for electronic equipment. Hammering into such material or into plasterboard is also quick and easy and does not require more force than twos and threes can muster. Older children need plentiful amounts of soft wood to work with. This is commonly available as scrap at construction sites and at some lumber mills. Cabinet shops are also good sources of wood; however, many of their scraps are hardwood and are more suitable for gluing than carpentry because they are too tough for children to saw through. Plywood is too tough and hard to be satisfying for children to manipulate. An old tree stump is great fun for children to pound countless nails into.

Some Suggested Variations for Woodworking

- Remember to vary the tools the children use as their skill (and self-control) increases.
- Purchase a variety of nails by the pound, not by the little box, from a hardware store. Children love an assortment of these. They can be set out in small foil pie plates to keep them from getting mixed up. Some schools nail these pie plates to a long board to prevent spilling.
- Offer various kinds of trims to go with woodworking, such as wire, thick colorful yarn, and wooden spools (with nails long enough to go through the spool).
- Offer round things for wheels, such as bottle caps, buttons, or the lids of 35mm film containers.
- Provide dowels of various sizes that will fit the holes made by the different sizes of bits.
- As previously mentioned, children like to paint what they have made, but this must be done another day or supervised by a second person because *it is vital to stay right beside the carpentry table at all times.*

Creative, Self-Expressive Dancing

Dancing offers another kind of self-expressive opportunity that is of great value in the lives of children. A full discussion of how to present a successful, free dance experience is included in chapter 9.

Fostering Pretend Play

No matter what else is discussed in relation to the various selves of the child, discussions of play keep cropping up in almost every chapter. This is because play is the great medium through which children learn and understand their world. In this chapter, once again, it is essential to talk about play to explain how it contributes to the development of the creative self. (The reader also may wish to review chapter 3 at this point.)

Benefits of Imaginative, Pretend Play

Creative, dramatic play provides limitless opportunities for children to imagine and pretend themselves into roles ranging from parents to babies to ogres to bears. Within a matter of minutes, their imaginations can transform a simple object such as a piece of wood into a little car, a baby bottle, a gun, or a bit of roof. Thus, imagination enables children to become in play what they cannot be in real life, and doing this exercises their intellects, since there is an obvious mental operation involved in substituting symbols for reality (Gowen, 1995; Piaget, 1962, 1976; Smilansky, 1991). Such play allows children to be masterful. It permits them to experiment with tentative solutions to problems, and it provides unparalleled opportunities for them to use their own ideas.

In their classic work, Sylva, Bruner, and Genova (1976) list some additional characteristics of play that are worth noting here because they apply particularly well to a discussion of the creative aspects of play. As they phrase it, "The essence of play is the dominance of means over ends" (p. 244)—a statement that certainly sounds familiar and comfortable to process-not-product devotees. Other characteristics of play cited by them include a lessening of the risk of failure and an increased "freedom to notice seemingly irrelevant detail" because people involved in play are less preoccupied with specific, focused tasks and so are more open to the world around them. Finally, the authors point out that play is voluntary and self-initiated; that

is, it comes from within the person. These qualities of freedom and self-initiation are what teachers wish to favor in creative play situations. The problem for beginning teachers is how to translate these high-sounding purposes into actual, down-to-earth practice. Fortunately, providing for such play need not be expensive, as Table 14–7 illustrates.

TABLE 14–7
Sources of Free or Almost Free Materials for Imaginative, Dramatic Play

Materials	Sources
Large appliance boxes for houses, markets, trains, or whatever; also nice for group painting projects	Appliance stores — kitchen, radio, and TV stores
Discarded furniture, cut down and repainted, for pretend-play corner — high chairs, small beds, and so forth	Attics, rummage sales, thrift stores
Sandbox and housekeeping equipment	Rummage sales, thrift stores; ask families to donate extras.
Telephones for promoting social interaction in play	Often on loan from public relations office of telephone company
Props for play, such as used envelopes, aged typewriters, pieces of hose, rope, discarded backpacks, hats of all descriptions	Families, paint stores, fast food places, workers, thrift stores, garage sales
Used gift wrappings— fun to use to play birthday party	Ask families to save.
Dress-up clothes—provide a good assortment of clothes for both sexes; add multiethnic touches if possible; cut garments down to reasonable size so children can move freely in them.	Ask families to save; garage sales, thrift shops.
Large outdoor blocks	Milk companies sometimes donate old cases; computer packers and shippers sometimes donate foam, packing blocks.
Crutches, braces, canes, blindfolds, ear plugs for hearing aids, and wheelchairs	Sometimes hospital rental supply places will donate worn equipment, or it can be borrowed temporarily.

Some Practical Ways to Encourage Imaginative, Creative Play

- Provide a background of actual experiences that may suggest possibilities for the children to pretend, such as a trip to a doctor's office.
- Provide plentiful equipment of the right kind (unstructured materials lend themselves to imaginative play most readily).
- Allow children to use this equipment in creative, possibly unconventional, but harmless ways to meet the needs of their play.
- Provide accessories to enhance play when children request them or to suggest a possible theme for play.
- Provide unusual rearrangements and juxtapositions of equipment to stimulate and extend play (combining the unit and hollow blocks, for example).
- Keep the play area appealing and the materials accessible.
- Most important of all, support but do not dominate the children's play by offering whatever assistance is necessary to continue or enrich it.

I have already used the housekeeping corner as an example of how a play area can foster social development and provide emotional relief (chapter 12, Table 12–2), so the following discussions will use hollow and unit blocks to illustrate how the practical principles for supporting creative play listed here can be put into practice in the preschool.

Unit Blocks

Unit blocks are those small hardwood blocks so dear to the hearts of children and so filled with potential for creative play. Designed by Caroline Pratt more than half a century ago, they remain one of the most enduring media for early childhood education. She described their value in comprehending the social world so clearly in the following paragraph that it is well worth quoting:

> I couldn't have asked for a more appropriate demonstration of my belief in the serious value of children's play. Michael was so deeply absorbed, so purposeful in his construction that he might have been a scientist working out an experiment in a laboratory. The likeness was no accident. He was precisely that, on his own level. He was not merely pushing blocks around: he was not even merely learning what could be done with blocks. With blocks to help him, he was using all his mental powers, reasoning out relationships—the relationship of the delivery wagon to the store, the coal cart loaded from the barge in the river and carrying its load to the home—and he was drawing conclusions. He was learning to think. (1948, p. 32)

Blocks are valuable because they suit the developmental needs and capabilities of a wide range of children, and they lend themselves to achieving large, spacious effects rather quickly. In imaginative play, unit blocks have another special quality that they share with models of animals and dolls. To use them for pretend purposes, children must project their imaginations even more than they do when involved directly in housekeeping play, because blocks are less structured. Table 14–8 includes many additional ways all the selves of the child may benefit from using this wonderful equipment.

Hardwood blocks are expensive but well worth the investment, and a children's center should add more every year, if at all possible, until they have a plentiful supply and a variety of shapes available. The various-sized blocks should always be multiples of each other to facilitate comprehension of mathematical concepts of equality and to make building with them more satisfactory. If new blocks are waxed with heavy-duty paste wax upon arrival, they will stay much cleaner and more appealing over the years.

A temporary set can be made from softwood with an electric saw, but unit blocks undergo such vigorous use that these softwood substitutes are not permanently satisfactory because they splinter and their corners get knocked off. In a real financial pinch, teachers can use flat-topped milk cartons or sealed detergent boxes for blocks rather than offer no blocks at all.

Presentation. *Unit blocks should always be stored, same size together, long side in view, on shelves—not in tubs or bins.* If they are dumped in bins, children cannot find just the size they want when they need it; they also have no opportunity to perceive the relationships between the different sizes.

If children are taught to build slightly away from the shelves, fighting and stress will be reduced as other youngsters try to reach in for blocks also. The construction area needs to be shielded from traffic to discourage children from delivering a kick at some treasured structure as they pass by, and it should be as large as possible and capable of being extended when necessary. A carpeted space is nice to use for this activity because it is warmer to kneel on while working and also quieter for play. The carpet has to be very flat and tight so that the blocks stand up easily.

According to Harriet Johnson (Provenzo & Brett, 1983), who wrote a classic pamphlet on block play, this kind of play progresses through a series of stages, beginning with simply carrying blocks around and progressing to stacking, simple bridging, and then to building enclosures with them. Following that, children begin to add decorative touches and also to use the structures for imaginative play. Ultimately they attempt to replicate actual buildings with which they are familiar (this stage is rarely seen at the preschool level).

I have visited many schools where I have seen unit blocks just sitting on shelves and not generally used by the children. Sometimes teachers even complain to me that the children have no interest in them. I suspect two reasons for this: the teachers have made such a chore of picking them up that the children have learned to avoid the area, or the children are unfamiliar with the joys of blocks, since many homes do not offer them, and the teachers do not know how to get such play started.

Getting Play Started. It often does require attention from the teacher to draw children into block play. One way of doing this is to use the "nest-egg" approach—perhaps setting out a few of the cars on the beginning of a road made of blocks or stacking up some of the blocks in an inviting way before the children arrive. This is not intended to provide a model for the children to copy but to attract them and prompt the beginning of their play.

The teacher who quietly pulls up a chair and sits near the block corner while keeping an eye on the room in general will also draw children to that area and can encourage the play with an occasional supportive comment or question. Drawing diagrams occasionally of their constructions (using carbon paper so that one copy can be kept in the portfolio as a developmental record and the other sent home) also stimulates such play. One school I know of even takes Polaroid shots of the children's work from time to time.

Tabletop blocks of various descriptions cultivate the use of smaller muscles, facilitate eye-hand development, and foster creative play, particularly if they are combined with little, plastic figures of animals and people. Lego toys, log-type blocks, and similar toys appeal to fours and fives, and Bristle Blocks can be used even with twos and threes because the pieces fasten together in such an easy, satisfactory way. Once again, it is important to have a large enough supply of these so that children can really build something with them and not run out of what they require.

Cleanup. The block area is much more appealing if blocks are not allowed to accumulate in a jumbled mess, so it makes sense that the children be encouraged to pick them up before leaving the area. Yet if this rule is enforced too rigidly or if the teacher refuses to help with the task, it certainly does discourage play. It seems better to strive for a general effect of tidiness without being disagreeable about it—thanking the children who do help and pitching in oneself to provide a good example. Children do not mind picking up so much if they can make a game of

TABLE 14–8
What Can Children Learn from Playing with Large and Unit Blocks?

Physical	Emotional	Social	Creative	Cognitive/Language
Encourages development of:	Encourages children to:	Encourages children to:	Encourages:	Encourages:
Eye-hand coordination	Play through emotional concerns	Share space	Use of imagination and pretend play	Use of symbols to replace reality (emergent literacy skill)
Fine-muscle control	Express feelings safely	Share resources	Generation of large, creative effects quickly	Use of comparison to determine same or different (matching — emergent literacy skill)
Large-muscle control	Relieve aggression safely (knocking blocks down)	Play together and co-operate (negotiate, bargain, wait, accept other people's ideas)	Problem solving ("If I can't build it this way, maybe I could . . .")	Conceptualization of ideas
Specific perceptual motor skills, such as stacking, grasping, lifting, shoving	Feel masterful because of potential for achieving large results quickly	Practice the art of persuasion	Generation of creative ideas in three-dimensional space	Use of language to explain ideas to others
Sense of spatial relationships	Exercise patience to try again when blocks collapse	Put their ideas of how social world operates into concrete form (highways, trains, houses, etc.)	Aesthetic pleasures of handling beautiful wood	Understanding principles of physics: balance, gravity, momentum, cause-effect
Following safety rules (stack blocks no higher than head, except for cardboard ones)	Feel delight with structures they build	Do meaningful work together (cleanup)		Understanding of mathematical/Piagetian concepts of equality — transitivity, conservation (4 is 4 no matter how blocks are arranged), reversibility
		Enlarge their gender roles (both girls and boys can build block structures)		Use of estimation ("How many blocks will it take to . . . ?")
				Planning what to build in advance (older children)

320

delivering the blocks to the shelves on trucks or shoving them over, train style, and they do experience satisfaction in getting them all marshalled neatly back in place.

Some Suggested Variations for Unit Block Play

- Widen the variety of shapes of blocks as the year progresses—include cylinders, pillars, and ramps, gothic arches, switches, and triangular blocks.
- Add cubical counting blocks; the touches of color these provide are exquisite.
- Use a dollhouse and furniture and dolls to go with it.
- Offer little cars and trucks.
- Provide a small wood train and tracks (a wonderful accessory for such play).
- Include additional transportation toys, such as boats and airplanes.
- Include wooden or rubber animals.
- Combine unit blocks with blocks of other kinds; they work well with both larger and smaller ones.
- Suggest that children incorporate tables into their block structures, particularly when combining them with smaller blocks.
- Offer the long boards as accessories.
- Move the block cases to other areas in the room; this often stimulates play by children who have not been attracted to them before.
- Remember that there is a tremendous variety of blocks (Provenzo & Brett, 1983), ranging from Bristle Blocks to Legos; all have their place in the playful, learning activities children enjoy.

Large Hollow Blocks and Boards

Simply nothing matches the value of boards and large hollow blocks for fostering creativity in play. Their manipulation requires children to involve both their minds and bodies together in a total way as they lug them about and hoist them into position. Their very nature and size suggest construction of structures large enough to play in when completed. Play periods should be long enough that there is time for this activity, as well as for actual building (Tegano & Burdette, 1991).

Hollow blocks are expensive and do require protection by using them either on carpeting inside or on grass or some other resilient material outdoors. (One center, e.g., uses artificial grass laid over cement as a cushioning surface to keep the blocks from breaking when they fall.) If used outdoors, they also require sanding and painting once a year with quick-drying lacquer, such as Deft, to preserve them.

Presentation. Once again, the nest-egg approach can prove useful as a starting point for large block play. The "egg" can be as simple as arranging four boards leaning against a few blocks to suggest a ramp or setting up a ladder to bridge two walls.

Providing accessories, such as ropes, lengths of hose, ladders and telephones, dolls, or housekeeping furniture, will also suggest possibilities and attract children. If the blocks are used in conjunction with other outdoor equipment, such as a boat, trikes, or a climbing gym, or are used around the sandbox to make a house, play in those areas will increase rapidly.

The teacher should be attentive to what is going on and be willing to serve as helper and supplier of needs rather than as dominator and controller of ideas. It facilitates play if such objects as sawhorses, hats, telephones, and old bedspreads are stored nearby so they can be produced at a moment's notice. To tell a child, "I can't get it right now—you'll have to wait until tomorrow," is unsatisfactory, since it is likely that the play will have moved on to something else by then.

Hollow blocks and boards should be used both indoors and out, because they generate different kinds of play when moved around (Cartwright, 1990). A nice, inexpensive large block that is satisfactory for use indoors where it is dry is the kind made of corrugated cardboard. Children can help assemble these and glue them closed, and a goodly supply can be obtained for a reasonable sum of money. Some computer firms also ship their products wedged between large blocks of spongy plastic (about 2 feet × 1½ feet × 1 foot). These make very light, surprisingly tough blocks.

Boards

Boards are one of the most useful and underrated pieces of equipment in a children's center. They should be made of ⅜- or ¾-inch all-weather plywood and cleated on the ends so that they hook safely over the edge of blocks and A-frames. They should be cut to fit other playground equipment when this exists. For example, it increases their usefulness if they hook across the bars of climbing gyms so that the children can use them to build floors within the gym for "tree houses."

Recently I have seen children use our set of boards in the following ways in their creative play: as an extension of the slide; as roofs for block structures; as decking on the row boat; as a network of roads on an elevated roadway; as a table in the sandbox; as part of an intricate, child-constructed obstacle course; as a ramp for climbing up to the A-frames; as a corral to keep bad horses out; and as a cage to keep bad lions in.

Boards are indispensable, and their usefulness is increased even more when sawhorses, barrels, tires, and large boxes are provided along with them. An adequate supply consists of 25 to 30 boards, of whatever two lengths adapt best to existing equipment. All it takes is one bake sale to raise enough money to purchase the wood and a handful of adults to cut, make, and finish them. The children's delight should be ample repayment for this effort.

Storage and Cleanup. Blocks and boards are cumbersome to move, although children are often of considerable help in doing this, particularly if they use a wagon. There are large, low carts made for this purpose, and if these materials must be stored far from the play area where they are used, such a cart can be a worthwhile investment. It is ideal to have the storage closet near a large, level area appropriate for large block play; it is also best to store the boards in racks, tray style, along one side of the storage wall rather than behind the blocks, so they will be used more freely. For added convenience, ladders can be hung on the wall also and sawhorses and A-frames stacked nearby.

Summary

Young children express their originality and creativity primarily through the use of self-expressive materials, imaginative play, and creative thought. This chapter discusses methods of fostering creativity by means of expressive materials and imaginative play.

Some general principles of teaching that foster creative self-expression include (a) maintaining a climate that encourages children to feel creative, (b) remembering that process is more important than product, (c) encouraging children to make choices, (d) interfering as little as possible with the children's creative activities but offering support and encouragement when necessary, (e) providing enough variety to the activities and keeping them developmentally appropriate, and (f) making certain that the activities are genuinely creative.

More specific recommendations related to the presentation of particular materials are presented for easel painting, finger painting, various drawing materials, printing and stamping, dough and clay, collage and assemblage, and woodworking. The chapter concludes with a discussion of the value of play as an imaginative, creative activity. It uses hollow and unit blocks to illustrate how to provide play opportunities that will enable children to make the best use of their creative powers.

Self-Check Questions for Review

Content-Related Questions

1. How is creativity usually expressed by young children?

2. Compare American and Reggian attitudes toward creativity by naming at least two differences in teacher attitudes.
3. The text lists six general principles that underlie successful presentation of most creative activities. Name what these are and explain why each is important.
4. What did Amabile and Gitomer find out in their research study on providing choices to children?
5. Select one of the self-expressive activities listed in Table 14–1 and describe how you would expect children of various ages to respond to it.
6. Imagine you are preparing to present easel painting or finger painting to the children in your group. How can you set it up most efficiently? What are some variations you could use to add variety to the experience? Answer the same questions for dough, collage, and woodworking.
7. Review the benefits of imaginative, pretend play for children, and use block play to illustrate some practical ways to encourage such play.
8. The principal of your school has asked you to explain why you want to purchase blocks for your classroom. Think of each of the child's five selves (physical, emotional, social, creative, and cognitive) and list at least two ways block play would help each of those selves develop.

Integrative Questions

1. The text points out there is a difference between suggesting that a child bear down on a brace and bit and telling her where to drill the hole. Please explain just what the difference is.
2. Refer to Table 14–2. What are the basic differences between Column 1, 2, and 3 activities? Which column provides the greatest opportunities for children to be creative? Why is this true?
3. What is the difference between *creating* something and *making* something? Explain how carpentry could be presented to fit either of these verbs.
4. Can you find examples of the principles for fostering creative play actually illustrated in the discussion on creative block play? Are all the principles there, or are some of them left out?
5. Suppose there was a child in your class who is very afraid of thunder and lightening. He has drawn a picture of a thunderstorm (consisting of purple and black patches and lots of little specks of black for raindrops). How could you honor the American value of using his painting to relieve his fears and also incorporate some of the cognitive values reflected in the Reggian Approach?

Questions and Activities

1. It is hard to really appreciate the individual merits of the dough recipes unless they are actually available for inspection and experimentation. As a class project, have volunteers make them up and bring them to class to try out.
2. As a class, brainstorm a list of "creative" activities appropriate for young children and then go back and decide whether they belong in Column 1, 2, or 3 of Table 14–2.
3. Suppose a bad fairy has waved her wand and ruled that you could only select three basic types of creative self-expressive activities to use for a whole year in your preschool. Which three would you select and why?
4. Suppose that same bad fairy has waved her wand again and now you are allowed to *purchase* only paint and glue (no paper, even!) for your creative curriculum. How limiting is this? What self-expressive activities would you actually be able to offer under these circumstances? How might you go about acquiring the necessary free materials to make them possible? Be specific.
5. Every community has its own special resources for free self-expressive materials. Gather these tidbits of information from members of the class and compile a resource list of these for everyone to use.
6. Copy some of the children's block constructions and ask the class to identify which developmental stage the construction represents.

References for Further Reading

Overviews

Amabile, T. (1989). *Growing up creative: Nurturing a lifetime of creativity*. New York: Crown. This delightful book is full of sensible recommendations of ways parents and teachers can foster creativity in children. *Highly recommended.*

Schirrmacher, R. (1997). *Art and creative development for young children* (3rd ed.). Albany, NY: Delmar. Schirrmacher's comprehensive approach deals with theory as well as practice. *Highly recommended.*

Seefeldt, C. (1995). Art—A serious work. *Young Children*, 50(3), 39–45. Seefeldt provides a good introduction to how graphic languages are used in the schools of Reggio Emilia for delight and enlightenment.

Self-Expressive Materials for Children with Disabilities

Anderson, F. E. (1994). *Art-centered education and therapy for children with disabilities*. Springfield, IL: Thomas. Preschool teachers will find the chapter on art adaptations for children with disabilities to be particularly helpful.

Spodek, B., & Saracho, O. N. (1994). *Dealing with individual differences in the early childhood classroom*. New York: Longman. This is a very good book about working with children who have special needs. The authors include a rare chapter on "Fostering Creative Expression" that covers movement education, music, and art.

Money Savers

Kohl, M. A. F., & Gainer, C. (1991). *Good earth art: Environmental art for kids*. Bellingham, WA: Bright Ring. Many of the creative ideas here use "trash" or recyclable materials. Each idea is coded according to appropriate age and includes variations. Activities are product oriented but could be used in freer approaches as well.

Drew, W. F. (1995). Tools for creative thinking: Recycled materials. *Scholastic Early Childhood Today*, 9(5), 36–43. Rather than listing specific materials, this article offers useful suggestions of places to find free/discarded items. *Highly recommended*.

Collections of Creative Activity Suggestions

Newcomers to the field of early childhood education should bear in mind that, when looking for resource books of creative activities, it is strictly buyer beware. Many so-called creative books are really collections of highly structured craft ideas that leave little or nothing to the child's imagination. The books included here are happy exceptions to this problem.

Bos, B. (1982). *Please don't move the muffin tins: A hands-off guide to art for the young child*. Roseville, CA: Turn the Page. Nicely illustrated, this book has many practical suggestions and draws a clear distinction between crafts and art.

Chenfield, M. (1995). *Creative experiences for young children* (2nd ed.). Orlando, FL: Harcourt Brace. In this very good book, Chenfield divides activities according to topics such as bodies or people we meet. She suggests creative activities, including art, movement, and discussion activities related to the topic. Excellent bibliographies for children and adults complete each chapter.

Kohl, M. A. (1994). *Preschool art: It's the process, not the product*. Beltsville, MD: Gryphon House. A wide range of not very craftlike self-expressive visual art activities are arranged by season. Each activity is coded according to age, amount of required preparation, how much teacher help is necessary, and so forth.

Olshansky, B. (1990). *Portfolio of illustrated step-by-step art projects for young children*. West Nyack, NY: Center for Applied Research in Education, Simon & Schuster. These activities are suitable for preschool-aged children on up. There is great variety, and activities are carefully explained—outstanding because the descriptions often show how to make the material simple or more challenging.

Painting

Smith, N. R., Fucigna, C., Kennedy, M., & Lord, L. (1993). *Teaching children to paint* (2nd ed.). New York: Teachers College Press. The title of this book is misleading because the intention is not so much teaching as *enabling* children of various ages to use paints with satisfaction.

Clay

Gandini, L. (1996). Teachers and children together: Constructing new learning. *Child Care Information Exchange*, 108, 43–46. For a delightful description of how children might be drawn into investigating clay à la Reggio, this article is *highly recommended*.

Kohl, M. F. (1989). *Mudworks: Creative clay, dough, and modeling experiences*. Bellingham, WA: Bright Ring. A tremendous variety of mixtures are included together with estimates of appropriate age, palatability, and variations.

Miller, S. A. (1994). *Learning through play: Sand, water, clay & wood*. New York: Scholastic. Many activities and suggestions for presentation are included here.

Topal, C. W. (1996). Fostering experiences between young children and clay. *Child Care Information Exchange*, 108, 51–55. This article provides a practical source of information about clay presented in a rather "instructional" sort of way.

Woodworking

Skeen, P., Garner, A. P., & Cartwright, S. (1984). *Woodworking for young children*. Washington, DC: National Association for the Education of Young Children. At last, a truly practical book about woodworking for teachers and young children. This book deals with everything from how to tell soft and hard woods apart to describing how tools should be used and nails straightened. *Highly recommended*.

Blocks

Church, E. B., & Miller, K. (1990). *Learning through play: Blocks: A practical guide for teaching young children*. New York: Scholastic. Church and Miller provide many practical recommendations for presenting block play effectively. Once again, it includes material related to children with disabilities.

Hirsch, E. S. (Ed.). (1996). *The block book* (3rd ed.). Washington, DC: National Association for the Education of Young

Children. This is the most comprehensive discussion of block play presently available.

Provenzo, E. F., Jr., & Brett, A. (1983). *The complete block book*. Syracuse, NY: Syracuse University Press. Lavishly illustrated, *The Complete Block Book* covers the history, as well as the potential uses, of blocks in the curriculum. Moreover, it reprints Harriet Johnson's famous pamphlet.

Dance

Please refer to the references at the end of chapter 9.

Creativity in Play

Hendrick, J. (1996). *The whole child: Developmental education for the early years* (6th ed.). Upper Saddle River, NJ: Merrill/Prentice Hall. Chapters 13 and 14 discuss fostering creativity by means of self-expressive materials and fostering creativity in play. These chapters contain additional information on theory and research that is not possible to include in *Total Learning*.

For the Advanced Student

Amabile, T. M. (1996). *Creativity in context: Update to the social psychology of creativity*. Boulder, CO: Westview/Harper-Collins. Written by *the* authority in the field, this book endears itself to me by its own creative approach—namely, all the new research and ideas that have occurred since original publication in 1983 are identified by a special symbol. An indispensable reference that is *highly recommended*.

Davis, J., & Gardner, H. (1993). The arts and early childhood education: A cognitive developmental portrait of the young child as artist. In B. Spodek (Ed.), *Handbook of research on the education of young children*. Upper Saddle River, NJ: Prentice Hall. This is a scholarly discussion of current cognitive theory as it is applied to understanding children's drawings.

Gardner, H. (1989). *To open minds*. New York: Basic Books. Gardner presents an interesting cross-cultural comparison of American and Chinese attitudes toward creativity—delightful, thought-provoking reading.

Golumb, C. (1992). *The child's creation of a pictorial world*. Berkeley: University of California Press. Golumb uses her extensive research as the basis for an exhaustive analysis of how children's drawings develop. Included are discussions of gifted child artists and the use of art for diagnostic purposes. Fascinating reading.

Isenberg, J. P., & Jalongo, M. R. (1996). *Creative expression and play in the early childhood curriculum* (2nd ed.). Upper Saddle River, NJ: Merrill/Prentice Hall. Isenberg and Jalongo present a lengthy, comprehensive discussion of the theoretical and practical aspects of creativity—*the best in the field*.

Runco, M. (Ed.). (1996). Creativity from childhood through adulthood: The developmental issues. *New Directions in Child Development*, 72, 1–95. The cutting edge of creativity theory is presented here—difficult but interesting reading.

Starko, A. J. (1995). *Creativity in the classroom: Schools of curious delight*. New York: Longman. Starko offers a good review of theoretical approaches and descriptions of creative persons. The suggested applications would most easily be applied for use with older children.

Thompson, C. M. (Ed.). (1995). *The visual arts and early childhood learning*. Reston, VA: National Art Education Association (1016 Association Dr., Reston, VA 22091). The approaches to art education advocated here come from a slightly different angle because most of the chapters are written by art educators. Valuable reading, particularly in the area of fostering appreciation of other people's artistic expressions.

15

Developing Verbal Competence

Have you ever

- Worked in a multiethnic classroom and wondered whether you should make all the children speak English all the time?
- Worried what to do about a 3-year-old who hardly ever says a word?
- Wished that you could get the children to sing more?
- Wanted to include more emergent literacy activities in your curriculum?

If you have, the material in this chapter will help you.

There is no better play material in the world than words. They surround us, go with us through our work-a-day tasks, their sound is always in our ears, their rhythms on our tongue. Why do we leave it to special occasions and to special people to use these common things as precious play material? Because we are grownups and have closed our ears and our eyes that we may not be distracted from our plodding ways! But when we turn to the children, to hearing and seeing children, to whom all the world is as play material, who think and feel through play, can we not then drop our adult utilitarian speech and listen and watch for the patterns of words and ideas? Can we not speak in rhythm, in pleasing sounds, even in song for the mere sensuous delight it gives us and them even though it adds nothing to the content of our remarks? If we can, I feel sure children will not lose their native use of words: What's more, I think those of six and seven and eight who have lost it in part—and their stories show they have—will win back their spontaneous joy in the play of words.

Lucy Sprague Mitchell (1948)

How Do Children Learn to Talk?

Arguments continue over how children actually acquire the ability to use language, and no definitive answer has been settled on yet (Bloom, 1996). However, it is valuable for teachers to be acquainted with the current state of theories of language acquisition, because this field of study is very active at present and the conclusions about how language is learned have important implications for teaching.

What is known so far is that the development of language is a gradual process that proceeds in predictable order and that parents and teachers (as representatives and conveyers of culture) can be powerful influences in fostering the acquisition of vocabulary and the growth of fluency as they help children acquire concepts and attach words to those concepts.

One school of thought favors the importance of imitation and reinforcement as the most probable acquisition device (Bandura, 1986; Skinner,

1957, 1974; Whitehurst & Valdez-Menchaca, 1988), but many people feel that these theorists have difficulty explaining how children can produce novel, previously unheard utterances by means of these processes. Another group postulates that children develop a language in accordance with a basic, universal linguistic structure inherent in all people that is gradually acted on by different cultures to produce diverse languages (Chomsky, 1987; McNeill, 1970). According to this linguistic theory, novel utterances are the result of applying abstracted linguistic rules rather than merely imitating what has been heard. Still another theory is that children simply derive abstract rules of language structure as they use it and hear it spoken around them (Maratsos, 1989). Such formulations of rules are not deliberate and consciously determined. It is impossible to picture little children saying to themselves, "If I want to tell my mother I see more than one cat, I must add an *s* at the end of *cat.*" As Herriot (1987) puts it, "They use the rule though they cannot describe it" (p. 427).

Because anyone who has worked with little children can cite numerous examples of their acquiring language through imitation and equally numerous examples of spontaneous, novel speech, it seems probable that several factors operate together in language learning and that teachers should take them all into account (Genishi, 1992; Stewig & Jett-Simpson, 1995). If imitation and reinforcement play a part in language acquisition, it behooves teachers to provide good examples for children to imitate and to make the process of using language to communicate satisfying for them. Such gratifications need not be elaborate. Paying attention to what children are saying, for instance, is a very effective way of encouraging them to continue speaking. If teachers also believe that children use experience with language to somehow arrive at linguistic rules for speaking, they will want to expose them to hearing a great deal of language and encourage them to use language in return. They should also encourage the children to use it in expressive, spontaneous ways as often as possible.

Teachers also need to have in mind a developmental timetable of when various language skills appear. Table 15–1 provides a list of readily observable behaviors that can help teachers and parents identify children who are lagging too far behind or who are exceptionally advanced. These youngsters can then be offered the special help and opportunities they require.

Black English and Bilingualism in the Children's Center

Because many youngsters come to preschool programs speaking only the language of their homes, which may differ from what is spoken at school, it is important for teachers to be well informed about Black English and bilingualism.

Black English

Because the structure of Black English differs from that of Standard English, in the past some teachers have assumed that it was an inferior form of Standard English (C. A. Hill, 1977). However, Black English has been analyzed and shown to possess a sophisticated grammatical structure different from, but not necessarily inferior to, that of Standard English (Labov, 1970; Owens, 1992).

Such research has helped teachers understand that this lect has a definite place in the culture of African American people and that it is not "baby talk." Actually, anyone who has been privileged to be included in the conversations, vivid and friendly insults, and other verbal games that go on between older African American children or adults really cannot fail to acknowledge the quickness of verbal wit and humor displayed at these times (Baugh, 1994; Hale, 1992). Unfortunately, most white teachers do not have this kind of contact with the children they teach, nor is this kind of verbal gamesmanship evident in children of preschool age. The reader can gain at least a partial idea of this humor by watching some of the television programs featuring casts of African American actors.

Teachers must also be aware of the negative effect that disapproval of something so personal as the child's means of expressing herself could have on her self-image. Because Black English is not an inferior form of Standard English, and because it is important to sustain the child's self-esteem, many authorities now suggest that teachers not deplore or attempt to suppress this form of speech (Hale, 1992).

Perhaps the most effective way for white, middle-class teachers to regard Black English is to think of it as being another language instead of a lower-class lect. To function successfully in our world today, African American children need to acquire proficiency in both Black and Standard English, because, as they mature, they will need to shift gears back and forth between them depending on whom they

TABLE 15–1
Milestones in the Development of Language Ability in Young Children

Average Age	Question	Average Behavior
3–6 months	What does he do when you talk to him?	He awakens or quiets to the sound of his mother's voice.
	Does he react to your voice even when he cannot see you?	He typically turns eyes and head in the direction of the source of sound.
7–10 months	When he can't see what is happening, what does he do when he hears familiar footsteps? The dog barking? The telephone ringing? Candy paper rattling? Someone's voice? His own name?	He turns his head and shoulders toward familiar sounds, even when he cannot see what is happening. Such sounds do not have to be loud to cause him to respond.
11–15 months	Can he point to or find familiar objects or people when he is asked to? **Example:** "Where is Jimmy?" "Find the ball."	He shows his understanding of some words by appropriate behavior; for example, he points to or looks at familiar objects or people, on request.
	Does he respond differently to different sounds?	He jabbers in response to a human voice, is apt to cry when there is thunder, or may frown when he is scolded.
	Does he enjoy listening to some sounds and imitating them?	Imitation indicates that he can hear the sounds and match them with his own sound production.
1½ years	Can he point to parts of his body when you ask him to? **Example:** "Show me your eyes." "Show me your nose."	Some children begin to identify parts of the body. He should be able to show his nose or eyes.
	How many understandable words does he use—words you are sure *really* mean something?	He should be using a few single words. They are not complete or pronounced perfectly but are clearly meaningful.
2 years	Can he follow simple verbal commands when you are careful not to give him any help, such as looking at the object or pointing in the right direction? **Example:** "Johnny, get your hat and give it to Daddy." "Debby, bring me your ball."	He should be able to follow a few simple commands without visual clues.

are talking to. As is true in other bilingual situations, teachers must realize that for Black children to acquire Standard English as their second language, it is not necessary for them to abandon their first one (Pflaum, 1986; Smitherman, 1977, 1994).

Bilingualism

The subject of bilingualism and bilingual education is simply too vast to be discussed in detail in a general education text of this kind. We must content ourselves here with pointing out that

Average Age	Question	Average Behavior
2 years, *cont'd*	Does he enjoy being read to? Does he point out pictures of familiar objects in a book when asked to? **Example:** "Show me the baby." "Where's the rabbit?"	Most 2-year-olds enjoy being "read to" and shown simple pictures in a book or magazine, and they will point out pictures when you ask them to.
	Does he use the names of familiar people and things such as *Mommy, milk, ball,* and *hat*?	He should be using a variety of everyday words heard in his home and neighborhood.
	What does he call himself?	He refers to himself by name.
	Is he beginning to show interest in the sound of radio or TV commercials?	Many 2-year-olds do show such interest, by word or action.
	Is he putting a few words together to make little "sentences"? **Example:** "Go bye-bye car." "Milk all gone."	These "sentences" are not usually complete or grammatically correct.
2½ years	Does he know a few rhymes or songs? Does he enjoy hearing them?	Many children can say or sing short rhymes or songs and enjoy listening to records or to mother singing.
	What does he do when the ice cream man's bell rings, out of his sight, or when a car door or house door closes at a time when someone in the family usually comes home?	If a child has good hearing, and these are events that bring him pleasure, he usually reacts to the sound by running to look or telling someone what he hears.
3 years	Can he show that he understands the meaning of some words besides the names of things? **Example:** "Make the car go." "Put the block in your pocket." "Find the big doll."	He should be able to understand and use some simple verbs, pronouns, prepositions, and adjectives, such as *go, me, in,* and *big.*
	Can he find you when you call him from another room?	He should be able to locate the source of a sound.
	Does he sometimes use complete sentences?	He should be using complete sentences some of the time.

speaking two or more languages often opens the doors to lucrative employment opportunities for adults, which makes preserving the home language an important educational asset to protect during childhood. Then, too, language is such an important part of identity that it is vital to honor it just as we do other aspects of children's cultural heritage (NAEYC, 1995). Respect for their native language also helps children maintain closeness to their families by supporting the cultural values of the home—a very worthwhile goal (Gonzalez, 1991; Wong Fillmore, 1991).

TABLE 15–1
continued

Average Age	Question	Average Behavior
4 years	Can he tell about events that have happened recently?	He should be able to give a connected account of some recent experiences.
	Can he carry out two directions, one after the other? **Example:** "Bobby, find Susie and tell her dinner's ready."	He should be able to carry out a sequence of two simple directions.
5 years	Do neighbors and others outside the family understand most of what he says?	His speech should be intelligible, although some sounds may still be mispronounced.
	Can he carry on a conversation with other children or familiar grown-ups?	Most children of this age can carry on a conversation if the vocabulary is within their experience.
	Does he begin a sentence with *I* instead of *me, he* instead of *him?*	He should use some pronouns correctly.
	Is his grammar almost as good as his parents'?	Most of the time, it should match the patterns of grammar used by the adults of his family and neighborhood.

Note. From *Learning to Talk: Speech, Hearing and Language Problems in the Pre-School Child* by the National Institute of Neurological Diseases and Stroke, 1969, Washington, DC: U.S. Department of Health, Education, and Welfare.

At the preschool level, this is usually accomplished by employing teaching staff who are bilingual. In earlier years, the skills of such staff were most often used for interpretation rather than for preservation of the children's native tongue. It frequently happened that, as the children gained facility in English, the school dropped the use of the other language.

Now in some areas of the country there is more of an attempt to operate truly bilingual classrooms, in which a genuine effort is made to teach and sustain both languages and to perpetuate other cultural values, too. This kind of bilingual education is often termed a *maintenance bilingual model* (Pease-Alvarez, Garcia, & Espinosa, 1991). Barrera (1996) describes this succinctly: "In *maintenance* programs, both languages are equally valued and equally maintained throughout the education. Sometimes these are called *dual lan-guage* programs" (p. 46). A variation of this is the two-way model in which native English speakers learn a second language while native Spanish or French speakers acquire English (Zanger, 1991). Still another model uses only the child's dominant language while providing a family-centered, quality educational program. When children reach kindergarten age, they transfer into a transitional bilingual education model (Campos, 1995).

Even though such programs may still be relatively rare in public schools, this need not be the case for children's centers, which have much greater opportunities for autonomy. If teachers so choose, they can make a point of combining the multiethnic educational model and environment discussed in chapter 13 with a balanced bilingual program, thereby providing good-quality language maintenance programs for the children they serve (Cazden, 1984; Soto, 1991).

Children need practice in both talking...

and listening.

At the very least, as Umberto Eco (1993) advocates:

> Work needs to be done among the young, from a very early age, three or four onwards, if only to teach them that there are different languages, so that they grasp the idea of diversity, to show them, for example, that in different languages there are many different names for a rabbit, and that those who call a rabbit by some other name are not necessarily barbarians. (p. 4)

The Child Who Is Not Fluent in Any Language

The foregoing discussion assumes that children who are not speaking Standard English do speak some other language or lect fluently. However, some youngsters arrive at the center who are not verbal at all. Teachers must be on the lookout for such youngsters and not make the mistake of assuming, for example, that they must be fluent in their "home" language just because they do not speak in English. This is not always the case. It is particularly valuable to check about such nonverbal behavior with the children's families. This will help determine whether they do not talk at school but *do* talk at home or whether they say very little in either circumstance.

Children who are generally nonverbal both at home and at school need special attention and stimulation to develop their verbal and mental capacities. When these are provided, they often make very dramatic progress at school. However, if they are still not talking after 2 to 3 months of regular attendance, it is vital to seek the help of specialists, because there is often a significant reason for the delay.

Perhaps the child is hard of hearing or is developmentally delayed in some way (Patterson & Wright, 1990). Referrals should be made to the child's pediatrician, an otolaryngologist (a physician specializing in diseases of the ear, nose, and throat), or a speech pathologist. If retardation is suspected, referral should be made to a child psychologist for testing. Once the reason for the delay in speech has been determined, a plan for remediation should be developed, and the teacher should make certain the specialist provides information about what should be done to help carry the plan out. The sooner these conditions are identified, the sooner they can be treated. *Teachers must never wait an entire year with a nonverbal 3- or 4-year-old in the hope that she will suddenly blossom forth and begin talking.* All too often this fails to happen.

Good Teaching Habits That Foster Children's Use of Language

Chapter 11 on emotional health has already discussed how important it is for the teacher to "hear" the children's feelings and, by describing these to them, let them know that he understands what is going on inside them. This kind of interested concern is also a fundamental way of encouraging children to talk, because the teacher who truly listens draws forth conversation from children as a magnet attracts iron.

Of course, if teachers have packed the day too full so that everyone must be pushed from one activity to the next or if there is not enough teaching staff, the leisure that good conversational opportunities require is hard to come by. But even in centers where these circumstances prevail, teachers can encourage children to chat with them, if they realize how valuable such opportunities are for encouraging verbal fluency.

Learn to Conduct a Conversation, Not an Interrogation

Teachers frequently see themselves as being primarily information givers and getters; that is, they are forever telling children important facts or asking them questions so the children will prove they already know the facts or are thinking about them. Good conversation, however, rarely dwells on such matters.

Witness the following variations on the same topic, then ask yourself which of the two you would prefer to take part in if you were the child. Also, ask yourself what the child *learned* from each of the two encounters and which one fostered the greater fluency and development of thought.

Example 1

Child: Guess what, Teacher, I got new shoes!
Teacher: No kidding! My, my! They're real pretty!
Child: They got chuckles!
Teacher: Chuckles?
Child: Yeah, *you* know! *Chuckles!* Here on the side. (points to buckles)
Teacher: (light dawning) Oh, you mean *buckles!* That word sounds like buck-buck-buck-buck-buck-buck-a-luck *b*uckles!
Child: (amused) Buck-buck-buck-buck-buck-a-luck buckles!
Teacher: That's right—*b*uckles. (pause) Are they hard to get through that hole? (meaning the straps)
Child: Yeah, but I don't mind. I just worm 'em through!
Teacher: Yeah, just wiggle the edge that way—into the side place!
Child: I can do it! Into the side place! (pause) They make marks on my socks!
Teacher: Oh, yeah, I see. Does it hurt?
Child: Nope. My foot's sweaty, that's all—makes the red come off.
Teacher: You take those shoes off at night, you'll still have little red feet on!
Child: (thinks this over, laughs) Well, yeah—little *pink* feet! Just like wearing shoes to bed! (laughs) My momma sure won't like that, no way! (runs off to play)

Example 2

Child: Guess what, Teacher, I got new shoes!
Teacher: Yes, I see you did. They're pretty, Tania. What color do you think they are?

Learn to conduct a conversation, not an interrogation.

Child: (pause) Red.

Teacher: And what else is special about them?

Child: (shakes head) I don't know.

Teacher: Oh, yes, now—think a minute. What's that on the side of your red shoe? Right there? (pointing to the buckle)

Child: It makes red marks.

Teacher: That isn't what I mean! What's *this* called? (pointing to the buckle again)

Child: Don't know.

Teacher: It's called a *buckle*. Buckle—can you say that?

Child: Fix it for me!

Teacher: What's the magic word?

Child: (pause) Please.

Teacher: Please what?

Child: Please fix that.

Teacher: (persistently but not unpleasantly) What's that called? I just told you.

Child: (says nothing)

Teacher: (patiently) Buckle—remember? That's a buckle!

Child: Buckle!

Teacher fixes the shoe while child stands silently, then runs off.

I hope the reader concludes from comparing these examples that there is a place for fun in talking with children and that it is not always necessary to use high-pressure techniques to obtain valuable educational results. Note also how in example 1 the ideas build on each other and the talk flows freely and increases in quantity. These are the most important goals to work toward when building language skills in young children. They are certainly more important than driving and driving to add one new word, *buckle*, to the child's vocabulary.

Learn to Listen as Well as Talk!

Of course, to conduct a genuine conversation, it is essential to pay real attention to what the child is saying—both with her body and with her words. Sensitive teachers (when working with children from most but not all cultures) show they are listening by bending down and looking eye to eye, providing a pause of "wait time" for the child to formulate her reply, and not *preforming* what to reply before the youngster has even had a turn to speak.

Learn How to Ask Questions That Invite Children to Respond

Questions should relate to topics that children are interested in and that they know something about—preferably, even more than the teacher does. For example, "Where did you get that wonderful hat?" "How come you like this book so much?" and "I saw you helping your mama in the market yesterday. Were you telling her what to get?" all invite replies that will tell the teacher something he does not already know, and they cast the child in the role of the authority.

If these invitations to chat are coupled with nonjudgmental replies to what the children say, they will encourage talk even further. For example, consider the effect of the two kinds of teacher responses in the following dialogues:

Example 3

Teacher (playfully picking up the child and hugging her): I saw you helping your mama in the market yesterday. Were you telling her what to get?
Child: Yeah! I told her to get pickles, and ice cream, and sugar buns!
Teacher: Why did you do that? You know that isn't good for you! You ought to tell her to get cereal and vegetables and the things that we talked about at lunch that are good for you to eat! They'll make you grow up strong like your brother!
Child: (says nothing—just wiggles to get down)

Example 4

Teacher (playfully picking up the child and hugging her): I saw you helping your mama in the market yesterday. Were you telling her what to get?
Child: Yeah, I told her to get pickles, and ice cream, and sugar buns!
Teacher: I guess you were really hungry!

Child: I sure was—and those little crackers, and chicken, and corn. . . .
Teacher: That's what makes you grow—good stuff like that. [meaning chicken and corn]
Child: And shoe polish!
Teacher: Shoe polish! (playfully) I don't want to eat that!
Child (grinning and with great emphasis): And *shoe polish*! We had shoe polish frosting for dessert!
Teacher (laughs): Yum, yum. It must have looked like chocolate!
Child: Yeah, chocolate shoe polish frosting. (laughs) Dyn-o-*mite*!
Teacher: Well, it's *real* chocolate pudding for lunch today. Want to set out the napkins?
Child: Sure! (wiggles to get down)

Learn to Use an Attractive Speaking Voice

When teachers are under stress, their voices sometimes rise in pitch or take on a hard, nasal quality that is unpleasant to listen to and that creates tension in the children, too. Other teachers may have monotonous voices and thereby fail to attract or hold the children's attention.

The best remedy for these problems is for teachers to tape-record themselves regularly during group or lunchtime and actually listen to what they are saying and how they sound while saying it. This is because it is impossible to correct a voice-quality problem until they are aware of it. The next step is catching themselves in the act and consciously modulating the tone of voice to a more pleasant level. One way teachers can keep track of voice quality is to put five pennies in a pocket at the beginning of the day and transfer one to another pocket every time they hear their voices rising too far. It only takes a few days to keep all the pennies in the beginning pocket.

Presenting Materials and Resources

As we have seen, the basic tool for developing language in children is the way teachers use

Research Study

Does Talking with Children Really Make Any Difference?

Research Question   In a previous study, Hart and Risley found that even though they could easily increase the amount of vocabulary that low-income children acquired at preschool, the *rate* the low-income children added words to their vocabulary remained markedly slower than did the rate of the professor's children. This difference in rate produced an ever-widening gap between the abilities of the two groups.

The question the researchers then asked was "What causes these differences in the growth rate of the children's vocabularies?"

Research Method   To find out the answer, the research team spent 2 ½ years observing 42 families for an hour each month to learn about what typically went on in the homes with their 1- and 2-year-old children while they were learning to talk. They selected only adequate, well-functioning families to study. Thirteen were classified as professional (higher socioeconomic status [SES]), 23 working-class (middle/lower SES), and 6 welfare families. Seventeen families were African American, and some of them were included in each of the SES groups. About half the children were girls. Taped and written records were transcribed and entered on a computer and coded for such features as vocabulary growth rates and family interaction patterns.

Research Results   The similarities between the families is best summed up in the observers' own words:

> Though we were aware that the families were very different in lifestyles, they were all similarly engaged in the fundamental task of raising a child. All the families nurtured their children and played and talked with them. They all disciplined their children and taught them good manners and how to dress and toilet themselves. They provided their children with much the same toys and talked to them about much the same thing. Though different in personality and skill levels, the children all learned to talk and to be socially appropriate members of the family with all the basic skills needed for preschool entry. (pp. 46, 47)

And yet analysis of the vocabulary words once again clearly showed growing differences between the groups of children (see Figure 15–A).

Because the families had so much in common, what was different about them that accounted for such differences in vocabulary development?

The answer became obvious when the frequency and kind of parental responses were analyzed. Parents from the professional group averaged 487 utterances addressed to the child per hour in contrast to 301 utterances in working-class families and 178 utterances in families on welfare. Not only did the professional families talk more to the children, but they also used many more different words and more elaborate language structure. The higher-SES parents were a lot more positive in their attitude, too, only giving about 5 prohibitions per hour to the children, whereas welfare parents used an average of 11—more than twice as many as the professional families did. The higher-SES families also used a guidance style of asking rather than demanding and were more responsive to the child's behavior.

Implications for the Children: When reevaluated at ages 9 and 10, all the children were developing within the normal range, but the children who had had less vocabulary at age 3 still had less vocabulary and also scored lower on reading comprehension (reading for understanding) scores. (There was no association between vocabulary growth and third-grade

FIGURE 15–A.
Rate of Increase in Vocabulary Acquisition by Age 3

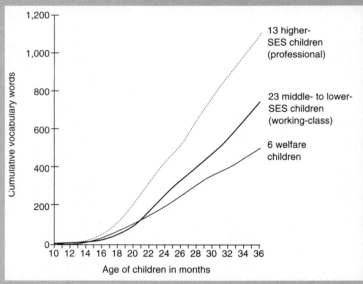

"At each month the average number of vocabulary words recorded in that and all prior months for three groups of children from the time the children were 10 months old until they were 36 months old. The children were grouped by the socioeconomic index assigned to the occupation of their parents. The 13 higher-SES children (dotted line) were in professional families, 23 middle- to lower-SES children (heavy solid line) were in working-class families, and 6 welfare children (light solid line) were in families receiving welfare" (Aid to Families with Dependent Children).

Note. From *Meaningful Differences in the Everyday Experience of Young American Children* (p. 234) by B. Hart and T. R. Risley, 1995, Baltimore, MD: Brookes. Used by permission.

academic skills scores of reading, writing, spelling, and arithmetic.) Hart and Risley point out that these differences in reduced vocabulary and reading comprehension abilities will become more and more serious as the youngsters approach high school and find increased difficulty comprehending more advanced textbooks.

Implications for Families: The researchers advocate increased mentoring of needful parents to encourage the use of language and development of more positive attitudes with their children, but such recommendations must overcome many obstacles such as prohibitive cost, differing cultural values, and potential privacy violations to be effective.

Implications for Preschool Teachers: Hart and Risley calculate that teachers do not have enough hours in the day to supply the necessary language interactions to completely fill the vocabulary gap they identified. But does this mean we cannot make a difference? Of course not! It *does* mean we must admit this difference exists and do everything we can to build language richness into our programs. We should begin with the children and their families as early as possible. We can be constantly aware of how important it is to generate language

Books—a never-ending source of true delight!

and discussion between ourselves and the children. We can make certain we talk with every child, individually, every day. We can extend their vocabulary by reading to them and champion consistent reading at home by establishing a library of good, inexpensive books for home use. We can help educate parents about the value of talking with and listening to their children.

Note. From *Meaningful Differences in the Everyday Experience of Young American Children* by B. Hart and T. R. Risley, 1995, Baltimore, MD: Brookes.

their time with them to generate satisfying episodes of dialogue. Preschool also abounds with additional opportunities for emphasizing more specific language activities, and the re-mainder of this chapter discusses principles related to their presentation. Group time, which is discussed in chapter 16, also provides many opportunities for building language skills.

Language Without Experience and Experience Without Language Is Almost Meaningless to Children

The work of Eve Clark (1983) on how children learn to attach meaning to words reminds us of the importance of tying experience to language. She points out that children originally establish word meanings on the basis of salient perceptual features of objects: shape, movement, size, sound, taste, and texture—all sensory experiences. The moral for early childhood teachers (even though they are dealing with children slightly older than the ones in Clark's studies) is that they must be careful to offer language activities related to those tangible, concrete things children know about because of their direct sensory experience with them (French, 1996).

It makes no sense to read a poem about snow to California children, many of whom have no idea of what it is, unless teachers also liken it to hail and include such experiences as taking them to visit an ice skating rink, showing them pictures of snow, and talking about how it feels when they put their hands in the refrigerator. Even then, these children do not really have the meanings associated with snow that youngsters in wintry climates do. Just because children can mouth a word does not mean they necessarily grasp the concept.

Auditory Discrimination Activities

Auditory discrimination is simply a fancy term for teaching children to pay attention to sounds and encouraging them to become discriminating so they can tell when the sounds are alike and when they are different. Being able to distinguish between sounds is an important skill because it can help sensitize children who do not speak clearly to differences in the way words are pronounced. It is also a helpful emergent literacy skill to foster because it helps children tell words apart.

Unfortunately, many schools seem unaware of the value of sharpening children's ears. Perhaps they feel this skill can only be taught through a lot of drill work, but this is untrue. There are many activities that can be used to build auditory discrimination skills and are just plain fun. Actually, anything that encourages children to listen closely to sounds and to signal in some way that they distinguish between them comes under this heading. The following are some suggestions:

- Let the children pull pictures of animals or model animals out of a "secret box." Next, make various animal sounds. When each child hears "her" animal, she jumps up and shows it to the other children. This activity can be made somewhat more challenging by using a tape recording instead of making the sounds yourself. This helps emphasize the aspect of sound more strongly.
- Tape-record various common household sounds—a car starting, a toilet flushing, food frying, door shutting, an electric mixer, and so forth—and ask children to guess what they are hearing.
- Make up paired sets of sound canisters (35mm film cases are good free containers to use) with different contents, and see if the children can pair the ones together that sound just alike. (Experience proves that it is important to seal the tops of these so that children use their ears, not their eyes or fingers, to determine the source of the sound.)
- Fill a set of sturdy glass jars with different amounts of water, and encourage the children to strike them gently with a spoon and arrange them from lowest to highest tone. (This activity is appropriate for older fours and requires careful supervision because of the glass containers.)
- Divide a few children into two groups. While one group hides behind a sheet or screen, have one of them say something out loud and ask the other group to guess who is talking. Asking them to say a nursery rhyme will help overcome their self-consciousness about what to say.

- Let the children think up ways to make sounds using their bodies (such as stamping or clapping or yawning), and ask the other children to shut their eyes and guess what they are doing.

More Difficult Discrimination Activities

- Have a small group of objects or even pictures and ask children to pick out the one that begins with "buh" or "a-a-a." A more advanced form of this activity is to ask them to look for something in the room that starts with a particular sound and point it out or ask the children to point out something that starts with the same sound as "baby" or "Mama."
- Have children listen to a series of words that are the same or almost alike, such as *dog, log, fog, dog, dog*. Every time they hear the same word they can take a marble from the pot. See how soon the children can empty the pot.

Songs and Records

Music should be part of the life of the school throughout the day and definitely not relegated just to group time. The use of a simple, familiar song can ease transitions between activities and deepen pleasure in activities themselves. Such a simple thing as singing the words, "Swing, swing, swingy, swing" to the tune of "Row, Row, Row Your Boat" can enchant a 2 ½-year-old, for example. Singing can pass the time while waiting for lunch or bind a group of parents and children together at a party. It can introduce the children to their cultural heritage, whether it be early American folk songs or ones from Africa or Germany or Japan. It is the perfect medium for opening group time, since children can join in as they arrive without feeling they are interrupting or that they have been left out.

Choosing a Good Song

A good song for little children is one that is simple, short, and repetitive. It should have a range of only a few notes. If it can be personalized by inserting the children's names, so much the bet-

ter. Careful thought should be devoted to the quality of the song, also. There is no need to settle for trivial material when we have people like Raffi (1987), Thomas Moore (1991), and Hap Palmer (n.d.) providing good-quality pieces.

Traditional music should be included also. Many children today no longer hear nursery rhymes unless they are presented at school, yet many of these are set to tunes that have stood the test of time and are already familiar. "Twinkle, Twinkle Little Star," "Jack and Jill," and "Mary Had a Little Lamb" come instantly to mind.

American folk songs, although less familiar to some of us, offer another rich resource for singing with children. These are often written in a minor key—a useful quality, because it extends the children's "ear" for melody. Some folk songs are surprisingly funny and frank, also qualities that both children and adults appreciate (Seeger, 1980).

Remember, too, that many children hear music all day long in their own homes where radios or television sets are continually turned on. Although one might not want to use all such material, there certainly are many popular songs that will fit in; and because popular music is so much a part of the life of the children's homes, it makes sense to include it.

Finally, singing simple songs from many cultures offers an excellent way of fostering positive feelings toward other peoples. A child can glow with importance when the teacher mentions that a particular song comes from Puerto Rico—the same place his own family comes from. The records of Ella Jenkins are prime examples of how various cultures can be presented to young children in a pleasureful, participatory way, but it is desirable to explore even further than that. There are many records and tapes available today that are authentic and appropriate to use with children. Adding musical instruments that come from the same culture as the song is a delightful touch. These need be neither elaborate nor expensive.

Here are four excellent books containing appropriate music for young children:

Bayless, K. M., & Ramsey, M. E. (1991). Music: A way of life for the young child (4th ed.). Upper Saddle River, NJ: Merrill/Prentice Hall.

Haines, J. E., & Gerber, L. L. (1996). Leading young children to music (5th ed.). Upper Saddle River, NJ: Merrill/Prentice Hall.

Jenkins, E. (1966). The Ella Jenkins song book for children. Woodstock, NY: Beekman.

Seeger, R. C. (1980). American folk songs for children. Garden City, NY: Doubleday.

The first two works listed here go far beyond presenting songs per se. They are also rich resources of information on presenting all forms of music to young children, with the added advantage of providing *very simple* arrangements scored for piano and Autoharp. The Seeger book, which is still in print, is an authentic resource for folk songs.

Teaching a Song to Children

Be prepared to repeat a song several times on several days for the children to learn it well enough to enjoy singing it freely. This is one of the primary reasons for choosing simple, repetitive songs of good quality. However, the children will be able to join in right away if there is a short chorus in which first the leader and then the group sing the same refrain (Wolf, 1994).

Sing slowly, and teach only one verse at a time. It will contribute to the pleasure if the song is accompanied by an instrument, such as a guitar or an Autoharp, but this is not essential. Indeed, unless done with care, using something like a piano can be more trouble than it is worth if it means the teacher must turn her back on the children while playing it. The advantage of using an Autoharp is that children can be invited to strum it in time to the singing, since all one must do to control the note is press down firmly on the correct key. (Incidentally, *anyone* can easily learn to play an Autoharp. Bayless and Ramsey provide helpful instructions for doing this in Appendix C of Music: A Way of Life for the Young Child.)

Remember, too, that one of the nicest things about singing with children is the freedom it gives the teacher to improvise and adapt a song to the circumstances of the day. Clare Cherry's book (1971) on movement is full of examples of how topical words can be set to tunes everyone knows.

Poetry

Like singing, poetry should not be reserved just for group time, although it should always be part of the experience (Andrews, 1988). Teachers who take the trouble to commit some short poems to memory and who can quote these as the occasion arises can make literature an integral, pleasureful part of the children's lives. I grew up in a school system that required us to learn a certain amount of poetry by heart, and that habit and those poems have never left me. Because of my own experience, I freely recommend the value of memorizing poetry to the reader. It can be a source of real delight for the children.

For teachers who do not wish to memorize verse, a poetry file is recommended as the quickest and best way to obtain access to poetry as it is needed. Relying on books as a resource really does not work out well. It is too hard to find just the right poem at the right time. Also, I have yet to find a completely satisfactory anthology of verse for preschool children, although if I were restricted to only one, I would choose Arbuthnot and Root's *Time for Poetry* (1968) because the majority of the poems are short and in excellent taste, and they are arranged by topic headings.

Our staff types out or photocopies appropriate, good-quality poetry as they come across it and mounts it on mat board obtained as "scraps" from picture frame shops. This preserves the poem on a durable, hard-to-lose background and also makes it easy to file by topic so it can be immediately located when needed. Then when we need something on rain, or worms, or going to sleep, or shadows, we can put our hands right on it.

We have found the poetry of Dorothy Aldis, Marchette Chute, Aileen Fisher, Myra Cohn

The children loved telling the story over by themselves after listening to it during group time.

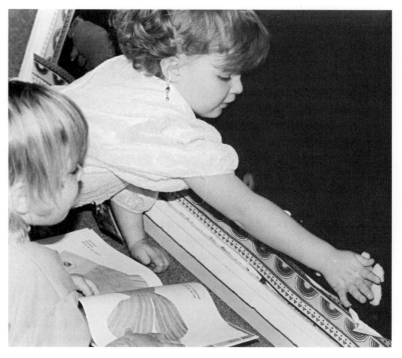

Livingston, Walter de la Mare, Miriam Clark Potter, Christina Rosetti, and Robert Louis Stevenson particularly appropriate—and of course Mother Goose should not be forgotten. Many fine editions of her rhymes are available. My favorite is the one with quaint, old-fashioned illustrations edited by Eulalie Osgood Grover (1971) based on Frederick Richardson's original edition, which has been reprinted by Hubbard Press.

No matter how complete the file, there will inevitably be times when no poem can be found that exactly suits a particular occasion. When this happens, try writing one yourself. The children will appreciate its timeliness. Its appropriateness for the occasion more than makes up for any potential lack of literary merit.

Finger Plays

Although the poetic quality of finger plays often leaves much to be desired, their ability to involve children instantly makes them a valuable addition to the language development arsenal. It is the old story of doing while saying—linking language and action—that helps children learn and enjoy this activity.

Finger plays, like songs, are excellent ways to begin a group time, because they are so attractive to children. They also can provide relief in the middle of a group time by offering a change of pace and recentering their attention. Finger plays make good "time fillers" when the schedule goes awry and the children have to wait awhile for something to happen. If the same one is presented repeatedly, they also enjoy saying it along with the teacher as they go through the actions. The actions themselves need not be limited just to fingers. Many successful "finger plays" actually involve larger muscles, such as getting up and sitting down. They can either be sung or recited.

Books and Stories

Reading Stories

Teachers often think of reading stories to children as being primarily a receptive language sit-

uation where the children are expected to sit quietly and "receive" the story, but it should be both a receptive and expressive language opportunity. If stories are presented with this goal in mind, teachers no longer have to struggle to keep the children quiet. Instead, they can welcome the children's comments and questions and invite discussion about what may happen next in the story.

Teachers should read with expression and enthusiasm and should be familiar with the text so that they do not stumble over words. They should take time to enjoy what is happening with the children and allow them to add their own comments. Bos (1983) describes this process well:

> Slowly I started letting the children discuss many pages of the book as I read. I would stop. We would examine a picture, asking questions about what they could see. Often they would see details I hadn't. If I would ask them what they thought would happen next, they could frequently come up with wonderfully creative ideas. As this process continued, I began to see marvelous results. I started to see the children themselves emerging—attempting *their* language, attempting to communicate with me—and at the same time I could see that they were discovering that they were capable of complicated and delightful communication.
>
> I have often been asked in my workshops how we can allow time for such interruptions—such a slow pace—when there's so much to do. My answer is that if the interruption doesn't happen, it is very likely that learning isn't happening. We need to translate *interruption* as the child's entering the process. If we genuinely believe that language development is at the heart of the learning process, then we must allow time. Not only allowing for it, but planning for interruptions is our whole purpose. (p. 7)

Of course, a balance is needed between encouraging children's comments and maintaining the momentum of the plot. Sometimes saying something such as "Just one more comment and then we'd better find out whether the Circus Baby could really sit on that chair" or "Well, let's go on now and see what's on the next page" will usually lead the children back to the book without hurting anyone's feelings.

Good books for young children generally have brief texts, beautiful pictures, and subject matter that is interesting to children and presented in good taste. When possible they should have a multiethnic or nonsexist approach. Excellent books also have that extra note of originality combined with quality writing and a good story that enshrines them in the hearts of children forever. Some outstanding examples are *Alejandro's Gift* (Albert, 1994), *Curious George* (Rey, 1941), *Owl Moon* (Yolen, 1987), *Bedtime for Frances* (Hoban, 1960), *The Girl Who Loved Wild Horses* (Goble, 1978), *Stellaluna* (Cannon, 1993), *Anansi the Spider* (McDermott, 1972), *Mirette on the High Wire* (McCully, 1992), *Madeline* (Bemelmans, 1939), *Cats Know Best* (Eisler, 1988), *The Goat in the Rug* (Blood & Link, 1976), *Mary Betty Lizzie McNutt's Birthday* (Bond, 1983), and *Abuela* (Dorros, 1991).

Books should be readily available throughout the day and should be varied from time to time—new ones brought out and more familiar friends put away. Variety is as close and inexpensive as the nearest public library.

Particularly in full-day centers, it is important to provide a cozy oasis where children can withdraw and leaf through their favorites without interruption. Opening a book to an especially beautiful or interesting picture and placing it in a holder by the bookshelf often entices children to that area. Preschoolers should be taught to handle books with care. *Never* permit them to leave books lying on the floor for children to walk on or otherwise abuse.

Reading stories is a good example of an activity in which volunteers can excel with only a moderate amount of instruction from the staff. Encourage them to settle down in a comfortable place with several well-chosen books. This provides wonderful opportunities for one-to-one and one-to-two contacts that both children and volunteers find meaningful and satisfying.

Encouraging Children to Tell Stories

We have already spoken of the value that telling stories can have for children in terms of express-ing their feeling and clarifying their ideas (chapter 11). Providing them with opportunities for doing this also develops language fluency.

To avoid long, rambling accounts at group time, which usually produce uncontrollable restlessness in the other children, it is best to pick times during the day when child storytelling can be done on a one-to-one basis between a staffperson or a volunteer and youngster. Children particularly enjoy dictating stories in their own special books that the teacher has made by stapling a few sheets of paper together. As they approach kindergarten age, they may even enjoy adding illustrations to emphasize what they mean.

There are various ways of starting things off with the child. The teacher can simply ask what she wants to tell about today, inquire if she wants to have him write down how her puppy learned to stop barking, or even begin a story himself for the child to continue, perhaps using those magical words, "Once upon a time. . . ."

Another way to encourage children to tell stories is to use pictures from the picture file. Younger children tend to use such single pictures more as opportunities simply to tell what is happening in the picture itself than as a starting point for a more extended story (Hough, Nurss, & Wood, 1987). Older children can go beyond that limited approach. Many times a picture of two little girls on a climbing gym or a lonely-looking boy holding a puppy can spark a long tale that uses the illustration as a take-off point, particularly if the teacher encourages such storytelling by asking occasional questions or making comments such as "Then what do you think happened?" or "After she caught the fish, what did she do next?"

Suggestions for Telling Stories

Like the children, teachers can also learn to tell stories with a little practice.[1] This often has a liberating, creative effect, since it allows them to

---

[1] Two good books about the art of storytelling are *Handbook for Story Tellers* by C. F. Bauer (Chicago: American Library Association, 1977) and *Just Enough to Make a Story: A Sourcebook for Storytelling* by N. Schimmel (Berkeley, CA: Sisters' Choice, 1978).

tailor the tale exactly to the requirements of the youthful audience. Telling stories also offers the opportunity to include the children themselves as characters. It can recapitulate something the children themselves have done, or it can be based on one of the teachers' experiences that they think the children will enjoy. Stories can be based on books, as well as on personal experience, and this is a particularly useful technique to employ when the illustrations are delightful but the text too difficult for the children to comprehend. Learning to "edit" as they go along is also a useful strategy for teachers to cultivate when material is sexist or conveys an undesirable racist slant. (Guidelines on identifying sexist and racist materials are found in Appendix E.)

If you are insecure about storytelling, remember that children's librarians are often excellent storytellers and can frequently be prevailed on to present story hours for visiting preschoolers. Furthermore, many of them are also happy to impart their skills to other teachers if invited to participate in training workshops for this purpose.

Discussion and Conversation

Some examples of possible discussion openers include asking children to offer suggestions ("Visiting day is coming up. What activities do you think we should set up for your brothers and sisters to do? What would they enjoy?"), to consider alternatives ("It's such a beautiful day! Do you think we should have water play after snack, or would you prefer to walk to the park?" "Would you rather have Officer Thompson visit us at school or go to the police station and meet her there?"), to make plans in advance ("You know, Cynthia is bringing her puppies to visit again tomorrow. Let's put our heads together and make a plan to keep them from being handled too much."), and to solve social problems ("We've been having so many fights over that trike with the license plate on it. I want to know what you children think we should do about it.").

Note that most of these gambits also require follow-up questions that encourage children to give the reasons for their opinions. Once all the possibilities, opinions, and reasons have been aired, it is best to reach a democratic group consensus—working out compromises where possible and, in the end, following the democratic principle of doing what the majority thinks best.

These decision-making opportunities should only be offered when the choices are real and are truly appropriate for children to evaluate. For example, it would *not* be appropriate to ask the children to decide what to do about a youngster who is wetting his pants or to expect them to make a decision on whether school fees should be raised, but it would be within their ability to ask them to suggest a number of ways Halloween might be celebrated or how they would help their friend Cindy feel better because her puppy died.

An alternative to taking the risk of abiding by a group decision, if you feel the children are too immature to reach an adequate one, is to tell them you want some ideas and suggestions that will help *you* arrive at a fair or good decision.

Link Language to the Printed Page

Parents often think of reading as being the first and fundamental building block of school success, and in a way, they are right. The ability to read and to grasp the meaning of what is read *is* basic to school success.

What they may fail to realize is that reading is actually just one link in a long developmental chain of broader literacy skills the child must forge from infancy onward, and that the concept of literacy extends far beyond the conventional idea of being able to read (Fields & Spangler, 1995; Strickland & Morrow, 1989).

Learning to substitute symbols for reality, for example, is a major step toward reading. Every time a child looks at a picture and talks about what it represents or pretends that something is something else—that is part of becoming literate, just

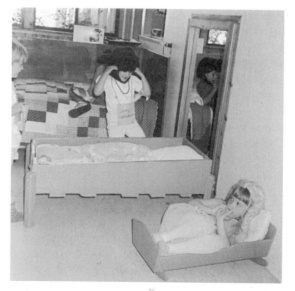

Acting out a beloved story: A wonderful way to add meaning to the printed page and a good example of an effective emergent literacy activity.

as understanding how to hold a book right side up is also part of that process. Indeed, all of the skills described earlier in this chapter—singing, telling stories, doing finger plays, and chatting with the teacher—are all important aspects of acquiring the language skills that underlie the later ability to read.

In addition to these more broadly based approaches to fostering the development of language and, ultimately, reading skills, there are many more specific ways to draw children's attention to the value of the printed word.

Reading aloud to children, which should be done both at home and school, is the most significant and satisfying way to convince children that print is important. It is true that when parents are encouraged to make a point of reading to their children and talking over what they are reading, children increase their language skills and do better in school (Halsall & Green, 1995; Nurss, 1991).

Unfortunately, only about one-third of 3- to 8-year-old children are read to by family members daily (*Young Children*, 1996). When we consider the Hart and Risley research reported earlier in this chapter, which reveals the distressing differences in the amount of vocabulary possessed by upper- and middle-SES children compared with youngsters on welfare, *the value of encouraging lower-income parents to read to their children takes on added importance.* It is such a relatively simple way to enrich the children's vocabulary and foster the foundations of literacy at the same time (Matthias & Gulley, 1995). Sometimes it is also necessary to offer literacy programs for the grown-ups to help that happen. This may be because the parent cannot read in any language (Darling, 1989) or because the parent comes from a bilingual background (Quinteror & Verlarde, 1990).

Additional informal strategies that draw attention to the importance of print and reading can also take place at home as well as at school, as Figure 15–1 demonstrates so clearly. Note the range of ages that are included in the examples and the way the activities are integrated into the life of the home.

When writing a child's name on his painting, call attention to the fact that you are starting on the left and printing toward the right. Use both uppercase and lowercase letters.

At school the strategies can also be casual and fun. They might be as simple as pointing out the convenience of labeling a child's picture, so "we'll know I should give it to you when it's time to go home," or as complex as writing down a story the group dictates describing where the rabbit hid when he got out. Or perhaps the teacher can say, "Just a minute—I have to read the directions so I'll know how to put it together," or "Here, let's write a note to your mother telling her you went down the slide for the first time." Or the teacher might set out a picture recipe for the children to follow on their own as they make individual fruit milk shakes.

It is also important to provide children with opportunities to use writing materials themselves as they move from scribbles, to pictures, and gradually incorporate the additional symbolic forms of

FIGURE 15–1
Selected Home-Based Literacy Events from Studies of Five Children

---

Child #1 (four-and-a-half-year-old)

1. Sorted Valentines for family members.
2. Drew lines with a ruler to make budget like mom's. Asked mom to help her make the words for her budget.
3. Marked days on the calendar with pictures or words to indicate coming events.
4. Checked cards in the pockets of library books. Checked calendar to see when due date was—how many more days.
5. Mom read directions to child from a cake box about how to test for doneness.
6. Played waitress in the kitchen while mom prepared dinner. Mom wrote drink choices on a piece of paper. Child circled drink dad wanted.
7. Watched mom write a letter in cursive. Asked mom to write her name in cursive. Child then wrote her name in three ways: Caps, lowercase, and cursive (mom helped with this one).

Child #2 (three-and-a-half-year-old)

1. Wrote letter to her dad in scribble writing.
2. Older brother read about 10 books to her at her request.
3. Read the letters she saw on road signs, while in the car.
4. Watched Sesame Street. Then, she and her mother tried to think of words that begin with "C." Mom thought of most of them.
5. Added words in her own scribble writing to grocery list on the oven door.
6. Asked about Dead End sign she saw while at grandmother's house. Recognized another Dead End sign a few days later.
7. Helped mom put laundry in the washer. Figured out, with mom's help, the words "cold," "warm," and "hot."

Child #3 (four-year-old)

1. Noticed the letter R on his sister's bike.
2. Took a box which had the numeral 2 on it out of the trash. Ripped the box to tear off the part with the numeral, and gave it to his mom.
3. Picked up the mail and tried to see if there was any mail for him. Mom showed him a piece with his name and address on it.
4. Looked through the Sunday newspaper to see the funnies and toy ads.
5. Looked at an alphabet book and wanted to know why there were 2 letters on each page. (Upper and lowercase letters were shown.)
6. Asked mom in the grocery store to read the signs posted above the vegetables.
7. Went to the bank with his father. Wrote on back of deposit slips as if doing a transaction. Asked father to write "bank open" and "bank closed."

FIGURE 15–1

continued

Child #4 (three years, two months old)

1. Asked mom to give her some mail to read after they had picked up the mail.

2. Found the letters A and F on the menu at a restaurant.

3. Watched Sesame Street and read the numerals on the screen. Then she counted from 1–8 by herself.

4. Traced over the names that mom had written on birthday bags for friends invited to birthday party.

5. Wrote on the order form of the sales catalogue. Carefully filled each box on the order form with writing.

6. Went to the theater to watch "Sleeping Beauty." Asked what it said in the credits on the screen.

7. Read the numerals and letters on the calendar in bathroom while she was sitting on her toilet seat. Mom read each day for her, and she repeated it: "Monday, May 15. Tuesday, May 16," etc.

Child #5 (five-year-old)

1. Mom made blank book for child to draw and write in (like a book), at child's request.

2. Mom covered milk cartons with brown paper to make buildings for a model city. Child asked mom for the spelling of "library" and other words.

3. On trip to New York, child asked mom to spell "American flag," "red," "green," and "yellow." (Markers and papers had been packed for the trip.)

4. Dad read books to daughter, at her request.

5. After visiting the Children's Museum, child wrote "fish." Mom helped by making the "fff" sound for "F" and by reminding her that the letters "s" and "h" are used to represent the sound at the end of the word "fish." Mom told her to write the letter "i" in the middle of the word.

6. Asked Dad to write "Joseph" and "Mike," the names of friends, for her to copy.

7. Mom baked letter cookies to spell "Happy Birthday." Made each letter out of dough as child said the letters one by one. Child knew how to spell "Happy Birthday" because she had written it on many birthday cards for friends, when she was invited to a party.

Note. From "Preschoolers and Academics: Some Thoughts" by J. A. Schickedanz, S. Chay, P. Gopin, L. L. Sheng, S. M. Song, and N. Wild (1990), *Young Children, 46*(1), p. 6. Data included came from four sources: (1) A study done by J. Schickedanz and M. Sullivan, some of which was reported in J. Schickedanz & M. Sullivan (1984), "Mom, What Does u-f-f Spell?" *Language Arts, 61*(1), 7–17 (children 1 and 2); (2) Paula Gopin (1989), case study of home-based literacy events (mimeo) (child 3); (3) Soo-Mi Song (1989), case study of home-based literacy events (mimeo) (child 4); (4) Soyoung Chay (1989), case study of home-based literacy events (mimeo) (child 5).

letters and numbers in their work. Felt-tip pens, crayons, old typewriters, and possibly computers can be used to good advantage in this regard (Morrow, 1995). Inclusion of writing materials during play is still another way to draw attention to the value of the printed page. Perhaps when the children are playing "McDonald's," order forms and play money can be included or letters can be addressed and mailed for Valentine's Day. All of these activities help children understand that there is a useful relationship between the printed word and what happens in life (Morrow, 1990).

Summary

One of the most important skills children acquire in the years before primary school is the ability to use language effectively. For this reason, teachers need to do all they can to facilitate such growth. Strategies include encouraging children to put their ideas into words as frequently as possible, maintaining the children's *home* languages in the school, and being aware of developmental timetables so that children who require special help can obtain it promptly. Conducting conversations rather than interrogations and asking questions that tend to prolong conversations are additional ways of facilitating the growth of language.

Specific curriculum activities to promote such growth include the use of auditory discrimination games, songs and records, poetry and finger plays, and books and stories.

It is also vital to link language to the printed page to help children forge still another link in the chain of literacy skills. Ways of weaving these activities into an attractive group time are suggested in chapter 16.

Self-Check Questions for Review

Content-Related Questions

1. List some average, "milestone" language behaviors typical for 2-, 3-, and 4-year-old children. Why is it important for teachers to know what these "milestones" are?
2. What are the three different theories explaining how children acquire language? Is there anything teachers can do, according to these theories, to help children acquire language?
3. Should teachers look down on children who speak Black English or require bilingual children to speak only English while they are at school?
4. Explain what teachers should do about the child who is not fluent in any language.
5. Think of a situation in which a teacher is talking with a child and practice including comments that would draw the child into more extended chatting.

6. Name three skills teachers should develop that will foster the development of children's language skills.
7. This chapter provides many suggestions for presenting language activities in seven areas. What are these areas? Be sure to include some specific recommendations for making each area more effective with children.
8. Does "literacy" mean that someone knows how to read? Be sure you can explain your answer and supply examples of skills young children must acquire before actually learning to read from the printed page.
9. In the Hart and Risley study about vocabulary acquisition, which socioeconomic class of children had the largest vocabulary and which had the smallest?
10. Does the difference in amount of vocabulary and comprehension become increasingly important in high school? If it does, why is that the case?

Integrative Questions

1. Suppose that two 4-year-olds are investigating the let's-find-out table. They are using ice cubes, putting them in tubs of warm and cold water to see which temperature water makes the ice melt faster. They are also sucking on the ice cubes from time to time. Give several examples of controlling comments the teacher might make. Then cite some additional information that the teacher could give or ask instead.
2. Heather and Allison are talking with you about Christmas and making grandiose plans about their presents. Then Allison says, "And if my little brother gets *anything*—even *one* thing—I'm gonna take it away and flush it down the toilet!" Give an example of a reply that would be moralistic and would probably put an end to further conversation. Then give two examples of replies that would extend the conversation further.
3. Pick out a song you think would be appropriate to teach young children. Then explain why you selected it, basing your explanation on the criteria recommended in the book for selecting children's songs.
4. Since the Hart and Risley research found out that differences in the amount of vocabulary growth in very early childhood were not related to the children's performance on reading, writing, spelling,

and arithmetic scores in the third grade, does this mean, according to those researchers, that the differences in vocabulary and comprehension also present in the third grade really do not matter?

Questions and Activities

1. You are teaching in a Head Start center, and you have a 4-year-old Mexican girl in the group who only replies in single English words when asked a question. What factors and possibilities would you want to consider before deciding how to deal with this behavior?
2. Many interesting questions arise when bilingual education is discussed. For example, the following question has been a hot topic in recent years: Do you think that staff members who are able to speak two languages (both of which are needed in the particular children's center where they teach) should receive additional compensation because they possess this special skill? Why or why not?
3. Imagine that some 4-year-olds you know have begun a conversation with you with the following statements: "Teacher, Teacher, Mindy had puppies last night." (Mindy is a cat!) "Guess what, Teacher, it's raining, and I got my head all wet!" "My Mother says I don't have to go outside today!" Now make up two conversational scripts for each of the children's statements—one script that you feel would deaden the conversation and one that would encourage children to continue it.
4. Is it possible to ask children too many questions? What might be some alternative ways of keeping conversation going instead of always asking questions?
5. Go to the corner drugstore or discount store and look over the inexpensive books offered there for children. Select and purchase a desirable and undesirable one and bring them to class. Be ready to explain their weak and strong points.

References for Further Reading

Overviews

Baron, N. S. (1992). *Growing up with language: How children learn to talk*. Reading, MA: Addison-Wesley. Baron provides us with an interesting, chatty book based on recent research about language development. She includes many practical suggestions about ways to facilitate its growth.

Jalongo, M. R. (1988). *Young children and picture books: Literature from infancy to six*. Washington, DC: National Association for the Education of Young Children. The joy of really good picture books is captured here. The author explains how to select quality books and how to present them so effectively that children will fall in love with them and with reading, too. *Highly recommended*.

Rice, M. L., & Wilcox, K. A. (Eds.). (1995). *Building a language-focused curriculum for the preschool classroom. Vol. 1: A foundation for lifelong communication*. Baltimore, MD: Brookes. This book and its companion volume by B. H. Bunce (1995)—*Building a language-focused curriculum for the preschool classroom. Vol. 2: A planning guide* (Baltimore, MD: Brookes)—are filled with sensible advice and examples of ways to incorporate a rich infusion of language stimulation into an otherwise "typical" children's center. The material is based on the Language Acquisition Preschool at the University of Kansas. *Highly recommended*.

Fostering Conversation

Bos, B. (1983). *Before the basics: Creating conversations with children*. Roseville, CA: Turn the Page. Bos's book is an utter delight! It is mostly about generating happy, wholesome relationships with children through the medium of music, conversation, and movement.

Jalongo, M. R. (1996). Teaching young children to become better listeners. *Young Children, 51*(2), 21–26. This article offers many concrete suggestions to teachers about how to become better conversationalists and listeners themselves as well as teaching those skills to children.

Bilingual and Multilectical Information

Smitherman, G. (1994). *Black talk: Words and phrases from the hood to the amen corner*. Boston: Houghton Mifflin. This is primarily a dictionary of current usage but also includes a helpful introductory essay. *Highly recommended*.

Soto, L. D. (1991). Research in review: Understanding bilingual/bicultural young children. *Young Children, 46*(2), 30–36. Soto reviews some myths about bilingualism and then outlines research-tested, effective approaches for teaching bilingual children.

Poetry[2]

Arbuthnot, M. H., & Root, S. L. (1968). *Time for poetry* (3rd ed.). Glenview, IL: Scott, Foresman. This book is a treasure. It is filled with poetry (most of which can be used at the preschool level) arranged by topic, and it also contains a valuable chapter on sharing poetry with children.

---

[2]Finger plays are listed in chapter 16.

Prelutsky, C. (Ed.). (1986) *Read aloud rhymes for the very young*. New York: Knopf. Delightfully illustrated, these poems *are* simple. They are also conveniently arranged somewhat according to subject.

Enjoying Books Together—Linking Home and School

Gottschall, S. M. (1995). Hug-a-Book: A program to nurture a young child's love of books and reading. *Young Children*, 50(4), 19–35. This is an inspiring description of practical ways to link home and center to books in an enhancing way.

Halsall, S., & Green, C. (1995). Reading aloud: A way for parents to support their children's growth in literacy. *Early Childhood Education Journal*, 23(1), 27–35. The authors provide many practical suggestions for encouraging families to include books in their lives. *Highly recommended*.

Mathias, M., & Gulley, B. (Eds.). (1995). *Celebrating family literacy through intergenerational programming*. Wheaton, MD: Association for Childhood Education International. This practical book provides many examples of ways to value families and include them in literacy activities. There is particularly helpful information on the Navajo point of view. *Highly recommended*.

Trelease, J. (1989). *The new read-aloud handbook*. New York: Penguin. A sensible, easy-to-read paperback that is filled with good advice for parents and teachers on enjoying books with children. Excellent bibliography.

Bibliographies of Children's Books

Kotlus, E., & Gellert, S. (1994). *Helping children love themselves and others: Resource guide to equity materials for young children* (rev. ed.). Washington, D.C.: Children's Foundation (725 Fifteenth St., N.W., Suite 505, Washington, DC 20005-2109). The books annotated here are identified by appropriate reader age, gender, race/culture, multiethnic background, and disabilities. Also includes resources for adults. *Highly recommended*.

McGowan, M., McGowan, T., & Wheeler, P. (1994). *Appreciating diversity through children's literature: Teaching activities for the primary grades*. Englewood, CO: Teacher ideas Press/Libraries Unlimited. This valuable reference includes material on dealing with aging, disabilities, gender, and ethnicity.

Fostering Literacy

Fields, M. V., & Spangler, K. L. (1995). *Let's begin reading right: Developmentally appropriate beginning literacy*. (3rd ed.). Upper Saddle River, NJ: Merrill/Prentice Hall. This book discusses the underpinnings of literacy and then discusses the development of reading and writing with older youngsters. *Highly recommended*.

Morrow, L. M. (1995). Literacy all around. *Scholastic Early Childhood Today*, 9(4), 34–41. Numerous examples are provided that illustrate how reading, writing, and oral language can be incorporated into self-select activities in a developmentally appropriate way.

For the Advanced Student

Crawford, P. A. (1995). Early literacy: Emerging perspectives: *Journal of Research in Childhood Education*, 10(1), 71–86. This is the best, clearest summary of historical and current approaches to developing literacy I have ever seen. *Highly recommended*.

Duchan, J. F. (1995). *Supporting language learning in everyday life*. San Diego: Singular. The chapter "The Influence of Culture on Children's Language Learning" raises many excellent points about how important it is to be sensitive to differing cultural values and their effects on children's speech.

Dyson, A. H., & Genishi, C. (1993). Visions of children as language users: Language and language education in early childhood. In B. Spodek (Ed.), *Handbook of research on the education of young children*. Upper Saddle River, NJ: Prentice Hall. The authors stress the role of socialization in children's language development.

Flavell, J. H., Miller, P. H., and Miller, S. A. (1993). *Cognitive development* (3rd ed.). Upper Saddle River, NJ: Prentice Hall. A readable yet thorough review of research on language acquisition is provided here. *Highly recommended*.

Garcia, E. E., & McLaughlin, B. (1995). *Meeting the challenge of linguistic and cultural diversity in early childhood education*. New York: Teachers College Press. This book focuses almost entirely on bilingual Mexican children. It covers subjects ranging from assessment to social development and would be most suitable for the advanced student.

Hecht, M. L., Collier, M. J., & Ribeau, S. A. (1993). *African American communication: Ethnic identity and cultural interpretation*. Newbury Park, CA: Sage. The authors provide a wide-ranging analysis of various components of African American communicative style.

McNamme, G. D. (1990). Learning to read and write in an inner-city setting: A longitudinal study of community change. In L. C. Moll (Ed.), *Vygotsky and education: Instructional implications and applications of sociohistorical psychology*. New York: Cambridge University Press. I hope readers will not be put off by the title—actually the chapter is a delightful account of how Head Start staff and community people worked with an adviser to increase developmentally appropriate literacy activities in their centers. *Highly recommended*.

Stott, J. C. (1995). *Native Americans in children's literature*. Phoenix: ORYX. Books written by Native and nonnative authors are

thoughtfully reviewed and discussed in relation to standards that should be applied when selecting them—
scholarly in tone.

Teale, W. H., & Sulzby, E. (1996). Emergent literacy: New perspectives. In R. D. Robinson, M. C. McKenna, & J. M.
Wedman (Eds.), *Issues and trends in literacy education*.
Boston: Allyn & Bacon. This is a reprint of an influential,
classic article defining the subject of emergent literacy
and recommending how to apply that approach in the
classroom.

Putting It All Together for a Good Group Time

Have you ever

- Wanted to offer more than songs and stories in group time but did not know what else to include?
- Worried about how to control restless children while you were reading to them?
- Needed help in planning language experiences for two different age groups?

If you have, the material in this chapter will help you.

Responding to children's spontaneous impulses to speak at the story table seems preferable to suppressing speech at one time and trying to draw it out at another. Remarks in the middle of a story may add to its significance for everyone, and if a discussion then developed, that would be the time to give language expression preference.

Elinor Fitch Griffin (1982)

Language-enhancing experiences should be present throughout the day, as we have seen in chapter 15. In addition to this continual interweaving of language with activity, a discussion of group time is included here because group time presents the opportunity par excellence for putting all the language and cognitive activities together in an integrated way, while also nourishing the child's social self.

We should bear in mind that the fundamental purpose of group time is to generate an occasion when everyone enjoys being together. It should be a happy time, not one marred by constant reprimands, unpleasantness, and struggles for control.

Well-presented group times provide opportunities for learning to do many things. Children are expected to focus their attention, to listen while others speak, to participate in discussions, to control wiggly impulses, and to keep themselves from being distracted by rambunctious neighbors. This is a great deal to expect from such young human beings. Fortunately, there are many things that teachers can do to help children meet these expectations and promote harmony as well.

Structuring the Group for Success

Keep the Groups as Small and Stable as Possible

The larger the group, the less personal attention each child receives, the fewer opportunities he has to participate, and the more waiting he must do. If this were stated as an equation, it would look like this:

$$\text{Less personal attention } + \text{ More waiting } =$$

$$\begin{array}{ccc} \text{Reduced} \\ \text{learning} \end{array} + \begin{array}{c} \text{Increased} \\ \text{discipline} \end{array} + \begin{array}{c} \text{Control} \\ \text{problems} \end{array}$$

Some teachers try to solve this by having a second adult do "police duty" on the fringes of the group, but it is more effective to split the group and give half of them to the other person.

If the same children are divided into the same groups each day, it is easier to continue interests from time to time as these build. Keeping the group population stable also fosters a sense of belonging among the children.

Choose a Time and Place That Minimize Tension and Distractions

Just before lunch is about the most stressful point of the day to offer group time. It is much better to choose a time when the children are rested and not hungry. For example, many teachers begin the day with this experience as soon as all the children have arrived.

Stress can also be reduced by locating groups as far away from each other as possible. Try to shield each group from the others by placing a low barrier between them, such as a screen or bookcase.

Choose a place that offers few distractions. If

you sit in front of a shelf of toys, for example, children's eyes are bound to wander to the delights on the shelves behind you. It is also wise to seat the children far enough away from any equipment so that it is out of their reach. An ideal site is a cozy corner with rugs and a feeling of softness about it.

Plan Carefully and Be Flexible

An important part of promoting harmonious learning at group time is being relaxed yourself. *Nothing fosters this as much as careful planning and advance preparation.* Always assemble the ingredients of the group-time curriculum beforehand, and have them in reach but as much out of the sight of the children as possible. Be sure to read books and poetry all the way through in advance to make certain that they are what you really want and to familiarize yourself thoroughly with the material.

Peace of mind is increased if more materials are selected than there will be time to use (two cognitive activities, for example, or several books), because it is almost impossible to know, in the beginning, what will be effective in group time and what will not. There is no sin in simply setting a book aside that the children do not enjoy and going on to something else.

Readiness to extend or contract an activity, to change the order of presentation, and to improvise spontaneously in response to the children's interests as needed are the hallmarks of the truly master teacher.

Start Group Time as Soon as Children Begin to Gather

Do not expect the children to sit quietly and wait until the last straggler appears. Having to wait encourages youngsters to think of all kinds of things to do! It is far better to begin group immediately with a song or finger plays. These activities are so attractive that laggards will want to hurry over. Moreover, these particular activities are easy for children to join in as they arrive.

Prepare Children for What You Intend to Present Next

The children will participate more if they understand what is going to happen next during group. So many times I have watched inexperienced teachers suddenly launch into song or pick up a book and begin reading without introducing it first. The look of bewilderment on the children's faces as they struggle to shift gears makes it obvious that a simple introduction is helpful. Perhaps the teacher can say, "Now we're going to sing that funny song about 'Hop Se Hi.' Do you remember what we did yesterday while we sang it?" or "I'm going to share a story with you today I bet a lot of you have heard before. It's a story about a little rabbit named Peter who has a special adventure in Mr. MacGreagor's garden."

Present Difficult or New Experiences Early

Decide in advance what activity is likely to require the most concentration or effort by the children. Perhaps this is the cognitive game or learning a new song. Present this early when the children are still fresh and attentive.

Change the Pace and Include Variety

Group time should generally be upbeat; do not allow anything to drag on too long. Since it is so taxing for young children to sit still for extended periods, some kind of exercise and movement should be provided as part of this experience. Typically this takes the form of finger plays and body movement ideas. It also might involve a relaxation exercise in which the children practice stretching out and letting go.

Encourage Discussion Among the Children

It seems that new teachers in particular fear being interrupted by the children during the group experience, so they read breathlessly through a book, brushing the children's interested comments aside as distractions. This is probably because they dread losing control, but allowing the children to respond to questions and volunteer information increases their interest in what is happening. It also encourages them to put their ideas into words and to share experiences with the group (Conlon, 1992).

Kindergarten teachers often plan for this deliberately by including a sharing time when every child contributes something. At the preschool level, doing this usually causes the other children to fidget and lose interest because it takes too long. For this reason, it seems best to allow time for children to interject spontaneous remarks and comments as group progresses. Often such remarks can be developed into a valuable discussion that involves many of the children. When it is time to return to the story, all the teacher has to do is say, for example, "Well, that certainly was interesting hearing about how Anselmo caught that fish. Now let's go back to Curious George and see if he caught one, too."

Move with the Children's Ideas

Of course, it is not always possible to shift the group time focus immediately in accord with an interest expressed by the children. However, if the teacher is paying close attention to what the children say, sometimes their discussions reveal an interest that is both unanticipated and surprising. Such an event can be a godsend when thinking about where the curriculum should move next.

Draw the Group to a Close Before It Falls Apart

It is always better to stop a little too soon than to go on and on until the children end up frantic to get away. Quit while you are ahead; then everyone will want to come back next time.

What to Do When a Child Continues to Distract the Group

Even when all these strategies are practiced faithfully, all teachers encounter children from time to time who are unable to conform to reasonable standards of behavior during group. The first thing to consider under such circumstances is whether the child is physically *able* to conform. Does he see well? How is his hearing? Consider also whether he might be developmentally younger than the other children so that the material presented is inappropriate for his interests.

When such problems create group-time difficulties, special plans have to be made that will enable the child to participate. Perhaps he needs to sit closer to the teacher to see or hear, or perhaps he can be dismissed early from the group or be read to by himself. Sometimes a number of such youngsters can be gathered into a separate group by another staff member so that the material is more appropriate to their age and interests.

Many children, however, do not seem to suffer from any of these problems, but they continue to be disruptive. The solution to this depends a lot on the philosophy of the particular teacher. Some teachers believe it is acceptable for children who do not want to be part of group time to play by themselves, as long as they are quiet and do not disturb the group. It is often, but not always, the case that such youngsters gradually return and join with the others as they become aware of the fun going on in the group.

Other teachers feel that this time of being together is so important that all children should attend. They have the restless one sit beside them, separating him from particular friends who may be drawn into misbehavior and then giving him a special role in the group. Perhaps he can turn the pages during story reading or hold the flannel board while others put on special items. Firm expectations of desirable behavior have to be projected to such a child as well.

If all else fails, it is occasionally necessary to have another adult remove the obstreperous one from the group. That person should explain to the child that he has lost the privilege of staying and may only return when he has made up his mind to be more cooperative. (This essentially is an application of the six learning steps described in chapter 12.)

Finally, Enjoy the Children

There is no substitute for your interest and enthusiasm. Be well enough prepared that you do not have to worry about how group time will go. Forget about the little, irritating things that do not really matter, and concentrate on relaxing and letting the children know you like them and that you are excited about what you are going to do together. This will make group time a pleasure for everyone.

Planning the Curriculum for Success

What Should a Good Group Time Include?

The basic educational goals of a good group time should be the development of receptive and expressive language, the enhancement of thinking processes, and the provision of a positive social experience for the children.

At first, planning a comprehensive group time may seem overwhelming because there are so many things to take into account. However, these basically boil down to just two considerations: the variety of content to include and the reason for including each item.

Contents of a Good Group Time

To provide variety of content in group time, each of the following ingredients should be included at least once during the week—and the more of them that can be used every day, the better.

1. Practice in auditory discrimination skills and listening
2. Songs
3. Poetry
4. Stories (not necessarily a book)
5. Finger plays and action activities
6. Discussions
7. Practice in a cognitive activity (discussed in chapters 17 and 18)
8. Something that is multiethnic or nonsexist

Unfortunately, as the research by McAfee (1985) reveals, all too often this kind of variety is not provided during group time. This is a shame because a well-planned group experience offers opportunities for a multitude of language, social, emotional, and cognitive learning experiences that are unsurpassed during the center day.

Basic Curriculum-Planning Principles

The following are fundamental principles to remember when planning a curriculum for group time:

- It is fun and helps tie learning together if you include one or two activities in group time that are related to the focus of interest for the week.
- *Always* be sensitive to the importance of including multicultural and nonsexist materials—and *always* check the materials you are using for possible bias before presentation.
- Keep the materials appropriate for the age with which you are working. (Note how the same subject matter, rabbits, is presented for young threes and older fours in Table 16–1 on pages 362–363, and Table 16–2 on page 365.
- Group times are precious—do not waste them. Be certain there is a valid reason for including every item you have selected.
- One selection can serve several purposes. For example, *Stellaluna* (Cannon, 1993), a delightful story about bats and birds, provides a wholesome message about sameness and differentness, while also presenting bats in a sympathetic light, including some information

Do Plans and Practice Match?

Research Study

Research Question   McAfee asked, How do teachers think about, plan, and conduct group time activities?

Research Method   In this exploratory study, 35 teachers teaching children from ages 2 ½ through kindergarten were interviewed, and five classrooms from that group were selected for intense observation. The programs all met the standards for good quality, with adequate or better than adequate adult/child ratios. About half of the teachers had a degree in early childhood education, child development, or a related area.

Teachers were asked to list types of activities commonly used during group times and to also include the most frequent difficulties they encountered while leading group times. Then during group time each classroom was observed for 48 1-minute time samples, and the results were recorded.

Results   The teachers listed 14 types of activities commonly used during group time. These were books/stories, music, songs, movement, finger plays, discussion, sharing/show-and-tell, lessons and demonstrations, traditional opening activities, planning and review, dramatizations, games, films, poetry and "other" (such as relaxation and news time).

However, when the analysis of the observations was completed, it turned out that the only activities usually included were books (33% of the time), music (10% of the time), sharing/show and tell (23% of the time), and traditional opening activities such as calendar and taking roll (13% of the time). The kinds of activities did not vary according to the children's ages. Advance planning in order to realize long-term educational goals was not typical.

When listing management difficulties, the teachers said that some children's disruptive behaviors and the need to balance individual needs with group needs were the hardest things to cope with. The teachers reported that 75% of the time the reasons for these problems were beyond their control; they ascribed the difficulties to developmental levels, emotional or behavioral problems, home background, or classroom conditions such as too many children.

about how they live, all presented in the context of a beautifully illustrated, good story.

- Good group times require not only careful planning and advance preparation but also the freedom to deviate from the plan when something special comes up.
- Practice may not make perfect, but doing group time over and over really helps. Seize every opportunity you can to practice this valuable skill.

Planning for Older 2- and Young 3-Year-Olds

A group of threes (or twos) does best with short and simple stories, large picture books, and con-

siderable repetition of material. This group also appreciates beginning with a familiar activity each time—perhaps "Head, Shoulders, Knees, and Toes" or "Where Is Thumbkin?" Group times should be kept fairly short for such young children and should use active participation whenever possible. Remember, there should be a sound reason for including every piece of material (see Table 16–1).

In Table 16–2 the focus of interest for this group of young threes is on dogs (carried over from the previous week) and rabbits, and materials were selected accordingly. A nonsexist component is not included because the material is about evenly divided between male and fe-

---

Implications for Teaching   If this sample, which was admittedly exploratory, is typical of what happens in most preschool and kindergarten classrooms, the news is not good. Teachers who rely on the same repetitive routines of calendar, weather, books, and songs are depriving themselves and the children of wonderful opportunities to expand their worlds. Moreover, using some of these strategies with children as young as 2 or 3 years of age is inappropriate. No wonder the children were restless and inattentive and that control situations proliferated.

It is clear from the original list that the teachers knew of many activities that should be included in group times, and it is just as clear from the observations that they did not include them. We must ask ourselves why those teachers did such a mediocre job when they knew and would probably have liked to do better. Most likely, the poor quality was due to a number of factors such as fatigue, pressure to keep moving from one thing to the next during the day, and apathy.

Providing educationally worthwhile group times takes self-discipline and energy combined with the sincere convictions that group time presents invaluable opportunities to promote thinking and reasoning skills, as well as developing language and social expertise. It requires self-discipline to sit down and plan such experiences in advance, energy to carry the plans out once they have been made, and sufficient conviction that group time is valuable to make careful planning a consistent part of the program. To ensure the success of group time, sustained effort is required not just once in a while, but daily.

Finally, teachers need to see themselves as being more in control of the situation than did the teachers in the sample. For example, rather than blaming the children for misbehaving because they are immature, it makes better sense to adjust what the teacher is doing and to suit the activities being offered to the age of the children instead of making impossible demands on them to behave better.

Note. From "Circle Time: Getting Past 'Two Little Pumpkins'" by O. D. McAfee, 1985, *Young Children*, 40(6), pp. 24–29.

---

male animal stories or the animal's sex is not discernible.

Planning for Older 4-Year-Olds

Older fours can sit for fairly long periods of time, especially when they are interested in the material. They enjoy some repetition but also relish diversity. They are thirsty for information per se and can deal with experience on a more verbal level. For example, they can grasp the idea that different languages can have different words for the same thing, and they enjoy learning some of these words. They are also partial to "nonsense" rhymes. Fours are able to talk about their feel-

ings and can deal with simple social discussions of such things as the pleasures and perils of giving and receiving gifts. They are also interested in the concept of growing up, and they are developing strong ideas about appropriate sex roles. The materials in Table 16–3 (pp. 366–367) have been selected with these characteristics in mind.

In Table 16–4 (pp. 368–369) the focus of interest for this group is rabbits and doing things for other people—in this case, making and receiving gifts. The tonsillectomy material is included to meet the need of a particular child and alleviate the anxiety of the group about what might happen to him.

TABLE 16–1

Analysis of Reasons for Selection of Literary Materials to Use with Young Threes (listed in the order of the days as they appear in Table 16–2)

Resource *	Reasons for Selection
Books	
Angus and the Cat Written and illustrated by Marjorie Flack (1931)	Beloved classic; continues dog focus from last week
Raindrops and Rabbits Written and illustrated by Jim Aronovsky (1997)	Good picture of how rabbits live underground and make other animals welcome
What Whiskers Did Written and illustrated by Ruth Carroll (1965)	A storytelling book that features a rabbit, uses no words, and requires children to tell story
Freckles the Rabbit Written by J. Burton (1989)	Accurate photographs of rabbits and how they live and develop; simple text
Where's the Bunny? Written and illustrated by Ruth Carroll (1950)	Another very simple book that requires children to hunt for hidden bunny (bunny is easy to find); also has dog, which continues dog focus
Whistle for Willie Written and illustrated by Ezra Jack Keats (1964)	Features a small African American child and his dog and deals with a universal experience; provides multiethnic experience; ties in with focus of previous week
What's Your Name? Written and illustrated by Zhenya Gay (1955)	Lists characteristics of familiar animals and asks children to guess their identity — a good review of what children have learned this week about rabbits
Animals on the Farm Feodor Rojankovsky (1982)	Simple, handsome pictures; presents concept of farm animals per se
Goodnight, Moon Written by Margaret Wise Brown, illustrated by Clement Hurd (1947)	A classic beloved by young children; story focuses on rabbit going to sleep; helpful to relax children; children must search carefully for little mouse that is hiding in the room (mouse is hard to find)
The Snuggle Bunny Written by N. Jewell, illustrated by March Chalmers (1972)	About rabbits and also about loneliness, caring, and older people

Resource *	Reasons for Selection
Poetry and Finger Plays	
"Listening" Miriam Clark Potter (1955)	For fun; short enough for children to learn; talks about mother-child relationship; flannel board provides variety and helps children remember as they say the poem
"My Rabbit"	Appropriate subject matter
A Tale of Tales Written by Elizabeth MacPherson, illustrated by Garth Williams (1962)	Charming illustrations; presents simple concept combined with poetry and has rabbit in it; might add song "Why Rabbits Have Bright Shiny Noses," if children can sit still that long
Songs	
"Head, Shoulders, Knees, and Toes"	Opening activity for the children
"Bye, Baby Bunting" and "Where Oh Where Has My Little Dog Gone?"	Rabbit and dog themes; familiar childhood songs
"Hop Se Hi"	Fits rabbit theme and provides the relief of large-muscle exercise for children
"Bingo"	Scottish American folk song about dogs — repeat from previous week

All the books for young threes and older fours have been selected with the criterion of age appropriateness in mind. They have also been selected because of their outstanding illustrations and good literary quality. The full names of authors and illustrators are given whenever possible because teachers should get to know these creative people as familiar, treasured friends of children.

*See material in the section "Examples of Poetry, Finger Plays, and Songs for Group Time" below.

Examples of Poetry, Finger Plays, and Songs for Group Time

Poetry

Listening[1]
Miriam Clark Potter

This is Mrs. Rabbit's house
    Up the stairs perhaps,
Hear the little bunnikins

Taking sniffy naps.
Sniffy naps, small sniffy naps,
    With their eyes shut tight.
Mrs. Rabbit's listening,
    To hear if they're all right.

The Rabbit[2]
Elizabeth Madox Roberts

When they said the time to hide was mine,
    I hid back under a thick grapevine.
And while I was still for the time to pass,

[1]Adapted from "Mrs. Bunny's House" from *Sleepy Kitten* by Miriam Clark Potter. Copyright 1938 by E. P. Dutton, renewed 1966 by Miriam Clark Potter. Reprinted by permission of E. P. Dutton, a division of New American Library.

[2]From *Under the Tree* by Elizabeth Madox Roberts. Copyright 1930, renewed 1958 by the Viking Press, Inc. Reprinted by permission of Viking Penguin Inc.

Good groups can happen any place!

TABLE 16–2 A Weekly Plan for Group Time with Young Threes (main topics are rabbits and dogs)

	Monday	Tuesday	Wednesday	Thursday	Friday
Stories to Read and Tell	*Angus and the Cat* Flack (1931) *The Big Red Barn* Brown (1989)	*What Whiskers Did* Carroll (1965) *Freckles the Rabbit* Burton (1989) *Rabbits and Raindrops* Aronovsky (1997)	*Where's the Bunny?* Carroll (1950) *Whistle for Willie* Keats (1964)	*What's Your Name?* Gay (1955) *Animals on the Farm* Rojankovsky (1982) *Goodnight, Moon* Brown (1947)	*The Snuggle Bunny* Jewell (1972) *What's Your Name?* Gay (1955) (repeated)
Poetry and Finger Plays	"Listening" Potter (1955) (flannel board)	*A Tale of Tales* MacPherson (1962) "Listening" (repeated)	"My Rabbit" (finger play)	"My Rabbit" (finger play, repeated)	"Listening" (flannel board, repeated)
Auditory Training		Children pull animal pictures out of "secret box," then give them to teacher when they hear her make animal's sounds.	Use tape recording of familiar household sounds, then children identify them.	With *Animals on the Farm*, teacher makes two animal noises for each picture, and children decide which is the correct one.	Play recordings of very familiar household sounds; children identify them (repeated).
Songs	"Head, Shoulders, Knees, and Toes" "Bingo Was His Name-O" (goes with Angus story) "Hop Se Hi" (action song)	"Bye Baby Bunting" (stand up and rock baby) "Hop Se Hi" (song and movement, repeated) "Where Oh Where Has My Little Dog Gone?"	"Head, Shoulders, Knees, and Toes" (repeated) "Hop Se Hi" (repeated) "Where Oh Where Has My Little Dog Gone?" (repeated)	"Head, Shoulders, Knees, and Toes" (repeated) "Bingo Was His Name-O" (repeated) "Bye Baby Bunting" (repeated)	"Hop Se Hi" (repeated) "Bye Baby Bunting" (repeated) "Bingo Was His Name-O" (repeated)
Discussion and Cognitive Games	Matching game: simple lotto game matching rabbit pictures cut from gift paper mounted on stiff cards to a second identical set	*What Whiskers Did* Whiskers has no words; have children tell story.	Children hunt for hidden bunny in Carroll's book, *Where's the Bunny?*	Guess animals in Gay's book, *What's Your Name?* Hunt for mouse in *Goodnight, Moon.*	Use pictures of children of various cultures eating with their families, and ask children how they are alike, and so forth. Guess animals in Gay's book, *What's Your Name?* (repeated)
Multiethnic Component	Pass around dolls brought back from Mexico by one of the children's families "Bingo," a Scottish American folk song		*Whistle for Willie*; features an African American youngster	"Bingo," a Scottish American folk song	Pictures of families of different cultures eating together

TABLE 16–3

Analysis of Reasons for Selection of Literary Materials to Use with Older Fours (listed in the order of the days as they appear in Table 16–4)

Resource *	Reasons for Selection
Books	
A Story, A Story Written and illustrated by Gail Haley (1970)	African "Ananse" folk tale; Caldecott winner; good story with multicultural value
The Tale of Peter Rabbit Written and illustrated by Beatrix Potter (1903)	Timeless classic; rabbit focus
A Starlit Somersault Down Hill Written by N. Willard, illustrated by J. Pinkney (1993)	Beautiful illustrations tell the story of a bear who invites rabbits to hibernate with him, but rabbits need to be free to relish winter delights.
Animals Every Child Should Know Written by Dena Humphreys, illustrated by Rudolf Freund (1951)	Handsome illustrations — all wild animals; contains many facts about wild rabbits that fours like to know; continues theme of Coatsworth poem nicely from previous day
A Letter to Amy Written and illustrated by Ezra Jack Keats (1968)	A story with African American children as the central characters; universal theme of boys and girls getting along together and a birthday party that carries out the gift theme
Annie and the Old One Written by Miska Miles, illustrated by Peter Parnall (1971)	Navajo girl's relationship with an older person, her grandmother, shows caring for others, accepting death as part of the life cycle; a rather long book but worthwhile
The Nicest Gift Written and illustrated by Leo Politi (1973)	About Christmas in the barrio of Los Angeles; portrays life as many of the children in our center know it; interpolates familiar Spanish words and Mexican customs; out-of-season topic, but included because of gift theme and ethnic character
Tops and Bottoms Written and illustrated by Janet Stevens (1995)	An updated trickster tale beloved by African American storytellers about a smart rabbit who fools a lazy bear. A Caldecott Honor book—wonderful illustrations
Curious George Goes to the Hospital Written and illustrated by H. A. and Margaret Rey (1966)	Included because one of the children is anticipating a tonsillectomy
Staying Home Alone on a Rainy Day Written and illustrated by Chiharo Iwasaki (1968)	Exquisite illustrations by a Japanese artist; talks about growing up, fear, and loneliness, a universal experience all children undergo sooner or later
Ten Little Rabbits Written and illustrated by V. Grossman and S. Long (1991)	This delightful counting book features authentic Indian tribes for each of the 10 numbers.

Resource *	Reasons for Selection
Books, *continued*	
A Hospital Story: An Open Book for Parents and Children Together Written by Sarah Stein, photographs by D. Piney (1974)	One of a series that includes other books on children with disabilities, death, and so forth; contains text and pictures for children and also comments written for adult reading the story; selected because of impending tonsillectomy
No Roses for Harry Written by Gene Zion, illustrated by M. B. Graham (1958)	An amusing book used here partly to balance *A Hospital Story* and partly to provide an opening for a discussion of the social problem of what to do when someone bestows an unwanted gift on you
Mr. Rabbit and the Lovely Present Written by Charlotte Zolotow, illustrated by Maurice Sendak (1962)	Accent in this story is about genuine caring for another person and about selecting a truly thoughtful gift; reviews colors; shows male (rabbit) in caring role
Poetry and Finger Plays	
"The Rabbits' Song Outside the Tavern" Elizabeth Coatsworth	A rather long, difficult poem; asks children to think about pros and cons of being wild and tame; beautiful language and images. Repeats theme of *A Starlit Somersault Down Hill*
"Once There Was a Bunny" traditional	Finger play — for fun
"The Rabbit" Elizabeth Madox Roberts	Captures a momentary encounter between child and rabbit; good poetry that carries out rabbit theme
"Listening" Miriam Clark Potter	For fun — easy for children to memorize
Songs	
"Little Peter Rabbit Had a Fly upon His Ear"; "Pedro El Conejito con la Mosca en Su Nariz" (same song, translated)	A funny song that also uses motions; use of English and Spanish desirable; gradually eliminating words as song is repeated causes children to concentrate on what they're doing
"Hop Se Hi"	Large-muscle movement song; carries out rabbit focus; provides relief from sitting still
"Why Rabbits Have Bright Shiny Noses"	Finger play — for fun

*See material later in this chapter for actual poems, songs, and finger plays.

TABLE 16-4 A Weekly Plan for Group Time with Older Fours (main topics are rabbits, gifts, caring for others, and tonsillectomy)

	Monday	Tuesday	Wednesday	Thursday	Friday
Books and Stories to Read and Tell	*A Story, a Story* Haley (1970) *The Tale of Peter Rabbit* Potter (1903)	*A Starlit Somersault Down Hill* Willard (1993) *Letter to Amy* Keats (1968) *Animals Every Child Should Know* Humphreys (1951)	*Annie and the Old One* Miles (1971) *The Nicest Gift* Politi (1972) *Tops and Bottoms* Stevens (1995)	*Curious George Goes to the Hospital* Rey and Rey (1966) *Staying Home Alone on a Rainy Day* Iwasaki (1968) *Ten Little Rabbits* Grossman & Long (1991)	*No Roses for Harry* Zion (1958) *A Hospital Story* Stein (1974) *Mr. Rabbit and the Lovely Present* Zolotow (1962) (use flannel board with colors of felt to go with colors in story)
Poetry and Finger Plays	"Listening" Potter "Once There Was a Bunny" (finger play)	"The Rabbits' Song Outside the Tavern" Coatsworth "The Rabbit" Roberts	"Once There Was a Bunny" (finger play, repeated)	"Listening" Potter (flannel board, repeated) "The Rabbit" Roberts (repeated)	"The Rabbits' Song Outside the Tavern" (repeated)
Auditory Training	Teacher puts different objects in box while holding it behind her back and then lets one child shake box; others guess what is inside by identifying sound.	Child goes behind low screen with teacher, selects object for sound box, and shakes it for other children to identify.	Each child has box, shakes and listens to sound, and matches it to teacher's box when they sound the same (develops auditory memory).	Name all the children, using the "Carolyn, Bombarolyn" nonsense rhyme	Repeat the "Carolyn, Bombarolyn" rhyme
Songs	"Little Peter Rabbit Had a Fly upon His Ear" sung in English and Spanish	"Hop Se Hi" (song with movement)	"Why Rabbits Have Bright Shiny Noses" (song with finger play)	"Little Peter Rabbit" in Spanish and English (repeated) "Hop Se Hi" with movement (repeated)	"Why Rabbits Have Bright Shiny Noses" (repeated) "Little Peter Rabbit" in Spanish and English (repeated) "Hop Se Hi" (repeated)

	Monday	Tuesday	Wednesday	Thursday	Friday
Discussion and Cognitive Activities	Classification activity: Which objects would be best presents for baby, parent, dog, child, rabbit? Have five children wear appropriate hats or animal ears; others draw out pictures of gifts from bag and give the appropriate gift to correct person or animal.	Comparisons: Ask children their opinion—who was smarter: Bear or Rabbit in *A Starlit Somersault Down Hill*? How are the rabbits alike in *The Rabbits' Song Outside the Tavern* and *A Starlit Somersault Down Hill*?	Matching sound boxes: Show a few "storytelling" pictures, and ask children what is happening in them; discuss gift giving. Cause and effect: Discuss gift giving.	Have you ever been in the hospital? What was it like?	Temporal ordering: Measure rabbit and compare it with previous measurements; discuss gift giving — unwanted gift (*Harry*) and thoughtfulness (*Mr. Rabbit and the Lovely Present*).
Multiethnic Component	*A Story, a Story* (African American) "Little Peter Rabbit" in Spanish (Mexican American) Talk about rabbits' viewpoint of people and animals inside tavern	*Letter to Amy* (African American)	*The Nicest Gift* (Mexican American) *Annie and the Old One* (Navajo) *Tops and Bottoms* (folklore)	*Staying Home Alone* (point out lovely pictures are by a Japanese artist) *Ten Little Rabbits* (honors 10 different Indian tribes)	
Nonsexist Component	Classification game deliberately nonsexist	*Letter to Amy* stresses boys and girls getting along together.	*Annie* has girl as heroine and presents women in strong roles. *Nicest Gift* has boy expressing feelings.	*Ten Little Rabbits* has material about Native Americans *Curious George* has a boy monkey feeling uncertain in hospital.	*Mr. Rabbit and the Lovely Present* has both male (rabbit) and female (girl) being thoughtful and caring. *Hospital Story* has a girl feeling uncertain.

A little gray thing came out of the grass.
He hopped his way through the melon bed
　　And sat down close by a cabbage head.
He sat down close where I could see.
　　And his big still eyes looked hard at me.
His big eyes bursting out of the rim.
　　And I looked back very hard at him.

Nonsense Naming Rhyme[3]
Eula Mullins

This naming rhyme comes from the childhood of one
of our center teachers and is much relished by 4-
year-olds, who appreciate the silliness of it. In
essence, the last one, two, or three syllables of the
child's name are added to "bomb . . ." "see . . ." and
"gof . . . ." For example:
Carolyn bombarolyn, seearolyn, gofarolyn!
Tee-legged, tie-legged, bow-legged Carolyn!
　　or
Betty, bombetty, seaetty, gofetty!
Tee-legged, tie-legged, bow-legged Betty!
　　or
Peter, bombeter, seacreter, gofeter!
Tee-legged, tie-legged, bow-legged Peter!

The Rabbits' Song outside the Tavern[4]
Elizabeth Coatsworth

We, who play under the pines,
We, who dance in the snow
That shines blue in the light of the moon,
Sometimes halt as we go—
Stand with our ears erect,
Our noses testing the air,
To gaze at the golden world
Behind the windows there.
Suns they have in a cave,
Stars, each on a tall white stem,
And the thought of a fox or an owl
Seems never to trouble them.
They laugh and eat and are warm.
Their food is ready at hand,

While hungry out in the cold
We little rabbits stand.
But they never dance as we dance!
They haven't the speed nor the grace.
We scorn both the dog and the cat
Who lie by their fireplace,
We scorn them licking their paws,
Their eyes on an upraised spoon—
We who dance hungry and wild
Under a winter's moon.

Finger Plays

My Rabbit
(Traditional)

My rabbit has two big ears
　　(hold up first two fingers to make ears)
And a funny little nose
　　(join together all five fingers to make a pointy "nose")
He likes to nibble carrots
　　(make nibbling motions with fingers)
And he hops wherever he goes.
　　(make hopping movements with entire hand)

Once There Was a Bunny
(Traditional)

Once there was a bunny
　　(make ears with first two fingers of left hand)
And a green, green cabbage head.
　　(make a cabbage head with right fist)
"I think I'll have some breakfast," the little bunny said.
　　(move bunny toward the cabbage)
So he nibbled and he nibbled,
　　(move fingers on left, "bunny," hand)
Then he turned around to say,
"I think this is the time I should be hopping on my
way!"
　　(make left, "bunny," hand hop away)

Songs and Musical Finger Plays

Little Peter Rabbit Had a Fly upon His Ear
*(sung, with gestures if desired, to the tune of "Battle Hymn of
the Republic")*

Little Peter Rabbit had a fly upon his ear,
Little Peter Rabbit had a fly upon his ear,
Little Peter Rabbit had a fly upon his ear,
And he flicked it and it flew away!

---

[3]Kindness of Eula Mullins, mother of Head Teacher Carolyn
Mullins Mathews, Santa Barbara City College Children's
Center.

[4]Reprinted with permission of Macmillan Publishing Co.,
Inc. from *Away Goes Sally* by E. Coatsworth. Copyright 1934 by
Macmillan Publishing Co., Inc., renewed 1962 by Elizabeth
Coatsworth Beston.

HOP SE HI

Words and music by K. BAYLESS

With a hop se hi and a hop se ho, With a

hop se hi and a ho, ho, ho, With a hop and a "bop" and a-

way we go, Hop se hi and a ho! ho! ho!

From *Music: A Way of Life for the Young Child* (3rd ed.) by K. M. Bayless and M. E. Ramsey, 1987, Upper Saddle River, NJ: Merrill/Prentice Hall.

(repeat, leaving off "ear," next verse; next verse leave out "fly" and "ear" and so forth)

Pedro el conejito con la mosca en su nariz,
Pedro el conejito con la mosca en su nariz,
Pedro el conejito con la mosca en su nariz,
La espanta y se asusta.

Why Rabbits Have Bright Shiny Noses
Author unknown
(*sung to the tune of "My Bonnie Lies over the Ocean"*)

All rabbits have bright shiny noses
I'm telling you now as a friend,
The reason they have shiny noses—
Their powder puff's on the wrong end.

Chorus
Wrong end, wrong end, wrong end,
 wrong end, wrong end, wrong end.
Wrong end, wrong end, wrong end,
 wrong end, wrong end, wrong end.

BINGO

Scottish song

Arranged by K. BAYLESS

There was a farm - er who had a dog, And Bin - go was his

name - O. B - I - N - G - O, B - I - N - G - O,

B - I - N - G - O, And Bin - go was his name - O

Suggestions: Sing the song as written. Then repeat it and clap or tap instead of singing the letter "B" in "B-I-N-G-O." On the next repetition substitute clapping the letters "B" and "I," etc. (This song is excellent for helping develop concentration.)
From *Music: A Way of Life for the Young Child* (3rd ed.) by K. M. Bayless and M. E. Ramsey, 1987, Upper Saddle River, NJ: Merrill/Prentice Hall.

Summary

A well-presented group time provides opportunities for children and staff to come together in a pleasant, harmonious way if the time is carefully structured so that it is easy for the children to function together. Some elements of structure that facilitate this include keeping groups small and stable, choosing a time for presentation when the children are rested and comfortable, planning carefully while retaining flexibility, beginning group as soon as children gather, keeping the pace upbeat, including sufficient variety, and drawing the group to a close before it falls apart.

HEAD, SHOULDERS, KNEES, AND TOES

Action song

Head, shoul-ders, knees, and toes, knees and toes, Head, shoul-ders, knees, and

toes, knees and toes and Eyes and ears and

mouth and nose, Head shoul-ders, knees and toes, knees and toes.

From *Music: A Way of Life for the Young Child* (3rd ed.) by K. M. Bayless and M. E. Ramsey, 1987, Upper Saddle River, NJ: Merrill/Prentice Hall.

In addition to songs and stories, group time curriculum should include opportunities for children to participate in discussions, to practice cognitive skills, to develop their ability to tell various sounds apart, and to be exposed to a multicultural, nonsexist point of view. Because these times are so precious, teachers should think carefully about what materials they wish to include and always have a genuine reason for adding every one.

Self-Check Questions for Review

Content-Related Questions

1. List several different kinds of things children have the opportunity to learn during group time.
2. There are some fundamental principles to bear in mind when presenting group times that will help make them more successful. What are these principles?

3. List the eight ingredients that should be included as often as possible during a week of group times. Do most teachers include them when presenting group time? Why or why not is this the case? Why should they be included?
4. What are some important points to remember when planning a group time for young 3-year-olds? How would planning for a group of old fours differ from the plan for the younger children?

Integrative Questions

1. If you were the director of a center and realized that the teachers under your supervision were relying only on stories and songs for group time, how would you go about changing their behavior? Would just telling them they should do better be enough? If not, what kinds of practical help and motivation could you offer?
2. How do you expect the behavior of 2- and 4-year-olds to differ from each other during group time? Based on these differences, explain how you would adjust your group time plans to take those differences into account.

Questions and Activities

1. Students usually know more resources for group time activities than they realize they do. How many resources do *you* know? For practice, have the class choose a focus of interest for group time and then brainstorm in the group for sources of songs, poems, stories, auditory discrimination activities, multiethnic materials, and so forth, that would fit that focus.

2. You have a little girl in your group who constantly interrupts what you are saying in group time. You believe children should participate in that experience, but this is too much! How would you solve this problem?

3. You want to present some group times that focus on water play, but you cannot find even one poem or finger play on that topic. Take 20 minutes and write one to share with the class.

4. You are now a director of a full-day center, and an inexperienced teacher comes to you and says she just cannot keep the children quiet during group time. What practical suggestions and help would you share with her that could make everyone's life easier during that period of the day?

5. Because the research shows that so many teachers present very limited activities during group time, is it possible that they are right and that the recommendations for including additional activities are too elaborate and should be ignored?

References for Further Reading

Overviews

Briggs, D. (1993). *Toddler storytime programs.* Metuchen, NJ: Scarecrow. This exceptionally helpful book lists group times by topic and includes books of good quality, finger plays, a flannel board activity, and a suggested—mostly Column 2–type (see Table 14–2)—craft activity. Helpful because it includes flannel board patterns that are not overly "cute."

Child Care Information Exchange. (1996). Beginnings workshop: "Circle time." *Child Care Information Exchange,* 109, 39–58. A number of very sensible articles about group time are included in this issue. *Highly recommended.*

Ernst, L. L. (1995). *Lapsit services for the very young: A how-to-do-it manual.* New York: Neal-Schuman. If you really want to know how to conduct a worthwhile group time featuring good literature, librarians are the ones to ask. This book begins with practical suggestions about how to engage the world's toughest group-time members (namely, library visitors aged 1–3!), but, of course, the advice also works with older children. It includes some sample programs. *Highly recommended.*

Hut, V., Dennis, B., Koplow, L., & Gerber, J. (1996). Lesson plans for emotional life. In L. Koplow (Ed.), *Unsmiling faces.* New York: Teachers College Press. The authors include innumerable examples of meeting-time activities. Emphasis is on topics appropriate for children who need to build particular emotional and social relationship skills. *Highly recommended.*

Sutherland, M. (1994). Group meeting time: Making it work for everyone. *Scholastic Early Childhood Today,* 8(6), 28–35. In this concise article, Sutherland presents practical advice plus a checklist for evaluating *teacher* behaviors that may be contributing to inattentiveness in children.

Using Story Books Effectively

Beaty, J. J. (1994). *Picture book storytelling: Literature activities for young children.* Fort Worth, TX: Harcourt Brace. This book features suggestions for group times based on specific topics and offers particularly appropriate follow-up activities.

Raines, S. C., and Canady, R. J. (1989). *Story s-t-r-e-t-c-h-e-r-s: Activities to expand children's favorite books* and *More story s-t-r-e-t-c-h-e-r-s.* (1991). Mount Rainier, MD: Gryphon House. In addition to providing a wonderful selection of really *good* books, Raines and Canady offer extensive ideas for ways to tie them to other activity areas. *Highly recommended.*

Finger Plays[1]

Dowell, R. I. (1987). *Move over, Mother Goose: Fingerplays, action verses & funny rhymes.* Mount Rainier, MD: Gryphon House. This nice mix of materials is divided into topics such as animals, family, and so on.

Redleaf, R. (1993). *Busy fingers, growing minds: Fingerplays, verses and activities for whole language learning.* St. Paul, MN: Redleaf. Simple, brief, relevant verses and group-time activities contributed by a very experienced teacher are included here.

Singing with Children

Ball, W. (1995). Nurturing musical aptitude in children. *Dimensions of Early Childhood,* 23(4), 19–24. Ball provides research-grounded information on ways to encourage young children to sing—very helpful.

Honig, A. S. (1995). Singing with infants and toddlers. *Young Children,* 50(5), 72–78. According to the author, it is never too early to begin singing to and with children. She ex-

---

[1]Resources for poetry are included in Chapter 15.

tols the benefits of beginning early and offers practical suggestions about how to do this.

Jalongo, M. R. (1996). Using recorded music with young children: A guide for nonmusicians. *Young Children*, 51(5), 6–14. This article provides suggestions and a rich array of suggestions of appropriate music. *Highly recommended.*

Bibliographies

Lima, C. W., & Lima, J. A. (1993). A *to zoo: Subject access to children's picture books* (4th ed.). New Providence, NJ: Bowker. Have you ever hunted desperately for a book about a particular subject that has caught the children's interest? If so, this reference is the answer to your prayers. *Highly recommended.*

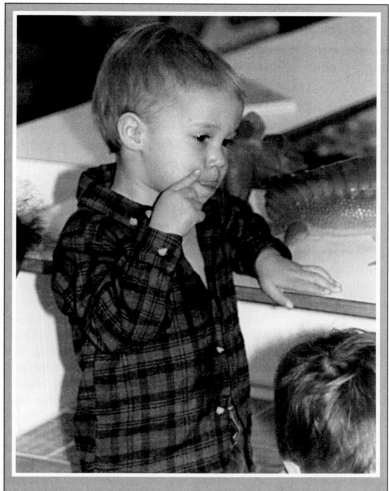

Have you ever

- Heard the words *emergent curriculum* and wondered what they meant?
- Heard the words *Reggio Emilia* and wondered what *they* meant?
- Wondered just who Vygotsky was and why people are talking about him?
- Thought that teaching facts was not enough but did not know how else to get the children to think?

If you have, the material in this chapter will help you.

Embalmed curriculum originates . . . with the teacher and all her years of experience. She started out with enthusiasm—writing her lessons plans, collecting her resource materials, working every night and all weekend. She can't work like that every year—so for every set of fresh faces, she brings it all out and dusts it off and is ready to roll. It is, after all, new to *them:* they're not being shortchanged by her shortcuts. That she may be shortchanging herself only occasionally crosses her mind as she wonders where her energy has gone and remembers how challenging teaching used to be before she was so good at it.

Elizabeth Jones and John Nimmo (1994, p. 77)

One of the most interesting aspects of teaching young children lies in the area of mental development, because young children usually come to school filled with curiosity, wonder, and the wish to learn. This eagerness makes cognitive education a delight for both teachers and children, *if the teachers have a clear idea of the children's capabilities and how to develop these further in an appropriate way.*

To accomplish this most effectively, teachers must take time to clarify their own educational values and decide for themselves what the real purpose of educating the children's cognitive selves should be. Should mental development consist only of learning a large array of facts, recognizing the alphabet, and parroting memorized replies to questions? Or should such education foster the ability to think and reason, to generate new ideas, to relish learning about a fascinating world, and to feel confident and enthusiastic when approaching new intellectual challenges?

While acknowledging the value of factual knowledge, the majority of teachers would want to include opportunities for thinking and reasoning in the curriculum, too. They want to nourish that spark of intellectual curiosity, develop that ability to think, and sustain that interest in the world and all it contains, as well as provide the children with facts and information.

Approaches to Fostering Mental Abilities

This book takes the position that there are three ways to foster the development of mental abilities. And, as Table 17-1 makes clear, they each enhance different kinds of mental processes and abilities in the children.

The first, most typical approach is engaging children in acquiring facts about their world and so is called the *information approach.* The second is termed the *emergent creative approach* and fosters the development of higher-order mental abilities such as problem solving. The third approach is termed the *conventional approach* because it focuses on some skills already familiar to many early childhood teachers. It provides practice in some midlevel mental abilities that form a foundation for later success in such academic areas as reading and certain mathematical processes. The conventional approach is discussed in detail in chapter 18.

A Comparison of the Approaches

The Information Approach

To begin with, we must acknowledge that many well-intentioned preschool teachers still see cognitive learning as mainly helping the children

TABLE 17-1
A Comparison of Cognitive Learning Opportunities Using the Three Approaches

	Information Approach	Emergent Creative Approach for Teaching Creative Thinking and Problem Solving	Conventional Approach for Teaching Midlevel Abilities
Value of approach	Provides information base needed as foundation for midlevel and problem solving skills. Widens knowledge of world.	Allows children to develop full range of mental powers. Encourages application of prior knowledge to solving new problems. Empowers children to try out ideas and explain what they know to other children and adults.	Makes certain diversified practice in applying midlevel mental ability skills (concepts) is provided. These are valuable emergent literacy and mathematical skills.
Examples of kinds of mental ability skills developed by approach	Pay attention. Process information. Retain information. Recall information. Reconstruct information.	Generate ideas on own. Form hypotheses (reasons) why something happens and try them out. Assess and evaluate possibilities. Pursue interests in depth.	Apply specific concepts to specific activities: matching, grouping, perceiving common relations, seriated and temporal ordering, cause-and-effect relationships, and conserving.
Teacher's role	Supply information to children and/or help them find information for themselves.	Listen to children; follow their lead to select pathway to investigate. Plan curriculum ahead but alter and adjust plans as direction of pathways become apparent. Encourage generation of ideas by "provoking" children to consider problems and solve them. Develop opportunities with children to try out their ideas.	May use children as source to determine interest around which to build a theme. Plan ahead to think up and present activities and experiences for children that provide opportunities for practice and application of specific concepts.
Child's role	Soak up interesting information and store it in memory. Be able to recall, reconstruct, and repeat information when needed.	Collaborate (toss ball of ideas back and forth) with teacher to pursue interests. Think up ways to express ideas and solve problems. Try ideas out. Express ideas and what is found out through language, graphics, and child-constructed models.	Participate in learning activities provided by teacher, thereby practicing various midlevel mental ability skills. Acquire mental ability concepts and apply them by reasoning. Express what he knows by manipulating teacher-provided materials.
Examples of typical questions	What color is this? What did we talk about last time? Tell me what happened? Can you find the round one?	Your opinion is that . . . ? How could we . . . ? What could we use to . . . ? What would happen if . . . ?	Is this the same? What belongs together? What should come next? What made that happen?

379

TABLE 17–2

Example of Using Three Approaches Together to Facilitate Learning for the Cognitive Self

Source of Interest	Information Approach Featuring Acquiring Facts	Emergent Approach Featuring Problems to Solve	Conventional Approach Featuring Midlevel Cognitive Skills

White, pink-eyed baby rabbit donated to center's 4-year-old group by one of the families	**What do children already know and/or think is true?**
	• Rabbits can hop straight up in the air.
	• They like lettuce.
	• They have long ears and a fluffy tail.
	• All rabbits are white and have pink eyes.
	• Rabbits hatch from Easter eggs.
	
	Additional facts they might acquire:
	• Rabbits are easily frightened.
	• There are many different kinds and colors of rabbits.
	• They can be housebroken.
	• They like to gnaw on things.
	• They are mammals—mothers give birth to babies.
	• Rabbits have strong hind legs and can scratch if frightened.
	• Rabbits get sick if they eat too many greens at one time.
	• Rabbits are very good diggers and like to make tunnels to live in.
	• There are different words meaning "rabbit" in different languages.
		Basic question: How can we take very good care of this young rabbit and make him happy?
		
		Children's concerns and potential solutions:
		• He misses his mother.
		  Borrow his mother to visit.
		  Put guinea pig in same cage.
		  Act friendly and be gentle with him ourselves.
		• His cage is so small—he needs to hop around some more— . . . but if we let him out, we can't catch him!
		  Build corral of blocks indoors.
		  Build rabbit pen outdoors.
		  What would it look like? Can we draw something (or model it from sticks or clay or something) to show how we could make it?
		  What can we make it out of?
		  How can we find out how much chicken wire to buy?
		  How many stakes will we need?
		  How high must it be to keep him from jumping out?
		  What if he digs under the fence?
		• What could we use temporarily outside until the pen is ready? Would the wading pool work? A big box?
			Matching: Play "Bunny Bingo" made from Easter rabbit stickers.
			
			Grouping: Are all rabbits white with pink eyes? Compare a variety of pictures of rabbits to several pictures of guinea pigs. Why do rabbits belong in one group and guinea pigs in another?
			
			Common relations: Pair live rabbit with picture in book. Pair baby animal pictures with mother animals—who goes with which mother?
			
			Temporal ordering: Use documentation board of children's plans, comments, and progress during pen building to show progress over time.
			
			Seriation (graduated ordering): Keep track of how far rabbit can hop as he matures. Compare to how far the children can hop.
			
			Cause and effect: Why *do* rabbits have long ears and big hind legs? What makes rabbits run and hide? What makes the rabbit cuddle down in your lap?

acquire a lot of interesting facts about a subject, and it is true that if you are going to think about something, you really *do* need facts to base your thinking on.

For example, suppose a rabbit has come to school (Table 17–2). The teacher might get out a book that talks about characteristics of rabbits or share an amusing story about them. She might also encourage the children to try feeding him various things to find out what he eats and help them dig his droppings into their garden for fertilizer.

The benefit of the information approach is that the children are probably interested, and they are acquiring factual information. The drawbacks are that it can lead to branching out in a helter-skelter kind of webbing in which topics are at best moderately and at worst too loosely related to the subject of rabbits so a central focal point is lost. For instance, "rabbits" might lead to "springtime," and "spring" to "rainy weather" and "what makes thunder," and then to "way to keep our feet dry so we stay healthy," and so on and so on.

Moreover, teachers who use only this approach are cheating the children because preschoolers are capable of doing so much more thinking beyond learning facts. If given the opportunity, they are also capable of having creative ideas, solving problems, and acquiring some midlevel figuring-out skills as well.

The Emergent Creative Approach

As we see in Table 17–1 and the discussion of the Reggio Emilia schools, this approach is characterized by the teacher and children collaborating together to pursue a common interest. The teacher contributes her ideas and information and also listens carefully to the children's comments and questions. She bases decisions about what should happen in the curriculum for the cognitive self as well as for the other selves on what these comments and behaviors reveal to her. That is why this approach is termed *emergent*—it develops gradually (kind of the way a water turtle first pokes his head out of the water and then gradually becomes more visible as his body emerges).

When this equipment arrived at school in pieces, the children and teacher figured out together how to assemble it. A nice example of the constructivist approach!

Like the information approach, the emergent approach makes use of webbing, but in this case the webbing is more focused and has more direction because the teacher keeps it within bounds. This more logical, closely linked kind of webbing can provide a richly developing focus of interest and projects lasting for weeks or even months.

Occasionally the emergent approach is misinterpreted by novices who conclude that all the ideas must come from the children and that the teacher blindly follows wherever they lead, "just letting the children do whatever they want." But that is not actually the way it works. What really happens, as Tables 17–1 and 17–2 indicate, is that the teacher may (or may not) have in mind some possibilities to begin with. She discusses potentially interesting subjects with the children and pays careful attention to their comments and questions. Then she analyzes what these reveal so she can selectively choose what she thinks might be the most productive possibilities to pursue further. As the project develops, she repeats this process many times and adjusts the curriculum accordingly.

Perhaps the children comment they think the rabbit is unhappy because he keeps bumping his head as he tries to jump in his cage. Then the teacher could ask them how to make his home better for him, which in turn could lead to taking the rabbit out on the grass, and the problem would need to be solved about how to confine him there. Perhaps a pen of chicken wire would work—what would that look like? How will we know how much wire to buy? And what can we use to hold the chicken wire up? What could we use for his home until we can build that enclosure?

Although this project has stemmed from the children's concern for the rabbit's well-being, it is the teacher who poses the problems "What can we do to make him happier?" and "How could we keep him from bumping his head?" and who foresees the learning opportunities that could come from needing to figure out how the children might draw or model their suggestions, how to measure the amount of chicken wire required, how to keep the rabbit warm at night, and so forth.

The Conventional Approach

Returning to Table 17–1, we see that in contrast to the emergent approach, the conventional approach is much more teacher determined. The teacher decides in advance which midlevel skills (such as matching or grouping) should be included in the curriculum, and she plans theme-related activities for the children to enjoy that provide opportunities to practice those skills.

Because the activities that make this approach possible are discussed in more detail in chapter 18, we will only take space here to describe it as an approach that singles out a handful of specific mental abilities and provides opportunities for practicing those abilities by including theme-related activities for the children

to use. Although this approach *is* valuable and definitely a step up from only emphasizing facts, it really does only part of the mental development job because it does not make use of the children's ideas and creative intellectual capabilities. Therefore, it is best used when it is included along with the more stimulating emergent approach.

Contributions of Lev Vygotsky

Vygotsky (1978) was a Russian psychological theoretician and teacher whose works have become increasingly well known in the West in the past few years. His interest in the effect of the sociocultural world on the child's development and its implications for the role of the teacher, in addition to his emphasis on the significance of language in fostering cognitive development, have provided a balance to the Piagetian view that children construct knowledge from within themselves.

Because many of his ideas are a "good fit" with the current interest in emergent curriculum, which emphasizes collaboration between teacher and child, it is helpful for early childhood teachers to understand some of his basic premises, so some of his most relevant ideas are briefly presented here. Readers who desire more in-depth information are referred to several excellent references at the end of this chapter.

The Impact of Society on the Child's Development

Fundamental to Vygotsky's theory is the assertion that all knowledge is socially constructed and that learning cannot be separated from the social context in which it takes place. For this reason, the influence of both adults and peers is seen as crucial to facilitating the child's development. It is what they say and do and what the child does in response to this that facilitates his mental development.

The Concept of the Zone of Proximal Development

Perhaps the best-known aspect of Vygotskian theory is what he termed "the zone of proximal development" (often spoken of as the ZPD). By this he means that children's abilities exist along a continuum of development within a zone of possible achievement. At one end of the continuum is what they are capable of doing on their own. At the other end, which is nearly (or proximately) within their reach, is the level they could move on to with the guidance of another more informed person. Each child has his own personal, unique zone of readiness that the teacher must detect to guide him most effectively in that direction.

The Role of the Teacher

Vygotsky's emphasis on the significance of external influences on the child's advancement emphasizes a particular aspect of the teacher's role—the importance of being a sensitive observer and guide. The ideal teacher is envisioned as being exquisitely aware of what the child already knows, what could be proposed next to further his learning, and how to conduct a dialogue that would fa-

cilitate that next step. By offering this support or *scaffolding*, she empowers the child to actualize his potential (Berk and Winsler, 1995). As the child gains competence, this support is gradually withdrawn, leaving him able to operate at a higher level than he was formerly capable of achieving by himself.

What Can the Teacher Do to Encourage Development?

During the preschool and early elementary years, children are shifting from what is termed *lower mental functions* (abilities held in common with other mammals) to *higher mental functions*, which are unique to human beings. These include the use of mediated *perception* (typically using language to gain understanding), focused attention, deliberate or intentional memory, and symbolic thought (using words to think with).

How Can the Preschool Teacher Encourage the Development of These Higher Mental Functions?

The teacher facilitates the development of these abilities by providing *leading activities*; at the

When teachers ask the right kinds of questions, they help children reach the leading edge of their zone of proximal development.

preschool level, Vygotsky maintains that the primary leading activity is play. He sees play as being particularly valuable because during play the child is always extending himself and moving beyond his usual operating level of development (Bodrova & Leong, 1996). Play fosters the development of self-regulation, focused attention, and deliberate memory. But for it to enable the child to move toward the growing edge of his understanding and ability, Vygotsky maintains it must be play of a particular kind. Namely, it should involve imaginary situations in which the child participates in role playing and uses language and social rules as components of that experience.

In addition to providing opportunities for imaginative pretend play to take place, the teacher can facilitate development in a second way. This is using discussion between the child and the adult and with other children to explore and share ideas on a subject. For example, the group might share their ideas about why leaves fall (Cadwell & Fyfe, 1997) or how shadows differ from real people (Bambini a Reggio Emilia, 1990). This could be followed by trying out some of the ideas—are shadows always attached to the person who makes them? Does everything have a shadow? And so forth.

It is this emphasis on teacher/child collaboration that we see put into practice in the emergent curriculum of the Reggio Emilia schools.

The Municipal Schools of Reggio Emilia: An Example of Emergent Curriculum

In the chapter on designing the environment (chapter 5), I described the lovely atmosphere I saw in the children's centers of a small Italian city named Reggio Emilia. Part of that ambience was due to planning and good design selected by adults, but part of it was the result of the beautiful things the children had made. The schools abounded with remarkable murals, collages, clay figures, and other constructions all done by children aged 3 to 6.

The attractive results convey an impression of beauty and happiness that entices visitors from abroad to seek answers to such questions as, How is it possible for such young children to produce such beautiful and advanced work? Is this really the work of teachers, not the children? How are these children taught, and what do they learn?

Although space does not permit a complete explanation of how these centers operate, I will attempt to answer these questions by describing my personal impression of the philosophy and practice that underlie the preschools of that city. For more detailed information, the reader is referred to a number of references listed at the end of this chapter.

Despite the abundant evidence of artistic creativity, it is important to understand that the Reggio Emilia children's centers are not intended to be art schools. Rather, Loris Malaguzzi, the founder, intended them to be places where children and teachers interact—listening and talking with each other—to explore subjects in depth by exchanging ideas and trying those ideas out. That is the reason I have placed the discussion of the Reggio philosophy in this chapter on cognitive development rather than in the chapter on creative self-expression.

The results of these joint investigations between teachers and children are then transformed by the children into visible results to communicate what they know to other people. As the staff often says, "You don't know it until you can express it." Because the children are too young to write, the staff encourages them to express what they know by using all sorts of other "languages." It might be the language of paint, or clay, or cardboard structures, or concoctions of bent wire bedecked with tissue paper or shadow plays acted out behind a lighted screen. That is why the exhibit of their work currently touring the United States is termed "The 100 Languages of Children." It illustrates the almost numberless ways children can use various materials to express what they know if only they are provided with that opportunity (Edwards, Gandini, & Forman, 1993).

But what kind of opportunity is it that the teachers provide? Part of it is the point of view of the teachers, described by Rinaldi (1993) as seeing the child as being strong, rich in potential, competent (capable of constructing his own thought), and having great potential to offer the world. The teacher is not seen as a transmitter of knowledge (a doer *to*) but as someone with whom the child collaborates in figuring things out (a doer *with*). The teacher helps the child construct a situation in which she can use her own competencies combined with the competencies of other children to explore experiences and reach conclusions. In this approach, the teacher becomes a compass that may point the child in a particular direction, and education is seen as a process that cannot be predetermined in advance because it develops organically. Close and repeated observation of the natural world is encouraged and accompanied by a wealth of self-expressive materials that are readily available for the children's use. Parents are a vital part of this process and are expected to participate very actively in these experiences.

As I visited the Reggio schools and studied their approach, it helped me to think of the way such learning proceeds as being investigative *pathways* down which the children, teachers, and parents venture together, hand in hand. Sometimes the direction of the pathways is anticipated in advance by the teachers; sometimes the direction shifts in unanticipated ways as the interests of the children point to a particular direction and the teachers pick up on that change.

But this sensitivity to the children's interests should not be interpreted as permissively letting them do whatever they wish. As I understand the process, what the teachers do is select an aspect of the children's interests to develop further. Ideally, that aspect is one that presents problems for the children to consider and solve. For example, their comments about the battered condition of a worktable might lead to figuring out how to explain to a volunteer carpenter what to build to replace it. This, in turn, might require deciding on units of measure, how to "write"

down the ensuing dimensions, and how to draw diagrams to clarify their vision.

Although not pursued every day, the majority of these interest pathways continue for a long time, sometimes as long as several months. How different this is from our American way of having a theme a week and providing children with what Katz (1992) characterizes as teaching a "smattering of information."

The teachers take the principle of following the children's lead very seriously for, as they say, "If you wish to follow, you have to see where the children are going." Therefore, they listen with close attention to what the children say, often recording discussions and meticulously analyzing them after school with other teachers. This requires a great deal of time and dedication, but the results are worth it because such careful listening provides insight into what the children are thinking and understanding. The result is a day-by-day development of a truly emergent curriculum.

The closest analogy to American education I can draw on is to think of the Reggio Approach as using a kind of "project approach." But we must take care when using the word *project* because in many American schools *project* means making something the teacher has thought up for the children to do, such as making suet balls for the birds or get-well cards for a sick friend. This kind of "project" is typically teacher instigated and controlled.

When using *project* in the emergent curriculum context, as Katz and Chard do (1991), we mean something quite different from that. In this context *project* means an ongoing investigation of a topic agreed on by the children and teacher together that develops gradually over a period of time. This kind of project should be pictured as a pathway along which everyone journeys together.

An example of how such a project emerged in one of the Reggio schools began when the children saw a puppet show that featured a monster—always an attractive, intriguing subject to 4- and 5-year-olds. The children produced a number of monster puppets of their own, and then some of them recalled the myth about the minotaur who was hidden in a labyrinth (or maze) on the nearby island of Crete. Much discussion about labyrinths and mazes ensued. The teachers encouraged the children to develop their interest further by making maps of pathways in their own classroom as being a kind of maze. Some youngsters used clay to do this; others used strips of tape or colored pens. They were also encouraged to develop plans for pretend mazes as well. After much discussion and some controversy, the group settled on a maze drawn by a particular child to translate into an actual maze out on the playground. Here a difficult problem developed. It was how to turn a plan, a diagram on paper, into an actual larger maze—how to change a symbol back into a real maze they could walk through. Ultimately the children solved this problem by requesting a ladder on which some of them stood so they could look at the plan and then direct their friends where to set the markers and draw the chalk lines to indicate the walls of the maze. The teachers said the final step would be for a group of parents to use the same plan to construct a three-dimensional maze in front of the school for everyone to enjoy.

As the children's investigations progressed, the teachers regularly took photos of what they were doing. These pictures were mounted on "documentation boards" to remind the children of what they had already accomplished and to keep parents informed of what was happening. These documentation boards are an integral part of the Reggio approach (Tarini, 1997).

Some Food for Future Thought

Of course, the cultures of the United States and Italy have their own unique aspects, and it would be neither desirable nor even possible to replicate that entire Reggio model over here. For example, it is difficult to even imagine there would be a city in the United States willing to devote a substantial portion of its municipal budget to the education of its young children! However, it is always possible for us to learn from each other, particularly when both approaches hold many values in common.

For example, the labyrinth investigation described earlier involved the children and teachers in many higher-order mental processes and skills. Translated into "Americanese" educational terms, the skills include fostering creativity, child-centered learning, cooperative learning, learning by doing, problem solving, basing learning on real experience, observing, reflecting on what has been learned, predicting outcomes, hypothesis

Here are the monster puppets and examples of maps and mazes devised by the children during the maze investigation.

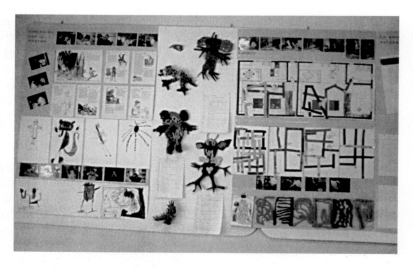

forming and testing, using symbolic representation, inquiry learning, and so forth.

With so much in common, why then is the Reggio approach so newly admired by many American preschool teachers? What do the teachers in that small Italian town do that is so inspiring and different from the American approach? Four major differences come to mind. The Reggio teachers see preschool children as being more competent than we do. They depend on the almost daily assessment of the children's ideas and concerns to plan what should happen next in the way of learning, they present related learning opportunities that extend over much longer periods of time, and they use documentation boards to keep continuing records of projects as they develop.

The children of Reggio are seen as competent, strong, and powerful. For many years preschool teachers in the United States have fought and *must continue* to fight the war against push-down curriculum that focuses on learning the alphabet, using work sheets, and so forth (Bredekamp & Shepherd, 1990). That necessity has made us so wary of pushing children out of their depth (Elkind, 1990a, 1990b) that we may have underestimated what they *can* do. The Italians are also wary of developmentally inappropriate curriculum but at the same time have retained an openness to young children's abilities

The plan for the playground maze drawn by the children is shared with a group of teachers touring one of the schools in Reggio Emilia.

And here is how the children translated their symbolic drawing of the maze into reality.

and a willingness to guide them to the edge of their ZPDs that Americans have not shared. By following their intellectual leads, proposing problems for them to solve, and encouraging them to use developmentally appropriate kinds of symbolization to express what they have learned, the teachers have empowered the children while not straining them beyond their capacities.

The curriculum in the Reggio schools is truly an emergent one. Although many early childhood teachers in the United States make a point of selecting a theme of genuine interest to the children, all too often that theme remains the same year after year—transportation, baby animals, or dinosaurs, for example. Although this generic approach has certain conveniences, it is a far cry from the recording and transcribing the children's comments that is done on a daily basis in Reggio Emilia. That close listening and consequent analysis is what enables the Reggio teachers to tailor curriculum to the children's concerns as these emerge and generate plans to further stimulate their thinking.

The curriculum in the Reggio schools encourages the children to pursue a subject in depth. The focus on the emergent, dynamic development of investigatory pathways (projects) emphasizes and makes possible a third difference in educational approach between American and Reggio Emilian preschools. As one teacher put it, the Italian children know a lot more about less than do their American peers. Because we cannot possibly teach any child a little about every subject in the world, why not concentrate on fewer subjects and experience the satisfaction of knowing more about a particular one in depth? The topic might be "Who Measures What in Our Town?" (Katz, 1992) coupled with how to measure a table and convey the results to an adult who will make a new one for the school (Scuola Diana, 1991), or how to make an amusement park for the birds involving making a fountain that actually works (Gambetti, 1992; Sandini, 1997), or an investigation of shadows, or making puddles disappear, or any number of other possibilities. As we see in this and the following chap-

Ah-ha! Four short blocks equal one long one—a good example of how practical experience can be used to foster the emerging mathematical concept of equality.

ter, any subject can be used to provide practice in all sorts of broad and/or more closely targeted thinking and reasoning skills—so why settle for the smattering of information Katz deplores?

Careful documentation is an important part of the Reggio Approach. As projects develop, recordings of the children's discussions are made and transcribed. These are used for two purposes. The first is that careful study of the written transcriptions often helps teachers spot interests and ideas they might otherwise have overlooked while the discussion was taking place. The second purpose is keeping track of the progress of projects as they develop. Children's and teacher's comments are included on documentation boards along with photographs and other graphics contributed by the children that explain what is happening. It cannot be emphasized enough that these boards form an integral part of the learning and assessment process because they record *ongoing* experiences, not just the final result. Parents and visitors are kept current by this means, teachers are more aware of what is happening, and the boards are used with the children to help them recognize what they formerly thought or are currently pursuing. In addition, the presence of these aesthetically pleasing boards, which are hung at strategic points in the school, adds a spirit of engagement, enthusiasm, and beauty to the environment that is very different from the materials usually seen on American bulletin boards.

Applying Emergent Curriculum Principles in American Schools: Some Recommendations

Be Prepared to Take Risks

Allowing curriculum to "emerge" sounds so easy in theory but actually can make teachers *un*easy in practice because they dread the insecurity of not knowing what they should plan ahead of time. This anxiety can be alleviated if the teacher realizes that allowing curriculum to emerge does *not* mean she does not plan in advance. The teacher *does* plan, but she remains sensitive to the children's concerns and adjusts her plan to pursue those concerns in an educationally beneficial way.

The real risks involved, then, do not lie in foregoing planning. It seems to me to have more to do with the teacher's underlying point of view about children. Does she really risk trusting them, relying on them to be competent and to collaborate with her in making decisions about the learning process? Or does she see them as fundamentally incompetent, helpless beings who require constant control and guidance to make sure they really learn something? Is she really able, as Confrey (1995) advocates, "to walk softly, ask without

telling, and rely on the child's actions as much as on his or her words" to determine the direction the curriculum should take (p. 205)?

Keep Cognitive Learning Appropriate to the Children's Age and Abilities

For those of us who are able to see children as truly competent, there remains a delicate balance between challenging and empowering young children to think, reason, and express their understanding through a variety of media and not overstressing them by driving them too hard.

If we are not careful, we can easily be led astray. For one thing, most of us went to elementary schools that may have used overly academic models of instruction, and we tend to repeat what we learned there—particularly in the academic realm. For another, the pressure of other non-early childhood teachers, administrators, and parents to conform to an academically inappropriate model can be difficult to resist for someone who is newly employed.

Nowadays still a third factor may lead us astray if we are not careful. Some people misinterpret what Vygotsky intended. They overlook his emphasis on the importance of imaginative play and the value of sensitive interchanges between child and teacher that allow the teacher to empower the child to reach a slightly more advanced level. The result can be (and in some instances already has been) domineering teachers providing inappropriate, too-difficult curriculum in the name of advancing the child's ZPD.

We must remember that there is a risk to misinterpreting an individual child's zone of potential development. Pushing children beyond their depth breeds discouragement, saps motivation, reduces opportunities for learning what the children should be learning at that particular age, and results in tension and unhappiness (Elkind, 1981; Rescorla, Hyson, & Hirsh-Pasek, 1991; Steffe & Gale, 1995). (For a developmental chart that includes cognitive skills, see appendix A.)

On the other hand, curriculum that is developmentally appropriate intrigues children and leads them to express further interest (Bredekamp & Copple, 1997). Some good indicators of developmental appropriateness are whether children are attracted to a subject or activity when it is presented, whether they persist in working on it, whether they show progress in learning to master it, and whether they contribute their own ideas to continue the interest. In short, cognitive curriculum should be difficult enough to invite interest but not so difficult it produces despair.

Keep Cognitive Learning a Part of Real Life

This book frequently extols the virtue of basing learning on concrete, actual involvement with the physical manipulation of materials—a position that is well supported in the literature (Kamii, 1985; Piaget, 1983; Vygotsky, 1978). Besides actual involvement, a second aspect should be emphasized when discussing cognitive learning. Intellectual learning should not only be based on the physical manipulation of materials but also be integrated into the everyday, real life of the center whenever possible. This is best achieved by selecting the focus of interest for developing thinking opportunities based on the children's current concerns. The way the labyrinth topic developed from the Italian children's concerns with monsters provides a good example of how such an interest could emerge for them because of their cultural knowledge base about the minotaur.

For American children, the subject might be camping because some families have just returned from vacation trips, or they could be interested in weather because school has been closed during a snowstorm. Perhaps a youngster has brought a grasshopper to school, which sparks their interest in insects, jumping, and how to compare distances various living things can travel.

As we can see in this chapter and the next, any of these topics could be used to develop higher-level and midlevel thinking abilities, and all will assuredly be relevant because they come from the youngsters themselves.

Keep Feelings a Part of the Experience

Remember, too, that part of reality is having feelings. Feeling and knowing properly belong together. Even when the accent is on developing an intellectual skill, whenever human beings are involved, feelings are there, also. Indeed, unless the emotional life of the child is reasonably calm and she has been able to achieve some degree of peaceful social coexistence with the other children, it is unlikely that she will be free to focus much of her energy on the more difficult task of intellectual learning. Therefore, teachers should be prepared to recognize feelings as they arise and not try to brush them aside "because we're playing lotto now." Teach ers should also appreciate the opportunities for special emotional or social learning that some subjects afford and deliberately include these as part of that curriculum area. *Learning should take place for many selves on many levels at the same time.*

Model Joy and Interest in Learning Yourself

The verve and interest in a subject that teachers feel themselves are among the most valuable ways to encourage children's enthusiasm for cognitive learning. When teachers are excited about whatever topic is used as a basis for developing mental ability, the children sense this and respond to it with their own enthusiasm.

One of the best rewards for using the emergent, evolving method of curriculum development is that it keeps the interest of the teacher as well as the children stimulated because there are always unanticipated, fresh elements to pursue as new pathways develop.

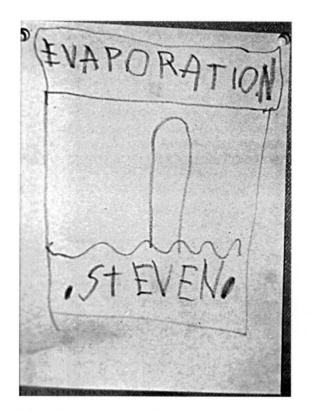

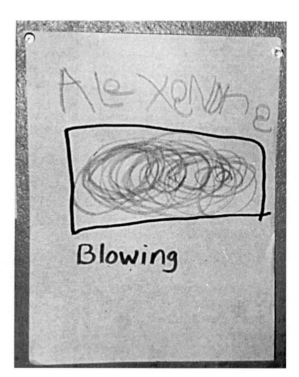

These pictures are the result of first attempts by some American children to illustrate their ideas graphically.

Encourage Children to Show You as Well as Tell You What They Mean

Many times when children are developing an idea about how things work or how they might solve a problem by making something work, words fail them. But anyone who has seen "The 100 Languages of Children" exhibit knows there are many ways besides language to express what one knows. In that display, everything from paints and drawing materials to bent wire, modeling clay, and dance are used to explain the children's ideas.

Moreover, as we all know, it is one thing to talk about something and quite another to represent it in graphic, visual form. We often think of using symbolic language as the highest form of understanding, but moving from one symbolic system such as language to another representational sys-

tem, the way the Reggio youngsters did in their maze project, is a very advanced form of mental activity and should always be encouraged. Of course, this also means that a wide variety of materials, teacher support, and the time to use them must be consistently available to the children.

Use Language to Promote Discussion

Because the remainder of this chapter concentrates on using questions in appropriate ways, it is important to emphasize here, as we did in chapter 15, that there is a difference between having a conversation versus conducting an interrogation. Discussions are *not* question-and-answer sessions—they should be talks in which everyone shares their ideas and opinions together. This means, as Berk and Winsler (1995) point out, that the teacher needs to concentrate on understanding what the child is trying to explain, not on whether what he says is right.

In American schools the most likely opportunities for such interchanges are during self-select activity times when the teacher can move about and talk individually or with small groups of children or, perhaps, during large-group time, though it can be very difficult to follow individual lines of thought from the children under such circumstances.

Special provisions are made in the Reggio Emilia schools for numerous small-group discussions in which interested children will pursue a particular topic over weeks or months—returning again and again to recall past work and ideas as well as to pursue new material.

Use Questions to Facilitate Learning

When Asking Questions, Keep the Pace Reasonably Slow

A teacher can ask the best, most interesting, and age-appropriate questions in the world and still experience discouragement if he fails to allow enough time for the children to reply before rushing on to the next question or, worse yet, answering it himself.

Rushing ahead of the children's ability to think is more typical of teachers than we would like to believe. As the work by Rowe in the chapter research study reveals so clearly, there are tremendous benefits for the children when teachers discard this pressured approach and substitute a more extended period of wait time between questions. Wait time can even be longer than a few minutes. When teachers at Reggio speak of wait time, they sometimes mean waiting several days while ideas percolate in the children's brains.

Encourage Children to Ask and Answer Questions Themselves

Coe (1987) puts it well when he says, "The best school, after all, for the world of childhood is not the school where children know the most answers, but the school where children ask the most questions" (p. 70).

Teachers can do several practical things to encourage question-asking and wondering behavior in their classrooms. Staying open and listening for questions are fundamental parts of such encouragement. Sometimes, particularly when the question is not clear, the teacher might ask the child to repeat or rephrase it, which helps both child and teacher understand what is being asked. Finally, as Rowe's research reminds us, *waiting and resisting the impulse to provide the answer oneself can stimulate the child to answer and ask more questions on her own.*

These responses are highly desirable because every time a child figures out an answer for herself, she has gained independence, confidence, and a good feeling about herself because she has been able to rely on herself instead of on someone else. Of course, sometimes there is just no way for a child to learn something unless she is told—names of things or certain facts fall into this category. But there are many other times when, *if the teacher asks the right question*, in reply to a question the child can have a pleasureful "Aha!" experience as she discovers or thinks through an idea on her own. These learning experiences are to be cherished, because they contribute much to the child's sense of happiness and feeling of intellectual competence.

With little children, such opportunities should be uncomplicated and straightforward. When something is tried out, the experiment will be most successful if it provides chances to figure out the answers to such questions as "Why do you think that happened?" "What would happen if . . . ?" or "How could we find out if . . . ?" These questions should be followed by, "Let's try it and see!"

The experiments can be as informal as seeing how a dog reacts when scratched in different places, or finding out how to make a kitten purr, or discovering what happens when red and yellow are mixed together. Perhaps it is a hot day, and the metal slide is hot, too. The teacher might ask the children, "How can we cool the

Research Study

How Long Is Long Enough?

Research Question   Rowe wanted to find out why a variety of science programs used in elementary school were not as effective in fostering inquiry skills as their developers had hoped.

Before beginning the study reported here, she had already analyzed hundreds of tapes of teachers talking with children in elementary school while they were teaching science units. She found out the differences in the inquiry abilities of the children were not due to lack of materials or scientific knowledge, group size, types of science curricula, age of children, or regionalism because she had controlled all these variables. The one thing almost all of the programs had in common was that the pace of instruction was very fast. When she measured the amount of time teachers waited for children to reply after asking a question, she discovered the wait time was only 1 *second*! It was so short she couldn't use a stopwatch to time it but had to use special mechanical equipment instead.

Rowe began to wonder if this short wait time could be the reason why the children were not responding well and developing their inquiry skills satisfactorily. To find out the answer, she posed the following research question: What would happen if teachers waited a little longer for the children to reply after asking a question? What if they did not interrupt so quickly? Would that affect the quality of the children's replies?

Research Method   Twelve classroom teachers working with children of various ages participated, using the same science lessons grouped into differing sequences. During the year of the experiment, the classes were recorded with audio- and videotape, and the teachers were trained to provide more wait time—allowing at least 3 seconds instead of the typical 1 second for replies.

Research Results   When the post training tapes were analyzed and compared with prior tapes, the results showed that as the teachers allowed more time for the children to think, the length of the children's responses increased, the number of unsolicited but appropriate responses increased, failures to respond decreased, incidence of speculative responses increased, child-child debate increased, conclusions increased, the number of children's questions increased, and children rated by teachers as being "slower" gave more responses. The quality of the teachers' follow-up replies changed, too. Their replies were more flexible (i.e., their follow-up comments more frequently related to what the children had said), they asked better questions, and their expectations of the children previously rated as "slow" rose.

Implications for Teaching   Although this research deals with school-age children, it seems highly probable that teachers of preschool-age children also need to increase their wait time between questions and answers. If anything, younger children require even longer to formulate their replies because it takes more effort for them to put ideas into words.

A glance at the second hand of a watch illustrates how surprisingly brief 1 second actually is. Surely, once the matter is raised to a conscious level, it is relatively easy to remember to wait those few additional seconds—precious seconds that enable children to gather their thoughts together and put them into words. That brief pause can make the difference between allowing children to feel competent or undercutting their sense of ability.

Note. From "Wait-Time and Rewards as Instructional Variables, Their Influence of Language, Logic, and Fate Control: Part One—Wait-Time" by M. B. Rowe, 1974, *Journal of Research in Science Teaching*, 11(2), 81–94.

slide?" If the children suggest pouring water down it, the teacher might respond, "Well, let's find out. How can we get the water there? What if the hose won't reach? Then what?" These opportunities for thinking and reasoning abound for the teacher who is on the lookout for them.

Remember that part of the learning experience should always include having the children put their conclusions into words. ("Well, what *did* make the kitten purr?" "Did the squirt bottle or the bucket of water work better? How come, do you think, the bucket was better?")

The following are examples of spontaneous situations in which the children could formulate reasons (hypotheses) for something happening:

- What makes the play dough so sticky? How could we make it drier?
- Can we turn Jell-O back to water? And then back to Jell-O again?
- How did you make that shadow? Can you make it go away?

The children may need to be helped along in their thinking by questions posed by the teacher or by other children, but the test of a truly successful experiment is that the children can answer most of their own questions as a result of their experience trying out possibilities with the materials.

Use Children's Questions to Help Them Learn

Answering a child's information-seeking questions requires two skills. First, it requires asking the right kind of question in reply to the child's query. Second, it requires waiting for the child's reply. Witness the differences in the following dialogues:

Example 1

The children, who have returned from a visit to the veterinarian, have found the doctor's kit all set up for them in the housekeeping corner. The teacher begins to unpack it.

Erin (to the teacher): What are you doing with those things?

Teacher: I'm getting out the stethoscopes. They help us hear noises in our bodies. Doesn't your doctor ever listen to your chest with one of these?

Erin: He listens to my heart. Where *is* my heart?

Teacher: In your chest. (He points.) Right there! Here, Erin, listen! (He puts the stethoscope on the child's chest.)

Erin (whining): I can't hear it. What does it sound like?

Teacher: Listen to mine. Don't you hear it go thump-thump?

Erin: Oh, yeah, now I do. It *does* go thump!

Teacher: Now listen to yours. What does *it* do?

Erin: It goes thump, too.

This situation may not seem limiting to the child, until you contrast it with the following one.

Example 2

On the way back from a trip to the veterinarian, Hank and Maggie decide they want to play hospital when they return to school. Upon arrival, they hurry to get out the medical kits.

Maggie (to the teacher): What's in that box?

Teacher: This one? Want to look? (hands the box to Maggie)

Maggie: Oh, it's that thing my doctor uses. It's a—what's it called?

Teacher: Anybody know? (total silence) It's called a stethoscope (pause). Does it tickle when your doctor uses it?

Maggie: Yes, and it's cold, too. What good is it anyway?

Hank: He listens to your heart. I've heard it—it goes kuh-thump. There, I'll show you. (They listen to each other's hearts and to the teacher's, too.)

Teacher: But how come the dog doctor had one?

Maggie: Do dogs have hearts?

Teacher (pause): Well, *you* know a dog. (The children's center is frequently visited by a forbearing springer spaniel named Lady.)

Hank: Lady! Let's get Lady! (The children proceed to the director's office where, providentially, Lady is stretched out, snoring.)

Teacher: Now, don't surprise her. Speak to her first.

Maggie: Hi, there, Lady, old girl. (Lady looks up and wags her tail.) (To Hank) Where's her heart?

Hank (authoritatively, pointing to Lady's hindquarters): Down there!

Teacher: Is it?

Maggie (putting stethoscope on Lady's rear): I don't hear nothing. She hasn't got one!

Teacher: Are you sure?

Hank: Let me listen! Nope, nothing there.

Teacher: Gee, I thought dogs had hearts. Where could it be?

Hank: On her back maybe.

Maggie: I want a turn. Let me do it. (She slides the stethoscope around Lady's chest.) I hear it! I hear it! Here it is! (Lady, gratified by the attention, licks her hand.) Yuck, her mouth is sticky—yuck, yuck! I gotta wash.

Hank: But lemme hear her heart first. (Maggie runs off, but Hank continues to listen, ultimately distinguishing the sounds of the dog's breathing and stomach growling, also.)

Note that this kind of teaching does not mean that the teacher never provides information or never makes a suggestion in the form of a guiding question (the teacher in example 2 did both), but it does mean that he continually asks himself the question, "How can I help the children discover the answer for themselves?"

The teachers in Reggio Emilia speak of this approach as *provoking* thought among the children. A delightful example of this was provided by Rea Baldridge, an artist who participated with our Oklahoma children when "The 100 Languages of Children" exhibit came to Omniplex, our children's science museum. She transcribed the following dialogue that happened during one of the hours she worked with the children.

Rea began by asking them what they already knew about shadows:

- Everywhere you go, your shadow goes.
- Your shadow is still with you even if you can't see it because it's invisible.
- You can never lose your shadow because it is stuck to your body.
- Sometimes your shadow can be asleep if you leave it under the covers.
- At night it goes inside you, but it comes back out in the daytime.

- When you're outside, your shadow is always in front of you.
- Shadows don't have eyes, but they still can see you.
- Shadows don't have tongues.
- Shadows are made out of dark air.
- My hair has a shadow.
- When you get in another shadow, you can't see yours.
- My dad's shadow is bigger than mine.
- Actually, a child's shadow is bigger than a grown-up's!

After listening respectfully to the children's ideas, Rea recorded the following dialogue and experiments.

Rea: How do you know so much about shadows?

Children: Because we look at them.

Rea: How can we find out more about shadows?

Children: We could turn out the lights.

Rea: If we turn out the lights, will we see our shadows?

Children: Yes! Yes!

(We turn out the lights.)

Children: I can't see my shadow! I can't see my shadow!

(We turn the lights on.)

Rea: What now? How can we see our shadows?

Children: You have to have a little light.

Children: You have to have a flashlight.

Children: Could we use that light? (pointing to a clip-on spotlight)

Rea: Yes.

(The spot is turned on, the room lights off. But the spot is aimed at the ceiling—no shadows.)

Rea: Where are our shadows?

Children: We only need a little light.

Rea: Well, yes, but the room is much darker.

Children: Turn the light down.

(The light is tilted down toward the floor.)

Children: Your shadow! I see your shadow!

Children: I see my shadow—it's behind me!

Children: It's on the floor!

Rea: How can we make shadows on the wall?

(Children scurry toward the wall trying to find their shadows, which they do.)

Rea: Great, but they're pretty small—how can we make bigger shadows?

Children: If you put the light on the ceiling!

Rea: But I can't reach that high.

Children: You could get on a ladder.

Rea: Yes, but we don't have one in here.

Children: You could get on that box.

Rea: Do you think it would hold me?

Children: Yes—maybe.

Rea: OK. If you bring it over here, I'll try it.

(Four children drag over a heavy wooden box.)

Rea: OK. Now look—what's happening?

Children: They're [shadows] getting littler.

Children: They're going on the floor!

Rea: What will happen if I do?

Children: I don't know.

Children: The shadows will get bigger?

Rea: You mean because your shadows got smaller when I put the light up high, they will get bigger if I put the light down lower?

Children: Yes! Yes!

Children: It might.

(As the light is lowered, the children's shadows grow on the wall.)

Children: They're getting bigger! They're getting bigger! (squeal)

(The light continues down until it is pressed against the floor; the room is dark.)

Children: Our shadows filled up the room!

Children: They got bigger than the whole room!

Children: She turned out the light!

Children: No, there it is—it's just covered up.

(The light is raised to a shadow-neutral position.)

Rea: OK. What happened?

Children: When the light got down, our shadows got bigger.

Children: They covered up the light.

Children: The light came up on the floor and made them get bigger.

Rea: You mean that the position of the light has something to do with the size of the shadows?

Children: Yes! 'Cause if the light is down on the floor, our shadows are bigger.

Rea: Is that the only way to make your shadow big?

Children: Yes! No! Yes! No!

Rea: Who said no? What else might make a big shadow?

Children: My dad turned a flashlight on me in the garage.

Rea: How did he do it?

(The children are cleared away from the wall.)

Children: He shined it on me.

Rea: OK. Let's see how that works. You stay there and I'll shine the light on you.

But what if we pull up the shade? What will become of the shadow then?

Children: Josh's shadow!

Children: OK, Josh, how do you make your shadow bigger?

(Josh walks toward the wall; his shadow gets smaller.)

Children: Go the other way! Back the other way!

Children: Go toward the light! The light!

(Josh comes closer to the light. His shadow gets bigger and bigger until at last he covers the light, his shadow filling the room.)

Children: (squealing and clapping): I want to try it! I want to try it! Let me! Let me!

The excitement and learning that resulted from that experience should inspire us all.

Ask Children to Think of Ways to Solve Problems and Propose Alternative Possibilities

One final function of asking questions must be added. To encourage the generation of ideas, teachers should cultivate the ability to ask questions that cause children to think about how to solve problems or even to propose alternative solutions. The foregoing dialogue about making shadows provides many examples of these strategies. Such questions are intended to encourage original solutions and so are called *creative thought questions* (Fisher, 1990).

Creative thought questions are characterized by having more than one "right" (alternative) answer because a number of possible replies may be of equal worth. This sort of open-ended thinking has been christened *divergent thinking* by Guilford (1967, 1981). Guilford contrasts it with its opposite, *convergent thinking*, which could be defined as thinking in which only one correct answer is possible. When teachers are developing *convergent* thinking in children, they ask questions that require information in reply. Such questions as "How old are you?" "What's your name?" "What's that picture on your T-shirt?" and "What's that called?" anticipate one correct, factual response. Note that much "discovery" learning, which fosters reasoning and process thinking, also produces convergent replies. For example, in the dialogue about finding Lady's heart, the children figured out the *facts* that a dog does have a heart and that it is located in its chest. However, if the children had been asked to figure out additional ways to hear Lady's heart, then it would have been an example of creative problem solving.

The following are examples of questions that stimulate *creative* problem solving and *divergent* thinking:

- How could we fix it?
- What else could we do?
- What do you think would happen if . . . ?
- But what if that won't work. What else could we use?
- What could you use to make it?
- What do *you* think? What's your opinion?

Such creative thought questions invite a multitude of answers and possibilities.

Four-year-olds, in particular, relish thinking about funny problems (what if everybody had a tail like a monkey, or what if we lived under water the way fish do?) as well as solving more serious ones (how can we keep the rabbit from getting too warm, or where should we hang all the bulky coats now that winter is here, or what is the best way to dry the dog after her bath?).

Little children usually come up with one idea each, but if these single ideas are pooled in a group discussion, they can learn to appreciate that there is often more than one good way to solve a problem.

Reinforce the Production of Creative Ideas by Recognizing Their Value

Holman, Goetz, and Baer (1976) summarize considerable research that supports the importance of providing positive recognition for children who are producing many different ideas, are engaging in other forms of original, creative behavior, or are doing both. It is all too easy for adults, who have had so much more experience, unintentionally to discourage creative thinking by evaluating the results too critically too soon, or by applying unreasonably high standards of accomplishment to what the children are doing, or by showing amusement at the unexpected novelty of a suggestion. Children are extraordinarily sensitive to these "put-downs" and quickly learn to hold their tongues and stop sharing their ideas when this occurs. Perhaps they may even stop thinking up alternative solutions to problems when subjected to such negative responses or, worse yet, to what they sense is subtle ridicule.

On the other hand, children will continue to be adventurous if teachers provide positive reinforcement by paying attention to their ideas, treating them with serious respect, encouraging them to try their suggestions out whenever possible and offering help when needed. Even an idea that does not turn out to be practical can have a beneficial result if it is used to teach the children that making an attempt is worthwhile and that failure just means it is time to propose another alternative.

Often, of course, the children's ideas are sound ones, and when this is the case and the group adopts the suggestion, the delight of the children is obvious. Their self-esteem, as well as their mental ability, has been enhanced.

Summary

When curriculum is generated for the cognitive self, the most important goal toward which to work is helping children feel confident, happy, and enthusiastic when engaged in mental activity.

There are three approaches to developing cognitive curriculum, all of which have merit. They include teaching facts to provide a foundation of information, using the emergent approach to facilitate the development of thought, and including practice in some midlevel mental ability skills that underlie later academic learning.

Emergent curriculum, which advocates that curriculum be based on the children's evolving interests and abilities combined with thoughtful support and guidance by their teacher, should provide the overall framework in which cognitive learning takes place. Using that approach provides the most interesting challenges for the children while making it possible for them to acquire information and practice midlevel skills at the same time. The municipal schools of Reggio Emilia and the educational philosophy of Vygotsky provide interesting examples and a theoretical base showing how this can be achieved.

Some practical points to remember when developing emergent curriculum include being

prepared to take risks, keeping cognitive learning appropriate to the children's age and abilities, keeping it part of real life, keeping feelings a part of the experience, and modeling joy and interest in learning yourself. Encouraging children to show as well as say what they mean and using language to promote discussion and deal with questions are additional important ingredients in sustaining effective cognitive learning.

Self-Check Questions for Review

Content-Related Questions
1. Explain why children should not be pushed beyond their depth in any area of learning.
2. Define *emergent curriculum*. Explain why the Reggio Emilia curriculum is said to be *emergent*.
3. List three ways the author states that the Reggio Emilia curriculum differs from the curriculum of the majority of American preschools.
4. What are three important things teachers can do that will help children enjoy cognitive learning?
5. What are the names of the three approaches to cognitive development? What are the primary benefits of using each of them?
6. Explain what the zone of proximal development is. What is the name of the educational theorist who developed that concept?
7. What are three purposes documentation boards are used for in the Reggio Emilia schools?
8. List four practical points to remember when developing emergent curriculum.

Integrative Questions
1. Explain why the staff of Reggio Emilia maintains that children have a hundred languages at their disposal.
2. Provide an example of an emergent possibility you have come across in recent weeks while working with children. How was that possibility handled at school (or home)? Would you describe the curriculum in your current school as emergent or conventional?
3. The children have been playing with beanbags, and one of the bags has got stuck in a tree beyond reach. Propose a dialogue between teacher and child that would discourage the child from thinking of a way to retrieve the beanbag. Now rewrite the dialogue demonstrating how the teacher might ask

a series of questions that could help the child figure out ways to retrieve the beanbag.

4. Compare the potential pitfalls and benefits of using "webbing" to build cognitive curriculum.

5. Use "ice" as a topic to investigate how the role of the teacher and the role of the children would differ if you used the information approach or if you used the emergent approach.

6. What is the difference between an interrogation and a conversation? What might be the value of using either or both of these in a discussion with young children?

7. Review the description of how the topic "mazes" developed as an emergent project in the Reggio Emilia setting and then describe how a teacher who was basing cognitive learning on teaching facts might present the same subject.

Questions and Activities

1. In examples 1 and 2 on page 394, identify the teacher's statements that provided factual answers. Were some of these necessary? Is it any better for another child to tell a child a fact than for the teacher to do it? Consider the incorrect information Hank gave Maggie about the location of Lady's heart—do you think the teacher should have said anything about that?

2. Movement education offers many opportunities for creative, alternative solutions to problems—for example, "If you couldn't use your arms at all, is there another way you might catch a ball?" Take a few minutes with the class and produce some more questions related to movement education that would be fun to pose to the children about turtles.

3. Try some brainstorming yourself. What else might a potato masher be used for? A rubber tire? A piece of cloth? A box of matches, contents included? Try to go beyond ordinary uses: have fun, take risks! (And if this exercise is especially difficult for you, analyze what has made it so hard and *not* fun. What are ways you can use these insights when teaching children in order to foster a more positive response from them?)

4. Do you think that waiting longer for preschool children to respond to questions might improve the quality of their replies? Propose an experiment that could help you find out if this is true.

References for Further Reading

Overviews

Cassidy, D. J., & Lancaster, C. (1993). The grassroots curriculum: A dialogue between children and teachers. *Young Children*, 48(6), 47–51. This delightful article describes how teachers developed an emergent curriculum in a preschool class serving 10 sighted and 5 visually impaired youngsters. *Highly recommended.*

Hendrick, J. B. (Ed.). (1997). *First steps toward teaching the Reggio way.* Upper Saddle River, NJ: Merrill/Prentice Hall. *First Steps* includes descriptions by many American teachers describing their attempts to develop emergent curriculum based on the philosophy of Reggio Emilia.

Jones, E., & Nimmo, J. (1994). *Emergent curriculum.* Washington, DC: National Association for the Education of Young Children. This book describes the agony and the ecstasy of providing emergent curriculum for a group of young children throughout a year. Honest and inspiring.

Wien, C. A. (1995). *Developmentally appropriate practice in "real life": Stories of teacher practical knowledge.* New York: Teachers College Press. Descriptions of five teachers and their varying degrees of incorporating developmentally appropriate practice into their classrooms are combined with an analysis of social constraints also operating in their environments—provides food for thought for teachers considering changing their teaching styles.

Information About Vygotsky

Berk, L. E., & Winsler, A. (1995). *Scaffolding children's learning: Vygotsky and early childhood education.* Washington, DC: National Association for the Education of Young Children. This readable book clearly explains the basic principles of the theory, cites recent research related to it, and explains how it can be applied to preschool and early elementary school. *Highly recommended.*

Steffe, L. P., & Gale, J. (Eds.). (1995). *Constructivism in education: Concerns about Vygotsky's theories.* Hillsdale, NJ: Erlbaum. This book provides helpful evaluations of some less desirable possibilities related to the interpretation of Vygotsky's theories.

Information About Reggio Emilia

The following articles provide quick, helpful introductions to this subject.

Abramson, S., Robinson, R., & Ankenman, K. (1995). Project work with diverse students: Adapting curriculum based on the Reggio Emilia approach. *Childhood Education*, 71(4), 197–202.

Edwards, C., & Springate, K. (1995). "The lion comes out of the stone": Helping young children achieve their creative potential. *Dimensions of Early Childhood*, 23(4), 25–29.

Gandini, L. (1996). Teachers and children together: Constructing new learning. *Child Care Information Exchange*, 108, 43–46.

Kennedy, D. K. (1996). After Reggio Emilia: May the conversation begin! *Young Children*, 51(5), 24–27.

Project Work

Edwards, C., Gandini, L., & Forman, G. (Eds.). (1993). *The hundred languages of children: The Reggio Emilia approach to early childhood education*. Norwood, NJ: Ablex. Although the entire book is of great value, the several chapters describing actual projects may be the most helpful ones for teachers who are striving to implement the emergent approach in their own classrooms.

Hartman, J. A., & Eckerty, C. (1995). Projects in the early years. *Childhood Education*, 71(3), 141–148. The authors describe a successful project done with elementary-age children.

Katz, L., & Chard, S. C. (1991). *Engaging children's minds: The project approach*. Norwood, NJ: Ablex. Katz and Chard provide practical suggestions of ways to shift from what they term *systematic instruction* to more flexible *project work*. Very helpful.

Asking Helpful Questions and Solving Problems

Forman, G. (1989). Helping children ask good questions. In B. Neugebauer (Ed.), *The wonder of it: Exploring how the world works*. Redmond, WA: Exchange Press. Examples from the "100 Languages of Children" exhibit are used to illustrate how teachers should interact with children to foster their quest for understanding.

Morse, P. S., & Brand, L. B. (1995). *Young children at home and in school: 212 educational activities for their parents, teachers, and caregivers*. Boston: Allyn & Bacon. An excellent book for the parent shelf, this volume is charmingly illustrated and offers many preschool age activities that incorporate learning opportunities while also being fun.

Sigel, I. E., & Saunders, R. (1979). An inquiry into inquiry: Question asking as an instructional model. In L. G. Katz (Ed.), *Current topics in early childhood education* (Vol. II). Norwood, NJ: Ablex. This wonderful chapter presents a list (with examples) of all sorts of questions teachers ask or *should* ask. *Highly recommended*.

For the Advanced Student

Bodrova, E., & Leong, D. J. (1996). *Tools of the mind: The Vygotskian approach to early childhood education*. Upper Saddle River, NJ: Merrill/Prentice Hall. Another valuable contribution to understanding Vygotsky's theory is presented here.

Flavell, J. H., Miller, P. H., & Miller, S. A. (1993). *Cognitive development* (3rd ed.). Upper Saddle River, NJ: Prentice Hall. The chapters on infancy and early childhood offer excellent summaries of how cognitive developmental theory, particularly in the areas of theories of mind, has changed in the past decade. *Highly recommended* for the serious student.

Vygotsky, L. S. (1978). *Mind in society: The development of higher psychological processes* Cambridge, MA: Harvard University Press. Originally written in 1934, this book sets forth some of Vygotsky's most fundamental ideas about learning.

Additional Resources of Particular Interest

Innovations in Early Education: The International Reggio Exchange. Merrill-Palmer Institute: Wayne State University, 71-A East Ferry Ave., Detroit, MI 48202 ($20/year). This quarterly newsletter encourages the exchange of ideas from around the world that are related to the Reggio Approach. Includes information on conferences and the "100 Languages" exhibit. *Highly recommended*.

Rechild: The Reggio Children Newsletter. Reggio Children srl, Via Monzermone 14, 42100 Reggio Emila, Italy. Published three times a year, this newsletter from Reggio Emilia itself provides information in English and Italian about various aspects of the municipal schools of Reggio Emilia. *Highly recommended*.

Building for Future Academic Competence

Developing Midlevel Mental Abilities

Have you ever

- Heard people refer to Piaget but did not really understand why his theories are so valuable?

- Wondered how to go about developing mental abilities in the children without pushing them beyond their depth?

- Wished that you knew more about presenting "pre-academic" skills so the children would find them fun?

If you have, the material in this chapter will help you.

Among the major contributions of Piaget's work has been the now widely accepted recognition that young children actively construct their own understanding of concepts and "operations" (such as cause and effect, number, classification, seriation and logical reasoning). This constructivist perspective in cognition emphasizes the child's need to act on objects, interact with people, and think and reflect on their experiences.

Sue Bredekamp and Carol Copple (1997, p. 110)

In addition to helping children sustain a zest for intellectual learning by fostering the emergent global skills of investigation and problem solving, it is also valuable to incorporate curriculum that targets some narrower, more specific midlevel mental abilities in young children. These include the skills of *matching, grouping, seeing common relationships, seriated and temporal ordering, and having a rudimentary understanding of cause/effect relationships*.

These midlevel cognitive skills are valuable to include because they are skills that Piaget and some other theorists maintain form the foundation for the development of more advanced thinking and reasoning skills as children mature.

Contributions of Jean Piaget

To understand more about such mental abilities, it is first necessary to review the most basic conclusions of Jean Piaget, because his work has made such a significant contribution to what is known about the development of cognitive structures in childhood.

Piaget has long maintained that children's mental growth is the result of dynamic *interaction* between children and their environments and that the activity of play and actual, involving experience are vital ingredients in fostering mental development. He also maintains that the thought processes of children differ from those of adults

and that these processes pass through a series of developmental stages as the child matures. He has demonstrated the truth of this contention quite convincingly in several areas, the most familiar being his demonstrations of preschoolers' inability to master the principle of conservation (the fact that the total amount or quantity of material remains unchanged even though the shape or number of parts may be altered). Young children will maintain stoutly, for instance, that the amount of water in a tall, thin beaker is greater than an identical amount of water in a squat jar, even though they may have just witnessed that the quantities were originally the same. As Charles (1974) puts it, preschool-age children lack "the ability to consider, at the same time, the whole and various arrangements of its parts" (p. 14). In our culture, it is not until about age 7 that children grasp the principle of "reversibility" and can, in their mind's eye, return a substance to its original state while viewing it in its altered state. This is, of course, only one of numerous examples Piaget and other scholars of the Genevan school have investigated over the past 60 years that demonstrate the perception-bound quality of thinking characteristic of preschool-age children. For children of this age, seeing is, quite literally, believing.

Piaget's research is very different in style from the other research studies cited in this book. For this reason an actual excerpt of his approach is included in this chapter in the Research Study. To study children's thinking, he used a combination of interview and observation to develop and then confirm his theories.

He has been criticized because it is not possible to repeat a Piagetian experiment exactly (Centre for Educational Research and Innovation, 1977). This is because his data often lack precise ages and numbers and are not statistically analyzed. Moreover, instead of using control groups and carefully presenting exactly the same situation to every child, he thought it was more valuable to conduct open-ended discussions with children on a one-to-one basis so every interview was somewhat different since he followed the child's lead as he formulated his questions.

Despite these criticisms, Piaget's clever investigations have blazed new trails in the study of children's development, particularly in the realm of cognition. Nowadays this approach has acquired new admirers as we gain an added appreciation of his ability to sense and follow the development of children's ideas by asking them suitable and ingenious questions. Teachers as well as children owe him a debt of gratitude for the remarkable insights he contributed.

Stages of Mental Development

Piaget has divided mental development roughly into four stages, as shown in Table 18–1. Although the age of onset and discreteness of these stages varies somewhat from culture to culture, the order in which the stages occur appears to be fairly regular (Kamii & Ewing, 1996; Siegler, 1991). The main value for the teacher of knowing about such stages and the characteristics of children who are in them lies in perceiving how children gradually construct their understanding of the world and in suiting learning opportunities to what they are able to grasp at each stage.

All children benefit from such learning opportunities, but it is particularly important to offer them to children who come from families of

the poor (Almy, Chittenden, & Miller, 1966; Golden, Bridger, & Martare, 1974; Sigel & Cocking, 1977), because these kinds of activities may not be part of the culture of their homes. Special attention should also be paid to other children whose life experiences may have been restricted because of such things as extensive hospitalization or overexposure to television.

Conditions That Favor Optimal Development

According to Piaget, development is influenced by (a) physical maturation, (b) experience, (c) interaction with other people (socialization), and (d) equilibration. This information has important implications for teachers and parents, because adults can influence all these elements, at least to a degree, thereby helping ensure the most favorable climate for the child's growth.

For instance, although physical maturation depends primarily on built-in timetables, the role of good nutrition, adequate health procedures, and ample physical activity should not be ignored. The Romans summed this up to perfection when they spoke of the importance of *mens sana in corpore sano*—a sound mind in a sound body.

The significance of experience—in particular concrete, tangible experience—has been stressed throughout this book as being a fundamental essential component of teaching young children, yet it must be mentioned once again in this discussion of mental growth, lest the reader be tempted to suddenly abandon the real world for the solely verbal-visual one.

The third enhancer of growth, social interactions, requires a bit more comment (DeVries & Zan, 1996). Although teachers of young children are usually well aware of the kind of *social* benefits children gain through interaction with other children, they tend to be less familiar with Piaget's idea that discussion and argument (in the sense of debate) among children is an important avenue of *mental* growth. It is very helpful for children to discuss reasons and thinking

TABLE 18–1
Summary of the Piaget Model

Basic Stages	Behavior Commonly Associated with the Stage
Sensorimotor stage (0–2 years) Understanding the present and real	Composed of six substages that move from reflex to intentional activity involving cause-and-effect behavior Involves direct interactions with the environment
Preoperational stage (2–7 years) Symbolic representation of the present and real Preparation for understanding concrete operations	Uses signifiers: mental images, imitation, symbolic play, drawing, language Understands verbal communication Believes what he sees — is "locked into" the perceptual world Sees things from his own point of view and only one way at a time ("centering") Thinking is *not* reversible Busy laying foundations for understanding concrete operations stage, which involves grasping concepts of conservation, transitivity, classification, seriation, and reversibility
Concrete operational stage (7–11 years) Organization of concrete operations	Has probably acquired the following concepts: conservation, reversibility, transitivity, seriation, and classification; that is, now believes that length, mass, weight, and number remain constant; understands relational terms such as "larger than" and "smaller than"; is able to arrange items in order from greatest amount to least amount; can group things, taking more than one quality into account at the same time
Formal operational stage (11–15 years) Hypothesis making Testing the possible	Age of abstract thinking Able to consider alternative possibilities and solutions Can consider "fanciful," hypothetical possibilities as a basis for theoretical problem solving Sees the world not only as it *is* but as it *could* be

problems among themselves, as well as directly with teachers. This encountering of experience together, combined with putting their ideas about it into some kind of symbolic form such as words or pictures and engaging in back-and-forth comparison of their thoughts, is a productive mode of learning that teachers should make greater use of as a teaching method.

Finally, the process of equilibration, or bringing ideas into balance with reality, is valuable to understand. Piaget maintains that there are two ways children deal with information; they either assimilate it or accommodate to it, and both of these processes contribute to equilibration. Quite simply, when children *assimilate* information, they add new facts to what they know already; when they *accommodate* to information, they change what they know to fit the new experience, thereby achieving a new balance or equilibrium.

For example, when some of the teachers at Reggio Emilia were talking with the children about shadows, some youngsters maintained that the

Research Study

A *Piagetian Experiment*: Conservation of a Discontinuous Quantity

Research Question   After Piaget conducted his pouring experiment with liquids and found out that children of preschool age were unable to master the principle of conservation, he wondered, What if pieces of solid material were used in place of liquids? Would the children reason differently about whether *that* material stayed the same even if put into different-sized containers?

Research Method   To determine the answer, Piaget substituted red and green beads in place of liquid and proceeded as follows. While the child watched, he poured the red beads into one container and then filled up an identical container to the same level with green beads. Next, as the child watched, he transferred the red and green beads into containers of differing sizes. During the experiment he asked the child questions phrased in the following manner. (Piaget's queries are in quotation marks, and the child's replies are italicized.)

[Subject is a child aged 5 years, 10 months.] "What are these?" *Little green and red beads.* "Is there the same amount in the two glasses?" *Yes.* "Why?" *Because there's the same height of green and red.* "If we put the beads in there, what would happen?" [The investigator points to a tall, thin glass.] *They would be higher.* "Would there be the same amount?" *No.* "Where would there be more?" [Child points to tall, narrow container.] *There.* [The investigator pours the red beads into the container.] "Do you really think there are more beads there than here?" *Yes.* "Why?" *Because it's narrow and they go higher.* "If I poured them all out [pretends to pour the red beads on one side and the green on the other], would they be the same or not?" *More red ones.* "Why?" *Because that one is narrow.* "And if I make a necklace with the red beads and one with the green beads, will they be the same, or not?" *The red one will be longer.* "Why?" *Because there'll be more in there.* [The investigator pours the red beads back into the original container.] "And now?" *They're the same height again.* "Why?" *Because you've poured them into that one.* "So are there more red ones or green ones?" *The same.* (Piaget, 1952, p. 26)

The experiment is repeated once more, with identical responses from the 5-year-old, demonstrating that the child judges quantity based on the appearance of the quantity in the container, not on the inherent amount of material.

On the other hand, when this experiment is carried out with older children (ranging in age from 6 to 9 years), they are no longer beguiled by the shape of the container. They are able to "conserve" the idea of quantity by concurrently remembering its previous state and understand that the actual amount of beads has not changed despite the fact that the taller cylinder makes it look like there are now more of them. Therefore, they answer correctly that the number of red and green beads remains the same, no matter how the shape of the container changes.

Implications for Teaching   Nothing demonstrates more clearly than Piaget's numerous investigations that children really do reason differently from adults and that their mental abilities develop sequentially as the child matures. When teachers understand this fact, it becomes apparent how important it is to suit learning to the correct developmental level. Otherwise instruction becomes a waste of time for the teacher and a source of frustration for the children in her care.

Note. From *The Child's Conception of Number* by J. Piaget, 1952, New York: Humanities Press.

Discussion between children is an important avenue for generating mental growth.

reason shadows moved was because shadows of living things moved whereas the shadows of non-living things did not. The teachers encouraged the children to try out their idea by outlining the shadow cast by a column in the morning and then returning to see what had become of the shadow in the afternoon—had it moved, or was it still where they had drawn it? The fact it had moved contradicted what the children thought they knew and required them to accommodate their knowledge about shadows to fit the observable facts. The movement of the shadows was not related to whether the shadow caster was alive. What then could have made the shadow move? Figuring that out was the next step.

Mental activity usually involves a combination of accommodation and assimilation working together, For example, years ago I had a child in my day-care group who found his little dog lying dead in the gutter one day, run over by a car. Weeks later, his mother reported that he was insisting on walking along the edge of the curb every time they went somewhere, and this almost fanatical preoccupation was driving her crazy! In approved counseling style, I asked her

how long he had been doing this and what else had happened or changed in his life at about the same time. At first she maintained that nothing much had changed, but upon thinking it over, she commented that he had begun doing that about the same time his grandfather had died. It turned out that the reason he had been so insistent on walking along the curb was that he was looking for his beloved grandpa. Once his mother realized this, she explained to him that dead people are not generally found in gutters and that Grandpa had been buried in the cemetery, which they then visited. This anecdote illustrates that this little boy had formerly *assimilated* his grandfather's dying (i.e., he interpreted it in the light of what he knew of death). The additional information required him to *accommodate* to it by changing his prior knowledge to include new experience. The new situation required new learning and a rebalancing of what he already knew about the world with what he had just learned.

Much learning involves this process of rebalancing, and teachers tend to accept this fact routinely. What they may be insensitive to, however, is that sometimes accommodating to new information also requires considerable tact by teachers so that the child can save face while he literally is changing his mind.

A Brief Comparison of Piaget's and Vygotsky's Points of View

Perhaps having read the brief introductions to Piagetian and Vygotskian theory, included in the cognitive chapters, you are wondering, "Well, who is right?"

Before answering that question, we should realize that, despite a number of differences, both Piaget and Vygotsky favor the constructivist point of view. That is, they agree that learning is generated (constructed) by the child and that, as children mature, a progressive structuring of cognitive processes takes place. They also agree that as that growth takes place, the thought processes become increasingly complex. Both theorists also acknowledge that play is the primary mode by which young children acquire learning.

Where they disagree is in the significance they attribute to the importance of external influences. Piaget sees the child as having the crucial role in constructing his understanding; sometimes this is spoken of as the "child as the little scientist," constructing hypothesis after hypothesis as he assimilates and accommodates information from the world. Because of his emphasis on the individual's role as he constructs what he knows, Piaget is sometimes spoken of as a *cognitive constructivist*. But remember that Piaget does not say that this learning takes place in isolation. As we see in his championing of dialogue and debate, he also acknowledges the influence of society on that learning.

On the other hand, though agreeing the children can attain some cognitive concepts spontaneously (on their own), Vygotsky looks at learning from a different point of view. He stresses the influence society has on children's development and so is sometimes spoken of as being a *social constructivist*. He argues that more difficult concepts can only be acquired by children because of the leadership provided by an adult or better-informed peer. For the child to attain a higher level of conceptualization, instruction is essential. The teacher is an essential part of the learning process as she provides the "scaffolding" that supports the child as he figures something out. She does this by using questions, prompts, and challenging examples that arouse the child's interest and cause him to advance beyond what he can do "on his own," thereby reaching the leading edge of his zone of proximal development. But this should not be envisioned as a one-way street—Vygotsky places considerable emphasis on the importance of *inter*action between child and teacher as they exchange information and ideas.

So the answer to the question "Who is right?" really depends on your point of view because both men have contributed valuable ideas we should bear in mind when discussing the child's cognitive self. Piaget's emphasis that learning is done by the child and has to be done for himself lies at the heart of our early childhood philosophy. Nor can we argue with Vygotsky's contention that children require other people to help them learn—that society and the cultural history it transmits preselect what knowledge children are exposed to and hence are able to acquire. Really, as Fosnot (1996) points out, the two constructivist viewpoints are inseparable: you cannot have individuals without society, and society would not exist were it not for the individuals who comprise it.

Which Mental Abilities Are Particularly Important?

As you progress through this chapter, you will no doubt realize that you occasionally *do* provide some practice in one or more of the midlevel abilities discussed here. Perhaps you play bingo with the children or provide Montessori graduated cylinders for them to use. The trouble is that such practice is often haphazard—fortuitous—rather than deliberately planned so that some skills are practiced and other, equally important ones are ignored. The remedy for this is to become aware of what the fundamental skills are and plan for their consistent inclusion rather than depending on "happy accidents" to provide spotty coverage of them.

Piaget (1983) identified various mental abilities that form the foundation for later concrete operational thought in older children. Constance Kamii (1972), who has had an important role in implementing Piagetian principles in early childhood classrooms, lists these early forms of concrete operational abilities as including (a) classification, (b) seriation, (c) structuring of time and space, (d) social knowledge, and (e) representation.

Ways of gaining social knowledge and using such symbols as language and imaginative play to represent reality have already been discussed in previous chapters, so we will concentrate here on how to develop the beginning skills that underlie classification, seriation, and structuring time and space.

These skills include

- matching,
- pairing common relations,
- grouping,
- graduated ordering (seriation),
- temporal ordering, and
- determining simple cause-and-effect relationships.

You will find the activities recommended later in the chapter for developing the various cognitive abilities to be simple ones. These have all been used successfully, not only in our own children's center and Institute but also in many other preschool settings, such as Head Start, so we know that young children enjoy them and are able to perform them satisfactorily.

Relationship Between the Mental Abilities and Later School Success

The mental abilities selected for discussion have great value in themselves because they encourage children to use their mental powers without asking them to do things that are beyond their grasp to achieve. These abilities are also valuable because they can help lay a foundation for later success in developing reading, mathematical, and scientific skills. Table 18–2 illustrates some of the links that exist between these abilities and later competence at a higher academic level.

General Principles for Working on Specific Mental Abilities

Make a Plan (But Be Prepared to Seize the "Teachable Moment")

To make certain these mental abilities are included regularly in the curriculum, it is very helpful to keep a list of them handy to remind yourself to fit them in as you plan.

Admittedly, with so many aspects of curriculum to consider, remembering to provide practice in these abilities can be difficult for the beginning teacher to do. The only effective way to make it easier is to discipline yourself to take the time and effort of learning to identify and develop the appropriate activities every time you develop a pathway so you can include them. The more you do it the easier it becomes to blend mental ability activities into the rest of the center day and to make use of spontaneous opportunities as they arise, also.

Table 18–3 shows how these midlevel abilities might be included as part of an ongoing gardening experience for 3- and 4-year-olds. Although the table includes only the cognitive self and stresses midlevel skills, remember that curriculum activities should develop and emerge gradually as teacher and children question and find things out together and that activities should educate *all* the selves, not just the cognitive one.

TABLE 18–2
Links between Mental Abilities and Later School-Related Skills

Ability	Value
Matching: Can identify which things are the same and which things are different *Basic question:* Can you find the pair that is exactly the same?	The ability to discriminate is crucial to development of other mental abilities. An important aspect of gaining literacy: discriminate between letters (such as *m* and *w*). Promotes understanding of equality. Encourages skill in figure/ground perception (separating a significant figure from the background).
Grouping: Can identify common property that forms a group or class *Basic question:* Can you show me the things that belong to the same family?	Fosters mathematical understanding: set theory and equivalency. Children must discriminate, reason, analyze, and select in order to formulate groups. Regrouping encourages flexibility of thought. Depending on manner of presentation, may foster divergent thinking—more than one way to group items. Requires use of accommodation and assimilation. Classification is a basic aspect of life sciences: allows people to organize knowledge.
Common relations: Can identify common property or relationship between a *nonidentical pair* *Basic question:* Which thing goes most closely with what other thing?	Fosters mathematical understanding: one-to-one correspondence. Fosters diversity of understanding concepts: many kinds of pairs (opposites, cause-effect, congruent). Can teach use of analogies and riddles.
Cause and effect: Can determine what makes something else happen: a special case of common relations *Basic question:* What makes something else happen?	Basis for scientific investigations. Conveys sense of order of world. Conveys sense of individual's ability to be effective: act on his world and produce results, make things happen. Encourages use of prediction and generation of hypotheses. Introduces child to elementary understanding of the scientific method.
Seriation: Can identify what comes next in a graduated series *Basic question:* What comes next?	Fosters mathematical understanding. Relationship between quantities: counting (enumeration) with understanding, one-to-one correspondence, equivalency, estimation. If teacher presents series going from left to right, fosters basic reading skill.
Temporal ordering: Can identify logical order of events occurring in time *Basic question:* What comes next?	Fosters mathematical understanding. Conveys a sense of order and a sense of time and its effect. Relationship between things: cause-effect and other relationships. Prediction. Requires memory: what happened first, then what happened?
Conservation: Can understand that a substance can return to its prior state and that quantity is not affected by mere changes in appearance *Basic question:* Are they still the same quantity?	Idea of constancy (reversibility) is fundamental as a foundation for logical reasoning, basic for scientific understanding; it is also the basis for mathematical calculations involving length, volume, area, and so forth.

Note. From *The Whole Child: Developmental Education for the Early Years* (6th ed., p. 519) by J. Hendrick, 1996, Upper Saddle River, NJ: Merrill/Prentice Hall.

For example, perhaps the children have been digging in the sandbox and have found, to their surprise, that some grass has sprouted there—this awakens their interest in where it came from and why it has those white, cold strings at one end. At that point the teacher thinks of a number of possible directions the curriculum path might take. She might think of starting beans in jars, or maybe it would be interesting to plant some vegetables or flowers or take a different investigative pathway altogether and find out what else is under the ground, such as worms, pipes, moles, or rabbits. The children continue their interest in the grass and also find some dandelions that are coming up, so she decides to pursue gardening as the extended activity to build on.

Once that focus is selected, she makes a point of incorporating related experiences that nourish *all* the selves, not just the cognitive one, in her plans. For example, gardening helps develop the physical self by fostering small- and large-muscle development as youngsters dig and weed, and generates social learning by providing opportunities to do meaningful work by both boys and girls working together. When vegetables that are favorites of families from differing cultural backgrounds are included, even more richness is added to social learning. Finally, a lot of emotional satisfaction is involved in just mucking about with mud, sand, and water as well as feeling satisfaction when the plants come up, mature, and are eaten.

As the interests emerge over the weeks, the teacher thinks of ways to "provoke" the children into thinking of many creative solutions to various problems: How can we keep the garden watered enough so that the plants will grow? How can we water the seeds lightly enough that we do not wash them out of the ground? How do we figure out which plants are weeds we should pull out and which we should leave in the ground to grow? What shall we do with the extra vegetables—take them home? Give them to the homeless shelter down the street? Freeze them to use later? Is it a good idea to pick the tomatoes when

the are still hard, green balls? And so forth.

Finally, as Table 18–3 illustrates, the teacher consistently uses the topic of gardening to provide opportunities to practice various midlevel mental ability skills. (Note that another example of incorporating midlevel skills into the curriculum is included in Table 17–2).

Consider Using a Science Table as an Alternative Approach to Planning for the Inclusion of Midlevel Skills

Ideally, as illustrated in table 18–3, opportunities to ask and answer thought-provoking questions, investigate possibilities, foster problem-solving skills, and practice midlevel mental abilities should be incorporated throughout the curriculum and throughout the day in accord with the children's developing interests.

However, many conscientious teachers prefer offering a special activity area during self-select time that provides a particular focus on cognitive learning. These are often called "sciencing tables" or "let's-find-out-tables." Hopefully, these, too, draw their inspiration from the children's concerns.

The drawbacks to providing such an area are that it may be overly teacher determined and inflexible because it is set up by the teacher ahead of time and because it may focus on teaching facts and information. The cardinal advantage is that such tables *can* go beyond teaching facts and encourage the children to practice some thinking skills if they are well planned. An additional advantage is that they combine a number of different learning materials in one place and can draw the children's interest and attention to a subject in a specific way.

Topics That Can Be Used Successfully for Let's-Find-Out Tables

The subject matter used for science tables is often some kind of natural history, but physical science subjects, such as pulleys, levers, and ob-

TABLE 18–3
Example of How Midlevel Mental Abilities Could Be Included in the Topic of Gardening

Midlevel Ability	Basic Question to Answer	Related Activity
Matching	Are these the same or are they different?	Weed the garden, leaving only lettuce and radish seedlings.
Pairing common relations	Which two things go most closely together?	Offer cooked foods at lunch and ask children to decide which raw vegetable came from: potato/mashed potato; spinach/cooked spinach; tomatoes/tomato sauce; peas in pod/cooked peas. Or pair can labels with what is inside the can.
Grouping	Which things belong in the same group or family?	At group time or snack time have many samples of food (real or pictures), and ask children to place them in groups and then explain why they grouped them together.
Seriation (graduated ordering; ordering in space)	What comes next?	In the garden, ask children to water first the smallest, then find the medium, and then water the largest plants.
Temporal ordering (ordering in time)	What happens next?	Put together a sequential pumpkin puzzle showing its life cycle, or dance through the life cycle of plants at dance time. Ask children how could they be a seed. Roots?
		Tell "Jack and the Bean Stalk," encouraging children to tell what comes next in the story.
Cause and effect	What made that happen?	Start bean seeds in pots, some in dark with and without water, some in light with and without water.
		Observe tender plants after a hard frost. What happened to them? What made it happen? (Try putting lettuce in the freezer section of refrigerator.)
		What if we did not weed the garden? (Leave a section and find out.)

jects that sink and float, are also effective. Some topics used by our staff in the past include these:

- How are rabbits, gerbils, and guinea pigs the same and different?
- How fast do plants grow? How could we find out?
- What's alive and what isn't? How can we tell?

- What do plants need to grow? Can we make them stop growing?
- Can you make water run uphill? Mix with oil? Mix with food coloring? Mix with salt?
- What makes shadows? Can we make them change shape or go away?
- What do birds eat? Do all birds like to eat the same things?

- Do balls roll faster down steep or shallow ramps? How about rolling *up* ramps? Which lets balls roll faster then?
- How heavy is it? How come some little things are heavy and some big things are light?

Some Basic Principles to Apply When Setting Up a Let's-Find-Out Table

1. It is much more satisfactory for children to learn about something when they can learn from real experience and by doing. For example, the inclusion of live animals, such as turtles,[1] enhances both interest and learning.
2. For the sake of comparison and asking questions, it is generally helpful to provide a contrast of some kind—such as between guinea pigs and turtles or between two species of turtle.
3. Provide activities the children can do with what is displayed. For turtles and guinea pigs this might include offering them food, analyzing which animal eats what, taking them out and holding them, and watching them move.
4. Unless you happen to know a lot about a particular subject already, it will be necessary to do at least a little reading about the topic.
5. Be prepared to offer some especially interesting tidbits of information, as well as basic facts, about what the children are studying. For example, did you know that the oldest known turtle lived 152 years? And did you know that in Peru, guinea pig is considered a delicacy? A nearby reference shelf of a few books is a real help.
6. Have in mind various questions you might ask the children to help them think up ways of finding out the answer.

7. Be as prepared as possible to let them try out their ideas and suggestions.
8. Do your best to combine beauty with learning: neat printing, beautifully illustrated books, pictures, and touches of color all do their part in making the let's-find-out area appealing. *National Geographic* publishes an outstanding series of natural history books suitable for young children. Librarians are also more than willing to help teachers locate appropriate support materials.
9. Remember to change the contents of the table as the interests of the children develop. Rather than setting out everything about turtles at once, for instance, it would sustain interest more effectively to introduce the turtle one day with some getting-acquainted activities about what it eats and does, then add guinea pigs for comparison toward the middle of the week, and perhaps add the large turtle shell after that for the children to try out being turtles themselves.
10. The let's-find-out area can also be tied nicely into the rest of the curriculum plan to extend learning further. For example, the children would enjoy moving like turtles and guinea pigs at dance time. Threes would appreciate hearing the story *Turtle Tale* (Asch, 1978), and fours would like *Molly's Woodland Garden* (Rockwell & Rockwell, 1971) or *Let's Get Turtles* (Selsam, 1965).

Using the Let's-Find-Out Table to Provide Practice in the Midlevel Skill of Understanding Cause and Effect
One of the joys of providing a let's-find-out table is the practice it may afford in figuring out cause-and-effect relationships because children can try out their ideas and do simple experiments to find out whether their ideas are correct. Trying ideas out introduces them to the concept of the scientific method, which involves (a) making observations, (b) thinking of possible reasons why things happen, (c) trying out these reasons or potential causes, (d) observing the results, and (e) then drawing conclusions.

---

[1]The health department has assured me that it is only the little, green turtles that sometimes spread the disease salmonella and that should not be used in child-care centers. Land turtles are all right because they are dry. They also suggest it is wise to wash hands after handling any animal.

This let's-find-out area provided the children with many different items to weigh and many ways to weigh them. The basket was used to hold stones so that investigators could find out how many stones it took to equal their body weight.

To encourage this approach, have some questions in mind to get the children started thinking. For example, if turtles are being investigated, the teacher might ask, "Are all turtles the same size?" The children need only look at the assortment of shells, pictures, and live animals provided to figure out the answer for themselves.

What is even more interesting (and fun) is to ask them a question and then follow up with, "How could you find out?" Remember, it is this kind of question that leads to simple experiments in which ideas are tried out and the answer is obtained. Of course, the experiments have to be supervised by the teacher to protect the animals from harm, and they need to be spread out throughout the week's time for the same reason. The following are some questions about turtles that could be answered by simple experimentation:

- Do turtles really move slowly when compared with guinea pigs? When compared with snails?
- What do they like to eat? What won't they eat?
- Do they act differently when they feel warm or cold?
- Are they afraid of guinea pigs?
- Do turtles talk?
- What frightens turtles?
- How do turtles protect themselves?

Although the chance to experiment and determine the reason that something happens is the most desirable skill to cultivate in the sciencing area, it is also possible to include additional activities there that provide practice in the other midlevel skills, such as these:

- *Matching:* Make a lotto game with pictures of turtles. (Turtles are easy to draw, and the drawings can be easily photocopied; stickers or duplicate sets of wildlife stamps also work well.)

- *Grouping*: This could be handled through discussion, comparing the qualities that animals have in common with the qualities of inanimate objects, or comparing turtles with animals that live only in water or that can fly.
- *Pairing common relations*: Looking up the visiting animal in a book and finding a picture of the turtle that goes with the live animal is a good example of one kind of common relations, relating two- to three-dimensional objects. It answers the question, "What picture goes with which turtle?"
- *Seriation*: Do big turtles eat only big things and small turtles only small things? Arrange several lettuce leaves in order from large to small and find out if the size of the leaf makes any difference to the turtle.
- *Temporal ordering*: A filmstrip on how turtles reproduce and grow would help the children understand that process as it occurs through time.

Keep It Fun

In chapter 17 we spoke of the importance of helping children feel confident and happy in the cognitive realm by providing them with mental challenges that are appropriate for their developmental level, by relating cognitive learning to their interests and real life, and by enabling children to solve problems and figure out answers for themselves. All these factors contribute to the basic pleasures and rewards related to intellectual learning. Besides these fundamental principles, there are a few additional ones teachers should apply when working with more specific midlevel skills so that the children's pleasure in that experience will be increased.

Integrate practice in mental skills into regular activities and play situations whenever possible. Many ordinary daily activities at school provide opportunities for practice in various midlevel skills. Using them for that purpose helps integrate them into the lives of the children and

keeps practice informal and pleasureful at the same time.

For example, when making whole-wheat muffins, gradations of sweetness could be compared by allowing the children to taste the flour, honey, and raisins and decide which is sweetest (graduated ordering—seriation), or the children could arrange recipe cards in order according to the steps in the recipe (temporal ordering), or the children could think about cause-and-effect relationships when figuring out it is the heat in the oven that turns the soft sticky dough into firm moist muffins.

It is important to realize that just doing activities will not provide sufficient learning. It is necessary also to talk about what the children are doing, so they are aware while they are doing it. Otherwise learning is likely to remain on the intuitive level longer than need be. For example, while putting the blocks away, you

Putting a puzzle together provides concrete experience in practicing common relations.

might use terms that young 3-year-olds understand and speak of putting away all the big "daddy" blocks first, the medium "mommy" ones next, and the little "baby" ones last to encourage the concept of graduated (seriated) ordering.

Make as Many Materials as You Can Yourself

Although much cognitive learning need not rely on tabletop or small-group activities for its implementation, sometimes table materials, such as lotto boards or puzzles, can be very effective learning accessories. When they are used, try to make as many of them yourself as possible.

There are several reasons for advocating this approach. First, such materials are usually much less expensive to make (if you do not include the teacher's time in the calculation), and making them provides creative satisfaction for the teacher as well as pleasure for the children. Second, the materials can be designed to fit a particular interest as it wells up from the children. (Just try to find a classification game that deals with camping, for instance, or with going to the hospital.) Finally, teacher-made materials are usually more attractive than commercial ones. I am always impressed by the color and spirit of the ones my own students concoct, and the children find them irresistible. Teachers seem to have a better idea of what will actually appeal to little children than most manufacturers do.

When making such materials, remember that durability is important. Glue pictures to a sturdy cardboard backing. Rubber cement works best as the adhesive, and mat board is both colorful and strong. Take time to spray the results with clear acrylic spray or cover them with clear contact paper to keep the materials permanently fresh and attractive.

It is easy to make inexpensive materials by drawing pictures or by using rubber stamps or paper stickers. Gift wrapping paper is a fine, frequently overlooked resource that is especially useful when making materials with a holiday theme. Catalogs, which are often arranged by category, are particularly good sources for sets of grouping pictures. Inexpensive "picture dictionaries" are still another source of colorful, attractive illustrations. Once made, the items can either be stored in neat boxes with a picture on the top so that children can tell what is inside or popped into ziplock bags where the contents are readily visible.

Provide Plentiful Opportunities for Practice

Repeated practice is necessary to learn any skill, and mental skills or abilities are no exception to this rule. Not only should opportunities for practice be repeated, using the same materials, but practice in the same skills should be provided over a long span of time, using different topics or themes and offering a range of levels of difficulty so that the children may progress as they become more proficient.

To Keep Activities Appropriate, Understand How to Make Them Very Simple and Also More Difficult

Very young children and ones who are just beginning to work on developing skills need to start with very simple activities, but they become quickly bored by these as their expertise increases. For this reason, each discussion of specific abilities offers suggestions for designing practice opportunities that range from easy to difficult.

Consider these basic ways to increase the challenge or difficulty of these skills:

- Increase the number of items the child has to work with at one time, such as providing two lotto boards to scan instead of one.
- Require that memory be used as part of the process—turning cards over so that the children have to remember which one is where is enjoyed by many 4-year-olds.

- Shift to a different sensory modality, such as moving to activities that require touching instead of seeing or matching by tasting alone.
- Increase the amount of detail that has to be analyzed while figuring out the answer.
- Asking children to give verbal reasons for their decision will certainly make the activity more challenging, and such answers may be within the ability of many 4-year-olds. However, an extensive explanation will probably be beyond the ability of most of them.

Curriculum Suggestions for Developing Specific Mental Abilities

Matching

To understand matching, children must be able to understand the concepts *same* and *different*. Teachers need to understand this, too. *Same* should mean "just the same" or identical. If one item is a two-dimensional picture of a dog, for example, the item it matches must be the same two-dimensional picture, not a three-dimensional little model of a dog.

The questions and directions that go with this activity should be, "Is this just the same?" or "Find me the one that is just the same," or "Show me the one that is different, or not the same."

Matching is the easiest of the mental skills described here for children to acquire. For that reason, matching activities are particularly appropriate to use with older twos and young threes, although older preschoolers also enjoy these activities. When developing specific mental abilities, it is desirable to begin with teaching this concept of same versus different, because children must be able to perform this basic discrimination task before they can learn the more difficult discriminations required for successfully accomplishing relational, grouping, and ordering skills. Moreover, the ability to perceive sameness and differentness is a vital element in learning to read, since children must be able to perceive

such subtle differences as the one between *d* and *b* or *m* and *w* to tell the difference between *dog*, *bog*, *God*, and *gob* or *mood*, *wood*, and *doom*.

Matching Activities That Children Enjoy

- Throw beanbags with pictures pinned on them into boxes with matching pictures.
- Put stickers on hands and have the children hunt for a matching child to sit with at lunch.
- Use "mirror" dancing in which one child imitates the actions of another as closely as possible.
- Put identical objects mixed in with other objects in a feel box or bag and have the child identify the identical pair by feel.
- Put one item in the bag or box and put three choices where the child can see them. The child matches the item in the box or bag with one of the three choices.
- Duplicate handclap patterns.
- Match sets of identical pairs of sound shakers.
- Match tastes or smells.
- Cut up varieties of apples and ask children if they can match the pieces by taste. (This is really hard!)
- Match paired pieces of various white vegetables, such as radishes, turnips, jicama, sunchokes, and potatoes.

Suggestions for Making the Task More Challenging
The difficulty level for matching activities can be increased by adding more detail to the pictures or making the differences less conspicuous. Using other sensory modalities adds challenge, too. For example, even children as young as 3 enjoy using their hands to search out the differences between two or possibly three objects in a feel bag, with the goal of identifying the one in the bag that is just the same as the one the teacher is holding.

Pairing Common Relations

It is easiest to grasp the difference between common relations and matching skills if one realizes that, although relations always involve pairs of items (as matching does), these are *never identical* pairs. Instead, they are pairs because they have some common element or bond between them that associates them. Perhaps they are opposites, such as up and down or hot and cold, or perhaps they are items that usually go together as do shoes and socks, pots and lids, cords and sockets, hats and heads, and flowers and vases. (Some of these relationships are the very simplest examples of what Piaget terms "one-to-one correspondence.") The basic question the children must be able to answer to succeed in these activities is "What belongs most closely or goes most closely together?"

Children really enjoy paired associate activities. Learning to see the relationships between things underlies the ability to appreciate riddles at a later age. It also prepares the way for the mental leap necessary to grasp analogies, such as "Hat is to head as lid is to . . ." or "Belt is to waist as ring is to . . .?" or "Two is to four as three is to . . .?" Such analogies are thought to be excellent tests of genuine reasoning and thinking abilities. (Witness the fact that the Miller Analogies Test is one of the most frequently used criteria for admission to graduate school.)

Common Relation Activities That Children Enjoy

- Children love to pore through a box of mixed items and put pairs together, such as salt and pepper shakers, leash and toy dog, nuts and bolts, and shoe and sock.
- Develop a game that involves putting picture and object together, such as ball with pictured ball and comb with pictured comb. (This provides valuable symbolization practice.)
- Use pictures of things that go together, such as animals and their homes or mothers and babies.
- Use flannel-board sets of pairs, such as raincoat with hat or swimsuit and cap.
- Put nonsense pairs together and ask children to identify what is wrong with the pair.
- Have children hold a particular item at group time, then wait suspensefully until you or an-

other youngster draws its pair from a box or from behind their backs, at which point they can shout its name out loud.
- Give children a particular picture of an animal and, as you produce a picture of its correct food, have them get up and "feed" their animal its dinner.

Grouping

Grouping involves being able to identify what a number of items, either pictures or objects, have in common. Thus, basically, the children's task is to "Show me which things belong together" or (the opposite task) "Show me what does not belong to this group or family."

Note that grouping differs from common relations because grouping always involves just

How might a collection of buttons be used to offer practice in matching? And how could it be used to practice grouping?

what the word says: dealing with a group rather than a pair. At least three or four items possessing a common property, as well as some that do not, are needed for the children to successfully determine what the group has in common. Grouping differs from matching because in grouping none of the items are identical; matching items are always exactly the same.

Grouping is a beginning form of the more sophisticated hierarchical classification identified by Piaget (1983) as being the intellectual prerogative of children who have attained the concrete operational stage of development. The concept of grouping is valuable to understand because the ability to perceive common properties not only underlies all the classification systems of science but also contributes to understanding set theory in mathematics. However, its greatest value is that grouping requires reasoning and thinking even at the preschool level, although children of that age may not always be able to put the reasons for their placing items into particular groups into words. (Piaget speaks of such grouping activity as being on the intuitive level—an apt description of how the children proceed. They appear to determine the reasons for the grouping as they do it rather than determining the common property in advance. This partially accounts for the fact that the basis for forming the group often shifts as the activity progresses.)

Many opportunities arise during the day for such grouping activities. If children are asked to sort all the foods they think should go into vegetable soup onto one tray and the ones for fruit salad onto another, that is a grouping activity. Or if they fish all the goldfish out of the aquarium and leave in the others, that too is grouping. If they take a field trip to the dog show and return with the concept that there is a large category "dog" composed of many subclasses, such as poodles, spaniels, and terriers, once again they are exposed to the idea of grouping according to common properties. In all these situations, the basic question the children must answer is "Which things belong to the same group or family?" and, possibly, "Why do they belong together?"

Be Careful to Talk About the Result

Simply doing the activity is not enough. The teacher should clarify what the children have intuitively perceived by asking questions about why things do or do not belong to the same group. For example, she might ask why German shepherds are different from poodles or inquire whether poodles and shepherds are cats—and if not, why not. She also might ask why cats are cats and dogs are dogs. The children will be able to give only very simple answers, such as "Dogs bark and cats meow," or "Dogs eat dog food, and cats eat cat food," or "Dogs are bigger than cats." Any of these answers should be accepted by the teacher without a lot of hairsplitting, because they are the result of the children identifying some attribute or quality generally possessed in common by one group and not possessed by the other one.

One of the most frequently used strategies for providing practice in classification or grouping is for adults to identify the group first and then ask the children to add things that belong to this category or to remove items that do not belong. For example, teachers frequently direct children to "Find all the things with fur on them" or to "Give me all the red beads." Unfortunately, this kind of teaching requires almost no thinking on the children's part. They only have to know what *red* means or what *fur* is and pick out all the items that possess this quality.

The way to elicit more thinking from children is to ask them to identify the common quality themselves and to sort items or pictures according to that property. For example, children love to sort buttons of all descriptions, and the opportunities buttons offer for composing groups according to differing properties is large indeed. Younger children will most likely sort them according to color or size or shape, but older ones may sort according to whether the buttons are plastic, metal, or shell or according to how many holes they possess. It is often obvious to the teacher what the basis of the grouping is, and if the children are too young to put it into words themselves, she can clarify what they have done by saying, "It looks to me as if you are putting all the red ones here and all the blue ones there. Is that your idea?"

Slightly older children also enjoy the challenge of guessing what should be added to an already existing group. The teacher might set out pictures of furniture on the flannel board without telling the children the common property (namely, furniture) and then ask the children to select the item that belongs to that same group from an additional group of pictures consisting of a table, a dog, a baseball, and a house.

Grouping Activities That Children Enjoy

- Use the dollhouse and ask children what furniture belongs in which room.
- Supply a large number of wildlife stamps, mounted on cardboard, and ask the children to sort which animals belong together.
- Acquire a large number of buttons, each one different, and encourage the children to sort the buttons into whatever categories appeal to them (egg cartons or muffin tins make good sorting trays).
- Dismiss the children according to whether they are wearing a particular color. To make it more difficult, dismiss according to stripes, plaids, and so forth.
- Provide a grocery store and have the children set it up by sorting empty boxes and cans onto the shelves as "they go together."
- Let them pin up, in one place (such as on a bulletin board), the animals they saw at the dog show and, in another place, the things they did not see there.
- Provide them with flannel-board groups, such as vegetables and other foods, and ask them to remove what does not belong.
- At dance time, ask the children what they can do with their arms that they cannot do with their feet.
- There are also many commercially made classification games that can be used to provide practice in this concept.

What midlevel mental ability concept are the children using here as they put the dinosaurs away?

Suggestions for Making the Task More Challenging
The easiest grouping activities are ones in which the common property or attribute is very obvious, such as color or shape. The less obvious the property, the more difficult is the category; thickness, for instance, is an attribute much less commonly identified by little children than color (Hendrick, 1973). Asking the children to name the category also increases the degree of difficulty; so does asking them to regroup the materials another way or to group them according to several properties at the same time.

Ordering

There are two systems of arranging things according to some form of order or regularity that are valuable to include in cognitive curriculum for preschool children. One is arranging items according to some form of *graduated order* (termed *seriation* by Piaget), and the other is arranging them according to the order in which they occur in time (*temporal ordering*). In both cases, the basic question the children must answer to perform these thinking tasks successfully is "What comes next?"

Seriation

Seriation, or arranging items according to a graduated order, is most frequently thought of in terms of gradations of size. Montessori cylinders are good examples of a regular change of dimension, and any kind of nested equipment can be used to teach the same concept. Measuring cups, measuring spoons, nested blocks, or those little wooden dolls or eggs that fit inside each other are all examples of seriated ordering. Nuts and bolts come in a wonderful array of sizes, too, and children enjoy arranging these in order and also performing the one-to-one correspondence involved in screwing the right-sized nut onto the correct bolt.

To teach the concept in a broader sense, it is also possible to teach gradations of color (ranging from palest pink to deep red, e.g.), taste (sweet to sour), or sound (loud to soft).

Cuisinaire rods and unit blocks whose sizes are all based on multiples of one basic unit measurement can also be used to teach seriation, if they are stacked in regular order beside each other for comparison. These are particularly valuable because they help children grasp the idea that 2 is composed of two 1s, 3 of three 1s or one 2 and one 1, and so forth. This results in a much more meaningful concept of enumeration than merely learning to parrot "1, 2, 3, . . ."

Seriation Activities That Children Enjoy

- Make a slot box with slots for different-sized and -shaped objects—a small circle, a larger square, a still larger rectangle, and so forth.
- Gather as many nested objects from around the house or school as possible (e.g., sets of spoons and cups), and offer them during house play or at the water table. Talk about how one fits inside another.
- When putting things away, hang them up in graduated order (e.g., in the house play area

hang up all the cooking spoons in order from small to large).
- Offer varying shades of the same color paint at the easel, from light to dark.
- Offer a feeling game in which various grades of sandpaper, mounted on cardboard, are put in the bag, then the children try to draw out the smoothest first, the next smoothest, and so forth.
- Ask the children to line up according to size and record the order. Repeat during the year to see if there is any change in the relationship.
- Throw beanbags or balls into larger and gradually smaller rings drawn on the cement.
- Build a family of snowmen according to size.
- Fill plastic eggs with differing amounts of beans or pebbles. *Seal tightly.* Have children arrange these in an egg carton according to the volume of sound they make when shaken. Have older children do this activity with their eyes shut.

Suggestions for Making the Task More Challenging

The easiest kind of what-comes-next seriation problem is asking youngsters to continue a trend by showing you what comes at the end of an established row or what comes at its beginning. The problem becomes much more difficult for them to solve as the number of choices is increased or if all the items are presented jumbled together. More difficult still is having them fill in the spaces left unfilled in a series.

Temporal Ordering

Temporal ordering is the logical order of events as they occur through time. Sometimes a change in size, as well as an advance in time occur, when it involves the life cycle. For example, as babies mature, they also become larger, as do young plants and animals. When not dealing with the life cycle, temporal ordering is exemplified in such things as following a recipe (the cake cannot go in the oven until the ingredients have been measured, mixed together, and put in a pan), sliding down a slide (you have to climb up before sliding down), or taking a bath (you have to get wet before you get dry). Remember that children should be encouraged to work from left to right when developing these sequences to help them acquire the left-to-right habit necessary in our culture for learning to read.

Temporal Ordering Activities That Children Enjoy

- Take pictures of a field trip the children went on, have each child draw one picture out of a hat, then ask them to arrange themselves with pictures in hand in a line according to what happened when.
- Be on the lookout for comic strip stories that can be mounted and used for temporal ordering sequence practice. ("Peanuts" is a good source for these.)
- Encourage children to tell stories that involve events happening in order—"The Three Little Pigs," for example, or "The Three Bears." (The latter teaches both graduated and temporal ordering.)
- Plan with the children in advance what the steps in a process will be and illustrate it as they tell you what these are—carving a pumpkin is easily drawn on a blackboard, for instance.
- Make a time line, such as showing how the baby rat changes as it grows.
- For church-related schools, advent calendars can be fun. Nonreligious calendars can also be made to help children anticipate how many days are left until some important event takes place (but do not start too soon).
- Use some of the commercially made sequence puzzles; these are quite good and show such sequences as getting dressed and making a snowman.
- Make illustrated recipe cards so children may prepare a snack by following these in order on their own.

Suggestions for Making the Task More Challenging

Temporal ordering depends partly on a knowledge of circumstances and partly on reasoning and common sense. Difficulty can be increased by adding more stages in the sequence and by asking children to interject events into the middle of the sequence. Older fours particularly enjoy being asked to arrange events backward (and for this reason they relish Ruth Krauss's book *The Backward Day* [1950]). They can also be challenged by out-of-order, "silly" questions, such as "What would happen if we ate the birthday cake and then the children came to the party?" or "What would happen if we frosted the cookies before we put them in the oven?"

It stimulates the use of memory and makes the task harder if the children are asked to recall exactly which step in a process they actually did first. The older children in school also enjoy simple, illustrated sequences that they can "read" by looking at the pictures as they follow a recipe. Such a chart for making soup, for example, might show pictures of meat cut up in pieces, a frying pan, 4 cups of tomato juice, and a number of vegetables and their needed quantities. Experienced older fours love the independence of "reading" such recipes entirely by themselves, assembling the ingredients, and following the illustrated steps with little or no additional guidance from the teacher.

Determining Cause-and-Effect Relationships

Children begin to understand the relationship between cause and effect in infancy when they first determine that shaking their crib makes a little, attached bell jingle, for example. But as Piaget points out, the distinction of which event is the cause and which is the effect remains confusing for many years. For this reason, when providing cause-and-effect learning experiences for preschoolers, keep them uncomplicated and quite obvious—obvious in the sense that the cause and the results can be readily observed.

Cause-and-effect learning is often thought of as being part of the world of science, and many illustrations of such scientific cause-and-effect relationships are included in the discussion of developing the let's-find-out table in chapter 17. However, many additional, simple cause-and-effect relationships occur everywhere and should be discussed with children.

Cause-and-Effect Relationships That Children Enjoy

Here are some common actions that can be used to help children realize that a particular act brings about a particular result:

- Squeeze whipped soap through a pastry decorator.
- Blow a whistle.
- Turn on a flashlight.
- Use a garlic press.
- Blow soap bubbles or a pinwheel.
- Squeeze an oil can.
- Use wind-up toys (such as little paddleboat bath toys).
- Grind nuts in a grinder.
- Shoot a squirt gun.
- Use a flashlight to make shadows come and go.
- Weigh objects on a balancing scale.
- Push a swing.
- Turn a kaleidoscope.

Children use these items every day but probably remain unaware of cause-and-effect relationships unless the teacher queries them about the relationships. The questions should be very simple ones, such as, "What makes the picture change in the kaleidoscope?" or "What makes the garlic come out?" The teacher should not expect highly technical explanations about energy and force in reply, nor should she attempt to provide these. However, the children are perfectly capable of answering that the picture changes because they are turning the cylinder or that the garlic is coming out because they are squeezing the handle.

In cause-and-effect learning situations, the basic question to ask the children is "What do you think made it happen?" and the basic question for the teacher to ask herself is "How can I help the children figure out the answer?"

Summary

During the past half century, Jean Piaget has made a tremendous contribution to our understanding of how young children think. He has maintained that children's understanding of the world and the way they think about it varies at different ages, that the development of thought results from dynamic interaction between children and their environments, that play is an important means of learning, and that movement from one stage to the next depends on maturation, experience, socialization, and equilibration.

Among the skills identified by Piaget as being significant are those related to classification, seriation, and understanding cause and effect. This chapter emphasizes how to provide cognitive learning opportunities for preschool children that contribute to their later under-

How could we make the sand come out faster? What would make it come out slower?

standing of these more sophisticated concepts, as well as to their success in school. These learning experiences should include work on the midlevel cognitive skills of matching, pairing common relations, grouping, graduated and temporal ordering, and understanding simple cause-and-effect relationships. The ideal way to integrate practice of these skills into the curriculum is to spread them throughout the day, but some teachers prefer to concentrate opportunities for practice in one activity area, often called the "let's-find-out table." Basic principles for planning such a table are included.

No matter which approach is used, to make learning midlevel skills a positive experience for teachers and children, it is necessary to formulate a curriculum plan, make certain the activities are fun for the children, provide plentiful opportunities for practice, and offer both simple and more taxing activities to sustain the children's interest and continue their growth. The chapter discusses each skill in detail and also includes many examples and suggestions for activities that meet those criteria.

Self-Check Questions for Review

Content-Related Questions

1. Name two ingredients Piaget feels are vital components in fostering mental development.
2. List each of the basic stages of cognitive development according to Piaget, and give examples of behavior that are commonly associated with each stage.
3. Explain what teachers can do to facilitate the conditions Piaget says are necessary for optimum development to take place. These include physical maturation, experience, interaction with other people, and equilibration.
4. What is the difference between *assimilation* and *accommodation*?
5. The six mental abilities discussed in detail in the chapter include matching, pairing common relations, grouping, seriated ordering, temporal ordering, and determining cause-and-effect relationships.

Define each of these abilities; explain how each of them is linked to later school-related skills.
6. Describe an activity you could use with the children that would provide practice in each of the six mental abilities discussed in detail in the chapter. Explain how you would make each one very easy for younger children and more challenging for older ones.
7. Although many preschool teachers already provide some practice in midlevel mental ability skills, why does the author maintain that doing that is not enough?
8. According to Piagetian theory, explain why the midlevel skills of grouping and seriation are important mental ability skills for young children to acquire.

Integrative Questions

1. Explain how the experiment described in the research study supports Piaget's sequential theory of cognitive development.
2. What is the difference between grouping, matching, and pairing common relations? How can one tell these particular mental abilities apart from each other?
3. Select an area such as housekeeping or outdoor play and propose activities that could take place there that would provide practice in each of the six mental abilities discussed in detail in chapter 18.
4. How could you use the material from this chapter to defend your curriculum when worried parents come to you and ask, "Why aren't the children learning the alphabet and how to count so they will be ready for school?"
5. Is it accurate to say that we should not pay attention to Piaget's theories any longer because Vygotsky's theory contradicts what Piaget thought? Explain why or why not this statement is true.
6. Some preschool teachers prefer to use a let's-find-out table while others prefer to spread practice in midlevel mental ability skills throughout the curriculum. What are the advantages and disadvantages of each of these approaches?
7. Explain what the scientific method is, providing an example showing how a preschool child could be expected to use it when figuring out a cause-and-effect relationship.

Questions and Activities

1. At one of the parent meetings, some of the parents say that they love the school but are worried because they have heard that the kindergarten teacher at their neighborhood school expects every child to be able to count to 20 and read his name and address as he enters kindergarten. How would you reply to this concern?
2. Select a holiday that is coming up and discuss with the class some ways that the mental abilities outlined in this chapter could be practiced using the holiday as the focus of interest.
3. Bring a commercially produced or teacher-made cognitive learning activity to class and explain how you might vary the presentation of the basic materials to make it simple enough for young threes or difficult enough for older fours to enjoy.
4. Appoint a committee to watch *Sesame Street* for two or three programs. Are opportunities provided to learn thinking skills, as well as the alphabet and rote counting? What do you think of television as a learning medium for such skills?
5. You have just purchased some attractive wrapping papers that have lots of little valentine and birthday pictures. Explain how you might use these papers to construct a matching game and a grouping game. What would be different about the way the two games are designed?

References for Further Reading

Explanations of Piagetian and Constructivist Thought

Bybee, R. W., & Sund, R. B. (1990). *Piaget for educators* (2nd ed.). Prospect Heights, IL: Waveland. It is delightful to welcome this useful book back into print. It is filled with clear explanations of Piaget's theory combined with many examples of Piagetian tasks.

DeVries, R., & Zan, B. (1994). *Moral children, moral classrooms: Creating a constructivist atmosphere in early education*. New York: Teachers College Press. DeVries and Zan illustrate how constructivist theory can be generalized to make classroom management consistent with Piagetian theory. *Highly recommended.*

Wadsworth, B. J. (1989). *Piaget's theory of cognitive and affective development* (4th ed.). New York: Longman. A good, clearly written introduction to Piaget that also deals with implications for teaching.

Midlevel Mental Ability Activities

Baratta-Lorton, M. (1972). *Workjobs: Activity-centered learning for early childhood education*. Reading, MA: Addison-Wesley. Photographs accompany every suggested activity, showing how a wide variety of cognitive materials can be made and used by the teacher.

Graves, M. (1989). *The teacher's idea book: Daily planning around the key experiences*. Ypsilanti, MI: High/Scope. Based on the Piagetian-based High/Scope curriculum, this book offers hands-on suggestions for such midlevel cognitive skills as seriation, classification, and others.

Hohmann, M., & Weikart, D. P. (1995). *Educating young children*. Ypsilanti, MI: High/Scope. This book is rich with examples of activities suitable for activities related to midlevel mental abilities.

Mickles, S. J. (1995). Developing young children's classification and logical thinking skills. *Childhood Education, 72*(10), 24–28. Readers who desire an overview will find it helpful to read this description of the longer process by which children grasp advanced classification insights.

Resources for Science Experiences

Harlan, J. C., & Rivkin, M. S. (1996). *Science experiences for the early childhood years: An integrated approach* (6th ed.). Upper Saddle River, NJ: Merrill/Prentice Hall. I recommend this book as a particularly rich source of additional curriculum-related ideas, including music, finger plays, lists of children's books, creative ideas, and even some examples of "thinking games."

Neugebauer, B. (Ed.). (1989). *The wonder of it: Exploring how the world works*. Redmond, WA: Exchange. This is a delightful collection of articles about teaching science. Topics range from cooking as science to how to ask good questions and set up a science table. *Highly recommended.*

Sprung, B. (1996). Physics is fun, physics is important, and physics belongs in the early childhood curriculum. *Young Children, 51*(5), 29–33. Long active in the women's equity movement, Sprung makes a plea for all children to "do" physical as well as other kinds of science. [Note the Woodard reference below.] *Highly recommended.*

Williams, R. A., Rockwell, R. E., & Sherwood, E. A. (1987). *Mudpies to magnets: A preschool science curriculum*. Mount Rainier, MD: Gryphon House. Another first-rate book that suggests many investigatory science experiences that are arranged according to topic and age. *Highly recommended.*

Woodard, C., & Davitt, R. (1987). *Physical science in early childhood*. Springfield, IL: Thomas. This book is replete with *appropriate* examples of exploratory activities that illustrate basic principles of physics. It includes suggestions for extending the experiences and for simplifying them for very young children. *Highly recommended.*

For the Advanced Student

Bodrova, E., & Leong, D. J. (1996). *Tools of the mind: The Vygotskian approach to early childhood education*. Upper Saddle River, NJ: Merrill/Prentice Hall. Of particular relevance to chapter 18 is the authors' comparison of Vygotsky with Piaget and other influential theoreticians such as Freud.

Duckworth, E. (1987). *"The having of wonderful ideas" and other essays on teaching and learning*. New York: Teachers College Press. Duckworth's thoughtful essays on Piaget and on other aspects of teaching are well worth reading.

Flavell, J. H., Miller, P. H., & Miller, S. A. (1993). *Cognitive development* (3rd ed.). Upper Saddle River, NJ: Prentice Hall. This book is filled with citations of current research and examples—a readable book on a potentially difficult subject that is *highly recommended*.

Fosnot, C. T. (Ed.). (1996). *Constructivism: Theory, perspectives and practice*. New York: Teachers College Press. This book presents a nice combination of theory accompanied by practical examples illustrating how theory can be translated into practice classroom teaching.

Piaget, J. (1983). Piaget's theory. In P. H. Mussen (Ed.), *Handbook of child psychology* (4th ed.), W. Kessen (Ed.), *Vol. I: History, theory, and methods*. New York: Wiley. This work by the master himself is a reprint from *Carmichael's Manual of Child Psychology*, 1970 edition. A classic.

Thomas. R. M. (1992). *Comparing theories of child development* (3rd ed.). Belmont, CA: Wadsworth. This invaluable book discusses a range of theories including that of Piaget. *Highly recommended* for its clarity and comprehensiveness.

$$\begin{array}{c} \smallsmile 19 \smallsmile \end{array}$$

Making Special Celebrations Part of the Life of the School

Have you ever

- Wondered how to help children enjoy holidays without having them become overtired and cranky?
- Needed ideas for holiday activities that enhance the children's creative selves?
- Wanted to know how to run a trouble-free potluck dinner for the families in your school?

If you have, the material in this chapter will help you.

> When we make choices about what to celebrate, let us be very conscious of who we are doing it for. . . . If we are doing it for the children, let us be conscious of all the subtle messages inherent in what we do and choose things to celebrate that are meaningful, developmentally appropriate, and healthy for them.
>
> Bonnie Neugebauer (1990, p. 42)

The celebration of days having special significance for children offers great opportunities to enrich the social, emotional, and creative aspects of the early childhood curriculum, and the end result of such celebrations can be wonderful—or absolutely terrible—depending on how much foresight and common sense the staff brings to these celebrations.

The holidays most widely observed in the United States have been singled out for discussion here, but I *hope that staff will add other celebrations as well that are appropriate to the ethnic and cultural backgrounds of the children in their particular schools.* The following suggestions are offered in the interest of keeping these occasions the cheerful, caring experiences teachers and families prefer.

Keeping Holidays Satisfying and Meaningful for Children and Families

Decide Which Values You Want Children to Learn from the Holiday, Then Plan Curriculum Accordingly

Unfortunately, just about all major holidays in the United States have developed an aura of commercialism that can pervert their true value and purpose if we do not resist this influence.[1] Think, for example, of the stress on candy that is associated with everything from Halloween to Mother's Day, Easter, and even chocolate cherries for Washington's Birthday. Or consider the emphasis on gluttony at Thanksgiving or the deluge of toy advertisements before Christmas.

Surely these are not aspects of holidays we want to emphasize with children, when so many other more wholesome values abound. At Thanksgiving it is just as easy to dwell on the plenitude of the earth and our gratitude for its bounty by sharing a snack of fruits and vegetables from each family as it is to lead discussions about how much you plan to eat on "Turkey Day." Or the school may share by sending each family a little pot of cranberry-orange relish for the Thanksgiving table. Either of these experiences is more genuine and meaningful for 3- and 4-year-olds than discussing the Pilgrims, and both reach the heart of the Thanksgiving experience (Neugebauer, 1990).

---

[1]To provide the widest possible application for this chapter, I have deliberately avoided discussion of religious teachings associated with church, temple, and mosque holidays. In my opinion, religiously oriented schools are indeed fortunate that they can include such aspects of holidays in their curriculum, because such inclusions do much to retain the basic meaning in holidays so often neglected in secular schools.

While speaking of the values we want children to learn, we should also ask ourselves whether we really want children to conclude that holidays are times when adults become irritable and there is increased stress between people. All too often poor planning and too much stimulation produce this result. *It is important to understand that excitement is not the same thing as enjoyment* (Katz, 1975). Allowing plenty of time for unhurried, simple holiday pleasures and at the same time not beginning so early that the children are kept in a dither of anticipation are important keys to keeping all these occasions pleasureful. A week of preparation is about the longest period of time that children can endure without going to pieces.

Stress during that week can be held to a minimum by reasonably observing routines, by deliberately including tension-reducing activities such as water play and vigorous outdoor exercise, and by not stuffing the day full of too many unusual activities.

How to Teach These Values

Once again, I want to emphasize the truth that children learn best through participation and firsthand experience. We all know this, yet holidays can lead us into thinking we have done a good job of teaching when actually we are depending on words and concepts that may have little or no real meaning for the youngsters. For this reason, preschool teachers must make special efforts not only to consciously choose the values they wish to teach but also to ask themselves how they can turn these experiences into more than words. Certainly they can tell simple stories to children about Martin Luther King, Jr., and what a great man he was, but real valuing of African American people is more likely to result from the children's daily encounter with their own firm but kind African American teachers.

Help Parents Think
Their Values Through

During the early years, parents of young children are often in the process of establishing family philosophies and traditions that they will follow all their lives. Teachers can contribute to this process by helping families think their values all the way through. For example, it could be worthwhile to plan a parent meeting before Christmas to discuss various ways to make the holiday truly meaningful and satisfying for everyone. Perhaps the group would want to spend an evening discussing ways young children can do something positive to help the family enjoy the holiday season. Ideas could be shared about simple gifts even quite little children can make, ways they can participate successfully in trimming the tree with homemade decorations, or simple, thoughtful things they could do for someone they care about.

Families may also want to talk over their expectations of their children's behavior at that time. Perhaps they are unintentionally burdening the children with the expectation of overresponse; the expression "being overjoyed" has real meaning in this context. Perhaps they want to learn how to deal with their children's unrealistic expectations of being given everything in the world. Then, too, the matter of what are safe and appropriate toys can be touched on, or suggestions for holding fatigue to a minimum can be presented.

Sharing family traditions is still another way everyone's lives can be enriched, as these shared bits of fun spark ideas for possibilities in young families who may be just beginning to build traditions into their family lives. And, of course, there is no better way to widen people's cross-cultural horizons than to exchange descriptions of family customs for the holidays (Wardle, 1990).

Another valuable discussion topic could be the problem of depression during the holidays. Single parents appear to be particularly prone to this condition, but depression seems to strike almost everyone sometime, and many adults confess to feelings of hollowness or sadness from time to time during this season. Because everyone else may appear to them to be joyful, a real sense of hurt and isolation can accompany this feeling. One parent expressed this feeling to me this way: "There must be something wrong with me to feel this way. I feel like all I'm doing, doing, doing is for others, and nobody really cares about doing anything for me!" A tactfully led discussion with a group of sympathetic people can offer the comfort of sharing these feelings. It could also encourage people to take an active part in planning for their own happiness by getting out and doing something they really want to do instead of just feeling low. This sort of response ultimately increases the pleasure of both children and adults as holidays approach (Dyer, 1986).

Planning Holiday Curriculum with Various Selves in Mind

The Social and Emotional Selves

The opportunity for sharing joyful experiences together that holidays provide makes them particularly promising subjects for the development of the social and emotional selves. Because such events inevitably include the receiving of gifts, attention, and care, they can enhance the children's feelings of being wanted and recognized. Less obvious but of equal importance is the opportunity these occasions provide for children to do satisfying things for others, whether making valentines or helping arrange the room for a potluck dinner. Older fours also derive benefit from planning together for such events ("How can we fix it so that the younger children can find eggs, too?" or "What could we do to celebrate our director's birthday?"). Such experiences provide simple but valuable opportunities for children to be generous, helpful, and kind. These opportunities are sometimes overlooked by teachers who assume that preschool children are too young or

not skillful enough to do something for someone else. The research study included in this chapter provides interesting evidence that children as young as 3½ can learn to be helpful and kind if the proper atmosphere and teaching methods are employed.

Celebrating holidays from various cultures is often advocated as a desirable way to add multicultural learning to the preschool curriculum (Goodwin & Pollen, 1980; Warren & McKinnon, 1988), but unless such celebrations are chosen with great care, they can become—and typically *do* become—just another example of superficial tourist curriculum.

To make multicultural celebrations *truly* relevant, it is far better to concentrate on including holidays observed by the families in your particu-

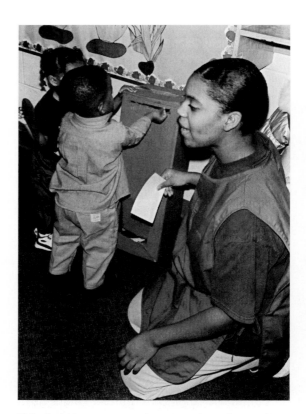

Valentine's Day presents a nice opportunity to do something loving for someone else.

lar group. For example, because our California center was blessed with several Mexican American children and many Mexican American student teachers, we were able to celebrate Cinco de Mayo with authentic verve (Derman-Sparks & the ABC Task Force, 1989). When I moved to Oklahoma, that holiday was no longer meaningful in the same way, and we celebrated quite different occasions such as the rivalry between the University of Oklahoma and Texas football teams.

Parents of various cultural backgrounds are often gracious about suggesting traditional ways for children to participate; some are willing to come to school and help with a special dish or tell stories of how they celebrated a particular holiday when they were young; they may even invite a group of children to visit their home. However, a thoughtful teacher should also bear in mind that holiday time means that the families observing them are already especially busy, so adjusting the date of the school celebration may make it easier for the family to participate.

In the emotional realm, holidays not only furnish special opportunities to experience love and caring but can also help children learn to deal with fear. Many children are afraid of Santa Claus or the Easter Bunny; Halloween, in particular, has a component of scariness, as well as pleasure, for young children. Advance preparation at group time, such as passing some of the more bizarre rubber masks around for inspection, may prevent a crisis of terror for an unprepared 3-year-old.

In addition, children need the opportunity to talk over important occasions afterward or play them through to clarify how they really felt about them. Once again, Halloween offers a particularly good example because of the thrill of going out in the dark to strange houses, the presence of mysterious visitors, and so forth.

The Creative Self

Frequently the social-emotional satisfaction of doing things for other people can be combined with doing something that satisfies the creative

aspect of the child's self, too. Usually this involves making something for someone she cares about. The pitfall here is that sometimes such gifts violate another principle to which early childhood teachers are usually devoted. This is the principle that children should be encouraged to be creative and self-expressive. Unfortunately, all too often as Mother's Day, Father's Day, or Valentine's Day approaches, mass production of identical gifts becomes the case. Most teachers are bothered by this contradiction of values and yet allow themselves to be trapped into such sweatshop activities time after time in the name of pleasing parents and including all the children.

One way to avoid this situation is to offer two or three different items for children to make and allow them to choose not only which one appeals to them the most but also which one they think the recipient may like the best. Uniquely self-expressive items such as finger painting can be given a holiday flavor if traditional color schemes are used. For example, red finger painting on white paper framed by green construction paper is very Christmasy. Or shaking gold or silver glitter on anything it will stick to can turn almost any object into a festive yuletide gift.

Anything the children can decorate themselves in their own way leaves at least some room for creativity. Iron-on crayons are a godsend for dish towels or pot holders, although these objects do have the drawback of requiring the teacher to hem the edges. Permanent felt-tip markers are excellent to use for this purpose, too, and their colors are particularly bright and clear. The use of collage for Valentine's Day is well known, and this technique can also be used to decorate simple frames for snapshots of each child for Mother's Day and Father's Day.

A good test of just how creative and child oriented the project is is how much the teacher has to do to complete it or how much teacher supervision and direction it requires. The more teacher participation, the less creative it is likely to be for the children. Remember that children also enjoy wrapping such gifts, and there are many ways to create attractive wrapping papers that allow individuality of expression.

The Cognitive Self

Although holiday curriculum's major strength lies in the areas of the social, emotional, and creative selves, as with any focus of interest, hol-

idays can and should be enriched with appropriate books, music, poetry, and flannel board stories. These contribute to language development, aesthetic appreciation, and the acquisition of factual knowledge.

Particular midlevel mental ability activities with a holiday flavor can easily be developed by using holiday stickers or pictures cut from wrapping paper. These lend themselves very well to

---

   Do Children Do as We Say or Do as We Do?

Research Study

Research Question   What are the most effective ways to teach kindness and altruism to young children?

Research Method   The sample consisted of 104 children aged 3½ to 5 who came from white, middle-class backgrounds. They were divided into two groups. During the hours of the experiment one group was taught by a nurturant teacher. (The nurturant teacher offered help, was sympathetic and protective, praised frequently, and paid attention to the children.) The other group was taught by a nonnurturant teacher. (The nonnurturant teacher acted reserved, responded matter-of-factly to children's approaches, tended to ignore requests for attention, and disregarded or critically evaluated the children's achievements. She acted aloof and did not involve herself in the children's play. The investigators state that "precautions were taken so that children would not experience undue anxiety.")

The children were subdivided into four groups. Group A1 had a nurturant teacher; group A2 had a nonnurturant teacher; group B1 had a nurturant teacher; group B2 had a nonnurturant teacher.

Groups A1 (nurturant) and A2 (nonnurturant) were taught about being kind and helpful, using little models of animals and people. For example, one setup had a monkey who could not reach his banana. Both nurturant and nonnurturant teachers of groups A1 and A2 modeled helping behavior by giving the monkey his banana and then letting the children repeat that action.

The children in the nurturant group B1 and nonnurturant group B2 used the same little models and situations to learn about kindliness, but they also participated in discussions of pictured incidents and witnessed examples of real-life situations in which the teachers acted kindly toward someone else. For instance, in one of the real-life situations, their teachers comforted another adult who bumped her head.

Following conclusion of the lessons, the children were tested for their ability to demonstrate kindly, helping behavior using models, pictures, and real-life situations. Groups B1 and B2 were retested in real-life situations 2 weeks later.

Results   Analysis of the first set of posttest results revealed no difference between the behavior of the children who had been in the nurturant environments and those in the nonnurturant environments. Apparently, the way the teachers acted toward the children did not affect the way the children behaved.

What *was* different about the groups was that the A1 and A2 children who had only worked with the little models did not transfer their learning about kindliness to either pictures or real-life situations.

the construction of matching and grouping games, and children love them. Since the events of many celebrations occur in a prescribed order, they are also excellent resources for practice in sequential reasoning: birthday parties, for example, often begin when the birthday child opens his presents, then games are played, and finally refreshments are served, with the party culminating in the arrival of the birthday cake.

The ability to recall the past can be stimulated by asking children to dictate stories such as "What I did on my birthday" or "What happened at the potluck dinner." Waiting a week or two and then reminiscing also helps children begin to develop a sense of time passing and exercise their capacity to remember. And, of course, holidays can be used as stepping-stones to new interests for the children—the living Christmas

On the other hand, the children in groups B1 and B2 who had been taught with the little models, pictures, and *real-life examples did* show positive changes in their responses to both model situations and pictures but not to real-life situations.

But the investigators did not stop at that point. They conducted a retest of group B1 and group B2 children 2 weeks later. That retest produced quite different and interesting results. At this time the children were presented with real-life situations that were conducted in a more natural, homelike setting. For example, they were provided with what appeared to be spontaneous opportunities to retrieve a baby's toys for him without being asked to or to pick up spools from a spilled workbasket.

That retest revealed significantly different results between the behavior of the children in group B1 who had been with a nurturant teacher, and the behavior of the children in group B2 who had been with the nonnurturant teacher.

When presented with the opportunity to be kind and helpful, 84% of the children who had worked with the nurturant teacher responded by retrieving the baby's toys or the spools without being asked, whereas only 43% of the children who had worked with the nonnurturant teacher did so. (Responses were significant at the .001 level.)

The investigators concluded that, when tested under more natural circumstances, it was evident that the modeling of helpfulness by the nurturant teacher had taken root and produced a behavioral as well as a symbolic change in the children's responses.

Implications for Teaching   This research provides evidence that it is possible to teach children even as young as 3½ to 5 years of age to reach out and do something kind and helpful for someone else if the correct methods of instruction are employed.

It also supports the idea that teaching the concept of kindliness on only a symbolic level by using models, pictures, and discussion is not sufficient if we want children to go beyond paying lip service to that ideal.

If we want young children to translate what they are told into action and become kind and helpful, we must provide them with real-life examples of that behavior. Moreover, if we want them to act spontaneously in a helpful and kindly way, then we need to combine that instruction with behaving in a kindly, nurturant way toward them ourselves. It is this nurturant approach that encourages them most effectively to do as we do rather than merely doing as we say.

Note: From "Learning Concern for Others" by M. R. Yarrow, P. N. Scott, and C. Z. Waxler, 1973, *Developmental Psychology*, 8(2), pp. 240–260.

tree can be planted outside, the Easter animals raised to maturity, and (my favorite!) the Halloween pumpkin allowed to rot and dug back into the garden.

Surefire Hints for Observing Special Days[2]

Special Celebrations

Primary Values
It is a pity to limit celebrating special days to particular holidays. Sometimes the very most satisfying—and certainly most genuinely relevant—celebrations happen almost spontaneously. Perhaps the children have finished the new rabbit enclosure and are delighted with their accomplishment and the bunny's pleasure in using it, or perhaps summer vacation is approaching and it is time at last to gather the greens from the garden and share them at snack, or perhaps the children want to celebrate the return of a loved teacher with her new baby. The primary value of such celebrations is that they provide opportunities to relish the delights of accomplishments and to recognize achievements by the children or by other people whom they love.

Things to Avoid
Avoid making overly elaborate plans that take too much preparation and make everyone tired before they start, feeling that every event requires an obligatory amount of recognition so the spontaneous joy goes out of the experience, and always doing the same thing to celebrate.

[2]The following material is included to illustrate how the suggestions in the previous discussion might be implemented in a children's center. Note that the emphasis here is on social, emotional, and creative growth; general methods of developing appropriate cognitive material are described in chapter 18. These suggestions should not be taken as gospel but only as possibilities that will stimulate teachers to develop similar experiences particularly suited to the children in their groups.

Activities
Eating something special together is such a fundamental aspect of most celebrations, it makes sense to suggest it here. Also, dressing up in some quick way can add to the fun; for example, perhaps the children would like to wear rabbit-ear hats for the bunny day. Most basically, an opportunity should be provided for the children and often their families to gather together and review the reason for the celebration. These events provide the place *par excellence* for sharing the pictures and comments from the children that have already been assembled on documentation boards or in memory books.

Birthdays

Primary Values
Honor the birthday child and mark her progress toward maturity (growing up is an idea dear to the hearts of most children).

Things to Avoid
Avoid placing undue emphasis on the number of presents expected and received, and who is and is not going to be invited to the birthday party; overlooking a child's birthday at school (this can really hurt feelings, so it is wise to keep a calendar of these events); and neglecting to celebrate the birthdays of children whose birthdays fall in the summer.

Activities
An activity that allows the child to assess her personal growth, such as measuring her or making a book about what she did when she was younger, is satisfying. Reviewing the assessment portfolios discussed in chapter 7 with the child and family is still another way of rejoicing over her growth.

It helps to keep a special box that has a variety of birthday things all assembled, such as a birthday puzzle, some stories and poems about birthdays, and cognitive games using that theme. If these are kept all in one place, it makes life much easier for the teacher, and the children look forward to the tradition of getting down the "birthday box" with great pleasure.

Singling the child out by making her a special crown to wear is usually much enjoyed. Parents can be encouraged to provide a special snack—ideally one with good nutritional value that is not as costly as an elaborately decorated birthday cake, which the child is likely to have at home, anyway.

Our staff also have a special tradition of celebrating their own birthdays with the children by bringing a special snack to share with everyone. The children are often surprised to discover that everyone gets older—even teachers!

Appropriate Books[3]

Bond, F. (1983). *Mary Betty Lizzie McNutt's birthday*. New York: Crowell. This is a little bitty book about a little bitty pig's birthday—delightful. (2 years and older)

Hertz, O. (1981). *Tobias has a birthday*. Minneapolis: Carolrhoda. One of a series, this is a simple story of how a child in Greenland celebrates his birthday. (4 years)

Keats, E. J. (1968). *A letter to Amy*. New York: Harper & Row. This is a story about a young boy who invites a little girl to his birthday party—a multiethnic book with a universal theme. (3–5 years)

Shiman, S. (1976). *A special birthday*. New York: McGraw-Hill. Here is a beautifully illustrated book without words. Children will enjoy following the ribbon to various gifts. (2½–5 years)

Uchida, Y. (1975). *The birthday visitor*. New York: Scribner's. This story focuses on a Japanese American family; in an unusual approach, it deals with both death and life. (4–6 years)

Halloween

Primary Values
More than any other holiday except birthdays, Halloween remains a children's day with all the fun of dressing up and carving pumpkins. If well handled, it can also help children learn to cope with halfway delicious fears.

Things to Avoid
Discourage prolonged glutting on candy, overstimulation, and wearing costumes to school.

Activities
Allow the children to draw the features on the jack-o'-lantern, but an adult should do the cutting. (Knives coated with pumpkin pulp are dangerously slippery.) The children can scrape out all the seeds, though. (One of our children commented, "Gee, teacher, it feels just like wet cobwebs inside!") They can also light the candle if long, hearth-type matches are provided.

Eat snack by pumpkin light; serve an orange-and-black snack (perhaps oranges and raisins and toasted pumpkin seeds, or orange-colored pancakes with raisin faces). Use an additional pumpkin to make cookies or pumpkin cake.

If the center is fortunate enough to have access to a pumpkin field, as is often true in warm climates, be sure to bring back a vine with flowers and green fruit still attached, or grow and harvest your own (this can be difficult to do if older children intrude on the playground from time to time). Keep one jack-o'-lantern and place it in a shallow pan and allow it to deteriorate. The mold is beautiful if examined with a magnifying glass, and digging the remains back into the soil helps children understand how the life cycle produces more life.

---

[3]Note that most of the books recommended for the following holidays emphasize wholesome social values as well as good stories and handsome illustrations.

Some schools have a tradition of a Halloween parade. I prefer to leave this to the grammar school crowd; however, if the staff wants to do this, remember to keep the parade short, do not make the children wait too long to participate in it, make certain every child has a costume (this usually requires extra adults around to help dress the children), and do not rely on paper costumes, which are too delicate for little children to wear successfully.

It is also a good idea to send a safety reminder home to parents about Halloween precautions. Parents should be encouraged to go with children for tricks or treats rather than sending them along with an older child. Remind them, too, about the dangers of candles combined with flimsy costumes and the unfortunate possibility that candy may be contaminated with pins, razor blades, or poison. Light reflecting tape stuck on costumes will increase the children's visibility and safety.

Afterward
Provide Halloween paraphernalia for imaginative play so that children can play through their feelings about this event. Plan a very easygoing day afterward if Halloween comes on a school evening.

Appropriate Books

Carlson, N. (1982). *Harriet's Halloween candy*. Minneapolis: Carolrhoda. Harriet's problems with sharing and eating her Halloween candy are presented in a humorous way that fours and fives will appreciate. The story has a wholesome message about the value of sharing versus being greedy. (4–5 years)

Kroll, S. (1984). *The biggest pumpkin ever*. New York: Scholastic. There is a wholesome moral included here about the joys of working cooperatively together. (3 years and older)

Miller, E. (1972). *Mousekin's golden house*. Upper Saddle River, NJ: Prentice Hall. The first, and in my opinion the best, of the Mousekin books focuses on what happens to a little mouse and the jack-o'-lantern in which he makes his home during the winter. (3–5 years)

Nerlove, M. (1989). *Halloween*. Morton Grove, IL: Whitman. This is a pleasant story about getting dressed in costumes and going trick or treating. (3 years and older)

Schweninger, A. (1984). *Halloween surprises*. New York: Viking Kestrel. The charming illustrations depict the joys of Halloween with almost no language. (3–5 years)

Sendak, M. (1963). *Where the wild things are*. New York: Harper & Row. A 4-year-old triumphs over a variety of horrifying monsters. (4–6 years)

Zimmerman, H. W. (1990). *Zero is not enough*. Oxford: Oxford University Press. This is a funny little counting book based on Halloween candy—delightful reading for fours.

Thanksgiving

Primary Values
The pleasure of families gathering together and sharing food together as a social experience; appreciating and being grateful for the earth's plenty; valuing the philosophy of many Native American cultures and their respect for the natural world.

Things to Avoid
Discourage overemphasizing how much everyone expects to eat, being obsessed only with turkeys (there are other valuable things to talk about in group besides these ungainly birds), relying mainly on discussing Pilgrims and Indians to make the day meaningful, encouraging racial stereotypes of Native Americans wearing paint on their faces and feathers in their hair, misrepresenting the relationship between Native Americans and Pilgrims, and misrepresenting the benefits to Native Americans of the invasion of their country by conquerors (Derman-Sparks & the ABC Task Force, 1989).

Activities

Make something at school to send home with the youngster to share on Thanksgiving Day, such as cranberry-orange relish, pumpkin bread, or a holiday decoration.

Children can be encouraged to bring an assortment of fruits and vegetables from home, which they can handle and talk about and then prepare together to share as a wonderfully varied Thanksgiving snack, or they can be taken to a large market to buy one of every kind of fruit and vegetable they find there for the same purpose.

Afterward

Ask the children to talk about the family and guests who came to share the holiday or tell where their family went to be with others. Children also enjoy picking out a variety of flannel-board family members (including pets, of course) who attended; a few older children may wish to attempt to describe how these people are related to each other ("She's my mother and she's my grandmother's daughter"), but this is usually too difficult for preschoolers.

Appropriate Books

Chief Seattle. (1991). *Brother eagle, sister sky*. New York: Dial. Beautiful illustrations accompany Chief Seattle's charge to white people to preserve the natural world. (4 years and older)

Child, L. M. (1974). *Over the river and through the woods*. New York: Coward, McCann & Geoghegan. Beautiful illustrations of an idealized 1890 family's trip to Grandmother's house accompany the familiar words of this poem-song. (4 years and older)

Gibbons, G. (1983). *Thanksgiving Day*. New York: Holiday House. Gibbons tells the Pilgrim story in simple language and ties it to current traditions. (4 years and older)

Nicola-Lisa, W. (1991). *1, 2, 3 Thanksgiving*. Morton Grove, IL: Whitman. This is a backward and forward counting book featuring Thanksgiving objects. (3–5 years)

Prelutsky, J. (1982). *That's Thanksgiving*. New York: Greenwillow. More simple, amusing poems by Prelutsky about Thanksgiving are included here. (4 years and older)

Spinelli, E. (1982). *Thanksgiving at the Tappleton's*. Reading, MA: Addison-Wesley. The plot focuses on how a family comes to realize that it is being together, not eating special things, that makes Thanksgiving a special time. (3–5 years)

Stock, C. (1990). *Thanksgiving treat*. New York: Bradbury. A little boy finds his place in the Thanksgiving festivities by helping his grandfather gather chestnuts for all the family to enjoy. (3–5 years)

Christmas

Primary Values

These include doing thoughtful and loving things for others; participating in various craft activities;[4] sharing in family customs and festivities (this is a particularly good time to share customs of other families, also). Remember that not everyone celebrates Christmas; be sensitive to the needs of children who do not and discuss this with their parents, asking for their suggestions and point of view (Gelb, 1987). For example, many Jewish families will graciously contribute to the richness of the holiday season by sharing their Hanukkah traditions with the children if they are invited to do this. This will help everyone understand that Hanukkah is not the Jewish equivalent of Christmas.

Afterward

Reminisce about the joys of this holiday, encouraging children to discuss a variety of satisfactions rather than just enumerating everything

---

[4]See, particularly, the recipes for the basic dough and ornamental clay in Table 14–6.

they received as gifts. If weather permits, plant a living Christmas tree outdoors.

Appropriate Books

Brett, J. (1990). *The wild Christmas reindeer.* New York: Putnam's. A young Lapland girl learns that love is the way to teach her reindeer to pull Santa's sleigh. (4 years and up)

Briggs, R. (1973). *Father Christmas.* New York: Coward, McCann & Geoghegan. Children will pore for hours over the odd little illustrations in *Father Christmas*; a truly one-of-a-kind book that should not be missed. (3–6 years)

Budbill, D. (1974). *Christmas tree farm.* New York: Macmillan. Nicely illustrated, *Christmas Tree Farm* is particularly enjoyed by fours, whose interest in facts is satisfied by this description of where Christmas trees come from.

Bunting, E. (1991). *Night tree.* New York: Harcourt Brace. Another good book about doing something for someone else—in this case a family decorating a tree with food for the animals to eat.

Ets, M. H., & Labastida, A. (1959). *Nine days to Christmas.* New York: Viking. Beautifully illustrated, this somewhat lengthy book deals with Christmas in Mexico. (4–6 years)

Fearrington, A. (1996). *Christmas lights.* Boston: Houghton Mifflin. Lovely pictures grace this simple text illustrating a family's evening trip to look at the Christmas lights. (2–5 years)

Hayes, S. (1986). *Happy Christmas Gemma.* New York: Lothrop, Lee. This book about an African American family describes how they prepare for and enjoy Christmas. (2 years and older)

Holnbird, K. (1985). *Angelina's Christmas.* New York: Clarkson. Kindly mice gather a lonely old postman into their family. (3 years and up)

Johnston, T. (1996). *The magic maguay.* New York: Harcourt Brace. A young Mexican boy saves the village's treasured maguay plant from destruction.

Kent, J. (1969). *The Christmas piñata.* New York: Parent's Magazine Press. Here is a delightful little book that describes a Christmas celebration in Mexico. (3–5 years)

Moore, C. C. (1961). *The night before Christmas.* New York: Grosset & Dunlap. The exquisite illustrations by Gyo Fujikawa make this a particularly attractive presentation of this old classic. (2 years and older)

Rogers, J. (1985). *King Island Christmas.* New York: Greenwillow. This is a story about how contemporary Eskimos celebrate Christmas on a remote Alaskan island. (4 years and older)

Spier, P. (1983). *Christmas!* New York: Doubleday. In a wordless, attractively illustrated book, Spier includes pictures having to do with preparations for, celebrations of, and the day after Christmas. Could be used with any age, with some judicious shortening for younger children.

Stock, C. (1984). *Sampson, the Christmas cat.* New York: Putnam's. Sampson is a cat who has some funny adventures on Christmas day as he adopts a family. (3–5 years)

Willson, R. B. (1983). *Merry Christmas: Children at Christmastime around the world.* New York: Philomel. The text is way too grown up for preschoolers, but information could be paraphrased. The book has exquisite illustrations of Christmas celebrations in many cultures.

Valentine's Day

Primary Values

These include the pleasure of telling someone else you like them and the pleasure of being liked, plus receiving letters—a rare, intense pleasure for many little children.

Things to Avoid

Avoid the popularity contest often inherent in having a Valentine's box at school—many early childhood teachers put up a tactful notice ahead of time explaining why this is not done at their school and how the holiday will be celebrated instead. Precocious comments on "boyfriends" and "girlfriends" are also inappropriate.

Activities

Valentine's Day calls out for pretty collage materials—white lace, red hearts, and so forth. Although costs of mailing can be prohibitive if the school must bear it alone, it *is* possible to ask each family to provide a stamp and then encourage the children to make a valentine that they can mail at the post office to their families.

It can be fun to carry out the holiday theme by having an all red and pink day, including easel paints, play dough, snack, and even lunch.

Children do love dramatic play involving sending and receiving mail. It can be worth the

When the eggs are bright enough, they can be lifted out and drained in an old egg carton with the child's name on it.

investment to have lots of cheap or recycled envelopes in the housekeeping corner that they can use for making and mailing valentines.

Appropriate Books

Bunting, E. (1983). *The Valentine bears*. New York: Houghton Mifflin. Bunting tells how Mrs. Bear attempts to wake Mr. Bear up to celebrate Valentine's Day. (Sophisticated humor makes it appropriate for older fours)

Schweninger, A. (1976). *The hunt for Rabbit's galosh*. New York: Doubleday. Various animals help Rabbit hunt for his galosh so he can mail a valentine to his mother. (3–5 years)

Easter

Primary Values

This is an excellent time to teach about the beauty of the renewal of life by celebrating such springtime rites as planting seeds and enjoying baby animals.

Things to Avoid

Try not to stress the omnipresent candy; letting children mix all the egg dye into one bowl of dull gray; and labeling each egg and trying to make sure each child gets that particular egg to take home!

Activities

It can be difficult to control the experience if everyone is allowed to crowd around and slosh eggs in the dye at the same time. The best way I have seen this presented was by a teacher at the Oaks Parent/Child Workshop who brought a tray to each snack table with enough eggs for two apiece and cups of various colored dyes from which the children could choose. When the eggs were bright enough, they were spooned out and put in cartons to dry.

If an egg hunt is planned, it is necessary to hide eggs in different areas for different-age children. Otherwise the fours find all the "easy" ones immediately and the threes have an unsatisfying time of it. At our center, we separate age groups and also explain in advance that each child may find two dyed eggs to keep and as many foil wrapped jelly beans (yes, I know they are made of sugar!) as they can locate. This works out all right for everyone but the 2-year-olds, who seem to think that anything wrapped in foil must be litter.

Wheat or corn may be planted in eggshell halves and sent home when sprouted; the shells are biodegradable and only need to be crushed a little when the plants are set out in the garden.

If planned in advance, the school rabbit will produce babies at this time, which has the added advantage of increasing the likelihood of their later adoption.

Appropriate Books

See also group time recommendations about rabbit materials in chapter 16.

Balian, L. (1974). *Humbug rabbit*. Nashville, TN: Abingdon. (Still in print). This is an amusing story about baby rabbits and Easter eggs. (3–5 years)

Chalmers, M. (1988). *Easter parade*. New York: HarperCollins. Rabbits thoughtfully deliver Easter baskets to everyone—even the ladybug. Lovely pictures. (2–3 years)

Milhous, K. (1950). *The egg tree*. New York: Scribner's. This story describes an Easter egg hunt and the old custom of using the eggs to decorate a tree. (4–6 years)

Tresselt, A. (1967). *The world in the candy egg*. New York: Lothrop, Lee & Shepard. Many animals look into this old-fashioned candy egg and see what they love best. (4–5 years)

Mother's Day and Father's Day

Primary Values

These holidays can contribute to an understanding and valuing of family relationships—and an opportunity to reciprocate parental affection by doing something for that parent. In our center, where so many of the parents are single, we have found that such days take on a very special meaning to parents, as well as to children, and a special sensitivity is required because of this.

Things to Avoid

Do not insensitively assume that all the children have both parents readily available (Hasson, 1996; Lewis, 1996). By that time of the year, teachers usually know who in the child's life might serve as a surrogate parent if the natural parent is not in evidence. Although acknowledging the relationship may not be the same, they can then propose that the youngster make a present for that person instead. Also to be avoided are presents that are more teacher than child made.

Activities

There are a variety of small gifts that can be simply made by a child for the parent. Among these are cards made from paintings the youngster has done with a dictated message inside about "What my mother does . . ." or "I like my father because. . . ." Or the card may describe in the child's words some special, kindly thing she intends to do for the parent on that special day.

Handprints made in plaster of paris are another longtime favorite. The plaster can be tinted any color the child prefers by adding tempera to the dry plaster, but the whole process has to be done very speedily, and it is wise to realize that some prints will have to be done more than once to obtain a clear one. Children also enjoy potting up small, quick-blooming plants, such as dwarf marigolds, for gifts.

Some of the best presents we ever made for parents of either sex were the soap balls described by Lewis (1975). Mix 2 teaspoons of hot water with liquid food color and scent if desired (such as lemon or clove). Add colored liquid to

½ cup soap flakes and mold and squeeze until it can be rolled into small balls. Or the material can be rolled out thick and cut with cookie cutters, or formed around colored heavy cotton yarn for a bath ball.

To go with the soap, we made bath salts composed of baking soda colored with several drops of food coloring and worked together with fingers or a spoon. These salts are nice to put in small baby food jars and give with the soap.

Appropriate Books

Just about any good book on family life will do here, depending on the children's favorites. Be sure to include alternative family styles.

Greenspun, A. A. (1991). *Fathers*. New York: Philomel. Photographs illustrate fathers of all descriptions. Very simple text. (2 or 3 years and older)

Holiday Books

A few additional books about holidays and seasons that may be of interest follow:

Coleridge, S. (1986). *January brings the snow*. New York: Dial. This old rhyme is beautifully illustrated by Jenni Oliver. It takes the reader through the year month by month. (4 years and older)

Friedrich, P., & Friedrich, O. (1957). *The Easter bunny that overslept*. New York: Lothrop, Lee & Shepard. This presents a review of major holidays throughout the year as the bunny attempts unsuccessfully to participate in each one of them with his Easter eggs. (4–5 years)

Parsons, V. (1975). *Ring for liberty*. New York: Golden. This attractively illustrated book tells the story of the signing of the Declaration of Independence as told through the eyes of a little boy. Although the children's grasp of this subject is necessarily limited, I would at-

tempt to use this book with older fours to help them understand that the Fourth of July is more than just fireworks.

Rockwell, A. (1985). *First comes spring*. New York: Crowell. Rockwell provides numerous charming pictures of what people do and wear at various seasons of the year. (Older threes–fives)

Zolotow, C. (1957). *Over and over*. New York: Harper & Row. Beautifully illustrated, this book also uses a simple story line to trace the progression of holidays throughout the year, including birthdays. (4–6 years)

Celebrating Holidays with Families by Having a Children's Program

Some schools like to make an occasion of holidays by having the children present a program for the parents to enjoy. If this can be a very simple occasion that involves a brief period of preparation, it can add to the pleasure of the holiday. However, if the program becomes so elaborate that it requires months or even weeks of practice, it not only places stress on everyone but may go stale long before the actual presentation takes place.

One approach our staff has found that works well is to teach the children a few songs or finger plays related to the particular holiday. When the adults have assembled, the children sit down together with their families and sing these for the parents. We also include copies of the words for the visitors to use and ask them to join in with us on the second time around. Following this, we provide a simple, festive snack for everyone. Such an event is enough of a "program" and is not too stressful for the young participants to enjoy. If costumes are thought to be necessary, hats are enough for the children to wear. These can be made at school so that parents are spared the problem and expense of producing elaborate costumes.

Suggestions for Managing a
Successful Family Picnic or Potluck[5]

Signing Up

To make adequate potluck plans, have an attractive poster available for signing up; otherwise, one can end up with all desserts and no hot dishes. These posters can also mitigate one of the real problems at potlucks: occasionally the food runs out before the people do. This situation can be alleviated by specifying clearly on the sign-up sheet how many people each dish should be expected to serve (e.g., "It should be a casserole for 6 or 8" or "Please bring enough for two families"). If there are going to be many children attending, it may be necessary to ask people to sign up for two items so there will be enough to go around. If families in the school are on slim budgets, it is wise to plan such dinners early in the month so that more people will feel able to participate. It is also helpful to be very definite on the sign-up sheet about details, such as "Bring your own table service," and to specify the exact time the meal will be served.

A poster will help catch people's attention, but it may also be necessary for teachers to invite individuals specifically. People are often shyly reluctant to participate in such events, particularly at the beginning of the year when they do not know other families or that the potlucks are fun. Of course, the more responsibility that is spread around, the more likely people are to come. For example, asking families to provide transportation for other families means that both will show up and that they will have become acquainted before arrival. This is especially helpful for single parents, who may otherwise dread being one of a

kind. (You might consider asking the single parent to do the picking up to avoid the connotation of being a "charity case.")

Choosing the Place

Some staffs never consider having any gathering away from the school site; however, we have found that there are real advantages to planning a potluck or picnic at a park when weather permits. Quite frankly, this is because there is a subtle difference in the attitude of the families when we move off school premises. When parties are held at the school, parents assume the teachers are in charge of the children and leave this responsibility, as well as more of the setting up and cleaning up, to the staff. As a result, the staff spends most of the next day recovering. When the gathering is "off campus," parents assume more of the responsibility. Besides this, if a park is selected, there is the advantage that some of the play equipment is larger and more appropriate for older children, and for family potlucks this is a real boon. On the other hand, having the event at school does present the different advantage of giving parents and older children an opportunity to see what the school itself is like.

Some Recommendations on Serving Food

A handful of people inevitably forget to bring either dishes, cups, silverware, or serving spoons, so it is a good idea to have some extras on hand to avoid embarrassing them. Serving will go faster if tables are arranged so that people can go down both sides at the same time. We have found it wise to bring out a few hot dishes and salads later so that people at the end of the line have fresh foods from which to choose.

Beverages can be offered most economically if hot water is heated in large coffee urns and instant coffee and tea provided to mix individually as desired. We always serve lemonade for the children (and for anyone else who wishes it), because red-colored juices stain if

---

[5]Detailed suggestions for potlucks are included here because I have never been able to find such suggestions elsewhere. Yet potluck dinners remain one of the most successful ways to draw families together, and the more planning and care that goes into them, the more delightful the outcome is likely to be for everyone.

spilled and milk has to be refrigerated. If it has been a hot day, almost everyone will prefer juice, and quantities should be adjusted accordingly.

Plan the Purpose of the Potluck Carefully

There are two kinds of potluck dinners: those with and those without children. The purpose of having such events varies accordingly, although the basic purpose should always be to help people get to know each other and feel comfortable with the staff. Eating together helps people become acquainted. Thoughtful introductions by the staff can provide parents with some common ground for conversation; for example, the teacher may say, "Maggie, I want you and your husband to meet the Smiths. Your Dorothy and their Emily have a mutual interest in our rabbit."

Picnics may not require any special focus other than having some simple equipment such as Frisbees available, but indoor evening potlucks do. If they are dinners with the children attending, it is helpful to have something for the children to do before dinner because this is when the adults are preoccupied with setting things up and the children are likely to be tired and hungry. Our staff has solved this problem by showing a couple of children's movies or videotapes while the crowd is gathering. Many Weston Woods films of high caliber fulfill this need admirably; many public libraries make these available at no cost. After dinner, because the children are so young, activities should be simple, if offered at all. Perhaps the evening can draw to a close with each group singing a few of their best loved songs for the parents.

We have also found that the parents appreciate having an occasional evening potluck when the children are left at home. After a quick cleanup, it is especially easy to move on to an evening program because people are already "warmed up" to participate.

Get into the Spirit of the Holiday Yourself!

Finally, I can do no better when discussing holidays than to close this chapter with the following suggestions that appeared in an advertisement for Bullock's Wilshire, a West Coast department store:

102 Gifts for Any Season, to Give with All Your Heart

1. Smile. 2. Provide a shoulder to lean on. 3. Pat someone on the back. 4. Say "thank you." 5. Give an unexpected kiss. 6. Or a warm hug. 7. Say "Gosh you look good!" 8. Rub a tired back. 9. Apply a cold compress. 10. Whistle when you're feeling down. 11. Keep the 55 mph speed limit. 12. Say "good morning" even if it isn't. 13. Mail a letter to an old friend. 14. Place a surprise phone call. 15. Wash the dishes when it's her turn. 16. Empty the trash when it's his turn. 17. Ignore a rude remark. 18. Help a friend move her piano. 19. Or clean his garage. 20. Or paint his house. 21. Make the coffee at the office. 22. Save the want-ads for a job hunter. 23. Write a nice letter to the editor. 24. Take Grandma to lunch. 25. Don't discuss the election with your mother-in-law. 26. Don't discuss the Superbowl with your father-in-law. 27. Send a "thinking of you" card. 28. Wave at a meter maid. 29. Just use one parking space. 30. Pay your doctor bill. 31. Give your used clothes to a needy person. 32. Pass on some good news. 33. Send a complimentary letter about a great product. 34. Buy the wine she likes. 35. But the cheese he likes. 36. Say something nice, instead. 37. Consider a different point of view. 38. Loan a favorite book. 39. Return a friend's favorite book. 40. Let him win at golf. 41. Let her win at tennis. 42. Play catch with a little boy. 43. Or a little girl. 44. Take a box of homemade cookies to work. 45. Visit an elderly shut-in. 46. Forgive an old grudge. 47. Talk to a lonely child. 48. Laugh at an old joke. 49. Laugh at a boring joke. 50. Tell him he's wonderful. 51. Tell her she's beautiful. 52. Take the kids to the park. 53. Or the zoo. 54. Or the show. 55. Serve breakfast in bed. 56. Make the music soft and the lights low. 57. Clean the house for Mom. 58. Share a dream. 59. Jog with her. 60. Walk with him. 61. Adopt a stray cat. 62. Or a lost dog. 63. Keep a confidence.

64. Try to understand a teenager. 65. Try to understand an adult. 66. Squeeze the toothpaste tube from the bottom. 67. Relay an overheard compliment. 68. Let someone ahead of you in line. 69. Say "You're doing a good job." 70. Send a friendly note to a computer. 71. Tell your optometrist he has pretty eyes. 72. Laugh when the joke's on you. 73. Say you were wrong. 74. Say someone else was right. 75. Say "please." 76. Say "yes." 77. Help someone change a tire. 78. Be quiet in the library. 79. Type a term paper for a friend. 80. Explain, patiently. 81. Tell the truth. 82. Encourage a sad person. 83. Take a problem upon yourself. 84. Spread a little joy around. 85. Remain calm. 86. Leave your mailman a little gift. 87. And your milkman. 88. Change someone's typewriter ribbon. 89. Cut the grass. 90. Tell a bedtime story to a little one. 91. Do a kind deed, anonymously. 92. Share your umbrella. 93. And your vitamin Cs. 94. Talk to a friend's plant. 95. Mail someone a poem. 96. Leave a funny card under a windshield wiper. 97. Tape a love note to the refrigerator. 98. Be quiet while he watches the game. 99. Be quiet while she watches the movie. 100. Give a flower you picked yourself. 101. Point out a beautiful sunset. 102. Say "I love you," often.

Summary

The celebration of special events at the children's center can make a rich contribution to the developing selves of the child, but such celebrations are of particular value to the social, emotional, and creative selves.

Many holidays present excellent opportunities to do things for other family members that are kind and thoughtful, and such actions should be encouraged. However, the most effective way to instill the impulse to be kind in the hearts of children is for the teacher to set an example of kindly nurturance toward the youngsters in her care.

Successful curricular usage of these festive occasions is ensured if the staff thinks carefully about what they want the children to gain from the experience and how they intend to commu-nicate these values. Many specific examples of how this can be accomplished for a variety of holidays ranging from Halloween to Father's Day are included.

Self-Check Questions for Review

Content-Related Questions

1. List several ways teachers can increase children's pleasure in celebrating holidays without increasing their level of stress to an intolerable degree.
2. Suggest some topics centering on holidays that could provide a focus for a parent meeting. Explain why each topic might be particularly valuable to present.
3. Suggest some holiday activities that would benefit the social and emotional selves of the children. Now suggest some activities that would benefit the creative and cognitive selves.
4. In the research study about learning concern for others, why was it important for Yarrow, Scott, and Waxler to conduct the second retest?
5. Select a holiday and give some examples of social values associated with that holiday that you feel are undesirable. Then identify additional social values you feel should be emphasized.

Integrative Questions

1. Select a holiday and, using it as your focus, outline activities you plan to include. Be sure to include a list of positive values you intend to teach, an analysis of any "creative" activities according to whether they should be classified as Column 1, 2, or 3 activities (see Table 14–2), and suggestions for relieving stress for adults and children as the holiday approaches.
2. Reread the Yarrow, Scott, and Waxler research study. If the investigators had stopped their research at the end of the first posttest, what conclusions might they have drawn from the experiment?

Questions and Activities

1. Do you think that Santa Claus and the Easter Bunny should be included as part of the curriculum for holidays? How about ghosts and witches? How do you plan to handle these subjects in your own school?

2. Are there special traditions observed by your own family for some particular holiday? For the pleasure of it, share these with the class.

3. Describe five Christmas craft projects that would be more *teacher* than child produced.

4. Review column 1, 2, and 3 activities described in Table 14–2, and decide in which column the holiday activities used at your school belong.

5. Take a look at the population of children where you teach. What cultural resources are available among these families on which you might draw to increase multicultural awareness and appreciation by the children as holidays approach?

References for Further Reading

Presentation of Holidays

Bos, B. (1982). *Please don't move the muffin tins: A hands-off guide to art for the young child.* Roseville, CA: Turn the Page. Bos's book has been already recommended in the chapter on self-expressive materials but merits mention here because of a sensible chapter on creative holiday activities.

Dyer, W. W. (1986). *Happy holidays! How to enjoy the Christmas and Hanukkah season to the fullest.* New York: Morrow. Dyer has filled this brief book with positive, practical suggestions of ways for adults to enjoy the holiday season.

Jones, E., & Nimmo, J. (1994). *Emergent curriculum.* Washington, DC: National Association for the Education of Young Children. Throughout this book, the authors raise the question of the meaningfulness that curriculum may or may not have for young children. Because they often consider various holidays from that aspect, the book is particularly relevant to this chapter. *Highly recommended.*

Kendall, F. E. (1996). *Diversity in the classroom: New approaches to the education of young children.* New York: Teachers College Press. Kendall provides a series of guidelines for holidays to be used in antibias programs.

Neugebauer, B. (1990). Going one step further—No traditional holidays. *Child Care Information Exchange, 74,* 42. Neugebauer reviews the problems inherent in celebrating holidays and suggests alternative events to celebrate such as the first tooth, the color red, or a grandparent's visit.

Wardle, F. (1990). Bunny ears and cupcakes for all—are parties developmentally appropriate? *Child Care Information Exchange, 74,* 39–41. An excellent case is made here for low-key holidays that feature cultural sensitivity and wholesome nutrition.

Activities and Resources

Gillis, J. S. (1992). *In a pumpkin shell: Over 20 pumpkin projects for kids.* Powhall, VT: Storey Communications. This small book offers information, recipes, and things to do with pumpkins for a variety of ages.

Goodwin, M. T., & Pollen, G. (1980). *Creative food experiences for children* (rev. ed.). (Available from Center for Science in the Public Interest, 1875 Connecticut Ave., Suite 300, N.W., Washington, DC 20009-5728.) Although not restricted to holiday recipes, this book does have a special section on appropriate holiday foods combined with an accent on sound nutrition.

Kladder, J. (1995). *Story hour: 55 preschool programs for public libraries* Jefferson, NC: McFarland. The desirable thing about book materials produced for librarians is that they recommend really good rather than "cute" books for children. This particular reference offers a particularly attractive list of books about holidays and seasons.

Warren, J., & McKinnon, E. (1988). *Small world celebrations: Around-the-world holidays to celebrate with young children.* Everett, WA: Warren. The authors provide a multicultural resource of holidays, ranging from a Vietnamese midautumn festival to a Native American intertribal ceremony. Stories, songs, crafts, and activities are included for each culture.

Wilmes, L., & Wilmes, D. (1982). *The circle time book.* Elgin, IL: Building Blocks. This book covers a wide variety of holidays and provides suggestions for language games, creative activities, poetry, books, and recipes.

Wilmes, L., & Wilmes, D. (1986). *Exploring art.* Elgin, IL: Building Blocks. The authors provide an abundance of reasonably self-expressive ideas to be used at various seasons and holidays.

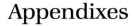

Appendixes

Chart of Normal Development:
Infancy to 6 Years of Age[1]

The chart of normal development on the next pages presents children's achievements from infancy to 6 years of age in five areas:

- Motor skills (gross and fine motor)
- Cognitive skills
- Self-help skills
- Social skills
- Communication skills (understanding and speaking language)

In each skill area, the age at which each milestone is reached *on the average* is also presented. This information is useful if you have a child in your class who you suspect is seriously delayed in one or more skill areas.

However, it is important to remember that these milestones are only average. From the moment of birth, each child is a distinct individual and develops in his or her unique manner. No two children have ever reached all the same developmental milestones at the exact same ages. The examples that follow show what we mean.

By 9 months of age Gi Lin had spent much of her time scooting around on her hands and tummy, making no effort to crawl. After about a week of pulling herself up on chairs and table legs, she let go and started to walk on her own. Gi Lin skipped the crawling stage entirely and scarcely said more than a few sounds until she was 15 months old. But she walked with ease and skill by 9½ months.

Marcus learned to crawl on all fours very early, and continued crawling until he was nearly 18 months old, when he started to walk. However, he said single words and used two-word phrases meaningfully before his first birthday. A talking, crawling baby is quite a sight!

Molly worried her parents by saying scarcely a word, although she managed to make her needs known with sounds and gestures. Shortly after her second birthday, Molly suddenly began talking in two- to four-word phrases and sentences. She was never again a quiet child.

All three children were healthy and normal. By the time they were 3 years old, there were no major differences among them in walking and talking. They had simply developed in their own ways and at their own rates. Some children seem to concentrate on one thing at a time—learning to crawl, to walk, or to talk. Other children develop across areas at a more even rate.

As you read the chart of normal development, remember that children don't read child development books. They don't know they're supposed to be able to point out Daddy when they are a year old or copy a circle in their third year. And even if they could read these baby books, they probably wouldn't follow them! Age-related developmental milestones are obtained by averaging out what many children do at various ages. No child is "average" in all areas. Each child is a unique person.

One final word of caution. As children grow, their abilities are shaped by the opportunities they have for learning. For example, although many 5-year-olds can

[1]From *Mainstreaming Preschoolers: Children with Health Impairments* by A. Healy, P. McAreavey, C. S. VonHippel, and S. H. Jones, 1978, Washington, DC: U.S. Department of Health, Education, and Welfare, Office of Human Development Services, Administration for Children, Youth and Families, Head Start Bureau.

repeat songs and rhymes, the child who has not heard songs and rhymes many times cannot be expected to repeat them. All areas of development and learning are influenced by the child's experiences as well as by the abilities they are born with.

TABLE A–1
Chart of Normal Development

MOTOR SKILLS

Gross Motor Skills

0 – 12 months	12 – 24 months	24 – 36 months	36 – 48 months	48 – 60 months	60 – 72 months
Sits without support	Walks alone	Runs forward well	Runs around obstacles	Walks backward toe-heel	Runs lightly on toes
Crawls	Walks backward	Jumps in place, two feet together	Walks on a line	Jumps forward 10 times, without falling	Walks on balance beam
Pulls self to standing and stands unaided	Picks up toys from floor without falling	Stands on one foot, with aid	Balances on one foot for 5 to 10 seconds	Walks up and down stairs alone, alternating feet	Can cover 2 meters (6'6") hopping
Walks with aid	Pulls toy, pushes toy	Walks on tiptoe	Hops on one foot	Turns somersault	Skips on alternate feet
Rolls a ball in imitation of adult	Seats self in child's chair	Kicks ball forward	Pushes, pulls, steers wheeled toys		Jumps rope
	Walks up and down stairs (hand-held)		Rides (that is, steers and pedals) tricycle		Skates
	Moves to music		Uses slide without assistance		
			Jumps over 15 cm (6") high object, landing on both feet together		
			Throws ball overhand		
			Catches ball bounced to him or her		

Fine Motor Skills

Reaches, grasps, puts objects in mouth	Builds tower of three small blocks	Strings four large beads	Builds tower of nine small blocks	Cuts on line continuously	Cuts out simple shapes
Picks things up with thumb and one finger (pincer grasp)	Puts four rings on stick	Turns pages singly	Drives nails and pegs	Copies cross	Copies triangle
Transfers object from one hand to other hand	Places five pegs in pegboard	Snips with scissors	Copies circle	Copies square	Traces diamond
Drops and picks up toy	Turns pages two or three at a time	Holds crayon with thumb and finger, not fist	Imitates cross	Prints a few capital letters	Copies first name
	Scribbles	Uses one hand consistently in most activities	Manipulates clay materials (for example, rolls balls, snakes, cookies)		Prints numerals 1 to 5
	Turns knobs	Imitates circular, vertical, horizontal strokes			Colors within lines
	Throws small ball	Paints with some wrist action. Makes dots, lines, circular strokes			Has adult grasp of pencil
	Paints with whole arm movement, shifts hands, makes strokes	Rolls, pounds, squeezes, and pulls clay			Has handedness well established (that is, child is left- or right-handed)
					Pastes and glues appropriately

COMMUNICATION SKILLS

Understanding Language

Responds to speech by looking at speaker	Responds correctly when asked *where* (when question is accompanied by gesture)	Points to pictures of common objects when they are named	Begins to understand sentences involving time concepts (for example, *We are going to the zoo tomorrow*)	Follows three unrelated commands in proper order	Demonstrates pre-academic skills

TABLE A–1
continued

0 – 12 months	12 – 24 months	24 – 36 months	36 – 48 months	48 – 60 months	60 – 72 months
Understanding Language, *continued*					
Responds differently to aspects of speaker's voice (for example, friendly or unfriendly, male or female)	Understands prepositions *on, in,* and *under*	Can identify objects when told their use	Understands size comparatives such as *big* and *bigger*	Understands comparatives like *pretty, prettier,* and *prettiest*	
Turns to source of sound	Follows request to bring familiar object from another room	Understands question forms *what* and *where*	Understands relationships expressed by *if . . . then* or *because* sentences	Listens to long stories but often misinterprets the facts	
Responds with gesture to *hi, bye-bye,* and *up* when these words are accompanied by appropriate gesture	Understands simple phrases with key words (for example, *Open the door. Get the ball.*)	Understands negatives *no, not, can't,* and *don't*	Carries out a series of two to four related directions	Incorporates verbal directions into play activities	
Stops ongoing action when told *no* (when negative is accompanied by appropriate gesture and tone)	Follows a series of two simple but related directions	Enjoys listening to simple storybooks and requests them again	Understands when told, *Let's pretend*	Understands sequencing of events when told them (for example, *First we have to go to the store, then we can make the cake and tomorrow we will eat it*)	
Spoken Language					
Makes crying and noncrying sounds	Says first meaningful word	Joins vocabulary words together in two-word phrases	Talks in sentences of three or more words, which take the form agent-action-object (*I see the ball*) or agent-action-location (*Daddy sit on chair*)	Asks *when, how,* and *why* questions	There are few obvious differences between child's grammar and adult's grammar
Repeats some vowel and consonant sounds (babbles) when alone or when spoken to	Uses single words plus a gesture to ask for objects	Gives first and last name		Uses models like *can, will, shall, should,* and *might*	
		Asks *what* and *where* questions			

Interacts with others by vocalizing after adult	Says successive single words to describe an event	Makes negative statements (for example, *Can't open it*)	Tells about past experiences	Joins sentences together (for example, *I like chocolate chip cookies and milk*)	Still needs to learn such things as subject-verb agreement and some irregular past tense verbs
Communicates meaning through intonation	Refers to self by name	Shows frustration at not being understood	Uses *s* on nouns to indicate plurals	Talks about causality by using *because and so*	Can take appropriate turns in a conversation
Attempts to imitate sounds	Uses *my or mine* to indicate possession		Uses *ed* on verbs to indicate past tense	Tells the content of a story but may confuse facts	Gives and receives information
	Has vocabulary of about 50 words for important people, common objects, and the existence, nonexistence, and recurrence of objects and events (for example, *more* and *all gone*)		Refers to self using pronouns *I or me*		Communicates well with family, friends, or strangers
			Repeats at least one nursery rhyme and can sing a song		
			Speech is understandable to strangers, but still has some sound errors		

COGNITIVE SKILLS

Follows moving objects with eyes	Imitates actions and words of adults	Responds to simple directions (for example, *Give me the ball and the block. Get your shoes and socks*)	Recognizes and matches six colors	Plays with words (creates own rhyming words; says or makes up words having similar sounds)	Retells story from picture book with reasonable accuracy
Recognizes differences among people. Responds to strangers by crying or staring	Responds to words or commands with appropriate action (for example, *Stop that. Get down*)	Selects and looks at picture books, names pictured objects, and identifies several objects within one picture	Intentionally stacks blocks or rings in order of size	Points to and names four to six colors	Names some letters and numerals
Responds to and imitates facial expressions of others	Is able to match two similar objects		Draws somewhat recognizable picture that is meaningful to child, if not to adult. Names and briefly explains picture		Rote counts to 10
					Sorts objects by single characteristics (for example, by color, shape, or size if the difference is obvious)

TABLE A–1
continued

COGNITIVE SKILLS, *continued*

0 – 12 months	12 – 24 months	24 – 36 months	36 – 48 months	48 – 60 months	60 – 72 months
Responds to very simple directions (for example, raises arms when someone says, *Come,* and turns head when asked, *Where is Daddy?*)	Looks at storybook pictures with an adult, naming or pointing to familiar objects on request (for example, *What is that? Point to the baby*)	Matches and uses associated objects meaningfully (for example, given cup, saucer, and bead, puts cup and saucer together)	Asks questions for information (*why* and *how* questions requiring simple answers)	Matches pictures of familiar objects (for example, shoe, sock, foot; apple, orange, banana)	Is beginning to use time accurately concepts of *tomorrow and yesterday*
Imitates gestures and actions (for example, shakes head no, plays peek-a-boo, waves bye-bye)	Recognizes difference between *you* and *me*	Stacks rings on peg in order of size	Knows own age Knows own last name	Draws a person with two to six recognizable parts, such as head, arms, legs. Can name or match drawn parts to own body	Uses classroom tools (such as scissors and paints) meaningfully and purposefully
Puts small objects in and out of container with intention	Has very limited attention span	Recognizes self in mirror, saying *baby,* or own name	Has short attention span	Draws, names, and describes recognizable picture	Begins to relate clock time to daily schedule
	Accomplishes primary learning through own exploration	Can talk briefly about what he or she is doing	Learns through observing and imitating adults, and by adult instruction and explanation. Is very easily distracted	Rote counts to 5, imitating adults	Attention span increases noticeably. Learns through adult instruction. When interested, can ignore distractions.
		Imitates adult actions (for example, housekeeping play)	Has increased understanding of concepts of the functions and groupings of objects (for example, can put doll house furniture in correct rooms), and part-whole (for example, can identify pictures of hand and foot as parts of body)	Knows own street and town	Concepts of function increase as well as understanding of why things happen. Time concepts are expanding into an understanding of the future in terms of major events (for example, *Christmas will come after two weekends*)
		Has limited attention span. Learning is through exploration and adult direction (as in reading of picture stories)		Has more extended attention span. Learns through observing and listening to adults as well as through exploration. Is easily distracted	

	Cognitive / Language				
	Is beginning to understand functional concepts of familiar objects (for example, that a spoon is used for eating) and part-whole concepts (for example, parts of the body)	Begins to be aware of past and present (for example, *Yesterday we went to the park. Today we go to the library*)	Has increased understanding of concepts of function, time, part-whole relationships. Function or use of objects may be stated in addition to names of objects Time concepts are expanding. The child can talk about yesterday or last week (a long time ago), about today, and about what will happen tomorrow		

SELF-HELP SKILLS

Feeds self cracker	Uses spoons, spilling little	Uses spoon, little spilling	Pours well from small pitcher	Cuts easy foods with a knife (for example, hamburger patty, tomato slice)	Dresses self completely
Holds cup with two hands; drinks with assistance	Drinks from cup, one hand, unassisted	Gets drink from fountain or faucet unassisted	Spreads soft butter with knife	Laces shoes	Ties bow
Holds out arms and legs while being dressed	Chews food	Opens door by turning handle	Buttons and unbuttons large buttons		Brushes teeth unassisted
	Removes shoes, socks, pants, sweater	Takes off coat	Washes hands unassisted		Crosses street safely
	Unzips large zipper	Puts on coat with assistance	Blows nose when reminded		
	Indicates toilet needs	Washes and dries hands with assistance			

TABLE A–1
continued

SOCIAL SKILLS

0 – 12 months	12 – 24 months	24 – 36 months	36 – 48 months	48 – 60 months	60 – 72 months
Smiles spontaneously	Recognizes self in mirror or picture	Plays near other children	Joins in play with other children; begins to interact	Plays and interacts with other children	Chooses own friend(s)
Responds differently to strangers than to familiar people	Refers to self by name	Watches other children, joins briefly in their play	Shares toys. Takes turns with assistance	Dramatic play is closer to reality, with attention paid to detail, time, and space	Plays simple table games
Pays attention to own name	Plays by self, initiates own play	Defends own possessions	Begins dramatic play, acting out whole scenes (for example, traveling, playing house, pretending to be animals)	Plays dress-up	Plays competitive games
Responds to *no*	Imitates adult behaviors in play	Begins to play house		Shows interest in exploring sex differences	Engages with other children in cooperative play involving group decisions, role assignments, fair play
Copies simple actions of others	Helps put things away	Symbolically uses objects, self in play			
		Participates in simple group activity (for example, sings, claps, dances)			
		Knows gender identity			

B

A Suggested Method for Preparing Summarizing Reports for Official Boards and Funding Agencies

With increasing frequency, teachers and directors of day-care centers are required to present annual summaries of the children's progress to justify continuation of funding. Many staff members are uncertain about how to present such information effectively even though they have faithfully kept track of the children's growth during the year. For this reason, the following information is included.

One useful method of summarizing such data that is relatively easy for all teachers, even those untrained in statistics, is the simple numerical summary of checklist material. In this method, answers are tallied for the various categories on the checklists, and the totals are converted to percentages to simplify drawing comparisons.

Computing a Numerical Summary for a Checklist

Only checklists of children who have remained throughout all three testing periods should be used. If there are more than 10 children in each age group, it may be worthwhile to sort the children into the smaller groups and compute the percentage for separate ages. This separation will demonstrate change between categories more clearly.

Step 1: Tally (count up) for each category on a master sheet. For example, tally all the answers in the "not able to observe" category for the Self-Confidence Pretest; next, tally answers for the "hardly ever" category, and so forth.

Step 2: Add the number of tallies in each column.

Step 3: Add the totals of the four columns for the pretest together to obtain the total number of answers given in all the columns. (This same total is used in the midtest and posttest calculations.)

Step 4: Find the percentage of replies for each column by dividing the number of answers in each column by the total number of answers for all the pretest columns.

Step 5: Repeat this process to calculate the percentage replies for the midtest and posttest.

Once the percentages have been calculated, they may be used to draw a variety of comparisons among the results of the test periods. Thus, if the chart shown in this appendix were used in a fiscal report, it could be pointed out that although only 38% of the children were rated as usually appearing to be self-confident in September, by May the percentage had increased to 62. Or the analysis might be phrased, "The percentage of 4-year-old children who rated high on measures of self-confidence almost doubled in the period from September to May."

Although the teacher will no doubt wish to attribute such a favorable change to the educational program, it must be emphasized that this method draws no comparisons between that group and a control group not undergoing instruction. Thus, it documents change but does not provide evidence that the change could not be due to other influences, such as maturation. To be on safer scientific ground, the teacher will need to use a control group and more sophisticated statistical methods to obtain such evidence.

Using Statistical Methods
for the Analysis of Data

It is important to know that methods that are vastly superior to the scheme proposed here exist for the statistical analysis of data. In particular, such techniques as *t*-tests and analysis of variance (ANOVA) are helpful. These methods are superior because they may be used to determine whether there is a signifi-cant difference among pretest, midtest, and posttest results or between the test results of the school population and those of a control group.

Although these techniques usually lie beyond the expertise of the center teachers, they should realize that such techniques have been developed and are of real value in assessing data. Occasionally, a statistician can be prevailed on to carry out such calculations should they be needed.

TABLE B–1

Computation of Percentage Representation in Various Categories of a Checklist

Self-Confidence	Pretest				Midtest				Posttest			
	Not able to observe	Hardly ever	About half the time	Usually	Not able to observe	Hardly ever	About half the time	Usually	Not able to observe	Hardly ever	About half the time	Usually
Able to hold her own when challenged (confident, not unduly intimidated)	1	2	7	5	0	2	7	6	0	1	6	8
Likes to try new things	2	2	6	5	0	0	8	7	0	0	6	9
Takes criticism and reprimands in stride (not overwhelmed or crushed)	0	4	4	7	0	3	3	9	0	2	2	11
Able to adjust to change in routines or people in the center	0	1	8	6	0	1	7	7	0	0	6	9
Number of tallies in each column	3	9	25	23	0	6	25	29	0	3	20	37
Column answer divided by total of all columns	0.05	0.15	0.42	0.38	0	0.10	0.42	0.48	0	0.05	0.33	0.62
Percentage of replies in each category	5	15	42	38	0	10	42	48	0	5	33	62

Number of participating children = 15

Total answers for pretest = 60

$$\text{Percentage} = \frac{\text{Number of answers in column}}{\text{Total number of answers in pretest, midtest, or posttest}}$$

459

Summary of Communicable Diseases

TABLE C-1

Disease	Agent	Incubation	Communicable Period	Transmission	Symptoms	Remarks
Chicken pox (herpes zoster; varicella; shingles)	Virus	2 – 3 weeks	1–5 days before rash; no more than 6 days after first vesicles	Direct contact with vesicle fluid, soiled articles, or droplets from respiratory tract	Sudden onset; slight fever; malaise; mild constitutional symptoms, followed by eruption of lesions; followed by fluid-filled blisters for 3–4 days; ending with scab	Very communicable; lesions, blisters and scabbed sores can exist at the same time; lesions are most common on covered parts of the body; vaccine available
Conjunctivitis (pink eye)	Bacteria	24–72 hours	Throughout course of infection	Contact with discharge from conjunctiva or upper respiratory tract, or objects contaminated by those discharges	Tearing and irritation of conjunctiva; lid swelling, discharge; sensitivity to light	Most common in preschoolers
Cytomegalovirus (CMV)	Virus	May be acquired during birth, but show no symptoms for up to 3 months after delivery	Virus may be excreted for 5–6 years	Direct/indirect contact with membranes or secretions; blood; urine	Usually no symptoms; may show signs of severe infection of central nervous system or liver	Most serious in early infancy; many apparently healthy children in day care have CMV in urine or saliva; *potentially serious for pregnant women*
Giardiasis	Protozoa (a cyst in the inactive form)	5–25 days	Entire period of infection	Hand to mouth transfer of cysts from stools of infected person	Chronic pale, greasy diarrhea; abdominal cramping; fatigue; weight loss	Frequently found in day care centers; carriers may be asymptomatic
Hepatitis	Several viruses	Hepatitis A: 15–50 days	Hepatitis A: A week before infection to one week after appearance of jaundice	Hepatitis A: Fecal/oral route; direct contact	Hepatitis A: Sudden onset with fever, lack of appetite, nausea, abdominal pain; jaundice follows in a few days	Hepatitis A: Common in day care; severity increases with age; infections in infants may be asymptomatic; vaccine available
		Hepatitis B: 45–180 days	Hepatitis B: From several weeks before symptoms until weeks after symptoms; may be a carrier for years	Hepatitis B: Contact with infected blood; saliva, and vaginal fluids; semen	Hepatitis B: Lack of appetite; nausea, vomiting, and later jaundice	Hepatitis B: May be present but asymptomatic in young children; HB vaccine available to prevent this type of hepatitis

461

TABLE C–1
continued

Disease	Agent	Incubation	Communicable Period	Transmission	Symptoms	Remarks
Measles (hard measles; red measles)	Virus	1–2 weeks before rash to 4 days after the rash appears	Communicable from before fever to 4 days after rash	Direct contact with nasal or throat secretions or freshly contaminated objects	Fever, conjunctivitis, cough, Koplik spots; rash appears on 3rd day—usually starting on face	Easily spread; very common in preschool populations; immunization available; potentially serious for ill or young children
Meningitis (viral)	Several viruses	Incubation varies by specific virus	Communicability varies with specific virus	Direct contact with respiratory droplets or excretions of infected person, or objects contaminated by these secretions	Symptoms vary by specific type of virus; usually sudden fever and central nervous system symptoms; may have rash	Symptoms last 10 days with residual symptoms for a year or more
Meningitis (bacterial)	Various bacteria	2–10 days	Until organisms are not found in discharge	Direct contact with respiratory droplets or excretions of an infected person or objects contaminated by these secretions	Sudden onset of fever; severe headache; stiff neck; rash	Early detection and treatment necessary to prevent death
Mumps	Virus	2–3 weeks	6 days before until 9 days after onset of illness	Direct contact with respiratory droplets or saliva of infected person	Fever, swelling and tenderness of one or more salivary glands	Meningitis occurs frequently; vaccine available
Pediatric AIDS	Virus	Unknown	Unknown	Contact with blood and blood contaminated fluids and objects; sexual contact with semen and vaginal fluids	Early symptoms are nonspecific: loss of appetite; chronic diarrhea; fatigue; symptoms progress to opportunistic infections and central nervous system symptoms	Use universal precautions

Pediculosis (lice)	Lice (adult, larvae or nits)	Eggs hatch in a week; sexual maturity is reached 8–10 days after hatching	Communicable as long as eggs and lice are alive on person or clothing	Direct contact with infected person or indirect contact with contaminated objects	Itching and excoriation of infected head and body parts	Common in school children; check with physician regarding use of over-the-counter products; some are not recommended for infants and young children
Ringworm	Fungus	4–10 days	Until lesions are gone and fungus is no longer on contaminated objects	Direct or indirect contact with infected persons or contaminated objects	Lesions appear flat, spreading, and ring-shaped; outer ring may be filled with pus or fluid; inside may be dry and scaly or moist and crusty	Infected children should be excluded from common swimming pools
Rubella (3-day measles)	Virus	2–3 weeks	From 1 week before to 1 week after onset of rash	Droplet spread or direct/indirect contact with objects soiled with nasal secretions, blood, urine, or feces	Symptoms may range from no symptoms to cold-like symptoms such as low grade fever, malaise, and runny nose; not all infections have a rash; if it does exist, it usually starts on the face and spreads to trunk and extremities	Easily spread; high incidence in preschool populations; immunizations available; resembles measles; *potentially serious for pregnant women*
Scabies	Mite	2–6 weeks in person with no exposure; 1–4 days after re-exposure	Until mites and eggs are killed; usually 1–2 courses of treatment, 1 week apart	Skin to skin contact, or contact with recently infected undergarments or bed clothes	Intense itching of head, neck, palms, soles in infants; may also involve other body creases	In persons with reduced resistance, infection will be generalized; check with physician prior to use of over-the-counter medications, because some are not recommended for infants and young children

Note. From *Preschool Children with Special Needs* (pp. 179–182) by M. T. Urbano, 1992, San Diego: Singular Publishing Group. Reprinted with permission.

Sample Daily Food Plans
for One Meal and Snack

TABLE D–1

Pattern	I	II	III	IV
Snack [*]	Orange juice Whole-wheat bread Butter	Apple wedge Cheese	Milk Banana	Hard-cooked egg Tomato juice
Lunch or supper [†]	Ground beef patty Peas Carrot strips Enriched roll Butter or margarine Milk	Roast turkey Broccoli Mashed potatoes Whole-wheat bread Butter or margarine Milk	Fish sticks Scalloped potatoes Stewed tomatoes Whole-wheat bread Butter or margarine Milk	Blackeyed peas with ham Mustard greens Purple plums Corn bread Butter or margarine Milk

Pattern	V	VI	VII	VIII
Snack	Celery stuffed with liver sausage Apple juice	Milk Wheat crackers and apple slices	Apple juice Cheese toast	Milk Raisins and orange wedges
Lunch or supper	Scrambled eggs Spinach Fried apples Biscuit Butter or margarine Milk	Oven-fried drumsticks Corn on the cob Sliced tomato/green pepper rings Whole-wheat bread Butter or margarine Milk	Meat loaf Green beans Baked potato Carrot strips Enriched bread Butter or margarine Milk	Tuna sandwich on whole-wheat bread Tomato juice Raw cabbage (small pieces) Apricots Milk

Pattern	IX	X	XI	XII
Snack	Grapefruit juice Finger-size pieces of leftover meat	Raw carrots, celery, green pepper with cottage cheese dip	Tomato juice Flour tortilla with melted cheese	Fresh fruit in season (strawberries, melons, tangerines, etc.)
Lunch or supper	Pinto beans with melted cheese Chili peppers, chopped tomato, onion, lettuce Flour tortilla Milk	Meatballs in tomato sauce over spaghetti Zucchini Peaches French bread heated with butter or margarine Milk	Liver fingers Sweet potato Apple, banana, and orange salad Fry bread Milk	Swiss steak cubes Cauliflower Cooked carrots Whole-wheat roll Butter or margarine Milk

Note. Modified from *Nutrition: Better Eating for a Head Start* by U.S. Department of Health, Education and Welfare, 1976, Washington, DC: Author.

[*]Include one or more of the following: milk, fruit, vegetable, juice, or protein-rich food; may include a bread or cereal product in addition.

[†]Protein-rich food, vegetable and/or fruit (at least two kinds), bread, enriched or whole grain, butter or margarine as needed, milk.

10 Quick Ways to Analyze Children's Books for Racism and Sexism[1]

Both in school and out, young children are exposed to racist and sexist attitudes. These attitudes—expressed over and over in books and in other media—gradually distort their perceptions until stereotypes and myths about minorities and women are accepted as reality. It is difficult for a librarian or teacher to convince children to question society's attitudes. But if a child can be shown how to detect racism and sexism in a book, the child can proceed to transfer the perception to wider areas. The following 10 guidelines are offered as a starting point in evaluating children's books from this perspective.

1. Check the Illustrations

Look for stereotypes. A stereotype is an oversimplified generalization about a particular group, race, or sex, which usually carries derogatory implications. Some infamous (overt) stereotypes of Blacks are the happy-go-lucky watermelon-eating Sambo and the fat, eye-rolling "mammy"; of Chicanos, the sombrero-wearing peon or fiesta-loving, macho bandito; of Asian Americans, the inscrutable, slant-eyed "Oriental"; of Native Americans, the naked savage or "primitive" craftsman and his squaw; of Puerto Ricans, the switchblade-toting teenage gang member; of women, the completely domesticated mother, the demure, doll-loving little girl, or the wicked stepmother. While you may not always find stereotypes

in the blatant forms described, look for variations which in any way demean or ridicule because of their race or sex.

Look for tokenism. If there are non-White characters in the illustrations, do they look just like Whites except for being tinted or colored in? Do all minority faces look stereotypically alike, or are they depicted as genuine individuals with distinctive features?

Who's doing what? Do the illustrations depict minorities in subservient and passive roles or in leadership and action roles? Are males the active "doers" and females the inactive observers?

2. Check the Story Line

The Civil Rights Movement has led publishers to weed out many insulting passages, particularly from stories with Black themes, but the attitudes still find expression in less obvious ways. The following checklist suggests some of the subtle (covert) forms of bias to watch for.

Standard for Success

Does it take "White" behavior standards for a minority person to "get ahead"? Is "making it" in the dominant White society projected as the only ideal? To gain acceptance and approval, do non-White persons have to exhibit extraordinary qualities—excel in sports, get A's, etc.? In friendships between White and non-White children, is it the non-White who does most of the understanding and forgiving?

[1]Reprinted with permission from the *Bulletin* of the Council on Interracial Books for Children, Inc., 1841 Broadway, New York, NY 10023.

Resolution of Problems

How are problems presented, conceived, and resolved in the story? Are minority people considered to be "the problem"? Are the oppressions faced by minorities and women represented as causally related to an unjust society? Are the reasons for poverty and oppression explained, or are they accepted as inevitable? Does the story line encourage passive acceptance or active resistance? Is a particular problem that is faced by a minority person resolved through the benevolent intervention of a White person?

Role of Women

Are the achievements of girls and women based on their own initiative and intelligence, or are they due to their good looks or to their relationship with boys? Are sex roles incidental or critical to characterization and plot? Could the same story be told if the sex roles were reversed?

3. Look at the Lifestyles

Are minority persons and their setting depicted in such a way that they contrast unfavorably with the unstated norm of White middle-class suburbia? If the minority group in question is depicted as "different," are negative value judgements implied? Are minorities depicted exclusively in ghettos, barrios, or migrant camps? If the illustrations and text attempt to depict another culture, do they go beyond oversimplifications and offer genuine insights into another lifestyle? Look for inaccuracy and inappropriateness of the depiction of other cultures. Watch for instances of the "quaint-natives-in-costume" syndrome (most noticeable in areas like costume and custom, but extending to behavior and personality traits as well).

4. Weigh the Relationships Between People

Do the Whites in the story possess the power, take the leadership, and make the important decisions? Do non-Whites and females function in essentially supporting roles?

How are family relationships depicted? In Black families, is the mother always dominant? In Hispanic families, are there always lots and lots of children? If the family is separated, are societal conditions—unemployment, poverty—cited among the reasons for the separation?

5. Note the Heroes and Heroines

For many years, books showed only "safe" minority heroes and heroines—those who avoided serious conflict with the White establishment of their time. Minority groups today are insisting on the right to define their own heroes and heroines based on their own concepts and struggles for justice.

When minority heroes and heroines do appear, are they admired for the same qualities that have made White heroes and heroines famous or because what they have done has benefitted White people? Ask this question: Whose interest is a particular figure really serving?

6. Consider the Effects on a Child's Self-Image

Are norms established that limit the child's aspirations and self-concepts? What effect can it have on Black children to be continuously bombarded with images of the color white as the ultimate in beauty, cleanliness, virtue, and the color black as evil, dirty, menacing, etc.? Does the book counteract or reinforce this positive association with the color white and negative association with black?

What happens to a girl's self-image when she reads that boys perform all of the brave and important deeds? What about a girl's self-esteem if she is not "fair" of skin and slim of body?

In a particular story, is there one or more persons with whom a minority child can readily identify to a positive and constructive end?

7. Consider the Author's or Illustrator's Background

Analyze the biographical material on the jacket flap or the back of the book. If a story deals with a minority theme, what qualifies the author or illustrator to deal with the subject? If the author and illustrator are not members of the minority being written about, is there anything in their background that would specifically recommend them as the creators of this book?

Similarly, a book that deals with the feelings and insights of women should be more carefully examined if it is written by a man—unless the book's avowed purpose is to present a strictly male perspective.

8. Check Out the Author's Perspective

No author can be wholly objective. All authors write out of a cultural as well as a personal context. Children's books in the past have traditionally come from authors who are White and who are members of the middle class, with one result being that a single ethnocentric perspective has dominated American children's literature. With the book in question, look carefully to determine whether the direction of the author's perspective substantially weakens or strengthens the value of his/her written book. Are omissions and distortions central to the overall character or "message" of the book?

9. Watch for Loaded Words

A word is loaded when it has insulting overtones. Examples of loaded adjectives (usually racist) are savage, primitive, conniving, lazy, superstitious, treacherous, wily, crafty, inscrutable, docile, and backward.

Look for sexist language and adjectives that exclude or ridicule women. Look for use of the male pronoun to refer to both males and females. While the generic use of the word "man" was accepted in the past, its use today is outmoded. The following examples show how sexist language can be avoided: ancestors instead of forefathers; chairperson instead of chairman; community instead of brotherhood; firefighters instead of firemen; manufactured instead of manmade; the human family instead of the family of man.

10. Look at the Copyright Date

Books on minority themes—usually hastily conceived—suddenly began appearing in the mid-1960s. There followed a growing number of "minority experience" books to meet the new market demand, but most of these were still written by White authors, edited by White editors, and published by White publishers. They therefore reflected a White point of view. Only very recently in the late 1960s and early 1970s has the children's book world begun to even remotely reflect the realities of a multiracial society. And it has just begun to reflect feminists' concerns.

The copyright dates, therefore, can be a clue as to how likely the book is to be overtly racist or sexist, although a recent copyright date, of course, is no guarantee of a book's relevance or sensitivity. The copyright date only means the year the book was published. It usually takes a minimum of 1 year—and often much more than that—from the time a manuscript is submitted to the publisher to the time it is actually printed and put on the market. This time lag meant very little in the past, but in a time of rapid change and changing consciousness, when children's book publishing is attempting to be "relevant," it is becoming increasingly significant.

What Are Some Good Toys and Play Materials for Young Children?

TABLE F–1
What Are Some Good Toys and Play Materials for Young Children?

All ages are approximate. Most suggestions for young children are also appropriate for older children.

	Sensory Materials	Active Play Equipment	Construction Materials	Manipulative Toys	Dolls and Dramatic Play	Books and Recordings	Art Materials
2-Year-Olds and Young Threes	Water and sand toys: cups, shovels	Low climber	Unit blocks and accessories: animals, people, simple wood cars and trucks	Wooden puzzles with 4–20 large pieces	Washable dolls with a few clothes	Clear picture books, stories, and poems about things children know	Wide-tip watercolor markers
	Modeling dough	Canvas swing		Pegboards	Doll bed		Large sheets of paper, easel
		Low slide		Big beads or spools to string	Child-sized table and chairs	Records or tapes of classical music, folk music, or children's songs	Finger or tempera paint, ½" brushes
	Sound-matching games	Wagon, cart, or wheelbarrow	Interlocking construction set with large pieces	Sewing cards	Dishes, pots, and pans		Blunt-nose scissors
	Bells, wood block, triangle, drum	Large rubber balls		Stacking toys			White glue
		Low three-wheeled, steerable vehicle with pedals	Wood train and track set	Picture lotto, picture dominoes	Dress-up clothes: hats, shoes, shirts		
	Texture matching games, feel box		Hammer (13-oz. steel-shanked), soft wood, roofing nails, nailing block		Hand puppets		
					Shopping cart		
Older Threes and 4-Year-Olds	Water toys: measuring cups, egg beaters	Large three-wheeled riding vehicle	More unit blocks, shapes, and accessories	Puzzles, pegboard, small beads to string	Dolls and accessories	Simple science books	Easel, narrower brushes
		Roller skates	Table blocks	Parquetry blocks	Doll carriage	More detailed picture and storybooks	Thick crayons, chalk
	Sand toys: muffin tins, vehicles	Climbing structure	Realistic model vehicles	Small objects to sort	Child-sized stove or sink	Sturdy record or tape player	Paste, tape with dispenser
		Rope or tire swing	Construction set with smaller pieces	Marbles	More dress-up clothes		Collage materials
		Plastic bats and balls		Magnifying glass	Play food, cardboard cartons		

Xylophone, maracas, tambourine Potter's clay	Various sized rubber balls Balance board Planks, boxes, old tires Bowling pins, ring toss, bean-bags and target	Simple card or board games Flannel board with pictures, letters Sturdy letters and numbers	Airport, doll-house, or other settings with accessories Finger or stick puppets	Recordings of wider variety of music Book and recording sets	
Water toys: food coloring, pumps, funnels Sand toys: containers, utensils Harmonica, kazoo, guitar, recorder Tools for working with clay	Bicycle Outdoor games: bocce, tetherball, shuffleboard, jump rope, Frisbee	More unit blocks, shapes, and accessories Props for roads, towns Hollow blocks Brace and bits, screwdrivers, screws, metric measure, accessories	More complex puzzles Dominoes More difficult board and card games Yarn, big needles, mesh fabric, weaving materials Magnets, balances Attribute blocks	Cash register, play money, accessories, or props for other dramatic play settings: gas station, construction, office Typewriter	Books on cultures Stories with chapters Favorite stories children can read Children's recipe books	Watercolors, smaller paper, stapler, hole puncher Chalkboard Oil crayons, paint crayons, charcoal Simple camera, film

5- and 6-Year-Olds

Note. From *Choosing Good Toys for Young Children* by S. Feeney and M. Magarick, 1983, Washington, DC: National Association for the Education of Young Children. Copyright 1983 by National Association for the Education of Young Children. Used by permission.

G

Educational Organizations, Newsletters, and Journals Associated with Early Childhood

Educational Organizations

American Alliance for Health, Physical Education, and Recreation (AAHPER)
1900 Association Dr.
Reston, VA 22091

Association for Childhood Education International (ACEI)
Olney Professional Building
17904 Georgia Ave., Suite 215
Olney, MD 20832

Child Welfare League of America, Inc. (CWLA)
440 First St., N.W., Suite 316
Washington, DC 20001

Children's Defense Fund (CDF)
25 E St., N.W.
Washington, DC 20001

Children's Foundation
725 15th St., N.W., Suite 505
Washington, DC 20005

Council for Exceptional Children (CEC)
1920 Association Dr.
Reston, VA 22091

Day Care and Child Development Council of America (DCCDCA)
1401 K St., N.W.
Washington, DC 20005

Educational Resources Information Center on Early Childhood Education (ERIC/ECE)
805 W. Pennsylvania Ave.
Urbana, IL 61801

National Association for the Education of Young Children (NAEYC)
1509 16th St., N.W.
Washington, DC 20036-1426
(1-800-424-8777)

National Committee for the Prevention of Child Abuse
332 S. Michigan Ave., Suite 950
Chicago, IL 60604-4357

Southern Early Childhood Association (SECA) (formerly Southern Association for Children under Six [SACUS])
P.O. 55930
Little Rock, AR 72215-5930

Newsletters

The Black Child Advocate
Black Child Development Institute
1023 15th St., N.W., Suite 600
Washington, DC 20005-5002

Child Health Alert
P.O. Box 338
Newton Highlands, MA 02161

ERIC/ECE Newsletter
805 W. Pennsylvania Ave.
Urbana, IL 61801

Journals

American Journal of Orthopsychiatry
American Orthopsychiatric Association
49 Sheridan Ave.
Albany, NY 10010

Child Care Information Exchange
P.O. Box 2890
Redmond, WA 98073-2890

Child Development
Society for Research in Child Development
University of Chicago Press
5801 Ellis Ave.
Chicago, IL 60637

Childhood Education
ACEI
11501 Georgia Ave., Suite 315
Wheaton, MD 20902

Children Today
Superintendent of Documents
U.S. Government Printing Office
Washington, DC 20402

Day Care and Early Education
Human Sciences Press
72 Fifth Ave.
New York, NY 10011

Developmental Psychology
American Psychological Association
1200 17th St., N.W.
Washington, DC 20036

Dimensions of Early Childhood
Southern Early Childhood Association
P.O. Box 55930
Little Rock, AR 72215-5930

Early Childhood Education Journal
Human Sciences Press
233 Spring St.
New York, NY 10013-1578

Early Childhood Research Quarterly
National Association for the Education of Young
Children

Ablex Publishing Company
355 Chestnut St.
Norwood, NJ 07648

Exceptional Children
Council for Exceptional Children
1920 Association Dr.
Reston, VA 22091

Future of Children
David & Lucille Packard Foundation
Center for the Future of Children
300 2nd Street, Suite 102
Los Altos, CA 94022

Harvard Educational Review
Longfellow Hall
13 Appian Way
Cambridge, MA 02138

Innovations in Early Education: The International Reggio
Exchange
Merrill-Palmer Institute
Wayne State University
71-A East Ferry Avenue
Detroit, MI 48202

Journal of Children in Contemporary Society
Haworth Press
28 E. 22nd St.
New York, NY 10010

Journal of Research in Childhood Education
Association for Childhood Education International
11501 Georgia Ave., Suite 315
Wheaton, MD 20902

Nutrition Action
Center for Science in the Public Interest
1875 Connecticut Ave., Suite 300, N.W.
Washington, DC 20009-5728

Scholastic Early Childhood Today
555 Broadway
New York, NY 10012

Young Children
NAEYC
1509 16th St., N.W.
Washington, DC 20036-1426

References

Abramson, S., Robinson, R., & Ankenman, K. (1995). Project work with diverse students: Adapting curriculum based on the Reggio Emilia approach. *Childhood Education*, 71(4), 197–202.

Albert, R. E. (1994). *Alejandro's gift*. San Francisco: Chronicle.

Allen, J., McNeill, E., & Schmidt, V. (1992). *Cultural awareness for children*. Menlo Park, CA: Addison-Wesley.

Allen, K. E., & Marotz, K. (1990). *Developmental profiles: Birth to six*. Albany, NY: Delmar.

Allen, Lady of Hurtwood. (1968). *Planning for play*. Cambridge, MA: MIT Press.

Allen, M., Brown, P., & Finlay, B. (n.d.). *Helping children by strengthening families*. Washington, DC: Children's Defense Fund.

Almy, M., Chittenden, E., & Miller, P. (1966). *Young children's thinking*. New York: Teachers College Press.

Alpern, G., Boll, T. & Shearer, M. (1986). *The Developmental Profile–II*. Los Angeles; Western Psychological Services.

Amabile, T. M. (1983). *The social psychology of creativity*. New York: Springer.

Amabile, T. M. (1989). *Growing up creative: Nurturing a lifetime of creativity*. New York: Crown.

Amabile, T. M. (1996). *Creativity in context: Update to The Social Psychology of Creativity*. Bolder, CO: Westview/HarperCollins.

Amabile, T. M., & Gitomer, J. (1984). Children's artistic creativity: Effects of choice in task materials. *Personality and Social Psychology Bulletin*, 10(2), 209–215.

American Public Health Association/American Academy of Pediatrics. (1992). *Caring for our children: National health and safety guidelines for out-of-home child care*. Washington, DC/Elk Grove Village, IL: Authors.

Anastas, P. (1973). *Glooskap's children*. Boston: Beacon.

Anderson, F. E. (1994). *Art-centered education and therapy for children with disabilities*. Springfield, IL: Thomas.

Andrews, J. H. (1988). Poetry: Tool of the classroom magician. *Young Children*, 43(4), 17–24.

Arbuthnot, M. H., & Root, S. L. Jr. (1968). *Time for poetry* (3rd ed.). Glenview, IL: Scott, Foresman.

Arnheim, D. D., & Pestolesi, R. A. (1978). *Elementary physical education: A developmental approach*. St. Louis, MO: Mosby.

Arnheim, D. D., & Sinclair, W. A. (1979). *The clumsy child: A program of motor therapy* (2nd ed.). St. Louis, MO: Mosby.

Aronovsky, J. (1997). *Rabbits and raindrops*. New York: Putnam.

Aronowitz, V., & Turner, S. (1989). *Health wise quantity cookbook*. Washington, DC: Center for Science in the Public Interest.

Aronson, S. (1987). Health update. AIDS and child care programs. *Child Care Information Exchange*, 58, 35–39.

Aronson, S. (1991). *Health and safety in child care*. New York: HarperCollins.

Aronson, S. (1992). Is playground safety being taken seriously? *Child Care Information Exchange*, 85, 47–48.

Asch, F. (1978). *Turtle tale*. New York: Dial.

Axline, V. (1964). *Dibs: In search of self*. Boston: Houghton Mifflin.

Axline, V. (1969). *Play therapy* (rev. ed.). New York: Ballantine.

Axtmann, A., & Bluhm, C. (1986). Friendship among infants? Yes, indeed! In D. P. Wolf (Ed.), *Connecting: Friendship in the lives of young children and their teachers*. Redmond, WA: Exchange.

Babcock, F., Hartle, L., & Lamme, L. L. (1995). Prosocial behaviors of 5-year-old children in 16 learning/activity centers. *Journal of Research in Childhood Education*, 9(2), 113–126.

Bailey, D. B., & Wolery, M. (1992). *Teaching infants and preschoolers with disabilities* (2nd ed.). Upper Saddle River, NJ: Merrill/Prentice Hall.

Balian, L. (1974). *Humbug rabbit*. Nashville, TN: Abingdon.

Ball, W. (1995). Nurturing musical aptitude in children. *Dimensions of Early Childhood*, 23(4), 19–24.

Bambini a Reggio Emilia. (1990). *Tutto ha un'ombra meno le formiche*. Reggio Emilia, Italy: Commune di Reggio Emilia.

Bandura, A. (1977). *Social learning theory*. Upper Saddle River, NJ: Prentice Hall.

Bandura, A. (1986). *Social foundations of thought and action*. Upper Saddle River, NJ: Prentice Hall.

Banks, J. A. (1991). *Multiethnic education: Theory and practice* (3rd ed.). Boston: Allyn & Bacon.

Baratta-Lorton, M. (1972). *Workjobs: Activity-centered learning for early childhood education*. Reading, MA: Addison-Wesley.

Baron, N. S. (1992). *Growing up with language. How children learn to talk*. Reading, MA: Addison-Wesley.

Barrera, R. M. (1996). What's all the fuss? A frank conversation about the needs of bilingual children. *Child Care Information Exchange*, 107, 44–47.

Barton, M. L., & Zeanah, C. H. (1990). Stress in the preschool years. In L. E. Arnold (Ed.), *Childhood stress*. New York: Wiley.

Bauer, C. F. (1977). *Handbook for story tellers*. Chicago: American Library Association.

Baugh, N. (1994). New and prevailing misconceptions of African American English for logic and mathematics. In E. R. Hollings, J. E. King, & W. C. Hayman (Eds.), *Teaching diverse populations: Formulating a knowledge base*. Albany: State University of New York Press.

Baumrind, D. (1989). Rearing competent children. In W. Damon (Ed.), *Child development today and tomorrow*. San Francisco: Jossey-Bass.

Bayless, K. M., & Ramsey, M. E. (1987). *Music: A way of life for the young child* (3rd ed.). Upper Saddle River, NJ: Merrill/Prentice Hall.

Bayless, K. M., & Ramsey, M. E. (1991). *Music: A way of life for the young child* (4th ed.). Upper Saddle River, NJ: Merrill/Prentice Hall.

Beal, C. R. (1994). *Boys and girls: The development of gender roles*. New York: McGraw-Hill.

Bearer, C. F. (1995). Environmental health hazards: How children are different from adults. *The Future of Children: Critical Issues for Children and Youths, 5*(2), 11–26.

Beaty, J. J. (1994a). *Observing development of the young child*. Upper Saddle River, NJ: Merrill/Prentice Hall.

Beaty, J. J. (1994b). *Picture book storytelling: Literature activities for young children*. Fort Worth, TX: Harcourt Brace.

Beaty, J. J. (1995). *Converting conflicts in preschool*. New York: Harcourt Brace.

Beaty, J. J. (1996). *Skills for preschool teachers* (5th ed.). Upper Saddle River, NJ: Merrill/Prentice Hall.

Behrman, R. E. (Ed.). (1994). Children and divorce. *The Future of Children, 4*(1), 4–254.

Bemelmans, L. (1939). *Madeline*. New York: Simon & Schuster.

Benelli, C., & Yougue, B. (1995). Supporting young children's motor skill development. *Childhood Education, 71*(4), 217–220.

Bentzen, W. R. (1985). *Seeing young children: a guide to observing and recording behavior*. Albany, NY: Delmar.

Bentzen, W. R. (1991). *Seeing young children: A guide to observing and recording behavior* (2nd ed.). Albany, NY: Delmar.

Benzwie, T. (1987). *A moving experience: Dance for lovers of children and the child within*. Tucson, AZ: Zephyr.

Bereiter, C., & Englemann, E. (1966). *Teaching the culturally disadvantaged child in the preschool*. Upper Saddle River, NJ: Prentice Hall.

Bergen, D., & Moseley-Howard, S. (1994). Assessment perspectives for culturally diverse young children. In D. Bergen (Ed.), *Assessment methods for infants and toddlers: Transdisciplinary team approaches*. New York: Teachers College Press.

Berger, E. H. (1995). *Parents as partners in education: Families and schools working together* (4th ed.). Upper Saddle River, NJ: Merrill/Prentice Hall.

Berger, E. H. (1996). Communication: The key to parent involvement. *Early Childhood Education Journal, 23*(3), 179–183.

Bergin, C. A. C., Bergin, D. A., & French, E. (1995). Preschoolers' prosocial repertoires: Parents' perspectives. *Early Childhood Research Quarterly, 10*(1), 81–103.

Berk, L. (1994). Vygotsky's theory: The importance of make-believe play. *Young Children, 50*(1), 30–39.

Berk, L. E., & Winsler, A. (1995). *Scaffolding children's learning: Vygotsky and early childhood education*. Washington, DC: National Association for the Education of Young Children.

Berkowitz, L. (1993). *Aggression: Its causes, consequences and control*. Philadelphia: Temple University Press.

Berman, C., & Fromer, J. (1991a). *Meals without squeals*. Palo Alto, CA: Bull.

Berman, C., & Fromer, J. (1991b). *Teaching children about food: A teaching guide and activities guide*. Palo Alto, CA: Bull.

Bernal, E. M. (1993). Multicultural considerations for choosing a screening assessment instrument. *National Head Start Bulletin, 43,* 6–7.

Bernal, M. E., & G. P. Knight (Eds.). (1993). *Ethnic identity 1: Formation and transmission among Hispanic and other minorities*. Albany: State University of New York Press.

Betz, C. (1992). The happy medium. *Young Children, 47*(3), 34–35.

Beuf, A. H. (1977). *Red children in white America*. Philadelphia: University of Pennsylvania Press.

Birch, L. L., (1980). Effect of peer models' food choices and eating behavior on preschoolers' food preferences. *Child Development, 52,* 489–496.

Birch, L. L., Johnson, S. L., & Fisher, J. A. (1995). Children's eating: The development of food-acceptance patterns. *Young Children, 50*(2), 71–78.

Block, M. (1994). *A teacher's guide to including students with disabilities in regular physical education*. Baltimore, MD: Brookes.

Blood, C. L., & Link, M. *The goat in the rug*. New York: Parent's Magazine Press.

Bloom, B. (1964). *Stability and change in human characteristics*. New York: Wiley.

Bloom, B. S., Engelhart, M. D., Furst, E. J., Hill, W. H., & Krathwohl, D. R. (1956). *Taxonomy of educational objectives*. New York: McKay.

Bloom, P. (1996). Controversies in language acquisition: Word learning and the part of speech. In R. Gelman & T. K.-F. Au (Eds.), *Perceptual and cognitive development*. New York: Academic Press.

Board on Children and Families. (1995). Immigrant children and their families: Issues for research and policy. *The Future of Children, 5*(2), 72–80.

Bodrova, E., & Leong, D. J. (1996). *Tools of the mind: The Vygotskian approach to early childhood education*. Upper Saddle River, NJ: Merrill/Prentice Hall.

Bond, F. (1983). *Mary Betty Lizzie McNutt's birthday*. New York: Thomas Y. Crowell.

Bondurant-Utz, J. A., & Luciano, L. B. (1994). *A practical guide to infant and preschool assessment in special education*. Boston: Allyn & Bacon.

Bos, B. (1982). *Please don't move the muffin tins: A hands-off guide to art for the young child*. Roseville, CA: Turn the Page Press.

Bos, B. (1983). Before the basics: Creating conversations with children. Roseville, CA: Turn the Page Press.

Bos, B. (1990). *Together we're better: Establishing a coactive learning environment*. Roseville, CA: Turn the Page Press.

Boutte, G. S., Keepler, D. L., Tyler, V. S., & Terry, B. Z. (1992). Effective techniques for involving "difficult" parents. *Young Children, 47*(3), 19–27.

Bowman, B. (1995). Embracing all our children. *Scholastic Early Childhood Today, 10*(3), 40.

Boyer, E. L. (1992). *Ready to learn: A mandate for the nation*. Princeton, NJ: Carnegie Foundation for the Advancement of Teaching.

Bracken, B. (1987). Limitations of preschool instruments and standards for minimal levels of technical adequacy. *Journal of Psychoeducational Assessment, 4*, 313–326.

Brand, S. (1996). Making parent involvement a reality: Helping teachers develop partnerships with parents. *Young Children, 51*(2), 76–83.

Bredekamp, S. (Ed.). (1987). *Developmentally appropriate practice in early childhood programs serving children from birth through age 8* (expanded ed.). Washington, DC: National Association for the Education of Young Children.

Bredekamp, S., & Copple, C. (Eds.). (1997). *Developmentally appropriate practice in early childhood programs* (rev. ed.). Washington, DC: National Association for the Education of Young Children.

Bredekamp, S., & Rosegrant, T. (1992). *Reaching potentials: Appropriate curriculum and assessment for young children* (Vol. 1). Washington, DC: National Association for the Education of Young Children.

Bredekamp, S., & Rosegrant, T. (Eds.). (1995). *Reaching potentials: Transforming early childhood curriculum and assessment* (Vol. 2). Washington, DC: National Association for the Education of Young Children.

Bredekamp, S., & Shepherd, L. (1990). *Protecting children from inappropriate practices*. Urbana, IL: ERIC Clearinghouse on Elementary and Early Childhood Education (EDO-PS-90-9).

Breig-Allen, C. (1997). Implementing the process of change in a public school setting. In J. B. Hendrick (Ed.), *First steps toward teaching the Reggio Way*. Upper Saddle River, NJ: Merrill/Prentice Hall.

Brett, A., Moore, R. C., & Provenzo, E. B. (1993). *The complete playground book*. Syracuse, NY: Syracuse University Press.

Brett, J. *The wild Christmas reindeer*. New York: Putnam's.

Bricker, D. (1995). The challenge of inclusion. *Journal of Early Intervention, 19*(1), 179–194.

Bricker, D., & Cripe, J. J. W. (1992). *An activity based approach to early intervention*. Baltimore, MD: Brookes.

Briggs, D. (1993). *Toddler storytime programs*. Metuchen, NJ: Scarecrow.

Briggs, R. (1973). *Father Christmas*. New York: Coward, McGann & Geoghegan.

Brim, O., Boocock, S., Hoffman, L., Bronfenbrenner, U., & Edelman, M. (1975). *Ecology of child development*. Philadelphia: American Philosophical Society.

Brittain, G. (1979). *Creativity, art and the young child*. New York: Macmillan.

Brokering, L. (1989). *Resources for dramatic play*. Belmont, CA: Fearon.

Bronson, M. B. (1995). *The right stuff for children birth to 8: Selecting play materials to support development*. Washington, DC: National Association for the Education of Young Children.

Bronson, W. J. (1974). Competence and the growth of personality. In K. Connolly & J. S. Bruner (Eds.), *The growth of competence*. London: Academic Press.

Brown, M. W. (1947). *Goodnight, moon*. New York: Harper & Row.

Brown, M. W. (1989). *The big red barn*. Illus. by F. Bond. New York: HarperCollins.

Budbill, D. (1974). *Christmas tree farm*. New York: Macmillan.

Bunce, B. H. (1995). *Building a language-focused curriculum for the preschool classroom. Vol. 2: A planning guide*. Baltimore, MD: Brookes.

Bundy, B. F. (1991). Fostering communication between parents and preschools. *Young Children, 46*(2), 12–17.

Bunting, E. (1983). *The Valentine bears*. New York: Houghton Mifflin.

Bunting, E. (1991). *Night tree*, New York: Harcourt Brace.

Burton, J. (1989). *Freckles the rabbit*. Milwaukee: Gareth Stevens.

Buzzelli, C. A. (1992). Young children's moral understanding: Learning about right and wrong. *Young Children, 47*(6), 47–53.

Bybee, R. W., & Sund, R. B. (1990). *Piaget for educators* (2nd ed.). Prospect Heights, IL: Waveland.

Cadwell, L. B., & Fyfe, B. V. (1997). Conversations with children. In J. B. Hendrick (Ed.), *First steps towards teaching the Reggio Way*. Upper Saddle River, NJ: Merrill/Prentice Hall.

Campos, J. (1995). The Carpinteria Preschool Program: A long-term effects study. In E. E. Garcia & B. McLaughlin (Eds.), *Meeting the challenge of linguistic and cultural diversity in early childhood education*. New York: Teachers College Press.

Cannon, J. (1993). *Stellaluna*. New York: Harcourt Brace.

Caples, S. E. (1996). Some guidelines for preschool design. *Young Children, 51*(4), 15–21.

Carlson, N. (1982). *Harriet's Halloween candy*. Minneapolis: Carolrhoda.

Carr, R. (1980). *See and be: Yoga and creative movement for children*. Upper Saddle River, NJ: Prentice Hall.

Carroll, R. (1950). *Where's the bunny?* New York: Walck.

Carroll, R. (1965). *What whiskers did*. New York: Macmillan.

Carson, R. (1956). *The sense of wonder*. New York: Harper & Row.

Cartwright, S. (1990). Learning with large blocks. *Young Children*, 45(3), 38–41.

Cassidy, D. J., & Lancaster, C. (1993). The grassroots curriculum: A dialog between children and teachers. *Young Children*, 48(6), 47–51.

Cazden, C. (1984). *Effective instructional practices in bilingual education*. Washington, DC: National Institute of Education.

Centre for Educational Research and Innovation (CERI). (1977). *Piagetian inventories: The experiments of Jean Piaget*. Paris: Organization for Economic Co-operation and Development.

Chalmers, M. (1988). *Easter parade*. New York: HarperCollins.

Chandler, P. S. (1994). *A place for me: Including children with special needs in early care and education settings*. Washington, DC: National Association for the Education of Young Children.

Charles, C. M. (1974). *Teacher's petit Piaget*. Belmont, CA: Fearon.

Chenfield, M. (1995). *Creative experiences for young children* (2nd ed.). Fort Worth, TX: Harcourt Brace.

Cherry, C. (1971). *Creative movement for the developing child: A nursery school handbook for non-musicians* (rev. ed.). Belmont, CA: Fearon.

Cherry, C. (1976). *Creative play for the developing child: Early lifelong education through play*. Belmont, CA: Fearon.

Cherry, C. (1981). *Think of something quiet: A guide for achieving serenity in early childhood classrooms*. Belmont, CA: Pitman Learning.

Cheung, L. W. Y. (1995). Current views and future perspectives. In L. W. Y. Cheung & J. B. Richmond (Eds.), *Child health, nutrition, and physical activity*. Champaign, IL: Human Kinetics.

Chief Seattle. (1991). *Brother eagle, sister sky*. New York: Dial.

Child Care Information Exchange. (1996). Beginning workshop: "Circle time." *Child Care Information Exchange*, 109, 39–58.

Child Care Law Center. (1994a). *Caring for children with HIV or AIDs in child care*. San Francisco: Author.

Child Care Law Center. (1994b). *Caring for children with special needs: The Americans with Disabilities Act and child care*. San Francisco: Author.

Child Health Alert. (1996). Children, car seats, and air bags: Guidelines for safety. *Child Health Alert*, 14, 6.

Child, L. M. (1974). *Over the river and through the woods*. New York: Coward, McGann & Geoghegan.

Children's Defense Fund. (1994). *The state of America's children yearbook*. Washington, DC: Author.

Children's Defense Fund. (1995). *The state of America's children yearbook*. Washington, DC: Author.

Children's Defense Fund. (1996a). Immunization rate up: One in four children still lacks full protection. *CDF Reports*, 17(6), 1–2.

Children's Defense Fund. (1996b). *The state of America's children yearbook*. Washington, DC: The Fund.

Children's Safety Network. (1996). *The Children's Safety Network: A resource for child and adolescent injury and violence prevention*. Rockville, MD: Maternal Child Health Bureau, Division of Maternal, Infant, Child, and Adolescent Health.

Chisholm, J. S. (1996). Learning "Respect for Everything": Navajo images of development. In C. P. Hwang, M. E. Lamb, & I. E. Sigel (Eds.). *Images of childhood*. Mahwah, NJ: Erlbaum.

Chomsky, N. (1987). Language: Chomsky's theory. In R. L. Gregory (Ed.), *The Oxford companion to the mind*. Oxford: Oxford University Press.

Christie, J. F., Johnsen, E. P., & Peckover, R. B. (1988). The effect of play periods duration in children's play patterns. *Journal of Research in Childhood Education*, 3/2, 123–131.

Christie, J. F., & Wardle, F. (1992). How much time is needed for play? *Young Children*, 47(3), 28–32.

Church, E. B. (1996). Your learning environment: A look back at your year. *Scholastic Early Childhood Today*, 10(8), 28–35.

Church, E. B., & Miller, K. (1990). *Learning through play: Blocks: A practical guide for teaching young children*. New York: Scholastic.

Cicchetti, D., & Beeghly, M. (Eds.). (1990). *The self in transition: Infancy to childhood*. Chicago: University of Chicago Press.

Cicerelli, V. G., Evans, J. W., & Schiller, J. S. (1969). *The impact of Head Start on children's cognitive and affective development: Preliminary report*. Washington, DC: Office of Economic Opportunity.

Clark, E. (1983). Meanings and concepts. In P. H. Mussen (Ed.,), *Handbook of child psychology*, J. H. Flavell & E. Markman (Eds.), *Vol 3: Cognitive development*. New York: Wiley.

Coatsworth, E. (1934). The rabbit's song outside the tavern. *Away Goes Sally*. New York: Macmillan.

Cobb, P. (1996). Where is the mind? A coordination of sociocultural and cognitive constructivist perspectives. In C. T. Fosnot (Ed.), *Constructivism: Theory, perspectives, and practice*. New York: Teachers College Press.

Coe, J. (1987). Children come first. *Childhood Education*, 64(2), 73.

Coleridge, S. (1986). *January brings the snow*. New York: Dial.

Confrey, J. (1995). How compatible are radical constructivism, sociocultural approaches, and social constructivism? In L. P. Steffe & J. Gale (Eds.), *Constructivism in education: Concerns about Vygotsky's theories*. Hillsdale, NJ: Erlbaum.

Conlon, A. (1992). Giving Mrs. Jones a hand: Making group storytime more pleasurable and meaningful for young children. *Young Children*, 47(3), 14–18.

Connolly, K., & Bruner, J. (Eds.). (1974). *The growth of competence*. London: Academic Press.

Conroy, M. A., Langenbrunner, M. R., & Burleson, R. B. (1996). Suggestions for enhancing the social behaviors of preschoolers with disabilities using developmentally appropriate practices. *Dimensions of Early Childhood*, 24(1), 9–15.

Cooper, T. T., & Ratner, M. (1980). *Many friends cooking: An international cookbook for girls and boys*. New York: Philomel.

Coopersmith, S. (1967). *The antecedents of self esteem.* San Francisco: Freeman.

Copage, E. V. (1991). *Kwanzaa: An African-American celebration of culture and cooking.* New York: Morrow.

Copeland, M. L. (1996). Code blue! Establishing a child care emergency plan. *Child Care Information Exchange, 107,* 17–22.

Cox, B., & Jacobs, M. (1991). *Spirit of the harvest.* New York: Stewart, Tabori, & Chang.

Cratty, B. J., & Martin, M. M. (1969). *Perceptual-motor efficiency in children: The measurement and improvement of movement attributes.* Philadelphia: Lea & Febiger.

Crawford, P. A. (1995). Early literacy: Emerging perspectives. *Journal of Research in Childhood Education, 10*(1), 71–86.

Crawford, S. H. (1996). *Beyond dolls & guns: 101 ways to help children avoid gender bias.* Portsmouth, NH: Heinemann.

Crocker, B. (1993). *Betty Crocker's Mexican made easy.* Upper Saddle River, NJ: Prentice Hall.

Croft, D. (1967). *Recipes for busy little hands.* Palo Alto, CA: De Anza College.

Crosbie-Burnett, M. (1994). The interface between stepparent families and schools: Research, theory, policy, and practice. In K. Pasley & M. Iniger-Tallman, (Eds.), *Stepparenting: Issues in theory, research, and practice.* Westport, CT: Greenwood.

Crosser, S. (1994). Making the most of water play. *Young Children, 49*(5), 28–32.

Crump, D. J. (1983). *Creatures small and furry.* Washington, DC: National Geographic Society.

Cuffaro, H. (1995). *Experimenting with the world: John Dewey and the early childhood classroom.* New York: Teachers College Press.

Curry, N. E., & Arnaud, S. H. (1982). Dramatic play as a diagnostic aid in the preschool. *Journal of Children in Contemporary Society, 14*(4), 37–46.

Curry, N. E., & Arnaud, S. H. (1995). Personality difficulties in preschool children as revealed through play themes and styles. *Young Children, 50*(4), 4–9.

Curry, N. E., Johnson, C. N. (1990). *Beyond self-esteem: Developing a genuine sense of human value.* Washington, DC: National Association for the Education of Young Children.

Darling, S. (1989). *Kenan Trust family literacy project guidebook.* Louisville, KY: The Trust.

Davidson, J. I. (1996). *Emergent literacy and dramatic play in early education.* Albany, NY: Delmar.

Davis, J., & Gardner, H. (1993). The arts and early childhood education: A cognitive developmental portrait of the young child as artist. In B. Spodek (Ed.), *Handbook of research on the education of young children.* Upper Saddle River, NJ: Prentice Hall.

Day, B. (1994). *Early childhood education: Development/experiential teaching and learning* (4th ed.). Upper Saddle River, NJ: Merrill/Prentice Hall.

deBarona Santos, M., & Barona, A. (1991). The assessment of culturally and linguistically different preschoolers. *Early Childhood Research Quarterly, 6*(3), 363–376.

Derman-Sparks, L. (1987). "It isn't fair!": Anti-bias curriculum for young children. In B. Neugebauer (Ed.), *Alike and different: Exploring our humanity with young children.* Redmond, WA: Exchange.

Derman-Sparks, L. (1992). Reaching potentials through anti-bias, multicultural curriculum. In S. Bredekamp & T. Rosegrant (Eds.), *Reaching potentials: Appropriate curriculum and assessment for young children.* Washington, DC: National Association for the Education of Young Children.

Derman-Sparks, L. (1995). Children and diversity. *Scholastic Early Childhood Today, 10*(3), 42–45.

Derman-Sparks, L., & the A.B.C. Task Force. (1989). *Anti-bias curriculum: Tools for empowering young children.* Washington, DC: National Association for the Education of Young Children.

DeVries, R., & Kohlberg, L. (1990). *Constructivist early education: Overview and comparison with other programs.* Washington, DC: National Association for the Education of Young Children.

DeVries, R., & Zan, B. (1994). *Moral children, moral classrooms: Creating a constructivist atmosphere in early education.* New York: Teachers College Press.

DeVries, R., & Zan, B. (1995). Creating a constructivist classroom atmosphere. *Young Children, 51*(1), 4–14.

DeVries, R., & Zan, B. (1996). A constructivist perspective on the role of the sociomoral atmosphere in promoting children's development. In C. T. Fosnot (Ed.), *Constructivism: Theory, perspectives, and practice.* New York: Teachers College Press.

Diffily, D., & Morrison, K. (1996). *Family-friendly communication for early childhood programs.* Washington, DC: National Association for the Education of Young Children.

Dolinar, K. J., Boser, C., & Holm, E. (1994). *Learning through play: Curriculum and activities for the inclusive classroom.* Albany, NY: Delmar.

Dorros, A. (1991). *Abuela.* New York: Dutton.

Dowell, R. I. (1987). *Move over, Mother Goose: Fingerplays, action verses & funny rhymes.* Mount Rainier, MD: Gryphon House.

Drew, W. F. (1995). Tools for creative thinking: Recycled materials. *Scholastic Early Childhood Today, 9*(5), 36–43.

Driscoll, A. (1995). *Cases in early childhood education: Stories of programs and practices.* Boston: Allyn & Bacon.

Duchan, J. F. (1995). *Supporting language learning in everyday life.* San Diego: Singular.

Duckworth, E. (1987). *"The having of wonderful ideas" and other essays on teaching and learning.* New York: Teachers College Press.

Dunkle, J. L., & Edwards, M. S. (1992). *The no leftovers child care cookbook.* St. Paul, MN: Redleaf.

Dunst, C. J., Trivette, C. M., & Deal A. G. (Eds.). (1994). *Supporting & strengthening families: Vol. 1: Methods, strategies and practices.* Cambridge, MA: Brookline.

Dyer, W. W. (1986). *Happy holidays! How to enjoy the Christmas & Hanukkah season to the fullest.* New York: Morrow.

Dyson, A. H., & Genishi, C. (1993). Visions of children as language users: Language and language education in early childhood. In B. Spodek (Ed.), *Handbook of research on the education of young children*. New York: Macmillan.

Education Week. (1995, October 15). By the numbers: Family portrait, p. 4.

Ebel, R. L. (1970). Behavioral objectives: A close look. *Phi Delta Kappan*, 171–173.

Edelstein, S. (1992). *Nutrition and meal planning in child-care programs: A practical guide*. Chicago: American Dietetic Association.

Edwards, C., Gandini, L., & Forman, G. (1993). *The hundred languages of children: The Reggio Emilia approach to early childhood education*. Norwood, NJ: Ablex.

Edwards, C. P., & Ramsey, P. G. (1986). *Promoting social and moral development in young children: Creative approaches for the classroom*. New York: Teachers College Press.

Edwards, C., & Springate, K. (1995). "The lion comes out of the stone": Helping young children achieve their creative potential. *Dimensions of Early Childhood*, 23(4), 25–29.

Eisenberg, N. (1992). *The caring child*. Cambridge, MA: Harvard University Press.

Eisenberg, N., Fabes, R. A., Carlo, G., & Karbon, M. (1992). Emotional responsivity to others: Behavioral correlates and socialization antecedents. *New Directions for Child Development*, 55, 57–73.

Eisler, C. (1988). *Cats know best*. New York: Dial.

Eisner, E. (1969). Instructional and expressive educational objectives: Their formulation and use in curriculum. In W. J. Popham, E. W. Eisner, H. J., Sullivan, & L. L. Tyler. *Instructional objectives*. Chicago: Rand McNally, American Educational Research Association.

Elicker, J., & Fortner-Wood, C. (1995). Adult-child relationships in early childhood programs. *Young Children*, 51(1), 69–78.

Elkind, D. (1981). *The hurried child: Growing up too fast, too soon*. Reading, MA: Addison-Wesley.

Elkind, D. (1990a). Academic pressures—Too much, too soon: The demise of play. In E. Klugman & S. Smilansky (Eds.), *Children's play and learning: Perspectives and policy implications*. New York: Teachers College Press.

Elkind, D. (1990b). *Miseducation: Preschoolers at risk*. New York: Knopf.

Endres, J. B., & Rockwell, R. E. (1993). *Food, nutrition and the young child*. (4th ed.). Upper Saddle River, NJ: Merrill/Prentice Hall.

Engel, B. S. (1995). *Considering children's art: Why and how to value their work*. Washington, DC: National Association for the Education of Young Children.

Erikson, E. H. (1963). *Childhood and society* (2nd ed.). New York: Norton.

Erikson, E. H. (1982). *The life cycle completed: A review*. New York: Norton.

Erikson, E. H. (1996). A healthy personality for every child. In K. M. Paciorek & J. H. Munro (Eds.), *Sources: Notable selections in early childhood education*. Guilford, CT: Dushkin.

Ernst, L. L. (1995). *Lapsit services for the very young: A how-to-do-it manual*. New York: Neal-Schuman.

Essa, E. L., & Murray, C. I. (1994). Research in review: Young children's understanding and experience with death. *Young Children*, 49(4), 74–81.

Ets, M. H., & Labastida, A. (1959). *Nine days to Christmas*. New York: Viking.

Eyre, L., & Eyre, R. (1984). *Teaching children joy*. New York: Ballantine.

Faber, A., & Mazlish, E. (1980). *How to talk so kids will listen, and listen so kids will talk*. New York: Avon.

Fagot, B. I. (1994). Peer relations and the development of competence in boys and girls. *New Directions for Child Development*, 65, 53–65.

Farish, J. M. (1995). *When disaster strikes: Helping young children cope*. Washington, DC: National Association for the Education of Young Children.

Farnhham-Diggory, S. (1992). Head shakers and mind benders. *Child Care Information Exchange*, 85, 54.

Fearrington, A. (1996). *Christmas lights*. Boston: Houghton Mifflin.

Feng, J. (1994). *Asian-American children: What teachers should know*. Urbana, IL: ERIC Clearinghouse on Elementary and Early Childhood Education.

Fenwick, K. (1993). Diffusing conflict with parents: A model for communication. *Child Care Information Exchange*, 93, 59–60.

Feree, M. J., & Groppe, C. C. (1975). Balanced food values and sense. In F. Cook, C. Groppe, & M. Feree (Eds.), *Balance food values and cents*. (Report 2220). Berkeley: University of California, Division of Agricultural Science.

Ferreira, N. (1982). *Learning through cooking: a cooking program for children two to ten*. Palo Alto, CA: R & E Associates.

Fields, M. V., & Spangler, K. L. (1995). *Let's begin reading right: Developmentally appropriate beginning literacy* (3rd ed.). Upper Saddle River, NJ: Merrill/Prentice Hall.

Fiese, B. (1990). Playful relationships: A contextual analysis of mother-toddler interaction and symbolic play. *Child Development*, 61, 1648–1656.

Finkelhor, D. (1994). Current information on the scope and nature of child sexual abuse. *The Future of Children*, 4(2), 31–53.

Fisher, R. (1990). *Teaching children to think*. Oxford: Blackwell.

Flack, M. (1931). *Angus and the cat*. Garden City, NY: Doubleday.

Flack, M. (1932). *Ask Mr. Bear*. New York: Macmillan.

Flavell, J. H., Miller, P. H., & Miller, S. A. (1993). *Cognitive development* (3rd ed.). Upper Saddle River, NJ: Prentice Hall.

Flax, E. (1991, October 23). New guide calls for broad approach to sex education. *Education Week*, p. 12.

Food Research and Action Council. (1995). *Hunger*. Washington, DC: Council on Childhood Hunger Identification Project.

Forman, G. (1989). Helping children ask good questions. In B. Neugebauer (Ed.), *The wonder of it: Exploring how the world works*. Redmond, WA: Exchange.

Fosnot, C. T. (1996). *Constructivism: Theory, perspectives, and practice*. New York: Teachers College Press.

Foster, S. M. (1994). Successful parent meetings. *Young Children, 50*(1), 78–80.

Fox, J. E., & Tipps, R. S. (1995). Young children's development of swinging behaviors. *Early Childhood Research Quarterly, 10*(4), 491–504.

Fox, S. S. (1985). *Good grief: Helping groups of children when a friend dies*. Boston: New England Association for the Education of Young Children.

Fox-Barnett, M., & Meyer, T. (1992). The teacher's playing at my house this week. *Young Children, 47*(5), 45–50.

Frank, L. (1968). *Play is valid*. Wheaton, MD: Association for Childhood Education International.

Frankenburg, W. K., Dodds, J., Archer, P., Bresnick, B., Maschka, P., Edelman, N., & Shapiro, H. (1990). *Denver-II*. Denver: Denver Developmental Materials.

Franklin, M. B., & Biber, B. (1977). Psychological perspectives and early childhood education: Some relations between theory and practice. In L. G. Katz (Ed.), *Current topics in early childhood education* (Vol. 1). Norwood, NJ: Ablex.

French, L. (1996). "I told you all about it, so don't tell me you don't know": Two-year-olds and learning through language. *Young Children, 51*(2), 17–20.

Freud, S. (1962). *Three essays on the theory of sexuality*. New York: Basic Books.

Friedrich, P., & Friedrich, O. (1957). *The Easter bunny that overslept*. New York: Lothrop, Lee & Shepard.

Frost, J. (1996). Joe Frost on playing outdoors. *Scholastic Early Childhood Today, 10*(7), 26–28.

Frost, J. L. (1992a). *Play and playscapes*. Albany, NY: Delmar.

Frost, J. L. (1992b). Reflections on research and practice in outdoor play environments. *Dimensions of Early Childhood, 20*(4), 6–10.

Frost, J. L., & Strickland, E. (1985). Equipment choices of young children during free play. In J. L. Frost & S. Sunderland (Eds.), *When children play: Proceedings of the International Conference on Play and Play Environments*. Wheaton, MD: Association for Childhood Education International.

Fuerst, J. S., & Fuerst, D. (1993). Chicago experience with an early childhood program: The special case of the Child Parent Center Program. *Urban Education, 28*(1), 69–96.

Furman, E. (1990). Plant a potato—learn about life (and death). *Young Children, 46*(1), 15–20.

Furman, R. (1995a). Helping children cope with stress. In E. Furman (Ed.), *Preschoolers: Questions and answers: Psychoanalytic consultations with parents, teachers, and caregivers*. Madison, CT: International Universities Press.

Furman, R. (1995b). On preparation: "New" perspectives. In E. Furman (Ed.), *Preschoolers: Questions and answers: Psychoanalytic consultations with parents, teachers, and caregivers*. Madison, CT: International Universities Press.

The Future of Children. (1994). Sexual abuse of children. 4(2) (entire issue). Los Altos, CA: Packard Foundation.

Gabbard, C. C. (1991). Early childhood physical education: The essential elements. In K. M. Paciorek & J. H. Munro (Eds.), *Early childhood education 91/92*. Guilford, CT: Dushkin.

Gallahue, D. L. (1995a). Transforming physical education curriculum. In S. Bredekamp & T. Rosegrant (eds.), *Reaching potentials: Transforming early childhood curriculum and assessment* (Vol. 2). Washington, DC: National Association for the Education of Young Children.

Gallahue, D. L. (1995b). *Understanding motor development: Infants, children, adolescents, adults*. Dubuque, IA: Brown & Benchmark.

Gambetti, A. (1992, November). *An amusement park for the birds*. Paper presented at the National Association for the Education of Young Children Conference, New Orleans.

Gandini, L. (1996). Teachers and children together: Constructing new learning. *Child Care Information Exchange, 108*, 43–46.

Gandini, L. (1997). Foundations of the Reggio Emilia Approach. In J. Hendrick (Ed.), *First steps toward teaching the Reggio Way*. Upper Saddle River, NJ: Merrill/Prentice Hall.

Garber, H. L. (1989). *The Milwaukee Project: Preventing mental retardation in children at risk*. Washington, DC: American Association on Mental Retardation.

Garcia, E. E., & McLaughlin, B. (1995). *Meeting the challenge of linguistic and cultural diversity in early childhood education*. New York: Teachers College Press.

Gardner, H. (1989). *To open minds*. New York: Basic Books.

Gardner, H. (1993). *Multiple intelligences: The theory in practice*. New York: Basic Books.

Gartrell, D. (1995). Misbehavior or mistaken behavior? *Young Children, 50*(5), 27–34.

Garvey, C. (1983). Some properties of social play. In M. Donaldson, R. Grieve, & C. Pratt (Eds.), *Early childhood development and education: Readings in psychology*. New York: Guilford.

Gaspar, K. (1995). Liberating art experiences for preschoolers and their teachers. In C. M. Thompson (Ed.), *The visual arts and early childhood learning*. Reston, VA: National Art Education Association.

Gatto, J. (1992). *Dumbing us down*. Philadelphia: New Society.

Gay, Z. (1955). *What's your name?* New York: Viking.

Genishi, C. (1992). Developing the foundation: oral language and communicative competence. In C. Seefeldt (Ed.), *The early childhood curriculum: A review of current research* (2nd ed.). New York: Teachers College Press.

Gesell, A., Halverson, H. M., Thompson, H., Ilg, F., Costner, R. M., Ames, L. B. & Amatruda, C. S. (1940). *The first five years of life: A guide to the study of the preschool child*. New York: Harper & Row.

Gesell Institute. (1987). The Gesell Institute responds. *Young Children, 42*(2), 7–8.

Gestwicki, C. (1995). *Developmentally appropriate practice: Curriculum and development in early education*. Albany, NY: Delmar.

Gibbons, G. 1983. *Thanksgiving Day*. New York: Holiday House.

Gillis, J. S. (1992). *In a pumpkin shell: Over 20 pumpkin projects for kids*. Powhall, VT: Storey Communications.

Glascoe, F. P., & Byrne, K. E. (1993). The accuracy of three developmental screening tests. *Journal of Early Intervention*, 17(4), 368–379.

Goble, P. (1978). *The girl who loved wild horses*. Scarsdale, NY: Bradbury.

Godwin, L. J., Groves, M. M., & Horm-Wingerd, D. M. (1994). Separation distress in infants, toddlers, and parents. In L. Paciorek & K. G. Munro (Eds.), *Early childhood education 94/95*. Guilford, CT: Dushkin.

Goelman, R., & Jacobs, E. V. (Eds.). (1994). *Children's play in child care settings*. Albany: State University of New York.

Goffin, S. G. (1987). How well do we respect the children in our care? *Childhood Education*, 66(2).

Golden, M., Bridger, W. H., & Martare, A. (1974). Social class differences in the ability of young children to use verbal information to facilitate learning. *American Journal of Orthopsychiatry*, 44(1), 86–91.

Goldhaber, J., Smith, D., & Sortino, S. (1997). Observing, recording, understanding: The role of documentation in early childhood teacher education. In J. Hendrick (Ed.), *First steps toward teaching the Reggio Way*. Upper Saddle River, NJ: Merrill/Prentice Hall.

Golinkoff, R. M., & Hirsh-Pasek, K. (1990). Let the mute speak: What infants can tell us about language acquisition. *Merrill-Palmer Quarterly: Journal of Developmental Psychology*, 36(1), 67–91.

Golumb, C. (1992). *The child's creation of a pictorial world*. Berkeley: University of California Press.

Gonzalez, G. (1991). Language acquisition: Research in Mexican-American children: The sad state of the art. *Early Childhood Research Quarterly*, 6(3), 411–425.

Gonzalez-Mena, J. (1993). *The child in the family and in the community*. Upper Saddle River, NJ: Merrill/Prentice Hall.

Goodman, J. F. (1992). *When slow is fast enough: Educating the delayed preschool child*. New York: Guilford.

Goodwin, M. T., & Pollen, G. (1980). *Creative food experiences for children* (rev. ed.). Washington, DC: Center for Science in the Public Interest.

Gordon, T. (1976). *P.E.T. in action: Inside P.E.T. families. New problems, insights and solutions in Parent Effectiveness Training*. New York: Wyden.

Gordon, T. (1989). *Discipline that works: Promoting self-discipline in children*. New York: Wyden.

Görlitz, D., & Wohlwill, J. F. (Eds.). (1987). *Curiosity, imagination, and play*. Hillsdale, NJ: Erlbaum.

Gotts, E. E. (1989). *HOPE, preschool to graduation: Contributions to parenting and school-family relations: Theory and practice*. Charleston, WV: Appalachia Educational Laboratory. (ED 3-5, 146)

Gottschall, S. M. (1995). Hug-a-Book: A program to nurture a young child's love of books and reading. *Young Children*, 50(4), 29–35.

Gould, J. S. (1996). On teaching and learning in the language arts. In C. T. Fosnot (Ed.), *Constructivism: Theory, perspectives, and practice*. New York: Teachers College Press.

Gowen, J. W. (1995). The early development of symbolic play. *Young Children*, 50(3), 75–84.

Grace, K., & Shores, E. F. (1991). *The portfolio and its use: Developmentally appropriate assessment of young children*. Little Rock, AR: Southern Association for Children under Six.

Graham, A. (1976). *Foxtails, ferns and fish scales: A handbook of art and nature projects*. New York: Four Winds.

Gratz, R. R., & Boulton, P. J. (1996). Erikson and early childhood educators: Looking at ourselves and our profession developmentally. *Young Children*, 51(5), 74–78.

Graue, M. E. (1992). Social interpretations of readiness for kindergarten. *Early Childhood Research Quarterly*, 7, 225–244.

Graue, M. E. (1993). *Ready for what? Constructing meanings of readiness for kindergarten*. Albany: State University of New York Press.

Graves, M. (1989). *The teacher's idea book: Daily planning around the key experiences*. Ypsilanti, MI: High/Scope.

Greenberg, J. (1996). Seeing children through tragedy: My mother died today . . . When is she coming back? *Young Children*, 51(6), 76–77.

Greenberg, P. (1991a). Avoiding "Me against you" discipline. In J. H. Munro (Ed.), *Early childhood education 91/92*. Guilford, CT: Dushkin.

Greenberg, P. (1991b). *Character development: Encouraging self-esteem & self-discipline in infants, toddlers, & two-year-olds*. Washington, DC: National Association for the Education of Young Children.

Greenberg, P. (1992). Why not academic preschool? Pt. 2. Autocracy or democracy in the classroom? *Young Children*, 47(3), 54–64.

Greenman, J. (1988). *Caring spaces, learning places: Children's environments that work*. Redmond, WA: Exchange.

Greenspun, A. A. (1991). *Fathers*. New York: Philomel.

Greenstein, D., Miner, N., Kudela, E., & Bloom, S. (1995). *Backyards and butterflies: Ways to include children with disabilities in outdoor activities*. Cambridge, MA: Brookline.

Grief, E. B. (1980). Sex differences in parent-child conversations. *Women's Studies International Quarterly*, 3, 253–258.

Griffin, E. F. (1982). *Island of childhood: Education in the special world of nursery school*. New York: Teachers College Press.

Gronlund, N. E. (1995). *How to write and use instructional objectives* (5th ed.). Upper Saddle River, NJ: Merrill/Prentice Hall.

Grossman, V., & Long, S. (1991). *Ten little rabbits*. San Francisco: Chronicle Books.

Grover, E. O. (Ed.). (1971). *Mother Goose: The classic Volland edition* (originally by F. Richardson). Long Beach, CA: Hubbard.

Guilford, J. P. (1967). *The nature of human intelligence*. New York: McGraw-Hill.

Guilford, J. P. (1981). Developmental characteristics: Factors that aid and hinder creativity. In J. C. Gowan, J. Khatena,

& E. P. Torrance (Eds.). *Creativity: Its educational implications* (2nd ed.). Dubuque, IA: Kendall/Hunt.

Gullo, D. F. (1994). *Understanding assessment and evaluation in early childhood education*. New York: Teachers College Press.

Haigh, K. (1997). How the Reggio Approach has influenced an inner-city program. In J. Hendrick, *First steps toward teaching the Reggio Way*. Upper Saddle River, NJ: Merrill/Prentice Hall.

Haines, J. E., & Gerber, L. L. (1996). *Leading young children to music* (5th ed.). Upper Saddle River, NJ: Merrill/Prentice Hall.

Hale, J. E. (1986). *Black children: Their roots, culture, and learning style* (2nd ed.). Baltimore, MD: Johns Hopkins University Press.

Hale, J. E. (1992). Dignifying black children's lives. *Dimensions*, 20(3), 8–9, 40+.

Haley, G. E. (1970). *A story, a story*. New York: Atheneum.

Halsall, S., & Green, C. (1995). Reading aloud: A way for parents to support their children's growth in literacy. *Early Childhood Education Journal*, 23(1), 27–35.

Hammet, C. T. (1992). *Movement activities for early childhood*. Champaign, IL: Human Kinetics.

Harlan, J. C., & Rivkin, M. S. (1996). *Science experiences for the early childhood years: An integrated approach* (6th ed.). Upper Saddle River, NJ: Merrill/Prentice Hall.

Harms, T. (1972). Evaluating settings for learning. In K. H. Baker. (Ed.), *Ideas that work with young children*. Washington, DC: National Association for the Education of Young Children.

Harms, T., & Clifford, R. M. (1996). *Early childhood environment rating scale*. New York: Teachers College Press.

Harris, F. W. (1990). *The racial attitudes of Black preschoolers: An exploratory study*. Ann Arbor, MI: UMI Dissertation Services.

Hart, B., & Risley, T. R. (1995). *Meaningful differences in the everyday experience of young American children*. Baltimore, MD: Brookes.

Harter, S. (1983). Developmental perspectives on the self system. In P. H. Mussen (Ed.), *Handbook of child psychology* (4th ed.), E. M. Hetherington (Ed.), *Vol. 4: Socialization, personality, and social development*. New York: Wiley.

Hartman, J. A., & Eckerty, C. (1995). Projects in the early years. *Childhood Education*, 71(3), 141–148.

Hartup, W. W. (1983). Peer relations. In P. H. Mussen (Ed.). *Handbook of child psychology*, E. M. Hetherington (Ed.), *Vol. 4: Socialization, personality, and social development*. New York: Wiley.

Hasson, J. B. (1996). Grandparent's day: What to do for children who don't have a grandparent. *Young Children*, 52(3), 28–31.

Hayes, D. S. (1978). Cognitive bases for liking and disliking among preschool children. *Child Development*, 49, 906–909.

Hayes, S. (1986). *Happy Christmas Gemma*. New York: Lothrup, Lee.

Hecht, M. L., Collier, M. J., & Ribeau., S. A. (1993). *African American communication: Ethnic identity and cultural interpretation*. Newbury Park, CA: Sage.

Heitz, T. (1989). How do I help Jacob? *Young Children*, 45(1), 11–15.

Helburn, S., Howes, C., Bryant, D., & Kagan, S. L. (1995). *Cost, quality, and child outcomes in child care centers: Executive summary* (2nd ed.). Denver: Economics Department, University of Colorado.

Hendrick, J. (1973). *The cognitive development of the economically disadvantaged Mexican-American and Anglo-American four-year-old: Teaching the concepts of grouping, ordering, perceiving common connections and matching by means of semantic and figural materials*. Unpublished doctoral dissertation, University of California, Santa Barbara.

Hendrick, J. B. (1996). *The whole child: Developmental education for the early years* (6th ed.). Upper Saddle River, NJ: Merrill/Prentice Hall.

Hendrick, J. (Ed.). (1997). *First steps toward teaching the Reggio Way*. Upper Saddle River, NJ: Merrill/Prentice Hall.

Hendrick, J., & Stange, T. (1991). Do actions speak louder than words? An effect of the functional use of language on dominant sex role behavior in boys and girls. *Early Childhood Research Quarterly*, 6(4), 565–576.

Henninger, M. L. (1985). Preschool children's play behaviors in an indoor and outdoor environment. In J. Frost & S. Sunderlin (Eds.), *When children play*. Wheaton, MD: Association for Childhood Education International.

Herriot, P. (1987). Language development in children. In R. L. Gregory (Ed.), *The Oxford companion to the mind*. Oxford: Oxford University Press.

Hertz, O. (1981). *Tobias has a birthday*. Minneapolis: Carolrhoda.

Hewitt, D. (1995). *So this is normal too?* St. Paul, MN: Redleaf.

Hildebrand, V., Phenice, L. A., Gray, M. M., & Hines, R. P. (1996). *Knowing and serving diverse families*. Upper Saddle River, NJ: Merrill/Prentice Hall.

Hill, C. A. (1977). A review of the language deficit position: Some sociolinguistic and psycholinguistic perspectives. *IRCD Bulletin*, 12(4), 1–13.

Hirsch, E. S. (Ed.). (1996). *The block book* (3rd ed.). Washington, DC: National Association for the Education of Young Children.

Hoban, R. (1960). *Bedtime for Frances*. New York: Harper & Row.

Hoban, R. (1964). *Bread and jam for Frances*. New York: Harper & Row.

Hodges, W. (1987). Active listening. *Dimensions*, 15(4), 13.

Hoffman, M. L. (1970). Moral development. In P. H. Mussen (Ed.), *Carmichael's manual of child psychology* (3rd ed., Vol. 2). New York: Wiley.

Hohmann, M., & Weikart, D. (1995). *Educating young children: Active learning practices for preschool and child care programs*. Ypsilanti, MI: High/Scope.

Hollins, E. R., King, J. E., & Hayman, W. C. (1994). *Teaching diverse populations: Formulating a knowledge base*. Albany: State University of New York Press.

Holman, J., Goetz, E. M., & Baer, D. M. (1976). The training of creativity as an operant and an examination of its generalization characteristics. In B. C. Etzel, J. M. Le Blanc, & D. M. Baer (Eds.), *New developments in behavioral research: Theory, method, and application.* Hillsdale, NJ: Erlbaum.

Holnbird, K. (1985). *Angelina's Christmas.* New York: Clarkson.

Honig, A. S. (1983). Sex role socialization in early childhood. *Young Children,* 38(6), 57–70.

Honig, A. S. (1995). Singing with infants and toddlers.*Young Children,* 50(5), 72–78.

Honig, A., & Wittmer, D. S. (1982). Teachers and low-income toddlers in metropolitan day care. *Early Child Development and Care,* 10(1), 95–112.

Hough, R. A., Nurss, J. R., & Wood, D. (1987). Making opportunities for elaborated language in early childhood classrooms. *Young Children,* 43(1), 6–12.

Houle, G. B. (1987). *Learning centers for young children* (3rd ed.). West Greenwich, RI: Consortium.

Howe, D. (1995). IEP social goals found lacking: Surprise, surprise! *Journal of Early Intervention,* 19(4), 286–287.

Howe, N., Moller, L., & Chambers, B. (1994). Dramatic play in day care; What happens when doctors, cooks, bakers, pirates and pharmacists invade the classroom? In H. Goelman & E. V. Jacobs (Eds.), *Children's play in child care settings.* Albany: State University of New York Press.

Howes, C., & Clements, D. (1994). Adult socialization of children's play in child care. In H. Goelman & E. V. Jacobs (Eds.), *Children's play in child care settings.* Albany: State University of New York Press.

Howes, C., Unger, O. & Matheson, C. C. (1992). *The collaborative construction of pretend.* Albany: State University of New York Press.

Humphrey, J. L. (1988). *Teaching children to relax.* Springfield, IL: Thomas.

Huyghe, F. B. (1993, June). Interview with Umberto Eco. UNESCO *Courier.*

Humphreys, D. (1951). *Animals every child should know.* New York: Grosset & Dunlap.

Hut, V., Dennis, B., Koplow, L., & Ferber, J. (1996). Lesson plans for emotional life. In L. Koplow (Ed.), *Unsmiling faces.* New York: Teachers College Press.

Hwang, C. P., Lamb, M. E., & Sigel, I. E. (Eds.). (1996). *Images of childhood.* Mahwah, NJ: Erlbaum.

Hyson, M. C. (1994). *The emotional development of young children: Building an emotion-center curriculum.* New York: Teachers College Press.

Hyson, M. C., Whitehead, L. C., & Prudhoe, C. M. (1988). Influences on attitudes toward physical affection between adults and children. *Early Childhood Research Quarterly,* 3(1), 55–75.

Igoa, C. (1995). *The inner world of the immigrant children.* New York: St. Martin's.

Isbell, R. (1995). *The complete learning center book.* Beltsville, MD: Gryphon House.

Isenberg, J. P., & Jalongo, M. R. (1996). *Creative expression and play in the early childhood curriculum* (2nd ed.). Upper Saddle River, NJ: Merrill/Prentice Hall.

Iwasaki, C. (1968). *Staying home alone on a rainy day.* New York: McGraw-Hill.

Jacobs, N. L. (1992). Unhappy endings. *Young Children,* 47(3), 23–27.

Jacobson, E. (1976). *You must relax* (5th ed.). New York: McGraw Hill.

Jacobson, M., & Hill, L. (1991). *Kitchen fun for kids.* Washington, DC: Center for Science in the Public Interest.

Jalongo, M. R. (1988). *Young children and picture books: Literature from infancy to six.* Washington, DC: National Association for the Education of Young Children.

Jalongo, M. R. (1996a). Teaching young children to become better listeners. *Young Children,* 51(2), 21–26.

Jalongo, M. R. (1996b). Using recorded music with young children: A guide for nonmusicians. *Young Children,* 51(5), 6–14.

James, J. C., & Granovetter, R. F. (1987). *Waterworks: A new book of water play activities for children ages 1 to 6.* Lewisville, NC: Kaplan.

Javernick, E. (1988). Johnny's not jumping: Can we help obese children? *Young Children,* 43(2), 18–23.

Jervis, K. (1996). *Eyes on the child: Three portfolio stories.* New York: Teachers College Press.

Jewell, N. (1972). *The snuggle bunny.* New York: Harper & Row.

Johnson, J. E. (1990). The role of play in cognitive development. In E. Klugman & S. Smilansky (Eds.), *Children's play and learning: Perspectives and policy implications.* New York: Teachers College Press.

Johnson, J. E., & Ershler, J. (1982). Curricular effects on the play of preschoolers. In D. J. Pepler & K. H. Rubin (Eds.), *The play of children: Current theory and research.* Basel: Karger.

Johnston, T. (1996). *The magic maguay.* New York: Harcourt Brace.

Jones, D. P. H., & McGraw, J. M. (1987). Reliable and fictitious accounts of sexual abuse to children. *Journal of Interpersonal Violence,* 2(1), 27–45.

Jones, E. (1977). *Dimensions of teaching-learning environments: Handbook for teachers.* Pasadena, CA: Pacific Oaks.

Jones, E., & Derman-Sparks, L. (1992). Meeting the challenge of diversity. *Young Children,* 47(2), 12–18.

Jones, E., & Nimmo, J. (1994). *Emergent curriculum.* Washington, DC: National Association for the Education of Young Children.

Jones, E., & Prescott, E. (1978). *Dimensions of teaching/learning environments. 2: Focus on day care.* Pasadena, CA: Pacific Oaks.

Jones, E., & Reynolds, G. (1992). *The play's the thing: Teachers' roles in children's play.* New York: Teachers College Press.

Jones, R. (1996). Producing a parent newsletter parents will read. *Child Care Information Exchange,* 107, 91–93.

Kagan, S. L., & Weissbourd, B. (Eds.). (1994). *Putting families first: America's family support movement and the challenge of change.* San Francisco: Jossey-Bass.

Kamii, C. (1972). A sketch of the Piaget-derived preschool curriculum developed by the Ypsilanti Early Education

Program. In S. J. Braun & E. P. Edwards (Eds.), *History and theory of early childhood education.* Worthington, OH: Jones.

Kamii, C., & Ewing, J. K. (1996). Basing teaching on Piaget's constructivism. *Childhood Education, 72*(5), 260–264.

Kampe, E. (1990). Children in health care: When the prescription is play. In E. Klugman & S. Smilansky (Eds.), *Children's play and learning: Perspectives and policy implications.* New York: Teachers College Press.

Katz, L. (1975). *Second collection of papers for teachers.* Urbana: College of Education, University of Illinois.

Katz, L. (1992, April). *The Reggio Approach: Hundred Languages of Children Conference, Oklahoma City.*

Katz, L., & Cesarone, B. (Eds.). (1994). *Reflections on the Reggio Emilia Approach.* Urbana, IL: ERIC Clearinghouse on Elementary & Early Education.

Katz, L., & Chard, S. (1991). *Engaging children's minds: The project approach.* Norwood, NJ: Ablex.

Katz, L., & McClellan, D. E. (1991). *The teacher's role in the social development of young children.* Urbana, IL: ERIC Clearinghouse on Elementary and Early Childhood Education.

Katzen, M., & Henderson, A. (1994). *Pretend soup and other real recipes: A cookbook for preschoolers and up.* Berkeley, CA: Tricycle.

Keats, E. J. (1964). *Whistle for Willie.* New York: Viking.

Keats, E. J. (1968). *A letter to Amy.* New York: Harper & Row.

Kendall, F. E. (1996). *Diversity in the classroom: New approaches to the education of young children* (2nd ed.) New York: Teachers College Press.

Kendrick, A. S., Kaufmann, R., & Messenger, K. P. (Eds.). (1995). *Healthy young children: A manual for programs* (3rd ed.). Washington, DC: National Association for the Education of Young Children.

Kennedy, D. K. (1996). After Reggio Emilia: May the conversation begin! *Young Children, 51*(5), 24–27.

Kennedy, M., & Ing, J. S. (1994). *The single-parent family: Living happily in a changing world.* New York: Brown Trade.

Kent, J. (1969). *The Christmas piñata.* New York: Parent's Magazine Press.

Kessler, S. (1991). The teaching presence. *The Holistic Education Review, 4*(4), 6.

Keubli, J. (1994). Young children's understanding of everyday emotions. *Young Children, 49*(3), 36–47.

Kinnear, K. L. (1995). *Childhood sexual abuse: A reference handbook.* Santa Barbara, CA: ABC-CLIO.

Kinsey, A. C., Pomeroy, W. B., & Martin, C. E. (1948). *Sexual behavior in the human male.* Philadelphia: Saunders.

Kinsey, A. C., Pomeroy, W. B., Martin, C. E., & Gebhard, P. H. (1953). *Sexual behavior in the human female.* Philadelphia: Saunders.

Kladder, J. (1995). *Story hour: 55 preschool programs for public libraries.* Jefferson, NC: McFarland.

Klugman, E., & Smilansky, S. (1990). *Children's play and learning: Perspectives and policy implications.* New York: Teachers College Press.

Knutson, J. B., & Bower, M. E. (1994). Physically abusive parenting as an escalated aggressive response. In M. Potegal & J. F. Knutson (Eds.), *The dynamics of aggression.* Hillsdale, NJ: Erlbaum.

Kohl, M. J. (1989). *Mudworks: Creative clay, dough and modeling experiences.* Bellingham, WA: Bright Ring.

Kohl, M. J. (1994). *Preschool art: It's the process, not the product.* Beltsville, MD: Gryphon House.

Kohl, M. A., & Gainer, C. (1991). *Good earth art: Environmental art for kids.* Bellingham, WA: Bright Ring.

Kohn, A. (1993). *Punished by rewards: The trouble with gold stars, incentive plans, A's, praise, and other bribes.* Boston: Houghton Mifflin.

Kontos, S., & Wells, W. (1986). Attitudes of caregivers and the day care experiences of families. *Early Childhood Research Quarterly, 1,* 47–67.

Koplow, L. (1996). *Unsmiling faces: How preschools can heal.* New York: Teachers College Press.

Koralek, D. (1992). *Caregivers of young children: Preventing and responding to child maltreatment.* Washington, DC: U.S. Department of Health and Human Services, Administration on Children, Youth and Families, National Center on Child Abuse and Neglect.

Kotlus, E., & Gellert, S. (1994). *Helping children love themselves and others: Resource guide to equity materials for young children* (rev. ed.). Washington, DC: Children's Foundation.

Kramer, D. C. (1989). *Animals in the classroom: Selection, care, and observations.* Menlo Park, CA: Addison Wesley.

Krathwohl, D. R., Bloom, B. S., & Masia, B. B. (1964). *Taxonomy of educational objectives: Handbook 2.* New York: McKay.

Krauss, R. (1950). *The backward day.* New York: Harper & Row.

Krauss, R., & Johnson, C. (1971). *The carrot seed.* New York: Scholastic.

Kritchevsky, S., Prescott, E., & Walling, L. (1996). How to analyze play space. In K. M. Paciorek & J. G. Munro (Eds.), *Sources: Notable selections in early childhood education.* Guilford, CT: Dushkin.

Kroll, S. (1984). *The biggest pumpkin ever.* New York: Scholastic.

Kruger, H., & Kruger, J. (1989). *The preschool teacher's guide to movement education.* Baltimore, MD: Gerstung.

Labov, W. (1970). The logic of nonstandard English. In F. Williams (Ed.), *Language and poverty.* Chicago: Markham.

LaFontaine. (1966–1991). *The hare and the tortoise.* Oxford: Oxford University Press.

Lamme, L. L., McKinley, L. (1992). Creating a caring classroom with children's literature. *Young Children, 48*(1), 65–71.

Larson, N., Henthorne, M., & Plum, B. (1994). *Transition magician: Strategies for guiding young children in early childhood programs.* St. Paul, MN: Redleaf.

Lawler, S. B. (1991). *Teacher-parent conferencing in early childhood education.* Washington, DC: National Education Association.

Lazar, I., Darlington, R., Murray, H., Royce, J., & Snipper, A. (1982). Lasting effects of early education: A report from the Consortium for Longitudinal Studies. *Monographs of the Society for Research in Child Development, 47*(2–3), no. 195.

Lazear, D. (1991). *Seven ways of knowing: Teaching for multiple intelligences: A handbook of techniques for expanding intelligence* (2nd ed.). Palatine, IL: Skylight.

Lee, F. Y. (1995). Asian parents as partners. *Young Children, 50*(3), 4–9.

Lee, V., & Gupta, P. D. (Eds.). (1995). *Children's cognitive and language development.* Oxford: Blackwell.

Leifer, A. D., & Lesser, G. S. (1976). *The development of career awareness in young children: NIE papers on education and work* (No. 1). Washington, DC: United States Department of Health, Education, and Welfare: National Institute of Education.

Leight, L. (1988). *Raising sexually healthy children: A loving guide for parents, teachers and care-givers.* New York: Avon.

Lemley, V., & Lemley, J. (1976). *Zucchini cookbook.* Cave Junction, OR: Wilderness House.

Levine, J. A., Murphy, D. T., & Wilson, S. (1993). *Getting men involved: Strategies for early childhood programs.* New York: Scholastic.

Lewis, A. G. (1975). *Lotions, soaps, and scents.* Minneapolis: Lerner.

Lewis, E. G. (1996). What mother? What father? *Young Children, 52*(3), 27.

Lewit, W. M., & Baker, L. S. (1995). School readiness. *The Future of Children: Critical Issues for Children and Youths, 5*(2), 128–139.

Liaw, F. R., Meisels, S. J., & Brooks-Gunn, J. (1995). The effects of experience of early intervention on low birth weight, premature children: The Infant Health and Development program. *Early Childhood Research Quarterly, 10*(4), 405–431.

Lima, C. W., & Lima, J. A. (1993). *A to zoo: Subject access to children's picture books* (4th ed.). NJ: Bowker.

Linder, T. W. (1993). *Transdisciplinary play-based intervention: Guidelines for developing a meaningful curriculum for young children.* Baltimore, MD: Brookes.

Lively, V., & Lively, E. (1991). *Sexual development of young children.* Albany, NY: Delmar.

Logan, S. L. (Ed.). (1996). *The black family: Strengths, self-help, and positive change.* Boulder, CO: Westview/HarperCollins.

Lopez, A. (1996). Creation is ongoing: Developing a relationship with non-English-speaking parents. *Child Care Information Exchange, 107,* 56–62.

Lubeck, S. (1985). *Sandbox society: Early education in Black and White America.* Philadelphia: Falmer.

Lystad, M. (1973). *Halloween parade.* New York: Putnam's.

Maccoby, E. E., & Martin, J. A. (1983). Socialization in the context of the family. Parent-child interaction. In P. H. Mussen (Ed.), *Handbook of child psychology* (4th ed.), E. M. Hetherington (Ed.), *Vol. 4: Socialization, personality, and social development.* New York: Wiley.

Macpherson, E. H. (1962). *A tale of tails.* New York: Golden.

Mager, R. F. (1984). *Preparing instructional objectives* (2nd ed.). Belmont, CA: Pitman Learning.

Mallory, B. L., & New, R. S. (Eds.). (1993). *Diversity & developmentally appropriate practices: Challenges for early childhood education.* New York: Teachers College Press.

Marion, M. (1995). *Guidance of young children* (4th ed.). Upper Saddle River, NJ: Merrill/Prentice Hall.

Maratsos, M. P. (1989). Innateness and plasticity in language acquisition. In M. L. Rice & R. L. Schiefelbusch (Eds.), *The teaching ability of language.* Baltimore, MD: Brookes/Cole.

Mash, E. J., & Barkley, R. Q. (Eds.). (1989). *Treatment of childhood disorders.* New York: Guilford.

Masters, W. H., Johnson, V. E., & Kolodny, R. C. (1994). *Heterosexuality.* New York: HarperCollins.

Mathias, M., & Gulley, B. (Eds.). (1995). *Celebrating family literacy through intergenerational programming.* Wheaton, MD: Association for Childhood Education International.

Maxim, G. W. (1993). *The very young: Guiding children from infancy through the early years* (4th ed.). Upper Saddle River, NJ: Merrill/Prentice Hall.

May, R. (1977). *The meaning of anxiety* (rev. ed.). New York: Norton.

McAfee, O. D. (1981). Planning the preschool program. In M. Kaplan-Sanoff & R. Yablans-Magid (Eds.), *Exploring early childhood: Readings in theory and practice.* New York: Macmillan.

McAfee, O. D. (1985). Circle time: Getting past "Two Little Pumpkins." *Young Children, 40*(6), 24–29.

McAfee, O. & Leong, D. (1994). *Assessing and guiding young children's development and learning.* Boston: Allyn & Bacon.

McClenahan, P., & Jaqua, I. (1976). *Cool cooking for kids: Recipes and nutrition for preschoolers.* Belmont, CA: Fearon Pitman.

McClosky, R. (1948). *Blueberries for Sal.* New York: Viking.

McCollum, J. (1995). Social competence and IEP objectives: Where is the match? *Journal of Early Intervention, 19*(4), 283–285.

McCully, E. A. (1992). *Mirette on the high wire.* New York: Putnam's.

McDermott, G. (1972). *Anansi the spider.* New York: Holt.

McGowan, M., McGowan, T., & Wheeler, P. (1994). *Appreciating diversity through children's literature: Teaching activities for the primary grades.* Englewood, CO: Teacher Ideas/Libraries Unlimited.

McNamme, G. D. (1990). Learning to read and write in an inner-city setting: A longitudinal study of community change. In L. C. Moll (Ed.), *Vygotsky and education: Instructional implications and applications of sociohistorical psychology.* New York: Cambridge University Press.

McNeill, D. (1970). The development of language. In P. H. Mussen (Ed.), *Carmichael's manual of child psychology* (3rd ed., Vol. 1). New York: Wiley.

Meisels, S. J. (1987). Uses and abuses of developmental screening and school readiness testing. In K. M. Paciorek & J. H. Munro (Ed.), *Sources: Notable selections in early childhood education.* Guilford, CT: Dushkin.

Meisels, S. J. (1992). *The work sampling system: An overview.* Ann Arbor: Center for Human Growth and Development, University of Michigan.

Meisels, S. J., & Atkins-Burnett, S. (1994). *Developmental screening in early childhood: A guide.* Washington, DC: National Association for the Education of Young Children.

Meisels, S. J., Liaw, F., Dorfman, A., & Nelson, R. F. (1995). The Work Sampling System: Reliability and validity of a performance assessment for young children. *Early Childhood Research Quarterly*, 10(3), 277–296.

Merahn, S., Shevlov, S., & McCracken, G. H. (1988). Special report: AIDS: What teachers, directors, & parents want to know. *Pre-K today*, 2(6), A1–A7.

Messer, D. J. (1993). *Mastery motivation in early childhood.* London: Routledge.

Mickles, S. J. (1995). Developing young children's classification and logical thinking skills. *Childhood Education*, 72(10), 24–28.

Miles, M. (1971). *Annie and the old one* Boston: Little, Brown.

Milhous, K. (1950). *The egg tree.* New York: Scribner's.

Miller, B. L., & Wilmshurst, A. L. (1984). *Parents and volunteers in the classroom: A handbook for teachers* (2nd ed.). San Francisco: R & E Associates.

Miller, E. (1972). *Mousekin's golden house.* Upper Saddle River, NJ: Prentice Hall.

Miller, K. (1989). *The outside play and learning book: Activities for young children.* Mount Rainier, MD: Gryphon House.

Miller, R. (1996). *The developmentally appropriate inclusive classroom in early education.* New York: Delmar.

Miller, S. A. (1994). *Learning through play: Sand, water, clay & wood.* New York: Scholastic.

Milord, S. (1992). *Hands around the world: 365 creative ways to build cultural awareness & global respect.* Charlotte, VT: Williamson.

Mindes, G., Ireton, H., & Mardell-Czudnowski, C. (1996). *Assessing young children.* Albany, NY: Delmar.

Mitchell, G. (1982). *A very practical guide to discipline with young children.* Marshfield, MA: Telshare.

Mitchell, L. S. (1948). *Here and now story book.* New York: Dutton.

Mize, J. (1995). Coaching preschool children in social skills: A cognitive-social learning curriculum. In G. Cartlegde & J. F. Milburn (Eds.), *Teaching social skills to children and youth* (3rd ed.). Boston: Allyn & Bacon.

Mize, J., & Abell, E. (1996). Encouraging social skills in young children: Tips teachers can share with parents. *Dimensions of Early Childhood*, 24(3), 15–23.

Moglia, R., & Welbourne-Moglia, A., & Haffner, D. W. (1989). *How to talk to your children about AIDS.* New York: SEICUS.

Molitor, F., & Hirsch, K. W. (1994). Children's toleration of real-life aggression after exposure to media violence: A replication of the Drabman and Thomas studies. *Child Study Journal*, 24(3), 191–195.

Moll, L. (ED.). (1990). *Vygotsky and education: Instructional implications and applications of sociohistorical psychology.* New York: Cambridge University Press.

Moller, D. W. (1996). *Confronting death: Values, institutions, and human morality.* Cambridge: Oxford University Press.

Monahon, C. (1993). *Children and trauma: A parent's guide to helping children heal.* New York: Free Press.

Monighan-Nourot, P., Scales, B., Van Hoorn, J., with Almy, M. (1987). *Looking at children's play: A bridge between theory and practice.* New York: Teachers College Press.

Moore, C. C. (1961). *The night before Christmas.* New York: Grosset & Dunlap.

Moore, R. C., Goltsman, S. M., & Iacofano, D. S. (1992). *Play for all guidelines: Planning, design and management of outdoor play settings for all children* (2nd ed.). Berkeley, CA: MIG Communications.

Moore, T. (1991). *My magical world: I am special. Singing, moving and learning.* Charlotte, NC: Thomas Moore Records.

Morrow, A. O., Benton, M., Reves, R. R., & Pickering, L. K. (1991). Knowledge and attitudes of day care center parents and care providers regarding children infected with human immunodeficiency virus. *Pediatrics*, 87(6), 876–883.

Morrow, L. M. (1990). Preparing the classroom environment to promote literacy during play. *Early Childhood Research Quarterly*, 5(4), 537–554.

Morrow, L. M. (1995). Literacy all around. *Scholastic Early Childhood Today*, 9(4), 34–41.

Morse, P. S., & Brand, L. B. (1995). *Young children at home and in school: 212 educational activities for their parents, teachers, and caregivers.* Boston: Allyn & Bacon.

Moyer, J. (Ed.). (1995). *Selecting educational equipment and materials for school and home.* Wheaton, MD: Association for Childhood Education International.

Murphy, L. B. (1987). Further reflections on resilience. In E. J. Anthony & B. J. Cohler (Eds.), *The invulnerable child.* New York: Guilford.

Murphy, L. B., & Moriarty, A. E. (1976). *Vulnerability, coping, and growth from infancy to adolescence.* New Haven, CT: Yale University Press.

Nash, J. M. (February 3, 1997). Fertile minds: Special report. *Time*, 48–56.

National Association for the Education of Young Children. (1988). NAEYC position statement on standardized testing of young children 3 through 8 years of age. *Young Children*, 43(3), 42–47.

National Association for the Education of Young Children. (1990). NAEYC position statement on school readiness. *Young Children*, 46(1), 21–23.

National Association for the Education of Young Children. (1991). *Accreditation criteria and proceedings of the National Academy of Early Childhood Programs.* Washington, DC: Author.

National Association for the Education of Young Children. (1995). *NAEYC position statement: Responding to linguistic and cultural diversity: Recommendations for effective early childhood education.* Washington, DC: Author.

National Association for the Education of Young Children. (1997). NAEYC position statement on the prevention of child abuse in early childhood programs and the responsibilities of early childhood professionals to prevent child abuse. *Young Children*, 52(3), 42–46.

National Association for the Education of Young Children Information Service. (1991). *Facility design for early childhood programs: An NAEYC Resource Guide.* Washington, DC: Author.

National Association for the Education of Young Children and the National Association of Early Childhood Specialists in State Departments of Education. (1991).

Guidelines for appropriate curriculum content and assessment in programs serving children ages 3 through 8. *Young Children, 46*(3), 21–37.

National Guidelines Task Force. (1992). *Guidelines for comprehensive sexuality education.* New York: SIECUS.

National Institute of Neurological Diseases and Stroke. (1969). *Learning to talk: Speech, hearing, and language problems in the pre-school child.* Washington, DC: U.S. Department of Health, Education and Welfare.

National Pediatric HIV Resource Center (in cooperation with the Region II Head Start Resource Center). (1992). *Getting a Head Start on HIV: A resource manual for enhancing services to HIV-affected children in Head Start.* Newark, NJ: Author.

Neill, M., Bursh, P., Schaeffer, B., Thall, C., Yohe, M., & Zappardino, P. (n.d.). *Implementing performance assessments: A guide to classroom, school and system reform.* Cambridge, MA: Fair Test, National Center for Fair & Open Testing.

Neisworth, J. T., & Buggey, T. J. (1993). Behavior analysis and principles in early childhood education. In J. L. Roopnarine & J. E. Johnson (Eds.), *Approaches to early childhood education* (2nd ed.). Upper Saddle River, NJ: Merrill/Prentice Hall.

Nelson, E. (1987). Learned helplessness and children's achievement. In S. Moore & K. Kolb (Eds.), *Reviews of research for practitioners and parents.* Minneapolis: Center for Early Education and Development, University of Minnesota.

Nelson, M., & Clark, K. (Eds.). (1986). *The educator's guide to preventing child sexual abuse.* Santa Cruz, CA: Network.

Nerlove, M. (1989). *Halloween.* Morton Grove, IL: Whitman.

Neugebauer, B. (1988). Raising the issue. *Child Care Information Exchange, 69,* 31.

Neugebauer, B. (Ed.). (1989). *The wonder of it: Exploring how the world works.* Redmond, WA: Exchange.

Neugebauer, B. (1990). Going one step further—No traditional holidays. *Child Care Information Exchange, 74,* 40–44.

Neugebauer, B. (1992). A manner of speaking. *Child Care Information Exchange, 86,* 50.

Newberry, C. T. (1942). *Marshmallow.* New York: Harper.

Newborg, J., Stock, J. R., Winek, L, Guidabaldi, J., & Svinicki, J. (1984). *Battelle Developmental Inventory Screening Test.* Allen, TX: DLM–Teaching Resources.

Nicola-Lisa, W. (1991). *1, 2, 3 Thanksgiving.* Morton Grove, IL: Whitman.

Nieto, S. (1992). *Affirming diversity: The sociopolitical content of multicultural education.* New York: Longman.

Notari-Syverson, A. R., & Shuster, S. L. (1995). Putting real-life skills into IEP/IFSPs for infants and young children. *Teaching Exceptional Children, 27*(2), 29–32.

Nourot, P. M., & Van Hoorn, J. L. (1991). Symbolic play in preschool and primary settings. *Young Children, 46*(6), 40–50.

Nucci, L. (1994). Mothers' beliefs regarding the personal domain of children. *New Directions for Child Development, 66,* 81–97.

Numeroff, L. J. (1985). *If you give a mouse a cookie.* New York: Harper & Row.

Nurss, J. R. (1991). Reading together: Times worth remembering. *Dimensions, 19*(4), 21–23.

Olshansky, B. (1990). *Portfolio of illustrated step-by-step art projects for young children.* West Nyack, NY: Center for Applied Research in Education, Simon & Schuster.

Ortiz, F. I. (1988). Hispanic-American children's experiences in classrooms: A comparison between Hispanic and non-Hispanic children. In L. Weis (Ed.), *Class, race and gender in American education.* Albany: State University of New York Press.

Overby, L. Y. (Ed.). (1991). *Early childhood creative arts: Proceedings of the International Early Childhood Creative Arts Conference.* Reston, VA: American Alliance for Health, Physical Education, Recreation and Dance.

Owens, K. (1995). *Raising your child's inner self-esteem: The authoritative guide from infancy through the teen years.* New York: Plenum.

Owens, R. E. (1992). *Language development: An introduction* (3rd ed.). Upper Saddle River, NJ: Merrill/Prentice Hall.

Oxford Scientific Films. (1980). *The wild rabbit.* New York: Putnam's.

Palmer, H. (n.d.). *Getting to know myself: Learning basic skills through music: The feel of music.* Freeport, NY: Educational Activities.

Palmer, H., & Cheney, M. (1984). *Happy song.* Topanga, CA: Hap-Pal Music.

Papadatou, D., & Papadatos, S. C. (Eds.). (1991). *Children and death.* New York: Hemisphere.

Parham, V. R. (1993). *The African-American child's heritage cookbook.* South Pasadena, CA: Sandcastle.

Parkinson, K. (1986). *The enormous turnip.* Niles, IL: Whitman.

Parsons, V. (1975). *Ring for liberty.* New York: Golden.

Parten, M. B. (1932). Social participation among preschool children. *Journal of Abnormal Psychology, 27,* 243–269.

Parten, M. B. (1996). Social participation among preschool children. In K. M. Paciorek & J. H. Munro (Eds.), *Sources: Notable selections in early childhood education.* Guilford, CT: Dushkin.

Patterson, K., & Wright, A. E. (1990). The speech, language, hearing-impaired child: At risk academically. *Childhood Education, 67*(2), 91–95.

Pease-Alvarez, L., Garcia, E. E., & Espinosa, P. (1991). Effective instruction for language-minority students: An early childhood case study. *Early Childhood Research Quarterly, 6*(3), 347–361.

Pellegrini, A. D. (Ed.). (1995). *The future of play theory: A multidisciplinary inquiry into the contributions of Brian Sutton-Smith.* Albany: State University of New York Press.

Pellegrini, A. D., & Boyd, B. (1993). The role of play in early childhood development and education: Issue in definition and function. In B. Spodek (Ed.), *Handbook of research on the education of young children.* Upper Saddle River, NJ: Prentice Hall.

Pepler, D. J. (1982). Play and divergent thinking. In D. J. Pepler & K. H. Rubin (Eds.), *The play of children: Current theory and research.* Basel, Switzerland: Karger.

Perrone, V. (1991). On standardized testing. *Childhood Education, 67*(3), 132–142.

Peterson, C., Maier, S. F., & Seligman, M. E. P. (1993). *Learned helplessness: A theory for the age of personal control.* New York: Oxford University Press.

Petrakos, H., & Howe, N. (1996). The influence of the physical design of the dramatic play center on children's play. *Early Childhood Research Quarterly, 11*(1), 63–77.

Pflaum, S. W. (1986). *The development of language and literacy in young children* (3rd ed.). Upper Saddle River, NJ: Merrill/Prentice Hall.

Pfluger, L. W., & Zola, J. M. (1972). A room planned by children. In K. R. Baker (Ed.), *Ideas that work with young children.* Washington, DC: National Association for the Education of Young Children.

Piaget, J. (1952). *The child's conception of number.* New York: Humanities Press.

Piaget, J. (1954). *The construction of reality in the child.* New York: Basic Books.

Piaget, J. (1962). *Play, dreams and imitation in childhood.* New York: Norton.

Piaget, J. (1976). Symbolic play. In J. S. Bruner, A. Jolly, & K. Sylva (Eds.), *Play: Its role in development and evolution.* New York: Basic Books.

Piaget, J. (1983). Piaget's theory. In P. H. Mussen (Ed.), *Handbook of child psychology,* W. Kessen (Ed.), *Vol. 1: History, theory, and methods.* New York: Wiley.

Piaget, J., & Inhelder, B. (1969). *The psychology of the child* (trans. Helen Weaver). New York: Basic Books.

Pipes, P. L., & Trahms, C. M. (1993). *Nutrition in infancy and childhood.* St. Louis, MO: Mosby.

Poersch, N., Adams, G., & Sandfort, J. (1994). *Child care and development: Key facts.* Washington, DC: Children's Defense Fund.

Politi, L. (1973). *The nicest gift.* New York: Scribner's.

Potter, B. (1903). *The tale of Peter Rabbit.* New York: Warne.

Potter, M. C. (1938). *Sleepy kitten.* New York: Dutton.

Potter, M. C. (1955). *The golden book of little verses.* New York: Simon & Schuster.

Powell, D. (1990). Home visiting in the early years: Policy and program design decisions. *Young Children, 45*(6), 65–69.

Powell, D. R. (1989). *Families and early childhood programs.* Washington, DC: National Association for the Education of Young Children.

Pozen, A. S. (1995). HIV/AIDS in the schools. In A. Boyd-Franklin, G. L. Steiner, & M. G. Boland (Eds.), *Children, families, and HIV/AIDS: Psychosocial and therapeutic issues.* New York: Guilford.

Pratt, C. (1948). *I learn from children: An adventure in progressive education.* New York: Simon & Schuster.

Prelutsky, J. (1982). *That's Thanksgiving.* New York: Greenwillow.

Prelutsky, C. (Ed.). (1986). *Read aloud rhymes for the very young.* New York: Knopf.

Prescott, E., Jones, E., & Kritchevsky, S. (1972). *Environmental Inventory.* Pasadena, CA: Pacific Oaks.

Pressma, D., & Emery, L. J. (1991). *Serving children with HIV infection in child day care.* Washington, DC: Child Welfare League of America.

Pristine, J. S. (1993). *Helping children cope with death: A practical resource guide for "Someone Special Died."* Carthage, IL: Fearon Teacher Aids.

Provenzo, E. F., Jr., & Brett, A. (1983). *The complete block book.* Syracuse, NY: Syracuse University Press.

Quackenbush, M., & Villarreal, S. (1988). *Does AIDS hurt? Educating young children about AIDS.* Santa Cruz, CA: Network.

Quintero, E., & Velarde, M. C. (1990). Intergenerational literacy: A developmental bilingual approach. *Young Children, 45*(4), 10–15.

Rab, V. Y., & Wood, K. I. (1995). *Child care and the ADA.* Baltimore, MD: Brookes.

Raffi. (1987). *Down by the bay.* New York: Crown.

Raines, B. (1991). *Creating sex-fair family day care: A guide for trainers.* Philadelphia: CHOICE, Office of Research and Improvement, U.S. Department of Education; Newton, MA: WEEA Publishing Center.

Raines, S. C., & Canady, R. J. (1989). *Story s-t-r-e-t-c-h-e-r-s: Activities to expand children's favorite books.* Mount Rainier, MD: Gryphon House.

Raines, S. C., & Canaday, R. J. (1991). *More story s-t-r-e-t-c-h-e-r-s: Activities to expand children's favorite books.* Mount Rainier, MD: Gryphon House.

Ramsey, P. (1986). Racial and cultural categories. In C. P. Edwards & P. G. Ramsey (Eds.), *Promoting social and moral development in young children: Creative approaches for the classroom.* New York: Teachers College Press.

Ramsey, P. (1991). *Making friends in school.* New York: Teachers College Press.

Ramsey, P. (1995). Research in review: Growing up with the contradictions of race and class. *Young Children, 50*(6), 18–22.

Rasmussen, M. (1979). *Listen! The children speak.* Washington, DC: Organization Mondiale pour l'Education Préscolaire, U.S. National Committee, Region 3.

Read, K. H. (1996). Initial support through guides to speech and action. In K. M. Paciorek & J. H. Munro (Eds), *Sources: Notable selections in early childhood education.* Guilford, CT: Dushkin.

Readdick, C. A., & Bartlett, P. M. (1995). Vertical learning environments. *Childhood Education, 71*(2), 86–90.

Rechild: The Reggio children newsletter. Reggio Emilia, Italy: Reggio Children.

Redleaf, R. (1983). *Open the door: Let's explore: Neighborhood field trips for young children.* Mount Rainier, MD: Gryphon House.

Redleaf, R. (1993). *Busy fingers, growing minds: Fingerplays, verses, and activities for whole language learning.* St. Paul, MN: Redleaf.

Rescorla, L., Hyson, M. D., & Hirsh-Pasek, K. (Eds.). (1991). Academic instruction in early childhood: Challenge or pressure? *New Directions for Child Development,* 53 (entire issue).

Rey, H. A. (1941). *Curious George*. Boston: Houghton Mifflin.

Rey, H. A., & Rey, M. (1966). *Curious George goes to the hospital*. Boston: Houghton Mifflin.

Rice, J. A. *The kindness curriculum: Introducing young children to loving values*. St. Paul, MN: Redleaf.

Rice, M. L., & Wilcox, K. A. (Eds.). (1995). *Building a language-focused curriculum for the preschool classroom. Vol. 1: A foundation for lifelong communication*. Baltimore, MD: Brookes.

Rinaldi, C. (1993). The emergent curriculum and social constructivism. In C. Edwards, L. Gandini, & G. Forman (Eds.), *The hundred languages of children: The Reggio Emilia Approach to early childhood education*. Norwood, NJ: Ablex.

Rinaldi, C. (1994, May). *The philosophy of Reggio Emilia*. Paper presented at the Study Seminar on the Experience of the Municipal Infant-Toddler Centers and Pre-Primary Schools of Reggio Emilia, Reggio Emilia, Italy.

Rivkin, M. W. (1995). *The great outdoors: Restoring children's right to play outside*. Washington, DC: National Association for the Education of Young Children.

Roberts, E. M. (1922). The rabbit. In *Under the tree*. New York: Viking.

Rockwell, A. (1985). *First comes spring*. New York: Crowell.

Rockwell, A., and Rockwell, H. (1971). *Molly's woodland garden*. Garden City, NY: Doubleday.

Rockwell, R. E., Williams, R. T., & Sherwood, E. A. (1992). *Everybody has a body: Science from head to toe: Activities book for teachers of children ages 3–6*. Mount Rainier, MD: Gryphon House.

Rodriguez, J. L., Diaz, R. M., & Duran, D., & Espinosa, L. (1995). The impact of bilingual preschool education on the language development of Spanish-speaking children. *Early Childhood Research Quarterly, 10*(4), 475–490.

Rogers, J. (1985). *King Island Christmas*. New York: Greenwillow.

Rojankovsky, F. (1982). *The great big animal book*. New York: Golden.

Roopnarine, J. L., Bright, J. A., & Riegraf, N. B. (1994). Family dynamics and day care children's peer group participation. In H. Goelman and E. V. Jacobs (Eds.), *Children's play in child care settings*. Albany: State University of New York Press.

Roopnarine, J. L., & Johnson, J. E. (1993). *Approaches to early childhood education* (2nd ed.). Upper Saddle River, NJ: Merrill/Prentice Hall.

Roopnarine, J. L., Johnson, J. E., & Hooper, F. H. (Eds.). (1994). *Children's play in diverse cultures*. Albany: State University of New York Press.

Rothman, R. (1990). Survey reveals wide latitude in reporting abuse. *Education Week, 9*(23), 28.

Rowe, M. B. (1974). Wait time and reward. Pt. 1: Wait time. *Journal of Research on Science Teaching, 11*, 81–94.

Rubin, K. H. (1977). The play behaviors of young children. *Young Children, 32*(6), 16–24.

Rubin, K. H. (1982). Early play theories revisited: Contributions to contemporary research and theory. In D. J. Pepler & K. H. Rubin (Eds.), *The play of children: Current theory and research*. Basel, Switzerland: Karger.

Rubin, K. H., & Asendorpf, J. B. (1993). *Social withdrawal, inhibition and shyness in childhood*. Hillsdale, NJ: Erlbaum.

Rubin, K. H., & Howe, N. (1986). Social play and perspective taking. In G. Fein & M. Rivkin (Eds.), *The young child at play: Reviews of research* (Vol. 4). Washington, DC: National Association for the Education of Young Children.

Runco, M. (Ed.). Creativity from childhood to adulthood: The developmental issues. *New Directions for Child Development, 72*, 1–95.

Russ, S. S. (1996). Development of creative processes in children. In M. Runco (Ed.), Creativity from childhood to adulthood: The developmental issues. *New Directions for Child Development, 72*, 31–42.

Sadker, M., & Sadker, D. (1994). *Failing at fairness: How our schools cheat girls*. New York: Simon & Schuster.

Saiffer, S. (1990). *Practical solutions to practically every problem: The early childhood teacher's manual*. St. Paul, MN: Toys 'n Things Press.

Sallis, J. F., Patterson, R. L., McKenzie, T. L., & Nader, P. R. (1988). Family variables and physical activity in preschool children. *Journal of Developmental and Behavioral Pediatrics, 9*(2), 57–61.

Saltz, R. (1997). The Reggio Emilia influence at the University of Michigan-Dearborn Child Development Center: Challenges and change. In J. Hendrick (Ed.), *First steps toward teaching the Reggio Way*. Upper Saddle River, NJ: Merrill/Prentice Hall.

Samalin, N. (1991). *Love and anger: The parental dilemma*. New York: Viking.

Samalin, N., & Jablow, M. M. (1989). *Loving your child is not enough*. New York: Viking.

Santos, de Barona, M., & Barona, A. (1991). The assessment of culturally and linguistically difference preschoolers. *Early Childhood Research Quarterly, 6*(3), 363–376.

Satter, E. (1987). *How to get your kid to eat . . . but not too much*. Palo Alto, CA: Bull.

Schaefer, D. J. (1988). Communication among children, parents, and funeral directors. In H. M. Dick, E. P. Roye, P. R. Buschman, A. H. Kutscher, B. Rubinstein, & F. K. Forstenzer (Eds.), *Dying and disabled children: Dealing with loss and grief*. New York: Haworth.

Schaefer, D. J. (1987). The status of parent-child communication on death and early-stage grief and loss. In J. E. Schowalter, P. Buschman, P. R. Patterson, A. H. Kutscher, M. Tallmer, & R. G. Stevenson (Eds.), *Children and death: Perspectives from birth through adolescence*. New York: Praeger.

Schickedanz, J. A. (1994). Helping children develop self-control. *Childhood Education, 70*(5), 274–275.

Schickedanz, J. A., Chay, S., Gopin, P., Sheng, L. L., Song, S. M., & Wild, N. (1990). Preschoolers and academics: Some thoughts. *Young Children, 46*(1), 4–13.

Schirrmacher, R. (1997). *Art and creative development for young children* (3rd ed.). Albany, NY: Delmar.

Schwartzman, H. B. (1978). *Transformations: The anthropology of children's play.* New York: Plenum.

Schweninger, A. (1976). *The hunt for Rabbit's galosh.* New York: Doubleday.

Schweninger, A. (1984). *Halloween surprises.* New York: Viking Kestrel.

Schweinhart, L. J., Barnes, H. V., & Weikart, D. P. (1993). *Significant benefits: The High/Scope Perry Preschool Study through age 27.* Ypsilanti, MI: High/Scope.

Scuola, Diana. (1991). *Scarpa e metro: I bambini e la misura.* Reggio Emilia, Italy: Author.

Seefeldt, C. (1973). *A curriculum for child care centers.* Upper Saddle River, NJ: Merrill/Prentice Hall.

Seefeldt, C. (1995). Art—A serious work. *Young Children, 50*(3), 39–45.

Seefeldt, C., & Barbour N. (1994). *Early childhood education: An introduction* (3rd ed.). Upper Saddle River, NJ: Merrill/Prentice Hall.

Seefeldt, C., & Warman, B. (1990). *Young and old together.* Washington, DC: National Association for the Education of Young Children.

Seeger, R. C. (1980). *American folk songs for children.* Garden City, NY: Doubleday.

Selman, R. L. (1971). Taking another perspective: Role-taking development in early childhood. *Child Development, 42,* 1721–1734.

Selsam, M. (1965). *Let's get turtles.* New York: Harper & Row.

Sendak, M. (1963). *Where the wild things are.* New York: Harper & Row.

Serbin, L. A. (1980). Play activities and the development of visual-spatial skills. *Equal Play,* Fall, 6–9.

Serbin, L. A., O'Leary, K. D., Kent, R. N., & Tonick, E. J. (1973). A comparison of teacher response to preacademic and problem behavior of boys and girls. *Child Development, 22,* 796–804.

Sharmat, M. (1980). *Gregory the terrible eater.* New York: Four Winds.

Shearer, D. E. (1993). The Portage Project: An international home approach to early intervention of young children and their families. In J. L. Roopnarine & J. E. Johnson (Eds.), *Approaches to early childhood education* (2nd ed.). Upper Saddle River, NJ: Merrill/Prentice Hall.

Shefatya, L. (1990). Socioeconomic status and ethnic differences in sociodramatic play: Theoretical and practical implications. In E. L. Klugman & S. Smilansky (Eds.), *Children's play and learning: Perspectives and policy implications.* New York: Teachers College.

Sheridan, M. K., Foley, G. M., & Radlinkski, S. H. (1995). *Using the Supportive Play Model: Individualized intervention in early childhood practice.* New York: Teachers College Press.

Shiman, S. (1976). *A special birthday.* New York: McGraw-Hill.

Shure, M. B. (1994). *Raising a thinking child: Helping your young child to resolve everyday conflicts and get along with others.* New York: Holt.

Siegler, R. S. (1991). *Children's thinking* (2nd ed.). Upper Saddle River, NJ: Prentice Hall.

Sigel, I. W., & Cocking, R. R. (1977). *Cognitive development from childhood to adolescence: A constructivist perspective.* New York: Holt, Rinehart & Winston.

Sigel, I. E., & Saunders, R. (1979). An inquiry into inquiry: Question asking as an instructional model. In L. G. Katz (Ed.), *Current topics in early childhood education* (Vol. II). Norwood, NJ: Ablex.

Skeen, P., Garner, A. P., & Cartwright, S. (1984). *Woodworking for young children.* Washington, DC: National Association for the Education of Young Children.

Skeen, P., & Hodson, D. (1987). AIDS: What adults should know about AIDS (and shouldn't discuss with very young children). *Young Children, 42*(4), 63–71.

Skinner, B. F. (1954). The science of living and the art of teaching. *Harvard Educational Review, 24,* 86–97.

Skinner, B. F. (1957). *Verbal behavior.* New York: Appleton-Century Crofts.

Skinner, B. F. (1974). *About behaviorism.* New York: Knopf.

Slavin, R. E., Karweitz, N. L., & Wasik, B. A. (Eds.). (1994). *Preventing early school failure: Research, policy, and practice.* Boston: Allyn & Bacon.

Smilansky, S. (1968). *The effects of sociodramatic play on disadvantaged children.* New York: Wiley.

Smilansky, S. (1991). Foreword: A conversation with Sara Smilansky about the value of dramatic play. In N. J. Hereford & J. Schall (Eds.), *Learning through play: A practical guide for teaching young children.* New York: Scholastic.

Smilansky, S., & Shefatya, L. (1990). *Facilitating play: A medium for promoting cognitive, socioemotional and academic development in young children.* Gaithersburg, MD: Psychosocial & Educational Smith.

Smith, C. (1993). *The peaceful classroom: 162 easy activities to teach preschoolers compassion and cooperation.* Beltsville, MD: Gryphon House.

Smith, M. S., & Bissell, J. S. (1970). Report analysis: The impact of Head Start. *Harvard Educational Review, 14,* 51–104.

Smith, N. R., Fucigna, C., Kennedy, M., & Lord, L. (1993). *Teaching children to paint* (2nd ed.). New York: Teachers College Press.

Smith, P. K., & Connolly, K. J. (1980). *The ecology of preschool behavior.* Cambridge: Cambridge University Press.

Smith, S. L., Fairchild, M., & Groginsky, S. (1995). *Early childhood care and education: An investment that works.* Washington, DC: National Conference of State Legislatures.

Smitherman, G. (1994). *Black talk: Words and phrases from the hood to the amen corner.* Boston: Houghton Mifflin.

Snyder, M., Snyder, R., & Snyder, R., Jr. (1980). *The young child as a person.* New York: HarperCollins.

Solter, A. (1992). Understanding tears and tantrums. *Young Children, 47*(4), 64–68.

Sorti, C. (1989). *The art of crossing cultures*. Yarmouth, ME: Intercultural Press.

Soto, L. D. (1991). Research in review: Understanding bilingual/bicultural young children. *Young Children, 46*(2), 30–36.

Southern Association for Children under Six. (1990). *Developmentally appropriate assessment: A position statement*. Little Rock, AR: Author.

Southern Regional Education Board. (1994). *Getting schools ready for children: The other side of the readiness goal*. Atlanta: Author.

Spier, P. (1983). *Christmas!* New York: Doubleday.

Spinelli, E. (1982). *Thanksgiving at the Tappleton's*. Reading, MA: Addison-Wesley.

Spodek, B., & Saracho, O. N. (1994). *Dealing with individual differences in the early childhood classroom*. New York: Longman.

Sprang, G., & McNeil, J. (1995). *The many faces of bereavement: The nature and treatment of natural, traumatic, and stigmatized grief*. New York: Brunner/Mazel.

Sprung, B. (1975). *Non-sexist education for young children: A practical guide*. New York: Citation.

Sprung, B. (1996). Physics is fun, physics is important, and physics belongs in the early childhood curriculum. *Young Children, 51*(5), 29–33.

Stangl, J. (1975). *Fingerpainting is fun*. Camarillo, CA: Educational Techniques.

Starko, A. J. (1995). *Creativity in the classroom: Schools of curious delight*. New York: Longman.

Steffe, L. P., Gale, J. (Eds.). (1995). *Constructivism in education: Concerns about Vygotsky's theories*. Hillsdale, NJ: Erlbaum.

Stein, S. B. (1974). *A hospital story: An open book for parents and children together*. New York: Walker.

Stephens, K. (1993). Making the most of outdoor play: A bounty of ideas to motivate the hesitant teacher. *Child Care Information Exchange, 91*, 49–54.

Stephens, K. (1988). The First National Study of Sexual Abuse in Child Care: Findings and recommendations. *Child Care Information Exchange, 60*, 9–12.

Stevens, J. (1995). *Tops and bottoms*. New York: Harcourt Brace.

Stewig, J. W., & Jett-Simpson, M. (1995). *Language arts in the early childhood classroom*. Belmont, CA: Wadsworth.

Stinson, S. (1988). *Dance for young children: Finding the magic in movement*. Reston, VA: American Alliance for Health, Physical Education, Recreation, and Dance.

Stinson, W. J. (Ed.). (1990). *Moving and learning for the young child*. Reston, VA: American Alliance for Health, Physical Education, Recreation and Dance.

Stock, C. (1984). *Sampson, the Christmas cat*. New York: Putnam's.

Stock, C. (1990). *Thanksgiving treat*. New York: Bradbury.

Stone, S. J. (1995). Wanted: Advocates for play in the primary grades. *Young Children, 50*(6), 45–54.

Stonehouse, A. (1995). What's love got to do with it? *Child Care Information Exchange, 102*, 18–21.

Stott, J. C. (1995). *Native Americans in children's literature*. Phoenix: Oryx.

Strickland, D. S., & Morrow, L. M. (1989). *Emerging literacy: Young children learn to read and write*. Newark, DE: International Reading Association.

Sullivan, H. S. (1940). *Conceptions of modern psychiatry: The first William Alanson White Memorial Lectures*. Washington, DC: William Alanson White Psychiatric Foundation.

Sullivan, M. (1982). *Feeling strong, feeling free: Movement exploration for young children*. Washington, DC: National Association for the Education of Young Children.

Sutherland, M. (1994). Group meeting time: Making it work for everyone. *Scholastic Early Childhood Today, 8*(6), 28–35.

Sutton-Smith, B. (1987, December 9). Commentary: The domestication of early childhood play. *Education Week*, p. 28.

Swadener, B. B., & Lubeck, S. (Eds.). (1995). *Children and families "at promise": Deconstructing the discourse of risk*. Albany: State University of New York Press.

Swick, K. J. (1989). Understanding and relating to transformed (blended) families. *Dimensions, 17*(4), 8–11.

Swick, K. J. (1991). *Teacher-parent partnerships to enhance school success in early childhood education*. Washington, DC: National Education Association.

Swick, K. J. (1992). *An early childhood school-home learning design: Strategies and resources*. Champaign, IL: Stipes.

Sylva, K., Bruner, J. S., & Genova, P. (1976). The role of play in the problem-solving of children 3–5 years old. In J. S. Bruner, A. Jolly, & K. Sylva (Eds.), *Play—Its role in development and evolution*. New York: Basic Books.

Tarini, E. (1997). Reflections on a year in Reggio Emilia: Key concepts in rethinking and learning the Reggio Way. In J. Hendrick (Ed.), *First steps toward teaching the Reggio Way*. Upper Saddle River, NJ: Merrill/Prentice hall.

Taylor, B. J. (1995). *A child goes forth: A curriculum guide for preschool children* (8th ed.). Upper Saddle River, NJ: Merrill/Prentice Hall.

Taylor, S. I., & Morris, V. G. (1996). Outdoor play in early childhood settings: Is it safe and healthy for children? *Early Childhood Education Journal, 23*(3), 153–158.

Teale, W. H., & Sulzby, E. (1996). Emergent literacy: New perspectives. In R. D. Robinson, M. C. McKenna, & J. M. Wedman (Eds.), *Issues and trends in literacy education*. Boston: Allyn & Bacon.

Teets, S. T. (1985). Modification of play behaviors of preschool children through manipulation of environmental variables. In J. L. Frost & S. Sunderlin (Eds.), *When children play: Proceedings of the International Conference on Play and Play Environments*. Wheaton, MD: Association for Childhood Education International.

Tegano, D. W., & Burdette, M. P. (1991). Length of play periods and play behaviors of preschool children. *Journal of Research in Childhood Education, 5*(2).

Tegano, D. W., Moran, J. C., DeLong, A. J., Brickey, J., & Ramassini, K. K. Designing classroom spaces: Making the most of time. *Early Childhood Education Journal, 23*(3), 135–141.

Thelen, E., Ulrich, D., & Jensen, J. (1989). The developmental origins of locomotion. In M. Woolacott & A. Shumway-Cook (Eds.), *A development of posture and gait: Across the lifespan.* Columbia: University of South Carolina Press.

Thomas, R. M. (1992). *Comparing theories of child development* (3rd ed.). Belmont, CA: Wadsworth.

Thompson, C. M. (1995a). Transforming curriculum in the visual arts. In S. Bredekamp, & R. Rosegrant (Eds.), *Reaching potentials: Transforming early childhood curriculum and assessment* (Vol. 2). Washington, DC: National Association for the Education of Young Children.

Thompson, C. M. (Ed.). (1995b). *The visual arts and early childhood learning.* Reston, VA: National Art Education Association.

Tobias, E. (1994). The play behaviors of special needs children in integrated and non-integrated child-care settings. In H. Goelman & E. V. Jacobs (Eds.), *Children's play in child care settings.* Albany: State University of New York Press.

Topal, C. W. (1996). Fostering experiences between young children and clay. *Child Care Information Exchange, 108,* 51–55.

Trawick-Smith, J. (1988). "Let's say you're the baby, OK?": Play leadership and following behavior of young children. *Young Children, 43*(5), 51–59.

Trelease, J. (1989). *The new read-aloud handbook.* New York: Penguin Books.

Tresselt, A. (1967). *The world in the candy egg.* New York: Lothrop, Lee & Shepard.

Trostle, S. L. (1988). The effects of child-centered group play sessions on social-emotional growth of three- to six-year-old bilingual Puerto Rican children. *Journal of Research in Childhood Education, 3*(2), 93–106.

Tyler, R. W. (1950). *Basic principles of curriculum and instruction.* Chicago: University of Chicago Press.

Uchida, Y. (1975). *The birthday visitor.* New York: Scribner's.

UNICEF. (1993). *Child malnutrition: Progress toward the world summit for children goal.* New York: UNICEF, Statistics and Monitoring Section.

Villarruel, F. A., Imig, D. R., & Kostelnik, M. J. (1995). Diverse families. In E. E. Garcia & B. McLaughlin (Eds.), *Meeting the challenge of linguistic and cultural diversity in early childhood education.* New York: Teachers College Press.

Viorst, J. (1972). *The 10th good thing about Barney.* New York: Atheneum.

Vygotsky, L. (1966). *Thought and language.* Cambridge, MA: MIT Press.

Vygotsky, L. (1978). *Mind in society: The development of higher psychological processes.* Cambridge, MA: Harvard University Press.

Wadsworth, B. J. (1989). *Piaget's theory of cognitive and affective development* (4th ed.). New York: Longman.

Wallinga, C., & Skeen, P. (1996). Siblings of hospitalized and ill children: The teacher's role in helping these forgotten family members. *Young Children, 51*(6), 78–83.

Wang, M. C., & Gordon, E. W. (1994). *Educational resilience in inner-city America: Challenges and prospects.* Hillsdale, NJ: Erlbaum.

Ward, C. D. (1996). Adult intervention: Appropriate strategies for enriching the quality of children's play. *Young Children, 51*(3), 20–25.

Wardle, F. (1990). Bunny ears and cupcakes for all—Are parties developmentally appropriate? *Child Care Information Exchange, 74,* 39–41.

Warren, J., & McKinnon, E. (1988). *Small world celebrations: Around-the-world holidays to celebrate with young children.* Everett, WA: Warren.

Wasik, B. H., Bryant, D. M., & Lyons, C. M. (1990). *Home visiting: Procedures for helping families.* Newbury Park, CA: Sage.

Wasserman, S. (1990). *Serious players in the primary classroom: Empowering the young child through active learning experiences.* New York: Teachers College Press.

Wassom, J. (1995). Turning bad press into prestige. *Child Care Information Exchange, 101,* 69–72.

Webb, N. B. (Ed.). (1993). *Helping bereaved children: A handbook for practitioners.* New York: Guilford.

Weber, S., & Mitchell, C. (1995). *That's funny, you don't look like a teacher.* London: Falmer.

Weikart, P. (1987). *Round the circle: Key experiences in movement for children ages 3 to 5.* Ypsilanti, MI: High/Scope Press.

Weikart, P. (1988). *Movement plus rhymes, songs and singing games: Activities for children ages 3 to 7.* Ypsilanti, MI: High/Scope Press.

Weill, J. L. (1992). *Early deprivation of empathic care.* Madison, CT: International Universities Press.

Weinstein, C., & David, T. (1987). *Spaces for children: The built environment and children's development.* New York: Plenum.

Weissbourd, R. (1996). *The vulnerable child: What really hurts America's children and what we can do about it.* Reading, MA: Addison-Wesley.

Wellesley College Center for Research on Women. (1992). *How schools shortchange girls—The AAUW report: A study of major findings on girls and education.* New York: Marlowe.

Wellhousen, K. (1993). Children from nontraditional families: A lesson in acceptance. *Childhood Education, 69*(5), 281–288.

Wellhousen, K. (1996a). Do's and don't's for eliminating hidden bias. *Childhood Education, 73*(1), 36–39.

Wellhousen, K. (1996b). Girls can be bull riders, too! Supporting children's understanding of gender roles through children's literature. *Young Children, 51*(5), 79–83.

Wenar, C. (1990). *Developmental psychopathology: From infancy to adolescence* (2nd ed.). New York: McGraw-Hill.

Werner, P., Timms, S., & Almond, L. (1996). Health stops: Practical ideas for health-related exercise in preschool and primary classrooms. *Young Children, 51*(6), 48–55.

Werner, R. H., & Simmons, R. Q. (1990). *Homemade play equipment.* Reston, VA: American Alliance for Health, Physical Education, Recreation, and Dance.

Wesson, C. L., & King, R. P. (1996). Portfolio assessment and special education students. *Teaching Exceptional Children, 28*(2), 44–48.

Westmoreland, P. (1996). Coping with death: Helping students grieve. *Childhood Education*, 72(3), 157–160.

White, E. B. (1958). *Charlotte's web*. New York: Harper & Row.

White, R. W. (1968). Motivation reconsidered: The concept of competence. In M. Almy (Ed.), *Early childhood play: Selected readings related to cognition and motivation*. New York: Simon & Schuster.

Whitehurst, G. J., & Valdez-Menchaca, M. C. (1988). What is the role of reinforcement in early language acquisition? *Child Development*, 59, 430–440.

Wien, C. A. (1995). *Developmentally appropriate practice in "real life": Stories of teacher practical knowledge*. New York: Teachers College Press.

Wildsmith, B. (1985). *Give a dog a bone*. New York: Pantheon.

Williams, D. C., & Kantor, R. (1997). The challenge of Reggio Emilia's research: One teacher's reflections. In J. Hendrick (Ed.), *First steps toward teaching the Reggio Way*. Upper Saddle River, NJ: Merrill/Prentice Hall.

Williams, R. A., Rockwell, R. E., & Sherwood, E. A. (1987). *Mudpies to magnets: A preschool science curriculum*. Mount Rainier, MD: Gryphon House.

Williams, S. R. (1990). *Essentials of nutrition and diet therapy* (5th ed.). St. Louis, MO: Mosby.

Willard, N. (1993). *A starlit somersault downhill*. Boston: Little, Brown.

Wilmes, L. M., & Wilmes, D. (1982). *The circle time book*. Elgin, IL: Building Blocks.

Wilmes, L. M. & Wilmes, D. (1986). *Exploring art*. Elgin, IL: Building Blocks.

Wilson, M. (1989). *The good-for-your-health all-Asian cookbook*. Washington, DC: Center Science in the Public Interest.

Wilson, M. N. (Ed.). (1995). African American family life: Its structural and ecological aspects. *New Directions for Child Development*, 68 (entire issue).

Wilson, R. A. (1995). Nature and young children: A natural connection. *Young Children*, 50(6), 4–11.

Wilson, R. A., Kilmer, S., & Knauerhase, V. (1996). Developing an environmental outdoor play space. *Young Children*, 51(6), 56–61.

Wilson, R. B. (1983). *Merry Christmas: Children at Christmastime around the world*. New York: Philomel.

Wilt, J. V. (1996). Beyond stickers & popcorn parties. *Dimensions of Early Childhood*, 24(1), 17–20.

Wing, L. A. (1995). Play is *not* the work of the child: Young children's perceptions of work and play. *Early Childhood Research Quarterly*, 10(2), 223–247.

Winter, S. M. (1995). *Outdoor play and learning for infants and toddlers*. Little Rock, AR: Southern Early Childhood Association.

Wittmer, D. S., & Honig, A. S. (1996). Encouraging positive social development in young children. In K. M. Paciorek & J. H. Munro (Eds.), *Early childhood education 96/97*. Guilford, CT: Dushkin.

Woodard, C., & Davitt, R. (1987). *Physical science in early childhood*. Springfield, IL: Thomas.

Wolery, M., & Wilbers, J. S. (Eds.) (1994). *Including children with special needs in early childhood programs*. Washington, DC: National Association for the Education of Young Children.

Wolf, D. P. (Ed.). (1986). *Connecting: Friendship in the lives of young children and their teachers*. Redmond, WA: Exchange.

Wolf, J. (1994). Singing with children is a cinch. *Young Children*, 49(4), 20–25.

Wong, Fillmore, L. (1991). When learning a second language means losing the first. *Early Childhood Research Quarterly*, 6(3), 323–346.

Workman, S., & Anziano, M. C. (1996). Curriculum webs: Weaving connections from children to teachers. In K. M. Paciorek & J. H. Munro (Eds.), *Early Childhood Education 96/97*. Sluice Dock, CT: Dushkin.

Wortham, S. 1995. *Tests and measurement in early childhood education* (2nd ed.). Upper Saddle River, NJ: Merrill/Prentice Hall.

Woteki, C. E., & Filer, L. J. (1995). Dietary issues and nutritional status of American children. In L. W. Cheung & J. B. Richmond (Eds.), *Child health, nutrition, and physical activity*. Champaign, IL: Human Kinetics.

Yarrow, M. R., Scott, P., & Waxler, C. Z. (1973). Learning concern for others. *Developmental Psychology*, 8, 240–260.

Yolen, J. (1987). *Owl moon*. New York: Philomel.

York, S. (1991). *Roots and wings: Affirming culture in early childhood programs*. St. Paul, MN: Redleaf.

Young Children. (1996). TV-turnoff Week—April 24–30, 1996. *Young Children*, 51(3), 25.

Zanger, V. V. (1991). Social and cultural dimensions of the education of language minority students. In A. N. Ambert (Ed.), *Bilingual education and English as a second language: A research handbook*, 1988–1990. New York: Garland.

Zeanah, C. (Ed.). (1993). *Handbook of infant mental health*. New York: Guilford.

Zimmerman, H. W. (1990). *Zero is not enough*. Oxford: Oxford University Press.

Zion, G. (1958). *No roses for Harry*. New York: Harper & Row.

Zolotow, C. (1957). *Over and over*. New York: Harper & Row.

Zolotow, C. (1962). *Mr. Rabbit and the lovely present*. New York: Harper & Row.

Zuckerman, M. P. (1992). Editorial: George Bush: Evening in America. *U.S. News & World Report*, 113(10), 88.

Zukowski, G., & Dickson, A. (1990). *On the move: A handbook for exploring creative movement with young children*. Carbondale: Southern Illinois University Press.

Author Index

Subject Index

Acknowledgements for
Chapter Opening Quotes

Chapter 1

From A. Stonehouse (1995), What's love got to do with it? *Child Care Information Exchange*, 102, p. 20.

Chapter 2

From P. Anastas, *Glooskaps' children* (Boston: Beacon Press, 1973), pp. 14-15. Copyright © 1973 by Peter Anastas. Reprinted by permission of Beacon Press.

Chapter 3

From P. Monighan-Nourot, B. Scales, J. Van Hoorn, with M. Almy (1987), *Looking at children's play: A bridge between theory and practice.* (New York: Teachers College Press), p. 9.

From L. Vygotsky, *Thought and language.* (1962). (Cambridge, MA: MIT Press), p. 16. Used by permission.

Chapter 4

From O. McAfee, Planning the preschool program. In M. Kaplan-Sanoff & R. Yablans-Magrid (Eds), *Exploring early childhood: Readings in theory and practice* (New York: Macmillan, 1981).

From C. Breig-Allen (1997), Implementing the process of change in a public school setting. In J. B. Hendrick (Ed.), *First steps toward teaching the Reggio way.* (Upper Saddle River, NJ: Merrill/Prentice Hall), p. 128.

From Y. Berra, as quoted in M. Zuckerman, 1992, Editorial: George Bush: Evening in America, U.S. *News & World Report*, 113(10), p. 88.

Chapter 5

From K. Haigh (1997), How the Reggio approach has influenced an inner-city program. In J. B. Hendrick (Ed.), *First steps toward teaching the Reggio way*. (Upper Saddle River, NJ: Merrill/Prentice Hall), p. 161.

Chapter 6

From "Animal School" (anonymous).

Chapter 7

From K. Haigh (1997), How the Reggio approach has influenced an inner-city program. In J. B. Hendrick (Ed.), *First steps toward teaching the Reggio way*. (Upper Saddle River, NJ: Merrill/Prentice Hall), p. 164.

Chapter 8

To be sung to the tune "Short'nin Bread." From "Happy Song" by H. Palmer and M. Cheney (Topanga, CA: Hap-Pal Music, 1984). Reprinted by permission.

Chapter 9

From L. Eyre and R. Eyre, *Teaching children joy* (New York: Ballantine Books, 1984), p. 26. Used by permission.

Chapter 10

From R. Snyder, M. Snyder, & R. Snyder, Jr., *The young child as a person* (New York: Human Sciences, 1989), pp. 33–34. Used by permission.

Chapter 11

From S. Kessler (1991), The teaching presence, *Holistic Education Review*, 4(4), p. 6.

From J. Elicker & C. Fortner-Wood (1995), Adult-child relationships in early childhood programs, *Young Children*, 51(1), p. 76.

Chapter 12

From K. Owens (1995), *Raising your child's self-esteem: The authoritative guide from infancy through the teen years.* (New York: Plenum Press), p. 194.

From J. A. Rice (1995), *The kindness curriculum: Introducing young children to loving values.* (St. Paul, MN: Redleaf Press), p. 1.

Chapter 13

From B. Bowman (1995), *Scholastic Early Childhood Today*, 10(3), p. 40.

From B. Neugebauer (1992), A manner of speaking, *Child Care Information Exchange*, 86, p. 50.

Chapter 14

From J. Coe (1987), Children come first, *Childhood Education*, 64(2), p. 73.

Chapter 15

From L. S. Mitchell (1948), *The here and now story book* (New York: Dutton; republished by Fields, Spangler & Lee, 1991).

Chapter 16

From E. F. Griffin (1982). *Island of childhood: Education in the special world of nursery school* (New York: Teachers College Press).

Chapter 17

From E. Jones and J. Nimmo (1994), *Emergent curriculum* (Washington, DC: National Association for the Education of Young Children), p. 77.

Chapter 18

From S. Bredekamp & C. Copple (Eds). (1997), *Developmentally appropriate practice in early childhood programs* (rev. ed.). (Washington, DC: National Association for the Education of Young Children), p. 110.

Chapter 19

From B. Neugebauer (1990), Going one step further—No traditional holidays, *Child Care Information Exchange*, 74, p. 42.

Author Profile

Joanne Hendrick is an emeritus professor of early childhood education from the University of Oklahoma. In addition to raising four children of her own, her practical experience includes working with children at the Stanford Speech and Hearing Clinic, directing a parent-child workshop, working in Head Start, and chairing the early childhood areas at Santa Barbara City College and the University of Oklahoma. She holds an undergraduate degree from Stanford University in disorders of speech and hearing and graduate degrees from the University of California in counseling and early childhood education. She is past president of the California Association for the Education of Young Children.

Her current interests include serving on the editorial board for *Innovations in Early Childhood: The International Reggio Exchange*, traveling to exotic places, writing about young children, and enjoying her ten grandchildren.